OUR CALLING AND GOD'S HAND IN HISTORY

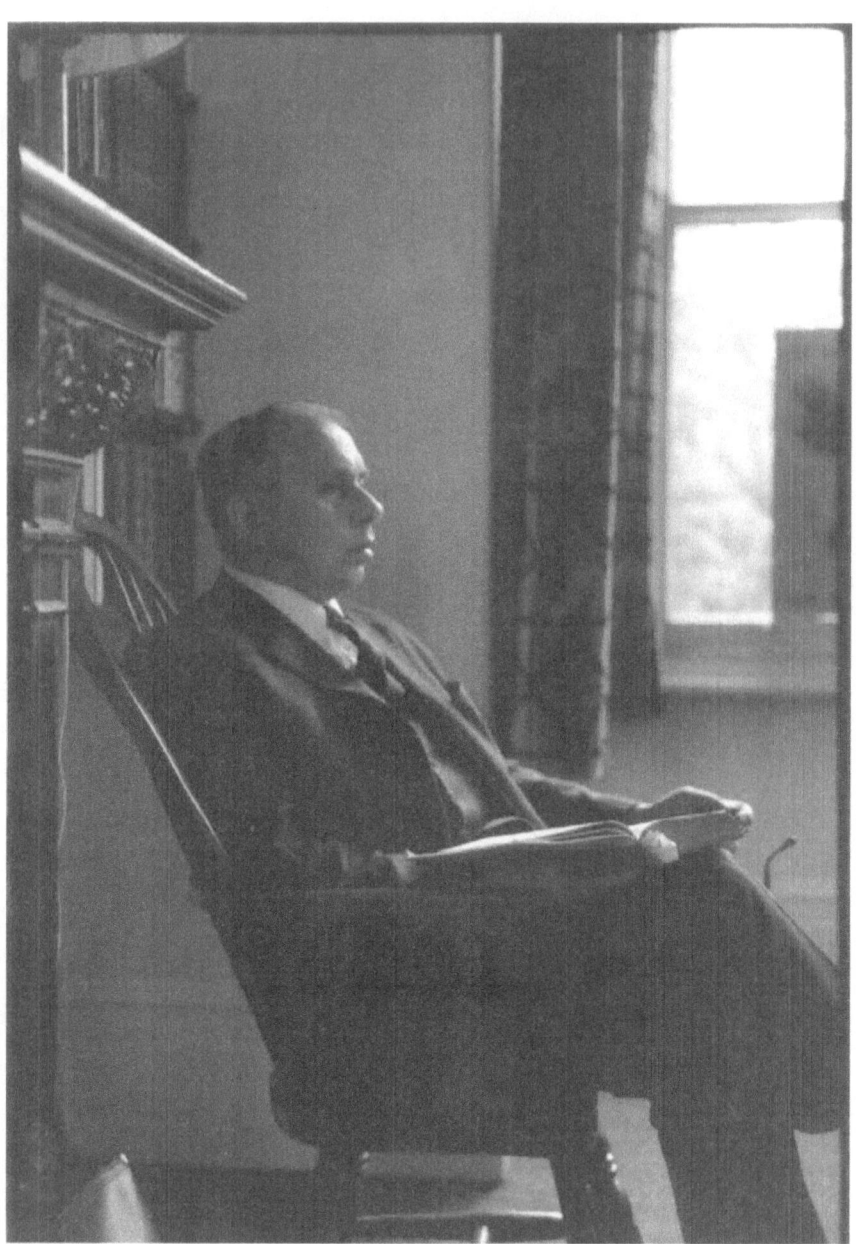
Photograph by Sylvester Jacobs, 1976.

OUR CALLING AND GOD'S HAND IN HISTORY

The Complete Works of Hans R. Rookmaaker

Volume 6

Edited by
Marleen Hengelaar-Rookmaaker

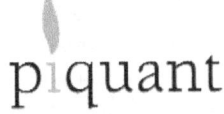

Copyright © 2003 by Marleen Hengelaar-Rookmaaker

This edition copyright © 2021 by Piquant Editions in the UK

Piquant Editions
Website: www.piquanteditions.com

First edition 2003
Paperback edition 2021

ISBN for this volume: 978-1-909281-85-1

The right of Marleen Hengelaar-Rookmaaker to be identified as author of this work has been asserted by her in accordance with the Copyright, Designs and Patents Act, 1988.

All Rights Reserved. No part of this publication may be reproduced, stored in a retrieval system or transmitted, in any form or by any means, electronic, mechanical, photocopying, recording or otherwise, without the prior written permission of the publisher or the Copyright Licensing Agency.

'*God's Hand in History*', copyright © 2002 by
Colin Duriez and Marleen Hengelaar-Rookmaaker
Lectures, articles and interviews, copyright © by H.R. Rookmaaker;
copyright © 2000 by Marleen Hengelaar-Rookmaaker
'*Hans Rookmaaker: An Open Life*', copyright © 2003 by Laurel Gasque
Unless otherwise stated or the author's own paraphrase is used,
Scripture quotations are from the HOLY BIBLE, NEW INTERNATIONAL VERSION ®
NIV®, copyright © 1973, 1978, 1984 by the International Bible Society.
Scripture quotations in 'God's hand in History' are from THE HOLY BIBLE,
ENGLISH STANDARD VERSION, copyright © 2001 by Crossway Bibles, a division of
Good News Publishers. Used by permission. All rights reserved.
All rights reserved.

British Library Cataloguing-in-Publication Data
A catalogue record of this book is available in the UK from the British Library.

ISBN 978-1-909281-85-1

Cover art: Marc de Klijn, detail from
Monuments in the (pre)history of modern art (2000)
Cover design: Jonathan Kearney

Piquant Editions actively supports theological dialogue and an author's right to publish but does not necessarily endorse the individual views and opinions set forth here or in works referenced within this publication, nor guarantee technical and grammatical correctness. The publishers do not accept any responsibility or liability to persons or property as a consequence of the reading, use or interpretation of its published content.

Contents of Volume 6

List of Photographs ix
Acknowledgments xi

Part I: God's Hand in History, edited by Colin Duriez

Preface by Colin Duriez 3
Introduction by H.R.R. 5
1. The Bible's Portrait of History: Announcing the Themes 7
    A forgotten theme of Scripture (7); Blessing and judgment in Deuteronomy 28–30 (9)
2. Blessing and Judgment in the Life of Israel 16
    The prayer of Solomon (17); God's acting in the seen world (18); God's acting in the unseen world (19); The warnings of the prophets (20)
3. Refinement 1: Good People in a Time of Wickedness 25
    Why do the godly suffer? (25); Do the principles no longer hold? (28)
4. Refinement 2: When God has to Judge, What Happens to Mercy? 33
    Waiting for God (34); What happens when judgment is inexorable? (36)
5. Refinement 3: The Hidden God 40
    Hidden Christianity? (42); Science versus faith (43); Love versus judgment? (44); When God is absent (48)
6. Blessing and Judgment in the New Testament 50
    Jesus affirms the Old Testament themes (52); The apostles affirm the Old Testament themes (53)
7. Reading the Book of Revelation 58
    Meaning or fact? (58); A book of consolation (61)
8. The Active Centre of History 63
    The nature of visions (63); The opening of the seals (68); The seventh seal (76)
9. Christians in the World Today 79
    The woman and the dragon (Revelation 12:1–6) (80); War in heaven (Revelation 12:7–12) (81); Pursued into the wilderness (Revelation 12:13–17) (83)

Part II: Articles and Interviews

Prophecy in the Old and New Testaments: God's Way with Israel   91

The prophet (91); Two kinds of prophecy (92); The subject prophecy addresses (92); Revelation of John (93); Symbolism (94); Evil, sin, sorrow (98); Chronological analysis (98); Conclusion (118)

Articles on Evangelism   120

Child Evangelism (120); On witnessing (122); Evangelization (125)

Interviews   131

Interview by Marc de Klijn (131); Interview by C.A. Delhaas-Kraan and J. Boelema (145); Interview for Crusade (150); Interview for Right On (154); Broadcast interview by Jan van Capelleveen (156)

Part III: The L'Abri Lectures

Our Calling in a Postchristian World   163

A world without God (163); Downfall of norms (164); Demasking of values (166); Christians in a world without God (167); Nature and grace (169); Our calling in a world without God (170); The world is God's world (171)

A Dutch Christian View of Philosophy   174

Life is a unity (174); Groen van Prinsterer (175); Kuyper and Christian scholarship (176); Dooyeweerd and L'Abri (178); Dooyeweerd's basic ideas (179); Structures and sphere sovereignty (181); The tragedy of modernity (183)

Jazz and Revolution   185

The revolutionary tide (185); Black music as iron pill (187); Two ways of listening (189); Tragedy (190)

Rock and Protest   192

From Paul Whiteman to rock-and-roll (192); From Hobbes to Dylan (193); From Diderot to Paul Simon (195); From Freud to Leonard Cohen (196); From Franz Marc to Velvet Underground (197); From P.F. Sloan to James Taylor (199); Four possibilities (201)

What is Reality?   203

Inexhaustible meaning (203); Opening eyes (204); Santorio (205); Galenus, Mundinis, Vesalius and Harvey (206); Before the change (207); A new way of seeing (209); Reduced reality (210); Science falsifies reality (212); Rediscover reality (213)

Genesis 1: Creation versus Evolution   215
    *Christians and science (215); Darwin (217); Truth (218);
    Matthew 1 (219); Genesis 1 (221); The evolution theory (222);
    Fullness of reality (223)*
To Do the Truth in Art   225
    *Beauty (225); Reality (226); Art today (228); Truth (230); To do
    the truth (232); Choice (234)*
Hermeneutics of Art   236
    *Introduction (236); The quest for certainty (238); Art as the
    obscure (241); The loss of meaning (244); Meaning (245);
    Causing ripples (248)*
Ultranaturalism   252
    *A new view of reality (252); Cold facts (254); Ultranaturalism
    (256)*
Christianity and Music   259
    *Should we aim to be a subculture? (259); Misplaced optimism
    (260); Keep the good things (261); It is our mentality that
    counts (262); Music makes the person (263); The influence of
    music (264); The debasement of entertainment music (265); Rock
    and pop (266)*
The Christian Artist   269
    *Calvinism and art (269); Pietism and art (270); Gnosticism,
    stoicism and cynicism (271); The role of faith (272); The
    Christian artist (274)*
The Problem of Christian Themes in Art   276
    *Natural and supernatural (276); Early solutions (276);
    Renaissance tensions (278); Reformation and Counter-
    Reformation responses (279); Seventeenth-century Dutch directions
    (281); Nineteenth-century snapshots (283); Sunday school
    pictures (284); Twentieth-century diversity (286)*
Predestination   288
    *Ephesians 1 (288); Determinism and freedom (289); Two answers
    (290); Implications (291)*
Love is the End: Sermon on 2 Peter   294
    *The salutation (294); Life and godliness (294); Divine nature
    (295); God's scaffolding (296); Love (297)*

Part IV: Hans Rookmaaker: An Open Life, by Laurel Gasque

Preface	301
Acknowledgments	304
1. Impact	307
2. Childhood	318
3. Youth	325
4. Conversion and Calling	331
5. Family and Career	337
6. Friendships	358
7. Passions	374
8. Legacy	384
Appendix I: Chronology	413
Appendix II: Sources	417
Notes to Volume 6	431
Appendix A: Bibliography of Published Writings about H.R.R.	434
Appendix B: Hans Rookmaaker Papers at Wheaton College	447
Publishers' Afterword	471
Errata	473
Complete Contents of all 6 Volumes	475
Scripture Index to all 6 Volumes	483
Concordance of Names	497

List of Photographs

1 H.R.R.'s mother, Theodora Catharina Heitink, at age 16
2 H.R.R.'s father, Henderik Roelof Rookmaaker, in the 1930s
3. One-year-old Hans (Hansje) and his sisters on board the *Prins der Nederlanden* in 1923
4. A family photograph from 1924
5. The active interest that Hans's father took in plants and animals created an appreciation of rare creatures right at home
6. The Rookmaaker family home in Sumatra
7. A family photograph, c. 1926
8. Hans was welcome in his father's office, c. 1930
9. Hans with his mother and sisters on leave in the Netherlands
10. A rather anxious-looking Hans with his mother in 1932
11. Hans's sisters adored him
12. H.R.R. and his father, c. 1938
13–15. Hendrika Beatrix (Riki) Spetter had sparkle!
16. Captain J.P.A. Mekkes, one of the most influential and faithful friends of H.R.R.
17. In 1948 Hans became engaged to Anna Marie (Anky) Huitker
18. A group of VGSA members at the University of Amsterdam
19. The wedding of Hans and Anky on 1 June 1949
20. Kees, Marleen and Hans, junior Rookmaaker
21. A family photograph from around 1966
22. The Rookmaaker family on vacation in Vancouver, 1970
23. Some announcement leaflets
24 & 25. Francis and Edith Schaeffer visiting H.R.R. and Anky in Leiden around 1960
26. H.R.R. and Francis Schaeffer
27. H.R.R., Anky and Wim Rietkerk at Dutch L'Abri
28 & 29. H.R.R. had no scruples about smoking his pipe
30. H.R.R. guiding a group through an art gallery
31. *Black tea (for H.R. Rookmaaker)* by Peter S. Smith

The publishers acknowledge with thanks permission to reproduce photographs from the following copyright holders: Laurel Gasque, Marleen Hengelaar-Rookmaaker, Sylvester Jacobs, Peter Smith, and John Walford.
Photograph 16, copyright Fotostudio Joh. van Hespen, The Hague

Acknowledgments

During my childhood we usually went on family nature hikes or cultural excursions on Sunday afternoons. After a while my brothers and I often grew tired, bored and convinced that we could not possibly take another step (or another church or painting). One of the ways in which my father dealt with this situation was to propose that we do a race, not an ordinary one which he would never have stood a chance of winning, but a three steps forward, two steps back race. The trick is of course to make the three steps forward as big as possible, and the two steps back very small. The work on these Complete Works has sometimes reminded me (and the other participants in this race, I am sure) of this game: it has been fun, but at times also frustrating, and the speed was never as great as we wanted it to be.

Volume 6 has however materialized, and the race is run. In this volume we have included the L'Abri lectures, of which Colin Duriez edited the two series of tapes on 'God's Hand in History' and 'Revelation'. My father had asked him to take this job upon himself and Colin had already started to work on it while my father was still alive. Now this project could be completed and the material could be given its rightful place among the other L'Abri lectures. I want to thank Colin for his dedication and good work. Colin proposed to also take up my father's notes on 'Prophecy in the Old and New Testament', which he wrote as a prisoner of war in 1943 for his Jewish fiancé Riki Spetter, who however would not survive the war. It is the earliest piece of writing in these volumes. It shows that the theme of God's hand in history was fundamental to my father's thinking, one that was very close to his heart from the time he became a Christian till the end of his life when he was looking for ways to offer what he found out about this subject to a bigger audience in the form of a book.

The other fourteen lectures were given at either Dutch L'Abri, Swiss L'Abri or at one of the L'Abri conferences in the USA. The lecture on the hermeneutics of art was held in England for the Arts Centre Group. I want to thank Peter Smith for giving it to me, as it is a valuable addition to the rest of the lectures. Some lectures were published earlier and can be found in the other volumes. A number of lectures formed the basis for *The Creative Gift* (see volume 3).

The transcription of the unedited lectures proved to be a big job in itself that asked for a lot of perseverance. Two people stuck with it. They deserve a big word of thanks: Marga van Gent-Petter and Ruth Slater. For anyone interested in the typed versions of the lectures or the cassettes, these may be ordered from Dutch L'Abri (labri@labri.nl).

This volume concludes with a new biography written by Laurel Gasque. The former biography written by Linette Martin has been out of print for a long time (Hodder and Stoughton, 1979). While Linette's concern was mainly with my father's personal history, Laurel focuses on the development of my father's thinking in relation to the course of his life. I want to express my gratitude to Laurel for a biography which betrays great accuracy and empathy, but most of all for being a faithful friend not only to my father but also to me.

The materials that needed translation in this volume (interviews, articles, the notes on prophecy) have been translated by Herbert Donald Morton. Again, many thanks.

The six volumes together come close to 3000 pages. Have all HRR materials now been put into print? The answer is 'no'. In these *Complete Works* we have restricted ourselves to materials of which we were certain that they had been published before, and knew where. There is a long list of articles of which we have only the typed manuscripts, in addition to radio talks, a series of art-historical lectures, notes on record sleeves (Fontana/Riverside series), letters and other miscellanea. For those who want to do research beyond these six volumes, these materials are available from the Special Collections section of the Buswell Memorial Library of Wheaton College (special.collections@wheaton.edu). But our job has ended with this volume.

Ad maiorem gloriam Dei,

Marleen Hengelaar-Rookmaaker
Ommen, The Netherlands

Part I

GOD'S HAND IN HISTORY

edited by COLIN DURIEZ

Preface

I came to know Hans Rookmaaker while I was a student studying English literature and philosophy. He kindly commented on an unpublished manuscript of mine and engaged me to edit material he called 'God's Hand in History', which existed as tape-recorded lectures. He told me his thinking on this theme had begun as a prisoner of war in Poland around the time he had become a Christian. As he read through the Bible he had started to note what the Bible had to say about the principles behind what happens in human history. When I started to make notes for the project I listed all the biblical references, from the beginning to the end of the Bible. On a visit to see him in Eck en Wiel, Holland, I happened to show him the list. 'Let me show you something,' he said. He took me over to a filing cabinet and pulled out two (I think) time-stained notebooks with similar lists to mine. These were his original notebooks from that wartime period. At that time he made a study of these principles. The typewritten script[1] was dedicated to his then fiancé, Riki Spetter, a Jewish woman he afterwards discovered had failed to return from Auschwitz. A few years later he married Riki's best friend, Anky Huitker. He told me in a letter: 'For me, this book is very important: it is my life's work' (unpublished letter, December 24, 1976).

Rookmaaker's idea was that I make an English text out of his words, without distorting the meaning, rather than merely transcribing the audio tapes.[2] The introduction was revised by him and he expressed his satisfaction with the rough draft of chapter one. While I was working on a second chapter, my mind full of Rookmaaker's thought, I was interrupted by a phone call from a friend to say that he had died suddenly from a heart attack. It was a deep loss. I knew well how rare his insights were. Not only was he trying to rehabilitate an understanding of one of the major biblical themes but he was also exploring radical insights into the nature of symbolism and metaphor as a foundation for the human knowledge of reality. There was no one like him with whom one could discuss these things, though there were parallel insights scattered in the writings of C.S. Lewis, J.R.R. Tolkien and Owen Barfield. He also owed much to the philosopher Herman Dooyeweerd. I determined to press on with the task without the benefit of his guidance and spent many months making notes and writing up the taped material. In vain I tried to secure a publisher.

As the years progressed many events confirmed Rookmaaker's main thesis expressed here. When the Berlin Wall was dismantled, for instance, I immediately recalled how he used to say, 'If these biblical principles are true then one day even the Iron Curtain will fall.' What happened on 11 September 2001 in New York confirmed that some events have a particular symbolic significance and provide a representative insight into the course of history that goes far beyond the cold statistics of casualties and damage. Like apocalyptic events they are key historical moments. Though mine is an imperfect rendition of Rookmaaker's understanding of these great biblical principles, and must be read as such, I am delighted, after all these years, to make them public. I hope they will challenge and shape the thinking of many Christians just as they have shaped mine. Though these insights bring deep struggles and pain, it is essential to understand what is happening in the stories of cultures, societies and civilizations. Like many important contemporary writers and thinkers, Rookmaaker was shaped by the horrors of modern warfare, holocaust and genocide and tried to respond to them with integrity. We owe it to those who have suffered not to hide our delicate eyes.

Hans Rookmaaker saw that in addition to the themes of Creation, Fall, and God's provision of salvation, the theme of God's dealing in history is basic for a biblical understanding of reality. God is alive and active in our history and cannot be ignored, though sometimes he appears to hide himself. In fact, God's withdrawal is one of his prime judgments. Some modern theologians of Rookmaaker's time spoke of a 'hidden' or even a 'dead' God. Incidentally, Rookmaaker outlined many of the signs of God's withdrawal from Western culture in his *Modern Art and the Death of a Culture*, which in a way is a case study for his reflections on divine judgment in history. The biblical books of Deuteronomy and Revelation are key to the thesis of Rookmaaker. Undoubtedly his wartime experience, particularly the suffering of his country and the grievous fate of the Jewish people, was the matrix out of which his reflections on God's hand in history grew.

Colin Duriez
Leicester, August 2002

Original Introduction by H.R.R.

If a Christian today was asked what the essence of Christianity is, he or she might well stress three vital themes: God's creation, humankind's fall into sin, and God's provision of salvation. But a fourth theme, equally important, is neglected and radically misunderstood by Christians in our day. This theme is God's dealing in history.

Just as the Bible devotes particular chapters to the three well-known themes (as well as expressing them here and there throughout its books) so too it expresses, and devotes key chapters to, this neglected theme. In particular chapters 28 to 30 of Deuteronomy lay down the fundamental principles by which God works in history.

There are definite reasons why contemporary Christians neglect and misunderstand the theme of God's hand in history. But by coming to terms with our blindness, Christians today could open themselves to the richness and freedom of life that God's word promises. Only such a consoling promise can sustain us in the darkness of this period of God's judgment on our Western world with its dying culture. Christians who do not understand the clear biblical principles of God's dealing in history, however, will lose their voices in the characteristic chaos and confusion of such a period of judgment.

According to how they use or misuse their God-given responsibilities on group or social levels, people reap *real*, not so-called 'spiritual', blessing or judgment from God: either such things as an adequate food supply, a good standard of living with health, peace and security; or terror, war, pollution and the like. Thus history (and culture) is composed, in its very texture, of human obedience and disobedience to God: it is essentially a battle between good and evil fought in the fields and streets, homes and factories of our common and familiar world. All people are responsible in freedom to God, for he has chosen to work out his will through us. The events of history are the result of both human doing and God's special acting in judgment or blessing. A text that often comes to my mind is Isaiah 9:19. This speaks of people providing the fire of wickedness but God setting the flame alight: 'Through the wrath of the Lord of Hosts the land is burned, and the people are like fuel for the fire; no man spares his brother.' So in history there is real cause and effect, and we can understand bad situations as the result of mismanagement or evildoing. But at the same time there is an extra, a something more, which cannot be understood merely by our reasoned analysis. This is God's working in history. It is not that we just fill the gaps in our knowledge by reference to God. The situation is deeper and more real than this. It means that God is acting, and that we can see that he is: or rather, we *ought* to see that he is. As Deuteronomy 29:29 states, the things that are revealed are for us to use in order to understand. Belonging to these revealed things, as that Bible chapter makes clear, are

God's blessing and cursing. In the past people understood this matter of God's acting in history. In 1586, for instance, the British and Dutch knew that they could not stop the gigantic fleet of the Spaniards. Therefore they prayed to God who, in answer, shipwrecked the Armada against the coast of Scotland. People saw God working as in biblical times. Are we to say that they were wrong in this understanding? Are we so restricted in our faith? Are we unbelievers, even while we profess to love Christ?

My study of God's hand in history really began as a prisoner of war in Poland, when I read through the whole Bible, including the Revelation of John. As a result I became a Christian. Only when I returned to Holland from captivity and came into contact with Christian churches for the first time did I discover with gladness that what I had found and come to believe in the Bible was the orthodox position. There are some points, of course, on which orthodox Christians might differ, but they are relatively minor in my opinion. (It also convinced me that orthodoxy is not merely an approach or way of thinking that one is brought up to accept. I had discovered it independently.) Indeed, the first lecture that I ever gave in my life was on this subject of God's hand in history.

For many years now one of my greatest concerns has been the whole question relating to the meaning of culture, which is very closely involved with the meaning of history. Some of the key biblical texts that suggest answers to this question are to be found in the much neglected and misunderstood Bible book of Revelation. In particular the beautiful descriptions of the opening of the sealed scroll by the Lamb of God give at once the essential meaning of history and offer the deepest consolation for Christians who question the significance of our lives in the present temporal world.

One of the most pressing problems that we must confront today is the meaning of our involvement in this temporal world. Our neglect of that problem is related to our neglect of the theme of God's hand in history. I believe that a proper understanding of, and response to, the revealed principles of God's dealing in history substantially resolves the problem, or should I say that it sets the Christian's living and working in the right direction. That is not easy. But applying the truth rarely is.

1
The Bible's Portrait of History: Announcing the Themes

In the modern world, people speak of Christianity as a 'religion', which means that it is a subjective matter, something created by the human mind. But Christianity is not in the first place a religion or a private matter. It is rather an assertion of the truth that God lives and acts.

What lies behind the view of Christianity as religion is a conflict between the biblical viewpoint on reality and the new view, which originated in the Enlightenment. That new view, which influences Christians as well as non-Christians, has reduced reality and truth to what we can see or experience with our senses and what we can understand by our 'natural' reason. Such a view of truth conflicts with the biblical idea of truth. Biblical truth starts from the assertion that God does exist. Not only that, but he is interested in his creation and acts in, and into, it. In particular God is interested in human history: indeed, he has become part of it by becoming human.

The principles of the modern world really mean apostasy from the God of Scripture. This might seem an extreme statement. But the Christian churches have been guilty of not taking the matter seriously enough. We have too easily accepted the modern labelling of Christianity as a 'religion', a completely subjective, personal matter to be kept out of public life, scholarly discussions, political decisions and everyday life. As a result life is divided into a spiritual realm, where the biblical content is real and true, and the realm of nature, where people act practically out of their common sense, where people live by their natural lights in a more or less neutral world. This attitude leads to a misreading of God's very Word itself.

Christians turn to the Scriptures because we believe that God is the same in all ages – then as now, now as for ever. We turn to them also because we believe that human beings are basically the same in all ages, even though frameworks change, forms differ and knowledge increases or decreases.

A forgotten theme of Scripture

When we turn to the Scriptures, we usually accept easily enough the basic points of Scriptural revelation: Creation, the fall of humanity, redemption, judgment, and the promise of a new earth. But we often and easily forget the revelation that our God is the Lord who looks after his people. We forget that such chapters as Deuteronomy 28 to 30 are equally basic for understanding the teaching of both the prophets of the Old Testament and the apostles of the New Testament. These chapters – and parallel chapters in Leviticus and elsewhere – teach us how God deals with his people and all people either in blessing or in judgment. And we should not neglect to notice that these blessings and judgments are not 'spiritual' ones: in Scripture there is no such differentiation between 'spiritual', on the one hand, and 'secular' or material, on the other. These blessings and judgments are very real indeed. They have a bearing upon the fullness of life in all its aspects, not just in one religious respect. In fact, what these chapters teach is how God acts in history. They are concerned with the very centre of biblical truth: that God is, and that he acts. They explain the basic assumptions of all the prophets, men like Jeremiah and Isaiah. They tell us to be careful not to forsake the Lord, the source of our life, not to abandon his ways. We are to fear his curse, his very real and tangible judgment in history.

Many Christians today forget this; often these matters are not even taught in our congregations. Thoughts along these lines may be pushed out of the way by an assumption that such principles apply only to Old Testament times. But did not our Lord Jesus himself say that 'if salt has lost its taste . . . it is no longer good for anything except to be thrown out and trampled under people's feet' (Matthew 5:13)? Furthermore, in Matthew 23 he repeated his 'woe unto you' many times; and in the following chapter told of the tribulations to come as a fulfilment of his curse. We must remember that these prophecies did happen with the fall and destruction of Jerusalem a few decades later by the order of the Roman Emperor Titus. Also we may think of the very real woes that Revelation speaks about, and of many passages in the apostolic letters. Indeed, as Hebrews 10:31 vividly puts it, it is a fearful thing to fall into the hands of the living God!

God, of course, is a God of love. His judgment must always be seen in relation to his love. Yet this does not mean that the theme of judgment can be ignored. The whole relationship between judgment and love, and how this relationship relates to God's active working in history, is beautifully expressed in Exodus 34:6,7. These verses are also remarkable because here, most unusually, God speaks directly to his people:

> The Lord passed before him and proclaimed, 'The Lord, the Lord, a God merciful and gracious, slow to anger, and abounding in steadfast love and faithfulness, keeping steadfast love for thousands, forgiving iniquity and transgression and sin, but who will by no means clear the guilty, visiting the iniquity of the fathers on the children and the children's children, to the third and the fourth generation.'

There are a number of important points that can be drawn from these verses. Most importantly, they tell us above all that God loves people and is positive towards them, wanting to help them. He is willing to forgive sin and he helps the bad as well as the good. Yet the side of God's judgment is also made clear. He will not accept a mentality of wrongdoing in a people. He will certainly act in judgment in such a case. On the one side there is God's love, but on the other side is his judgment when a people does not repent. In these verses, love and judgment go together; there is no loveless judgment, which would be harsh, tyrannical and arbitrary. Rather, an active fight against, and resistance to, evil is implied as a direct consequence of God's love. God acts in judgment because he loves life, beauty, goodness, and his own creation.

Blessing and judgment in Deuteronomy 28–30

God's revelation always contains the two sides of blessing and cursing. This is first revealed in God's fundamental promise of national blessing or cursing for the Israelites – a 'light to the nations' – depending upon their obedience or disobedience. The promise can be found, for instance, in Deuteronomy 4:25–31. Earlier in the same chapter the writer of Deuteronomy points out that a society that listens to God will eventually be great in the sight of the nations (Deuteronomy 4:5–9). Their very growth and quality of life will be a sign of the reality behind their godly faith.

It is fundamental to the teaching of Deuteronomy, and indeed of the whole Bible, that God provides the only proper foundation for the life of a society; if he is rejected, the very source of life is removed. Thus obedience to God is a matter of life in all its fullness or death in all its emptiness. God wants us to have life for our *own* sakes as well as for *his* sake. When a society receives God's blessing in reward for obedience, ungodly nations will acknowledge what a great nation it is, what a good system it has, how humane its laws are, and so forth. On the other hand, a society that disobeys God will certainly deteriorate and disintegrate, becoming a by-word. In fact, if its proper life is thwarted, God could put a stop to a nation completely (Deuteronomy 6:14, 15). At the very centre of the biblical message then is a living God who loves human beings and who is good. He is the Head of the universe and will stand no rival. If a society leaves God out, inexorably life vanishes: death and decay results. God makes it clear that if a nation does not allow him to help it, if it does not rely fully upon him for its life-support, then that nation will die.

This sober message makes it clear that we must take Deuteronomy 28 to 30 as key chapters of the Bible, to be placed in importance alongside Genesis 1 and 2 and other chapters concerned with Creation and the other central biblical themes. The prophets continually refer to these chapters, as do the apostles, and our Lord himself emphatically taught the message of God's blessing and cursing in history. If these chapters are neglectfully missed out, the reader fails to understand much of the Bible.

Deuteronomy, in which these key chapters occur, presents the final discourses of Moses before he died. These speeches are given at the end of the forty years' wandering in the wilderness, before the Israelites go in to possess the land of Canaan. Moses recapitulates the recent history of Israel and the principles of their history. To use an analogy, it is as if he starts painting a vast and beautiful portrait, to which the later books of the Bible add detail, refining the broad strokes presented here. By the time the book of Revelation is finished, the picture is full and rich and many details have been added, such as the complex matter of the individual in a period of general blessing or cursing: What is the fate of a good person in the time of great national wickedness? Why do the innocent suffer? It is clear that the Bible in such historical matters is dealing with some of the deepest and most painful questions people ask – questions about war and peace, about suffering and the significance of doing good when it all appears to be meaningless.

Our attention in Deuteronomy 28–30, however, is drawn not to individuals but to groups and societies. It refers back to the very beginning of history, as we are told in Genesis, immediately after the Fall, when we discover a battle between two groups of people: the seed of woman (or true humanity) and the seed of the enemy of humanity, the Devil. Genesis 3:15 prophecies that human thought, life and personality (which is essentially good) will eventually flourish, but that in the meantime the Devil will severely cripple and disfigure the 'good' group. That is, in the battle between good and evil – which is a fundamental principle of human history – there are *real* scars and wounds. This battle is first expressed in the conflict between Cain and Abel, in the tragic consequences as brother kills brother (Genesis 4:6, 7).

In the final chapters of Deuteronomy, bringing this matter right down to their present situation, Moses tells the assembled Israelites that the reason why the land of Canaan is to be taken from the Canaanites is because, as a nation, they have settled into a hardened mentality of wrongdoing. However, the Israelites, who are to be given the land in place of them, cannot claim any glory for possessing it (Deuteronomy 9:4). They are not to boast, for God is taking the land from the Canaanites in response to the pitch their wickedness has reached; the removal of their land is to be seen as God's judgment. The Israelites are not allowed to take any land they choose; this is expressly forbidden (e.g. Deuteronomy 2:5, 9). Rather, they are given the land of Canaan, and they are to remember that God could as easily take it from them again in judgment.

Chapters 28 to 30 contain a most explicit and systematic statement of the principles by which God deals with societies and nations in history. God states quite categorically to the Israelite congregation (and indeed to any nation or society) that if they listen to God's command, if the people love and obey him with all their heart, then that nation or society eventually will be prosperous and grow in a *real* sense: they will have good crops, peace, security, health and the like. But if they refuse to walk in God's way, he'll set himself against them. The enemy will overcome them if the people persist in not keeping God's commands, which are for their benefit. God will take their land from them. (The removal of a nation's land is a basic theme throughout the Bible.) Their culture and their country will come to an end. But if they will return to God and choose once more the right direction for their lives, he will listen; he will hear their cries for help.

The attitude of these chapters is far from the often secularized, unbiblical attitudes of Christians today. We often see only two possibilities and never dream that there are more. In the first place we think a period of prosperity is the result of either sheer luck or the fact that as individuals we have been good or 'spiritual'. In the second place, when hardship occurs we tend to think this is either the result of bad luck or of the fact that individually we have been bad or 'unspiritual'. But the Bible shows us another possibility, for the Bible does not deal merely with individuals (and their personal prosperity) or with their 'spiritual' life (the Afterlife, and so forth). The Bible is preoccupied with what the living God is doing in all the rich fullness of human history and culture. What Deuteronomy expresses here is a momentous and heart-stirring theme that demands our courage and all-out response.

Moses starts his discourse with the words: 'And when all these things come upon you, the blessing and the curse, which I have set before you, and you call them to mind among all the nations where the Lord your God has driven you' (Deuteronomy 30:1). Thus the guiding principle is set forth. Everything is conditional upon obedience to, and thoughtfulness before, the living God. First the nation must listen to, and then they must attempt to practise, the commandments. The truth is to be heard and then *done*. What Moses is presenting is a social attitude. This attitude or mentality of listening and heeding is vitally important because, indeed, life itself is at stake. All the fullness of human reality – the total engagement of our minds and our bodies – is involved. Yet if we sometimes sin, he will forgive us. But where our whole mentality is at fault, where we neither listen to nor practise the truth, the vital condition of national life and beauty is violated. Thus the condition of social life is centrally one of a mentality.

And when we as a nation or society listen to what God has to say, he will do great things for us. For instance, he will bless our lives with substantial elements, with things that can be seen and are tangible: riches, flocks, health and the like (Deuteronomy 28:8). The previous verse (28:7) tells the assembled Israelites that, as one of the real consequences of his blessing, God will rebuff their enemies. As Moses vividly puts it: 'They shall come out against you one way, and flee before you seven ways.' God will help a godly nation in time of war; at such a time, godly and understanding people need not fear. This principle is true not only in biblical times but throughout history.

Let me give a positive and a negative example of this principle at work in recent history. The first concerns the Pilgrim Fathers: a hundred or so godly people went to America, seeing the continent as theirs. Historically we can see the blessing of God upon that group of Pilgrims as the New World opened up. The second example concerns an incident from more recent history and it illustrates the converse, namely that when a nation or society is disobedient and heedless, God helps its enemies. In the African Congo all areas of public life were dominated by whites. But when one schoolteacher stood up and spoke out against the regime, the rulers fled in panic. There was no big racial battle. Just a few words were a sufficient attack upon the status quo. A thousand people were indeed conquered by one man.

Not only will God rebuff the enemies of a nation that heeds his commands, but he will also exalt that nation to a position of international leadership: it will be like a light on a hill. Deuteronomy 28:17 suggests that other nations will look to it for guidance. They will notice the 'real blessings' of less crime, justice, a good quality of life and an integrated society that have come as a result of an attitude of listening and attending to God's desires for human life. Such leadership is one of the consequences of obedience, and it shows the implications of God's plan in the area of politics.

This statement about the political implications of a national response to God's commands effectively ends this short first section of Deuteronomy 28, which has been concerned with the blessings that God has to give. The long remaining section of the chapter is concerned with the converse, the judgment that God will give where a society is disobedient, heedless and unresponsive to his good plan for its life. Like the blessings, these are real judgments; they are not merely 'spiritual'. They concern war, disease, famine, lack of security and the possibility of a nation's losing their territory. The sheer length of this negative section is very human; people not only have to be presented with the results of choosing life and blessing but also have to be soundly warned of the consequences of rejecting God's beneficial plan. Human freedom and responsibility are respected:

> But if you will not obey the voice of the Lord your God or be careful to do all his commandments and his statutes that I command you today, then all these curses shall come upon you and overtake you. Cursed shall you be in the city, and cursed shall you be in the field. Cursed shall be your basket and your kneading bowl. Cursed shall be the fruit of your womb and the fruit of your ground, the increase of your herds and the young of your flock. Cursed shall you be when you come in, and cursed shall you be when you go out.

> The Lord will send on you curses, confusion, and frustration in all that you undertake to do, until you are destroyed and perish quickly on account of the evil of your deeds, because you have forsaken me. The Lord will make the pestilence stick to you until he has consumed you off the land that you are entering to take possession of it (Deuteronomy 28:15–21).

Perhaps the most telling verse in this quotation is verse 20, with its emphasis upon *confusion* as one of the judgments that God inflicts when people turn from him and choose the wrong direction. There will be confusion in the land, and destruction will result from that. The main point, however, is that when matters start to go drastically wrong, and the sorts of things that are graphically described in these verses happen, they are to be taken as the judgments of God. They are real. There is chaos and confusion in the land, not simply difficulties to be overcome. The results are devastating and unavoidable.

While the reality of these judgments must be emphasized, they must not be regarded as merely 'natural' matters. That is as great a mistake as to regard them as merely 'spiritual'. The judgments are not simply a matter of natural historical effects, as when hatred leads to murder, the loss of life, and sorrow for the family of the murdered. This 'natural' level is only one level of the meaning of judgment. There is clearly a level that is richer and higher, and that contains the same sort of mystery as the centre of our own lives and motives. On this higher level it is quite clear that these judgments are the direct working of God in history. An enemy, for example, may conquer our land, as happened to Holland in the Second World War. The invasion can also be seen as God's direct action in history. Then God's direct action in history and natural historical cause and effect are equally involved in the reality of judgment. Without divine action, it would not be meaningful to call these events judgments of God; they would simply be 'unfortunate events'.

Verse 28 repeats the fact that one of the curses is 'confusion of mind'. Other nations (v.37) will be horrified by the state of confusion existing in the cursed nation. Confusion is an important theme in the Bible. The New Testament, for instance, speaks of confusion or delusion coming as a result of a refusal 'to love the truth' (2 Thessalonians 2:10, 11). Thus when we find a state of confusion in a nation we should not think it strange and unnatural but rather ask ourselves whether this is not a result of God's judgment.

When such things as the drastic failure of crops happen to a nation (as in 28:38) there is a reason for this. People are meant to see that God is doing something in history, as a special act of judgment. There are not only the historical snowballing effects of wrongdoing, such as bad crops from a misuse of land resources and defeat in war because of lack of 'moral backbone' and 'morale'. There is also something *more* a nation's or society's mentality plays a part, in that God is actively responding to that according to his promise of judgment. Historical events do not happen by themselves in a closed system – they are not 'in a box'. They come from God, and there is a reason why war, starvation, disease and such like, have arisen. It touches on a nation's or society's mentality. This is made clear in verses 45–48a, which points out that a cursed nation, falling prey to their enemies, become a negative proverb, a negative 'sign and a wonder' (v.46) to other nations.

God's final message about his curses comes in verse 64: he will eventually take away a nation's land from them. God is patient and continues to send his prophets to the nation, but he will eventually act decisively against a continual attitude of unrepentance.

In Deuteronomy 29, Moses returns to the theme of all the good things that the living God did for them during the wilderness wanderings; how he cared for them (29:5, 6). Then he points out that because God has given so much specifically to the Israelites, his anger against their disobedience and heedlessness to his commands will be that much more fierce (29:19, 20). When they see their destruction, other nations will understand that God has cursed them because they have forsaken him (29:24, 25).

Much has been said about God's commands, that they must be obeyed by a nation as the essential condition of its life. In Deuteronomy 30:11–14, Moses makes some important comments about these commands. They are not alien matters, far away from us, inaccessible and beyond our ability to accomplish. On the contrary, they are the nearest and simplest things for us; they accord with the very laws of our humanity; they are in deepest sympathy with our nature.

Moses emphasizes this and then concludes the whole section by presenting the gathered Israelites with a fundamental choice, a simple choice between life and death:

> See, I have set before you today life and good, death and evil. If you obey the commandments of the Lord your God that I command you today, by loving the Lord your God, by walking in his ways, and by keeping his commandments and his statutes and his rules, then you shall live and multiply, and the Lord your God will bless you in the land that you are entering to take possession of it. But if your heart turns away, and you will not hear, but are drawn away to worship other gods and serve them, I declare to you today, that you shall surely perish. You shall not live long in the land that you are going over the Jordan to enter and possess. I call heaven and earth to witness against you today, that I have set before you life and death, blessing and curse. Therefore choose life, that you and your offspring may live, loving the Lord your God, obeying his voice and holding fast to him, for he is your life and length of days, that you may dwell in the land that the Lord swore to your fathers, to Abraham, to Isaac, and to Jacob, to give them (Deuteronomy 30:15–20).

As we look over history, there are many matters that we could talk about in relation to these great principles connected with corporate and national life. What happens, for instance, if we look at the present Western world and at America with these principles in mind? What could we say about confusion in many lands? What about crops and the failures of crops? What about the ecological imbalance? What about rising criminality? What is really going on? The political systems in America, and in Europe on a smaller scale, are no longer coping. We could say that these matters are nothing new; they have been seen before. We could say that they are not accidental. We could say that they are not merely the natural progression of history.

To look at our present situation in this way would not be an easy matter. There are many complexities in the portrait of history set up by Moses in Deuteronomy. Many of these shall be considered in the following chapters, such as the issue of which matters are outside human control and which ones are caused by us. What do we say when an oil ship breaks up in rough seas and pollution results? The same problem relates to crop failures. On a political level, complications force us not to easily lay the blame on the US President or Mr Brezhnev or the Left or the Right. Questions concerning the social and national mentality arise and naturally complicate matters.

Many historical matters also can be related to principles outlined by Moses. It is true, for example, that Jewish people, sadly, were (and still are) a 'proverb', a 'sign and a wonder among the nations'. Israel as a state has stepped back into historical prominence since 1948.

If the principles of Deuteronomy 28–30 are truly the principles of history, then they can and must be applied to the present-day and recent history. They will yield the essential meaning of events, which our enquiries only on the level of natural cause and effect can never do. Without the discovery of the essential meaning, some of our deepest questions will remain unanswered.

2
Blessing and Judgment in the Life of Israel

In the book of Deuteronomy, Moses announced the principles behind the history of God's people up to the point of their entering the Promised Land. These principles are not only a reality for the Israelite people but for any nation or society. The principles of God's blessing and cursing are inviolable. In this chapter we shall see the principles at work in the history of the Israelites as a nation, beginning with the book of Judges.

Historically the testing place of these principles comes after the Israelites' crossing of the Jordan and their entering of Canaan. The Israelites under the judges fought for the possession of their Promised Land, then the kingdom divided into two, with Israel in the north and Judah in the south, and both these territories were eventually taken away from the Israelites by invaders as a result of God's judgment. In this chapter we will look at the period of possession under the judges and the time of the Israelite Kingdom, a period that dramatically reveals the outworking of the great principles expounded by Moses in Deuteronomy.

The period of the judges begins the history of Israel as a nation. Life at that time fell into a certain constantly repeated pattern, which is expressed in Judges 2:

> And the people of Israel did what was evil in the sight of the Lord and served the Baals. And they abandoned the Lord, the God of their fathers, who had brought them out of the land of Egypt. They went after other gods, from among the gods of the peoples who were around them, and bowed down to them. And they provoked the Lord to anger. They abandoned the Lord and served the Baals and the Ashtaroth. So the anger of the Lord was kindled against Israel, and he gave them over to plunderers, who plundered them. And he sold them into the hand of their surrounding enemies, so that they could no longer withstand their enemies. Whenever they marched out, the hand of the Lord was against them for harm, as the Lord had warned, and as the Lord had sworn to them. And they were in terrible distress.
>
> Then the Lord raised up judges, who saved them out of the hand of those who plundered them (Judges 2:11–16).

At this time there is both obedience and disobedience, and in direct response God sends judges to overcome the enemies he has sent in judgment. It is clear that when the people go after other gods and weaken themselves, the enemy does not overcome them as a result of natural causality alone. They are not overcome for simple reasons, which the eye can see and natural reason can determine. There are in fact deeply historical causes, not reducible to other kinds of causality. God is moving, and his hand is leading its enemies upon Israel in direct judgment. He also moves in sending judges – he is not indifferent to the hardship and sufferings of his disobedient people but is gracious. He is teaching his people a hard lesson, emphasizing the clear principles of his blessing and cursing that Moses had taught them. He teaches them a lesson using actual history, so that his people could know these things in their familiar, 'real' reality. Through the immediate and concrete actuality of their experience he brings these principles home, showing that he takes them seriously, whatever the cost. He forces his people to recognize that they are not being harassed and defeated by enemies because that is inevitable. It is not *natural* that this should happen. Rather, he forces them to recognize that he is putting the enemy on top of them as a result of their open disobedience; he is using the enemy as a tool. He is also showing that, because he is behind their enemies' triumph, there is no natural, human solution to the situation. Only God can rescue them. In this case he uses the judges he raises up. The people of Israel are entirely dependent upon God's blessing and cursing; he is the sole source of their national life and wellbeing.

The prayer of Solomon

Following the period of the judges and God's repeated lessons of blessing and cursing, the kingdom is established with first King Saul, then King David, and then David's son Solomon. With Solomon the high point of the national kingdom is reached as the Temple in Jerusalem is built and dedicated. Solomon was acutely aware of the principles of blessing and cursing, the principles of God's hand in history. This is nowhere more apparent than in his beautiful song, his lovely prayer at the dedication of the Temple (1 Kings 8:32–53). It is a prayer that every Christian organization or group should make its own. Solomon realized that the establishment of the Temple was a momentous event, and felt that it was appropriate to teach his nation this song. Obviously deeply moved, Solomon presents the theme of God's blessing and cursing in history as the most important matter for the life and beauty of the nation.

Solomon's prayer contains all the elements of the principles outlined in Deuteronomy 28–30. For example verses 31–34, which deal first with the individual and then with the nation, state the principle: if the enemy wins the battle, then the reason is sin and nothing else. It is not saying that the enemy has won because it has not sinned, as if it were good and in God's favour. On the contrary, God has used the enemy in his judgment for his own ends. At such a time of defeat, God's nation must come to him for forgiveness:

> When heaven is shut up and there is no rain because they have sinned against you, if they pray toward this place and acknowledge your name and turn from their sin, when you afflict them, then hear in heaven and forgive the sin of your servants, your people Israel, when you teach them the good way in which they should walk, and grant rain upon your land, which you have given to your people as an inheritance (1 Kings 8:35–36).

Solomon goes on to point out that when there is drought, it is not simply because the people happen to have bad weather; they have sinned and drought is a consequence (8:35, 36). The same is true of famine, plague, diseased crops and other calamities (v.37). Solomon's prayer is a thoroughly biblical prayer, full of understanding of the principles of God's working in history in blessing and cursing.

Solomon makes it clear that God listens to and takes serious note of people's prayers (8:28, 29). It follows that we cannot be hypocrites before him or play games with him. The king stresses that people are to think about what is wrong, go to the Temple and confess that they have sinned, for there is no one who does not sin. The same is true on a national level. Solomon clearly understood the necessity for repentance in times of sin and for obedience to God's good laws. If these principles are not followed, a society will bring itself into real calamities; Solomon mentions, for example, being taken captive by their enemies (v.50), a calamity that is in fact to take place in the future, unbeknown to him.

God's acting in the seen world

After Solomon, during the reign of his son Rehoboam, the nation divided into two kingdoms, one of which – Judah, in the South – was loyal to the chosen king and another – called Israel, in the North – following Jeroboam, the first of the Northern kings. The Northern Kingdom turned to idolatry (1 Kings 12:28–30). This came about by King Jeroboam's setting up two golden calves to be worshipped in place of worshipping God at his appointed place, the Temple in Jerusalem, which was in the territory of the Southern Kingdom. The golden calves, we are told, were acceptable to the people of the Northern Kingdom, but 'became a sin' (v.30); in my Dutch Bible it says that the calves were the *cause* of sin.

In the chapters which follow, dealing with events in the Northern Kingdom, there appears a kind of refrain, that King Jeroboam 'made Israel to sin' (see 2 Kings 10:29,31, for example) on account of setting up these golden calves. Many prophets are raised up by God to criticize the sinful people of the Northern Kingdom and its successive kings. These prophets reiterate the great principles of God's blessing and cursing as set out in Deuteronomy. They care deeply about the life and quality of life in their society and see clearly the consequences of idolatry and disobedience.

One of the greatest prophets of the Northern Kingdom was Elijah. When there was a drought for many years, the king at that time, Ahab, blamed Elijah for that curse. In Ahab we have the first instance of individual apostasy in the Bible, and his reign is treated in some detail. The climax of Elijah's career as a prophet was the momentous event at Mount Carmel, where he challenged the prophets of Baal – the idol worshipped by Ahab and the people of the Northern Kingdom (1 Kings 18). Elijah declared that the true God – be he the Lord God of the Israelites or Baal – would kindle the appropriate altar, one being set up for Baal and one for the Lord. Baal's altar remained unlit as Elijah derided the prophets of Baal, but the Lord answered unequivocally with fire from heaven. When the people acknowledged the true God as Lord, rain came and the drought was ended.

Notice, however, that the rain did not come suddenly and sensationally. The fire from heaven that kindled the altar to the Lord God is the only 'miraculous miracle' that happened, if we might use such a term. We must not always expect 'miraculous miracles', like fire from heaven; generally the blessings of God are humble blessings, like rain. In the case of the events on Mount Carmel, all those centuries ago, the rain not only (and certainly) came in direct answer to Elijah's prayer, by the overruling hand of God in history, but it also came within the normal framework of cause and event. Elijah clearly expected nothing strange and outside the frame of ordinary reality; he did not expect rain to fall out of a clear blue, cloudless sky. On the contrary, he awaited the formation of natural rain clouds. He repeatedly told his servant to go up the slope of Mount Carmel and to look for clouds until, after several fruitless viewings, the servant finally saw a cloud as small as a man's hand rising out of the sea. Then, we are told, 'in a little while the heavens grew black with clouds and wind, and there was a great rain' (v.45).

The fire from heaven, falling upon the altar to the true God on Mount Carmel, was a 'miraculous miracle', out of the normal framework of common events. Not only do we occasionally have such special miracles recorded in the Bible, but also actual visions of the unseen world are recorded, things beyond the usual framework. These are *actual* visions because they are viewings of truly *real* matters; they are not merely metaphors and figurative language used to illustrate and enrich concepts and ideas. One of the most momentous of these actual visions of the world beyond the five senses happened in the lifetime of the prophet Elisha, who was Elijah's successor and pupil.

God's acting in the unseen world

An army of Syrians had come, under cover of night, to capture Elisha. They surrounded the city in which he and his servant were staying. Early in the morning the servant got up and saw this great army. In utmost fear he informed Elisha, who calmly told him not to be afraid because those 'with us' were more than those who are 'with them' (6:16). Elisha then prayed that God would open the servant's eyes: 'So the Lord opened the eyes of the young man, and he saw; and behold, the mountain was full of horses and chariots of fire round about Elisha' (v.17).

The young servant is allowed to see realities that lie outside or beyond the frame of ordinary experience. This sort of vision reveals the essential meaning of what we are considering in this study: God's hand in history. Elisha pointed out to his servant, and God allowed him to actually see it, that on the side of the faithful and wise is more than the eye can perceive. The young man's eyes are opened to the real meaning of history. In all wars, conflicts and national events there is more at work than the eye can see; there is an extra that cannot be naturally explained. The servant, using normal sight, had seen that the two of them were hopelessly outnumbered. But in reality that large army was insignificant in relation to the great angelic forces on their side. To understand reality, the principles of God's blessing and cursing have to be taken into consideration. These principles, and these principles alone, determine whether or not there is to be defeat or triumph.

The Bible records several such visions of the reality lying beyond the ordinary frame of the world. In particular, Daniel was shown something about what is really behind wars and battles, that there is far more than can be explained naturally. In Daniel 10, Daniel has a vision of the angel Gabriel, who reveals that he has been in conflict with various princes or guardian angels of nations and was helped by the angel Michael (verses 1, 5, 13). Daniel 12:1 reveals that Michael is the guardian angel of God's people. It is clear that there are real happenings in the unseen world, directly related to the course of history, which must be taken into account. Daniel is allowed to glimpse beyond this world, that is, beyond the ordinary framework of events as normally perceived. The same idea of guardian angels allocated to nations and involved with God's dealing in history is suggested in the Song of Moses (Deuteronomy 32:8), which declares that God has given each nation its country, 'according to the number of the sons of God'.

The warnings of the prophets

Another prophet whom God raised up to preach the theme of blessing and cursing in the Northern Kingdom of Israel was Amos. He reiterated that God had given a special blessing to the Israelites – they were his people. They had received more revelation than any other nation and thus were more responsible to live in a way that pleased God. In Amos 3, God declares through the prophet that he had brought the 'whole family' of Israel from Egypt and, he added: 'You only have I known of all the families of the earth; therefore I will punish you for all your iniquities' (v.2). They had turned from the true God to idols.

This statement of Amos's has direct application to our own day. If any nation in the Western world claims in any way to be a Christian nation, then it had better be on its guard, for God is certainly watching it in a closer way than he watches overtly heathen nations. 'Therefore' (v.2) his hand will move in history in judgment against it. The same idea is to be found in Isaiah 48:9–11. God's name is at stake when a nation claims to follow him; the worse for that nation if it transgresses God's laws.

Amos displays great understanding of the principles of God's working in history revealed in Deuteronomy 28–30. One passage (Amos 3:3–8) is about nature and history and, in momentous phrases, declares that there is always causality in some sense. Nothing happens by chance or luck. Hence, if something terrifying happens – such as invasion and occupation by an enemy – we are meant to ask why this is happening:

> Do two walk together,
>   unless they have agreed to meet?
> Does a lion roar in the forest,
>   when he has no prey?
> Does a young lion cry out from his den,
>   if he has taken nothing? (vv.3–4).

When we ask about the causes of events, we must take into account the principles of God's acting in history. An account of causes based upon ordinary vision and natural reason is simply not adequate. In situations of terrifying horror we are to see the hand of God in judgment (v.6); through his prophets – such as Amos, Elijah and others – God also reveals the principles behind his actions. There is always a reason for what happens, no matter how terrible that happening is.

In chapter 4, Amos declares that God has sent various troubles and afflictions upon the people of Israel in order to teach them a lesson. Indeed, many of their troubles and afflictions (famine and drought among them) were actually listed as examples of judgments in Deuteronomy 28–30. Yet, despite all these curses, the nation has failed to understand; it has not returned to God in repentance and renewed obedience. God speaks satirically through Amos about their numerous sacrifices at the chief sanctuaries; the futility of these is revealed by the continuance of God's judgments upon his people.

Many other prophets proclaimed God's judgment against the Northern Kingdom. Some of Hosea's prophecies and denouncements were both particular and universal as they dealt both with a particular situation and with the underlying principles. Perhaps only as little as fifty years ago, theologians and readers would not have understood the following passage (Hosea 4:1–3) as well as we understand it today with our heightened awareness of the curse of pollution and the importance of ecology:

> Hear the word of the Lord, O children of Israel,
>   for the Lord has a controversy with the inhabitants of the land.
> There is no faithfulness or steadfast love,
>   and no knowledge of God in the land;
>   there is swearing, lying, murder, stealing, and committing
>   adultery;
>   they break all bounds, and bloodshed follows bloodshed.
> Therefore the land mourns,
>   and all who dwell in it languish,
>   and also the beasts of the field
>   and the birds of the heavens,
>   and even the fish of the sea are taken away (Hosea 4:1–3).

Ecological problems do not come by accident. The hand of God, moving in history (in this case clearly in judgment) is behind them. It is not merely a natural event that 'the land mourns'; God is actively steering his people back to obedience, back to blessing instead of cursing.

Eventually the supreme social judgment came upon the Northern Kingdom for their hardened attitude of sin and rebellion against God. They lost their territory, an ultimate lesson about how seriously God takes the matter. In the ninth year of Hosea, the last king of the Northern Kingdom, the Israelites were subdued and carried away to Assyria. That this happened as a result of their sin is clear from 2 Kings 17, which catalogues their sins (v.7 ff.). God was angry; they had sinned against their Lord. They not only practised idol worship (v.16) but all manner of things associated with it, such as human sacrifice (v.17). As well as outlining the sins which led to this dire judgment the chapter emphasizes the extent of the clear warnings that God had given them. As a leading point it mentions that God had sent his prophets: 'The Lord warned Israel and Judah by every prophet and every seer, saying "Turn from your evil ways and keep my commandments and my statues, in accordance with all the laws which I commanded your fathers, and which I sent to you by my servants the prophets"' (v.13). In his love and care for their nation, God wished for the people to understand, to see the meaning of what was happening to them in history.

Both Israel and Judah were warned by prophets. It was to be some time before the Southern Kingdom, Judah, was also occupied and exiled – losing its territory in drastic judgment. An important event in the South was the reforms under King Josiah. Judah had completely forgotten God: the Bible (the extent of which then was probably the Books of Moses) had been neglected, left in some corner or attic, perhaps under rubbish.

In 2 Kings 22 (and a parallel passage in 2 Chronicles 34) we learn that the book, or scroll as it was, was rediscovered and read by the king.

Through reading it he discovered God's anger against national sin and disobedience; he discovered the principles of God's acting in history. He ordered some of his servants and the priest to enquire of a prophetess about it, for clarification and advice. She gave them a clear and unequivocal answer (2 Kings 22:15 ff.): firstly she confirmed that the king's understanding of the book was exactly right; God's curse was certainly coming against Judah, and it was fully deserved (16,17). Secondly she added that because the king had heeded the book, listened carefully to what it said and humbled himself, the judgment would not fall upon him, even though there certainly was to be a general judgment upon the nation eventually. In other words, the king would be blessed rather than cursed (vv.18–20).

A number of principles are reaffirmed here. The leading one is that if people and individuals listen to God, he will bless them; if they ignore his good commands, they will reap his curse. Another is that God sometimes makes exceptions in a time of social judgment to bless an individual. The following chapters will fill in more detail on God's dealing with individuals in a time of wickedness. The general, inviolable principle is that hearkening to God eventually results in blessing, while a heedless attitude will lead to cursing.

Jeremiah was a prophet in the Southern Kingdom of Judah from the time of his calling during the reign of King Josiah (626 BC) up to the fall of Jerusalem (587 BC). God raised him up to denounce the disobedience of the nation and to point out the significance of the curses that fell upon them. In Jeremiah 29, a remarkable chapter, there is an almost exact quotation from Deuteronomy 29 in which the prophet in vivid language describes the judgments falling upon Judah, such as famine and pestilence (Jeremiah 29:18). The idea is repeated that God has persistently sent his prophets to them, but that they have not been heeded (29:19).

It is a common emphasis throughout the periods of judgment that God sent his prophets to make it quite clear that he was working in history in these curses, just as he was working at times in blessing. The prophets reiterated the great principles of God's hand in history, along the lines of Deuteronomy 28–30, so that the nation would be without excuse – they could not blame other circumstances for their national misfortunes. God would not allow them, for instance, to blame their troubles upon magic (Jeremiah 29:8, 9).

The outcome of national disobedience against God for both the kingdoms of Israel and Judah was captivity and exile. He had promised many times that if his people did not believe, he would come with *real*, tangible judgments that would hurt – famine, pestilence, disease, and ultimately enemies that would overcome them. In Jeremiah 51 the nature of this victorious enemy is revealed: he is a cup in the hands of God, an instrument God uses, who too will ultimately be destroyed.

God's tool of judgment against Judah would be Babylon. Through Jeremiah, God declares:

> You are my hammer and weapon of war:
>   with you I break nations in pieces;
>   with you I destroy kingdoms (Jeremiah 51:20).

In modern terminology, it is as if God said, 'You are my gun.' His direct hand is behind the Babylon's oppression of Judah which resulted in captivity and exile. It is quite clear, however, that God, while using the enemy as his instrument of judgment, does not approve of war crimes. It is also absolutely clear that the enemy is not favoured by God (as was already made evident in Solomon's prayer). In fact, this chapter – Jeremiah 51 – contains also his judgment against Babylon; he judged the enemy of Judah even though he used them. Such disastrous happenings as invasion and defeat by an enemy are *never* accidental. Furthermore, these principles of God's hand in history still hold in our own day. Tomorrow the instrument in God's judging hand may be the Chinese.

In Ezekiel 22 the consequences of the great sins of Judah are declared: God's judgment is that through their enemies they are to become a joke; they are to be scattered among the nations and derided: 'Therefore I have made you a reproach to the nations, and a mocking to all the countries. Those who are near and those who are far from you will mock you, you infamous one, full of tumult' (vv.4, 5).

This principle does not apply solely to Judah. It applies throughout history. It applies to apostate societies and cultures today.

3
Refinement 1: Good People in a Time of Wickedness

It is a clear biblical principle that God's cursing or judgment, though it may not be immediate, most certainly comes as a direct and personal response to a society's disobedience and faithlessness, while his blessing with equal certainty comes in response to obedience and faithfulness. We must not be afraid of using the Old Testament term 'covenant'. God made a promise to, or covenant with, his people that had conditions: if you go my way, such and such will happen; if you do not go my way, something else will happen. God is Lord also of the non-covenant nations or societies (such as Assyria or Nineveh), that is, those nations or groups to whom he has not explicitly revealed his wishes in so many words. The principles of blessing and cursing apply to all societies and to all history. Clearly there are many refinements of, and details to, the biblical portrait of God's hand in history. The details are not the same, for example, for a believing nation as they are for unbelievers: a believing nation will reap greater judgment if they become apostate. Further refinements or details include the fact that, although judgment is very real and solid, God is always open to a repentant society: he is willing to accept sorrow, or 'mourning', and to forgive – those who mourn are blessed (Matthew 5:4). People are always free to alter history.

As the Old Testament unfolds, more and more details of and refinements to its portrait of God's dealing in history are brought out. Our next three chapters will consider some of these complexities. Many of them raise some of humanity's deepest questions: How does God deal with the individual as well as a society? What happens to a good individual (like Jeremiah) in a time of national judgment? What about a wicked person living in a good period of peace, godliness, security and the like? We must beware of oversimplification: the Bible gives a carefully balanced portrait of history that is neither individualistic nor communistic.

Why do the godly suffer?

Psalm 44 takes us into a characteristic and important refinement of the historical portrait. This Psalm is a cry to God for help, a group lament. It points out, in addressing God, that he has given them great things, huge blessings – notably their land. They praise him for this. Nevertheless, a strange note has crept in.

> But you have rejected us and disgraced us
> and have not gone out with our armies (Psalm 44:9).

Things have gone nightmarishly wrong: so bad, in fact, that they have become a byword to other nations.

> You have made us a byword among the nations,
> a laughingstock among the peoples (44:14).

This is odd, they point out, because they have not forgotten God, nor forsaken his way (vv.17, 18).

> All this has come upon us,
> though we have not forgotten you,
> and we have not been false to your covenant.
> Our heart has not turned back,
> nor have our steps departed from your way.

The Psalm ends in very great emotional appeal to God to help them in their national anguish.

What has happened? The people of this psalm have fulfilled all the conditions of obedience laid down in Deuteronomy 28–30, yet very real judgments rather than blessings have come their way. The answer to this problem is brought out in the Book of Isaiah.

> Because of the iniquity of his unjust gain I was angry,
> I struck him; I hid my face and was angry,
> but he went on backsliding in the way of his own heart.
> I have seen his ways, but I will heal him;
> I will lead him and restore comfort to him and his mourners
> (Isaiah 57:17–18).

These people are, in fact, a minority within the disobedient nation. Though most of the nation has disobeyed God's rules, some people have remained faithful to him. Yet the whole nation suffers the effects of the judgments, the punishments promised for a disobedient society. God, however, has not forgotten the group that 'mourn'; the group that are repentant and sorry before him. His judgments will not last for ever: he will eventually heal and console.

There are many recent examples of this principle in action. One could think of the Huguenots in France or, in the twentieth century, of the underground church in Eastern Europe. There are many other such minority groups – faithful, godly people who suffer for the sake of their apostate nations. When God is forgotten, his believers are likewise forgotten and suffer in various ways, sometimes overt persecution and death, sometimes the real curses that God is bringing against their society.

Psalm 73 reveals more of this particular refinement of the great principles of history. When a group of people hate God (expressed in disobedience and rebellion), they naturally hate the people of God around them. Even in a period of material prosperity, if the time is ungodly, believers may have a hard time:

> For I was envious of the arrogant
>   when I saw the prosperity of the wicked.
> All in vain have I kept my heart clean
>   and washed my hands in innocence.
> For all the day long I have been stricken
>   and rebuked every morning.
> If I had said, 'I will speak thus,'
>   I would have betrayed the generation of your children.
>
> (Psalm 73:3,13–15)

In history there are many records of Christians being killed at such times. This psalm sounds a different note from that of Psalm 44. It does not directly ask God for an explanation of the believers' suffering. It seeks its own answer within the course of the psalm. It does it like this: the psalmist, in a manner rather similar to the Job, reflects on the apparent contradiction that

> Truly God is good to Israel,
>   to those who are pure in heart, (v.1)

yet bad people, arrogant before God, are prospering in the world over which God is sovereign. (Job's problem is that of a good person suffering rather than of the wicked prospering.) The psalmist is tempted to doubt God's faithfulness: he has prayed and listened to God in vain – the whole thing seems meaningless. He has tried to understand but could not. The turning point comes in verse 17: he did something, and then he understood. He went into God's sanctuary (in modern terms, into the church):

> But when I thought how to understand this,
>   it seemed to me a wearisome task,
>   until I went into the sanctuary of God;
>   then I discerned their end (16–17).

He perceived that he had been shortsighted, not looking at how the wicked ended up. Though all looked good for the wicked, there was absolutely no security for them, for God was not the support of their lives.

Looking at Psalm 44 alongside the verses from Isaiah 57:17, 18 and this Psalm 73, we see that there are two factors to understand when asking about the predicament of the faithful in difficult times:

1. Look back in history to Abraham, Moses and others. The great principles always hold – blessing for obedience; cursing for faithlessness. A minority of good people, however, will inevitably suffer.

2. Consider the real finale of the wicked – not prosperity, success and self-sufficiency but worms and the real dust of what death ultimately means for them – futility.

Do the principles no longer hold?

The problem of believers' suffering, which apparently denies the great principles of history, continues to be explored in the book of Job. There, off-stage as it were, unknown to Job, God allows Satan, the enemy of humankind, to afflict Job. Satan argues that Job, a godly man, is only faithful because he is prosperous. Take away his prosperity and he will lose his faith along with it. This discussion in the unseen world is never revealed to Job, but he continues faithfully despite great physical and mental suffering and the loss of those closest to him.

Job asks: 'What is happening? Why am I suffering in this appalling way? What has happened to the principles I've lived by? Surely the rule is that if one is righteous, God will send blessing, and I have been godly.' Job's friends contradict him; they say that the answer to the problem is that he must have sinned against God. His sincere reply is that he is not a sinner in that sense; he has always confessed his sins in repentance. Had he sinned, he would have accepted the situation. The rules have not changed; the principles of God's acting in history held: that God rewards faithfulness with real blessings. Thus Job's real suffering, as a faithful man, presents a stubborn problem to him. The final conclusion, however, is God's vindication of Job. Job has been right all along; the principles hold. Job is no exception to the rule; his faithfulness has not led God to punish him. But the story goes deeper, for God points out that some things by necessity must be beyond human understanding. He asks Job where he was when God created the world. God as creator has full understanding of Job's case, but Job as a created being has only a limited insight into it. God points out, however, that Job was quite right to be puzzled and perplexed about his situation.

One of the sorest challenges to Job came from the friend who suggested to him that perhaps God had brought the trouble upon him to teach him something – a pious thought. It is noteworthy that God's vindication of Job includes his direct rejection of this seemingly pious suggestion.

The book ends with God's restoring his full blessing to Job. No repentance on Job's part is required. In fact, repentance would have shown a failure to trust in the principles of God's dealing with people in history. We, as readers, are allowed to see what is happening in the unseen world in Job's case, and thus to see (as he was not allowed to) why he suffered. We also see, as he only saw by faith, that the principles of blessing and cursing did not change in his case. Job's friends, however, relied upon their natural, reduced understanding of the situation and came to totally wrong conclusions.

We may well look at what goes on under the sun and think to ourselves, 'Look how the ungodly have such a good time, while people who stay faithful to God are often having a bad time!' The answer to our unspoken question is in Ecclesiastes: 'Because the sentence against an evil deed is not executed speedily, the heart of the children of man is fully set to do evil' (Ecclesiastes 8:11).

The point of this verse is that we must look closer still at the situation. What is really going on? Sometimes judgment is slow in coming, and people then presume that it will not come. The psalmist saw this when he reflected upon how the wicked end up. It is our vision that is wrong; the principles do not change. We always expect *immediate* judgment upon the ungodly and *immediate* blessing upon God's people. The rules, however, are in force and shaping events even when we do not see them worked out fully.

If we are living through a time of real blessing – all the good and full things of life which hearten a person – then thank God. But in times (like today) when the great rules or principles do not always seem to apply, we should take a closer look. We should understand what is really going on.

The prophet Habakkuk, preaching in the last days of the kingdom of Judah, vividly points out that their enemies are practising terrible things against the godly.

> You who are of purer eyes than to see evil
>   and cannot look at wrong,
> why do you idly look at traitors
>   and are silent when the wicked swallows up
> the man more righteous than he? (Habakkuk 1:13)

Why does God not see what they are doing, he asks, if God is ruler of the world? Habakkuk even takes himself off to the watchtower to see what God will do about the situation. God's response takes a long-term view. 'So you think that there will be no judgment? My judgment will eventually come – it is inexorable.'

> And the Lord answered me:
> 'Write the vision;
>   make it plain on tablets,
>   so he may run who reads it.
> For still the vision awaits its appointed time;
>   it hastens to the end—it will not lie.

> If it seems slow, wait for it;
> it will surely come; it will not delay (Habakkuk 2:2,3).

In other words, the great principles are reaffirmed: blessing upon the good, cursing upon the wicked. The basic point is that the godly must live by faith, not that they have *immediate* and automatic prosperity and security from terror. Eventually, indeed, the world will be 'filled with the knowledge of the glory of God' (v.14) in the final balancing. Even we in the late twentieth century have not seen this accomplished yet, though probably we see it more than Habakkuk did. But like him, first and foremost we must live by faith and not judge by the immediate, short-term situation.

This problem of the apparent contradictions of the great historical principles of blessing and cursing is taken up in the New as well as the Old Testament. To turn again to the metaphor of a painting, the refining of the grand lines of the biblical portrait of history is continued throughout the Bible. In Romans 1–8, Paul gives a summary of the whole gospel, ending with his triumphant song celebrating that nothing can separate us from the love of God in Christ (Romans 8:35–39). But then chapter 9 addresses the urgent question: What of the unbelieving Jews who were God's people under the covenant? What is their status now that Christ has come? God's promise to Abraham has not failed, Paul argues, as it was not merely to his *physical* descendants who are the true descendants of Abraham in whom God's promise is fulfilled. But his descendants include non-Jews from all ethnic groups and, indeed, many Jews are rejected; this has always been the case. It is not a contradiction of God's promised blessing. Esau, for example, rejected God's blessing; he was not chosen by God. The basic refinement of the portrait that is added here is that wherever God's people are found, God's choice is involved in the relationship. The same is true of those who are ungodly – those who disobey him and whom he judges according to the principles of Deuteronomy 28–30.

Now Esau voluntarily refused to accept God's blessing, so it is not the case that God *arbitrarily* 'hated' him (Romans 9:13). When in verse 15 Paul repeats God's declaration, 'I will have mercy on whom I have mercy,' what may we say? It appears to be predestination. Is God all-powerful in the way that he acts in history, so that what happens *must* happen?

Clearly, to be fatalistic at this point would be wrong. In the case of Esau, for example, he both refused to accept God's blessing and was rejected by God. We should be wrong to speak as if Esau's refusal was God's fault or to blame all wickedness on God. There are some matters and causal relationships which we simply cannot understand, even though the rules and principles of God's acting in history always apply. If we speak as if it all were God's fault, we are in fact implicitly saying: God, why did you not do things *this* way or *that* way? In other words we are judging the matter by our natural reason and according to natural causality; we are ignoring the hidden and richer level of God's acting in and from the unseen world. But then we judge from an inadequate view of what goes on behind a historical (as opposed to a merely natural) event. We reject the principles which control the very meaning of history.

Paul certainly does not take the view that God's choosing and acting is arbitrary. He admits in Romans 9:20: 'Will what is moulded say to its moulder, "Why have you made me like this?"' and at the same time points out that, as beings made by God, we have no right to argue that, because his will is irresistible, God cannot find fault with us and judge us. The book of Revelation, as we shall see, takes us a significant step further into the mysterious choices and actions of God in history. There is a mystery, a secret that belongs to God. An angel swears that there should be no more delay, so that 'in the days of the trumpet call to be sounded by the seventh angel, the mystery of God would be fulfilled, just as he announced to his servants the prophet' (Revelation 10:7).

Thus, although there is a mystery behind history, there will come a day when we shall understand. The secret will be revealed.

If we have a good relationship with God, as with any other person, there can be secrets. God does not have to tell us everything. It is only when there is something wrong in a relationship that we fear secrets. If we trust God, we will accept the fact that there are such secrets. In the end, we are promised, we shall see that what at present is secret is good. There are no dirty tricks behind God's dealing with us in history, either on an individual or a social level.

This necessity for trust, for acknowledging that the pot cannot comprehend the potter, that Hamlet cannot know everything about Shakespeare, is brought out in Ezekiel's words, which suggest how easy it is for us to have our eyes merely on the short-term. They suggest that sometimes God's blessing is so very long in coming that it seems too late before it comes. In human terms, there now seems no point in God doing anything, for the worst possible disaster has happened:

> For thus says the Lord God: 'How much more when I send upon Jerusalem my fourscore acts of judgment, sword, famine, evil beasts, and pestilence, to cut off from it man and beast! Yet, if there should be left in it any survivors to lead out sons and daughters, when they come forth to you, and you see their ways and their doings, you will be consoled for the evil that I have brought upon it.' (Ezekiel 14:21, 22)

The promise here is that if we were able to see the blessing of God that might follow even the very worst catastrophe, we should be consoled.

Clearly everything in history is not plain and obvious to our natural vision. We have to trust that God acts consistently and faithfully according to his own rules and principles: the great Deuteronomic principles of history presenting the life-and-death choice between blessing and cursing. We do not and cannot always see how what God is doing at a particular moment of history fits into these inviolable principles. We have to look to the future in hope, and to trust that God will do what he is doing in accordance with these principles. Then, like Job's, our faithfulness will be vindicated. But, like Job, we may have to suffer first.

4
Refinement 2: When God has to Judge, What Happens to Mercy?

Here we shall continue to add more details to refine the portrait of history brought out earlier. This will also prepare the way for a consideration in the next chapter of what it means to say that God is hidden – as, in some sense, he is – at our present moment of history.

The Old Testament records that the Jews were God's chosen people, yet in Isaiah God speaks of Judah as if the nation were the people of Sodom and Gomorrah, whom God could no longer endure!

> Hear the word of the Lord,
>   you rulers of Sodom!
> Give ear to the teaching of our God,
>   you people of Gomorrah! ...
> Your new moons and your appointed feasts
>   my soul hates;
> they have become a burden to me;
>   I am weary of bearing them.
> When you spread out your hands,
>   I will hide my eyes from you;
> even though you make many prayers,
>   I will not listen;
>   your hands are full of blood (Isaiah 1:10,14–15).

In verses 16 and 17 of the same passage, however, the prophet Isaiah urges a return to the Lord: if the people would come back to God, he will certainly forgive their wickedness and sin. God's horror at his people is tempered by the wonderful biblical teaching that he forgives, although this is far from being an automatic process, as if God were a forgiving machine, responding to the correct buttons being pressed. The stamp of God's character in his forgiveness is clearly spelled out in the book of Ezekiel, where there is a sort of refrain, 'You shall know that I am the Lord' (e.g. 16:62), that is, God's character stamps all his actions, including his forgiveness.

It is quite obvious that in such a period as is here described by Isaiah, when there is injustice and oppression of the poor and disadvantaged (cf. 1:17), many of the unpleasant features of life flow naturally from wrongdoing. High criminality, for example, restricts the freedom of the nation. Isaiah shows that there are not merely natural consequences, but that God is working in and directing events and will continue to do so over and above any natural process:

> If you refuse and rebel,
> > you shall be eaten by the sword;
> > for the mouth of the Lord has spoken (Isaiah 1:20).

Natural causality and divine action are both involved. In a bad period, when everyone is wicked, people become debased and their inhumanity to others increases (as we witness in our own day). There is cruelty and violation beyond thinkable imagination. But it is also God who brings people down, enmeshed in his curses. By the same token, it is God who lifts us up, as a mother lifts her fallen child and comforts him or her. God is angry when people walk in the wrong way, flouting the rules that make life possible and wholesome; but he is willing to forgive. His holiness and justice are terribly apparent when he comes in judgment, but it is justice and holiness with love. There is no tyranny on God's part, no law without love.

Again and again God declared: if you walk in my way, I will bless you with all the fullness of human life and experience. One reason for judgment is to show to people – stubborn and tending to learn our lessons the hard way – that God is a living, holy God. He acts in history and will take nothing but obedience, a humble attitude and repentance at such times as it is necessary. If we grasp the real meaning of a judgment and return to him, he will certainly accept us. There is no period of history in which God is not open to people returning to him.

Waiting for God

Isaiah is a difficult book to read. As readers we continually find ourselves asking: To whom is the prophet speaking? There are, in fact, two audiences being addressed. The one is the audience of those who do not love God and reveal their lack of love in disobedience, those who consequently receive a message of judgment. The other is the audience of those who fear God and therefore listen carefully to the prophet for advice and counsel on how to live. There is both a negative and a positive audience, a negative and a positive message.

One of those positive messages occurs in Isaiah 30, a chapter which points out the futility of Judah's military reliance upon Egypt. Isaiah, on the contrary, reveals that God's plan is for them to still themselves, trusting in him, and staying where they are.

> For thus said the Lord God, the Holy One of Israel,
> 'In returning and rest you shall be saved;
> > in quietness and in trust shall be your strength' (Isaiah 30:15).

God desires that they do not try to change the predicament that they face on account of Assyria's hostility. They are not to try to change their situation themselves; they are to wait as, in fact, God is doing something that is much too big for them to have done by themselves. He is coming with his judgment – Assyria is his instrument of judgment. The invader itself will be cursed, however (Isaiah 10:5, 6,12). Blessed are those who wait for his judgment (Isaiah 30:18) and its outcome.

Such waiting is very difficult. Patience, however, is an important principle in the Bible. It is very human to rush, but God sometimes waits hundreds of years before doing something. There are many stories in the Bible about waiting for God's time. Believers might find themselves waiting for God's judgment. This is not easy, as such a time is difficult for both Christians and non-Christians. The very fish in the sea may die (Hosea 4:3).

Isaiah 30:27–33 vividly describes the coming of God's judgment against mighty Assyria; the imagery speaks of storm and thunder: 'And the Lord will cause his majestic voice to be heard and the descending blow of his arm to be seen, in furious anger and a flame of devouring fire, with a cloudburst and storm and hailstones. The Assyrians will be terror-stricken at the voice of the Lord, when he strikes with his rod.'

It always happens that both believers and non-believers fail to see God working in this kind of judgment. He warns us in many places not to be too quick to assess the situation; not to be too hasty in denying that God's hand is behind it. The enemy can be his instrument, even though enemies are really enemies. In a time of judgment and of doubt and uncertainty, he will help the weak and give his strength to the faithful; he will truly console.

In Isaiah 30 we find again the two categories of people, the two 'races' which can be traced back to Seth and Cain, the godly and the ungodly. Both are addressed with the message of God's impending judgment, both hear it but they respond differently: positively or negatively. The setting is just before Israel's fall and exile, executed by Assyria, and Isaiah was forecasting this catastrophic event.

Jeremiah is a very different prophet from Isaiah. He prophesied in Judea in quite different circumstances. The Judeans eventually were made captive by the new conquerors, the Babylonians, and exiled. Jeremiah held a high place in his society. In modern terms, his status was something like that of a Prime Minister. On one occasion he had to write a speech twice because the King tore the original copy up (Jeremiah 36:32). He was, most of all, a prophet from God announcing the inevitability of judgment upon the nation. When Judah eventually was invaded, Jeremiah was not taken by surprise. God had warned his people centuries ago that they would lose their national territory if they persisted in sin.

Again and again in history people claim that they are not sinners. The Judeans – who of all people should have known better – were no exception and they even killed God's prophets, who pointed out their sin, and ignored the tell-tale signs of God's judgment:

> Why do you contend with me?
>> You have all transgressed against me,
> declares the Lord.
> In vain have I struck your children;
>> they took no correction;
> your own sword devoured your prophets
>> like a ravening lion (Jeremiah 2:29,30).

God does not come in history in judgment because people are sinners (we are all sinners), but because people claim that they have not done wrong even though they know that they have. A society might claim that it is righteous and 'Christian': in Judah's case, the people obviously persuaded themselves that they were entitled to kill the prophets who spoke against them. St Paul was referring to the same attitude when he pointed out that as people we suppress the truth in our unrighteousness (Romans 1:18).

What happens when judgment is inexorable?

In Jeremiah 15 we find a new and startling thought with deep implications. The Lord declares that *even if* Moses and Samuel were before him, pleading for Jerusalem, he would not relent and turn from his judgment, a judgment of famine, death and captivity.

> Then the Lord said to me, 'Though Moses and Samuel stood before me, yet my heart would not turn toward this people. Send them out of my sight, and let them go! And when they ask you, "Where shall we go?" you shall say to them, "Thus says the Lord:
>
>> Those who are for pestilence, to pestilence,
>>> and those who are for the sword, to the sword;
>> those who are for famine, to famine,
>>> and those who are for captivity, to captivity"' (Jeremiah 15:1-2).

Even though there were good people like Moses around – one of the greatest of all men – it would not make any difference. It is futile for people to point out to God that there are some righteous people in Judah. Even if Noah or Job were there, the judgment would not pass by: 'I will make you serve your enemies in a land that you do not know, for in my anger a fire is kindled that shall burn for ever' (Jeremiah 15:14).

Along these lines of the inevitability of God's judgment, is Jeremiah 45, a very brief, personal chapter that is one of the most beautiful in the Bible. It is addressed to Baruch, Jeremiah's secretary. He was a brilliant young man who had made his first step in a great career. But as he wrote out Jeremiah's words, he realized that, in fact, there was no future for him. He was to be a captive, at best. It is like my secretary reading in my work that we are all soon due to be transported to Siberia. (In the Second World War it might have been transportation to Poland, as happened to me.) Jeremiah has a special message of consolation for him, that he will not be killed in the holocaust:

> The word that Jeremiah the prophet spoke to Baruch the son of Neriah, when he wrote these words in a book at the dictation of Jeremiah, in the fourth year of Jehoiakim the son of Josiah, king of Judah: 'Thus says the Lord, the God of Israel, to you, O Baruch: You said, "Woe is me! For the Lord has added sorrow to my pain. I am weary with my groaning, and I find no rest." Thus shall you say to him, Thus says the Lord: Behold, what I have built I am breaking down, and what I have planted I am plucking up – that is, the whole land. And do you seek great things for yourself? Seek them not, for behold, I am bringing disaster upon all flesh, declares the Lord. But I will give you your life as a prize of war in all places to which you may go' (Jeremiah 45).

There is a lesson here for believers today. We are living in a time of judgment; for instance, we have affluence, but without joy. In these difficulties God takes personal care of us, his people, just as he had a special, personal concern for Baruch. He promises his care and concern, even though God's judgment is a difficult time for all of us: the judgment is *real* and it hurts.

Another instance of God's personal attention to, and care of, his own people occurs in Jeremiah 39:15–19. Jeremiah had been confined in a filthy cistern for his honest preaching of the inevitability of Jerusalem's downfall, but had been rescued by a certain Ebed-melech, an Ethiopian. In return, Jeremiah receives a special message from God for Ebed-melech that he will not be slain during the general judgment upon the city.

> The word of the Lord came to Jeremiah while he was shut up in the court of the guard: 'Go, and say to Ebed-melech the Ethiopian, "Thus says the Lord of hosts, the God of Israel: Behold, I will fulfil my words against this city for harm and not for good, and they shall be accomplished before you on that day. But I will deliver you on that day, declares the Lord, and you shall not be given into the hand of the men of whom you are afraid. For I will surely save you, and you shall not fall by the sword, but you shall have your life as a prize of war, because you have put your trust in me, declares the Lord"' (Jeremiah 39:15–18).

The book of the prophet Ezekiel takes us forward in time from Jeremiah's context to the captivity in Babylon. Ezekiel lived at the beginning of Judah's captivity. He points out that there is a purpose, meaning and reason behind the captivity: through it, God's nation (at least, those that survived death) will acknowledge their sin and disobedience.

> I will leave some of you alive. When you have among the nations some who escape the sword, and when you are scattered through the countries, then those of you who escape will remember me among the nations where they are carried captive, how I have been broken over their whoring heart that has departed from me and over their eyes that go whoring after their idols. And they will be loathsome in their own sight for the evils that they have committed, for all their abominations. And they shall know that I am the Lord. I have not said in vain that I would do this evil to them (Ezekiel 6:8–10).

God has not 'said in vain' that he would place this terrible judgment on them; it has meaning (v.10). It is not futile and wasted. This is a consolation for the believer (see also Ezekiel 14:21–23).

Ezekiel 18 deals at length with the theme of every individual's own responsibility – an important refinement of the principles of history. If a son and daughter are bad, yet their father is a good man, God will still judge the son and the daughter. Conversely, if there is a bad father, and a good son or daughter, God will accept the latter. God cares for the individual.

> You say, 'Why should not the son suffer for the iniquity of the father?' When the son has done what is just and right, and has been careful to observe all my statutes, he shall surely live. The soul who sins shall die. The son shall not suffer for the iniquity of the father, nor the father suffer for the iniquity of the son. The righteousness of the righteous shall be upon himself, and the wickedness of the wicked shall be upon himself (Ezekiel 18:19–20).

Repentance implies the reality of responsibility. The principle always holds that if an individual or nation (or other grouping) returns to God, he accepts us. But our repentance must be visible, must show through. God will help the repentant and give him or her strength. This does not contradict the principle of judgment.

Zephaniah prophesied earlier than Ezekiel, before the fall of Jerusalem and Judah. His book opens with an announcement that God's judgment is coming – the terrible catastrophe that Ezekiel was later to experience. Zephaniah also later in his book addresses the faithful in the light of this impending judgment. He tells them how they will seek righteousness, be humble and 'seek refuge in the name of the Lord':

> On that day you shall not be put to shame
>   because of the deeds by which you have rebelled against me;
> for then I will remove from your midst
>   your proudly exultant ones,
> and you shall no longer be haughty
>   in my holy mountain.
> But I will leave in your midst
>   a people humble and lowly.

> They shall seek refuge in the name of the Lord,
>   those who are left in Israel;
> they shall do no injustice
>   and speak no lies,
> nor shall there be found in their mouth
>   a deceitful tongue.
> For they shall graze and lie down,
> and none shall make them afraid (Zephaniah 3:11–13).

All this promise of consolation is very real to us, for we live in a time of deepening judgment. What are we to do as believers? What is our response? Clearly, we cannot put a halt to the judgment, for it is God's work and doing. On the other hand, we must not hasten it by becoming disengaged from the sorrows of our lands (if we even have that luxury). There are things we must continue to do: we have our conscience, our sense of responsibility, our feeling for suffering and human loss, our righteousness. We are just little people with limited possibilities, but we have to *practise* the truth according to our knowledge; we are to be full of wisdom. God is working, and we must be faithful. Meanwhile, it may be that God will save us from harm, just as he spared many of his people during the occupation of Judah and the fall of Jerusalem, people like Baruch and Jeremiah.

5
Refinement 3: The Hidden God

Malachi the prophet lived about four hundred years before Christ, yet what he writes about his day is remarkably similar to what we observe in our day. People then said that God is dead, or at least, that he is not working or that he can be safely dismissed from consideration. People then said, in effect, 'Why must we use old-fashioned words like "sin"?' Rather as people today do not like referring to 'blood' in religion, they then said that it makes no difference at all whether or not one is a believer, faithful to God:

> Your words have been hard against me, says the Lord. But you say, 'How have we spoken against you?' You have said, 'It is vain to serve God. What is the profit of our keeping his charge or of walking as in mourning before the Lord of hosts? And now we call the arrogant blessed. Evildoers not only prosper but they put God to the test and they escape' (Malachi 3:13–15).

In such a situation, what should the faithful reply?

> Then those who feared the Lord spoke with one another. The Lord paid attention and heard them, and a book of remembrance was written before him of those who feared the Lord and esteemed his name. 'They shall be mine, says the Lord of hosts, in the day when I make up my treasured possession, and I will spare them as a man spares his son who serves him. Then once more you shall see the distinction between the righteous and the wicked, between one who serves God and one who does not serve him' (3:16–18).

Malachi affirms that there is a difference between the believer and non-believer. Furthermore, God knows who's who: he keeps a book of Remembrance, recording the struggles of his faithful people. We shall come across this book again in Revelation.

This is a consolation to believers, because even the faithful sometimes lose hope. One day they will understand, when they see the real difference between the righteous and wicked, not as a theoretical matter but *see* it tangibly. God does not forget his people, even when he does not seem to be present and active.

There is a mistaken theology today that speaks of a 'hidden God'. It is a great mistake to fail to ask *why* God is *sometimes* (not always) hidden. This hiddenness is part of God's judgment. Temporarily it is as if there were no God. At such a time (and today is such a time) blessed are those who mourn, who are meek, who follow the other injunctions of Zephaniah we came across at the end of the last chapter.

People today say that the point of view of the Bible is something of the past. We live in a new world. The God of the Bible, of the Old and New Testament, is dead, which means that we need not look to him. People now think in a different framework. Religion is seen as something subjective, and 'God' is merely a name for the projection of their human thoughts, wishes, fears and hopes, outside of themselves. People argue, 'Isn't it a sacrifice of our intellects to believe in the miraculous things that the Bible talks about? Shouldn't we understand those things differently, now that we have come of age?'

Thoughts like these are the starting point of the modern theologians. They are concerned about Christianity in our world, and now they have invented a 'God' to their liking in the hope of meeting modern people on their own ground. But this new God is not the God of Scripture, and so there can be no faith that God's word will remain for ever. It is a capitulation to the world view of modern people, a compromise which leaves the Christian with nothing to say. Maybe it meets a human psychological and social need for religion – but Christianity is not in the first place a religion. It is an assertion of the truth that God lives, and that he acts.

The modern world has found that the reduction of the world to 'what it really is', the things seen or understood by natural reason and the five senses, has led to a technocracy in which human beings have become machines and have lost their personality and, in a way, their very identity. When people today say that the world is bad, that its basic principles are wrong and that things must be changed, they often go on to accuse Christianity of creating the problems, instead of understanding that it is not Christianity but the apostasy from Christianity that has led our world into its present condition. The principles of the Age of Reason, worked out in the French Revolution and followed in the same direction for a century and a half after that, have created the problems. That there are problems is true, but Christianity should not be blamed.

Or should it? A biblical 'walking in God's ways' cannot be blamed and, as I have said, the principles of the modern world really mean apostasy from the God of Scripture, but maybe Christianity in the sense of the Christian churches can be blamed. The church can be blamed for letting the world accept the view that Christianity is a 'religion', and as such a completely subjective personal thing, to be kept out of politics, scholarship, public decisions and day-to-day life. In humanistic ethics, however, much of biblical ethics still remained and so our culture did not collapse immediately. The spiritual force of tradition and the living faith of Christians in some places still were active. But in many ways Christians did withdraw.

Hidden Christianity?

The main reason why Christians withdrew may be found in the principle that has crippled Christianity for so many centuries, namely the idea of a division between nature and grace – that life is divided into a spiritual realm, where the biblical truth is real and true, and another realm, the realm of nature, where we must act out of common sense or live by 'natural revelation', the 'obvious' reality of the world around us, and where things are more or less neutral as long as one keeps the basic moral principles. On this basis many Christians have led a double life: being devout Christians but alongside that living another 'natural' life in their work as scientists, scholars, officials, managers, business executives, economists, artists and so on. Often they have felt that something was wrong, they had a bad conscience. Should one not live totally as a Christian? For that reason many have longed to be pastors or missionaries in order to work more fully 'for the Lord'. They did not see that they could, and should, work in their own fields as 'total' Christians, obeying their calling. For they did not see that those secular fields were not secular in the sense of 'unchristian' but secular in the sense of not being 'religious'. God is the God of all life, and the Bible talks about the whole of life – in that sense the Bible is not a 'religious book'.

As time went on and the unchristian principles of the Enlightenment were increasingly worked out in many fields, Christians more and more felt the problems of working in that atmosphere and, in a way, dropped out. They did not fight the battle on these frontlines, in science, in the humanities, in politics, in economics, in the arts, as they did not understand that there was a battle to be fought there in the name of the Lord. They did not understand that in fact there are no neutral realms of life; and that the real line dividing reality does not run between nature and grace, in the old traditional sense, but between good and evil, obedience and sin, right and wrong. The Christian should always be fighting at that frontier line, should always be found there standing firm on the side of God. His will is to preserve his creation, to build up, to do away with evil, captivity, injustice, lack of love and care.

Christianity has too long kept itself out of that battle. There were only a few who taught these things. Happily, here and there, individual Christians have done their work, despite sometimes being misunderstood by other Christians. But, as a whole, Christianity has not been the salting salt that it should have been.

Sometimes I think that this is a fulfilment of God's words at the beginning of history – that the seed of the woman would bruise the head of the serpent. That has been fulfilled by Christ on the cross and in his resurrection. But God added that the serpent would bruise the heel of the seed of the woman. That is part of the curse. The church – the body of God's people – has been weak, and Christianity has not really accomplished all that it should have brought into being. The life-giving insights and commands of the Lord have often not been followed. Christianity itself has been 'spiritualized' and in this way hindered from showing its fruits. This is even apart from the devastating results of sin still found within Christianity which break up the real unity of churches and bring in heretical ideas, such as the ones leading to modernist theology.

Science versus faith

Indeed, the conflict of our time between biblical Christianity and science is not a conflict between an old obsolete view of reality and new, better proven insights but rather one between a biblical understanding of reality and a shrunken, reduced world view – that of scientism. These are the problems many Christians struggle with today, expressed for instance in the Genesis vs. Evolution debate. In that respect we must understand that evolutionary theory as such is not proved at all but is rather a modernist belief, one that in fact provides too small an answer for a very big question. The question is: How did the world in which we live come into existence, with its manifold fauna and flora, with its ecological unity? To answer that question it is necessary first to have a clear answer to the question: What is true? Do we in that automatically ask for scientific truth? In that sense, we may never get to an answer about the beginning of our universe or our earth, as these things are as hard to trace as ever. We should remember also that the basic principles of modern science from the time of the Age of Reason onwards were defined in principle to exclude God, the Bible and the supernatural. Or do we, in looking for truth, ask for a fullness of truth? Do we ask in order to understand the basic principles of our world? In that case the Bible gives us a wonderful insight into reality as created by God, the God who also cares for his creation.

Science, it is popular for people to say today, shows that it is impossible to walk on water or to come alive again after death. But, in a way, science can never prove that these kinds of events are impossible. It can only say, correctly, that it almost never happens. The Bible does not contradict science here, and indeed is emphatically not anti-science. It says that usually people cannot walk on the water. Christ, however, did, and Peter – and that was quite exceptional (as Peter was only too aware!). Christ did rise from the grave; but that is a central fact of history and as such, totally unique. Again the Bible agrees with science. Until the Last Day, when Jesus comes back, people will not come back to life once they have died.

Christians today live in a world in which for many people scientific 'facts' are more true than biblical truths. For many people around us the God we believe in is at best a beautiful idea. We, God's children, have become a minority. But we must understand that this situation is not so very new. That is why I like to read Malachi, where we find that our fellow believers in the Old Testament times also knew about such problems. Our modern style of unbelief is not so new either.

Today, I feel, Christian preachers should speak like the prophets of old. Consider Hosea 4, where the Lord speaks through these words:

> Hear the word of the Lord, O children of Israel,
> for the Lord has a controversy with the inhabitants of the land.
> There is no faithfulness or steadfast love,
> and no knowledge of God in the land;
> there is swearing, lying, murder, stealing, and committing adultery;
> they break all bounds, and bloodshed follows bloodshed.
> Therefore the land mourns,
> and all who dwell in it languish,
> and also the beasts of the field
> and the birds of the heavens,
> and even the fish of the sea are taken away (Hosea 4:1–3).

When we read these words, do they not remind us of our own day? When we read on and hear that the priests, those who had to teach the people, are accused, do we not think of modernist theology and also of the ever growing lack of knowledge in the world around us about what the Bible teaches? If we think about the things that are happening around us, a world collapsing, an economy going wrong, ecology turning into a problem, are we not thinking about God's warning that he will come with his very real judgment?

Love versus judgment?

There is a great stress on God's love in preaching today, and that is right. The Old and the New testaments are full of it. But in the Bible, as well as in the reality in which we live (after all the Bible teaches us the truth about the world), we see there can be no love without righteousness and, if necessary, judgment. If we love something (and God loves his creation, and humankind, and his children in a very special way) then we must be able to defend it. If we only preach a God of love without adding this, we make a caricature of God. Out of that comes the question: How can God be a God of love if he allows murders, wars, famine, death, and so on? The answer must be that just because God is a God of love he does *not* accept these things but comes with his judgment, in a very real sense. That judgment can come in one's personal life or in the judgment after death, but it can also come upon peoples, nations, societies. There is, furthermore, another sense in which God does not accept suffering and death: Jesus Christ did in fact come to bring redemption, to save humankind from all this; and in his new world, when also the final enemy, death, definitely will have been overcome, these things will be no more.

So we can understand what we are told in the book of Malachi. Repeatedly we read how the prophets spoke about the Lord. The Lord uses their words to explain why he is coming with his tribulations, his curses, upon the people. We must note that there is little difference between the mentality of people in those days and in our day, just as there is no difference between the days before and after the Babylonian captivity, when Malachi was written. Frameworks may differ, and political and cultural circumstances may vary greatly but people speak in the same way.

In Malachi 1:2 the Lord says, 'I have loved you,' but the people answer, 'How have you loved us?' Do people not ask that same question today? Do they not see that the gospel was preached, and more than that, that God gave many blessings and riches; he gave wellbeing and political hegemony. But he gave it to be used in a right way. People say that religions can be found all over the world and that as such Christianity is a passing way of thinking. They can no longer see truth and God's love as specific and particular realities.

Today people say that religion is to no avail – it is a strictly private matter. They say that the Christian religion makes no difference. As a result, Christian ways of life have become obsolete and indeed the differences between Christians and non-Christians have become smaller – but certainly not because the world is getting better.

Malachi speaks of the priests who act wrongly.

> A son honours his father, and a servant his master. If then I am a father, where is my honour? And if I am a master, where is my fear? says the Lord of hosts to you, O priests, who despise my name. But you say, 'How have we despised your name?' By offering polluted food upon my altar. But you say, 'How have we polluted you?' By saying that the Lord's table may be despised (Malachi 1:6–7).

There are many church services today, but faith is lacking. There are many Christian meetings, but teaching is often shallow and repetitive, leaving many treasures of God's teaching aside. Yet people want to have God's blessing without any cost. They often say that God is love, which should be translated, 'He will accept when I do it my way. What I do does not matter to him.' But such people are wrong. Human life has meaning, certainly in the eyes of God.

Malachi also speaks of the religious leaders' misleading instruction: '"But you have turned aside from the way. You have caused many to stumble by your instruction. You have corrupted the covenant of Levi, says the Lord of hosts"' (Malachi 2:8). Is that not the same today? Biblical teaching is perverted through being deemed old-fashioned. Today we should think more horizontally, we are told. God is in our meeting with our fellow creatures. It is indeed true that we should love our neighbours, even those who are far away. We cannot, however, tamper with God's word without losing wisdom, insight, and his blessing. We are not allowed to speak about God and his Son in a new way, just as we do not have the freedom to make a God of our own liking. That is just as well, because we should be so much poorer for it.

The Lord is not blessing the land, and Malachi records the people asking why (2:13,14):

> You cover the Lord's altar with tears, with weeping and groaning because he no longer regards the offering or accepts it with favour from your hand. But you say, 'Why does he not?' Because the Lord was witness between you and the wife of your youth, to whom you have been faithless, though she is your companion and your wife by covenant (Malachi 2:13–14).

The answer is that there is lack of faithfulness in sexual matters. Do we not hear things like sexual faithlessness defended today, in the so-called new morality? Do we not see more and more divorces, even in church circles? God's laws, given so that we may live, are discarded carelessly.

People say that human beings have come of age. It is typical twentieth-century pride to think that we are wiser, better and 'further on' than people of the past, even the dim past of the days of Malachi. Perhaps we are just as foolish as they were. The Bible is not a childish book, and the people that it speaks to are not children or childlike. In fact, the Bible takes human beings very seriously and approaches them as responsible adults. This is true from the very beginning of history. Modern people, however, think that they have grown up, that they can act autonomously, that they know better and that they have gained freedom. The freedom, though, is the kind of freedom Peter speaks about: 'Speaking loud boasts of folly, they entice by sensual passions of the flesh those who are barely escaping from those who live in error. They promise them freedom, but they themselves are slaves of corruption. For whatever overcomes a person, to that he is enslaved' (2 Peter 2:18–19).

The new sex films come to mind, and so much of their kind. While the Bible does not ask for Victorian morals (they were legalistic and self-righteous), it does insist that to overcome sexual corruption we must not opt for lawlessness.

Malachi further reveals that people in that time stopped making value judgments: 'You have wearied the Lord with your words. But you say, "How have we wearied him?" By saying, "Everyone who does evil is good in the sight of the Lord, and he delights in them." Or by asking, "Where is the God of justice?"' (Malachi 2:17).

People today are very slow to pass judgment. Maybe it is a reaction to a legalistic way of judging in the past that was too quick and easy; a reaction against a pharisaic mentality. But the other alternative to legalism is not simply to suspend judgment. There are norms, and we can know them, even though one should not judge too quickly according to the laws of our making. This modern lawlessness, if not always in practice then in principle, is closely related to the fact that people do not see God any more as the judge. Maybe modern people talk like the 'scoffers' Peter refers to (2 Peter 3:3, 4), those who cannot see that day of final judgment coming. But even theologians are saying that Christ's coming has only an eschatological meaning, and in this sense often rob it of its deep reality and rob people of a hope for a better future. Indeed, these errors run deep today. We can understand that if we miss a view of the reality of the end as described by Paul in 1 Corinthians 15:24–28, we are left with becoming revolutionaries, wanting to bring into being a better world of our own making. Things were not different in the time of Malachi, and the answer is also the same. Look, God's messenger is coming, 'But who can endure the day of his coming, and who can stand when he appears? For he is like a refiner's fire and like fullers' soap' (Malachi 3:2).

Malachi tells us that every call to return to the Lord goes unheeded. 'From the days of your fathers you have turned aside from my statutes and have not kept them. Return to me, and I will return to you, says the Lord of hosts. But you say, "How shall we return?"' (Malachi 3:7). Perhaps each call to return to God is branded by its recipient as fundamentalistic or as old-fashioned. We must however understand that maybe a merely spiritual understanding of the phrase 'returning to the Lord' might well have put people off. In that case we, the Bible-believing Christians, could have been to blame. Turning back to God means that we change our hearts and our direction; it means that we accept again our God as Lord and take to our hearts what he has said in Scripture – which is what his children in all ages have understood clearly. There may be discussion about the details, but the teaching of the Bible is not dubious, dark, incomprehensible, and it certainly is not merely something for the 'spirit'. It is not just piety but means a whole attitude of returning to the ways of the Lord. The ways are specific, and Malachi discusses the specific demands of the Lord. We are to love the Lord, yes, but also to love our neighbours and to hunger and thirst for righteousness. We know that our Lord said that whatever we do to the smallest of his creatures we do to him. To serve him in spirit and truth is not a vague and pious act but a reversal of our way of life.

Malachi records how people in his time were saying, 'Look, what God says does not come true!' (Malachi 3:13–15). As we have already seen, many are recorded in the Bible as saying words like that. Sometimes we may even fall into that kind of reasoning ourselves. God considers it a very great sin to say that the Lord does not see what goes on (Ezekiel 9:9). In the New Testament we find a discussion of this mentality in Paul's second letter to Timothy (3:5), saying that such people have the form of religion but 'reject the power that could make them godly'.

When God is absent

In a way, the big question is not whether or not God exists (even the devils know that he does) but what he does, how he acts. The Bible gives clear teaching about that, yet people say that he is a hidden God, a God who is far away and not interested in human doings. Even if his existence is not denied, he is not taken into account in daily life. Some theologians even say that he is dead.

Really, we do not need to think about wicked people like gangsters, mobsters, thugs, blackmailers, pimps, drug dealers and smugglers. Merely look at an 'innocent' film or TV programme, something called entertainment, and see how nice folk in those 'sketches from life' do a little bit of wrong, some right, have a bit of fun and some tears, but never take into account for one moment that there is a God who is alive and active. Their lives are religionless and lived completely within a closed world, in which there may be a vague sentimental hope for a better future but never is an opening towards the great God Almighty, who is coming and is now already acting. Indeed, we see in these things the best proof that we Westerners have put God aside, have turned belief in God into a kind of private act that never interferes with the doings of human beings in the world today. Secularization? Just look around us.

The question is: Why? How is that possible? How can it be that people do not see God acting, in reality, in judgment, throughout our Western world, today? He is acting very directly, hitting us in those things in which we have put our hope: oil, wealth, technology, economics, science, psychiatry and its new modes of treating people, practices like sensitivity training. God is confronting us there.

Yet sometimes it seems as if God were hiding himself, as if he has let us go in our unrighteousness, in our self-reliance. The Bible knows of that situation and warns us to be careful; God is hiding himself, which in itself is already judgment. Should we not sing with the psalmist: 'How long, O Lord? Will you hide yourself forever? How long will your wrath burn like fire?' (Psalm 89:46). God replies that he is responding to human wickedness: 'Because of the iniquity of his unjust gain I was angry, I struck him; I hid my face and was angry' (Isaiah 57:17). It can even go so far, and in many instances has gone so far today, that

> With their flocks and herds they shall go
> to seek the Lord,
> but they will not find him;
> he has withdrawn from them (Hosea 5:6).

No, the Lord does not always answer at our call (Micah 3:4, 6, 7). Let us also not delude ourselves that that is only true of the Old Testament. Do we not read that 'God sends them a strong delusion, so that they may believe what is false' (2 Thessalonians 2:11), and yes, that 'God gave them up' to their own ways (Romans 1:24).

What does this mean for God's children in days which are difficult, when it sometimes seems as if only so very few are left, as if everybody has lost heart and joined the ranks of the unbelievers? What does it mean in such days, when God has to console his people saying 'There are left seven thousand more than you really suppose.' At such a time he says to the believer:

> Seek the Lord, all you humble of the land,
>   who do his just commands;
> seek righteousness; seek humility;
>   perhaps you may be hidden
>   on the day of the anger of the Lord (Zephaniah 2:3).

There, in these words, the Lord gives us a promise and also shows us the way to go. God's children have to go on in righteousness, keeping themselves clean, honest and true, and they must not look for great things such as changing the world and stopping its fall. They are rather to be meek, humble, knowing their own weakness (cf. Micah 7:7–10). This does not mean that they do not care what happens in the world; that they will not help if they can. It also does not mean that they should not hunger and thirst for righteousness. But it does mean that they know their place, and do not go on, singing with triumphant voices 'Onward Christian soldiers!', wishing to change the course of history. Maybe they weep with Jeremiah over the fall of their civilization, but they understand that if the Lord is acting they are meant to be still. We might remember Baruch, whose great career was to be broken off when the prophecies he had to write down as Jeremiah's secretary would come true. God told him not to look for great things but to trust that God would care for him, and not to be afraid (Jeremiah 45).

In Malachi we also read about God's care (3:16): 'Then those who feared the Lord spoke with one another. The Lord paid attention and heard them, and a book of Remembrance was written before him 'of those who feared the Lord and esteemed his name'. Indeed, it is a great consolation to know that the Lord does know, even if he seems to hide himself. He knows all that goes on. He also knows the fears, pains and sometimes seemingly fruitless work of his people, and he keeps a book of Remembrance. Yes, some day you will see, says the Lord, that whatever you have done has made a difference. There is a difference between serving the Lord and forgetting him, perhaps only paying lip service, sometimes. We should not, therefore, be afraid and should never compromise. We must keep up righteousness, but with meekness. In this way our faith will not be in vain. God stresses that we should remember his word and be obedient to what he tells us in it. Furthermore, as there was a future coming in the Old Testament, the coming Messiah, so there is still and again a future to look forward to, the coming again of our Messiah, when all the books will be opened and all things will be clear at last.

6
Blessing and Judgment in the New Testament

The New Testament does not cancel the principles of blessing and cursing, which are indeed the great principles of all history. They are plainly evident throughout the Gospels, Acts, Epistles, and the book of Revelation. Many Christians would object to the statements that I have just made. Many would not regard the Old Testament (or 'old covenant') as important in this respect any longer. But these objections (both against the importance of the Old Testament and against the continuance of the principles of blessing and cursing) are answerable:

1. Consider the sheer size, and thus importance and weight, of the Old Testament. If the Old Testament is no longer important as it stands, most of the Bible is no longer important.

2. There is a true sense in which the Old Testament is the Bible. Everything that is to be said was said essentially in the Old Testament. In this same sense, the New Testament only adds the glorious point that the Messiah has come. Christ himself declared that he had not done away with the old covenant in coming to the world. He never went against Moses; in fact, he often went much further than Moses did in his demands. Jesus pointed out that people often had misunderstood what Moses was teaching. Even though, obviously, with Christ's coming some things changed – sacrifices, for example, were abolished – this does not do away with the Old Testament.

3. Many events and matters prophesied in the Old Testament were not fulfilled in the New Testament times, not in Christ's life or in the days of the early church. This is why we have the book of Revelation, which collects together the prophecies yet to be fulfilled at the time of the late first century AD.

4. I have a strong feeling that the New Testament did not stress some important matters *because knowledge of the Old Testament was assumed.* The books of the New Testament were never meant to stand on their own, in a vacuum. There is, of course, a notable difference in flavour or atmosphere between the Old and New testaments. This difference merely comes from the refining quality of the latter. To continue the basic metaphor we have been using, the New Testament adds a coat of varnish to the portrait, but leaves the basic composition unchanged.

The Old Testament is very basic, and should not be neglected. In it God called his people and gave them his revelation. *Everything* is given there, such as how to live one's life and how to worship God. The Old Testament makes clear that we are sinful and gives us the promise of the coming Saviour. British Christians are especially prone to neglect the Old Testament and not to read it properly. It is wrong to see it as addressed to the individual Christian, except on rare occasions as in some psalms. The Bible is not dealing merely with individuals but with nations and groups of people. We often fail to see its meaning when we do not take this into account (as we saw when considering Isaiah). The social emphasis is important, also today. If one crosses the border from Holland into Germany, for instance, one can sense a difference after just ten miles. The houses look different, the history is different, and so on.

The situation in the New Testament is that the long-promised Saviour has come. The Gospels reveal three basic discussions: (a) questions asked by Christ's immediate followers; (b) questions asked by the people, the crowds in general; and (c) questions asked by Christ's opponents. All three groups had one common question to ask Christ: 'Are you the Saviour promised in the Old Testament?' Christ's reply is to tell them to look at the Scriptures. He added that, had they believed Moses, they would believe him. There had been many false deliverers and saviours but, Jesus told them, to know the truth about him they only had to examine the words of Moses. He took them back to Moses and all the prophets. One prophet had said that the Saviour would come riding upon an ass. There were to be other fulfilments. Some of the tokens or signs of his authenticity as Saviour were his miracles, as John showed.

After Christ's ascension, new questions arose. What about the Old Testament law? (Much of the Old Testament had looked forward to the Saviour, who had now come.) Another question concerned the place of the Temple and the blood sacrifices. Christ's coming had ended the localized Temple and annulled the necessity for sacrifice. All these Old Testament matters changed in their meaning, and questions concerning them are addressed in the apostolic letters. A letter of Peter deals with the question: How do we live in the present world? Can we eat pagan sacrificial meat? Now that everything has been completed by Christ's coming, these questions have an answer.

An important remaining matter, however, concerned the future. There was much not yet fulfilled in Christ's coming, and also principles still to be realized. One great unfulfilled matter was Christ's kingship: one day he will reign over all the earth, but that day is in the future; one day Christ will trample death, the final enemy, underfoot. Those matters regarding the future are the concern of Revelation.

The New Testament sees itself throughout as a continuation of the Old. That is plainly evident in the theme of God's hand in history as well as in the other key Bible themes.

Jesus affirms the Old Testament themes

Christ's famous statement about the salt in his Sermon on the Mount clearly emphasizes the theme of blessing and judgment: 'You are the salt of the earth, but if salt has lost its taste, how shall its saltiness be restored? It is no longer good for anything except to be thrown out and trampled under people's feet' (Matthew 5:13).

Christ is saying here that God's people are very important in the world. Their presence brings a blessing. Those who listen to the Sermon on the Mount, then and now, have a special task. We today do not understand the full significance of the term 'salt' as used then. From the days of Christ to sixty or so years ago, salt was a preservative for meat and other perishables: it stopped decay. Christ is saying, through this figure of speech, that his listeners then and now will keep this world healthy. If the salt loses its flavour – if you do not do what you should do – it loses its meaning – you lose your meaning – and will be 'trampled under people's feet' (close echoes of Deuteronomy 28–30) – just as in the Old Testament, you will be judged, cursed. The 'you' of this verse is a communal or plural 'you', another continuation of the Old Testament. Christ is addressing his followers, the people of God, as a group. Similarly in Revelation, Christ writes letters to the seven churches as groups or communities. Some he warns that he will punish them for not listening to him and for not doing what he said.

Later in the Sermon on the Mount, Jesus speaks about wolves in sheep's clothing, or 'false prophets':

> Beware of false prophets, who come to you in sheep's clothing but inwardly are ravenous wolves. You will recognize them by their fruits. Are grapes gathered from thornbushes, or figs from thistles? So, every healthy tree bears good fruit, but the diseased tree bears bad fruit. A healthy tree cannot bear bad fruit, nor can a diseased tree bear good fruit. Every tree that does not bear good fruit is cut down and thrown into the fire. Thus you will recognize them by their fruits (Matthew 7:15–20).

As in Old Testament times there are good and bad prophets – the rules have not changed. Christ declares that we should look at the fruit, at the results. Where there is bad fruit, the tree is cut down; this is a metaphor of judgment. The metaphor reveals that there is not only natural causality, but God specifically acts to remove the tree. He specifically acts in judgment, as in the Old Testament.

Further in the Gospel of Matthew we come across Christ saying, after instructing his disciples to go on a preaching mission to the Jews, 'And if anyone will not receive you or listen to your words, shake off the dust from your feet when you leave that house or town. Truly, I say to you, it will be more bearable on the day of judgment for the land of Sodom and Gomorrah than for that town' (Matthew 10:14–15). These are special instructions for when the disciples are not accepted in a place. There is to be terrible judgment on the 'house or town' that says 'no' to God's teaching. Where the gospel is heard and not received, there is a stronger judgment than where it has not been heard. This repeats the Old Testament emphasis that apostasy can lead to the judgment of the loss of a nation's territory. Christ says that it is to be worse for such towns than it was for Sodom and Gomorrah, which were merely immoral. The rejection of the gospel is a matter that concerns more than morals. Note that the 'day of judgment' upon the unreceptive towns is not the Last or final Judgment; it means *the time when judgment occurs.* This may well be before the Last Judgment. Christ is speaking of these very real matters in the here and now when he mentions judgment.

In Matthew 23, Christ utters a number of 'woes' against the religious leaders of the time and against the holy city, Jerusalem. These deeply sad and heartfelt 'woes' are uttered because something ominous and terrible is in store for them. They are not 'woes' without result, empty and futile, mere eloquence. Christ is warning of what is to happen inevitably; he is telling them to be dreadfully careful.

> Therefore I send you prophets and wise men and scribes, some of whom you will kill and crucify, and some you will flog in your synagogues and persecute from town to town. ... 'O Jerusalem, Jerusalem, the city that kills the prophets and stones those who are sent to it! How often would I have gathered your children together as a hen gathers her brood under her wings, and you would not! See, your house is left to you desolate. For I tell you, you will not see me again, until you say, "Blessed is he who comes in the name of the Lord."' (Matthew 23:34,37–39).

It speaks about 'this generation' (v.26). A 'generation' does not mean a range of twenty or thirty years but refers to the present period or era of history. At this time, the people and their religious leaders were going in a bad direction; they were killing the prophets – or the equivalent (one can kill without bullets or weapons). Christ points out that they did not want to receive him. He was the one who longed to console and protect them – truly like a mother. But they were going their own way, and Christ's judgment is that they shall have their way. They will no longer see him, the great prophet (he of course is soon to be executed and soon to leave them after that). Christ's judgment is exactly like the judgment in Old Testament times when God deliberately withdrew or hid himself. At such a time it seems as if God is not at work.

The apostles affirm the Old Testament themes

In Romans 11, Paul explicitly links his present, first-century time with the days of the Old Testament. He speaks of God's reply to Elijah when he felt desolate as prophet after prophet was killed by King Ahab and Elijah's life was sought. What was God's reply to him? 'I have kept for myself seven thousand men who have not bowed the knee to Baal.' So too at the present time there is a remnant, chosen by grace (Romans 11:4–5).

Not only does Paul make this link but it is obvious that this passage cannot be understood without knowledge of the Old Testament. Paul clearly felt that, as in the time of Elijah, very few people were listening to God. The word 'remnant' is an Old Testament word deliberately employed by Paul to stress the fact that the faithful are a minority.

The result of the majority being ungodly is revealed in Romans 11:11: 'So I ask, did they stumble in order that they might fall? By no means! Rather through their trespass salvation has come to the Gentiles, so as to make Israel jealous.' It is clear that God is still working with the Jewish people. He is still willing and ready to accept those who repent, as he was in the Old Testament. He has not given up on them.

In Hosea 2 there is a parable of sorts that is very relevant to the New Testament perspective. Hosea must receive back an adulterous and faithless woman he had married. This is a parable of God and his people. Hosea 3 records essentially the same story – Hosea restores Gomer, his faithless wife. This time the story refers to the future restoration of Israel in the New Testament. The Old Testament looks forward to the New Testament. The New Testament also looks back to the Old. The style of the following extract from Hebrews is difficult, as it is made up of quotations from the Old Testament familiar to its original readers (see Jeremiah 31:31–34), but it is important:

> For this is the covenant that I will make with the house of Israel
>   after those days, declares the Lord:
> I will put my laws into their minds,
>   and write them on their hearts,
> and I will be their God,
>   and they shall be my people.
> And they shall not teach, each one his neighbour
>   and each one his brother, saying, 'Know the Lord,'
> for they shall all know me,
>   from the least of them to the greatest.
> For I will be merciful toward their iniquities,
>   and I will remember their sins no more (Hebrews 8:10–12).

This extract shows that many Old Testament prophecies were fulfilled in the New Testament.

We have already seen Christ's reiteration in Matthew 10 of the Old Testament principle that to hear and to reject God's word is a great sin, bringing great punishment. In Hebrews 2 the apostolic writer also warns of this. The people of his day were without excuse. God had come in person with his message and they have known, with undeniable evidences, of God's salvation (Hebrews 2:1–4). How can they escape judgment if those Old Testament people, who had less knowledge than they have, did not escape? The New Testament emphasizes the same principle as the Old, but puts it stronger. It stresses that people should not rely upon their natural reason and view of the situation: 'Beloved, never avenge yourselves, but leave it to the wrath of God, for it is written, "Vengeance is mine, I will repay, says the Lord."' To the contrary, 'if your enemy is hungry, feed him; if he is thirsty, give him something to drink; for by so doing you will heap burning coals on his head' (Romans 12:19, 20).

There is to be vengeance and judgment, but it is not for us to do it. Judgment is God's prerogative. When we love our enemies, we are revealing God's truth to them; their rejection of this truth would add to their judgment. We cannot be involved in any persecution – this is never our prerogative. In the story of Noah, the ship slowly rises upon the floodwater. People are desperately swimming. Noah could not himself close the door upon them, as his desire obviously was to save people. God closed the door of the ark – it was his judgment.

We must never play God.

In 1 Corinthians 10:1–14, Paul points out that the ancient Jewish people ('our fathers') were 'all under the cloud, and all passed through the sea' in the Exodus from Egypt. God gave them many blessings, but they did not heed what he said. They did not listen, and so were judged in very real ways. Paul points out that 'these things [are] examples for us, that we might not desire evil as they did.' When we read these stories, Paul implies, we realize that we know so much more than they did in those days. And we, today, in the twentieth-century West, are even nearer to the end of the end. All these warnings apply even more to us than they did to the people living in Paul's time. Let us be careful.

The first letter to the Corinthians is not a comfortable, relaxing piece of prose. The passage just mentioned is characteristic of its tone. Paul is angry. He calls them foolish. They cannot go on as they have been doing. If God judges them (there has been illness in the church, and other afflictions), there is a reason for it, a meaning behind it. They are to listen and to observe carefully. The purpose of this judgment is that the Corinthian Church may turn back to God.

A similar stern warning against a church comes in Revelation, where Christ writes through John to the Christians in Ephesus: 'Remember therefore from where you have fallen; repent, and do the works you did at first. If not, I will come to you and remove your lampstand from its place, unless you repent' (Revelation 2:5). The church was not growing as it should, and Christ tells the Christians to remember and repent, or his judgment will come.

Christ's message to the church at Thyatira (Revelation 2:18–29) is quite different. He says that the church community is good, full of 'love and faith and service and patient endurance', but in the midst is a woman with wrong teaching (she is called a Jezebel). In verse 21, Christ says that he has given her time to repent but that she has failed to do so. Now he will punish her. As in the Old Testament, judgment from God comes upon individuals as well as groups, even in the midst of general blessing. The portrait of history includes both individuals and community. Also, as in the Old Testament, judgments (and blessings) are very real, not merely spiritual. Christ's judgment upon this false teacher is frighteningly real.

One of the greatest resonances of the Old Testament theme of blessing and cursing, however, comes in Revelation 9.

> The rest of mankind, who were not killed by these plagues, did not repent of the works of their hands nor give up worshiping demons and idols of gold and silver and bronze and stone and wood, which cannot see or hear or walk, nor did they repent of their murders or their sorceries or their sexual immorality or their thefts (Revelation 9:20–21).

The chapters surrounding these verses speak of trumpets being sounded. Each trumpet means a great deal of trouble for humankind (see below, chapter 8). Each speaks of God's judgment upon the world. There is good reason for judgment, as these verses show. For people must see that God is truly Lord and Ruler so that they may repent.

These verses raise the whole matter of war and peace, so important to the message of the Old Testament. Revelation tells us that there will be very many wars on earth, and that terrifying and horrific events will take place. There is no promise of a peaceful period in history. The permanence of war *does not mean*, of course, that the Christian, as a shaper of history, is free to initiate war, to be an aggressor. This is God's prerogative. If Christians take up the sword as aggressors, they will die by the sword. Christians rather should promote peace – they are peacemakers.

God's judgment comes in the form of war. My whole study of God's hand in history is making the point that war is not something resulting merely from natural causes (as it would be in the formulation: 'People are bad, therefore they make war'). War means more than this; an extra, vital factor is involved. Many wars are God's judgment coming to bear upon us, as was the case in the Old Testament. Someone said of the Korean War: 'The hand of God is heavy upon this land.' They understood this principle of history. We might never know the real reason for a war, the reason behind and greater than an assassin's bullet or perhaps the triggering of a nuclear weapon. In Holland before the Second World War somebody wrote to the effect that if the enemy should invade our country, we should not see this outside of the framework of God's judgment. Hitler's invasion was a judgment upon Holland: he was, like Assyria, God's *instrument* of judgment.

In the light of the sombre realities revealed clearly throughout the Bible, Christians must not proclaim 'Be saved' – thinking only of life after death or death after death. They must proclaim 'Repent!' – for God's judgment is upon us here and now. It is upon us in the last quarter of the twentieth century. In America, for example, which was once a prominently Christian country, God's judgment is taking place *now*. We saw that in the book of Hosea, God said that when he comes in judgment even the fish in the rivers and seas would suffer. Though Christians must resist wars, they must see God's hand in them and in other judgments: Revelation 10:7 speaks of the mystery of God, spoken to the prophets, being fulfilled or finished at the sound of the seventh trumpet of judgment. This links with Deuteronomy 29:29, which states: 'The secret things belong to the Lord our God, but the things that are revealed belong to us and to our children forever, that we may do all the words of this law.'

There are some matters – some meanings of wars and other historical events, for instance – that are hidden. To God's people, however, they are not secrets, for they are revealed through the prophets and they belong to us. So when we try to understand history, we are not confronted by mysteries but by what is revealed by God.

7
Reading the Book of Revelation

The last book of the Bible, Revelation, sums up all that has come before. This very important book is not read much by Christians today, and not read in the right way. Essential to it is the momentous theme of God's hand in history. This biblical theme is a key that unlocks its meaning.

By its very nature we must ask what Revelation is about. There are some basic questions to answer: How is it constructed? How should we read it? What is its basic message? What manner of expression does it use? What method does it use to get its message and content across?

Meaning or fact?

Revelation is a very difficult book for twentieth-century people, because we have lost the skill to understand it. There is a very deep break between us and the writer and readers of this book around the end of the first century AD. They would have found it exceedingly more easy to understand than we do. It appears very strange and unnatural to us today.

A tentative suggestion (we shall consider this more deeply later in the chapter) is that we, the twentieth-century readers, will have to greatly change our way of thinking. This is *not* to suggest that people today who think normally must jump out of that 'normality' in order to read Revelation, as if they had to put on a red cap, yellow shoes, odd socks and so on in order to understand it. Rather, my explanation would suggest that *we* today have lost 'normality' in our thinking and understanding. This loss goes right back to Renaissance humanism, where scientific thinking became the only way or exclusive model of proper thinking. It is summed up in the attitude that A or B is proved simply by an appeal to *facts*.

But what are *facts*? Let us suppose that I was giving a lecture in a room. One could spend a year making a precise and exhaustive inventory of every detail of the room, and of each person in it, such as their dates of birth, hair colour, height and weight. At the end of the year we should be very tired, but we would still not have touched upon a real knowledge or understanding of the room and its contents.

This is because facts, by their nature, are reductions or limited selections of full reality. They do not exist in and of themselves. Atoms and positrons do not exist as such. The same is true of things that seem as far apart as psychological feelings and the stars, which are many millions of light years away. The realities behind these matters exist in a far larger and richer sense. Atoms, statistics and censuses are abstractions. Reality is fuller, richer, and always concrete in meaning. Reality is the fullness of meaning of what exists.

What is wine? We might say that it is 98 per cent water and 2 per cent other constituents. But this does not do justice to the full weight of meaning of wine. Wine means celebration, Christian communion, a gift, enjoyment and much more. It is far more than merely the necessary chemical substances.

Even more basically, what is water? 'H_2O,' a scientist might answer. Yet water clearly is not H_2O. Rain is water falling. Water is the survival of a people. Water could be the cause of a war or could determine the fate of a nation. Its meaning seems almost limitless. The shades and resonances of its meaning are employed by the poet; the Bible often uses these meaningful features of water. Water, for example, is not only more than H_2O but also more than rain, snow, ice, a torrent, the sea or a cool drink for a thirsty person.

We people of the twentieth century are brainwashed against receiving the true reality, the fullness of meaning, of things – all things – ourselves included.

The first philosophy lecture that I heard made me never want to hear another, even though I love philosophy. The lecturer said, 'Do you see the rainbow? It is nothing but light being broken up.' I walked out of that lecture. The rainbow is more real than such an extremely limited view of it. It is true that for the rainbow to appear, light has to be broken up into a spectrum, but that is not the full story of the rainbow's existence. We are brainwashed into accepting, without question, an impoverished, reduced view of reality.

Nothing is real only as a fact; reality is fact plus meaning united into a coherent whole. It follows that fact is as dependent upon meaning as meaning is dependent upon fact to have a reality. In any real thing, fact and meaning are united and mutually dependent. We could express the real like this: *Reality = fact + meaning*.

Another way of putting this is that a fact is a tiny aspect of reality. We can never have meaning without fact, and no fact without some connection with meaning. Let me illustrate this basic and vital principle with a simple illustration.

If someone said to you, 'I love you, and because I love you I'll give you £10,000 with immediate effect,' and months later you are still awaiting the money, the statement still has meaning. But without the fact – i.e. £10,000 – it is an empty statement. On a deeper level, the avowal of love has been proved meaningless.

How important and basic this principle is to our understanding of the Bible can be seen in the matter of the crucifixion of Christ, so important to our faith and creed. The meaning of the Crucifixion is clearly not merely the fact that Jesus of Nazareth, the Christ, was crucified. Very many people, including many Christians in Nero's time, were executed by crucifixion; in this sense, Christ was only one of many.

We must understand that the Bible presents us with meaning as well as fact; in this case, the meaning of Christ's execution as well as the actual happening. This meaning is always weighted, articulate and distinctive. Biblical meaning is more than merely physical facts – it is meaning united with the facts of the matter.

Modern theology wishes for meaning without the rooting of facts. But theological statements without a basis in fact, crumble. This can be seen in the pivotal matter of the Genesis account of Adam and Eve. How many women, in the history of humanity, have eaten fruit while naked? In this sense Eve is only one of many women. We cannot have a meaningful account of Adam and Eve without an actual Adam and Eve. I shall return to this later.

The attempt to separate meaning from fact which occurs in modern theology, and which is the natural way for twentieth-century people to think, is related to our failure to understand historical events. When we only look at natural causality – when we only look for natural and commonsense explanations of why things happen – we are considering fact divorced from meaning. The vital extra factors – the hand of God and the hidden motives of the human heart – reveal the meaning of historical events, allowing us to properly understand them.

In a general sense, the book of Revelation concentrates on meaning rather than fact. It intends to give us general principles of meaning. If we do not read it in the light of this, we misunderstand it. Though Revelation is generally meaning alone, it would of course prove to be meaningless if its prophecies regarding events in the world were to stay unfulfilled.

Let us consider the passage that recounts John's vision of a scroll in God's hand (Revelation 5). Before books were produced, of course, writing was done upon scrolls, which could be sealed. No one could open this scroll in God's hand except Christ. He, the 'lion of the tribe of Judah', can open its seal. John, the writer of Revelation, looks again and sees a Lamb, who takes the scroll.

This passage is very important. It speaks about the very centre of history – what history is all about. We shall look at it more closely in the next chapter. All of life is recorded in a 'book' in God's hand, and God alone is worthy to open the scroll of history. The passage contains many symbolic words, to be understood in the light of the Old Testament – 'the root of David', the 'lamb', and others. The lamb was 'slain' because Christ was crucified – the Crucifixion is a fact with a wealth of historical coordinates. All that happens here can only happen because Christ died, in actual fact, in human history, in a particular place at a specific time. If seen without the rest of the Bible (the Gospel accounts of Christ's execution, for instance) this passage is only a strangely beautiful myth. The passage is characteristic of the book of Revelation. Meanings are given – the facts are given elsewhere in the Bible, some of them yet to happen, such as Christ's Second Coming or the fruition of his kingdom. Specifically, this passage presents the *meaning* of the crucifixion of

Christ. He is able and worthy to open the scroll of Life. Christ is the boss or governor of history. History – all of it, throughout all our times and in all places – is truly guided and shaped, and this is done by a person, Christ. He gives form to human history. This must of course be seen in connection with the biblical principles referred to in the earlier chapters, the principles of blessing and cursing which work out in the hard details of human events, such as those recorded for us by the biblical writers.

Another example of the method of the book of Revelation comes just after this passage in chapter 6. Horses and horsemen are spoken of, with the second horse referred to as the horse of War. What does this mean?

As Christ opens the seal of the book of Life, something truly happens in the world. But the reference to the bright red horse of War is not only making the general statement that there are wars. It is not only a meaningful statement because wars, in fact, do happen. Rather, the reference is to the whole *meaning* of war: why do wars happen? Although Revelation underlines that there is a real sequence to history (it is not an eternal cycle), it is not concerned as such with this or that war. The red horse may signify the bombing in Cambodia, the great battles of the Second World War or the battle between the Incas and the Aztecs. Rather, happenings in the world, facts, including wars, are 'full of history' – they are not the result of chance. Christ releases the horse of War, dreadful though it be. We are being told that when something like a war or a massacre happens, we can know why, because there is a meaning that we can know to every part of history. The book of Revelation reveals this meaning. It is the key to history, telling us what history means. One aspect of the meaning of history is the meaning of war. The central purpose of the book of Revelation is to point out which Old Testament prophecies are not yet fulfilled, and though these remain as prophecies from our twentieth-century perspective, they will eventually be fulfilled.

Taking into account that its symbols are not merely meanings bearing no relation to real events and life here and now, what is the content, the subject matter, of the book of Revelation? We have said that it is concerned with prophecies yet to be fulfilled at the end of the first century, and with the meaning of history. What is that about?

A book of consolation

The central event in the book of Revelation is Christ opening the scroll (or book) of Life. As he opens the seals, history unrolls. In fact, Revelation could be called the 'book of consolation'. What does it tell us that is so consoling?

That nothing which happens takes place by chance. There is no one person as such, no matter how powerful, who has the whole world in his or her hands. Horror and terror is real, and it is proper to respond to horror as horror. The Bible is totally realistic about that. God's 'woe to you' includes concern for the little bird that is flying in the sky. We must speak of the horror of war and its effect on those embroiled in it. Yet, at the same time, God does keep a very special eye upon his children. Revelation mentions a momentary 'silence in heaven' (Revelation 8:1). Heaven waits while God marks his people with a seal.

There is no promise that it will be easy to live in the world, for a great conflict is going on between God and the powers of evil. Evil has many senses and forms, such as the enemy of humanity, the Devil himself, wickedness, and demons opposed to angels. All nations and all individuals are involved in this great battle. Each of us has a cross to bear. There is a cosmic drama taking place in the heavenlies, on earth and 'under the earth'. But we are part of what the book of Revelation sets out: we have our place in this vast drama. Revelation teaches that history is important, that each little one of us is important. This confirms what we naturally feel about the significance of history. Why do we still speak of Michelangelo and of St Augustine? Why do we still speak of Louis XIV – the worst dictator in history – and his infamous revoking of the Edict of Nantes in 1685? We do so because these people remind us of things that are not random facts but meaningful events, 'full of history'.

As well as the central event of the Lamb opening the scroll of Life, we have the seven seals of the scroll of Life which are opened (Revelation 6:1–17; 8:1). This is the second set of visions. In them the veil, as it were, is taken away from the surface of life – the surface of bombs falling, people dying in masses, and other terrors. The meaning that is revealed is larger than the events and facts in themselves.

Following this, Revelation 12 and 13 reveal the meaning of the church – which touches upon the meaning of the Christian life today. The last chapters then give, from a different angle of vision, a portrait of how the end is to come about.

This is the basic content of the book of Revelation – consolation despite real, not merely spiritual, judgment. It is an important and beautiful book, not difficult to understand if one knows the Old Testament well and properly. It is only hard for us to read Revelation today because we have forgotten how to approach symbolic writing. For us, if something deals with meanings, it is unrelated to actual facts; if something deals with facts, it is unrelated to meaning. Consequently, there are today many fanciful explanations and interpretations of the book of Revelation, such as that it is only symbolic or that it gives a calendar in advance of what is to happen literally in the future. It is also hard for us to read it because we in the West have grown soft and naturally do not wish to be told that life is going to be very difficult for us. The book of Revelation offers no view of the past or the future through rose-tinted spectacles. It is, however, the key to the meaning of history.

8
The Active Centre of History

In the first chapter of the book of Revelation we learn that John the Evangelist is exiled on the island of Patmos (off the western coast of Asia Minor, modern-day Turkey). He is in exile because of the persecution of the churches.

Christ comes to him; and this involves seeing things which are not usually seen. In fact, few people in history have viewed such matters. Many of the Old Testament prophets belong to this small group of people. Very often we do not know what lies behind their characteristic statement, 'the Lord said . . .' Sometimes they might be referring to something that they saw that made the situation clearer. This is particularly true of Ezekiel, whose visions in Ezekiel 1 bear many similarities to those of John in Revelation, though there are important differences.

Ezekiel, like John in Revelation 4, sees God on the throne of the universe. But his vision was different from seeing, say, a tree by normal sight. It was something deeply and disturbingly supernatural. Naturally, he has no words to describe what he sees. Ezekiel gropes for words, which are always tentative, with the expressions 'likeness' and 'like' constantly recurring. He cannot straightforwardly identify features of the vision either literally or symbolically. This is because the visions, like John's, do not belong to the normal framework of the world. It is illuminating to compare Ezekiel's reactions with those of primitive people who, in the Second World War, saw aircraft for the first time. They were not astonished in the way that Ezekiel was. The aeroplanes, though novel and remarkable, belong to the normal world.

Ezekiel sees something which he can only describe, in all his honesty, as a figure like a man. The feet, for instance, are like molten bronze, which is not usual of course. Is Ezekiel speaking only symbolically? Is he actually seeing something that requires all his verbal skill to describe and even then only falteringly? John is much more at ease in describing the very similar visions he sees, drawing on the symbolic language used by Ezekiel and Daniel. But the same questions must be asked. Is it only poetry? Or does John see reality?

The nature of visions

Here we must return to the matter that forced itself upon us in the last chapter – our modern inability to bring together fact and meaning. This has direct bearing upon visions of the sort that Ezekiel, John, Elisha (2 Kings 2: 9–12), Elisha's servant (2 Kings 6:8–23) and many others have experienced.

When we talk about visions in the twentieth century, we automatically think of subjective or private hallucinations or of mass suggestion, but not of something that truly exists outside of the visionary somewhere in the world. This emphatically is neither the biblical meaning nor the meaning that people two or three hundred years ago would have perceived. It is not the meaning John's readers would have put to it. What is seen is definitely *outside of* John's mind and senses. Different terms and coordinates from the normal are employed. We are told, for example, that he was 'in the Spirit'. It was not like the native in New Guinea seeing an aircraft for the first time. Although the terms and coordinates differ, however, nothing is unconscious or trance-like for John – the events are not being played upon the stage of his unconscious mind. John is clearly acutely conscious of what he is seeing; he is not in a trance. He is told, 'Write this down,' from which it follows that there were things about which he was told, 'Don't write that down.' In one place (Revelation 10:4) he is actually told not to record the words of the voice of the seven thunders. He is in full possession of his critical and analytical faculties, able to discriminate and creatively give appropriate words and images to something very difficult to express in language. Yet he sees a world that is of another framework, not four-dimensional like ours but n-dimensional. It is 'where God lives' and where supernatural powers are visible, both terrible and beautiful; it is not our framework and not our world.

Connected with this is the description of God on his throne in Revelation 4. Here John is again trying to describe the indescribable. One element of the vision is human – yet under the throne are wheels. The vision is of something like an eagle and other beings, something that speaks. There are twenty-four elders. The proximity of the elders portrays the principle that God is not far off; he has a direct relationship with human beings. This is because the elders represent humankind. We are told the purpose of God's creation (Revelation 4:11). Though they are close to God, the elders are also creatures, part of creation. The cry of all creatures to God is, 'by your will all things are created.' They offer the creation to God; they declare that it is his.

The Lamb takes the scroll of history (Revelation 5). In Revelation we are given the heart of the Bible and the gospel in the form of principles. In both style and intention the book of Revelation aims to give such principles. It is not anything like history in our sense – what we read here is unlike the accounts in the Gospels of Christ's birth. If we had been present at his birth we could have looked at our watches, as it were. This is similarly true of Jesus' crucifixion and resurrection. They are all hard facts rooted in history. But behind all historical events, all facts, is a cardinal principle. While things really 'happen' in Revelation 5, they do not happen in a clock-time sense. This chapter of Revelation is not about the very beginning of history in that sense. In fact, the passage itself contradicts such a view – it mentions the Lamb 'standing, as though it had been slain' (v.6).

The taking of the scroll by the Lamb is a 'real symbol'. It is not simply factual – indeed, the events recorded cannot be pinned down to a moment in history. How it can be both symbolic and real is very hard for us today to understand, as we discussed in the previous chapter. Yet even we have retained many 'real symbols' – for example, the ring that is given in marriage. The ring is both real and symbolic. Such things are remnants or vestiges of what earlier ages perceived as 'real symbols'.

Though difficult for us, this passage is illuminated by the book of Daniel. In Daniel 12 we find out about the book of Life – that is, a scroll – which is mentioned a number of times in the Old Testament. Daniel rolls up the scroll (Daniel 12:4). In Revelation 5 the same scroll is unrolled, and we learn that the scroll has seven seals – it is a holy book. The great question of history is: Who is worthy to open that scroll?

What is the scroll of Life? It is two things: it is history itself; and it is the record of the names of those who are God's children. Daniel speaks of difficult times and of deliverance for those whose names are written in the book. But without the opening of the book there is no salvation, and also no history. It is the breaking of the seals upon the scroll that 'opens' history.

'One of the elders' is mentioned in Revelation (Revelation 5:5). Notice, in all the symbolism, the reference is to somebody specific. John's reference to the tribe of Judah is a special reference to Genesis, where Judah is given a special blessing. Then it becomes more specific – the family of David within the tribe of Judah is especially blessed: 'the Lion of the tribe of Judah, the Root of David'. Here we find symbolic names – the 'Lion', the 'Root'. But the very specific person the elder is referring to is neither a lion nor a root. Here there is, then, an instance of language being made up not only of metaphors but also of 'real symbols'. There is a distinction to be made – this is not simply poetic language. What is spoken of here is not in any way less than the literal, and it is at the same time much more than the metaphorical.

This is the central chapter of the whole Bible, for it tells us the true and final meaning of reality. The Gospels, on the other hand, tell us how it actually happened that God came and saved us. Revelation 5 is real, not merely metaphorical and spiritual. God gives a real book of Life to a real Christ, who really died. This giving of the scroll of history is deep reality and deep truth: while it is more than simple fact, it by no means excludes fact. Anybody present at Christ's crucifixion, for example, would have seen actual blood and could have got a splinter from the cross. Without the actual fact, nothing would have happened, not even spiritually. If this is all true, everything makes sense. There is then meaning. But if it is not true, then blowing up everything with an H-bomb would not matter. It being true, what I do has meaning. How come that people wonder whether or not what they do has any meaning? It happens because God has given all human beings a sense of meaning.

John in Revelation 4 and 5 is seeing visions, and he 'sees' God on the throne. But he is looking at a different world, a world outside of our world framework. Thus John has no words to describe what he sees. It is a world beyond comparisons. This is why he struggles to find analogies – even though they do not fully work. He has to employ the appearances of animals. God, he knows, is the Creator – there is nothing in John's description that God did not make; just as there is nothing, he confesses, other than himself that God did not make. God is the centre and source of all things, even the comparisons John uses to describe him. Yet the descriptions portray a deep reality, a symbolic reality that is true, highly articulate and accurate in its meaning.

What then is happening in this momentous chapter, in its symbolic reality? John is consoled as Christ enters as the centre of history. Certain facts are of highest historic importance as they are at the focal point of history, and these crux events are the death, resurrection and ascension of Christ. These facts are the centerpieces, not only of Christianity but of human history itself. It follows that if Christians are wrong in their beliefs, there is no centre to history. The world, then, is meaningless; the book of history cannot be opened. Tomorrow a gigantic meteor might hit the earth and destroy us along with all the records of our progress and of our civilizations. Or, on a different time scale, the world might eventually go cold. Either way, all human effort becomes meaningless. The book of history then is a toy of God or the play of chance.

Part of John's consolation is that the worthy One is revealed, the One who can open the scroll of history (5:6): 'And between the throne and the four living creatures and among the elders I saw a Lamb standing, as though it had been slain, with seven horns and with seven eyes, which are the seven spirits of God sent out into all the earth.'

The worthy One is the Lamb in the centre of the throne. Seven (seven horns, seven eyes, seven spirits) is the number of holiness. The 'seven spirits of God' is therefore the Holy Spirit active in this present world. Notice the Trinity here – God has the seven spirits, and Christ also has the seven spirits. The Holy Spirit goes from God to his people, throughout the world, through the Lamb, who is Christ. The Lion (5:5) also is Christ.

'The Lamb' is named in many places in the Bible – for example, in Isaiah 53, and in John the Baptist's statement, 'Behold, the Lamb of God, who takes away the sin of the world!' The same 'Lamb' of this statement goes back to the Passover in Egypt. Christ is the real Lamb, real in all history. Christ actually had to die, as the sacrificial Lamb is a real symbol, not merely a poetic one.

Though Christ's death is specific in time and place this passage of Revelation is nevertheless totally symbolic. In this sense, Christ is not really before the throne as a sacrificed lamb. In Daniel 7:9–14, for instance, Christ is pictured in a different way, as 'a son of man', and God is spoken of as the 'Ancient of days'. This passage provides an illuminating parallel with the passage in Revelation 5.

Daniel sees somebody 'like a son of man' who came to the Ancient of days (Daniel 7:13). This person is Christ: when in the New Testament he calls himself the 'Son of Man', he is quoting from this passage. Christ in Daniel, the son of man, is given dominion over all humanity, with a kingdom that is everlasting. Isaiah however gives the clearest prophecy of Christ:

> He was oppressed, and he was afflicted,
>   yet he opened not his mouth;
> like a lamb that is led to the slaughter,
>   and like a sheep that before its shearers is silent,
> so he opened not his mouth (Isaiah 57:7).

In Isaiah 59:15 we are given further insights into Christ's role:

> Truth is lacking,
>   and he who departs from evil makes himself a prey.
> The Lord saw it, and it displeased him
>   that there was no justice.

This verse must be read in its own context as usual. God sees that there is no justice. Who can accomplish justice? No man. But God himself can accomplish it:

> He saw that there was no man,
>   and wondered that there was no one to intercede;
> Then his own arm brought him salvation,
>   and his righteousness upheld him (Isaiah 59:16).

The domination of the 'son of man' of Daniel 7 and the necessary personal intervention of God here in Isaiah are identical. Christ can open the scroll of history because he has conquered sin and the Evil one. He 'has been slain'. John tells us that the holy Lamb, the Lamb with the seven eyes, takes the scroll (Revelation 5:7). At this, the creatures make adoring obeisance to him. A new song is sung (5:9). They realize that this is the moment of moments, the moment at the centre of history. The bowls of incense (5:8) are the prayers of the saints (the faithful believers). Our prayers are not in vain. What is recorded here is the very centre of history; and we are there at the very centre with our prayers. They who bow, sing that those the Lamb has ransomed will be made rulers (5:10). This song picks up on many Old Testament declarations.

So, in Exodus 19:5, 6 we read: 'Now therefore, if you will indeed obey my voice and keep my covenant, you shall be my treasured possession among all peoples, for all the earth is mine; and you shall be to me a kingdom of priests and a holy nation. These are the words that you shall speak unto the people of Israel.'

The people are set apart are from all ethnic groups and shall be 'priests'. This is brought out also in Isaiah 61:6:

> But you shall be called the priests of the Lord;
>   they shall speak of you as the ministers of our God;
> you shall eat the wealth of the nations,
>   and in their glory you shall boast.

Again in Isaiah 66:18 (note especially the phrase, 'all nations'): 'The time is coming to gather all nations and tongues. And they shall come and shall see my glory.'

When the song to the worthy Lamb is sung (5:12) it is not just the angels who sing this but all beings in the universe. In verse 13, the phrase 'under the earth' is not to be taken as a scientific reference, referring to burrowing animals, with the next phrase, 'in the sea', referring to fish. Rather, even the mountains and seas are included in this peon of praise. The whole of creation wants to sing God's glory. When God is praised the song is not only in heaven but also here on earth.

The opening of the seals

In the centre of heaven, then, is the Lamb who was slain. As the worthy One he unrolls the scroll. There were seals on scrolls because, in olden days, secure messages were carried in this way. Christ gradually removes the seals. In Revelation 6 the first seal is opened, and chapter 8 brings us to the end of the opening of the book, which marks the time for the Last Judgment (Revelation 6:1–8:5). Every removal of a seal is marked by events in history. The scroll is the book of history, the book of Life.

The accounts of the opening of seals do not give us history in the sense of dates. Rather, they name principles and meanings; they tell us about the structure and being of history – they tell us the way history is. A particular removal of a seal is not taking place on a particular date as such – each represents a meaning, a principle. The same is true of Christ as the centre of history, of course. He is not described here as the centre in a chronological sense, with so many years before the crucifixion, and so many years after. Instead, John's vision of him at the centre gives us the cardinal principle of history. The Bible is ultimately a book of consolation, even though history is often full of horror and terror. If living in the world were easy, we would not need consolation.

One of the living creatures around the throne calls to John, 'Come' (6:1). The apostle next sees a white horse. This is usually interpreted as Christ and the gospel: Christ coming in victory (cf. the same white horse in Revelation 19:11f). When he comes with the gospel, the Lord is not soft and sweet – he is forceful and warlike. The second horse he sends (v.4) is war; the third (v.5) is famine; the fourth (v.7) is death. Notice that the Christians are not taken out of this – there is no escape for us. It should not surprise us in the light of the biblical principles of history.

The coming of the terrifying horsemen is speaking of the world as it is now, in a time when we suffer wars and when there are both blessing and cursing, as we have discussed in earlier chapters. We saw that Deuteronomy makes it forcefully clear in relation to our lives that a choice is set before us, of obedience or disobedience. We are told that we will perish if we disobey. We are told to choose life and with it blessing (Deuteronomy 30:14–20). This choice is the very centre of all things that are happening; it is at the centre of history. There are both a positive and a negative side to events, and they are related. The consequences of evil are real, and the cleaning up of evil will necessarily be painful. Jeremiah too points out (Jeremiah 23:16–19) that everything will not be fine – especially verse 19:

> Behold, the storm of the Lord!
>   Wrath has gone forth,
> a whirling tempest;
>   it will burst upon the head of the wicked.

These things are as true now as they were in Jeremiah's time, and perhaps more true now. In Isaiah 66:15–24, as always in the Bible, two things are put together – the hope and the curse. Christ is not just a 'friend' or a 'mate' – he is also the person opening the book of history. There is judgment and war. God works not only through the blessings of the gospel but also through judgment and war, the other horsemen.

As Christ opens the second seal, the second living creature calls out to John, 'Come' (Revelation 6:3). He sees a red horse, and its rider is permitted to take away peace from the earth. People slay one another – it is effectively the wickedness of human beings that causes this war.

Jesus himself spoke clearly in Matthew 24:6 about the future: 'And you shall hear of wars and rumours of wars. See that you are not alarmed, for this must take place, but the end is not yet.' Earlier in the same passage (Matthew 24:3) we learn that the disciples on the Mount of Olives asked Christ about what was going to happen in the future. Jesus gave a partial answer to their question. Many believed that the world would become better, and some would falsely claim to be saviours. But Christ says, 'See that no one leads you astray.' He tells them not to be alarmed when there is war. Wars will happen. He describes times of war in the future as the beginning of a woman's inevitable labour pains.

Christians will face tribulation – wickedness will be multiplied. The future will not be sweet. In fact, he in effect is saying that there will be no time in history without wars, even though the time of the end will eventually come.

Thus Isaiah writes:

> Therefore hear the word of the Lord, you scoffers,
>   who rule this people in Jerusalem!
> Because you have said, 'We have made a covenant with death,
>   and with Sheol we have an agreement,
>   when the overflowing whip passes through
>   it will not come to us,
>   for we have made lies our refuge,
>   and in falsehood we have taken shelter;'
>   therefore thus says the Lord God,
> 'Behold, I am the one who has laid as a foundation in Zion,
>   a stone, a tested stone,
>   a precious cornerstone, of a sure foundation:
> "Whoever believes will not be in haste."' (28:14–16).

With people, wishful thinking surfaces again and again. But Christ is the only 'sure foundation' when God comes with his judgment. Outside him only sheer terror and discomfort are to be found.

> As often as it ['the overwhelming scourge'] passes through it will
>   take you;
> for morning by morning it will pass through,
>   by day and by night;
> and it will be sheer terror to understand the message.
> For the bed is too shorter to stretch oneself on,
>   and the covering too narrow to wrap oneself in (Isaiah 28:19, 20).

We can stand, because of the promise of the gospel. The Christian position is realistic; it says that living in the world will be hard. At the time that I began to study these things I was a prisoner of war. In a time of war, I discovered, we are not to be afraid, for God is working. In the end, good will win. The 'thousand year Reich' would eventually fall, as would all other future terrors.

As the third seal is opened (Revelation 6:5) the third living creature that is under the throne of God calls to John, 'Come.' This time it is a black horse he sees, the horse of Famine. This means that until Christ returns there will always be famine. 'The oil and the wine' of verse 6 are luxuries. In famine, simple staple goods become a luxury. This reference adds to the vivid reality of the depiction of famine.

Then the fourth seal is opened (verse 7), and again John is told, 'Come.' The fourth rider is Death, empowered to slaughter. This again refers to all history, not simply to a single date in time. It is not only about death in general, stating the truism that all will die. It is speaking of violent death, death from a disaster.

Jesus similarly spoke of violent events like famines and earthquakes (Matthew 24:7): 'For nation will rise against nation, and kingdom against kingdom, and there will be famines and earthquakes in various places.'

Here Christ tells of things to come. Masses of people will die at once. The prophet Hosea speaks of the same thing, namely death, as God's mouthpiece:

> Shall I ransom them from the power of Sheol?
>   Shall I redeem them from Death?
> O death, where are your plagues?
>   O Sheol, where is your sting?
> Compassion is hidden from my eyes (13:14).

Sheol is the grave. 'O Sheol where is thy sting?' refers to the fact that Christ (the ransom) removes the sting of death. Death is normal; this is not speaking of mere death, but death as a terrifying curse. One of the most beautiful passages in the Bible, Amos 3:1–8, concerns God's causal hand in fearful events like widespread death. The punishments of God's judgment have everything to do with basic Christian faith: they are a sign of God's working in history. He comes in judgment as well as in blessing. The punishment is for disobedience and iniquity. Furthermore, God works specifically in individual or particular situations. There is no neutrality here as anywhere else; wars are never neutral and automatic as far as God is concerned. A trumpet cannot blow in the city (announcing danger) without people becoming fearful. Similarly, in a modern war, the siren cannot sound without that same trepidation arising. God's actions are part of this causality. God has spoken about his actions; the prophet can but prophesy. God is doing something in history.

The opening of the fifth seal (Revelation 6:9, 10) marks a dramatic change: the souls of the slain cry out for vengeance and redress. The previous happenings were all naturally related – like famine and death. But now something occurs that surprises us, and it surprises us because our way of thinking is askew. The deaths of the martyred believers do matter. Thus they are right to ask God to do something about their deaths, to avenge them. It is a cry for justice as in the Old Testament (Habakkuk 1:2). The suffering of these believers has been unspeakable. 'The earth' here refers to the non-believing world, not to our planet. The 'white robe' (Revelation 6:11) refers to the consolation that the salvation of the martyrs will be completed. We have made a rotten world of it, and God is cleaning it up. Christ is the centre of history; he is the Lord of history. History therefore never passes out of God's hands. The optimism of Christianity is a hard optimism, not a soft one. We are exhorted 'Don't be afraid,' not 'Relax, it will be easy.'

One of the reasons I have made this study of God's hand in history is because people so often say that the gospel is tender and full of love. But that is not a true picture of the gospel. If our salvation were only that, I could well understand people revolting against it and saying that to believe in such a sort of God is outrageous; but when people revolt against that conception they are not revolting against the true God. It is not what the Bible says. The Bible speaks about the hard and bitter things of human life such as war, famine, disease and death (the four horsemen of Revelation). It forces us to reconsider and ask: What kind of God is our God?

In the midst of all the horrible things in history – war, famine and terror but also the force of the gospel – the martyrs under the throne cry out, 'How long?' God, in response, offers a real consolation to them. He gives each a white robe and tells them to be patient and to rest, for he is working in history.

John goes on to speak of the impact of the opening of the sixth seal in weighty, beautiful language (Revelation 6:12–17):

> When he [the rider of the pale horse of Death] opened the sixth seal, I looked, and behold, there was a great earthquake, and the sun became black as sackcloth, and the full moon became like blood, and the stars of the sky fell to the earth as a fig tree sheds its winter fruit when shaken by a gale. The sky vanished like a scroll that is being rolled up, and every mountain and island was removed from its place. Then the kings of the earth and the great ones and the generals and the rich and the powerful, and every one, slave and free, hid themselves in the caves and among the rocks of the mountains, calling to the mountains and rocks, 'Fall on us and hide us from the face of him who is seated on the throne, and from the wrath of the Lamb, for the great day of their wrath has come, and who can stand?'

The Bible is written in a kind of language that I would not use – it repeats itself constantly; there are digressions and asides; and there are apparent anomalies and inconsistencies. But, for all this, there is a wonderful condensation, compression and compactness to the Bible – a miracle in itself. For all its repetitions, passages such as the one I just quoted are far shorter than we today could write if we had to convey the same content.

Fact-crazy people, including Christians, take all in this passage as if it were happening literally, with great earthquakes and a darkening sun. Yet is the sun dark today, as these events take place? What is this passage actually saying? Is it speaking of great natural disturbances? Perhaps, but not necessarily. (We now know of the relationship between sun spots and terrestrial storms.) Are the stars going to literally fall? Perhaps – but only perhaps.

Natural disturbances, specifically the calamities related here, are not the central meaning of the passage – to see it so is to read it badly and improperly. Let us ask, rather, how Revelation sums up and encapsulates the Bible. How does it make the meaning of the Bible clear? Let us once more pick out some representative passages from throughout the Bible that are collated and summed up in Revelation.

'But in those days, after that tribulation, the sun will be darkened, and the moon shall not give its light, and the stars will be falling from heaven, and the powers in the heavens will be shaken' (Mark 13:24,25). Clearly, terrible things are going to happen in the future. There will be an 'abomination of desolation' (Mark 13:14). After these things however the Son of Man will be seen in all his glory (Mark 13:26). We have the same imagery here as we have in Revelation 6. Similarly we read Jesus' words in Luke 21:25–28:

> And there shall be signs in sun and moon and stars, and on the earth distress of nations in perplexity because of the roaring of the sea and the waves, people fainting with fear and with foreboding of what is coming on the world. For the powers of the heavens will be shaken. And then they will see the Son of Man coming in a cloud with power and great glory. Now when these things begin to take place, straighten up and raise your heads, because your redemption is drawing near.

Again we are told of terrible days to come. Christ talks of Jerusalem and of the distress of nations. After this, he says, the Son of Man shall be seen. *Perhaps* before he comes, something as described will literally happen to the sun, moon and stars. But here the Bible is speaking poetically of these bodies. However, to say this is poetic language is emphatically not to say that this is not real. This is as real as real can be.

There is also a prophecy of Daniel (Daniel 8) in which he looks into the future and speaks of a goat fighting a ram. Alexander the Great (356–323 BC) is the he-goat, while the ram is the Persian Empire. Out of the goat, four kingdoms grow. Reference is made to the 'glorious land', namely Palestine. Then Daniel 8:10, 11 reads: 'It [one of the kingdoms] grew great, even to the host of heaven. And some of the host and some of the stars it threw down to the ground and trampled on them . . . And the regular burnt offering was taken away from him, and the place of his sanctuary was overthrown.'

Notice the imagery of falling stars. This is the same symbolism as is used in Revelation, Mark and Luke. What is this prophecy of Daniel speaking about? It tells us of a great king who would stop sacrifices to God (verse 11) and substitute them with sacrifices to Jupiter – for this deity, a pig was slaughtered and there were even human sacrifices made. Stars are cast to the ground. This passage is not speaking of literal stars but of the people of God. The great king tramples them down. Revelation ties in with this outrage when it portrays the deaths of the martyrs. But Revelation is fulfilled at all periods of history – for example, the red horse of war is fulfilled in all ages. The prophecy is not only fulfilled in Daniel's time but in many other periods, for it speaks of the principles of history. Even as far back as in Daniel, the insight into history that is given is not simply into specific events. At the end of the book of Daniel, it speaks of the finale of history (Daniel 12). There is a Last Judgment, and the 'wise', the believers, are described as being like stars (Daniel 12:3).

The prophet Micah also speaks of a dark period when bad prophets make his people err (Micah 3:5–7). These prophets are mercenary; they prophesy according to the payment and food they are given; they can be bought. Because of them and their acceptance by the people, God says that he will not help the people and, consequently, it will be dark around them.

Amos too writes about such dark days in Amos 5:18–20. He speaks of the day of God's wrath, a day of darkness that will be a time of woe when he declares:

> Shall not the land tremble on this account,
>   and every one mourn who dwells in it,
> and all of it rise like the Nile,
>   and be tossed about and sink again, like the Nile of Egypt?
> 'And on that day,' declares the Lord God,
>   'I will make the sun to go down at noon
>   and darken the earth in broad daylight' (Amos 8:8,9).

Once again there are awesome prophecies of flooding and of the sun going down at noon.

Isaiah presents the same theme of the darkness of the Day of the Lord:

> Behold, the day of the Lord comes,
>   Cruel, with wrath and fierce anger,
> to make the land a desolation
>   and to destroy its sinners from it.
> For the stars of the heavens and their constellations
>   will not give their light;
> the sun shall be dark at its rising,
>   and the moon will not shed its light (Isaiah 13:9,10).

I have given a few quotations to convey a sense of the implications of this prophetic imagery. We find unremitting repetition: the stars will not give any light; the sun will not shine; there will be terrifying darkness. This is like our world today as the darkness increases. While God is not the author of evil, he does initiate punishment and judgment. His concern is for justice. He is active in wars such as what happened in Vietnam. The age-old prophecies are being fulfilled again and again.

Here are some more representative biblical passages seen through the eyes of the book of Revelation, and gathered and summarized there, beginning with Isaiah, who declares God's terrifying judgment:

> All the host of heaven shall rot away,
>   and the skies roll up like a scroll.
> All their host shall fall,
>   as leaves fall from the vine,
>   like leaves falling from the fig tree (Isaiah 34:4).

All this is very real, even if the mountains and the amount of blood are not literal. The heavens being rolled up like a scroll, the stars like falling figs, use the same words, ideas, metaphors and 'real symbols' as we encounter in Revelation. There are references to portents in the sky, and people fleeing and hiding from the wrath of God. All these are similar to what is found in Revelation.

a) Portents in the sky

The prophet Joel pictures astounding portents, or 'wonders', in the skies and on the earth:

> And I will show wonders in the heavens and on the earth, blood and fire and columns of smoke. The sun shall be turned to darkness, and the moon to blood, before the great and awesome day of the Lord comes. And it shall come to pass that everyone who calls on the name of the Lord shall be saved. For in Mount Zion and in Jerusalem there shall be those who escape, as the Lord has said, and among the survivors shall be those whom the Lord calls (Joel 2:30–32).

This passage tells about the future – the preceding verses tell of the coming of the Holy Spirit and were cited at Pentecost (Acts 2:17–21). The same wonders come into the fervent prayer of Habakkuk:

> The mountains saw you and writhed;
>   the raging waters swept on;
> the deep gave forth its voice;
>   it lifted its hands on high.
> The sun and moon stood still in their place
>   at the light of your arrows as they sped,
>   at the flash of your glittering spear (Habakkuk 3:10–11).

Habakkuk speaks of God coming with judgment. The sun and the moon stand still. He does not say that these things, which we see today, portents like war and calamity, are 'wonderful' in the usual sense; they are dreadfully disturbing. It is not Christian to be pleased about such horrors. Jeremiah's attitude was right when he wept over the fall of Jerusalem. His heartrending prayer vividly echoes the sorrow of Habakkuk (see Habakkuk 3:16).

b) Fleeing and hiding

John paints a scene in which our desire to hide from God (Genesis 3:8) is taken to its extreme when kings, presidents, prime ministers, military commanders, world leaders, great men, and the mass of humanity all hide themselves under rocks from the wrath of God (Revelation 6:15–17). This is very real when it speaks of people fleeing and hiding from God. In the Old Testament we have a similar scene:

> For the Lord of hosts has a day
>   against all that is proud and lofty,
>   against all that is lifted up—and it shall be brought low...
> And people shall enter the caves of the rocks
>   and the holes of the ground,
> from before the terror of the Lord,
>   and from the splendor of his majesty,
>   when he rises to terrify the earth (Isaiah 2:12,19).

The principle here is that the Lord shall be exalted; the high made low. Indeed, all hide in caves for fear of the Lord.

The seventh seal

As Christ takes the book of seven seals, his removing of the seals is history – but not what we think of as history. We think of this or that date of a war or a discovery or a new philosophy or a new idea as history. But there is something more behind it all. Here in Revelation, through John's depictions, the veil is lifted as we see Christ removing the seals. Though symbolic, this is very real. The removal of the last seal is the Last Judgment.

We must understand, in considering the trumpets, that Revelation is composed of cycle upon cycle of events rather than of a chronological sequence. With the opening of the seventh seal, after a silence in heaven for half an hour, there is the blowing of trumpets (Revelation 8:1). John finds the results hard to describe – in one place he describes the vision as 'something like' (8:8). The results are hard to describe even in symbols. An example of such a symbol is that one third of the trees, the seas and the green grass is destroyed or spoiled. The 'sun' and the 'moon' are symbolic words, as is 'great star' (8:10). With these trumpet sounds, Revelation is speaking of natural disasters. If there is famine in India or West Africa, we should not say, 'Too bad, there was a sunspot' (or something similar). Rather, we must see that famine has to do with God's judgment on our world. The visions of the trumpets are not merely of 'spiritual' significance. The veil of history is lifted and we are shown what the eye cannot see.

When there is silence for half an hour after the seventh seal is opened, everyone in heaven realizes that something immense is happening. I cannot explain why the pause is half an hour. This is beyond our knowledge; we are at the limits of what humans can understand. What does half an hour mean in heaven? It can only mean that God – and all the heavenlies with him – is interested in and aware of earthly happenings.

John speaks of an altar with a 'golden censor', based upon Old Testament imagery. The Roman Catholic Church still retains these symbols in worship. Probably there is no literal altar in heaven, but this description is nevertheless real. In fact, it does not matter whether there is a literal altar in heaven or not – these indispensable images are there to help us understand the meaning.

The prayers of the saints are described as an offering (Revelation 8:3–5). Sometimes, in the Old Testament, an illegitimate sacrifice was described as a 'bad odour' to God. The imagery here is the ancient imagery of the Old Testament, weighty with meaning. The prayers of the saints – our prayers – are there, before God.

Christ speaks of the end of the world in the same way as the book of Revelation does:

> Immediately after the tribulation of those days the sun will be darkened, and the moon will not give its light, and the stars will fall from heaven, and the powers of the heavens will be shaken. Then will appear in heaven the sign of the Son of Man, and then all the tribes of the earth will mourn, and they will see the Son of Man coming on the clouds of heaven with power and great glory. And he will send out his angels with a loud trumpet call, and they will gather his elect from the four winds, from one end of heaven to the other (Matthew 24:29–31).

Notice that angels with trumpets are mentioned. Furthermore Jesus describes the sun as being darkened – using the same image as in Revelation. God is working in all events like famine and war – they are not merely the Devil's work. God is not a sweet 'do-gooder'. God of course wishes to do good, but it must involve destroying evil. The resultant war – the battle between good and evil – makes up history. When our prayers are fulfilled and answered, this battle is carried forward, the battle against the misuse of women, against the wrong use of power, against enslavement and pollution and greed for gain. We should praise the Lord because he does something about these evils.

This work of God reminds us of the principles set out in Deuteronomy 28–30 and passages in Leviticus, Jeremiah and many other places we have looked at earlier. They tell us of both God's promise and his curse. His promise is of the Messiah and of our inheritance of the earth. Those who obey God are exalted and receive blessings. These are real blessings that are evident in the fields and rivers, and in the health and beauty of people, in children, cattle and other aspects of a full human life. God's blessing gives the 'good life'. His blessing is not only spiritual and psychological. However, the Bible also tells of God's judgments, in which often the innocent are caught up. Many more curses are mentioned than blessings, for we, being fallible, need to be reminded again and again of the negative side of our relationship with God.

Late twentieth-century Western people have undoubtedly become 'soft'. We have forgotten the harsh realities of life. Everything is cushioned, especially in America. We do not see fighting in the streets, empty food cupboards. We have forgotten that the world is in a terrible situation and in need of justice and judgment. We have to see God's judgment in this light: If you really love something, will you let it get beaten down? I heard a story once of a youth who claimed that he loved a girl, but when she was attacked by a gang he stood by and did nothing. Micah speaks of the reality of evil (Micah 7:1–7), and trusts in God to deliver him. His faith is that God is not indifferent to what is happening on earth.

> Woe is me! For I have become as when the summer fruit has been gathered,
>   as when the grapes have been gleaned:
> there is no cluster to eat,
>   no first-ripe fig that my soul desires.
> The godly has perished from the earth,
>   and there is no one upright among mankind;
> they all lie in wait for blood,
>   and each hunts the other with a net.
> Their hands are on what is evil, to do it well;
>   the prince and the judge ask for a bribe,
> and the great man utters the evil desire of his soul;
>   thus they weave it together.
> The best of them is like a brier,
>   the most upright of them a thorn hedge.
> The day of your watchmen, of your punishment, has come;
>   now their confusion is at hand.
> Put no trust in a neighbour;
>   have no confidence in a friend;
> guard the doors of your mouth
>   from her who lies in your arms;
> for the son treats the father with contempt,
>   the daughter rises up against her mother,
> the daughter-in-law against her mother-in-law;
>   a man's enemies are the men of his own house.
> But as for me, I will look to the Lord;
>   I will wait for the God of my salvation;
>   my God will hear me.

9
Christians in the World Today

Revelation, the last book of the Bible, gives a condensed view of history from the time that Christ left the earth till his return. This is a history that repeats the fundamental pattern of earlier ages. Revelation speaks about those great things that were prophesied in the Old Testament times but were not yet completely fulfilled by Christ in his first coming to the world to live among us. It shows how these yet to be fulfilled events are going to fill up this age of history between Christ's first and second coming, till the Last Day comes, when the final enemy, death, is decisively destroyed (1 Corinthians 15:26).

Revelation is a book full of terrible events, full of God's judgment, showing us what his curse really means. In stressing the gospel when preaching to non-Christians we often emphasize God's saving grace, his openness to accept repentant sinners – but our message is not complete and not totally true if we leave out that God, in his love for his creatures, really cannot fail to see iniquity and therefore does come also in judgment. We can then prophesy to those around us that God is active and concerned about what they do, so that they will be without any excuse (cf. Ezekiel 33:1–20).

The first twelve chapters of the book of Revelation form a unity. They tell of the opening of the seals of the special scroll, the book of history. The opening of the seals *is* history. One cycle of events starts at the beginning of chapter 6 and ends with the opening of the seventh seal, which is significant because it starts another parallel cycle, that of the seven trumpets. The seventh trumpet marks the end of the second cycle and also of the first half of the Revelation. The last trumpet, described in chapter 11, is the Last Judgment. We are told of 'thunder and lightning'. In this case, the thunder and lightning is a symbol or outward expression of God's greatness. The ark is a symbol of God himself. The energy and power of this ark is the thunder and lightning. This symbolism of the natural phenomena signifies something very specific.

This chapter speaks of the Last Judgment as the time when Christ is given the kingship over the world, when he is anointed to be King in all eternity (see also 1 Corinthians 15:20–28). There are, clearly, two sides to the Last Judgment. One side is about the judgment of humanity. The other side is about Christ becoming King. As it was in the beginning, so it will be at the end. The Last Judgment is both terrible and wonderful as the familiar is transformed into the unfamiliar.

As Christians, we can be confident at the Last Judgment. All bad things like pain, death, and tears, will be gone. God will truly be King.

We anticipate this with joy, even though, naturally, our feelings are mixed. When we pray, 'Your kingdom come,' we pray for that day. This can be compared with the end of Revelation, where John declares 'Even so, come Lord Jesus'. Something great is to come.

Revelation is a book of consolation for the Christian. It shows that God is there in the hard times; he is not out of it but is concerned to protects us in the midst of all the woes. And in chapter 12, God tells us what that means for us.

The woman and the dragon (Revelation 12:1–6)

In the Bible we often find the metaphor of a woman representing a community: God's people are his bride, they are the daughter of Jerusalem. If however the daughter of Zion is going astray and apostasy is taking place – as when the Israelites are following other gods – then it is said that she is a prostitute. She is a whore following other lovers rather than her rightful one, the lover of her youth who discovered her as a foundling and raised her to be his fiancée and bride (Ezekiel 16). And again we read about such a woman, the great whore sitting on the beast, or Babel (Babylon) in Revelation 17. She is the counterpart, the degeneration, of the woman prepared for Christ – she is the fallen woman.

The woman of Revelation 12 is described as clothed with the sun – God takes care of her. The moon is under her feet and on her head is a crown of twelve stars – a reference to the twelve tribes of Israel, twelve being the number of God's covenant. She is pregnant with a child who, as the next verses makes clear, is the coming Messiah. This woman is Israel, the people of God who in Old Testament times were full of the coming Messiah, looking forward to the event, indeed were 'pregnant' with it. Out of the flesh of his people, the promised seed was to come. Then we are told of the dragon – clearly Satan, the snake, the Evil one – who is threatening the woman, and trying to get the child in his power. But the child, Jesus Christ, who 'will rule them [the nations] with a rod of iron' (Revelation 2:27), was quickly snatched away up to God and his throne – referring back to chapters 4 and 5, and very concisely showing the real meaning and impact of the work of Christ. After delivering the child, the woman flees into the wilderness where she has a place prepared for her by God, 'in which she is to be nourished 1,260 days'. God takes care of his people in this period we inhabit, the time after Christ's first coming and ascension back to heaven. The woman, who is still his bride, is now full of anticipation for the return of her groom.

In these opening verses there is no reference to the seals and trumpets of earlier chapters. Something completely new is beginning. Nor is there any discussion of the meaning of the woman. It is clear however that she is the church of God and God's people of the Old

Testament. Verse 17 refers to the seed of the woman – Christ came out from humankind in fulfilment of prophecy. In the Old Testament childless women were actually scorned, as children had to be born in order to preserve the lineage from which the Messiah was to come.

We follow the story of the woman before and after the birth of her child, Christ. The child is quickly taken away from the woman and back to God – Christ's life on earth is a very short moment in history. All that is recorded in detail in the Gospels basically represents only three years. The meaning of the return of the child to God, to heaven, is found back in chapter 5: Christ is the Lamb who was slain, the King of history, alone worthy to open the scroll of the ages. We are told: 'She gave birth to a male child, one who is to rule all the nations with a rod of iron, but her child was caught up to God, and to his throne.' This child is going to rule over the world firmly, strongly and severely. It follows that we must not speak only of Christ as loving – that is only half the truth, and half the truth can be a lie. Particularly in the Anglo-Saxon evangelical world there is an emphasis on a certain kind of evangelism, in which Christ is pictured as sweet, effeminate and soft. Understandably, many reject this Christ as unreal. Christ does not only softly and tenderly say 'Come home' but he himself also emphasizes his terrifying judgment.

Francis Schaeffer's book *The God Who is There* points out the reality of God. When people accept God's reality, even the angels are joyful. But when he is rejected, the person who rejects him is worse off than before – it is a bad message, then, not Good News. Christ is not soft and tame. Christ *hates* death, sin and the evil happenings in the world. This hatred accounts for his coming again in power and in judgment.

Once, during a time I was at L'Abri, there was an international crisis making everybody tense and afraid that there might be another world war. But my advice to the students was not to be afraid, even if the Chinese or Russians or other forces should go war. Christ is the General above all generals, President above all presidents, the Prime Minister of all prime ministers. Even a formidable atheistic force is not ultimately strong. There are woes that are undeniably terrible, but Christ holds human history in his hands. He has the power to do good *and* to destroy evil – and one involves the other. The book of Revelation describes the cleaning up of the world – there is no desperation of mood in its pages. Christ suffered to save, but this is the way the world is to be cleansed.

War in heaven (Revelation 12:7–12)

After the woman flees to the wilderness, we read about a great battle between God's angels and the dragon and his angels, fallen angels. The dragon was thrown down as the fruit of the finished work of Christ, who overcame the powers of evil. This is the fulfilment of the promise in

Genesis 3 – that the seed of the woman shall bruise the head of the serpent. Here is another glimpse of the great implications of what it means when we say that Christ is the centre of history – this is the real meaning of his redemptive work, and Christ himself spoke about it: 'I saw Satan fall like lightning from heaven' (Luke 10:18). The next verses (Revelation 12:10–12) make up a magnificent song of rejoicing; it is the supreme hymn in which all the heavens and the earth tell of the implications and meaning of the great war in heaven:

> Now the salvation and the power and the kingdom of our God and the authority of his Christ have come, for the accuser of our brothers [and sisters] has been thrown down, who accuses them day and night before our God. And they have conquered him by the blood of the Lamb and by the word of their testimony, for they loved not their lives even unto death. Therefore, rejoice, O heavens and you who dwell in them! But woe to you, O earth and sea, for the devil has come down to you in great wrath, because he knows that his time is short!

'Now war arose in heaven'(v.7). The beginning of the Book of Job provides a glimpse into this event in the unseen world. This makes it very clear that the Devil is the accuser, and that he is on the attack. This view of an unseen battle is therefore not unique to the book of Revelation. The archangel Michael, guardian of God's people, fights the enemy of humankind. We read of this in Daniel, and more about the battle in Ephesians (6:12). But this is not part of our usual thinking; and therefore not part of our usual experience. We are not used to thinking that there is a battle in the heavens. We cannot literally see Michael fighting there, yet there is a certain blindness in *not* seeing it. The eyes of Elisha's servant were once opened, and he saw the angelic chariots of battle (2 Kings 6:15–17). Angels have some kind of body, evidently, even though these bodies are not like ours. It is better to say that they have some kind of body unknown to us than merely to say that they are 'spiritual'.

There is a war between the forces of Darkness and Light. Even if one is completely alone when one sins, a battle is lost because it is seen by the heavenly powers. Nothing that we do is meaningless. Even the small things are unimaginably important, for the consequences are endless.

We have already mentioned Christ's declaration, 'I saw Satan fall like lightning from heaven.' This appears in the middle of a passage that deals with the power of Satan (Luke 10:17–20). Now Satan is not in heaven any more but on earth. One of the tricks of the Devil is to get people to believe that he does not exist – this non-belief increases his power. In the work of L'Abri I have found that things always go wrong. This is not surprising, for the Devil is working to break it up. The battle is very real, for the Devil is really working.

I heard the story of a person who visited a university to take part in an evangelistic outreach event. A group of students had started to play with demonic powers, and that had frightened them. Reportedly they all became Christians during the mission. They had seen the reality of the unseen power of Satan.

In Tibet many strange, supernatural things are said to have happened. Apparently there have been magical happenings, such as arrows falling from the sky. Also, it is claimed that money can buy a death curse upon somebody. Is this obviously exaggerated and untrue? It is better to say that these sorts of things ring true, for they do occur. Similarly in countries where animism is practiced these sorts of things happen.

The Dohnavur Fellowship in India help difficult children from many backgrounds. In one of their homes a girl wrote a letter to a man in her home village. Soon sand and stones, apparently from nowhere, started to be thrown into the house. None of the other girls was doing it – it was an occult happening.

Christianity displaces evil forces. Since the Reformation, black magic has been subdued in Europe, not because it was just imaginary but because of the power of God. In a Christian country the Devil's power is reduced. But now it is again on the increase. These things are very real.

Pursued into the wilderness (Revelation 12:13–17)

The dragon, realizing that he has been thrown down to the ground, pursues the woman, namely God's people. But she is brought to the wilderness – the story, which has been left off at verse 7, is taken up again – to be nourished there for a time, times and half a time. 'Times, times and half a time' is a phrase that reminds us of other verses in the Bible. It means a time that is long, and is even much longer, but just when we begin to think it will go yet longer, it suddenly begins to come to an end. (In a comparable way in Revelation 11:11 we read about three and a half days. If we count times as years, these times mean 1260 days, or 42 months, as in Daniel 7:25 and 12:7; Revelation 12:6, 14 and 13:5). This is the time between the first and second comings of Christ, the great in-between age about which Revelation speaks.

The question is what 'wilderness' means in this context. Is it, after all, so that the Christian community is in a 'wilderness' or, as some translations have it, a 'desert', a place far away from cities, vineyards, cultivated fields, in short, far away from all culture? What does it mean that the woman – the communion of saints, the church of God, God's people, Christ's bride – is in the wilderness?

Certainly the wilderness is a place where the devil cannot follow her. He tries to sweep her away by means of a river, but the earth swallows the river and so saves the woman. Rivers, waters, often in Revelation indicate a mass of people, so maybe this force aimed at sweeping away Christianity is absorbed by the masses, perhaps those who are indifferent yet make a full and final persecution of Christians impossible. There is reason to think this might be the explanation here.

It is because the dragon loses the war in heaven that he turns upon the woman and persecutes her, pursuing her in the wilderness. But the earth helps her. These metaphors are difficult and we cannot understand all the details. We do not know the Bible well enough to understand all the connotations of the metaphors; we need to read the Old Testament attentively. The difficulty with these metaphors is to know where the boundaries are between the real and the metaphorical. This is especially true for us today, when we have little understanding of the nature of metaphor.

But this chapter is not difficult in its general thrust; only the details are difficult. The woman is brought to the wilderness and God gives her wings in order to flee.

Even though it is true that Christ has power over the Devil and has won the war in heaven – consider the fact that he drove out demons – yet the Christian has to fight against evil powers and has to be very careful. Not only are we told that our battle is against the powers from on high (Ephesians 6) – and in many places the apostles in their letters warn us not to give the Devil any opportunity (Ephesians 4:27; cf. 1 Timothy 6:12; 2 Timothy 2:26; James 4:7; 1 John 3:8) – but Jesus himself told us to pray: 'Lead us not into temptation, but deliver us from evil.' This prayer is very important. If we find in the countries of Western civilization that there is not much magic, dark powers, witchcraft and possession, in short, if it appears that here the power of the Devil is reduced, I believe this is in answer to the prayers of Christians. As soon as we leave the old world of Christianity, we find dark powers, magic and all kinds of occultism abound. But we also see these powers growing again today in the Western world and it is certainly not just by chance that that growth coincides with the waning of Christianity, with the fact that we are living in a postchristian world.

In the wilderness the Devil's power is frustrated, even if occult practices abound. The wilderness is mentioned many times in the Bible. It is of course the place where the Israelites lived for 40 years, a time of which we are told:

> [It was] the way that the Lord your God has led you ... that he might humble you, testing you to know what was in your heart, whether you would keep his commandments or not. And he humbled you and let you hunger and fed you with manna, which you did not know ... that he might make you know that man does not live by bread alone, but man lives by every word that comes from the mouth of the Lord. Your clothing did not wear out on you and your foot did not swell these forty years ... For the Lord your God is bringing you into a good land ... in which you will lack nothing ... (Deuteronomy 8:2ff; cf. 6:10 ff).

The wilderness is never the final goal; it looks forward to the fulfillment of the promise of all the good things of life – we are reminded here again of the words of Jesus, like a refrain in Matthew 6 (vs.4b, 6b, 18b, 33b).

The wilderness is a place of testing. We are reminded of the temptation of Christ by the Devil. Christ made it clear in his answer to the Devil – in Matthew 4:4, quoting from Deuteronomy 8:3 – that God feeds people; he will give us all we need, and we should not bow to the Devil in order to have 'the good life'.

The wilderness is also a place where God acts. The wilderness is a place of God's wrath until his longed-for promise is fulfilled and 'the wilderness and the dry land shall be glad' (Isaiah 35:1), and 'a highway shall be there' (Isaiah 35:6).

With Christ gone, the woman flees into the wilderness (verse 6). When the woman flees there it is a desolation. It is far away from human habitation and there is no shelter. It is an unfriendly place. This chapter seems to take us from its present time to somewhere near the end of time. What then is this wilderness or desolation?

Some have argued that it means 'lack of culture'. Christians should be plain-living; inhabiting a cultural desert; 'unworldly'. As someone very interested in the meaning of culture, I have thought much about this interpretation. Here are some points against this view:

1. Even if this interpretation *were* true, it may not be used as an excuse not to work in one's culture. Here is an analogy for not using such an excuse. During the argument between the Jewish leaders and Pilate, the leaders cursed, 'His blood be upon us and our children.' This sadly is a real curse that has proved to be horribly true. It is in fact one of the proofs of the truth of the Bible that there is a judgment from God upon the Jewish people. But this judgment can never be used as an excuse for anti-Semitism. Christians cannot deliberately be the instrument of the persecution of Jewish people. To the contrary, we should help them in their suffering. God is fulfilling his prophecies, not we. If it were not so, and we were to deliberately fulfil prophecy, prophecies would merely be suggestions, self-fulfilling and not miraculous. It has to be up to God alone to fulfil them by the very nature of their being prophecy. In a similar way, we cannot use an argument that excuses us for remaining in a cultural desert. We are not to actively contribute to a desolation.

Rather than the 'cultural desert' theory, the wilderness more likely means the normal situation of the church. It seems much more likely, and more natural, to mean that the church is persecuted. In a time of persecution no time may be left for cultural development; the priority would be to remain alive, to survive. So there is this possible explanation of a 'cultural desert', which may not be used as an excuse to fail to discover the cultural possibilities open to us.

2. The biblical context possibly gives a different connotation to 'wilderness'. The people of God are described in one place as being like a prostitute because of their backsliding (Hosea 2:13–15). God says that he will bring them into the wilderness. A wilderness here is a place where there is nothing, a place requiring a fresh start. God in fact has prepared something completely new for us; it is not a patch-up job.

God promises that he will act – the Spirit shall be *poured* down from upon high onto the wilderness; there will be broad rivers (Isaiah 32:12–16; 33:20,21). In both passages from Isaiah, the word 'wilderness' is not used negatively. It is a place to be made alive; it is meant to come alive. In the wilderness there will be growing fields. It is a place of unrealized potential. Christianity always requires that something be *done;* it does something, but the possibilities of what can be done are given by God. It is God's *doing through* Christians. God is an active God. There is always activity going on. We are to *do* the truth – living and doing wisely. Take the choice of Abraham and Lot respectively, early in the Old Testament story. Lot chooses what seems the 'best' – cultured people, fertile land, an easy life. Abraham however has to lead a nomadic existence in a place that is half desert, on the fringe of the Negev. But God used Abraham to shape history.

The wilderness of Revelation is not easy to grasp; it is many-sided in meaning. But the idea of a 'cultural desert' is a modern, not biblical, idea, I suspect. It does not really fit into the biblical connotation of wilderness. What Revelation is talking about is very real. The dragon tries to overpower the woman in the wilderness, but cannot. God however makes the wilderness to bloom and flourish. He makes it a place to live, and a place of life.

3. A third aspect of the wilderness and a Christian's cultural calling is this. The Bible makes it clear that Christian faith is not a soft option. The following verses make this very clear: 'They will deliver you up to tribulation and put you to death, and you will be hated by all nations for my name's sake' (Matthew 24:9); 'Beloved, do not be surprised at the fiery trial when it comes upon you to test you, as though something strange were happening to you. But rejoice insofar as you share Christ's sufferings, that you also may rejoice and be glad when his glory is revealed' (1 Peter 4:12,13).

Someone wrote to me that Christianity means the end to all difficulties, and yet he was facing very real difficulties as a Christian. He was perplexed. Christ provides the answer. If you are a child of mine, he says, then you must expect tribulation and suffering: 'Blessed are those who are persecuted' (Matthew 5:10).

We are to be as wise as serpents, and yet to be sheep among wolves. We are not tanks or armoured cars among wolves. (By the way, sheep are foolish and troublesome; they are not easy to handle. Sheep have almost no defensive weapons.) We are told not to fear those who kill the body. Perhaps you will have to face death. The worst that can happen, however, is not physical death. God's 'second death' is more terrible.

Christ also is the one who said, 'Do not think that I have come to bring peace to the earth. I have not come to bring peace, but a sword' (Matthew 10:34). Christians too readily say that the gospel means joy, peace, something we can be comfortable with. But peace doesn't mean sitting in a big soft armchair smoking a cigar (admittedly, a Dutch picture of happiness), having a big car like my neighbours and all the latest accessories. That *isn't* Christianity. Christianity brings upon itself many troubles, because God is setting the world right.

This is why Revelation is, in the first place, a book of consolation. It is *real* in what it says. If any age makes it clear that Revelation is true, our age does. Becoming a Christian does not introduce people to an easy, bed-of-roses life. We should not be optimistic about the future, especially here in the West. In a sense, troubles are normal. We have had, in the recent past, an abnormally easy time. Even Christians have begun to say, 'We can manage it ourselves.' When the woman becomes a prostitute, the wilderness becomes truly *desolate.*

Today, indeed, the people of God have a special place in the midst of hardships, when the four horsemen of Revelation 6 are passing over the earth bringing famine, war and death. We need not fear. Like God's people whose houses were sealed with blood on the eve of leaving Egypt, we too are sealed (Revelation 7:2, 3). The Lord has written in his book those who are his.

In the meantime we are called to 'Seek righteousness; seek humility' (Zephaniah 2:3), to act with integrity, obeying God's commands and not compromising with the idols of the world. There is no room for the pretension that we are to change history or even to save ourselves: our involvement in culture must not be with the idea that God needs the assistance of our great accomplishments. We are cast into the wilderness, and it is he who pours down his Spirit so that the wilderness lives. Humility implies looking to him for shelter in the day of adversity, as Zephaniah suggests, using words that are nearly identical to the words of Christ – to seek God's kingdom first, and the rest will follow.

Revelation is perhaps the most beautiful book ever written. It is weighty with meaning – we must open our eyes to it, even if we do not understand every word. We have eternity to study it and understand it. The vantage point that it offers on all of history, however, is ours now.

Part II

ARTICLES AND INTERVIEWS

Prophecy in the Old and New Testaments: God's Way with Israel

Dedicated to Riki Spetter
Stanislau, 19 September 1943

'Every part of the Holy Scriptures should be read in the same spirit as that in which it is written.' [3]

What do the Holy Scriptures prophesy? Is there a single great line in all the prophecies, and if so, what has been fulfilled and what still has to happen? What does Holy Scripture tell us about the future of Israel and Judah? Do the Scriptures give us an answer to the question, 'Why this wondrous course of events with Judah?' And what is Israel's role in connection with that? In a word, what is the course of humanity according to the Holy Scriptures, or does Holy Scripture only give religious 'ethical' truths and are the prophecies only 'poetic dressing'?

I hope to give an answer here to these questions. Our concern is with the larger picture. To the extent possible I have avoided passages that are difficult to interpret.

When I began this investigation I started out from an entirely unprejudiced position (or at least from as unprejudiced a position as possible). I set out with a desire to investigate exclusively and only the Scriptures. Only thereafter would it be possible to evaluate various persuasions such as the BIM[4] in respect of their being probable and scriptural. Isaiah 34:16: 'Look in the scroll of the Lord and read: None of these will be missing . . . his Spirit will gather them together.'

The prophet

Prophet is etymologically derived from 'speaking in the name of God'. Implicit in this 'speaking in the name of God' is the prophets' greatest problem: God has spoken with them, let them hear something, let them see, in short they have had a religious experience. Cf. Jeremiah 31:26, Ezekiel 40:1, Zechariah 1:8. How now to convert this, which cannot be expressed in words, into words, to put it into human language, to convert it into human images and concepts . . . this was the great problem. We can read how they solved the problem in the Old Testament, in the various prophets.

Concerning prophecy, we find the following texts: 'Surely the Sovereign LORD does nothing without revealing his plan to his servants the prophets' (Amos 3:7). See also Isaiah 48:4–5 and Ezekiel 12:21–25. 'Above all, you must understand that no prophecy of Scripture came about by the prophet's own interpretation. For prophecy never had its origin in the will of man, but men spoke from God as they were carried along by the Holy Spirit' (2 Peter 1:20–21).

It is however logical and necessary that God adjusts himself to the conceptual capacities of his servants; a prophet is not a typewriter or photographic negative. (Thus the prophets will explain what they 'saw' and did not understand in the words and images of their time, cf. Ezekiel 1.)

Two kinds of prophecy

We can distinguish two kinds of prophecy:

1. Instructional prophecy. In it God's will is revealed. In it religious truths are asserted or explained more fully. Thus we may interpret the representations of Jesus in the letters to the seven churches in Revelation 2–3 as instructional prophecy. In these letters we are shown how Christ empathizes with his church, whereby the fellowship between God and humanity is more fully explained and illuminated.

2. Historical prophecy. In it God's way with humanity is revealed. This shows us how God will lead the world and why. It shows us history in the light of God's eternal plan of salvation.

It is the latter that I wish to discuss in the continuation.

The subject prophecy addresses

The subject of prophecy is the mystery of God. In the prophecies he reveals himself. As to this mystery we can distinguish the following principal points:

1. Mystery of the divine operation in history.
2. Mystery of Israel: their ethical monotheism, their continuing dispersion and blindness.
3. Mystery of Christ and of his church; the mystery of the possibility of contact between God and people.
4. Mystery of the world: why sin, why strife?

People hear in the biblical prophecies the earth groaning under the feet of advancing humanity, a bit of history therein is explained to us. Even though it is not given us to read and know God's hidden decrees, to the extent that he wants us to have insight into the destiny of the nations we read here the righteous purpose according to which the events unfold. It is far from literature of sensation, which astonishes more than it edifies the reader. Here the earth creaks, here the caravan of humanity laments, yet here too prays the voice of the creature, of the penitent.[5]

We have a duty to pay attention to this; we may not ignore this as unimportant: 'We have the word of the prophets made more certain, and you will do well to pay attention to it' (2 Peter 1:19).

Revelation of John

Here still a brief word about the book of Revelation. Revelation is a further elaboration, a synthesis of what the old prophets already said earlier about the end of time. These old prophets all presented bits from the great series of events, they illuminated particular parts of it. Thus we find in Joel for example a description of the plague of locusts, which in Revelation (chapter 9) however is shown in connection with the other events, all of which together form God's way with humanity.

The Revelation of John is a book meant especially for Christians, most of them converted heathen; the role that Israel will play in all this is therefore not emphasized here as much as it is in the Old Testament. Yet everything said here about the congregation of Jesus Christ, about the ultimate salvation and kingship, also applies to Israel, as in Romans 11:25–27: 'I do not want you to be ignorant of this mystery, brothers, so that you may not be conceited: Israel has experienced a hardening in part until the full number of the Gentiles has come in. And so all Israel will be saved, as it is written . . .'

In Revelation stress is placed on God's having worked on earth throughout the whole of history, it presents the history of God's kingdom: 'Whereby world history becomes world judgment, which the prophet sees in his own time and which he sees increase in intensity till the end of days, when the final decision comes, thus, whereby history is set in the light of the counsel of God.'[6]

In Revelation Christ by the mouth of John wants to point out again emphatically that everything already said earlier about the end of the ages retains its full force. Mainly attention is called to the tremendous fight that must be fought, but – comforting and wonderful thought – God's spirit will triumph and the Devil will be defeated, as it is written: '"Not by might, nor by power, but by my Spirit," says the LORD Almighty' (Zechariah 4:6).

Revelation does not present a strict chronological order, but we must conceive of it as being built up from a single great underlying thought, which is then explained in the various parts. We are struck by the great agreement between the various parts (seven seals, seven trumpets, seven vials); again and again we wait after a part for the end, but no, there comes a new series of events that lead to the same end (the parts run parallel as it were with respect to the direction of the idea). We feel in it a certain restraining of God's wrath (which also comes out in each of the parts: thus in the visions of the seven seals a quarter and in the visions of the seven trumpets a third of humanity die; from this quarter and third great compassion speaks, but for all that, the closer we near the end, the worse things become, it proceeds by 'crescendo'). God is gracious, again and again he gives humanity a chance, again and again 'it' is postponed, but again and again the certainty of the end is shown.

Thus we find in the Revelation of John a certain 'synchronization', a further clarification and a summary of what the old prophets had already said and seen.

If we want to look at prophecy or revelation as a whole, we cannot do without any of the three: the old prophets, the words of Christ (and other references in the New Testament) and Revelation. They complement one another.

Symbolism

In prophecy use is often made of symbolism. Here I will present a short and by no means comprehensive survey.

A. Numerical symbolism

Certain numbers represent certain things, as follows:

- The number 2 indicates confirmation or emphasis, cf. Genesis 41:32: 'The reason the dream was given to Pharaoh in two forms is that the matter has been firmly decided by God, and God will do it soon.'

- The number 3 is the number of God and expresses the divine (cf. Holy Trinity).

- The number 4 is the number of the creation, God's work.

- The number 5 denotes an entity in itself, an in itself complete part of a whole; also the creation within sight of salvation (cf. the parable of the 5 wise and the 5 foolish virgins).

- The number 6 is the number of work, of the labour of humanity (cf. 6 workdays in a week).

- The number 7 = 3 + 4. It is the number of complete perfection (e.g. 7 days in a week, 7 seals etc. in Revelation; the Lord's Prayer that consists of 7 parts: 3 concerning the divine and 4 concerning the creation.)

- The number 8 represents grace (Genesis 17:1–17; Leviticus 9:1, 22; 1 Kings 8:66; Ezekiel 43:27).

- The number 12 = 3 x 4: Humanity under God's promise of salvation (cf. 12 tribes of Israel).

- The number 10 is perfection in power.
- The number 100 is perfection in space.
- The number 1000 is perfection in time and space.

'Through the entire cosmos run a number of great lines that cut through all spheres of the cosmos, so that everywhere we encounter the same numerical relationships, therefore numbers occupy a special place.'[7]

For the sake of clarification I will provide a few examples of the use of numbers. First, consider Revelation 13:18: 'for it is man's number. His number is 666.' The basic number is 6, which appears as a single number and as a multiple of 10 and as a multiple of 100 but is not carried through as a multiple of 1000. Six indicates work, being operative. Ten indicates perfection in power, 100 perfection in space, so that 666 expresses that the beast, during the period of its activity, performs this work with full force throughout the earth and brings it to full development.

Second, consider Revelation 20:4: 'They came to life and reigned with Christ for a thousand years' (the millennium, or kingdom of a thousand years). This is the fourth vision of the seven visions of the end of the world. In the third vision (Revelation 20:1–3) we are told how the dragon is bound for 1000 years (1000 = perfection in time and space). In this passage the dragon is also called the old serpent, the Satan, which means he has already existed throughout the whole of human history. He is bound, stopped in his activity; the number 1000 indicates that this has already continuously taken place in history. Because he has been stopped in his operation, the thousand-year kingdom is possible: we must not think of this as something at the end of time, it is a kingdom that exists 'since the ascension of Christ to the throne', yes, that was already there in the pre-messianic period, with all who lived with or out of the promised king of salvation. I think in this connection of Luke 17:21: 'for behold, the kingdom of God is among you.' Now, all this is to say that through faith, faith in Jesus Christ, the Devil is as if bound for us and no longer has any power over us. Everyone who believes in Christ, everyone who is a member of the 'invisible church' is at the same time one living in the millennial kingdom. I still want to refer in this connection to John 12:31: 'Now is the time for judgment on this world; now the prince of this world will be driven out.' We must be born again to be a member and inhabitant of that thousand-year kingdom, as John 3:7 states: 'You must be born again'.

B. Colour symbolism

I will mention a few colours:

- Fire red and brimstone: colours of judgment.
- Red: the colour of sin.

- Blue: the colour of God's faithfulness to his covenant.
- White: the colour of sinlessness and purity.

An example: In Revelation 9:17 it is said that the armies led by the three angels wear breastplates of fire, sapphire (ancient hyacinth blue) and brimstone, whereby it is indicated that the plague of this sixth trumpet is a judgment, that the three angels are avenging angels. The middle breastplates are sapphire (blue), whereby it is affirmed that God is faithful to his covenant: it is God's faithfulness that calls to conversion and uses this means to that end.

C. Symbols and metaphors

- The sun stands for the godhead, the source of light for souls, as well as God's power and authority on earth.
- The moon, an emblem of what changes and passes, signifies temporal authority or the lustre of divine glory enlightening human life en route to eternity, to God.
- Stars are spiritual lights, little suns, souls to enlighten and to lead other souls, leaders and teachers.
- Heaven is the abode of God, representing the spiritual world; heavenly forces are spiritual forces.
- Earth is the opposite of heaven; it is the realm of people, of the material.
- Hence earthquakes represent overthrows and revolutions in this world.
- The sea and water: these are often an image of humanity, grouped together in countless ways, principally in states, nations and multitudes. Thus we find in Revelation 17:15: 'The waters you saw, where the prostitute sits, are peoples, multitudes, nations and languages.'
- Jerusalem (also used in the sense of Israel), the Holy City, Zion: The kingdom of God, the centre of God's power on earth. Cf. Micah 4:2: 'The law will go out from Zion, the word of the LORD from Jerusalem' (see also Jeremiah 51:50). A comment: We often come across Jerusalem in the ordinary sense, but Zion almost never.
- Babylon, the city of blood, the wicked woman. Here we have the personification of the anti-divine powers and forces. When we read 'fallen is the great Babylon', then that is to say that the anti-divine is vanquished, that God is victorious. (We can say the same thing of Egypt, Edom, Tyre, etc.)
- Horns. Symbol of force and power (cf. Zechariah 1:18, Daniel 7:7).

Here too I would like to offer examples: Revelation 6:12: 'I watched as he [the Lamb] opened the sixth seal. There was a great earthquake.' Thus great upheavals will occur, in both the spiritual and the material realms.

Revelation 6:12–13: 'The sun turned black like sackcloth made of goathair, the whole moon turned blood red, and the stars in the sky fell to earth.' People no longer recognize God (the sun) or his word in witness (the moon), which vanish from their field of vision or are 'darkened', a result among other things of the stars of heaven falling to earth, humanity's leaders direct people's attention to materiality, while God and everything appertaining to God are reasoned away and the leaders fall back from a spiritual to a material standpoint. In place of spirituality, people will pursue material desires and 'ideals'. Cf. especially 2 Timothy 4:3–4.

In this connection I want to mention a passage from Dostoevsky's *Brothers Karamazov*:

> They follow their learning, they want to achieve it with their understanding, without God. They have already proclaimed that there is no sin, no crime ... The spiritual realm, the most exalted part of our human existence, they have driven off with hate and triumph. They have proclaimed that the world must be free ... It is no wonder that people instead of free have become slaves, instead of united they have been cast increasingly on themselves. ... They have attained their goal: they have amassed earthly goods, but they have lost their joy. (See also point I in the chronological summary below.)

It is, as argued above, a mystery why the world must be guided by means of labour pains towards the goal of the creation of a new heaven and a new earth. We can do nothing but believe that it is good as it is, because God is love and he guides the world: 'Nothing is deadlier for faith than to avert one's gaze the moment something appears that does not make sense,' says Miskotte correctly in his *Antwoord uit het onweer* [answer from the thunderstorm].

Prophecy teaches us that all this is not subject to chance but that God has so ordained it, that God guides the world, that God does not leave people to seek the way in their own strength but that he points the way, indicates the direction, propels the whole of history in the paths he desires, which lead to the great apotheosis, the creation of the new heaven and the new earth.

Much in prophecy has already been fulfilled (cf. Deuteronomy 18:22), so on this basis we already have a support in prophecy that gives us confidence in that which must still come, for it allows us to see that God conquers with his love. Again, why the road was chosen in this way we do not know, but then we can best think of Isaiah 55:8–9 ('"For my thoughts are not your thoughts, neither are your ways my ways," declares the LORD. "As the heavens are higher than the earth, so are my ways higher than your ways and my thoughts than your thoughts"') and 1 Corinthians 1:25 ('For the foolishness of God is wiser than man's wisdom').

Evil, sin, sorrow

God uses these to attain the intended goal. God has also created them or, better, made them possible (if not, then there would be something that God had not created, something that 'exceeded' him, such that God . . . would not be God). Here I want to refer to some passages from Miskotte's *Antwoord uit het onweer*: 'Why sorrow, death, temptation if God is love? Because God is love . . . if it agrees with God's power it agrees with his righteousness and if with his righteousness then also with his love.' And elsewhere: 'We are creatures and suffering is created . . . all taken together signs and seals of the mystery of God by whom life was and is and shall be, all of which taken together are revelations' and 'Therefore it is such a wholesome existing order . . . that we do not have the capacity to place ourselves at the standpoint of providence and so to understand the necessity of evil, the meaning of our trials' and 'that in the beginning everything was created "good" and at the same time that "good" escapes the human measure of good and evil while what we experience as evil is used by God for our good.' I think here of Job 2:10: 'Shall we accept good from God, and not trouble?' and Isaiah 45:7: 'I bring prosperity and create disaster' (= the chastisements and plagues).

People have always turned to the Bible in times of misery and said: 'The end is imminent.' Since the labour pangs work through the whole of history, people in every age can see that prophecy is fulfilled. Thus when we also see that today, it is perfectly correct, except that there is no proof that just now the end will come in the foreseeable future. The pangs steadily become worse, matters go 'crescendo'. Yet it is not impossible that we are now experiencing the 'apotheosis'. . . (Yet do keep in mind Matthew 24:32; Daniel 12:10, from which texts it is clear that we have a duty to see the signs of the times. And we are able, with God's word in hand, to understand and interpret them).

Chronological analysis

Now I want to use the following scheme to present the most important points of prophecy:

A. God's plan of salvation

B. Choosing of Israel

C. Promise of the Messiah

D. Israel's rejection: a. Separation of Judah and Israel; b. Diaspora

E. Rejection of the Messiah

F. Woes directed to the Jews: a. Diaspora; b. Pariah of the nations; c. Adversity

G. Proclamation of the gospel

H. Apostasy of the nations

I. Day of Jahweh I: Labour pains; Chastisement [of enemies, fall of Babylon]

J. Day of Jahweh II: Restoration of Israel; Nations acknowledge that God is the Lord

K. The Last Judgment

L. New heaven and new earth

We must not regard this as a static arrangement in which one part must be completed before the following can occur, but as dynamic, its elements intermeshed, sometimes coinciding with and sometimes resisting each other. Thus point 9 has been in progress ever since the first person took their first step, and 7 and 8 practically coincide and work against each other.

A. God's plan of salvation

At the beginning of everything stands God's eternal decree. Thus in Revelation 5:1: 'Then I saw in the right hand of him who sat on the throne a scroll with writing on both sides and sealed with seven seals.' These seven seals indicate that what is written in the book, namely the names of the elect (see Revelation 20:12), is fixed and will not be changed. The book is written on the inside and the outside, which is to say that most of it is almost entirely hidden from our eyes. Yet we can see something of it, even though only a very little. We can say that in it stands God's counsel, his decrees.

Next it is asked (Revelation 5:2) who is worthy to open the book, thus to break the seven seals or, as it were, to undertake the implementation of these decrees. This turns out to be (Revelation 5:5) the Lion of the tribe of Judah, the Root of David, the Christ. Thus Christ is appointed the executor of God's decrees.

Christ has been visible to us at one point in the history of the earth and then has showed us how he loves humanity, how he has wanted to take our sins upon himself, which he symbolized (showed) us in his death on the cross; but spiritually speaking he has always been there (cf. Micah 5:1), he has always taken our sins upon himself (the Holy Trinity also existed 'before' Christ). Thus it is possible that at the beginning of everything it is already said: 'because you were slain and with your blood you purchased men for God from every tribe and language and people and nation' (Revelation 5:9).

We must consider that God stands above time, so that when Christ at a certain moment in history takes sin upon himself on the cross, it may seem to human eyes that only thereafter can sins be forgiven, but for God this is an eternal and all-comprehensive given that has put its stamp on the entire path of humanity, from the earliest times until now (cf. Colossians 1:19, Isaiah 53).

In Christ the elect who stand in the book with the seven seals are sanctified; through his death on the cross they are bought with a price and become the bondservants of God.

B. Choosing of Israel

'When Israel was a child, I loved him, and out of Egypt I called my son . . . It was I who taught Ephraim to walk, taking them by the arms . . . I led them with cords of human kindness, with ties of love' (Hosea 11:1, 3, 4; see also Deuteronomy 20:25).

In connection with this Professor Bleeker says:

> When a father gets a child, there is in the first instance only a natural bond, a bond of caring, of the child's dependence. That must grow however into a bond of affection, of the child's trust – in all cases the father must begin by stooping to that child and, in his nurturing and training, adjust himself to the child's mental and emotional world. This is also the key to understanding God's ways with Israel. Whenever God connects with Israel it is not because this nation enjoys any merit or other privilege above other nations – we must not think that Israel already at the beginning of history was extended a system of truths, or granted a pure knowledge of God – that developed slowly.

'"Is not Ephraim my dear son, the child in whom I delight? Though I often speak against him, I still remember him. Therefore my heart yearns him; I have great compassion for him," declares the LORD' (Jeremiah 31:20).

Many texts can be cited, and many of these texts feature the promise of the Messiah, something that is of course inherent in the choosing of Israel. Thus we find in Genesis 12:2–3: 'I will make you into a great nation and I will bless you . . . and all peoples on earth will be blessed through you.'

This brings us to the next point.

C. Promise of the Messiah

The entire Old Testament is filled with it. Thus: 'He shall build a house for my name, and I will establish the throne of his kingdom forever. And I will be his father and he shall be my son' (2 Samuel 7:13–14). And further: 'But he (here the servant of the Lord can mean both Israel and Christ. Yet this makes no practical difference, inasmuch as the promise to Israel, the nation chosen to bring him forth, is fulfilled in Christ) was pierced for our transgressions, he was crushed for our iniquities; the punishment that brought us peace was upon him, and by his wounds we are healed' (Isaiah 53:5).

Also the place, Bethlehem, is given (Micah 5:1) together with other particulars of origin and walk. While the promise is given to the entire tribe of Jacob, it is given especially to Judah. We find that already in Genesis when Jacob blesses his twelve sons (Genesis 48:9–10), in

Revelation Christ is called among other things 'the Lion of the tribe of Judah' and furthermore: 'though you are small among the clans of Judah, out of you will come for me one who will be ruler' (Micah 5:2).

In the Old Testament a sharp distinction is made between the first and second coming of Christ. The second we may consider a continuation of the first: the first is the preparation and the second the completion of the kingdom of God (cf. e.g. Jeremiah 33:14). In this connection I want to refer also to Revelation 12:1: 'A great and wondrous sign appeared in heaven: a woman clothed with the sun, with the moon under her feet and a crown of twelve stars on her head'.

The woman referred to here is Israel (twelve stars) and also the church here on earth (consider Romans 11). Since the earliest times Israel has always been 'pregnant' with the messianic promise . . . just as the church of Christ is and must be still 'pregnant' with the idea of the return of Christ.

D. Israel's rejection

The Hebrew people acquired the name 'Israel' after their patriarch, the grandson of Abraham, Jacob, who received the name Israel at Peniel (Genesis 32:28–30). The total of twelve tribes, descendants of the twelve sons of Jacob, were called 'Israel'. 'Jews' is thus not a collective name for this entire nation, for round about 900 BC Israel was divided into Judah and Benjamin on the one hand (the Jews) and the other ten tribes on the other hand (Israel). In what follows here I will refer to the twelve tribes together as 'Israel', although thus perhaps not entirely correct.

Why was Israel rejected? We find the answer at many places in the Old Testament such as Isaiah 29:13: 'The LORD says: "These people come near to me with their mouth and honour me with their lips, but their hearts are far from me."' God himself confronts Israel with difficulties, see e.g. Jeremiah 6:21: 'I will lay stumbling blocks before this people' and 'Therefore once more I will astound these people with wonder upon wonder' (Isaiah 29:14). The purpose of this marvellous work is 'that the nations may know that I am the LORD.' For, '"you will be consoled regarding the disaster I have brought upon Jerusalem – every disaster I have brought upon it . . . for you will know that I have done nothing in it without cause," declares the Sovereign LORD' (Ezekiel 14:22–23).

With the rejection, the promise was not broken by any means. The assertion follows directly that Christ will come forth from Israel and that Israel will be accepted again: 'I will surely gather them from all the lands where I banish them in my furious anger and wrath; I will bring them back to this place and let them live in safety' (Jeremiah 33:24ff, especially verse 37). Jeremiah 33:14: 'For this is what the LORD Almighty, the God of Israel, says: Houses, fields and vineyards will again be bought in this land.'

Israel is tested. Just a 'remnant' will remain. Ezekiel 14:21–22: 'For this is what the Sovereign LORD says: How much worse will it be when I send against Jerusalem my four dreadful judgments . . . Yet there will be some survivors – sons and daughters who will be brought out of it' [Isaiah 1:9, 11:11, 16:14; Jeremiah 44:28; Ezekiel 6:8; Joel 2:32] (see also Jeremiah 31:20).

Pierson states in his book *Israël*:

> God desires to bring forth a people committed to God, filled with God, of all peoples his own, partakers in his dominion . . . God is not there for Israel but Israel for God. Practically speaking that means that what the people as a whole cannot realize must be done by a select company of the people through persistent purification and therefore by a remainder named a "remnant" (cf. also Romans 9:14–29; cf. Ezekiel 11:13, Isaiah 10:12).

By virtue of their being chosen, a heavy responsibility rests upon this people. 'You only have I chosen of all the families of the earth; therefore I will punish you for all your sins' (Amos 3:2).

We divide this punishment in two:

a. Separation between Judah and Israel. This separation, which dates to about 950 BC and follows the death of Solomon, pitted Judah against Israel: 'This is what the LORD says: Do not go up to fight against your brothers, the Israelites . . . for this is my doing' (1 Kings 12:24).

b. Diaspora. In about 600 BC a beginning was made with the dispersal of the entire people (Samaria 722, Jerusalem 597). Prophecy concerning that I will discuss further under 6 a. below.

Both nations, both of the groups into which the Hebrew nation was divided, were carried off into captivity. After 70 years, Judah (together with Benjamin) was returned to Palestine at the behest of Cyrus, the King of Persia. (We can read about that extensively in Ezra.) However, what became of the other ten tribes is not known, the writings provide no answer (See 2 Chronicles 35:18) while general archaeology says these tribes vanished without trace.

That leaves two possibilities: either (i) Judah is the remnant of Israel and the total promise including that of restoration devolves upon them (consider however Jeremiah 24:10); or (ii) Israel survives under a different name. This last possibility is advocated by among others the British Israel Movement, which holds that the Anglo-Saxon countries, the Netherlands, Denmark, Norway and northwest Spain would be Israel (England would be Ephraim; Manasseh would be America) (cf. also Genesis 48.) They can argue the case in a fairly compelling way. Israel would have left the land between the two rivers and migrated in a westerly direction through Europe. The peoples known from archaeology as the Scythes (think of Scots), Hittites and other peoples about whom little is known and who have vanished completely, are identified as these migrating people of Israel. (Dr Rademaker has written a valuable little book about all that entitled *Waar bleven de 10 stammen Israëls?* [what became of the 10 tribes of Israel?]). The proofs advanced suggest a high degree of probability, but we will leave it to the future to supply a definitive statement.

From a biblical standpoint we find support for this conception in Genesis 48, where Ephraim and Manasseh are blessed and told that they will become a multitude. If these peoples were to vanish entirely, then this prophecy would not be fulfilled (see again Deuteronomy 18:22).

That Israel has not vanished is highly probable since we find nothing about such a thing in prophecy, where there is mention however of Israel's restoration (cf. Jeremiah 31:1, Ezekiel 34, etc.). That we should read Israel = Christians is not very reasonable. Why should Israel mean Israel when there is talk of scandal and dispersal but suddenly mean Christians the moment there is talk of glory and restoration. We must guard against dragging any such wishes and notions into the Bible; we must not twist meanings in our favour, for then we are no longer expositing but importing.

It is logical that Judah should return to Palestine, since otherwise the promise of the Messiah could not be fulfilled.

E. Rejection of the Messiah

With the coming of Christ the promises concerning him are fulfilled, as many New Testament passages connected with Old Testament passages show. The Jews (Judah + Benjamin) have rejected him however, since God hardened them as it were with a spirit of deep sleep: 'But to this day the LORD has not given you a mind that understands or eyes that see or ears that hear' (Deuteronomy 29:4). In the New Testament too this is shown and stated.

We can even say, humanly speaking, that if the Jews had not been hardened, then they would have accepted Christ and he would not have been crucified, and then there would have been no satisfaction for sin . . . yes, even no Christianity.

When we find it said: 'Our fathers sinned and are no more, and we bear their punishment' (Lamentations 5:7), then this is in agreement with what the Jews cried out as Jesus stood before Pilate: 'Let his blood be on us and on our children!' (Matthew 27:25). ('For I tell you, you will not see me again until you say, "Blessed is he who comes in the name of the Lord"' – Matthew 23:39.)

If we now turn again to Revelation 12:1–6, we see that the woman who was pregnant (referred to toward the end of point C, above) brought forth a child: Christ was born as a fulfilment of the messianic prophecy. The dragon, the anti-god power, arrives directly to try and destroy this birth, just as he always persecuted the messianic idea. The child however was born after all and immediately kept safe from the claws of the dragon. The woman, the church, sojourns in the world now like someone who has fled into the wilderness, lonely and abandoned (Revelation of John 12:6). The power of the Devil has however been broken in principle; he can no longer do anything against God or Christ or his congregation (John 12:31).

F. Woes directed to the Jews

After Christ a more difficult period begins for the Jews. It begins directly in 70 AD: Titus destroys Jerusalem (predicted by Christ himself, Luke 21:24). Many disasters befall Palestine; the Jews are dispersed, in a word, prophecy is implemented in all its force and terror (cf. Isaiah 51:19–20).

These woes can be divided into:

a. Dispersal: 'So will I throw you out of this land into a land neither you nor your fathers have known . . . for I will show you no favour' (Jeremiah 16:13); and 'My God will reject them because they did not obey him; they will be wanderers among the nations' (Hosea 9:17). Many other texts say the same. That this prophecy has been entirely fulfilled needs no further argument.

b. Pariah of the nations: In this connection we find in Isaiah: 'You will leave your name to my chosen ones as a curse; the Sovereign LORD will put you to death, but to his servants he will give another name' (65:15). Here it is clear that they will be cursed, even by the 'chosen' of the Lord: they will no longer be the chosen (in any case temporarily, for there is still regular reference to restoration). These chosen will now be named by a different name; that too has been fulfilled, for are the chosen not now 'Christians'?

Jeremiah too is very clear when he says: 'I will make them abhorrent and an offence to all the kingdoms of the earth, a reproach and a byword, an object of ridicule and cursing, wherever I banish them' (Jeremiah 24:9). (Jeremiah 25:9.) Cf. for a. and b. also Deuteronomy 28:60ff. and 29:24ff.

c. Adversity: Concerning this we find: 'Whoever found them devoured them; their enemies said, "We are not guilty, for they sinned against the LORD, their true pasture, the LORD, the hope of their fathers"' (Jeremiah 50:7).

That the Jews are indeed persecuted and that their persecutors claim thereby to do good work is known to all of us; this prophecy too has turned out to be true in its full horror. The whole of point F can be summarized in the words of Jeremiah: 'For I am watching over them for harm, not for good' (Jeremiah 44:27).

G. Proclamation of the gospel

Before the end comes the gospel must be proclaimed everywhere. Those who accept the gospel are as it were added to Israel, as we can find described in the Romans 2 (see also Ephesians 3:6). In that discussion, amongst other things it is said: 'But if their transgression means riches for the world, and their loss means riches for the Gentiles, how much greater riches will their fullness bring?' (Romans 11:12; see also Isaiah 56).

I believe we should view the 'Jewish problem' from this vantage point: they are still always God's people, and Christians (not of Israelite blood) are only added to Israel by grace. Let us remember Paul's statement: 'provided that you continue in his kindness. Otherwise, you also will be cut off' (Romans 11:22). Indeed it is predicted and God's will is that all this should happen to the Jews, but . . . we do not need to give God a helping hand.

In this connection anti-Semitism – I want to refer to Nietzsche's saying: 'people do not hate what they disparage but only what they consider equal or above themselves.'[8]

Concerning the proclamation of the gospel we find many texts, including: 'to bring Jacob back to him and gather Israel to himself . . . I will also make you a light for the Gentiles, that you may bring my salvation to the ends of the earth' (Isaiah 49:5–6). And Christ himself says: 'And this gospel of the kingdom will be preached in the whole world as a testimony to all nations, and then the end will come' (Matthew 24:14).

Repeatedly Christ reminds his disciples of their task to shoulder the gospel; while God himself shows Peter emphatically in a dream that it is also for the heathen (Acts 10). Paul too calls attention to that again and again.

That this gospel is indeed proclaimed everywhere is a fact. No land in the world can say they have never heard of Christ.

But practically coinciding with this proclamation is a factor that works counter to it, namely:

H. Apostasy of the nations

Before the end comes many nations will fall away under pressure from the 'dragon and his two beasts'. Unbelief, scepticism and self-will will be at high tide, as we find in Revelation 6:12–13: 'The sun turned black like sackcloth made of goathair, the whole moon turned blood red, and the stars in the sky fell to earth.'

I will discuss this further in connection with the labour pains mentioned under point Ia below. Apostasy occurs contemporaneously, as said, with the proclamation of the gospel . . . only, the nearer to the end, the more severe the apostasy . . . towards the end the destructive stream increases in force, which is embodied in prophecy in the Antichrist, the dragon that will rage before the end, as we find it in Revelation 20.

People will cast off the ties that bind them to God: 'The kings of the earth take their stand and the rulers gather together against the LORD and against his Anointed One. "Let us break their chains," they say, "and throw off their fetters"' (Psalm 2:2–3). See also 2 Timothy 4:3–4: people are deceived by signs and wonders performed by lying prophets and false Christians. In the following part I want to discuss this more extensively.

If we think of Asia Minor, where the first Christian congregations arose and where today there is practically no Christianity to be found, and other similar examples, if we look around us and see how many people are now still really Christian (people therefore who belong to the 'invisible' church), then we see that this prophecy is well confirmed. To what extent, however, and whether it will become still worse, we do not know (at the moment something like 30 per cent of humanity are members of the Christian Church).

I. Day of Jahweh I

Before we discuss the 'labour pains' more extensively, a few preliminary remarks. When we look at the Revelation of John we see that, as I already said, Christ is appointed as the executor of God's eternal decree of salvation (*heilsraad*). To this end he opens the seven seals of the book of Life. Every one of these seals initiate pangs as its consequence. When we take a closer look at these pangs, we find that they have existed since the earliest times. Thus from removing the second seal (Revelation 6:4) there comes a rider on a red horse who will take away peace from the earth, and from the fourth seal a pale horse whose rider is Death. These pangs have occurred, as stated, since the first person took their first steps on earth. Thus we may see the labour pains as having been there from the earliest times to the present . . . only – and we find that again and again – it grows increasingly worse.

Because things worsen so slowly, people do not notice it and accommodate the situation as it were. Yet that things are moving 'fast' we can tell from the manifold use of the term 'haste, hastily'. We must see in this less the 'smallness' of the passage of time and more the tempo. The tempo is fast. Even if we do not perceive it, it is fast. (We can compare this with a cloud. Though to our eyes it may appear to move slowly, when we set out to measure its velocity we find that in reality it is moving very fast.)

People do not notice. Thus we find in Daniel 7:25, 26: 'The saints will be handed over to him for a time, times and half a time. But the court will sit, and his power will be taken away and completely destroyed for ever.' Then this all (the prophecy) shall be fulfilled. Cf. Revelation 11:11. See also Isaiah 47:6.

In that time, times and half a time we find the idea of a period that people increasingly experience as long until it seems endless, so that it cannot be surprising 'that in the last days scoffers will come, scoffing and following their own evil desires. They will say, "Where is this 'coming' he promised? Ever since our fathers died, everything goes on as it has since the beginning of the creation"' (2 Peter 3:3–4). The 'long' period however is suddenly broken off by surprise (hence the half time).

The Day of Jahweh is the final intervention of God in world history. Properly speaking then, the whole of history is the 'Day of Jahweh'. At the end God lets his hand be felt with full force. An image of this we can find in the great pyramid of Cheops: the entire system of passageways is constructed of a soft sort of stone. These passageways represent the way of humanity. The last part of the system of passageways, however, is constructed of granite, indicating that people can no longer change it at all.

How and why will this day of Jahweh be? There will be labour pains or spasms of distress: 'Take from my hand this cup filled with the wine of my wrath and make all the nations to whom I send you drink it . . . But if they refuse to take the cup from your hand and drink, tell them, "This is what the LORD Almighty says: You must drink it"' (Jeremiah 25 [cf. especially verses 15 and 28]).

The pangs are not local events but encompass everything and everyone (consider, for example, this present war, and how many lands that desired to avoid it were swept willy-nilly into the maelstrom)[9]. 'Men will faint from terror, apprehensive of what is coming on the world' (Luke 21:26).

From this we can see that the purpose of these pangs is to fill the world with terror; people will no longer know what to do. God uses the anti-God forces as a means to this end. The reason for all this is that people should come to understand that they cannot walk alone, that they need God's strength and guidance – thus the same thing is true here as in God's declaration to Israel just before their going into exile: 'When terror comes, they will seek peace, but there will be none. Calamity upon calamity will come, and rumour upon rumour. They will try to get a vision from the prophet; the teaching of the law by the priest will be lost, as will the counsel of the elders . . . Then they will know that I am the LORD' (Ezekiel 7:25–27). See also Revelation 11:13 'At that very hour there was a severe earthquake and a tenth of the city collapsed. Seven thousand people were killed in the earthquake, and the survivors were terrified and gave glory to the God of heaven.' This can be compared with what Luther said: 'Divine Love is also active in the storms of divine wrath.'

Of what then do the pangs consist? There will be catastrophes in the spiritual and material realm (including natural disasters etc., represented in the earthquake). See Revelation 6:12–14 and chapter 8. These revolutions and overthrows will have as their result that people will turn away from God, no longer believe in him (the sun) or his word and witness (the moon). Humanity's leaders will fall back upon the earthly standpoint. We can also say: people are no longer guided by spiritual ideals, they will be guided instead by earthly desires and wishes. Heaven recedes in that case, standing ever further away from people. 'Then the kings of the earth . . . hid in caves and among the rocks of the mountains' (Revelation 6:15).

It is the logical consequence of all this that they all no longer know where they should look for support. They no longer find a point of rest for their souls, the cosmos with all its mysteries and questions crashes down upon them, they no longer know what to do with it. 'The fear of the Lord is the beginning of knowledge' (Proverbs 1:7).

When people forget that, their only support, starting point and goal, in a word their guideline, is gone and thus it is entirely understandable that they all flee from the great problems, finally from God himself because they refuse to believe, flee into holes and clefts in the rocks. I think here of the positivists (Comte), who say that people must not cast themselves upon 'speculations concerning eternity', that they must restrict themselves to that which can be perceived by our senses and to the investigation of nature. Finally, when they no longer know a way out: 'They will flee to caverns in the rocks and to the overhanging crags from dread of the LORD and the splendour of his majesty, when he rises to shake the earth' (Isaiah 2:21).

At this point I want to refer to a passage from Dostoevsky's *Brothers Karamazov*. 'This freedom, their free reason and their science, these have confronted them with such wonders and such puzzles that the unbending and rebellious among them will destroy themselves and the other unbending but weaker natures will destroy each other.' And also to a passage from Huizinga's *De schaduwen van morgen* [the shadows of tomorrow]: 'Reason, which opposed faith, and thought to have destroyed it, must now resort to faith in order to save itself from destruction.'

The pangs of this sixth seal are also something that we must regard as existing and operative since people existed. Since the earliest times people have always had a penchant to give honour not to God but to themselves, to seek the ground of all this somewhere else. What, in contrast to the above, forms the 'certainty' of the 'elect' is laid out more fully in Revelation 7:9–16. These people, who sometimes stand with great difficulty and sacrifice in their hostile world, know where their salvation, their point of support is: 'he [the Lamb] will lead them to springs of living waters. And God will wipe away every tear from their eyes.' The fountain of life, the spiritual fountain from which we may derive our strength, we may conceive to be the Holy Spirit. 'They shall no longer hunger and thirst' after the knowledge of the ground of all this, because they 'know', because they believe.

In Revelation 9:1–3 the labour pains are described that attend the fifth trumpet: 'and I saw a star that had fallen from the sky to the earth. That star was given the key to the shaft of the Abyss . . . The sun and sky were darkened by the smoke from the Abyss. And out of the smoke locusts came down upon the earth and were given power like that of scorpions.'

A star falls from heaven to earth, an 'ideology' arises so to say, a worldly leader or system arises that opens the bottomless pit, that is responsible for the 'Sun' (figure for God) being hidden from the human eye. From the smoke that arises from the pit locusts swarm across the earth. These are the armies that march against the kingdom of God, against Jerusalem. This is thus a direct consequence of the ideas the 'star' has inculcated into them.

The image of 'dark clouds' we find already in the Old Testament, in Joel: 'Blow the trumpet in Zion; sound the alarm on my holy hill. Let all who live in the land tremble, for the day of the Lord is coming. It is close at hand – a day of darkness and gloom, a day of clouds and blackness' (Joel 2:1–2). And of the locusts Joel says: 'Before them the earth shakes, the sky trembles, the sun and moon are darkened, and the stars no longer shine' (Joel 2:10).

The goal of all this, namely conversion, is not directly reached: 'The rest of mankind that were not killed by these plagues still did not repent of the works of their hands' (Revelation 9:20).

The pangs are thus in both the spiritual and the physical material realm.

   a. The spiritual realm: This is indicated in prophecy by the stars falling, the bottomless pit opening, the sun darkening, etc. Humanity's leaders, the thinkers, the philosophers, direct people's attention to the material realm. God is or perhaps once was a useful concept, but truth? I think here of the positivists, of Nietzsche's 'Genealogy of Morality' in which he explains the concept of God in a psychological, way, and of materialism. See here also Ephesians 6:12: 'For our struggle is . . . against the powers of this dark world.' Cf. Jeremiah 5:4–5.

   b. The material realm: The 'ideologies' just mentioned produce wars and other external horrors as their result (I think here of the present war [WWII], of the absence of morality and ethics in Bolshevik Russia, of the consequences of the 'blood and soil' and racial theories in Germany, and so forth). Cf. Revelation 17:3–6: 'I saw a woman . . . she held a golden cup in her hand, filled with abominable things and the filth of her adulteries . . . THE MOTHER OF PROSTITUTES AND OF THE ABONIMATIONS OF THE EARTH. I saw that the woman was drunk with the blood of the saints, the blood of those who bore testimony to Jesus.' This is symbolized by the locusts that arise from the bottomless pit.

From the above it appears clearly that the anti-God powers and forces are the very causes of the pangs, of the spasms of distress, and that in precisely this way they contribute to the conversion of many and to the establishment of the kingdom, of the new heaven and the new earth: 'You are my war club, my weapon for battle – with you I shatter nations, with you I destroy kingdoms' (Jeremiah 51:20); and 'Babylon was a gold cup in the LORD's hand; she made the whole earth drunk' (Jeremiah 51:7); and 'You who have escaped the sword, leave and do not linger! Remember the LORD in a distant land, and think on Jerusalem.' (Jeremiah 51:50).

Taken as symbols of these anti-God powers in Revelation are the dragon, the beast from the sea, and the beast from the land. The dragon, the old serpent, Satan, as he is also called, we already find in Genesis when he seduces Eve, so we must think of him, as we must think of his two companions the two beasts, as active throughout the whole of history. From the earliest times he persecuted the messianic hope in people and tried to destroy it: 'And I saw a beast coming out of the sea... The dragon gave the beast his power and his throne and his great authority. One of the heads of the beast seemed to have had a fatal wound, but the fatal wound had been healed. The whole world was astonished and followed the beast' (Revelation 13:1–3). This beast according to this description is the anti-God power. He receives from the dragon his throne and his power. He also receives a great wound (the death of Christ on the cross in the preaching of the gospel?) but he recovers from that and the entire world follows him full of astonishment. 'Then I saw another beast, coming out of the earth ... he exercised all the authority of the first beast on his behalf ...' (Revelation 13: 11–16).

That he rose out of the earth indicates that the evil of the beast embodies itself in people. By means of miracles he made people follow the beast from the sea. (Does this not make one think of the fact that technology and science, by their great inventions and discoveries, the 'miracles of technology', sometimes render people arrogant and lead them astray from God? Not science but people are at fault who conclude that they therefore no longer need God.) The beast forced everyone to receive a mark, or sign, on their right hand and on their forehead, thereby indicating that both their work and their thoughts have come under the influence of Satan (forehead = understanding; right hand = work).

This threesome – the dragon, the beast from the sea, and the beast from the land – lead to a comparison with the Holy Trinity: The dragon is the antipode to God and is the founder, the source and instigator of all evil; the beast from the sea is the antipode to Christ and wields the power of the dragon and sits on the throne in his name – the anti-God powers gather around him in the same way as the church gathers around Christ; the beast from the earth is the antipode of the Holy Spirit, the one who magnifies and praises the dragon and the beast from the sea in the eyes of the people.

Remarkably, this threesome uses precisely the three powers capable of persuading people to follow them – I am reminded of the story of the Grand Inquisitor in Dostoevsky's *Brothers Karamazov* – namely miracles, mystery, and authority. Therefore miracles: 'Because of the signs he was given power to do . . . he deceived the inhabitants of the earth' (Revelation 13:14); and authority: 'He [the beast from the sea] was given power' (Revelation 13:5); and mystery: 'and upon her forehead was a name written: MYSTERY' (Revelation 17:5). Precisely these three means of getting people to follow him were scorned by Christ when the Devil offered them to him during the temptation in the wilderness (Matthew 4:1–11).

Thus God uses the anti-God powers as a means to reach the ends he sets. When however God no longer needs them for such purposes, their destruction is sure, since they no longer receive support of any kind from God. We find the demise of these powers in the chastisement of God's enemies and the fall of Babylon. 'The LORD will march out like a mighty man . . . and will triumph over his enemies' (Isaiah 42:13); 'Come, O Zion! Escape, you who live in the Daughter of Babylon!' (Zechariah 2:7); 'I am against you, O Sidon, and I will gain glory within you . . . Then they will know that I am the LORD' (Ezekiel 28:22).

An extensive discussion of the fall of the anti-God powers, personified in the fall of Babylon, are found in Isaiah 57, Jeremiah 50 and 51, Ezekiel 26 and 27 (which speaks of Tyre instead of Babylon) and finally in Revelation 17 and 18. Thus we read in Isaiah 47:10–11: 'You have trusted in your wickedness and have said, "No one sees me." . . . Disaster will come upon you, and you will not know how to conjure it away.'

Suddenly, in a day as it were, the lot of Babylon is reversed and an end comes to its anti-God disposition: 'Therefore in one day her plagues will overtake her' (Revelation 18:8; see also Isaiah 47:9).

God's people are warned at many places not to associate with her: 'Depart, depart, go out from there! . . . Come out from it and be pure, you who carry the vessels of the LORD' (Isaiah 52:11). The 'chosen' must therefore not have anything to do with these anti-God matters, these theories and practices. 'Flee from Babylon! Run for your lives! Do not be destroyed because of her sins' (Jeremiah 51:6). The false, godless ideologies thus come to nought; people will come to see that they were wrong, yet they will not turn directly to honour God for they still mourn the fact that the city is fallen; they had a lot of profit from her, lived in her in lechery and dissolution, and prospered there. Now they do not know where to look for succour, every certainty is gone.

Do we not see this in contemporary philosophy? Now that rationalism has fallen, people do not know where to turn: 'they will weep and mourn over her . . . they will stand far off and cry' (Revelation 18:9–10).

That this city, this Babylon, is the symbol for all that is anti-God, for all false ideologies that take no account of God and his love, appears clearly from among other passages Revelation 18:24: 'In her [Babylon] was found the blood of the prophets and of the saints, and of all who have been killed on the earth.'

To all lovelessness, deceit and arrogance, false ideologies and anti-God thinking there thus comes an end (Revelation 18:20).

It was God's will that Babylon should exist, he needed her to achieve his purpose; God disposed that the beast and the 'ten horns' should give their power to Babylon, that in this way Babylon could establish her power over them: 'For God has put it into their hearts to accomplish his purpose by agreeing to give the beast their power to rule' (Revelation 17:17). Although they bestow their power on Babylon, they nevertheless hate the 'abomination', the abominable one that rules over them. When God's words are fulfilled – 'The beast and the ten horns you saw will hate the prostitute. They will bring her to ruin . . . eat her flesh and burn her with fire' (Revelation 17:16) – God executes his judgment over the world city using the same powers that built it and made it great; thus this world power works at its own destruction. At some point the adherents of the false ideologies, the anti-God theories, by reasoning consistently and by thinking and acting accordingly will bring about their own demise (revolutions devour their own children) and people will perceive the fragility and transience of their own concoctions (cf. Isaiah 19:2). Thus Nietzsche asserted somewhere: 'Europe will go under due to the rise of nihilism. Why? Because all values are rendered problematical.' And I am reminded again of the passage from Huizinga's *De schaduwen van morgen*, referred to above: 'Reason, which opposed faith, and thought to have destroyed it, must now resort to faith in order to save itself from destruction.'

Yet how this change will take place so quickly – there is mention of an hour [Revelation 18:10, 17, 19] – is a great mystery to us. Is it not however comforting that these powers are working at their own destruction, that now 'the congregation has nothing to fear from her' (see Revelation 9:4; cf. also Zechariah 5:10–11, where Shinar = Babylon), nothing to do with her, therefore: 'Rejoice over her, O heaven! Rejoice, saints and apostles and prophets!' (Revelation 18:20). This destruction of Babylon we must not see as exclusively spiritual; in the physical, material realm too Babylon as the power and the people that are entirely anti-God, the enemies of Israel, will be defeated. This defeat will be the climax of the war or wars that will be waged at the end of the ages. In one battle, according to Joel, that will be waged in the valley of Jehoshaphat (Joel 3:12), Israel will defeat the armies of the enemy gathered to defeat Israel and lay waste to the world. We find the same discussed extensively in Ezekiel 38, where the following is said of 'Gog and Magog' (mentioned also in Revelation 20:8):

> This is what the Sovereign LORD says: I am against you, O Gog ... On that day thoughts will come into your mind and you will devise an evil scheme ... In days to come, O Gog, I will bring you against my land ... When Gog attacks

the land of Israel, my hot anger will be aroused ... I am against you, O Gog ... on the mountains of Israel you will fall ... I will send fire on Magog'. (Ezekiel 38:3, 10, 16, 18 and 39:1–5).

Here it is emphatically stated that it is God's will that this battle be fought. Gog will be defeated. Thus in both the spiritual and the physical, material realms the anti-God power will be destroyed.

In reality these two factors are naturally closely intertwined with each other. The contradiction in the spiritual realm will lead to this war, whereupon Gog's loss will lead people to see that God is the Lord and will be decisive for the already doubting and seeking multitudes of the anti-God camp. But Israel too will now let God lead them fully. See Ezekiel 34:30. Special texts: Isaiah 13:1–5; Jeremiah 6:22–26; Joel 3:1, 9 ff.; Daniel 11:40 ff.; Revelation 20:8; Ezekiel 28:6–7; Isaiah 34:1 ff.; Zechariah 12:1–9 and 14:12. Compare this with the influence of World War II on people's thinking: conceit vanished in a wink. Ezekiel 34:30: 'Then they will know that I, the LORD their God, am with them and that they, the house of Israel, are my people.'

What precisely the sequence of events will be and how the various situations will develop we cannot tell unambiguously from Holy Scripture. We can only conclude that there will be a great struggle. We could imagine that Israel would find itself in difficulty during this tremendous battle and transfer the leadership to God and so go on to win (see Isaiah 64:24, Nahum 3:3, Jeremiah 16:1–4, Ezekiel 36:14, Jeremiah 34:20).

We could summarize this section with: 'Light has come into the world, but men loved darkness instead of light because their deeds were evil' (John 3:19).

J. Day of Jahweh II

The events of this point coincide with those of the previous point. Israel, driven by the terrors caused by the birth pangs, will again seek God: 'In that day the remnant of Israel ... will truly rely on the LORD. . . a remnant of Jacob will return to the Mighty God' (Isaiah 10:21; see also Jeremiah 50:4). Even clearer is Hosea 3:4–5: 'Afterward the Israelites will return and seek the LORD . . . They will come trembling to the LORD their God and to his blessings.'

God will take away their heart of stone, he will be their God and they will be his people (Ezekiel 36:26–28). The curses, the chastisements that he once laid upon them will be taken away, as will sin, so that nothing will remain to separate them from God. Together with Christ, Israel will rule God's kingdom on earth: 'If you will walk in my ways and keep my requirements, then you will govern my house and have charge of my courts' (Zechariah 3:4–7); 'In those days ... the people of Israel and the people of Judah together will go in tears to seek the LORD their God' (Jeremiah 50:4).

As soon as God hears Israel, he will answer them and accept them again. Israel will seek God again, and that will happen because God will take away their hardness, 'How gracious he will be when you cry for help! As soon as he hears, he will answer you' (Isaiah 30:19); 'I will rescue you on that day, declares the LORD . . . I will save you . . . because you trust in me' (Jeremiah 39:17–18); see also Ezekiel 34:30 and Daniel 7:25.

Therefore there will be the restoration of Israel. In this we can distinguish:

a. Gathered again. They will be gathered again and return, the Diaspora will be lifted. '"The days are coming," declares the LORD, "when I will bring my people Israel and Judah back from captivity and restore them to the land"' (Jeremiah 30:3). God says to Israel: 'Do not be afraid, for I am with you; I will bring your children from the east and gather you from the west' (Isaiah 43:5–7).

As I already said, Israel is not yet back in the promised land, even Judah was only back for a brief period; the practically always added statement that it will be for ever shows us that this prophecy must still be fulfilled in the future.[10]

b. Rebuke removed. The indignity too is taken away: 'he will remove the disgrace of his people from off all the earth. The LORD has spoken' (Isaiah 25:8). This too is not yet fulfilled. The Jews are still 'despised' amongst the nations.

c. One nation again. The division between Judah and Israel will be cancelled: 'I will make them one nation in the land, on the mountains of Israel. There will be one king over all of them and they will never again be two nations or be divided into two kingdoms' (Ezekiel 37:22).

d. Stony heart softened. As we saw, the rejection of Christ and the wrong paths of this nation were the result of a hardening that God had brought upon them: (Isaiah 29:14).

Before they will acknowledge Christ, who will then rule over them as king (see Ezekiel 37:22) this hardening will be taken away: 'I will give you a new heart and put a new spirit in you; I will remove from you your heart of stone and give you a heart of flesh' (Ezekiel 36:26; see also Romans 11:25).

e. Christ acknowledged. 'They will look on me, the one they have pierced' (Zechariah 12:10; see also Matthew 23:39). At many places there is mention of one shepherd, of one king who shall rule over them, of David's root, who shall reign over them. Christ is thus recognized as being the son of God. 'I the LORD will be their God, and my servant David will be prince among them' (Ezekiel 34:24; cf. also Haggai 2:21–24).

f. Sin taken away. The last obstacle standing between Israel and God is now also taken away: 'I have swept away your offences like a cloud, your sins like the morning mist' (Isaiah 44:22); 'for I will forgive the remnant I spare' (Jeremiah 50:20). (This taking away of sin in order to make contact possible between God and people is really the foundation on which the whole of Christianity is built: Christ died on the cross so that sins might be forgiven and taken away and so that people might in this way appear before the face of God and approach him. Cf. Isaiah 59:1; see for this point also Zechariah 5:1–5.)

Now that Israel has been accepted again the nations will acknowledge that God is the Lord. Cf. Zechariah 8:13: 'As you have been an object of cursing among the nations, O Judah and Israel, so will I save you, and you will be a blessing.' Moreover, 'I will make known my holy name among my people Israel. I will no longer let my holy name be profaned, and the nations will know that I am the LORD am the Holy One in Israel' (Ezekiel 39:7).

In this way the nations, the 'heathen', will also have a part in the kingdom that stands under the leadership of Christ. This is really the logical consequence of the defeat of the anti-God powers (symbolized by the fall of Babylon). The anti-God persuasion is taken away. How that can happen we cannot even remotely understand. The renewed acceptance of Israel, the taking away of sin etc., and how these things will come about are all far beyond our powers of conception: ('"neither are your ways my ways," declares the LORD' (Isaiah 55:8–9).

People may not however be converted by force or violence, and if such are used they may only be a means to open people's eyes (Zechariah 4:6). God desires to bring us to subject ourselves to his guidance voluntarily. He wants all nations to follow him not out of fear but out of deep conviction. When this happens, then there will be a 'new earth and a new heaven' of which it is written: '"all mankind will come and bow down before me," says the LORD' (Isaiah 66:23); and 'And foreigners who bind themselves to the LORD . . . these I will bring to my holy mountain . . . for my house will be called a house of prayer for all nations' (Isaiah 56:6–7).

Here too sin is taken away: 'Then will I purify the lips of the peoples, that all of them may call on the name of the LORD and serve him shoulder to shoulder' (Zephaniah 3:9).

What is said above about Israel implies that Christians too will have a part in the 'kingdom', that they too will be 'kings' (see also Isaiah 56:6–7, cited above) for ever; for Christians, after all, are added to Israel and are spiritually speaking a part of Israel (cf. also Romans 11:11–27; Ezekiel 47:22 and Isaiah 56:1–8; and Ephesians 3:6).

We must understand well that God's way with Israel is intended to bring other nations too to see the light. The restoration of Israel will make such a tremendous impression that all nations will recognize the Lord. Thus it is written: 'It is not for your sake, O house of Israel . . . but for the sake of my holy name . . . Then the nations will know that I am the LORD, declares the Sovereign LORD, when I show myself holy through you before their eyes' (Ezekiel 36:22–23).

K. The Last Judgment

Now the final judgment is pronounced. The labour pains that have happened until now are already a judgment; through the victory over the dragon and his followers they have already been judged. Now however the sentence will be announced. Moreover, this victory occurs at the end of the ages. What then about the adherents of the dragon who followed him in remote or more recent times and vilified God? To this end the sea and the land give up their dead; we have the resurrection, we have judgment by Christ, who has received that authority (cf. Revelation 5 and affinitive passages). It is at this point that we have the second coming of Christ (See Matthew 24:25 and 29–31; Luke 17; and Revelation 20:11–15). The judgment can be pronounced because now, after the Day of Jahweh, the seven seals have been opened, and as these seven seals have been opened, one by one, the book mentioned in Revelation 5 is now open (see Revelation 20:12).

About this final judgment I want to say that I see it as, for example, in John 3:19: 'This is the verdict: Light has come into the world, but men loved darkness instead of light because their deeds were evil.' Hell is the place where people abide without God and without love because they will not give God the glory. Everyone who lives in this way, far from God, both here on earth and in the hereafter, finds him- or herself in hell. The Last Judgment, and hell, I see only in a symbolic sense. A judgment, a penalty in the human, juridical sense I cannot believe in, since these are all too human notions of things which are not so 'human' that we would be able to grasp them fully. Here I want to cite Miskotte's *Antwoord uit de storm*:

> To whom received an answer from the storm ... it may be that the goodness of God conquers all and that one must henceforth hold the doctrine of retribution for a form of apostasy, due to a new spiritual insight into the all-sufficiency of Christ ... to such an extent that it must even seem to one to be the acme of unbelief, with respect to one's life, even to think of punishment.' Naturally this also pertains to the present life and the 'life after death' of others.

'What is hell? The torture that one no longer has the capacity to love' (Dostoevsky). 'There is a judge for the one who rejects me and does not accept my words; that very word which I spoke will condemn him at the last day' (John 12:48). Through this judgment, however it may be, everything that separates people from God will be taken away, and then

'I the LORD will answer them; I, the God of Israel, will not forsake them
. . . so that people may see and know, may consider and understand, that
the hand of the LORD has done this, that the Holy One of Israel has
created it' (Isaiah 41:17, 20).

L. The new earth and the new heaven

Then 'the eyes of those who see will no longer be closed, and the ears of
those who hear will listen. The mind of the rash will know and
understand' (Isaiah 32:3–4). The earth will be full of the 'knowledge of
the Lord': 'No longer will a man teach his neighbour . . . saying, "Know
the LORD," because they will all know me, from the least of them to the
greatest' (Jeremiah 31:34). These are the days when 'God's law' shall be
the only law and nothing will remain that is in conflict with God: 'I will put
my law in their minds and write it on their hearts' (Jeremiah 31:33). In this
the apotheosis of the whole of world history, history as guided by God, is
reached. This is the time when Christ will hold universal sway, so that:

> Your eyes will see the king in his beauty ... your eyes will see Jerusalem, a
> peaceful abode, a tent that will not be moved ... It will be a place of broad
> rivers and streams ... For the LORD is our judge, the LORD is our lawgiver, the
> LORD is our king; it is he who will save us ... an abundance of spoils will be
> divided and even the lame will carry off plunder ... No one living in Zion will
> say, 'I am ill'; and the sins of those who dwell there will be forgiven (Isaiah
> 33:17–24).

Is this something entirely new, something 'out of the blue' as it were? I
think certainly not. This kingdom of God is something that has always
been: 'because the kingdom of God is within you' (Luke 17:21; cf. the
discussion of the thousand-year kingdom, above). The kingdom was a
kingdom that grew and grew, but opposed to it the power of the Devil
grew too. Thus we read: 'Let him who does wrong continue to do wrong;
let him who is vile continue to be vile' (Revelation 22:11). The existing
cleft between good and evil grows wider and wider . . . yet the kingdom
grows. As the end approaches the anti-God power will make things
difficult for 'Jerusalem': 'They marched across the breadth of the earth
and surrounded the camp of God's people, the city he loves' (Revelation
20:9). (This struggle will be waged on both spiritual and physical
terrains. Babylon, the spiritual enemy, will go under; they will also be
defeated physically, in a war, the outcome of which is described for us in
Ezekiel 38, Joel 3:1–3 and elsewhere.)

The dragon will leave nothing undone to bring members of the
'congregation' over to the camp of the godless, worse, of those who are
anti-God. But then the dragon, this Antichrist, will be defeated, even by
his own weapons, by his own forces (see above). And when the Devil is
vanquished, humanity will see the kingdom, 'Jerusalem', in all its power
and glory, for 'They shall know that God is the LORD, and the earth shall

be full of the knowledge of the LORD' [cf. Isaiah 11:9, Habakkuk 2:14]. And 'The moon will shine like the sun, and the sunlight will be seven times brighter, like the light of seven full days, when the LORD binds up the bruises of his people and heals the wounds he inflicted' (Isaiah 30:26).

This is the great apotheosis. Read Revelation 21. 'Rejoice with Jerusalem and be glad for her, all you who love her; rejoice greatly with her' [Isaiah 66:10].

Conclusion

The whole of prophecy shows us that it is God who has been active throughout all of history. Reference is made again and again to the special place Israel has in this history. Israel was hardened and therefore they rejected Christ, yet as a result Christianity became not a Jewish sect but a world religion, as it is written: 'if their transgression means riches for the world' (Romans 11:12). Those who accept Christianity are 'added' to Israel. They will have a part in the ultimate salvation and kingship of Israel (Romans 11:25).

Christ himself has told us to watch the signs of the times. Thus he says of the fig tree: 'As soon as its twigs get tender and its leaves come out, you know that summer is near . . . when you see all these things, you know that it is near' (Matthew 24:32–33). We do not know the precise moment (Matthew 24:36), but we know when we can expect it, therefore 'So you also must be ready, because the Son of Man will come at an hour when you do not expect him' (Matthew 24:44).

The pangs, the spasms of distress, do not come all at once; they have been present for a long time, but they are increasing in force and scope. Consequently people are not always keenly aware that matters are growing ever worse, for we adjust to circumstances as it were, so that it cannot be surprising that 'in the last days scoffers will come, scoffing and following their own evil desires. They will say, "Where is this 'coming' he promised?"' (2 Peter 3:3–4).

Therefore Christ comes in judgment unexpectedly; the end arrives almost unnoticed, 'as a thief' [1 Thessalonians 5:2, 4].

In prophecy, and very extensively in John's Revelation, reference is made to the heavy conflict that must be waged in both the spiritual and physical, material realms before the kingdom comes, but – comforting and tremendous thought – God shall triumph, the Devil shall go under, God's Spirit shall triumph, as it is written: '"Not by might, nor by power, but by my Spirit," says the LORD Almighty' (Zechariah 4:6).

Again, the Day of the Lord, Judgment Day, will come 'as a thief', so we must prepare ourselves for it and not say, 'after us the deluge.' 'Because of the increase of wickedness, the love of most will grow cold,

but he who stands firm to the end will be saved' (Matthew 24:12–13).
Therefore this prophecy – just to bring it home to our hearts – is meant to be a comfort and guide, a help and support to us in the midst of this world. What is said of the Revelation of John applies to the all of biblical prophecy, namely: 'Blessed is he who keeps the words of the prophecy in this book' (Revelation 22:7).

For, so it says in Ezekiel: 'It is coming! It will surely take place, declares the Sovereign LORD' (Ezekiel 21:7). 'You have seen correctly, for I am watching to see that my word is fulfilled' declares the Lord in Jeremiah 1:12. See also Ezekiel 12:28 and Habakkuk 2:2–3. (One finds everything summarized in Ezekiel 36:16–29.)

Stanislau, 22 September 1943

Articles on Evangelism

• Child evangelism[11]

'If you believe in the Lord Jesus but do something bad, can you still go to heaven?' a little boy asked, and this was the answer: 'If you really accept the Lord Jesus as your Saviour, you have also become a child in the great family of God, then you are God's child. And just as you will always remain the child of your own father for as long as you live, so you will also always remain the child of your Father who is in heaven. And then if you are naughty and do something you know our Father in heaven would not approve, you will feel sorry and then he will forgive you for that, just because the Lord Jesus already bore the punishment for this sin on the cross for you.'

Can earthly powers perhaps prevent us from giving to children this testimony of God's love? Perhaps. Yet if the child that heard it has accepted the word, then Romans 8 also holds for that child: that nothing shall separate us from the love of Christ, not even the possibly terrible future that may await that child. Then that child need not fear those who may be able to kill the body, having learned instead to fear him who is able to destroy both soul and body in hell but who will now keep her or him from it.

It is wonderful to be able to confess that and know that. Yes, but what then of all the children who never heard of God's love for sinners, for whom he even sent his only beloved Son to earth to bear their sin if they would believe in him? There are hosts of such children, in heathen countries, in Roman Catholic countries, yes, in our own neighbourhood. Worse still, there are thousands of children who at home, at school, perhaps even at a Sunday school are given poison instead of the milk of God's word, stones instead of bread, children who are taught to believe in the lie under the pretence that it is the word of God that is being proclaimed.

We often talk about apostasy and write about the disobedience, about the unbelief of the liberals and the Barthians and about the heresies and errors of the day; but then do we ever think about all the children who with full trust listen to their teachers and leaders only to receive and believe a lie? We must be just as moved by compassion for children who are misled in this way as we are for those who are born into the darkest paganism. The children are the victims of all these erring spirits because through them they learn to hold the truth in unrighteousness and through them the way to the Christ of the Scriptures is closed to them so that they do not know him.

If we see that the great day of the return of Christ is approaching, that the end of days when the church will be silenced and believers persecuted is near, then we ask ourselves: How much time do we still have? We have today at least, and therefore we must also do that work now: the work of telling the children in our immediate vicinity about the Lord Jesus Christ of the Scriptures – so that God may use us as instruments to draw them away from the power of the lies of communism, Barthianism, nominal Christianity, in a word, the power of unbelief, and to bring them to the fountains of living water, of saving faith in our Lord and Saviour.

If we can make our home a centre where the Way, the Truth and the Life is preached to the children from the immediate vicinity, from our own street, probably the little boys and girls who are friends of our own children, then we can also say that we have put the light on the candlestick, that we have not put the light we were given in grace under the bushel but have let it shine – then there is a possibility of saving children from the power of governments, from the powers and rulers of this darkness – for without God, that is what the world around us is. Perhaps the hearts of the parents can also be reached through these children.

And then it is not enough just to teach these children the gospel and to 'simply leave it at that'. As they grow older we must hold on to them by means of Bible classes and the like, so that they can learn to understand the doctrine of Truth not just in its principles but also can go on to understand it more fully and follow the path of the Christian life as a fruit of faith and even learn to know where to find a Bible-believing church in their own neighbourhood.

That last point is an urgent necessity, precisely because we live in a time of apostasy! It is not enough to tell about the Lord Jesus and leave it at that, we must also teach the difference between those who are really servants of God and those who have a form of godliness but deny the power of the gospel. If the parents, the mothers, cannot teach their children the difference between the true and false church, between believers and pseudo-believers, and they refuse to listen to us, then let us at least attempt to teach the children to distinguish between lies and the truth.

If we truly realize that God has placed us where we are, that he has called us to be ready always to give a defence of our faith, if we realize what it means to be the light of the world – Matthew 5: 14 – and if we then get to work, very simply with the gifts and possibilities that we have, and if the Lord blesses our work . . . just think of what that could mean for the children, for the church, for our country, for the world. If it is true that there are no immediate solutions for the problem of de-christianization and moral decline but only solutions such as we recently could read about,[12] then there is a work with perspective to be discerned in all this, the consequences of which we cannot foresee – although we know that the angels rejoice if one sinner, even a little one, converts. If later in wars and persecutions many victims fall, then we shall not have to reproach ourselves that once again so many have gone to hell whose blood is upon us because we kept silent and neglected to tell the children, whom we could have reached so easily, about the Truth and the Life (see Ezekiel 33:7–16). And this work is very simple.

Besides the children who are reached through the Sunday schools there are many thousands who are not reached and cannot be reached in that way. We receive them into our homes during the week, after school or on a free afternoon, and tell them what Holy Scripture is, what the parts of the Bible are, about Creation and the Fall, what sin is, in order then to tell them about the gospel. The method we use in doing so, which involves teaching the children directly how to use a 'big people's Bible' – they memorize Bible texts after having looked them up themselves – has proved very fruitful: the children really know what it means that Christ died for our sins, that we must believe in him in order to be saved, that the words of life in Scripture are readable, and that we can also find there what God asks us to do and not to do. After a year they really know the book of Luke with all its 'stories' and parables; in subsequent years we tell stories from other books.

It would carry us too far to discuss details of this method here. Suffice it to say that there is a task and that there are possibilities here for housewives and others who may have time available when the children are free. And everyone must seriously consider whether he or she has a responsibility here. It is very easy: good guidelines and materials are available, so that no one needs to think that they lack the ability to do it. We are always prepared to provide information and to help anyone who may be interested in getting started.

• On witnessing[13]

We are not going to talk about Bible clubs. Mine is unique and so is yours. Each of us has our own talents and possibilities. The ground rule is that every organizational structure must follow the facts, not the reverse. Do not organize ahead of time. Go to work and then organize to the extent that the work requires it.

How to witness for Christ today? Being a Christian is just a matter of being human. Christ came to make us human. The gospel is not for the soul only, not for Sunday only, not for heaven only but for human life: it is about walking with the heavenly Father.

The gospel is not an opinion but the truth, reality. It is not about ideas but about the living God. We should not compromise. However, we do need to connect with others and be a Jew to the Jews, a Greek to the Greeks. Make others feel at home and approach them in a way they understand, speak their language, not the terminology of the creeds, of the Three Formulas of Unity. They will not understand it.

You must also be able to listen. Witnessing to the gospel is not advertising for our business, our church, our clan. It is God's business, and it is about persons and not about our sacred hobby horses. Do not begin with secondary questions such as Sabbath observance, lifestyle, politics, church organization, ecumenism, Christian schools. But do give an honest answer to questions others may ask about these issues. These secondary matters are about the fruits of faith. Things that we experience as normal, morality, a way of living, are fruits of faith, and you cannot expect them of someone who lacks faith. We should talk about the problems that are of concern to the other person.

There is a dispute going on in our time about two views of the world. The biblical world view, in brief, is that there is a God, and that he created the cosmos with people, animals, plants and the like, and that he gave norms, laws for life. We can therefore speak meaningfully about good and evil. There are also angels, evil spirits and spiritual powers. Since the eighteenth century, for the last 250 years, this world view has been disputed. People said: 'God is definitely out of the picture. And when God disappears, norms also disappear. Who can tell what is right or wrong? Without God there is no norm.' That is what is being lived out all around us. We should not be optimistic in this respect. We have to reflect on this state of affairs. Before that change people based their thinking on the Bible: there is a God, who creates the cosmos and puts human beings into it. Those human beings have souls and bodies. And there are animals, and lowest of all there is matter. Today people have turned this thinking completely around: first there were atoms and through a long process of evolution the world evolved from those atoms and at the end of that evolution, at least for now, is humanity. Something has apparently gone awry with evolution, however, since people are crazy enough to think they need a God. They invented God. That means only the atoms are real, while all the rest originates from the atoms or are human concoctions.

When others raise questions, we must remember that they do so from the standpoint of their own view of the world. One person will ask: 'How do you know that that is all true?' I do not answer that question but rather say: 'What you want is proof based on the atoms or natural science, but then I have stepped into your world picture and God does not fit in that framework. Thus I cannot do that. Let us therefore pose the question differently.' That person must of course be given an answer. There are many people, bourgeois people if one may call them that, who live normal lives but without a basis. The ultimate norm of their lives is: What will the neighbours think? Underlying that is a strong element of emptiness and despair. Alas, many Christians are equally bourgeois, also fearful of the neighbours. There is considerable protest against that, sometimes with tears, as the church, which should have an answer, gives none.

Our aim in all that we do should be true humanness and the truth. See Romans 1 and 2. We live in an unnatural world where there is sin and death and sickness. The unnatural has become almost ordinary. We see it in films and read about it in novels. The other person lives with me in this same world. Our point of contact lies in our being human. We should try to show others that their certainties are not certainties; confront them with the truth of their being dead, here and now. Show them that what they want is impossible, but that the Bible provides an answer. It is essential to our humanity that we are able to choose between good and evil; that is our human freedom, but that also means that there is a judgment. God judges. We do not need to judge.

Righteousness and love go together. The righteousness that Scripture speaks about is something quite different from rigid adherence to the letter of the Law. God is a gracious God but also righteous. He does what is right and asks people to do what is right, taking circumstances into account, for that is what love inherently requires.

Christ did not come just to forgive sins. Much more: the power of sin is broken. Just read Romans 6 through 8. We have died with Christ, our sins have been forgiven, we have been buried with him and raised to a new life. That means we are new people. That is what the gospel is about, and that must be visible. Moreover, the Devil has been defeated. Becoming a Christian means passing from death to life.

God is the Creator and the Bible is God's word, which is not a strange book but rather one that deals with our ordinary world; it is not a religious book, but it is about ordinary reality and it gives answers to questions that concern that ordinary reality. If I believe in God, then at the deepest level I am really convinced that God exists, I am convinced of the truth of Scripture and of what God has done in history. Believing is simply walking with God, the living God, our Father. We must lead that life visibly, that is our witness: I trust in God, he has everything in his power. That is our gospel.

Now, prayer is tremendously important, also for your Bible club. If you want to do something, then begin with prayer: 'Lord God, let me do something, I want so much to do something, here I am and whatever you want me to do is up to you.' God will certainly hear that prayer. It really is the Lord that must do it. So do not force people but allow them to come in freedom to your club, in answer to your prayer. And you must pray concretely. We do not know how to do that as Reformed Christians (*Gereformeerden*), but we are certainly going to have to learn how to do it if the whole *Gereformeerde* world is to be kept from going under. Pray concretely, for your neighbours, for the lady or gentleman in the office who, if only she or he knew Christ, could be helped in their difficulties. Sometimes we do not give God a chance to answer our prayers; that is why our faith is sometimes so empty.

You want to witness. Now, you cannot witness just because God has commanded that, because then you would be a legalist and would do it only to gain favour with God. You must only testify out of love for the other person, who does not know the Lord and whom you see headed for disaster. The problems of another person must be of interest to you. Everyone is called upon to bear witness at an appropriate moment to her or his Lord and Saviour. But I do not think that everyone is called to this particular work [of evangelism]. That, namely, is something else. The Lord never requires something of you that goes against the grain of your own possibilities and talents. You must grow in the conviction that there is something that needs to be done, something you want to do, something that you cannot neglect to do. And then do it out of love for others. Begin by praying for others. God will provide the possibilities – perhaps not immediately. Sometimes the Lord wants to teach us through patience to expect things from him alone. Yet he will certainly hear your prayer.

• Evangelization[14]

When we set out to write about evangelization and when we begin by asking ourselves what Holy Scripture has to say about it, the first remarkable discovery is that nowhere do we find a command in this direction. Neither Paul nor any of the other apostles in their epistles urge believers to devote a great deal of special effort to propagating the gospel. Browsing through the Epistles, we come across many exhortations to lead a holy life, that is, to bring forth fruit through the power of the Holy Spirit (cf. Galatians 5:22, John 15:1–8), but we do not find injunctions to engage in anything similar to what we today know as evangelization. Acts 8:1 and 4 are no exception to this. Here we are told what members of the congregation did under certain circumstances, but one may not infer a general norm from that. As I see it, they were acting in the same way that is explained and illustrated in the continuation of this article.

What is the first thing that is asked of us? To love God and his Son. What is that, to love him? It is to keep his commandments, to bear fruit through the power of the Comforter (John 15:9–10; 1 John 5:3–4). In that way the kingdom of God can be righteousness, peace and joy through the Holy Spirit (Romans 14:7). The very first thing that is asked of us is to love God, to be his child, to seek our salvation in his grace, in the blood of the Cross, redeemed from the slavery of sin (Romans 6:22), not only to listen to his word and his commandments in general but also very particularly to seek the task and calling that he has planned for each one of us personally. The latter will never conflict with the former since each person has his or her own calling. To do what our hand finds to do, certainly, but our finding depends very much on our asking the Lord to show us the way to what he calls us to do.

I am not saying this in order to write pious words but to show the basis of all truly Christian endeavour. That does not consist in following a timeless commandment but rather in doing our specific calling, for which the Holy Spirit makes us willing and ready as we listen to the word and watch for God's answer to our prayer. Then we see that some are called in a special way to proclaim the gospel. That is what we read when Jesus himself says that he sends his disciples out to their field of labour and we read with how much emphasis Paul speaks about his own calling (e.g. Colossians 1:25).

To summarize all this briefly: we are all called to walk as children of God and to bear fruit in the power of the Holy Spirit, but only some are called particularly by the Lord to bring others to faith, to proclaim the gospel.

Let there be no misunderstanding, it is certain that each of us must be ready at all times to give a reason for our faith, for the hope that is in us (1 Peter 3:15); and there is no doubt that it is not for nothing that the Lord has called us to faith: he has called us to be his children in holiness, love and unity, so that (notice: so that) the world may believe that Christ is the One whom the Father has sent (John 17:21). When we do not demonstrate that we truly have been saved from the power of sin, thereby making the word of the Lord (Romans 6) to no effect, when we do not produce fruit (cf. John 15 and Galatians 5:22), then the world can correctly say that the Holy Spirit is not a renewing force leading in God's ways. In short, if we are not salt that salts and if we do not show the world by our works what justice, truth, love and unity in freedom are, then we are worthy of being cast away by the Lord. We must show through our lives, our actions in good times and bad, that we truly have been made free in Christ, free from every form of slavery, free from struggling to earn our own salvation through works, free from human opinions and commandments (cf. the entire epistle to the Galatians and Colossians 2:16). We must show that we desire to be good instruments in his hand, trusting that he protects, keeps and sustains us (Sunday 30), that he will always help us and that he will keep his often repeated promise to hear and answer our prayers (John 14:16 and 14:13; Matthew 7:7-12, etc.). Again, this is not intended as some sort of pious talk, no, it must be a reality in our lives, or else we do not need to speak of evangelization and the like at all.

Only on the basis of truly walking in the ways of the Lord can something like evangelization exist. It may be clear from what I have said thus far that personally I prefer not to use that term. It has such an organizational ring to it, a ring of 'in faithfulness to the generally obtaining principles we ourselves set to work to do something for the Lord' instead of waiting for the Lord to call us so that we may do something in his kingdom. Is this a passive attitude? Certainly, for we would rather allow our Father in heaven, who knows the times, occasions and possibilities better than we do, to decide the time and circumstances. Yes, passive, but do not think that that means it will be a light and easy task: God's servants are always busy, since he always gives us just as much work as we can handle. Working in his kingdom is not an unbearable task, not a heavy yoke, since he knows what he can require of us and what he can give us to do – yet it demands our entire person, all our gifts and all our energy.

Our calling

Now, what does all this mean practically speaking, you may ask. To be honest, we regard what we have written up to this point as the most practical thing there is. And everything that follows are at best suggestions or a further exchange of experiences. We even hesitate to go any further. For in this matter too God will call everyone individually to walk in his ways in their own particular freedom. That is one of the greatest wonders of God's work: the great diversity, the complete freedom that one finds in it, and at the same time the internal and external unity, the absence of all chaos, the harmony of all the parts and all the work. Thus be mindful that what we shall go on to say is nothing more than examples of personal experience. We write it down only because we hope to make clear to others what the principles explained above may mean.

Thus some are called to evangelization. Not everyone is automatically called to this work (cf. 1 Corinthians 12), also not the people who may be assigned this task by the church counsel, unless such an appointment has been based on a proper calling. Thus some are called. If they are, they are very well aware of that. No one else can determine that for them. They themselves are certain that God has a task for them in this. If someone desires such a thing, then let that person pray that God will make it clear to him or her whether such a task has been laid away for them. The Lord will certainly hear the prayer; he is a loving Father who grants his children what they ask in Christ's name, at least if that is good for his kingdom. Yet notice carefully: we must not dictate ways and methods to the Lord, just offer ourselves, our talents and possibilities, and ask him to show us the way in which we can make the best use of them. And then we must be prepared to do what he gives us to do. The means and ways to do that work, assuming the Lord has a task for us, we must neither determine nor set out to acquire for ourselves. Let us leave the leading to him so that he can work through us and the Holy Spirit can speak through us. Money, books, space, time, the right people, help, all these things we must not organize ourselves but wait until he shows us the way and provides them for us in answer to our prayers. That is moreover one more witness to unbelievers, namely that people take it seriously that God is the Living One who hears, who sees us, who helps us in our difficulties, who does not leave us, as it were, to 'row our own boat'.

That also applies to the people that God will send to us to hear his word. Never should we decide the time and the occasion ourselves in a forced way. We should instead seize whatever opportunity God may give us to bear witness to him, our Saviour and Redeemer. Certainly whenever we expect to receive a visit from an unbelieving neighbour or colleague, we should pray to the Lord beforehand, asking him to give us together with this opportunity also the wisdom to use it in the right way. And note well that if the occasion does not arise, then we should not take it but rather wait patiently, for the next time might be the right time. Perhaps you will have done something in the interim period that will have seemed important to the other person, perhaps you will have shown, for example in your everyday walk and in the serenity, joy and confidence you exhibit, that your life is different from that of others. If the person comes back another time he or she may therefore be better disposed to listen, and perhaps then God will give the opportunity to speak. And often with a wonderful result. So do not try to be tactical or to implement a strategy, just wait and use wisdom and insight, being open to the direction in which the conversation may lead by the questions and circumstances that arise. Speak freely and use all your knowledge of Scripture and all your experience of God's wonderful power to help his people and of his great deeds in our lives, and manifest the joy that is the result of your knowing him in whom all true love and freedom are rooted. If you want to do that, then naturally you can only do so if you know the Lord yourself, having studied his word daily, and if you trust him yourself in all the great and small issues of life.

The full biblical message

If at this point we wanted to summarize a few guidelines, we could do that as follows: a) We must leave the occasion to the Lord; b) He must send us the people whom he wishes to call through us; c) We are to have been prepared well ourselves through our own lifestyle, our trust in God and knowledge of the Scriptures, so that we really can tell something about him both from his word and from our own experience of his love; d) No conversation, no opportunity arrives out of a clear blue sky. The Lord gives us the opportunity in answer to our prayer. That strengthens us in our own faith too and teaches us to wait until he provides the right time. If we proceed in any other way, then we are more likely to mess things up than to serve the Lord.

I want to make a number of additional observations. In the first place, in our speaking with the people whom the Lord places along our way so that we may proclaim the good news to them, we must be utterly serious about God's word. We must not preach theology or the opinions currently prevalent in our own circle. We must not seek to be wiser than the wisdom God gives us in his word. Never try to reason something away because of the smallness of your own faith. If the Lord Jesus talks about always hearing prayer, then we must not try to 'save' the Lord when something does not turn out the way we think it should have done but rather take his words seriously and act on them and trust in them, and in that way let the unbelieving person understand that God does not need any justifying or excusing from our side, that although our faith may perhaps be small at times we are prepared nonetheless to entrust ourselves completely to him and his word. If the Lord Jesus speaks of the Comforter, the Holy Spirit bestowed upon every person who believes in him, then we should go on from there and not attempt to bind the Spirit of God to any church or synod or straitjacket whatsoever.

God's kingdom is never served except by righteousness, so never try to justify the sins (for example of the church) identified by unbelievers. Be honest and upright in everything.

God is a God of miracles: the Lord Jesus rebuked the winds and they were still. God protects his children. Sometimes it is necessary for him to open their eyes to let them see that the heavenly hosts are already here now (2 Kings 6:17). He raises the dead, heals the sick, yes, miracles without number are recounted of him. Shall we believe them? Know that we have the same God today who can still do today what happened then. The Bible tells us no fairy tales, lovely but alas old fairy tales, it tells us realities that can also happen in our time, and indeed that do happen, if we have eyes to see. To believe in miracles in our times, when people have been brainwashed by rationalism and the science ideal, is difficult. But without that we will never be able to convince anyone in all seriousness of the truth of the Scriptures.

In our conversations with people who do not know the Lord it is best to avoid getting into debates. The issue is not philosophical ideas, not interesting theories but the living God, the Saviour who truly saves, the Holy Spirit who really leads and reveals, the creation that is really his work, and humanity who are truly saved. It is best then, if that is possible, to read the Bible together with the other person, to submit ourselves to the Scriptures. Always live by this rule: that you want to know nothing apart from what has been revealed by God. Only what can be shown clearly in Scripture may you recount with certainty to another. The other person must also notice clearly that your wisdom is not from yourself.

There is another rule, if indeed we may speak of rules, that we definitely want to stress, namely that we must never preach anything but Christ and him crucified [cf. 1 Corinthians 1:23; 2 Corinthians 4:5]. Never preach the church or a Reformed Protestant lifestyle or a particular theology or a particular organization, not a particular political party like the GPV (*Gereformeerde Politiek Verbond*) or the AR (Anti-Revolutionary Party) or a particular journal like *Ruimte* or *Opbouw* or *De Reformatie*, do not preach against going to movies or travelling on Sundays or in favour of singing psalms exclusively. Those things may all be good or not good, they may be God's work or human work, but whatever they may be, we may never preach them. Christ and him crucified, God and his great love, God and his wrath against sin, the Second Coming of the Lord, the resurrection from the dead of believers and unbelievers, the judgment, eternal death and eternal life, all that and much more you may preach (not just hell and damnation but also God's gracious love in Jesus Christ for sinners, which is what we are, every one of us, believer or not), but never preach any human organizations or opinions. Show that Scripture (not our system of knowledge) truly answers all life's questions.

It can be clear that the approach set out briefly above is difficult to reconcile with today's familiar standard methods of evangelism. I can also say that I honestly do not believe in planned evangelization, barging into people's homes, seeking to attract people through advertising, trying to reach everybody and anybody while all too often forgetting the neighbour in one's own street or in the next chair at the office. If we want to engage in evangelization, let us pray that God will provide us with the opportunities and then, when he gives them, witness freely of the hope that is in us. With those whom we reach in this way, then, let us form Bible clubs (of two or three but a maximum of ten to fifteen people).

Yet we must never proceed unless God has called us. Not everyone is called to the task. And wait patiently to see how and when he will give the fruit. We are certain that if amongst us everyone were to look to the Lord and if everyone were to be true to her or his calling, a true reformation could be the result, if that is God's will. But then surely all the painstaking effort, so little edifying for our own belief and at times so little uplifting for the outside world, the consequence of working in our own strength, will be a thing of the past.

Another brief concluding word: if you enjoy the privilege of leading someone to faith, leave that person free and do not deprive anyone of the freedom gained in Christ by laying upon him or her all kinds of sectarian (*gereformeerde*) rules (Colossians 2:23)? With a gentle hand you may offer that person advice, to be sure, guiding him or her with prudent and loving patience to God's church. Yet be mindful that all Christian virtue that is worthy of the name is a fruit of belief and is gained in freedom. Let the fruit grow by itself and do not try to cultivate it artificially. The fruit of belief certainly will appear if only you abide by the rule to want to know nothing outside what is written in Scripture.

Interviews

• Interview by Marc de Klijn[15]

Personal faith
When and how did you come to personal faith in Christ?

During the Second World War, I was imprisoned in a German prisoner-of-war camp. In the officers camp we were relatively well off. We suffered no hunger and were not even allowed to work. Thus I had the opportunity to read the Bible and while reading I came to faith, because in it I found an answer to all the essential questions one can pose. Without books and without further help from the outside, I studied the Bible hard. My special interest concerned history, how God works in history, what God's plan is in history, questions about war, the place of Israel and the like.

God cannot be verified in a rationalistic manner, but reality and history are made transparent precisely by the Scriptures. Their capacity to make things clear and understandable, this rational approach is something that I recognized in the Calvinist tradition (after I had returned to Holland following the war), and so my faith and thinking became grafted onto the Reformational ground motive. Via the work of A. Janse, who emphasized that behind the German occupation of the Netherlands and the Nazi regime there might be God and his judgments and that we should therefore in the first instance be humble and modest in confronting the occupying power, I came into contact with Groen van Prinsterer and his powerful *Unbelief and Revolution* and *Handboek der vaderlandse geschiedenis* [handbook of the history of the Netherlands]. This last work was written like the Bible book of Chronicles and it has always appealed to me because of its prophetic view of history. The question of how God might have acted in it remains important. Naturally caution is called for in that matter, but it can also be imprudent simply to shove a prophetic view aside as irrelevant. Thus the question is not whether a prophetic view is speculative but whether it is true, and I believe that from a biblical standpoint it is legitimate to come to such a view as Groen's. I believe that his view, although corrections can be made in it here and there, is much richer than a view in which the approach to history is secularized.

Reformation and tradition
If you identify yourself with a tradition in that way, in this case the Reformational tradition, does that mean that you subscribe to the Doctrinal Standards and accept the tradition itself loyally and whole-heartedly as an imperishable good?

I have taken the position regarding the question of the Liberation in 1944[16] that the Reformed Synod made use of its power in an unchristian way and that the general course of events was indefensible. Thus I landed up at a rather early stage in the Liberated Reformed Churches. The Doctrinal Standards[17] also played a great role in 1967 in the suspension of preachers who accepted the Bible as the guideline for their preaching and pastoral work, to be sure, but who could not assign the Doctrinal Standards a place equal to or practically even above Scripture.

This illustrates tellingly on the one hand how a tradition that can be valuable in itself can be misused and impose a bond on people where there ought to be freedom, and on the other hand how a tradition can curdle and even petrify. For a tradition upheld for the sake of the tradition itself is a dead tradition. I do not deny that it is valuable to think and work in the line of a tradition (our tradition even begins with Abraham and Moses!) but in every generation there will be a need to think things through again. Not because our forefathers said silly things and we know so much better now, but because there should be a living contact with things, a living transmission that also always means, and brings, renewal. The contact with the past is important, but we have to determine our position in the present. Present-day thought and the sciences have brought forward new problems and also new facts that we can neither ignore nor accept straightaway, and we must take into account that we live in a changed situation. With respect to the Doctrinal Standards, we can say that they comprise an edifying document, produced in a rich age of Christian history, which we may admire greatly and from which we may learn a great deal. Yet it is also possible that people in those times did not ponder some of the problems we do have to think about today. However, it seems right to me that they did not pursue some of the problems that are suffocating us today. A tradition is a fallible piece of human work and personally I will never swear by it.

If you do not find an answer in the tradition for certain problems, in what direction do you look for an answer? Do you still seek connection with the tradition or do you set out to distance yourself from it?

I cannot give you a general answer to that. A tradition has taken shape and matured in a particular manner, and I can no longer alter that. I will only try to correct something if I think it is not quite right. For there are also instances where our tradition has petrified or is simply wrong. For example, in Reformed preaching it is a tradition to lay great stress on the condition of depravity (the inability to do any good) and on salvation in Christ alone. What is forgotten, however, is that it also says: unless one is born again. Rooted in Christ's finished work we are called to a new life, for we must not live out of the past, looking back at the Cross, but with the Cross behind us we must look towards the future, towards the return of Christ. That living and working out of our rebirth is something I have always missed in Reformed preaching, so to my mind such a tradition has grown out of shape and that is something that needs to be corrected.

That also applies to always singing the Psalms and a severely restricted repertoire. Something like that is a tremendous impoverishment that belongs to the Reformed tradition. If we were to sing a new song every week, that would be a lively affair, even if only one of the 52 new songs turned out to be of enduring importance.

L'Abri Fellowship

So you do not simply bow to tradition but you think the problems through for yourself. To what extent are you open to God's guidance and the 'dictates' of the Holy Spirit in your life and work?

The fact that Francis Schaeffer and I met each other in 1948 is something we have both regarded as God's guidance. We have had many discussions and talked about the need for a renewal in the church. To that end we found it essential to work from the finished work of Christ. Paul's Epistle to the Romans, chapters 6 and also 7 and 8, were decisive in that.

The Christian life in the Netherlands exerts itself through many and various organizations. Yet even with the greatest exertion and with the best Christian theory conceivable no fruitful Christian work is possible if the direct connection with God is missing. In the Netherlands we are insufficiently aware of the fact that the Christian life, besides being focused on the future, should also acquire concrete form here and now by being renewed in Christ and must also be visible because we are in Christ. That is why at L'Abri great emphasis is placed on prayer, not only personal prayer but also communal prayer, on praying together for one another, on prayer for direct needs and also on prayer for insight at times when it is no longer clear whether one is on the right path. For God can prevent something when he does not want it or when he does not find it necessary. That is a possibility we must be open to. Even a good way, according to the Scriptures, can be barred by God at a given moment, as when God said to Jeremiah: 'You do not have to pray for that any longer,' or 'I do not want you to speak to the people any longer.' That is a decision that no person should take just on the basis of his or her own insight, but God can lead people, send them or stop them.

This open relationship with God ought to be an essential part of the mentality from which every Christian organization works.

Does L'Abri as a Christian community satisfy the ideal you advocate more than the Christian churches in the Netherlands?

Here we must make a clear distinction. God has said that there will be a church, a fellowship of the saints, which to me means very simply Christians supporting one another, teaching and warning one another, and so forth. I believe that the church has been established by God and that it will be there until the end of time.

Besides that we see that alongside the church there are other institutions that come and go. There was perhaps a time when for some people it was a meaningful calling to set up cloisters for the preservation of civilization and so on. We have had the mendicant orders that resisted the lust for opulence and pleasure. There have been charitable, theological and educational institutions in every conceivable area. It can be a good calling to have a wonderful choir; in the time of the Reformation the singing of psalms meant a very great deal indeed. It can also be a calling to set up a political party, as happened in the Netherlands in the nineteenth century.

Yet all these institutions come and go because they respond to a particular situation in a particular time and therefore are not for all times. For that reason I also believe that L'Abri will not always continue to exist. Yet in the special context of many youth problems, of young people in despair, partly through the fault of the older generation – not only of the parents – the lagging behind culturally and societally of the churches, which have lost contact with the world, which do not keep pace with world developments and are rigidly traditional, in this constellation, then, I believe that L'Abri has had and still has a calling. I see no reason at all to suppose, however, that L'Abri is an enduring institution. I also feel no need at all to work towards L'Abri's lasting three hundred years.

A Christian's struggle

If the Christian life involves struggle, tribulation, suffering and oppression, can you say something about what a Christian has to fight against and the struggle you are engaged in yourself?

The struggle against sin of which the Bible speaks, involves, as I understand it, the struggle against injustice, the hungering and thirsting after righteousness. I just mentioned the fact that people in the Netherlands have constantly tried to articulate a special Christian theory for their Christian organizations. I believe however that one must struggle concretely against injustice wherever one finds it. If you do that with God, you attain insight and ways are shown to you. This is not only a matter of calling; I have gradually come to see that it is also a matter of competency.

I am outraged by President Nixon, who after news leaked out about the Watergate scandal failed to demand a radical investigation and did not punish the guilty, which he ought to have done immediately, but there is nothing I can do personally to change that since I am not competent. Many young revolutionaries often forget this. I also have many questions about South Africa. I am an opponent of racism and I do not know whether their policies are correct, even though they are Christians. I am not inclined simply to accept their actions, but I also do not find it necessary to organize protest marches here and to demand that people in South Africa adopt a different politics. In the first place the people there are responsible themselves to God and their fellow people. If I were invited to visit South Africa, I would in any case want to have the freedom to speak with black people and I would also want to do something for them to the extent that that is possible. I definitely would not want to be won over by the establishment.

Being a Christian is in the first place a matter of mentality and not a question of accepting a doctrine. It is walking with God. Christ preached this mentality in the Sermon on the Mount – the hungering and thirsting after righteousness, the peace making, the showing mercy, being meek, having a good attitude with respect to sexuality, in short, taking a stand in life. What Christians strive for and should strive for is to keep the world clean for God – that is how I translate serving the kingdom of God – and endeavouring to be salt that salts. We are not working to achieve a little Christian subculture, we are not working in the first place for a world of Christian organizations, although I am certainly not opposed to them, but our lives are always in the service of the world at large, of the general culture. We strive for a better culture and not for an elitist Christian community. I believe that the simple fruits of faith such as honesty, uprightness and the like enter into the general culture. Naturally there is also struggles in one's personal life. Of that I should like to say that we must learn to live with ourselves and to accept ourselves, faults and all. That means we must go to Christ with our infirmities and ask him to restore and set things right where we have made mistakes or to give us the strength to do better.

I gain the impression that the struggle you wage is rather introverted in character and that it does not accomplish much. You seem to assume that an exemplary Christian life simply will enter into the general culture. Protest actions seem clearer to me.

It is true that speaking in worldly terms there is an inherent pessimism built into the Christian approach to life, which neither believes nor expects that one can ever bring about a perfect world through one's own efforts. That is not to say however that it is right to simply accept the establishment, for the world is not good.

Now, that is precisely the point at which I differ with you! It is precisely that pessimism that cripples every initiative because it is already established beforehand that it will never be fully realized. Besides, any action about which people have such reservations lacks credibility as well.

The second half of Romans 8, where it says the creation is subjected to fruitlessness, that it eagerly waits for the revealing of the sons of God, that the whole creation groans and travails, seems clear enough to me. We have to recognize that we live in a broken and cursed world in which nothing will ever be realized fully. One can sometimes be particularly unjust when seeking to be too just. If I demand of someone 100 per cent good behaviour he or she will not attain 50 per cent, because my expectations exceed any person's capacity and take away his or her freedom, namely, the freedom to make mistakes. Accepting someone else's shortcomings in the knowledge that we are all sinful and imperfect people is not to say we are prepared to resign ourselves to those mistakes; rather, with prudence, tact and love we will endeavour to rectify them without boxing someone else's ears for their lapses. If we are competent we can also sometimes intervene, firing a person, for example, who does not treat his or her personnel correctly. A Christian lives in a permanent tension between accepting the brokenness of this world and opposing sin passionately wherever it may be; so it is a matter of insight and wisdom where to place the accent at any given moment. There are no general rules or guidelines.

The third way
But where do you differ concretely from the Marxist critique of society, which evinces just as little acceptance of the establishment and wants to radically change it?

Marxism proceeds from two principles that are to my mind radically mistaken. The first is the notion that we are indeed capable of fathoming and analysing evil – what is amiss in this world – in its depth and scope. The second is the idea that we would be capable of making a blueprint of an ideal world. Besides the fact that these optimistic notions are completely unattainable and entail an overestimation of human possibilities, Marxism is also a form of 'economism', an overvaluing of the economic aspect, so that its blueprint analysis presents a totally distorted picture of reality.

Marxism strives for a utopia and tries to realize this by violence or even in unfair ways when necessary. Everything must and shall change. I suppose that anyone with such a mentality must be as lost as one can be. For the end never justifies the means, and if we must do evil to achieve good, then the good has already been lost. Thus a Christian differs from a Marxist in that a Christian does not aspire to a utopia yet also does not acquiesce in the status quo or regard the establishment as the best imaginable world. Thus I distance myself expressly from a 'right-wing' mentality which simply accepts the world as it is and desires to maintain the status quo and so ignores possible evil. A Christian conservatism evincing rightist tendencies I consider absolutely unacceptable.

A Christian identifies evil in the world for what it is and ought not to be satisfied with it. However, a Christian's protest is protest in love. A Christian chooses neither left nor right but seeks another way, which Os Guinness has called 'the third way'.[18]

Can you make that more concrete by mentioning some examples of where you stand on social and political issues?

Before going on into that, I want to say that an enormously important good is at stake here: freedom. I am not one of those people who want to prohibit all bad films, ban all prostitution from public life and prosecute pornography. I believe that is not only foolish and unattainable but that it significantly threatens freedom and fosters censorship. Such a mentality arises from too little understanding of the fact that we always have to weigh our priorities. I think that we need to accept that there are temptations in our world. As I have said before, a Christian always lives in the tension between the brokenness of our world and our hungering and thirsting after righteousness, and I believe that this tension is good. If you want everything perfect, you end up with an absolute dictatorship.

Do you therefore also think abortion clinics should be allowed and that people should have the freedom to determine the fate of unborn lives?

I find the problem of abortion a difficult one. It is easy to say that abortion as such is wrong, but precisely because we live in a broken world it is ridiculous to think that with that we have posed the problem. Abortions are done, and situations are conceivable in which that could even be a good thing. And so the question is brought to the politician concerning what he must do concretely about that. I find myself sympathetic to there being a possibility for abortion, for example in cases of rape. I can understand it and fully accept it. I do not want to be legalistic or dogmatic about whether a foetus is or is not a person. That cannot be proved either with the Bible in hand or with a microscope. But in our thinking about this problem, to which I also reckon euthanasia and birth control, I want to take into consideration as well the general tendency of the time in which we live. It is one thing to talk about abortion in 1880 and it is something quite different to talk about it in 1974. Probably it would have been quite a good thing if the possibility of having an abortion had existed at that time, when all problems pertaining to sexuality were suppressed. People offered far too simplistic and legalistic solutions. Today however we are witnessing an ever more serious decline in respect for life. Steadily advancing technocratization brings with it a desire on the part of people to have everything as easy as possible and to suffer no more pain. I believe we must undergo pain and suffering because that is part of the brokenness of our world. God did not make the world with hospitals; we brought that about through sin. Yet the fact that hospitals are built, people nursed, cared for, operated on and made better shows that we accept this brokenness! Abstractly considered, I would not be opposed to abortion and abortion clinics because of the brokenness of this world. Yet in the present situation and considering the mentality behind the propagation of these clinics, I am more inclined to discourage rather than encourage the acceptance of abortion even if that means being labelled a conservative person.

Authority and freedom

I have the impression that your argumentation suffers shipwreck on the conflict between order and freedom. Do public order, authority and law really mean anything to you? At bottom, living in the contradiction you describe between resisting and accepting brokenness and injustice seems to me to resolve nothing.

When I talk about freedom I also have in mind a struggle for ethical purity. Freedom of the press means it must be possible to print and disseminate the gospel but also the messages of communism, of the Jehovah's Witnesses, of modernistic Catholic and Protestant theologians. But it also means that minority groups may not be oppressed. So, if free sex is preached, there must be a campaign for the institution of marriage. That is also a public health matter. Thus on the one hand I want to uphold freedom for myself and the gospel and give people the room to move freely, give new things a chance to arise, so that people can experiment and make mistakes. On the other hand, certain things cannot be tolerated because they put at risk the freedom of others or jeopardize the good. It is thus always a question of wisdom where you choose to be active and what you will deem tolerable or intolerable.

Yet in the conflict between order and freedom I would rather choose for freedom. That means that in today's situation that is my choice. I do not believe in 'order and authority' because I do not believe that a crisis of authority should be countered with the instruments of authority. That is also true for laws. I believe that laws are of a secondary order and can only prevent excesses. I believe personally that it is much more important to help to nurture a better mentality or to maintain a good mentality where it already exists. We must strive to work much more intrinsically. I would much rather be engaged in the spiritual struggle itself than with the regulative ordinances surrounding it. Perhaps that is also the reason why I have not become very involved in politics, because I do not believe laws are the answer. In L'Abri or at the Free University I am engaged in very long-term work – a change of mentality is a process of several generations and God's blessing is indispensable. Thus when we talk about building a better world I am not thinking about the police acting against theft but about preaching and working for a different mentality. Nevertheless, given the rise in crime I believe a more extensive police force would be justifiable, although that is a pity since a police force is expensive and only relatively useful. You can not use it to prevent developments.

But is it not precisely the lack of authority in our society that leads to your inner distancing of yourself from this society instead of your trying to preserve what is still standing?

I do not know if the general crisis of Western culture can be typified as a lack of authority. There seems to me to be much rather a total lack of values, or a lawlessness if you prefer, which can mean a crisis of authority as a consequence. I therefore would rather typify our society with a term like 'permissiveness'. However that may be, I am certainly fighting for the preservation of Western culture, of what is good in it. But I do not assume a priori that everything that has been passed on to us from the past is good. If something is truly dead, then you must not desire to resurrect it. That cannot be done. Bach's music was a high point in the history of music, but now I have to realize that Bach's music is dead. Naturally I can still enjoy this music and we should also fight for the possibility of listening to Bach's music, but we are no longer able to create such music ourselves. It is also the task of an art historian to preserve valuable cultural achievements. The preservation of old city centres I also see as such a task.

Western culture has sunk so deep that we may consider ourselves fortunate that we can still connect with the good things that remain here; perhaps in the course of two generations (during which we shall have to work hard and reflect seriously on various fields: legislation, medical ethics, morality, education, etc.) we may get onto a better track. But in that case what is needed first is a reformation of the church, and then out of that reformation we shall have to start working in society.

You once asserted, in your lecture on 'Authority and freedom',[19] that we as Christians have to understand that we form a small minority in society and can no longer – as in the past – influence government policy decisively. Is it really true that the cultivation of a new mentality depends on having majority status?

If you imagine a world in which everyone is a Christian, then it would be possible to make something lovely, not something perfect but something lovely. If 70 per cent or 60 per cent are Christians, in any case a majority, then to my mind this majority does not have a right on the political plane to impose a Christian pattern of life on the minority. That majority may at most influence the mentality, as we have already discussed above.

If these Christians are really wise and have organized their lives in a good manner, then I can imagine that others will enjoy the benefits as well. I believe that the seventeenth-century church and Christianity had a great deal of influence in the Netherlands, also in the lives of those who were by no means believers, bringing renewal of life and freedom. That is tremendous. That is formative. And that is acceptable, but coercion is not. Forced rest on the Sabbath is unacceptable to me. I am afraid that a good many Christians, if in the majority, would be dictators, and that is impermissible!

Now if there were 40 per cent Christians, you can imagine that they, organized via political parties for example, would endeavour to influence society and to make their contribution at the administrative level. People have every right in the world to do that and should make use of it.

Carrying our reasoning even further, you can imagine yourself entirely alone as a Christian in a non-Christian world. That is not so strange. When Paul and his companions landed in Corinth, they were the only Christians in that once mighty cultural empire. In such a situation it makes no sense to want to change a culture drastically. That is a *fata morgana*. One will have to observe the rules and customs of such a non-Christian society insofar as they do not violate God's law. But one preaches the gospel, and its effect after many years may be the transformation of such a culture. That to my mind is the way in which the spiritual struggle is waged. If from day to day I accept the plurality of our society, that is because in our Western world Christianity is no longer the leading religion but a religion alongside others. To me it is certainly *the* religion, in the literal sense, the only way to serve God, but I have to accept that there are people who think differently. Politically and culturally I may not ignore this fact. Yet that is something different from making a compromise with this world. For that would mean my accepting in an inner way that this world is good, and I do not do that. In this world, in which immorality reigns so extensively, I see it as a Christian's primary task to set an example and in that way to purify society. The only criterion is that always and everywhere you can say 'Lord, here am I!' with a good conscience and a firm conviction that you have tried to do good, for God's sake.

Art and social criticism
In 'Letter to a Christian Artist'[20] *you assert that the Christian community and the entire society are in urgent need of artists. What contribution do you believe artist should make to society and to the Christian community?*

The great problem of our Western culture is that art and the artist have really become unnecessary, a luxury by definition. We are saddled with a heritage from the time of the Enlightenment when people proclaimed art holy, a sort of religion, and adored the artist as the divine genius. At the same time art (like religion) was perfectly superfluous and stood outside reality. I fight on the one hand against this misguided tradition, in which Art is written with a capital letter, and try to bring art with all its branches and interweavements with life back to normal proportions. Yet on the other hand art and the artist are especially valuable in that they teach people to see, that they can open people's eyes to something that is going on in reality. In that respect I believe that film is the art most connected with reality. Film offers examples, offers ideals, puts forward a certain type of human being, a pattern of life that can exert great influence. That is precisely what I call 'essential' in the art of all ages, namely that in a certain manner it prompts something.

I believe, however, that we must not use art to show that Christianity is so good. That is Christian utilitarianism and as such awful, for art is not a means of evangelism. Yet out of the renewal of life, art can and must make something visible of this life and not restrict itself to a Christian subculture but place itself at the service of the general culture.

I have so often met people who, having become Christians, did not know what to do with their artistic talents. We have to understand that being an artist is no less Christian than being a missionary. Rembrandt never worried about how he could make his artistic skill useful for evangelization. Thank God he did not! And I say that without swearing. In *The Jewish bride* he painted the love of this one man for this one woman, and in doing so he served his culture and human culture more than he could ever have done had he preached every week of his life. Naturally this work of art should never be completely dissociated from all the sermons to which Rembrandt had listened or from his own Scripture reading, his own prayers and the prayers of others. But Christ died so that a painting like this can hang on the wall – not as a service to a mission organization but as a service to humanity!

As artists see through things and are capable of making them visible, should they therefore not screen society prophetically? Surely you believe that artists should understand their times and not bow before the spirit of the age? And that implies that they arrive at a judgment about society.

As it says in 1 Corinthians 12, there are diverse gifts and some are called to be prophets and others to be teachers. This list can be broadened: some are called to be artists, others to be healers, still others to be economists. At times an artist may well be able to say: that is God's will today; but then he or she will have received a special gift of the Holy Spirit that is not specifically tied to his or her being an artist.

An artist has received by nature a feeling, an instinct or gift for making beautiful things. In the first place an artist has received the talent to visualize things. That is thus something different from creativity, for being creative is not restricted to the artist. Creativity is typical of human life. Creativity as I see it is virtually identical with living, living human life in its fullness, making something of it. Creativity must be highly valued in the sense that it means creating something new. It facilitates the unfolding of human individuality. It means making use of the talents and possibilities God has given to human beings in every field. In this sense every person has creativity at his or her disposal, but in the case of a Christian it should attain full deployment. Christ died for that, so that we could be human. He was not out to make it possible for us to become Christians. To use the words of the Apostle Paul, Christians are human beings who, in the reality of their being new persons, are at last truly human beings. We have been freed, freed from the power of sin. It is the lie of the Devil that freedom means you must free yourself from the law of God. That would mean that the law of God is still placed like a wall across your path and that you smash yourself to pieces on it, while in fact it is only walking in God's ways – that is, according to his laws – that gives real freedom. Well then, in accepting this freedom as a given, I believe that every person has received special gifts to use to the best advantage, and an artist is in principle no different. He or she does not dispose over a special sort of creativity or one or another special sensibility.

But what artists do have to understand is that particular forms are very direct expressions of particular views and insights and that they must not become prey to particular kinds of modernism that do not belong to their own starting point. Perhaps I can clarify that with an example. Real Christians in the world of the African-Americans do not sing the blues. Mahalia Jackson has never sung the blues, for the blues is by definition not Christian. One knows that, one senses that, because it is built into the very structure of the blues. A blues song consists of three times four measures. There is something unfinished about it, something of a frustration in the song itself. When a Christian takes his or her inspiration from the blues anyway – there are some examples – then you see that some things are changed. People turn three times four into four times four, or they extend the blues song to thirty-six measures so that through its length the frustration is removed from the structure. Such refined changes show to my mind that people have understood what they could and could not do, and that is what I mean when I say that artists must know and understand their times. They must not try to preach, for they will overstrain themselves in doing so.

Christian aesthetics or truth in art

Can you suggest a number of principles for a Christian aesthetics, or a number of norms or guidelines on the basis of which such an aesthetics could be constructed?

First, I consider myself a student of Dooyeweerd's, who with his Philosophy of the Cosmonomic Idea as basic principle and philosophical approach has written one of the most powerful Christian works of recent centuries. He is and remains for me a signpost and as such valuable. However, that is not to say that I employ his 'system' schematically and pretend that by doing so I have reality in my grasp. A second point is that I have constantly endeavoured to think in an intrinsically biblical way. I have wanted to connect more directly and more closely with the language and thrust of the Bible itself. I believe namely that the Bible is not only normative for a number of considerations of faith but that the Bible is also normative for the way we think. If the Bible talks about wisdom, it means the wisdom directly connected with life, as in the Proverbs. I believe that is more important than making a closed system of thought in the rationalistic tradition that goes as far back as classical antiquity. Thus I am critical of philosophizing for the sake of philosophizing.

Finally, I believe that when people want to think about art, they must first know what art is. As an art historian I investigate not so much the subject of a work of art as its meaning and significance. To say it simply, one can analyse a certain Madonna. It is not enough to just recognize that the painting of Madonnas derives from a Roman Catholic tradition and Mariology. Looking at a Madonna one can perhaps conclude that a particular one is not so pious after all but that it celebrates the greatness of the man who had the chapel built.

Such questions, which place a work of art directly in the midst of life, I find essential. Naturally stylistic elements, iconographic, liturgical and possibly also economic and sociological elements all play a role. But in the end what interests me is what the work of art meant and still means, and I would rather postpone the formal analysis of a work of art until the primary and important questions have been answered. The question concerning the truth in art is more important to me than the abstract analysis of the structure of a work of art. Christ also says that we must do the truth. That is more concrete than a structural analysis that is perhaps so abstract that we can do nothing with it. On the other hand, we shall naturally also have to be able to elaborate our conclusions in structural analyses. Noncommittal chatter in the wind is worth nothing.

At what points do you diverge from an art historian like E. Panofsky, who likewise does not stick to the subject but investigates backgrounds?

When I read a book by someone else I never think: What is good and what is wrong in it? From someone like Panofsky I have learned a great deal and I have carried that over into my own work. What I value in him is that he does not occupy himself so much with stylistic analyses but instead poses questions in much the same vein as I do. Yet, he still does not get beyond analysing works of art and gets somewhat bogged down in iconography. Panofsky does not think through any further problems like, for example, the new experience of spatiality in the early Renaissance, which evoked resistance from many painters who did not integrate it at that time because it was evidently a life size problem for them. The struggle that took place around 1400 forms a parallel to my mind to the many discussions that have arisen around Genesis 1. At stake was a new way of approaching reality that was intrinsic to naturalism, by which Christian and also human values were put at risk. The same thing is involved in the naturalism of evolutionism. Here too realty is reduced to the 'natural' aspect. The same sort of struggle is going on between progressives who think in terms of evolution and more conservative souls who perceive that vitally important values are lost. But to return to Panofsky: he wrote an important work about Albrecht Dürer. I can still experience astonishment at the fact that someone of his allure grasps absolutely nothing of Dürer's Christian faith and his alignment with the Reformation. He dismisses it as a trifle, as if it would have played no role in his work! Perhaps that arises from Panofky's personal remoteness from the Reformation, for he did indeed say many meaningful things about Roman Catholic culture.

The Reformation as cultural renewal

You view the Reformation as the life and soul of Dutch art in the seventeenth century. But was Calvinism not much rather hostile to art? Did people not occupy themselves mainly with singing psalms and building ecclesiastical and political life?

The remarkable thing about seventeenth-century art is that there was not a great deal of theorizing about it. An art appeared that was so self-evident that no explanation was needed. Just think of the tremendous amount of literature that has arisen around the art of Cubism and Surrealism. That is precisely the opposite. Art that is strange in some way or that does strange things requires an explanation.

A landscape by Jan van Goyen is a splendid landscape. It is the landscape. This art is true, and truth requires no explanation – just as little as health requires an explanation. It is illness that needs explaining. Almost everything that has been investigated about the human body through the years is connected with sickness, although the healthy human is still a mightily interesting thing. It is something of this healthiness and this truth that I see in seventeenth-century art, and it is not only I who see it there, the people themselves experienced it that way at the time. This truth simply shines out at you, it is lifelike art. This healthiness is a fruit of the Reformation. People were not so concerned, I think, with political life or the liturgy but occupied themselves in the first place with the Bible, with the correct view of the relation between God and the world.

Calvinism strongly rejected the Roman Catholic nature-grace scheme and thereby opened the way for a better understanding of the world as a whole. In *Religion and the Rise of Modern Science*[21] Prof. R. Hooykaas has discussed the influence that the Reformational position had also on the beginning of the natural sciences. Here we see something of what I meant above when I spoke of a change of mentality. With respect to art this does not mean a number of theologians or preachers started to preach about these things or that a conscious campaign was waged for an improvement of the arts; even less that ecclesiastical leaders arrived at a unanimous decision that people should make better art. It means that these people who had attained a better view of reality, who had attained a grip on reality, simply tried to express that in their art, without laying any theoretical reflections at its foundation. They were much more involved with the actual production of art.

I am deeply convinced that the seventeenth century forms a high point in the whole of world history, in depth, in breadth, in richness in virtually every field. In art alone it is an incredibly rich time, particularly when you consider that the Netherlands still had less than three million inhabitants. Yet people were not 'aesthetistically' oriented[22] and they did not place art on an exalted plane, but I regard that as precisely a positive point. There was no overvaluation of art, it was just there. Similarly, in the fields of natural science, music, medicine and theology an enormous amount was accomplished by a relatively small number of people in a short period of time. The Reformation also influenced Roman Catholic culture and had an important part in the purification and renewal of what became known as the Counter-Reformation. The same is true for humanism, which in this time also had a breadth of vision and depth.

The Reformation was a breakthrough of diverse fruits of Christianity, not of Christianity itself but of its fruits. It is this rich culture that I have in mind when in my book *Modern Art and the Death of a Culture* I speak of the death of a culture. That came about through the new rationalism, the humanism that came into prominence in the line of Descartes and Locke, thus essentially the spirit of the Enlightenment that set God aside and glorified the human. Naturally that did not happen in a day, but our culture has been gradually torn down. When we speak today of art or science policy, then that is the proof that something is wrong, that there is chaos, the crisis of our culture. We must also not say that a healthy culture has become ill, but that it has been made sick. Historical personalities were responsible for that, people who consciously took certain decisions and switched the direction of the current of life. We must not fail to take note of this.

What for you is essential in being a Christian today?
I believe we must realize that being a Christian means redemption, including the strictly personal renewal of life and the promise that God will take care of us, but with that not everything has been said. Also demanded is a renewal of life that one may call the sanctification of life. A changed mentality – for example the preaching in the Sermon on the Mount – and a calling not only to evangelization but also to being fully human and to being salt that salts, in the community and with the community. In the present generation that could also mean that we are called to martyrdom or at least to significant persecution, as is the case in Russia today. Being a Christian must not be an escape. It is also not a promise of a comfortable life here and now. The Lord Jesus has warned us against that. But whatever the difficulties in which Christians may find themselves, there is always the promise of the new earth in which righteousness reigns. And this puts the Christian life into the perspective of patient endurance, an expectant hope that will be fulfilled one day, when Christ comes again.

• Interview by C.A. Delhaas-Kraan en J. Boelema[23]

> God made the world good. And in this world man has received the task of glorifying God. But sin has sown division. It has broken things and brought a curse. God has not forsaken his creation, but man finds himself in difficult circumstances. Now, the wonderful thing is that there is redemption in Jesus Christ. God is interested in his creation, and human beings may live out of the divine covenant. Then there is renewal of life.
>
> Our own cultural work can, if God wills it, mean much for the world.

On April 24, 1965 the Association of Christian Public Reading Rooms and Libraries in the Netherlands as it was then still called held its Annual Meeting in Utrecht. We can still remember this gathering very well, especially because of the fact that Prof. Dr Rookmaaker spoke on the subject of 'Christianity and Culture'.

The two citations placed at the head of this interview are from that address. On that occasion Professor Rookmaaker named three positions that a Christian can take with respect to the culture surrounding him or her: firstly, a gnostic-dualistic standpoint is taken by a movement that proceeds from a dualism, a dichotomy, to the effect that the creation is bad and it is a blessing to be freed from the world. Secondly, you can as a Christian adopt a synthetic standpoint, namely, the scheme of nature and grace. The third stance mentioned was called 'conversalism'. What is meant by that is described in the first citation above.

When we asked Professor Rookmaaker if we might have an interview with him, he agreed immediately. We were received on the eighth floor of the enormous Main Building of the Free University complex in Amsterdam-Buitenveldert where the professor has his office. At the Free University he teaches Art History, while Dr D. van Swigchem is responsible for Architecture.

Professor Rookmaaker was born in The Hague in 1922. In 1959 he completed his doctorate at the Municipal University of Amsterdam with a dissertation entitled *Synthetist Art Theories: Genesis and Nature of the Ideas on Art of Gauguin and His Circle.*[24] The following year his Dutch book *Jazz, blues, spirituals*[25] appeared. In 1962 the Dutch book *Art and Entertainment*[26] saw the light of day which formed the basis for the English publication of *Modern Art and the Death of a Culture*. In 1965 he delivered an address on the occasion of his acceptance of the post of professor at the Free University entitled 'The Artist as a Prophet?'.[27]

We began the interview with *Modern Art and the Death of a Culture*. 'There are two categories,' the professor told us, 'who appreciate my book: my friends, and people who are spiritually far removed from me. This latter category find themselves in crisis and despair and that is exactly what I write about. The ones who do not appreciate it are often those who are abandoning orthodoxy. They want complete freedom to devote themselves to modern art and find it annoying when someone confronts them with Christian concerns. They regard my book as unemancipated but fail to see that they themselves are still unfree, because they have not yet thought through certain problems. As I already said, my book enjoys an audience amongst those who are near despair, but those who are critical of my work have failed to see that this despair also lies at the end of their way, even though their view of life is optimistic and they believe that there is something good in people. It is worth noting that my book is well received in England, especially amongst those who are far removed from Christianity, who have landed up in negativity.'

Professor Rookmaaker told of a remarkable incident: 'I once held a lecture for the Inter-Varsity Fellowship (a Christian student organization that stimulates local student groups by organizing lectures, for example). This lecture is worked into my book *Modern Art and the Death of a Culture* and I showed in it how modern art could arise. I did not say a word about Christian faith. I spoke at length with these students; six of them became Christians. At a later meeting when I asked how they had come to that, they said: "You showed us what we were engaged in."'

An aspect that features strongly in *Modern Art* and also in other publications is that of Christian liberty. This is not so strange, for Professor Rookmaaker only became a Christian later in life, not through contact with other Christians but by reading the Bible. When he eventually found his way into the Reformed Churches he was surprised by the lack of freedom there ('and I have never got over my astonishment'): 'I encountered an enormous amount of legalism. Because of that I started to occupy myself intensely with this subject. I studied it extensively, especially what Paul says about freedom. I think it is precisely the great thing about being a Christian scientist that I may stand freely in the world, that there is nothing I have to be afraid of and that I may look into anything I wish.'

Do you then not take sin into account?

It is sin that took away freedom. The world as such is too grand for any person to comprehend, but the Bible provides the key to understanding reality, and then the door opens and you can investigate freely. But if you leave the key at home, the door stays shut and you kick as it were against a closed door. That is what we see in modern art: the closed world and absence of freedom. I want to go back in history a little way now. In the time of the Reformation something of this freedom became evident in the openness and freedom in the way painters worked. For example, there has never been such a rich array of genres in painting as there was then. Alas, Christianity has lost this freedom again under the influence of mystical movements and humanism. To focus on the latter: it is very idealistic, but one must always place some constraints on idealistic people. Humanism seeks general rules, therefore it often paves the way for the impersonal whereas the gospel finds precisely the personal important. And freedom and personality cannot be captured in rules. The recovery of this real freedom does not happen just as a matter of course. You cannot just say to someone who has tasted something of this freedom in the Bible: 'Now you must be free.' You can only say: 'Now you must try to realize this freedom in your life.' That too is creativity: 'What are you making of the possibility you have to be free?'

Professor Rookmaaker finds it difficult to answer our question whether his vision is well received by his students. 'Then you would have to step outside yourself as it were and look at yourself. In my lectures I am not evangelizing. Evangelization must be kept outside the university. However, just like everyone else I approach science from my own standpoint and background, as science is never neutral. But I just lecture and someone else will have to judge whether it has anything to do with Christianity. I have acquired wisdom from the Bible, and with it I have delved into reality. I have looked intensely at the work of Picasso and many others. Dismal often are the depths into which one must plunge, but there are sometimes also tremendous heights to attain. I try to understand the meaning and message of these works. I would like to put it this way: "You must confront your own spiritual bagage with that of the artist."'

Professor Rookmaaker endeavours always to inculcate in students that they must be open and honest in their discussions; they need not agree with the professors, but they need to have a standpoint! 'It is important to engage others in discussion at the same level and take them 100 per cent seriously, beginning with listening and looking. It is a fault of Christians that they too quickly start to criticize. Possibly another's analysis is superb, though one cannot agree with the solution that is offered. The greatest danger for Christians at the moment would be defending the establishment and allowing themselves to be polarized between the right and the left. We should not want to be right or left for then we should once again have lost our freedom.

'Much of the criticism from the left is dead on but the solutions proposed are usually incorrect. The economic and social structures are wrong, they say, and only if these are changed people will change as well. The mistake is that the left proceed from the notion that human beings are good and that evil arises only from the wrong structures. Only via a pure dictatorship can an immediate change in structures be achieved, but then freedom is taken away as well. Where there is a change of mentality, there can also be a change of structures.

'The tragedy of many young people is that they are in revolt against "the Christian world", as they say. Yet the world in which we live is not Christian. As a Christian I am in revolt against the same world as they are, for this world has become tangled up in its problems as a consequence of the Enlightenment. God was excluded again and again. Together we must return to the Source. That means that if a reformation comes we shall have to work very hard – possibly for three or four generations – before this world will be somewhat healthy again. At the same time we soberly need to take into account that a perfect world will never be attained here.

'Here and there something germinates but we must be patient. Things do not change from one day to the next; they have to grow out of the present situation. You can never begin something new without beginning in the here and now. If you want to cover a mile you have to cover every centimetre of it.'

We had an opportunity to ask Professor Rookmaaker about the Christian Cultural Study Centre, the CCS in Rijswijk. In the monthly magazine of the NCVB (December 1971) the director, Jan Sikko Siegers, describes the work of this association as follows: 'Engaging with the fundamental questions concerning art and culture, aiming at the Protestant Christian part of the population in particular. A centre where Christian artists, high school students, housewives, civil servants, members of Christian organizations throughout the land, and so forth, can go for information, orientation, study, reflection and forming.'

Professor Rookmaaker, as it turns out, is no longer a member of the board because of a difference in views on administrative policy. 'I think that a Christian organization with a well-defined goal can only really be creative if there is a deep-rooted spiritual unity. Then there can be things that are not yet clear as is the case in the thinking about art in Christian circles, but the starting point is more important. In shaping policy we need to agree as to the frontline matters of the moment. That is why I resigned from the CCS and that is the only light in which I wish to regard it. We have to be in agreement about our starting point, otherwise we cannot get on with our business and we end up in endless meetings and discussions.

'To clarify this: there was no discussion about whether in the CCS we wanted to work as Christians on the basis of Scripture. The differences arose in the implementation. I believed that we could only realize something if we would agree about a number of fundamental questions – and this meant, for example, that working and thinking from the modern theology of Professor Kuitert and his circle ought not to be accepted within the CCS. Others felt that the CCS should rather be a platform where all who as Christians (no matter how defined) occupy themselves with culture could meet. I see it more, however, as a creative, like-minded workgroup, albeit in an open forum. I favour a clearly formulated direction; be it in a broader set-up.

'The difference was thus at bottom one of policy, of direction and goal. In general, as I see it, the lack of vision and drawing power that plagues many Christian organizations today is a result of people wanting to be too broad and too relativistic, which results in the end in their being able to say very little. In the case of an association with a specific goal, it is acceptable to be quite precise in setting the boundaries. We are dealing here with an organization, not with the church. Entirely different rules obtain for the church. In the church there can be great openness and freedom with respect to differing standpoints. The present ecclesiastical boundaries are really outdated. Something like a new confession should be agreed upon with points that are open to discussion and points that cannot be discussed or only to a certain extent.'

With that we have arrived at an entirely different chapter, about which we could go on to talk with Professor Rookmaaker for a long time. Yet that lies beyond the scope of this article. We are grateful to him for granting this interview. Many of his ideas have now become much more clear to us.

• Interview for Crusade [28]

You have been accused [at the Royal Academy] of using your lectures and books as an excuse for propagating Christianity. What is your answer to that?

In a way everyone propagates his or her own viewpoint, and it is dishonest to call it 'propaganda'. This is because propaganda to most people means something negative and not honest, hypocritical even; it means building one's argument in one direction only, and leaving out anything that is against it. Propaganda in that sense is wrong. Yet when you feel that something is valuable, you promote it. One cannot escape this, because one is always fighting for or against something. That is human. Otherwise you promote the nothingness of complete neutrality, and everybody hates that.

You replied to one critic that you are interested in truth and reality, not in promoting your Christianity . . .

That is true. This is the complete honesty we must have, particularly if we are Christians. You are laying your own Christianity open upon the table, and you are asking the other person to lay open his or her position. Then we can try to find out which one is true.

What is truth?

What is true for me (and, I think, for everybody) is that which answers to reality, my own reality and the reality around me. Obviously, if somebody says, 'Christianity means that everybody has a red cap on,' and Christianity did say that, then Christianity is not true because I know that not everybody has a red cap on. But my Christianity is only my subjective reaction to what God has said.

Is the Bible only true because it says it's true?

Now I would say God's word is right because it is God's word. But being God's word (the same God who created this world) it must be the key to reality. If it does not fit, either I do not see it right or the Bible is not right.

I always like to say that you have to bow two times. First, you must bow before the reality of this world, and the God who made it. But, as soon as you agree: 'Yes, God made this world,' then you have to bow a second time, accepting God as Lord, as your personal Creator and Saviour. This second bowing only comes after the first discussion has finished. So, though I speak out of a conviction of knowing, when I come into a discussion I jump back to the first position and lay my Christianity open upon the table.

It is in these terms that you approach the message of modern art. You say that it is just like the ancient gnostic teaching. This denied one's emotions and physical desires in favour of an alternative 'spiritual' world. Modern people are refusing to accept the reality that has been given to them by God . . .

Yes. They see this world as completely evil; and in some ways they are right. If there were no God and no redemption, and we were therefore really caught in this world, then they are right. But we all know that is not right. The countryside that we are looking at at this present moment is beautiful. It does not fit that modern picture of evil. We always have to be open to everything, to the beautiful as well as the ugly. Christians do not think enough about the curse. There is much written on grace and redemption, but little on the curse. What does it mean and how far does it go? I am bound to say that the curse goes into the depth of every atom. It is not just something spiritual. That is why the genes of people can be so wrong that they are physically or mentally deprived.

What then do you mean by 'reality'?

Reality is something that is infinite. I do not mean this in the sense that there are still many things to discover: new kinds of trees, new kinds of animals, more molecules. But when I say that reality is 'infinite' I mean that reality is essentially open. We can create reality. There are new languages we can make, there are new words we can create. But we can never create outside of the possibilities open to us. God has given us a framework inside which we can do things. Let's say tomorrow you hit upon a new kind of music that expresses something which music has never done before. Then what you are doing is not making something out of nothing but realizing a possibility. This 'realization' is a human and free activity. We can 'realize' things that have never before been. Yet they are not inventions in the sense of having been made out of nothing. What people can do is to discover, but never to invent. We can never invent something for which the possibility was not already there. But we discover things when we create, because then we give form to them.

Can you give an example?

People discovered America. They at the same time began to create America. So now I look a couple of centuries later to see what we have done with that which was given there as an open possibility. I find we have developed it and have made it beautiful. We have opened it up, made roads through it, made parks and many things. But at the same time we have inflicted wounds and destroyed things that might have been possible; that is the negative side. So the America we now see is what people have done with the possibility.

Who would you say you have been helped by in the past? Have you been helped by the Dutch thinker Herman Dooyeweerd?

I am a pupil of Dooyeweerd. In fact, I am a pupil of a pupil of Dooyeweerd, namely of Professor J.P.A. Mekkes. What Dooyeweerd has discovered has given a better answer to many things than most other philosophies because it is more open; it is not such a narrow description of reality. Most philosophies try to approach everything either from history or from physics or from morality, etc. But in his philosophy all things have their own place. It is very wide and it is great for that reason. I do not think that all Christian philosophers should follow his exact terminology and system. But it is good to work in the same direction.

How exactly did he help you?

There are two sides to Dooyeweerd. Firstly he gives an interpretation of the history of philosophy, and secondly he made his own philosophy. When I became a Christian just by reading the Bible while I was a prisoner of war, there was nobody around to help me. At the same time as reading the Bible I was studying philosophy. So I came to the point where I said: 'Well the Bible gives me all the answers I need, but Kant[29] is very interesting. If I become a Christian, can I also be a Kantian?' In a way, this was the problem of the relationship between thinking and starting from the Bible.

Then somebody [Mekkes] pointed out, 'Why don't you read Dooyeweerd?' His first twenty pages utterly convinced me that Christianity was right, because they showed me that Kant had his own religious starting point. He was not just a neutral thinker using a neutral logic; he started from a point of view just as Christianity does. Knowing this liberates one to make an honest choice between points of view. I am very thankful to Dooyeweerd for this insight. I have worked along his lines rather freely.

Another man who has been important to me is someone whose books were never published in English, which is a surprise, for he was known in England. He gave lectures there. That was Groen van Prinsterer. He wrote a book in 1848 on revolution and unbelief, on the background of the French Revolution. In a way the thesis of my book [*Modern Art and the Death of a Culture*] is the same as his. He was warning the people of his day not to think that the French Revolution was over, for it was still around because the same mentality was still around, but that there would be many more revolutions to come. His book now reads like a prophecy.

How has your friend Francis Schaeffer been important to you?

We work together, we have learnt from each other, and I am very grateful for what he offered to me. It was in 1948 that I met Schaeffer. I was a bit dissatisfied with Dutch Christianity, which I felt was in some cases less than what it should be, particularly on the level of personal faith and walking with the Lord. On the other hand, I feel that Anglo-Saxon Christianity really lacks the intellectual insight we have developed in Holland. In a way what Dr Schaeffer and I have tried to do is to fuse the two things, to make them into something new.

Maybe the most important contribution of L'Abri – and this is particularly Dr Schaeffer's contribution – is that it has been trying to work out a point of view by which you can avoid compromise, where you are never relativistic, but where you can say to somebody 'You're completely wrong' and yet not break off the relationship. I think this is a great contribution because you see in Christianity fights between people, and jealousies, so that some almost destroy another's Christianity and all become very unfriendly. We have to be open and able to criticize someone without saying, 'You are nothing.' After all, we may be different but we are all one when we are Christians.

This is the balance of truth and love, the practice of truth, is it not? Human beings must be able to live with the truth if a person is not nothing.

Yes. We must understand we are all humans and fail. Maybe it would be wrong for somebody to change, even if your criticism of him or her were right. It might not fit his or her system or thoughts, and it would weaken his or her position. I do not think we need to be dismayed about this because one of the greatest enemies of Christianity is perfectionism. If we look for the perfect we better stop working.

We are working in a direction. Truth is not something final and closed. Truth is *doing* the truth. Of course, if you on purpose fail to think about things, then you are dishonest. But you may at a certain time say, 'Well, I must leave this out because I can't do everything.' I myself know many fields that I have never worked in because I am just human and finite.

Do you think it's because of the fact that Christians have not been practising doing the truth that they have not been producing in the arts and in the areas of culture?

That's maybe one little part of it. But I think that the most important part of the failure of much of Christianity, precisely in these fields, is the duality of nature and grace. Many evangelists go to a person and say: 'Be saved.' It means: get out of this world, and get yourself ready for heaven; keep your religion at home. They do not talk about how all nature is implied, and all the fullness of reality. As soon as people are saved, well, they leave them aside, because now they just have to wait to die. They have no life anymore.

But I feel that the moment you accept Christ, life *begins*. It means rethinking your whole position. You begin to work in the Christian community. You try to work out what it means that Christ is Lord in every field. You do it with love and patience and diligence and compassion, not just in a hard intellectual way. Why did God give us brains if we are not to use them?

• Interview for Right On[30]

Dr Hans Rookmaaker teaches Art History at the Free University of Amsterdam. He heads up L'Abri Fellowship in Holland, helps run aid programs in India and probably has the largest jazz collection in Europe. His books include *Modern Art and the Death of a Culture* and *Gauguin*. This interview was taped at Regent College in Vancouver where he taught a three-week course on 'Twentieth-Century Problems'.

In your book you say, in talking about a modern artist, that it's all very fine for him to express himself but when the cleaner comes in the following morning, does he or she understand what he's done. Does it matter that everybody understands a painting, is that a criterion?

No, of course not. Some things may be difficult. That all art is to be so simple that everybody understands it at first sight is not the criterion. It may have to be read twice or three times; there is a place for something that is difficult, on the one hand, but on the other hand what I wished to point out in the example of Mondrian, which you were talking about, is that he was so intellectual that there was nothing on the canvas. So when the cleaner comes, he or she sees only the white canvas and says that the man has done nothing, while he has been fighting an intellectual battle all afternoon. And what I was discussing in that part of my book is that much of modern art is so intellectual. I am an intellectual myself, so I am not against intellectuals, but I think that it is only intellectual. In a way the art has gone away and we have run into a kind of intellectualistic religion, and that's what much modern art is. Of course it is bound up with the neognosticism that is a kind of mysticism, but it is an intellectual mysticism. So in the world around us, let's say in the 'low' world of Pop and so on, we have very much non-intellectual or even an anti-intellectual mysticism. In the real field of modern art, people like Jackson Pollock and so on are really very intellectual mystics.

You said the other day that there are very few rationalists left. Does that relate to this whole mystical concept?

Yes.

Why do you think that there are so few rationalists left? That seems to be the whole starting point of Western civilization in a lot of ways?

That is the point that I discussed this morning about being 'in the box',[31] which means being dehumanized, and the artist in a way is the one who becomes aware of this and tries to find a solution by jumping out of the box. Much art today is the comment on the 'box', on being human but caught in society, in naturalistic laws and technology and all these things, in commercialism, Pop art or Romantic art.

People discredit the box and say 'no' to it, at the same time affirming the box, which is the point. They always say 'yes' to Cartesian logic and everything that comes out of that and then they say 'Yes, but I don't want to have it because it dehumanizes,' and then they try to jump out of it and there's a tension. They say 'yes' to something that they do not want to say 'yes' to, but then one has to try to get out of that by abstract art or Surrealism or other ways, just trying to find some meaning somewhere. So much of modern art may be termed, as one of my philosophy teachers would say, as 'meaninglessness giving meaning to the meaningless'.

You quote your philosophy, Professor, did not your own conversion come through private study of philosophy?

Yes, I studied the Bible at one point, just out of interest because I thought every cultured person should study the Bible. In studying the Bible I found that it gave answers to all my basic questions. Many of the basic questions were concerned with history, history of the Jewish people for instance, or the question of: Who are we today as Western Europeans? and many questions like that. So I found something true in that, but then at the same time I had begun to study philosophy, mainly the history of philosophy, and so at the end it came down to: people in history have philosophized; Christianity has a good answer; these philosophers are searching for an answer; so, can I be a Christian philosopher? As I phrased it in those days: Can I be a Kantian, a follower of Kant, and a Christian at the same time? Then people pointed me to Dooyeweerd and his philosophy, and he starts with this question and says 'no', because Kant is starting from different presuppositions, but you can be a Christian philosopher, and that is where I started to work.

You said the other day that the universe is held in freedom and yet from hearing you talk I would not think you would believe in anarchy, so how do you define 'freedom'? What do you mean by that?

I think that there are two concepts of freedom that are worthwhile talking about. There is the humanistic concept of freedom and the Christian concept of freedom. The humanistic concept is basically this, that people are their own gods, that they are their own kings and this is the mentality that wants to have everything at every moment, every wish fulfilled, no problems, no difficulties, everything smooth, no illness, every question answered immediately. Of course this freedom is a humanistic freedom – a human being is a great god and free to do everything that he or she wants, everything he or she feels – but then of course one gets into a conflict because, in a way, reality is standing in one's way. Such freedom asks for frustration, people want to have something which they cannot have, an impossible option, something out of this world. So you always end up with frustration or a feeling that those are just big ideas that do not work. In a way anarchism is the caricature of that. Everybody has to have his or her own thing, and everybody has to have freedom to do anything he or she wants to do. In the political field the frustration is biggest because there you end up with chaos – and chaos is the end of freedom because in chaos you cannot move at all Just suppose that there were no traffic rules – we would have a perpetual traffic jam.

There is another concept of freedom, the Christian concept that Paul talks about and that is freedom within a structure. God made people and gave them rules. For instance, in the field of marriage, people are completely free within the boundaries of marriage to move, but if they move out of it then they lose their freedom. If you were free to take a kind of orgy mentality then you have no freedom in the end. The answer to sexual prudishness is not an orgy. Orgies lead to the couch of a psychiatrist, and in the end everything is ugly because people have denied the first law, that there is one man and one woman who are to love each other. Now of course many Christians have forgotten this thing of freedom within the structure so that many people when you ask them what marriage is, say don't do this and don't do that. Those are all the boundaries. I do not think that marriage is 'no adultery'; I do not think that is the definition of marriage. Marriage is a beautiful relationship that a man can have with a woman within a structure, and the 'no adultery' only explains what does not belong to it, it is a limiting border. So you can have all the negatives, keep to all the don'ts, and yet not have fulfilled the freedom in which you could have moved. And then each couple, each marriage is different, because there are so many different people, and it can be beautiful just for that reason.

You can move in this world with freedom; you can make works of art and of course you have to follow some rules and those rules are not 'my' rules or anybody else's rules but they are rules that God made. That is the basic thing, in ethics, morals, language – how can I speak without keeping to the rules for language? If I keep the rules of language, then I am free to express myself, otherwise I run into the crazy Dadaist ways. It comes back to first principles: the Dadaists did not want accept the rules for language, so they made poems that go 'da da da, ding ding, bong bong bong' or they used strange language that is irrational: no laws, no structure. But then you lose communication – there are not many things you can really say in that way – and then you have lost all freedom to express anything.

•Broadcast interview by Jan van Capelleveen[32]

'Good morning. This is your Dutch host on the European Congress on Evangelism. And today will be the day to introduce the general subject entitled: "Youth in Revolt". The Frenchman, Charles Dideau, and the Dutch professor at the Free University of Amsterdam, Hendrik Rookmaaker, are here with me in our improvised studio.'

JvC: Dr Rookmaaker, in what way is youth now really different from youth, say, in the year 1930, before the Second World War?

I think that in general there is much more going on in the field of protest. Youth problems are much more violent than they were then. They were there but they were not as violent as now. My topic, as I raised it in my lecture, was 'Youth in Revolt, Youth in Trouble', and my question was, 'Who is to blame?'

JvC: And who is to blame?

I begin by saying that people give logical answers like affluence or just the course of history, and I think that things like this of course have to be accounted for, but they don't give the answer. I think there are three possible answers. Firstly, it is the youth itself that is wrong. And my short answer is, 'Of course, there are many things wrong.' But I think we should forget them in a way, because the problems are weighing so heavily on young people that they cannot understand them. Of course, there are many more young people in violent protest than those we see daily with their long hair and so on. There are many, many more who don't look like this but who are violent inside. And secondly, from a Christian point of view you can say it is the world that is to blame. I try to analyse this. I feel that there is really something happening in our world: dehumanization, alienation, technology that crushes people, and all these things have brought people into a very great predicament. This is something that all the protest singers are singing about. And the young people buy these records and they recognize it because it expresses their own feelings. Maybe it's not theoretically clear, but the feeling is there, very strongly. 'Who is to blame?' The third possible answer is that these things are happening due to the 95 per cent of the silent majority who in the 1930s, and even before then, has not tried to give answers to the real day-to-day problems of our time. So, if we're now hooked into a problem of ecology, it is because the last generation didn't do anything about that. They neglected all these great problems of dehumanization and so on. I remember, when I was young in the world in the years before the war, that we talked about this and the end of the talk was always, 'Well, anyway, let's hope that the next generation finds an answer,' or maybe, 'I'll live out my time.' And so we pass the real issues by. And I feel this silent majority is the real point of the trouble and the real generation that's to blame.

JvC: May I ask a question? Just at this moment you're speaking about the silent majority and the rebellious youth of our time. I sometimes have the feeling that we have passed the peak of rebellion and that a new type of youth is coming up during the last couple of months, and perhaps over the last year. Do you feel like that, too? Youth is searching perhaps more than rebelling?

Yes and no. On the one side I would say 'yes', the revolution already has been. We must realize that searching and rebelling are not opposites but very much the same thing. So the young generation is post-revolution youth, and in a way they try to cope with the new situation, in which all these things already have been and are not something to wait for. But some who are still in rebellious moods are so depressed because they feel that the society, the silent majority, the establishment and everything weigh so heavily on them that they are in double despair. One example, which is already old now, is that of a man like Bob Dylan, who was first a protest singer but is now turning to sweet songs. It is not something he is happy about . . . I feel it is a kind of double despair. He even despairs about despairing. And he feels, 'Well, let's try to make a nice life,' and that's all.

JvC: And that raises the question, how do we reach these youth in this day and age?

When I said it is the silent majority which may be to blame, I think that the church is not out. Maybe the church is where three quarters of the silent majority are. And I think that a real reformation of the church is needed: a real living up to what Christ asked of us . . . really going into the creeds and history and theology and thinking in general, as well as into the style of living, so that we live up to what Christ demands of us as living Christians. But one thing more about this matter of thinking: I feel that it's very important that we realize that it's not only theology, it's not only the church but the whole field of life we should study and think about as Christians. So we've got to think as Christians about literature, the arts, philosophy, economics, and we have to try and find Christian answers. I think young people are really waiting for this. And if we do not, they are not interested.

JvC: That means that we still have quite a task ahead of us.

LF: Sir, I'd like to ask you one or two more questions for this tape. And that is, would you care to comment on the impact of the Billy Graham crusades in Europe or Dr Graham's ministry itself, or his participation in any of the Congresses? I'm sure that you've thought this through and you probably have some ideas on this. Would you care to talk about it for just a few minutes?

Well, my impression is not too favourable. I'm not talking about Dr Graham himself. But I feel that the American way of evangelism is not quite up to the European situation. It often passes by the real issues. Sometimes people, especially young people in my surroundings, react very violently against it and we feel it's not giving the answers it should. And this ties up with the second objection that I have, and again it's probably not against Dr Graham himself, who I once heard in Mittersill when he gave a very good talk, in which I felt that he really spelt out the problems himself. But that is not on the TV screens and it's not in the big evangelistic campaigns. And that objection is that there is not quite the understanding that I should like to have seen in analysing first the youth's real predicament and situation. There are real problems, and our task is not just to say, 'I like Christ,' but rather to ask ourselves, 'How do we give the answers in the present situation.' And we should give them guidance after they become Christians on how to deal with the many problems of, let's say, philosophy . . . intellectual problems. Many young people go to universities and these are urgent and important questions for them. And I feel that generally in Europe, and particularly in Holland, we are very fortunate (may I phrase it like this): in Holland we have been busy for maybe 150 years or longer with studying these intellectual fields [from a Christian perspective]; and we have been very strong in this, and very good, I feel, and we have a great, great heritage in this. Now in a way we are throwing it away, because our church is growing weaker and weaker and our faith is waning. On the other hand, the Americans and English have been much stronger in evangelism, much stronger in personal Christian life but they have maybe disliked the intellectual side of the Christian life. What they lack is exactly what we have. And so I feel that bringing together the two traditions is maybe the best thing we can do in the future. I'm speaking out of experience. I know that those who have become Christians in recent years are in great trouble. And as far as I'm personally concerned, this has made me work on more than just making them Christians. It's what we do after they have become Christians that also counts, and if we want to reach the real intellectual young people, those who are going to be the leaders, we have to give answers to their real intellectual questions and not just say, 'Are you saved?' That is not enough. We have to ask questions: What about Europe? Is God's judgment upon Europe? And so, yes, what is our answer? And what about, let's say, ecology, and all of those other things? And what have they got to do with Christianity? Does Christianity have an answer? Things like that. So I have mixed feelings. In a way it is strange that I'm at the Congress. But that's another thing.

LF: Well, I think that we need all viewpoints. I think our world is having enough problems that everybody who thinks seriously about hem and who loves the Lord had better speak a word and try to do something about them, don't you?

JvC: I thank you very much. I appreciate your taking time and giving us your opinion on these aspects of intellectual Christian life in Holland. Thank you.

Part III

THE L'ABRI LECTURES

Our Calling in a Postchristian World

A world without God

We live in a postchristian world. The birth of the modern world took place somewhere around the beginning of the eighteenth century, when people said 'God we don't need you, please leave by the door. We can manage just fine by ourselves, we can use our brains and with our common sense build up a great world. Of course if some people want to sing a little hymn for you or pray a little prayer, they can do so. People can spend their Sundays any way they like. But when we talk about something important, God, we don't want you to enter in.' It was not the first time in history that this happened. Moses warned the Hebrew people in Deuteronomy 32 that in future, when they have conquered Canaan and have started to prosper, they should not forget the Lord, the Rock on which they were built. The Jews, however, did forget him and unfortunately Christianity in the Western world has done the same.

In the eighteenth century, during the Age of Reason, people very optimistically thought that nothing would change if they cut God out of the picture. But the last two and half centuries have shown that many things did change and that the changes have been fatal. What has changed? First people began to look at themselves as if they were completely autonomous, with no God to give account to as if they were their own God, standing on their own in an autonomous nature. Descartes was the first to look in this nature for eternal laws, laws that will always be true – like two and two is four – and the laws of physics. Through knowledge of these laws autonomous people could get a hold on reality and be the big boss, the God of this world. And so science received a new drive.

Before the change, philosophers were thinking in the line of ontology, the theory of being. They acknowledged that there is a God who created the world but questioned what this world is like and what place human beings have in it. Those were the big questions. But after the change autonomous people, standing before an autonomous nature, started to ask: How do I know something? How do I know that I know something? The focus shifted to questions of epistemology. Very soon science was allotted the task of providing people with true knowledge, and instead of the revelation of God they sought the revelation of science.

Van Leeuwenhoek, the great Dutch scientist of the seventeenth century, was the first to make a microscope and look through it. In his book he makes the following comment: 'I knew that God created the world, but after I had looked through the microscope I knew that God created two worlds.' He had discovered a new world just in a drop of water and stood in awe of God because of it. But later on people reacted rather like the Russian pilot who was on the way to the moon and said 'I went very high but I never saw God.' Science is there just to find out the eternal laws in order that people can control reality and play God. The tragedy, however, is that this reality includes humanity themselves, so that people too are placed 'in the box', in the box of science, which means that they have become just a bunch of atoms or are just like rabbits, completely determined by those eternal laws. The laws of economics, sociology and psychology govern human life and people have lost their humanity.

Already at the beginning of this new era people said there is no difference between human being and animals and plants and things. At first that was just a slogan, but then science began to prove it. Today people think they have proved it because, they say, in the beginning there were atoms and after a long period of time and through many strange 'jumps' human life came into being. And then people (it must have been a bit of a mistake of evolution) foolishly invented God. Such thinking involves a complete change in direction. Before the change everybody, not only Christians, thought like this: there is a God and he created humans and then animals and plants and then at the lowest level the material things. But now after the change it is commonly held that in the beginning there were atoms and then life came and plants and animals and then humans and lastly they invented God. But there is one problem: what is human being now, just a collection of atoms?

Downfall of norms

This reversal of thinking raised questions that are not just interesting theoretical issues to be discussed by philosophers and professors in the eighteenth century but they are everybody's problems today, voiced in the songs of for example Bob Dylan and Leonard Cohen. There are real human problems involved. For instance, is there right and wrong? How do we know that it is good not to steal? Hobbes in England and later Jean Jacques Rousseau in France spoke of a social contract, in which people invented norms and laws on the basis of their own reason and common sense. It is not basically bad to steal but it is just very inconvenient if everybody steals, so it is better not to steal. But if you can steal without serious repercussions, then why should you not? Laws are made by people and that means people can change them. And so we can understand the downfall of norms that is taking place today. Sartre said: 'If there is an old woman on the corner of the street, you can go and help her cross the street. But you can equally go and kill her, and there is no difference because there is no good and evil. The only thing is that you've got to do something.' Leonard Cohen says it like this in one of his songs: 'I can help you if I must, I will kill you if I can.' But he might equally have sung 'I must kill you if I must, I will help you if I can.' You can turn it around, it is all the same.

Lawlessness comes out of this. People want to be human and free and all seems to be fine. But they will find out the hard way that if you are lawless it does not work and that there will be psychological problems and people will be unhappy. It is very nice to say everybody is free, but what if your lover runs away? And what if you have twenty or thirty lovers who are psychologically able to cope with that? And life becomes aimless. What if I find a new girl in my bed tonight? It does not mean a thing. Everything decays and becomes completely meaningless. Life loses much of its reality, and in a way no one is aware of how deeply that has affected us all. Sometimes I have a little glimpse of it, and the more one studies history the more one sees what we have lost. Yet in a way it is not something you simply know, it is something you must feel. People have been reduced; they have become like little rabbits with brains or like thinking machines. C.S. Lewis talks about this in a beautifully written passage:

> The advance of knowledge gradually empties this rich and genial universe: first of its gods, then of its colours, smells, sounds and tastes ... As these items are taken from the world they are transferred to the subjective side of the account: classified as our sensations, thoughts, images or emotions. The Subject becomes gorged, inflated at the expense of the Object. But the matter does not end there. The same method which has emptied the world now proceeds to empty ourselves. The martyrs of the method soon announce that we were just as mistaken when we attributed souls, or selves, or minds to human organisms. We, who have personified all other things, turn out to be ourselves mere personifications. And thus we arrive at a result uncommonly like zero and the Subject is as empty as the Object.

Human beings have become empty shells. What about the human spirit? Our spirit has become something ghost-like, floating in the air with no contact with reality. What is religion? Religion is just something we invent; we psychologically need a God and that is why we make a God. Of course religion is very subjective and of course it is just for Sundays, and of course it is completely unrelated to truth. Religious truth does not exist, because the only things that are real are the things we can touch, measure and weigh. If I knock on this table it will make a certain sound, this I can prove whether I am a Roman Catholic or a Protestant or an atheist. Reality is where the atoms are, truth is what we can verify, what is 'eternal'.

Demasking of values

In the nineteenth and twentieth centuries people committed themselves to a 'demasking' of values, a taking away of the masks to look what is behind them. We should be very careful when people say 'after all it's just', for then something is always being lost. What is beauty? Beauty is just a psychological response – look in any modern book on aesthetics. What is love? Schopenhauer said in 1820: 'Love is just John having his hormones, and all the rest is nonsense.' Later on Freud talked about libido and everybody of course bow down before difficult terminology like that. Love is just a sexual urge. Love is just a beautiful façade we have invented to disguise the fact that there is sex.

Again, this is not just theory. To illustrate this I want to tell you a true story about a boy and a girl in Paris that happened about fifteen years ago. They were both pupils of Sartre, the great existentialist philosopher. They were sitting on a bench and they were weeping real tears. Why? Because they loved each other. What was wrong? Could they not go to bed with each other? No, because they had gone to bed with many boys and girls. The problem was precisely that they did not want to go to bed because they really loved each other, and that they wanted to say to each other 'I love you.' Three simple words which they could not say because that would only mean they felt a sexual urge. I am certain that this happened not only in Paris but also in Amsterdam and in many places in the USA and all over the world. Those tears prove that after all we are not just rabbits and sexual beings, and that love does exist.

What modern people have realized is that they are dead, living in an impersonal world that is also dead. They know that they are just 'rats in a maze', as Paul Simon puts it. Maybe tomorrow a comet will come and hit this world and destroy it. It can happen, but does it mean a thing? To modern people it does not, because they live in an impersonal world that is neither their enemy nor their friend but completely indifferent to them. Autonomous nature is only atoms. Pheasants, flowers and butterflies are only atoms. No wonder we become alienated from nature, no wonder there are ecological problems. It is because dead people stand in dead nature, which anyhow consists of dead atoms only.

There are many people, 95 per cent of people, who just pass by all these problems. They try to live as if everything is normal and evade the big questions. Their compass is: What will the neighbours say? How can I be respected? How can I have status? Let's pretend we are respectable and we build a façade. Paul Simon very aptly describes this bourgeois mentality when he says 'so we continue to continue to pretend that life will never end and flowers never bend with the rainfall.' Never talk about Vietnam, never talk about ecological problems, never talk about meaninglessness or a dying culture. Many people have asked me if I am not too pessimistic when I talk about the death of a culture. Are there not good things as well? Yes, there are positive things as well. But be careful if you ask me that question because you want to skirt around the problems of our culture; you better face the facts. Do not continue to continue to pretend that nothing has changed. For the change has affected us all in deep and diverse ways.

Christians in a world without God

All this is not just something happening outside the world of Christians, but we are involved as well. Who are the bourgeois after all? Are they not the Christians who have lost their faith? Are they not the Christians who try to live nice little lives? The Bible continuously speaks out against that type of mentality. Read Isaiah 1 and hear God speak to his people: 'You have your church and you bring your sacrifices, but you don't believe, you don't act upon it. You don't fight the real issues; you don't dare to. You just try to live comfortably.' In the Minor Prophets we read again and again: 'You are pious, but what does it mean? It's just traditionalism. You're only looking for a happy life.' And Jesus' greatest enemies were the Pharisees, the 'church' of the day. Jesus said 'Won't you come with me?' 'Oh,' they said, 'that is too dangerous,' and they did not want to go. But also in our own day and age Christianity has become just another word for the establishment.

That is true for a large part of Christianity, but hopefully not for all. For many of us Christianity has become absurd, a religion that is completely out of the world. 'I believe because it's absurd,' said Tertullian in the fourth century. I think he was wrong, I do not believe because it is absurd, for there is nothing absurd in the Bible. But in another sense it is true. In the present world Christianity has indeed become absurd. On Sunday morning the preacher will say 'Christ is alive. He is the only reality that counts,' but as soon as you come home you switch on your radio and hear the news: no God. You open a book: no God. You read the papers: no God. Whatever you do, there is no God. The preaching is not backed up by anything in the week. Is it really true that God created the world as is stated in Genesis 1 or is it more true what the scientists say today? We believe in creation without believing it; after all, science presents us with the facts.

The world around us is changing very quickly. There is a revolution going on, norms and values are rapidly losing ground. What does freedom mean? What does love mean? Are there things we should not do, and why not? The world asks those questions and we have to give answers. But in many instances it is just as if there has been no Christian before who has ever thought about these questions. We have no answers, and the great plight of many young Christian people is: What can I say to them? and: What can I say to myself? Many fall away from Christianity because Christianity has no answers. We have the word of God and we have the key to understanding reality but do we use the key? One thing we should keep in mind is that there is nothing neutral in this world, no neutral scholarship, no neutral art, no neutral politics, because all neutrality really means atheism and most probably antichristianity. So-called neutral culture is preaching, and it is proclaiming an antichristian message.

As to our relationship with this world, without God there are two ways in which we can take a wrong turn. Unfortunately the majority of Christians take one of these wrong turns. Firstly there is the answer of the modern theologian who says that if I want to communicate with the modern world I have to be a Greek to the Greeks and a modern to the moderns: so when I come to a modern person I am not going to ask him or her to believe something crazy, for instance Genesis 1 or the virgin birth of Christ or that Jesus walked on the water. Can I prove that somebody can walk on water? But Christians like these modern theologians have not understood that in their eagerness to communicate with modern people they have lost their message. Because modern people say, 'You take your Bible along but you have cut out so many pages that you're just an existentialist like I am. And after all your God is a God of your own making.' The compromise does not work and it can only weaken Christianity, although behind it there is a real eagerness to communicate. Secondly there are people who try to preserve their little churches and communities by building big walls around them, walls of do's and don'ts, in order to be safe within them. Do not read the newest modern theology, do not look at the newest films, do not listen to that music because you might fall over it. But they do not understand that those walls are really very strong and will perfectly prevent anyone on the outside from coming in. Moreover, the Bible tells us that we have to fight against the powers in the heavenlies, and what good are walls for that?

The problems of the present age have not come upon us by necessity. It is not the case that we unavoidably had to end up in the current malaise because we said 'no' to God. If that were true we would be caught in a really big box that includes even God. Rather, if we look at the situation of the world today we have to think about God acting. God is judging the Western world, just as in his word he said he would. The collapsing world in which we live is a world under God's wrath. Modern people speak about the hidden God. 'Yes,' says God in the Bible, 'I am indeed hiding myself, and it is because I am coming in judgment.' Revelation 8 tells us that angels will sound the trumpets and that the land and sea will be polluted. It is not just a result of bad industries or wrong human behaviour, it is much more: pollution belongs to God's judgment. And where is the church? God said to the church 'You ought to be salt that salts and if the salt is not salty it's worthless, ready to be thrown away and trampled upon.' Is the church ready to be thrown away because we have become so saltless and bourgeois? Maybe that is already happening, for the churches are growing emptier and emptier. God's judgment begins at home, as Peter said, it begins with the church.

Nature and grace

Why is it that Christianity has played such a small part in the developments since the seventeenth century? There have been great theologians and large revivals, but why is Christianity almost out of the picture when we speak about Western culture? Why did we not see all these problems a hundred or hundred-and-fifty years ago? Why did we not preach and prophesy about these things at that time? A few have, but their voices were lost in the lack of willingness to understand. The big and basic problem Christianity has to face is a legacy from a distant past, from the Middle Ages and even earlier, a problem that can be pinned down to a little scheme, that of nature versus grace. Christians have divided the world in two: nature and grace. What is grace? Grace is the realm of faith, but this realm is placed over against the realm of our bodies and the world. We have misunderstood the texts in which Paul speaks of the spirit over against the flesh to mean: the spirit is the realm of the soul, the higher things, where faith is. And the flesh is the realm of the lower things, where the body is. But Paul is speaking about that which belongs to God over against that which is sinful. We have made the realm of grace – the church, theology and all the things that pertain to faith – into something higher, out of this world. We have piety, yes, but that has nothing to do with our weekly work. And if one wants to do work for the kingdom of God, one has to be a missionary or evangelist, or the wife or secretary of an evangelist, otherwise one is not serving God.

So we have our world of faith on one side, but it is detached from the world of nature. Nature is an autonomous nature (where did we hear that before?) that has nothing to do with God. Maybe we say, very piously, that God created the world but we never study the world as God's creation; we study it like everyone else does. As scientists we keep God out of the picture, for what has God got to do with atoms after all? To give an example: what happened when Darwin produced his famous book more than a century ago? The Christian world said 'No, this is wrong, God says in Genesis 1 that he created the world.' But it was just an absurd statement, for they never tried to back it up. Why were there so few Christians who really went to the bones and animals that Darwin was studying and said 'We must look at the facts and do our own research. We will show that Darwin is wrong because if God's statement is right, it will be right in the bones as well and not only in the pulpit.' Christians did not do that because we thought just like Darwin that these are neutral facts. However, neutral facts do not exist.

We often did not understand that Christ said 'Whoever accepts me goes from death to life' – at that very moment. Many Christians are just waiting for the moment they die, for then life will begin. There is a question I read in one of the underground papers in New York that we have to answer for ourselves and for the world around us. Unless we answer this question positively, Christianity is dead. The question is this: Is there life before death?

Our calling in a world without God

Is there a way back? Our culture is in ruins, God's wrath is at work, and we are pouring out a spirituality that has no bearing on what is happening around us. Is there a way back? Do we care? Maybe we feel it only concerns the 'world', those bad people outside. It is not our problem. But are we not responsible for the people outside as well? Certainly the world has been looking for solutions. How can we change this world? How can we get people out of the box? How can we get a world that is good? The answer that has been given is that of Marx and Marcuse: that we need to change the structures of our society, by force and revolution if necessary. My answer to that is that they are simply too optimistic. It would be very nice if we could just change the structures and all would be fine. But I fear that they have not seen how deep the trouble is. A revolution is not the answer, because revolutionary hate will just reap more hatred and in that way we are not building up but breaking down. And structures do not mean a thing if there is not a living heart behind them. People themselves need to change first.

Let's think again of the boy and the girl in Paris who were sitting side by side weeping because there was real love between them. Is that not a very strange tale? Why could they not just love each other? I would say they could but it could not be done cheaply. It had as it were to be discovered and conquered back. We have to recapture the reality of reality. Love must be reconquered. God gave love to us, but we said 'no' to it and now we are in tears because there is something lacking. But it is still there: we have to win it back. Reality is not just something static that is, it is something we have to make and seize, an open possibility. Reality is a possibility that God gave to us, and we have to create the reality out of the possibility. Like the discovery of America: in 1492 one man discovered America and from that day on people went on discovering America, and in discovering it they were opening it up, forming it, doing good things and bad things, and in the end there is the great reality of America. In a similar way we have to rediscover and open up love. That is being creative: to reconquer reality. There are so many breaks in our reality that need to be healed, between art and daily reality, between love and sex, between the bodily and the spiritual, between culture and technology, between humankind and nature.

How can we go back and heal them? The answer is very simple: we need to turn back to the Lord and prophesy. If we do not prophesy about these things, then we just speak in vain. To save souls is not enough, because a saved soul will go to heaven after the person dies but we need to have people who live and know reality now. We need to turn back to the living God, because God is a God of life. The Bible is not a religious book – it does not talk about religion – for it talks about truth and walking with the Lord. It talks about the fullness of reality, about life, life before death. What does the Law of Moses speak about? About having a fence round your roof, otherwise somebody might fall off it. And God said it was legitimate to kill an animal for religious purposes, as a sacrifice, in Jerusalem but nowhere else. And if you went to Jerusalem to make your offering of thankfulness, you could do it for one, two or three days but never for a fourth day, because then it would become a stench in his nose. God does not want religious things to become everything: he wants life to be life.

Christ died in order that we might be living human beings. He did not die just simply to forgive sins but to achieve much more, to make us new men and women (Romans 6 and Colossians 2). Christ died in order to make normal human life possible, to make freedom and love possible, to make life meaningful. Yes, there is life before death because Christ came. Christ talked about the fullness of life in his Sermon on the Mount. Do these things in order that you may live. Christ never died in order to make us Christians. That is just too small: a few songs and a few prayers. No, Christ died in order that we could be human, that we could really be what he meant us to be when God created us in the beginning. And that was not cheap, that was very difficult. What we need is a reformation, to rethink the Scriptures and the big problems of life, to rethink the relationship between nature and grace, between our religion and our normal daily lives.

The world is God's world

And then we will need to get to work. We have to hunger and thirst for righteousness, which is to love in protest. We have to be salt that salts. Of course this will not be easy. We can never be just like a little straw floating down the stream of history. We have to go against the stream, and if we go together maybe the stream will be turned around to flow in the opposite direction. We will need to have strong faith and give ourselves to God with all our heart and all our body and all our soul and all our mind and understanding. For we are responsible, not just for souls but for the whole world around us. A girl once came to me and said 'You have a calling that's clear, but what's my calling?'

I asked her 'What kind of work do you do?'

She said 'Tomorrow I start a new job in an office but I'm there just as a secretary.'

I said, 'Your calling begins tomorrow when you enter that office. You may see that people are fighting with each other and you can be a peacemaker. You may help to bring renewal and a better life in that office. Maybe this has an influence on those around you. Maybe the whole office, maybe the whole company will change.'

Nobody knows what it will mean if you just do the little things God called you to do, but if you say 'This is a wicked world, I can do nothing about it, I'll just go to church and sing my little hallelujah song,' you can be sure that nothing will change. We have to understand that the world is God's world. Here I want to quote C.S. Lewis again:

> What we want is not more little books about Christianity but more little books by Christians on other subjects with their Christianity latent. It's not the books written in direct defence of materialism that make the modern man a materialist. It's the materialistic assumption in all the other books. In the same way it's not books on Christianity that will really trouble him but he would be troubled if, whenever he wanted a cheap popular introduction to some science, the best work on the market is always by a Christian. The first step to a reconversion of this country is a series produced by Christians which can beat the Penguin and the Thinkers Library on their own ground.

This means working towards a world in which there really is a God, in which one opens a book and it says God is there, in which one goes to university and God is there. How many Christians have said to me 'Isn't your new book very subjective? You brought Christianity into art history.' But I just tried to think of art as part of a world in which God is really there. I hope it is not a Christian art history in the sense that there is just a little Christian sauce poured over it.

We also have to avoid Christian utilitarianism, namely to do things just in order to promote the kingdom of heaven and not because God says they are good. Why do we work in science? Just to be able to talk to other scientists about Christ or because we love science and want to contribute to it in a worthwhile way? And if we evangelize, we should do it not just because we think we should but because we love the other person and want him or her to know about the fullness of life. Our evangelism is often so weak because the preaching is not backed up by the love and the life we talk about. Here is another true story. In L'Abri we had a group of people from Kenya and one of these people came up to Dr Schaeffer and he said to him 'In my part of the country we have a fine missionary couple, good people. But very few of us have become Christians and I'll tell you why. When we came to their house there was no beauty in the house and we felt that if Christianity was true there should have been beauty.' Was this African person asking that the missionaries should have Rembrandts hanging on their walls? No, of course not, he was just asking for beauty, care for the little things. If we preach that God is a living God and that he created the world, but we do not care for the flowers and we do not care about the things we have in our room – if we do not show what we preach, we can simply forget about proclaiming Christianity.

Is there a way back? Yes, but it may be difficult. I am not an optimist saying of course we will have a reformation and a renewal in our culture. Maybe God wants to do things differently. But let us be ready when the Lord should bring a reformation, just as the people in the sixteenth century were when Luther put his theses on the door of the church in Wittenberg. Let us be ready when the great reformer comes and God calls us. To be a Christian is not opting for an easy life. It may mean hardships, it may even mean persecution and death. It is a day-by-day walking with the Lord, walking like Peter on the water. It is going on an adventure with God, full of excitement and expectancy. A couple of weeks ago I gave a lecture to modern theological students and one of them asked me 'Don't you think it's tedious and boring to be a Christian?' And I said 'I became a Christian about twenty-five years ago and since that day life has been one great adventure and I really don't know what's happening next week and I really don't know where I will be going. But it's to live, to live a life before death.'

A Dutch Christian View of Philosophy

Life is a unity

Dutch Christian philosophy, as in the thinking of Kuyper and Dooyeweerd and kindred spirits, has its roots a long way back in Western history. Insights like theirs have never come about in a short time but take a long time and a lot of work. God respects us as people and therefore he does not hand ready-made notions to us on a silver plate. In the Bible not everything is said; we have to do our share of thinking as well, and what we can find out for ourselves we must find out.

The ideas I will discuss here go back particularly to the Reformation, but there were other people before that time who paved the way. Calvin understood that life is a unity and that there is no division between religion, or the devotional side of life, as something higher, and daily life as necessary but lower: we have to eat and do many other things in order to survive, but what really counts is that we go to church on Sunday and read our Bible. In this way a division has been made between the spiritual and the natural realm. Calvin said 'no' to this and stressed that the Bible speaks again and again about human life as a unity.

One place where this comes to the fore is in the Law of Moses. Moses says for instance that there is only one place where the Israelites should slaughter animals for sacrifice. Why? Because they were not to make all of life into religion. God also says that in order to thank him, people should go to the Temple to sacrifice and have a big feast. If they were really very thankful, they could do the same on a second day, and again on a third day, but they should never do it a fourth time, for then 'it is a stench in my nose.' God hates that. Why? Because he wants to keep religion in its place. On the other hand Moses makes it very plain that God is interested in everything we do, he talks about how to plough, how to care for the little birds and not be cruel to them, how to practise hygiene, how not to eat some animals (eating pigs in those days in that country was not safe). There were many such rules that God gave us through Moses because he cares for us.

In Isaiah 28:23–29, in the midst of very strong and awful prophecies about God's judgment, Isaiah stops and exclaims what a miracle it is that God gave us wheat and the possibility to make bread out of it – a kind of grass that can be turned into bread! – and he reminds the people that it was God who taught the farmers how to handle all the different crops. He stands in wonder that God cares about all these things. Religion is not something high but something that encompasses even the cultivation of our land and the baking of our bread.

Because of that Calvin emphasizes the importance of the covenant. God made a covenant with his people and he promised to bless them if they would walk in his ways. To walk in his ways is not only to pray, to read the Scriptures and so on, but it includes all of our life. Devotion is important, but it is only a part of life and the rest of our life is not outside of God but belongs to him just as well. These two sides of life belong together and there has to be a balance between them. We pray before we eat as an explicit statement of our thankfulness, but we cannot eat religiously, we just eat and enjoy it.

The greatest thing about the Reformation is that people began to understand that and act on it. We can see the fruits for instance in seventeenth-century Dutch art. But in the course of time this was forgotten again and the division returned in pietism: life became very pious on the one hand and very worldly and secular on the other. And then, around 1800, there was a man in Holland who began to think about these things again. He was a lecturer at the University of Leiden, and he had a pupil by the name of Guillaume Groen van Prinsterer.

Groen van Prinsterer

Groen van Prinsterer came from a wealthy family. He was a Calvinist, a very clever man and he became a historian. He got a job as curator of the archives of the family of the king, the House of Orange, and began to study them. At that time all the school history books dealt with the seventeenth and eighteenth centuries as if the House of Orange was always responsible for obstructing good. Those books were written by people who came out of the French Revolution with a completely secular Enlightenment approach to history. Groen van Prinsterer, who was particularly interested in the seventeenth century, began to read the documents in the archives and out of this grew a new book for elementary schools on the history of Holland. He made his readers understand that the Orange rulers and Christianity had been very important and positive factors in Dutch history. It is one of the most wonderful books on history that I have ever read. It was used in Dutch schools for a long time, from around 1850 up to 1920.

The book is written just like Chronicles or Kings in the Bible. It deals for instance with the year of disaster, 1672, when the French King Louis XIV, who wanted to stop all Protestant Christianity, was attacking the Netherlands from the East. The Dutch are used to stopping their enemies by breaking the dikes of the rivers so that whole regions become flooded, but now the rivers were all frozen and the enemy could just walk in. Groen van Prinsterer points out that there was a good reason for this as the Dutch were forgetting God, and he demonstrates when and how this was the case. But then, he says, they prayed to God and God answered and delivered them from their enemies. He shows that the future of Christianity was at stake at that time. In this way he quite naturally weaves into his account of history elements like prayer and God's judgment and blessing.

In another book, Groen deals with the French Revolution and the problems of his own time which he traces back to the change that took place in the eighteenth century Enlightenment when people turned away from God and wanted to be autonomous. He points out that even though the actual Revolution had died down forty to fifty years earlier, the spirit of the Revolution was still alive. He then gives an analysis of his own times and warns people that if they are not careful such and such will happen. It reads just like prophesy. Many of the problems we have today he wrote about more than a century ago, and the book had a great influence and people began to listen to him. One man who came to hear Groen van Prinsterer speak was a very liberal pastor in Amsterdam, and he changed and became van Prinsterer's pupil. His name was Abraham Kuyper. Kuyper and Groen started to work closely together in politics and many other fields because they understood that Christianity is not just religion, Christianity is not just the church, Christianity is not just a good feeling in your heart because you are saved and going to heaven, but Christianity is all of life and it is the covenant. We walk with God and he is taking care of his people and we should walk in his ways and look at the world with an open Bible and use the key that the Bible provides for us to understand the world, everything, not just religion but everything. And they talked about this and they founded a political party. This party was called the Anti-Revolutionary Party, which meant that they were anti the spirit of the French Revolution, which is the spirit of the Enlightenment, which is about autonomous human being, which I always talk about because I too am a pupil of Groen.

Kuyper and Christian scholarship

In 1880 Kuyper founded the Free University to have a place for Christian scholarship. This vision for Christian scholarship is quite different from what you will find in many of the American Christian colleges, where the teaching in philosophy, psychology and many other fields of learning is exactly the same as in the non-Christian college twenty miles away. The same theories and the same discussions fill the classrooms. Yet in the Christian college there is something special: at 10.30 a.m. the bell rings and everybody goes to chapel to sing a few hymns and say a few prayers; and that is the Christianity of the college. Maybe those colleges also have some rules that you should not drink alcohol or smoke, but what they do not do is to try and think about the problems of life and how to understand the world in a Christian way. What is a Christian approach to philosophy? Or to politics? Does Romans 13 give us a different view of the government because it tells us that our government is given to us by

God and is not a purely human institution as the people of the Enlightenment and the French Revolution believed? Can we just say 'no' to a government because we do not agree with it? When we start from the Bible our answers will be different. This is very obvious in biology, where we run into the evolution theory. I do not mean that we should not look at the facts; we should be open to all of the facts and we should not be afraid. Sometimes people ask me what the difference is between me and my non-Christian colleagues. In my opinion it is this: I do not need to be afraid and I have the freedom to go into everything because this is God's world. Non-Christian scholars always need to be wary because there are so many things they cannot answer and have to stay away from.

The great vision of Kuyper was to develop Christian scholarship and a Christian world view. Even though the Free University has not been a perfect school and has had its share of the crisis in all of Christianity, still there are some people and departments that are good. Bob Goudzwaard for instance – who also regularly comes to give lectures at L'Abri – is part of the politics department. Some years ago we had a conference within the Free University to discuss Christianity and scholarship and the interesting thing is that especially the science people said that they did not want to let go of the Christian identity of the university because then they would not be able to work as they did in the physics department. This department happens to be one of the best physics departments in Holland. Christianity makes a difference, not only in the humanities but also in the sciences.

The philosophy department has played a very crucial role in the Free University. Out of the work of Kuyper and Groen van Prinsterer grew the philosophy that was worked out especially by Dooyeweerd in the period between the two world wars. Another man who was involved in the development of this Philosophy of the Cosmonomic Idea was Vollenhoven. Vollenhoven was a pastor and before he became involved with philosophy he had written a book on the theology of mathematics. When he got his doctoral degree this book was published and one of the people in his congregation read the book and made all kinds of notes in the margin. Then he gave the book with his notes back to Vollenhoven to read. In his opinion Vollenhoven was talking about a God who was very different from the God of the Bible and his mathematics were far removed from commonsense mathematics and a biblical view of reality. Something great happened next: Vollenhoven came to see that he had been wrong, and from that time on he wanted to think as a man who starts with the Bible and with the world as God's creation. Together with his brother-in-law, Dooyeweerd, he then worked on a new philosophy.

After a number of years Dooyeweerd, who was a professor in law, used his philosophical insights in his first-year introductory course in law and several years later he wrote the book that was translated as *A New Critique of Theoretical Thought*.

Why does he call it a new critique? Because in his days, in the 1920s, the most important philosophy in Europe was neo-Kantianism. Kant's *Critique of Pure Reason* tried to answer questions like: What is theoretical thought? How can we think? What is reality? and so on. Dooyeweerd tackled the same questions while trying to show where Kant had gone wrong.

Dooyeweerd and L'Abri

When I was in a prisoner-of-war camp during World War II there was nothing much to do. I was in an officers camp and we were not supposed to work. As I wanted to be a cultured person, I thought it would be good to use this time to read the Bible. So I began to read the Bible and when I finished I was considering becoming a Christian. In the meantime I also had begun to study philosophy and I had one big question which was very crucial to me: If I become a Christian, could I be a philosopher at the same time? Or to put it differently: If I am a Christian, can I keep on thinking? I was discussing this with somebody and he advised me to go to a certain officer called Mekkes. I went to that officer, who later became a professor in philosophy, and he said, 'That's a very good question. Why don't you read this?' and he gave me Dooyeweerd's book. After thirty pages I was completely convinced that I could not be a Christian and a Kantian at the same time, as Kant starts from non-Christian presuppositions, but that it was very well possible to be a Christian and to think. This opened the way for me to accept Christianity.

I came out of the prisoner-of-war camp as a Christian and with quite a bit of training in philosophy. After the war I started my studies in art history and began to wrestle with the problems of modern art which I traced back to the existentialist outlook on life that lies behind modern art. In 1948, as a young student, I happened to meet Dr Schaeffer. Humanly speaking we met by chance. At an international conference in Amsterdam I was looking for an American who could answer some of my questions about Negro spirituals, so I was looking for an intelligent-looking American, and I came across Dr Schaeffer and said, 'May I speak to you?' He said, 'Yes, I have half an hour before we start again at 7 p.m.' So we went out of the building and he left my room the next morning at 4 a.m.! We just talked on and on. We discussed modern art and that brought us together.

In the course of the years Schaeffer and I discussed many things, among which philosophy and particularly Dooyeweerd's philosophy were favourite topics. Dooyeweerd's ideas have had an influence on Schaeffer and L'Abri in that way. Of course Schaeffer incorporated these ideas in his own thinking and continued on. Neither of us is a slavish pupil of Dooyeweerd. I make quite an effort not to use his difficult terminology, which in a way belonged to the style of the 1930s. So you will not find Dooyeweerd's vocabulary in our discussions at L'Abri, but his thoughts are there just the same.

Dooyeweerd's basic ideas

Dooyeweerd himself wrote a good and short introduction to his work called *The Twilight of Western Thought*. In the first part of that book he asks the question how Western thought is to be approached. Is it really Christian and if not, what is it? *Escape from Reason* is Schaeffer's version of what Dooyeweerd develops in those chapters. They both talk for instance about nature and grace and about the influence of Greek concepts. Dooyeweerd tries to trace the various ways of thinking in Western history to their starting points. A starting point can be defined as the basic answers that are given to basic questions like: What is the world? Who is God? or What is the source of this world? The answers given to those questions colour the answers that are given to all other questions. The second part of Dooyeweerd's book deals with a truly Christian approach to reality. Firstly it is basic to such an approach that we begin with a world that is created. Secondly we hold that this world is fallen, it is not perfect. But thirdly we say that this is not the end, there is redemption as Christ came to redeem this world. On the basis of these truths we can try to grasp reality and analyse how this world is made. Dooyeweerd then proceeds to give such an analysis.

With an eye to his analysis the following is important: when you read scientific books – in philosophy, the humanities or the sciences – you will find that people always say that everything can be reduced to this or that one thing. For instance to psychology, which means that all art, language or religion can be understood on the basis of psychology. Others say that history is the key to the understanding of all things, that religion, for example, is a historical phenomenon. Or that language is the key or that religion is key. Dooyeweerd began to think about this and in an attempt to do justice to the complexity of reality he began to develop his theory of modalities.

In reality there are numbers and there are certain laws concerning these numbers, and Dooyeweerd called this the modality or the 'law sphere' of number. This is one of the aspects by which reality presents itself to us. Then there is the physical sphere and it deals with things like energy and speed. There is life and life is bound to certain laws and this he called the biotic sphere. And there is a psychological side to life in that we have our senses, we can see and feel and touch and so on. There is also a logical sphere: we can discern, analyse and think. There is history, for we can make and give form to things (although I would rather call this creativity or the creative side of life). There is language and economics and beauty and law and then there is ethics, or the sphere of love, and the world of liturgy and dogma which is the sphere of faith. None of these spheres is more important than the others, none is the source or the main aspect to which the others can be reduced but they are all equally part of the fabric of life. That is the complexity of the world as God made it.

We can never have language unless there are norms or laws for language, because when I speak you must be able to understand me, and you can only understand me if I keep to the rules. So there are norms for language which are not made by human beings but which are made by God. We could never speak if God did not give us the possibility to speak, if he did not make the norms or laws for language. As human beings we discover those laws and apply them. But there is a certain freedom, we can (and this is the creative side of people) create different languages and give different forms to the laws. There are different languages or law systems. Each law system is a different positivization or realization of the basic laws. In the same way there are norms or laws in law (for instance that we must be righteous) that we give form to or positivize in different legal systems. Without these norms we would have no law. These norms are not humanly constructed but given to us by God as an open possibility.

We can speak because there are laws for language – these laws or structures of languages are what the linguist researches. But we would not be able to talk or use any language if there had not been a creative side to human life as well, so that we are able to give form to a language and develop it. And we could never have had a language unless we had been endowed with senses so that we can hear. In order to make sounds we must have a body and that is our biological side. There are all these different aspects of life and they are based one on the other. All these aspects are equal, none is deeper or higher or more important than the others: they are all interdependent.

Everything we do has all these aspects. If we cook an egg, for instance, there is a mathematical side to it: do we use one or two eggs? It has to be put in a pan, which is where space comes in. Then we heat the egg and that belongs to physics. An egg is a biological product that we eat with our body. The senses play a role as well, for the egg has a smell. Logic is involved as we can analyse and discuss what kind of egg is best. There is a creative side as some people somewhere in history discovered the possibility to have a fried egg: somebody somewhere must have had the bright idea to put some butter in a pan and put an egg in it – a fried egg is a cultural product. We invent a word for it, we call it fried eggs. The eggs fulfil a social role as we sit together at the table to eat them. They have an economic side, for the eggs may be expensive or cheap. Our fried eggs may be beautiful or messy and ugly, that is the aesthetical element. There is also an ethical side: we can express our love by frying eggs for someone else. There is a legal facet: if the other person throws the eggs in my face then maybe we would go to court. Before we eat the eggs we may pray and thank the Lord for the good food – that is the egg's religious aspect. A simple thing like the cooking of an egg participates in all of these fourteen spheres and so does everything else.

What is the difference between a lion and a human being? The difference lies in the number of spheres in which they are the subject rather than the object. A lion functions as a subject in the sphere of numbers: when it kills a deer it can only kill one deer at a time and not two. It is a subject in the modality of space: it has to cover a certain distance in order to get somewhere. It is a subject in the physical aspect of reality as it has to use force when it wants to kill the deer. Instinctively it knows the anatomy of the animal, it knows where to seize the deer and can smell the animal. However, the lion is not able to give a logical analysis. It is not able to create new things. It has no language, no economy, no love, and it does not pray before it eats the deer. It functions as a subject in the lower spheres ('lower' not in the sense of less important), but in the higher ones it is an object. It can be used as a symbol, it can be analysed. It can be given a name, there may be a legal fight over a lion. Nothing in this world is outside of any of these spheres, and any particular thing or being is a subject only in some spheres and an object in the others. Only human beings are subjects in all of the modalities. An animal is a subject in all spheres that are lower than the logical one. A plant has no senses and is a subject up to the biological sphere. An atom is a subject up to the physical sphere but in the biological sphere and higher it is an object.

Structures and sphere sovereignty

When God created the world, he first made the structure of this world with the modalities. This structure is very complex and we certainly have not yet uncovered all the little details. He also created the norms or laws that are valid in those spheres. Those are God's laws, his will, the way he wants his creation to function. Everything in reality is subject to those laws. There are for instance norms or laws for speaking: if we follow them we will express ourselves well. Artists are subject to the laws for beauty, otherwise they cannot make anything that is beautiful. There are different types of love – paternal love, filial love, husband-and-wife love, love for our neighbours, each of which in its own way is under the law for love. It is the summit of love that Christ, the King of the world, wanted to come down to earth and be obedient to the laws of his own creation. Those laws are universals that apply to everything in this world horizontally. But God moreover created another type of universals, which are vertical and go through all of these aspects or spheres: namely the structures. Those structures are again (just like the norms) given to us by God as possibilities. One of those structures is the state. God made the structure of the state and we have to fill it in. Other structures are marriage, the family, the church and any other institution. When we give form to a structure we have to follow the laws for that particular structure, otherwise it will not function well.

Just as there is no one dominant aspect to which all the others can be reduced (physics, psychology or history), there is no one dominant structure either. Each structure has its own sphere sovereignty. That means that you cannot just interchange them. The state is something different from the family and the family is something different from the church. If the state does something that must belong to the state's sphere. The state should never interfere in the sphere of the family. The state should not tell parents how to educate their children or order children to call their parents by their first names. Families differ in this. The parents can rightfully say, even to the highest king in the world, that they are in charge of their family. As to matters of the state, parents have to listen to the king, but in their families they are sovereign and free to make their own choices. The same holds for the church. A church can expel a person, but he or she should still get the protection of the state. And the state cannot tell the church to expel a particular member because he or she holds certain ideas. Each has its own sovereignty: the church has to keep itself pure and the state has to punish criminals. Maybe there are criminals in our church who have repented and accepted the Lord as their Saviour. Even though the state puts them in jail, they are still church members.

Let me give an example of the application of this principle of sphere sovereignty that has been very important in Dutch history. In the nineteenth century there were state schools in the Netherlands where the children were taught non-Christian views. The anti-revolutionairies, however, with Groen and Kuyper as their leaders, fought for Christian schools, as they held that the parents are responsible for the education of their children and have a right to say how they want their children educated in school. This fight lasted from around 1850–1880, for thirty years. It was engaged in a typically Calvinistic manner, for they did not in the first place battle for state support for the Christian schools only but rather for every person's right to state support as the education of the children belongs to the sphere of the family and not to that of the state or the church. So a group of parents should be able to come together and decide what character the school for their children should have. If Jewish parents come together they should be able to have a Jewish school and the same should apply to Roman Catholics, Protestants, socialists, etc. They fought for that freedom. The result is that in Holland all types of schools are supported by the state. In America the Protestants, who were in power in the nineteenth century, had their Protestant schools but forbid others to have their own special schools and told them all to go to the state school. Nowadays Protestants are a minority and they are in trouble.

The tragedy of modernity

We always have to follow the laws that God put in his creation. In order for a marriage to be a good marriage the husband and wife have to follow the laws that God made for marriage. If they do not, the marriage will not work: it will be a bad marriage. Since the Enlightenment people have tried again and again to make their own world, but they have never succeeded because they simply cannot. This is the tragedy of modernity. Even if you want to commit suicide because you hate God and his world there is only one way to commit suicide, and that is by using the laws God made for this world.

If there is a state with a dictator who rules his country very badly there will be all kinds of tensions. Why? Because there can never be a good state unless it follows the laws for the state that God made instead of laws made by people. Even if there is a state that is based on ideas of a social contract, in practice it does not work like that because in reality it just follows God's rules. One can say that there is no authority, but in reality there is authority. The state is not just made by people, and one cannot just abolish the state. What happens if we would all become anarchists and decide to have no state anymore? If we would look back in a few years, no in a few days, we would see that we may have abolished the word 'state' but that the state is still there because people need to be governed, things need to be organized, the criminals need to be taken care of and so on, and very soon you would have a new organization.

The French Revolution did not want to accept the world as it is. Many laws were changed. A new law was made, for instance, that we should drive on the right side of the road instead of on the left. But to drive on the left is actually more natural. Formerly you went on horseback and you rode left because then you could shake hands when you passed each other. But also, when you watch people going through a museum, you will see that they keep to the left. The French Revolution also decided to have kilometres instead of miles, and to have metres and so on. Was it just a change of name? No, the change involved much more. When you look at seventeenth-century buildings their proportions are good and those old rooms have a nice feeling, Why? Because they are based on feet and yards and inches which are human measures that were derived from the human body (the yard is the length of an arm and an inch that of a thumb). Even someone with a lot of experience like a carpenter will find it difficult to tell you exactly how much a metre is. Because it is completely arbitrary.

Out of the French Revolution eventually came the Russian Revolution and they wanted the state to rule everything while they did not recognize the state's boundaries. What is the great problem of the church in communist countries? That the state misuses the church for its aims. The Russians also took away the right of parents to form a family. The state was going to take care of the children. All kinds of problems came out of that. It does not work, because God made the family. Fifteen years later the country was flooded with children living in the streets without a mother or father and involved in all kinds of criminal acts. So the Russians said, 'Please let us have families.' And today they have families again.

It is very interesting that good things are very hard to expel. If something is good it will stay a long time; if something is not good it will not last long. For a century and a half all the revolutions have been teaching that free love is wonderful, but where do we see free love really practised? In some very strange little circles. Why? Because it is a strange human invention that does not work. Heretics were killed only for a very short time in Western history because most people felt this to be an injustice; people should be free to have their own ideas. Those principles or laws are imbedded in creation. They are not just our ideas or Christian ideas about how things should be, but they are true ideas that fit the way reality really is.

I wish more people would begin to study this philosophy, not just to follow Dooyeweerd, as he was not infallible, but because he went into a direction that was good and he opened up a view that no other philosophy has unlocked. We should think on the basis of those ideas: maybe say 'no' to some and expand others as I have done in my own field. I would never have been able to work on modern art the way I do if all this thinking had not been done by the previous generations. Each one in his or her own field – let us continue the good work.

Jazz and Revolution

The revolutionary tide

World War I sparked off a decade devoted to illusion and indulgence. Whether one looks at social behaviour or the arts, it is a period of extraordinary inventiveness with the common aim of systematically repudiating the past. The period between 1900 and 1930 was the first revolutionary age of our century and I want to deal with it here in relation to jazz. Just to give you a taste of the flavour of this time I want to read a nice little quote out of a magazine from the 1920s: 'The mother said to the girl. "Aren't you ashamed of yourself wearing so little clothing to a party?" The girl answered, "Goodness, no mother, if I were ashamed of myself I wouldn't wear so little clothing to a party."' This was the first wave of permissiveness. The second wave in the 1960s can be traced back to this time.

Scott Fitzgerald, who was a leading figure in this period between the two world wars, wrote an essay in 1932 called 'The Jazz Age' in which he paints a picture of this time. He observes that around 1930 the jazz age had come to an end. Here is a quote from his article:

> It was characteristic of the Jazz Age that it had no interest in politics at all. It was an age of miracles, it was an age of art, it was an age of excess and it was an age of sad time. We were the most powerful nation. Who could tell us any longer what was fashionable and what was fun. Isolated during the European War we had begun combing the unknown South and West for boat ways and pastimes and there were more ready to hand. The first social revelation created a sensation out of all proportion to its novelty. As far back as 1915 the unchaperoned young people of the smaller cities had discovered the mobile privacy of that automobile given to young Bill at sixteen to make him self-reliant. At first petting was a desperate adventure, even under such favourable conditions. But presently confidences were exchanged and the old commandment broke down ... Scarcely have the state or citizens of the republic caught their breath when the wildest of all generations, a generation which had been adolescent during the confusion of the war, brusquely shouldered by contemporaries out of the way and danced into the limelight ... By 1923 their elders, tired of watching the carnival with ill-concealed envy, had discovered the young liquor will take the place of young blood and with a whoop the orgy began. The younger generation was starred no longer. A whole race going hedonistic deciding on pleasure.

On the one hand there is a revolutionary generation and on the other hand there are the people with a bourgeois mindset who tried to shut their eyes to what was happening around them. Let's listen to Scott Fitzgerald as he talks about this:

The word 'jazz' in its progress towards respectability has meant first sex, then dancing, then music. It is associated with a state of nervous stimulation, not unlike that of big cities behind the lines of a war. There were entire classes, people over 50 for example, who spent a whole decade denying its existence even when its puckish face peered into the family circle. Never did they dream that they had contributed to it. The honest citizens of every class who believed in a strict public morality and were powerful enough to enforce the necessary legislation did not know that they would necessarily be served by criminals and quacks and do not really believe it today. Rich righteousness had always been able to buy honest and intelligent servants to free the slaves or the Cubans, so when this attempt collapsed our elders stood firm with all the stubbornness of people involved in a weak case, preserving their righteousness and losing their children. Silver haired women and men with fine old faces, people who never did a consciously dishonest thing in their lives still assure each other in the apartment hotels of New York and Boston and Washington that there is a whole generation growing up that will never know the taste of liquor. Meanwhile their granddaughters pass the well-thumbed copy of *Lady Chatterley's Lover* around the boarding school and if they get about at all know the taste of gin or corn at 16. But the generation who reached maturity between 1875 and 1895 continued to believe what they wanted to believe.

The people over 30, the people all the way up to 50, had joined the dance. We grey beards, to tread down FBA, remember the uproar in 1912: grandmothers of 40 tossed away their crutches and took lessons in the tango and the castle walk ... For a while bootleg Negro records with their phallic euphemisms made everything suggestive and simultaneously came a wave of erotic plays. Young girls from finishing schools packed the galleries to hear about the romance of being a lesbian and George G Nathan protested.

The Jazz Age has had a wild youth and a heady middle age ... In the second phase such phenomena as sex and murder became more mature, if much more conventional ... Finally skirts came down and everything was concealed. Everybody was in scratch now, let's go, but it was not to be. Somebody had blundered and the most expensive orgy in history was over. Now once more the belt is tight and we summon the proper expression of horror as we look back at our wasted youth. Sometimes though there is a ghostly rumble among the drums, an asthmatic whisper in the trombones that swings me back into the early 1920s when we drank wood alcohol and every day and every way grew better and better, and there was a first aborted shortening of the skirts and girls all looked alike in sweater dresses and people you didn't want to know said 'yes we have no bananas'. And it seemed only a question of a very few years before the older people would step aside and let the world be run by those who saw things as they were. And it all seems rosy and romantic to us who are young men, because we will never feel quite so intensely about our surroundings anymore.

The revolution of the 1960s is only part of a much larger revolution. If we feel that at this moment (in the 1970s) the impetus of this revolution is softening down as there are counter forces at work and romanticism is coming back again, then it is good to realize that the end is not yet reached and that there is much more to come. The revolutionary tide began to rise around 1900 and reached a peak in the 1920s, and then in the early 1930s it died down partly due to the Depression, but went up again after World War II with rock-and-roll in the 1950s, the Beatles, Bob Dylan and the riots and so on in the 1960s and now in the 1970s it dies down again and things become normal. People are left with a feeling of disillusionment, as described by Scott Fitzgerald, and they cling to the hope that in five, ten or maybe fifteen years the revolution will go much further and deeper, and that maybe someday it will reach the point that the whole world is changed and the older generation, the bourgeois, will be pushed out of the limelight.

Black music as iron pill

Why is this happening? My thesis is that in the eighteenth century something took place that was very deep when God and religion were taken out of the centre of life. Because of this something happened to human being. We see the life force go and people testify in the end that humanity are sick or even dead. Around 1900 one area of human expression, popular music, was really dead, having turned into the most horrible nothingness you can imagine. However, because people are human, they long for music that is good and deep and at the same time really joyful. This type of music still could be found in Western culture in the music of the African-Americans, who just because they were denied all kinds of education had not entered into this post-Enlightenment world. In a way they were still pre-Enlightenment. The Western world in need of an iron pill took the iron pill where they could find it, namely in black music. What I will try to show is that the whites who take this pill and try to swallow it, cannot swallow it because they are already too sick to truly take it in and revive. In a way the whole revolution of the 1920s as well the 1950s is a great tragedy because people revolted against the results of something that was in their own minds. They revolted but they had no foundation on which to build a better world, so whatever they did they always made things worse instead of better.

The first black music to attract the attention of the anaemic white culture was the ragtime of Scott Joplin, one of the greatest American composers of the twentieth century. In 1899 he made the 'Maple leaf rag', the first hit of our century, the first iron pill. People began to dance to this music. Here we have the first instance of the fusion of popular music and dancing. Up till that time people had always danced the old quadrilles to sweet music played by violins, but now they began to dance the cakewalk to this wonderful new music that is so full of life. If you listen to Scott Joplin it is not hard to imagine the excitement that must have accompanied this new rage. Of course Western society immediately commercialized this music and in bars all over the country it was played in a fashion that made it cheap and took all the depth and joy out of it.

Then comes the next phase when Jim Europe enters the scene, a very able musician who worked in New York. He was the first African-American musician to work the ragtime of Scott Joplin into black entertainment music for white people to dance to. His music was good and strong. He worked very closely together with Vernon and Irene Castle, a couple who danced and introduced new dances to New York like the castlewalk and the foxtrot. These dances very soon spread all over the States.

During World War I Jim Europe went to Europe to organize maybe the best military band that ever existed. He chose his line-up very carefully in such a way that he could send out little groups all over Europe. Those bands played Jim Europe's jazz (it was called jazz by now) and introduced jazz to Europe.

Various white musicians tried to imitate this music. Frisco, for instance, organized a jazz band and made a super hit in 1917 with his 'Umbrellas to mend'. Often songs were given very strange titles like 'Jazz bo jazz', 'Johnson jazz blues', 'Dada strain' or 'Shimmer shammer wobble'. The title 'Dada strain' is very interesting, for in 1917 a new art movement began in Europe that also called itself 'Dada'. Is there a connection? There is indeed. In both cases people try to get rid of the past and begin a new world, symbolized by 'dada' or baby talk.

The white jazz scene really takes off when in 1918 the Original Dixieland Jazz Band, a band from New Orleans, comes to New York, which is very much at the centre of all this. They had swallowed the iron pill of New Orleans jazz and they had swallowed it rather well, having compromised just a little bit in order to make the music more commercial. It is remarkable that the very first thing they say when people come up to them is that they cannot read music. And ever since that time that is what white jazz musicians will say. Of course this was not true for the Original Dixieland Jazz Band and it has not been true for any of the later artists. Why do they say it? Because they want to be original, immediate and direct. It reflects a 'Rousseau-ic' element – Jean Jacques Rousseau said culture is just a façade that covers up how things really are. Music becomes real only if you can express yourself immediately without culture. And so these people pretend that they are not cultured and do not know how to read music, and the Original Dixieland Jazz Band plays numbers with titles like the 'Tiger rag', the tiger being a symbol of everything that is strong, primitive and sexy. There is an element of anti-culture here, just as in 'dada'. There was also a strong shift in dancing in those days away from gentility, ballroom decorum and elegance of motion to a faster, jerkier and snappier kind of dance. In this we see the revolution moving on.

However, there were also people who found these developments a great pain in the stomach. They were the real bourgeois of those days, who transformed the iron jazz pill into the muzak of that time – not yet as bad as the muzak of today, for in time this type of music has only increased in banality.

Two ways of listening

In 1918 King Oliver came to Chicago from New Orleans and formed the King Oliver's Original Creole Jazz Band together with Louis Armstrong and various other important jazz musicians. They played in South Side Chicago, the black part of town, but many white people came to listen and tried to swallow this strong and deep music. There are two ways in which we can listen to it. One way is to listen to it as music coming out of a black culture that is untouched by Western culture, even though there are influences of white brass band music and so on. But it is music that comes out of a different mentality, out of a different world, it is pre-Enlightenment music. There are similarities with the music of Bach, although I am sure King Oliver never heard Bach. Most of these jazz musicians came from Christian families. They may not have been very strong Bible-believing, churchgoing people but they were certainly not antichristians, they were not part of the modern world. Being black they were not allowed to play in the respectable places and concert halls; they had to play in the nightclubs – but that was not their fault. This is dance music, yes, it has rhythm, yes, but it is wonderful music with a polyphony that was completely unknown in the Western world at that time, it is music that is deep and joyful at the same time. Nothing in the Western world since the Enlightenment has been deep and joyful: either it has been joyful and superficial or it has been deep and sad and despairing.

The other way to approach King Oliver is to listen to his music with a Western ear. What do you hear? This is Rousseau, this is a man who is real and completely free, this is rhythm, this is Africa, pre-cultural original authenticity. These are new sounds, irrational sounds, crazy sounds, going against everything that is considered to be music. People wanted to have an anti-cultural, lawless new music that would blow away the sickness of their own age. Of course they were mistaken because this music is anything but primeval and unrestrained, but that was how the young men in Chicago understood it as they sat down to listen to it.

I wish that in those days there would have been some very fine musically trained evangelicals who would have understood that this was not a type of 'Rousseau-ic' music but rather pre-Enlightenment music like that of Bach. I think music history and the world would have been different. I am sorry that it never happened. The Christians were probably still asleep under the old entertainment music and their nice little hymns.

In 1925 the electric recording was invented and recordings greatly increased in quality. Just then one of the most important black jazz musicians, Jelly Roll Morton, made his most important recordings. His records were very aptly sold under the name of Jelly Roll Morton's Red Hot Peppers as his music was considered hot and strong, music that burns in your mouth and your stomach – the 'hot pepper' being just another metaphor for the 'iron pill'. This is how the record company advertised these records: 'Foxtrot by coloured dance band, hot style, vocal refrain, sustained notes, wild, barbaric and loud, crude strong colour, good rhythm, many freak and mute effects', and so on. But if you listen to these records, there is nothing crude, loud and barbaric at all. It is rather very fine and refined music. To white post-Enlightenment, romantic ears it might have sounded wild but it was not intended to be wild, it was just fantastically real. Rudi Blesh who wrote a very good book on jazz in the early 1940s describes Jelly Roll Morton's music as follows: 'ragtime delicate yet strong, as precise, as dainty, as French as porcelain'.

Tragedy

What did the white entertainment music make out of this, after having tried to swallow a little bit of the iron pill? Although people had dreams about being lawless, wild and unrestricted, their music was often as sweet and trivial as can be. Still it was considered revolutionary and parents did not like their youngsters listening to it. I remember that when I was a boy of around ten years old, my aunt told me 'You know jazz – that's Paul Whiteman, the "King of Jazz" – is the wildest thing and becoming really popular. Do you know how he invented jazz? Well, he sat in his living room and he had glass doors and somebody came in and slammed the door and all the glass broke down and there was much noise, and he said "That is jazz." And that's how he made his music.' I was always trying to find this great noise that my aunt talked about, but I never found it. But is it not strange that people were talking about Paul Whiteman like that? It tells us something of the ideals of that time and the inability to realize them.

Louis Armstrong, one of the greatest of the black musicians, was well received by the whites and misused, in a way. They made him into a 'Rousseau-ic', exuberant, self-exhibiting musician. In 1926 he recorded the song 'Heebee jeebees' in which he included a section consisting of words like 'skit', 'skat', 'hoobie doobie' and so on. It was probably the first time in history that was ever done. And people would greet each other in the streets with words like that and the other person would answer with the song's next couple of wild words. Something of the unrestrained and free utterances of today we can trace back to that record. We also hear Louis Armstrong play very daring, forceful solos, at the edge of what is musically possible. It is strong music yet different from earlier black jazz, which was strong but also had a loving and a lilting, soft quality. This is strong and hard; it slaps you in the face. With Louis Armstrong we see the old pre-Enlightenment spirit changing into a post-Enlightenment one, though it is still just the beginning of the change. In all this we see that the revolution did not take place only in the elitist culture of Dada and Surrealism and so on. You just had to go down the street to the nearest bar or record shop and listen, and you would find the same thing.

Then Duke Ellington, another great African-American musician, came to the fore and he too played an important part in the translation of black jazz to the world of the whites. For many years he played in the Cotton Club in New York which was decorated as an African jungle where black semi-nude girls would dance their orgy-like dances and witch dances and play tom-toms in a primitive style. Ellington would play numbers like 'Jazz mania' and 'Dance mania' with jungle sounds deliberately worked in for Western ears. People looked for the real thing, but they were already too sick to stomach the really real thing. They ended up with quasi-African sounds, which were supposed to be authentic.

In 1929 the jazz age came to an end, the skirt hems dropped down again and much of the impetus of the search for something new and better died down. The first revolution was over and the tragedy of it was – just like in the 1960s – that people who were looking for life and something real did not succeed in finding it. They wanted to have strong music but it fell back into nothingness, into sweetness, banality or fake 'authenticity'. Why? Because there was no basis to build on. They were not able to truly understand black music and had to dilute it, and very soon it was commercialized and put into the capitalist mould of the establishment. It became plastic, a commodity sold in the supermarket. We can weep at the way Western culture made something so ugly and lifeless out of something that was so beautiful and so full of life.

Rock and Protest

From Paul Whiteman to rock-and-roll

I begin my story of rock somewhere around 1930, when the popular music of Paul Whiteman and Co. was sweet and safe, featuring songs in which girls always are very beautiful and always say 'yes' and the moon shines ceaselessly in the background. We can empathize with the boy who went to some second-hand record shop to search through the pile of 78 rpm records in order to find something different. He found a record by a man called Louis Armstrong that started out like this:

> Now I ain't rough and I don't bite

The boy would have thought to himself that his aunt would certainly say that this record was a little bit rough, upon which thought he would eagerly have continued to listen to the following lines:

> But the woman that gets me got to treat me right,
> 'cause I'm crazy 'bout my lovin' and I must have it all the time,
> it takes a brown-skin woman to satisfy my mind.33

The boy's aunt would no doubt have found this very shocking, with the obvious result that he took the record home and started to look for more black jazz records like this. All over the USA and Europe young people started to listen to this type of music and very soon the clever boys came in and began to commercialize, bourgeois-ize and streamline it so that by the end of the 1930s swing was all over radio, gramophone and film. Just to make you understand what swing meant, let me tell you a story about Artie Shaw. He was a man whose picture most girls in 1939 had above their beds. One day he was supposed to give a concert, but he did not turn up, and he never turned up again because he felt that everything was a big lie. This music was seemingly very fierce and strong, but the musicians knew they were just doing little tricks.

Then two things happened. On the one hand there were the black musicians who moved on to music that was more existential: they were the creators of modern jazz. One of them was Charlie Parker, who was very aware of the problems I want to deal with in this lecture. On the other hand part of the white audiences started to look for something more real and authentic. They went down to New Orleans and found that the original New Orleans jazz was still being played there. Others looked for music that was even more real and down to earth. They searched the deep South and found the folk blues of people like Leadbelly and the singing of prisoners working on the chain gang in the

Southern prison camps. These men were allowed to see their wives once a month. Well, if these men started to sing about their relationship to their women, it would certainly not be middle class. They found a new audience in these white adolescents.

However, the African-Americans did not like this because they felt that the whites were taking their music away from them. So just after 1945 they created something which was so rough, unintellectual and unmusical to a white person's ear that no white person would ever care to listen to it again. They called it rhythm-and-blues, a kind of down-to-earth blues.

What happened then is that many of the young people who listened to New Orleans jazz took up their clarinets and trombones and tried to make this music themselves. And very soon, in the early 1950s, the clever boys came in again and began to standardize and commercialize this music, and next we have Dixieland. And of course very soon some boys and girls again understood that this was very superficial music and started to look for something more real. They found what they wanted in rock-and-roll, which was a white adaptation of rhythm-and-blues. If you would take the New York subway and go from 120th Street in Harlem down to 4th Street in Greenwich Village, it would take you about half an hour. It took rhythm-and-blues about ten years to travel that distance. It arrived in 1954.

From Hobbes to Bob Dylan

After that you have a very confused and complex history, which for the most part takes place in England. We will just pass it by till we come to that great day in 1963 when the Beatles made their first record. It was a copy of a rhythm-and-blues record and it sold by the millions. It was actually not such a good record, but it had a wonderful title: *Roll over Beethoven*.

You may have understood that in all the jumps in this story there is protest implied. What is the protest about? In order to understand this we have to go back in history to the Enlightenment, or Age of Reason. At that time there were some great professors and they wrote books and had pupils and people read these books, and their pupils had pupils and so very soon their thinking filtered down to the upper middle class and then to the middle class and on to the lower middle class. At the same time it spread geographically from the cities in Europe where you had universities like Leiden, Oxford and specifically Edinburgh. This process goes on and on till you reach the year 1963 and then the thinking of those eighteenth-century professors reached the streets and became a worldwide phenomenon. There is no place excepted. Maybe there are some backward places that have not yet been reached, but they are just the last remnant and the last generation because now we have television, which is the book for those who do not read. Through television that thinking now reaches everyone in a diluted and soft form. And because the ideas are 'softened' people accept them.

In the continuation I want to deal with what happened around 1700 and shall illustrate this with records of the last ten years [roughly 1963–1973] in order to show that the problems that are on the street today are the same problems that those big professors were talking about then. Before the change, let's say before 1700, everybody, not just the intellectuals, not just the Christians but everybody looked at the world like this: there is a triune God and he created the universe and in this universe you have angels and devils and humans and animals and plants and things. And you have norms and laws and one of the norms is 'thou shalt not steal.' Now we know that if you say 'thou shalt not steal' some people do steal, so in this world you can make a distinction between good and evil. This little scheme was the basic approach to reality of everybody in the old world; it was very much influenced by biblical thinking.

Around 1700 this outlook started to stagger as the professors saw themselves confronted with a big problem: they wanted to put an end to the religious wars, which since the Reformation had swept over Europe for a century and a half. They came up with the following solution: from now on let's discuss all important things like science, politics and economics as human beings amongst human beings, using our brains, our common sense and our senses and only them. So they said to the Christians, you are quite welcome to sit around the table as we discuss these things but please leave that horrible little book at home, because as soon as that book comes on the table people begin to fight. I think it is a great tragedy that the Christians on that particular day said 'Okay, we will pray in the morning before the meeting starts and we will read our Bible in the evening after the meeting is over, but we will never refer to it during the meeting itself.' This is when secularism started to come in.

The people of the Enlightenment were very optimistic and they really thought that the world would not change too much because of this. What they did, in my little scheme, was this: they said very politely but very firmly, 'God please leave by the door, we don't need you anymore.' Then immediately the angels and the devils left the room too. What was more of a problem is that the norms left as well. The first man to talk about this was Hobbes. He asked, 'What do we base it on that we shall not steal?' Then he came up with the following story: in the beginning of history everybody was stealing and then they very soon found out that it does not work. Nobody could do anything at all because they all had to stay home in order to protect their things. So they called a meeting and discussed the problem and in the end there was a vote and everybody voted: we shall not steal. Hobbes called this a social contract, something that people have agreed upon once in history. It means that if tomorrow the intelligentsia will show that in the present economic situation it is much better to steal, we can all vote again and change it. In the communist countries it now has changed. If it is good for everybody that somebody's things are stolen, they are stolen. If it is good for everybody that somebody's life is taken, it is taken.

These things are much in discussion today because if there are no norms anymore but only things we have agreed upon in some contract, there is no good and evil anymore. That is what Bob Dylan is talking about when he sings:

> My guards stood hard when abstract threats too noble to neglect
> Deceived me into thinking I had something to protect
> Good and bad I defined these terms quite clear no doubt somehow
> But I was so much older then, I'm younger than that now[34]

I was so much older then, when I knew about good and bad; I am younger than that now. Sometimes people ask me whether I really feel that there is a kind of a generation gap. No, I do not believe in the generation gap but I do believe in a threshold that people cross over. Some people cross the threshold when they are sixteen, and some people when they are eighty. When you are older, terms like good and and evil are meaningful to you; when you are younger they have no meaning.

From Diderot to Paul Simon

Human being is also eliminated from my scheme. The first man to understand this was Diderot, who wrote in the French *Encyclopedia*, the 'Bible' of the Enlightenment, that there is no difference between human beings and animals and plants and things. This was a very violent antichristian statement and intended to be so. It was also a completely unproved statement. But since that day science has built on it and today scientists think they have proved it, for human beings after all consist only of atoms. Leonard Cohen talks about this. He says: 'If you call me brother now, forgive me if I enquire, just according to whose plan?' Who told you this? What do you base it on? And then he goes on: 'when it all comes down to dust,' if we are only atoms, 'I will kill you if I must, I will help you if I can.' And then he turns it around and says 'when it all comes down to dust, I will help you if I must, I will kill you if I can.' For when there is no good and bad there is no difference between killing and helping, it is just the same. And so he continues 'and mercy on our uniform, man of peace or man of war,' there is no difference, 'this peacock spreads his fan'.[35]

Paul Simon talks about this loss of humanity and meaning as well when he sings about the sound of silence: 'People talking without speaking, people hearing without listening, people writing songs that voices never share . . .'[36] Silence is an important concept in our day. Ingmar Bergman made a film called *Silence* with which he wanted to say that in this world of chaos there is no relationship between the separate things anymore. John Cage wrote a very thick book on music and he called it *Silence*. His most famous composition is four minutes and thirteen seconds of silence.

Almost all of my scheme has been erased by now, so that we can make a new scheme, a square (which I call 'the box') with all that is left: animals, plants and things. What is left is nature, the things we can investigate by science in a rational way. Out of science grew technology and a flourishing industry and then in the middle of the nineteenth century some people said, 'Why don't we apply science to human things, to the humanities, as well?' And they started to formulate economic and sociological laws, just like the laws of nature. And they said, 'If we know these laws of economics, maybe we can manipulate the economic reality just like we can manipulate nature.' But the more they began to do that, the more they were caught in the box. They became prisoners of the box because everything was now determined by all kinds of laws. From the moment of one's birth to the instant of death, Paul Simon says, a person is 'caught in patterns':

> Like a rat in a maze the path before me lies,
> The pattern never alters until the rat dies.[37]

We are rats in a maze: a typical twentieth-century way of approaching human being. We just breathe each breath until we die and that is all. We are caught in the box.

From Freud to Leonard Cohen

The last thing that brought us completely into the box is psychology. A great problem that has troubled people since the Enlightenment is What is love? Freud gave the answer: love is libido, a sexual urge. Of course if we start from our senses, that is completely true. If you take a gentleman rabbit and a lady rabbit and bring them together, and then go away and come back after some time, you find many little rabbits. What happens if you take a gentleman and a lady and leave them for a time? You come back and there are a number of little people. What is the difference? The only difference is that humans have erected a kind of façade behind which they cover this up.

I found a beautiful quote by a certain Przybyszewski, a Polish poet who worked in Berlin and was a very good friend of Edvard Munch, the Norwegian painter who worked there in the same period. He wrote a Mass for the Dead (*Totenmesse*) in 1893 and it begins like this: 'In the beginning was sex. Nothing was outside it, everything was in it. Sex is the basic substance of life, the inner being of evolution, and the essence of individuality.'

Sex is basic; everything else is just a covering up. Today we have come to a place where we really begin to see these things in practice. Many young people today declare that all sexual morals belong to the past generation, that we know better now and therefore should have free love. Examples of this reasoning abound in popular music. Listen to the Rolling Stones:

> Everybody wants some loving
> Everybody wants someone to love, to kiss, to squeeze, to please[38]

This is loud music, with protest built in. Some time ago there was an older gentleman who asked me: 'Do you really mean that this music in its very form and sound has protest in it?' I said: 'Yes.' It is not just in the words. If you would go to a discotheque tomorrow and open the door, a wall of sound would come at you. That wall of sound says this, even before you have heard any words: 'Gentleman, if you go through this wall you are in a world in which there are no gentlemen anymore, it's a different world with different clothes, different behaviour and different morals.' The same is true for this song of the Rolling Stones. Even if the words are not very deep, they speak about another world with a different concept of love and a different approach to life.

Some people are so clever that they know how to bring these thoughts even to people who do not want to go through the wall – one of them is Leonard Cohen. He writes a beautiful song about love, but there is venom in its tale, for the song ends with 'for a while', which means love is there just as long as it lasts, until it has become just 'a fine memory':

> Sometimes I see her undressing for me . . .
> I've got to remember that's a fine memory
> And I know from her eyes, and I know from her smile
> That tonight will be fine, will be fine, will be fine for a while[39]

Recently I gave this lecture in the Nursing School of the Free University and I played this record. And then I thought 'Isn't it strange that none of these girls is blushing and that I don't blush, I'm sure that five years ago I wouldn't have dared to play this record in such a surrounding.' So let us not think that these things only concern a faraway world, for they are here, within our hearts. They are our problem, not just their problem.

From Franz Marc to the Velvet Underground

If you visit the museum in Basle you will find a large picture there that at first sight seems to consist of cubistic patterns only. If you look more closely you see that there is a little deer in it and then you notice more deer till in the end you see that the picture is made up completely of deer caught in deer patterns. The picture is called *The fate of the animals* and was made in 1911 by Franz Marc, a German painter. In a letter he wrote 'all being is a flaming despair' and 'Human being is just like the animals, there is no difference but one, and that is that humans know that they are caught in patterns and are dying.' Human beings can get out of the box and look down into it and say 'Oh boy, look how caught I am.' It is very interesting that in 1911 an intellectual painter like Franz Marc was making these remarks while a couple of years ago Jimmy Hendrix, who is the complete opposite of an intellectual, deals with exactly the same things. In his 'Third stone from the sun' he looks at the world and says 'Scenes beautiful, grass so green' and so on and then he says 'I wish to see [these things] close when I'm in my thinking machine.' And as soon as he has said thinking machine, you hear the beautiful melody deteriorating, falling apart and running into complete chaos.

The Dutch painter Karel Appel, one of the Abstract Expressionists of the 1950s, gave expression to similar notions. He made very large canvasses which he painted with king-size brushes and very big brush strokes. In a way every stroke represents the destruction of all the things that were formerly painted, the little houses and trees and animals; all that is left are the brush strokes. In the early 1960s a film was made of him and while he is painting an enormous canvas he says 'I do not paint, I hit; painting is destruction.'

The modern jazz number 'Holy Ghost' (1965) by Albert Ayler was complete chaos to me when I listened to it for the first time. Later I listened to it again and it was not utter chaos to me anymore. That is what we have found over and over again in modern history: people come and destroy everything, but then very soon we find that something is still left standing. Many people say that this happens because we get accustomed to it, but I do not think that is true. My explanation goes like this: say you are standing in a building and you want to destroy the building. You take a bomb and you place it in the middle of the building, and it is destroyed. Then you come back the next day and what do you see? All the walls are still standing. So you phone the contractor and he takes away the walls. The next morning you walk past again and see that all the foundations are still there. So you phone the contractor again, and he digs out all the foundations. Now the building is really destroyed. The next morning you take a look again, but still you see traces of the foundations. It is very hard to destroy things; something is always left standing. That is what has happened in Western culture over the last three centuries.

In 1965 Albert Ayler's music was complete chaos. That was also the artist's intention. When it was first issued, the record was sent to the jazz magazine *Downbeat* and the editor listened to it in order to decide to which jazz critic he would send it. As he found it such a strange record he decided to send it to thirty different jazz critics. Then he printed all their criticisms. It is very interesting that all of them say that this record is sheer chaos, it does not seem to say anything, it is complete non-communication. Ten out of the thirty, however, add this: 'Yet it is a religious experience to listen to this music.' What are they saying? This music is irrational but it is religious, it talks about things that are beyond the box. They went to interview Albert Ayler and he said this: 'Music is a prayer, a message from God, it's freedom beyond the material.'

Many people want to get out of the box in order to be free human beings, because in the box we are just rabbits and atoms. But in order to get out we have to leave behind our rationality, we have to jump out of the box. In the past five years or so many have tried to jump out with the help of drugs. Velvet Underground talks about heroin like this: 'Heroin, be the death of me, heroin, it's my wife and it's my life . . . then I'm better off than dead, because when the smack begins to flow I really don't care anymore.'[40]

In the middle of this song there is a passage where there is only music, music that sounds just like Jimmy Hendrix and Albert Ayler. It is the same sound, the same reality out of the box.

From P.F. Sloan to James Taylor

I have found out that there are two types of people: optimists and pessimists. I will try to give a description of them both. In order to do so I follow them into the museum of modern art. First we follow the optimist, who comes to a painting and reads 'Picasso: *Head of a woman*', and thinks, 'Everybody says that Picasso is one of the greatest painters of Western history. All these great painters, Raphael, Titian and Rembrandt and so on, painted beautiful portraits of beautiful girls. Now Picasso is a great painter, so I'm sure he paints beautiful portraits of beautiful girls as well – yes, you see, the problem is I'm a little bit too old to understand all this and besides I had a very bad art teacher at school.' And so the optimist leaves the museum utterly convinced that Picasso made a beautiful head of a beautiful girl. There are many optimists. Once someone stood up after my lecture and said: 'You talk about all these problems of our time, don't you know that in history there are always ups and downs and now we are down but we will go up again.' They are the optimists and I tell them that theirs is a misplaced optimism.

Now the pessimist comes into the museum and does not need to look at the name beside the painting but knows it. And the pessimist says 'Yes, Mr Picasso, you are completely right, all beauty has burnt its face and all values are dead and gone. But I have to live in this time, what can I do? Yes, I can try to analyse what has happened and try to make everybody see.' And so there is quite a pile of books with analyses of our age written by the pessimists. Maybe the most intelligent and deepest and most beautifully written of those are by Jean-Paul Sartre.

The discussion between the optimist and the pessimist is the subject of the song 'Eve of destruction' by P.F. Sloan:

> Think of all the hate there is in Red China
> Then take a look around to Selma Alabama
> You may leave here for five days in space
> But when you return it's the same old place
> The pounding of the drums, the bride in disgrace
> You can bury your dead but don't leave a trace
> Hate your nextdoor neighbour
> But don't forget to say grace
> And yet you tell me over and over and over again, my friend
> That you don't believe we are on the eve of destruction

Of course Mr Sloan was one of those pessimists; he analyses the situation and sings a beautiful song about it. Yet many young people have come to the point that they say 'we have been protesting for fifty or hundred years and more now, we have written many books, painted many paintings, sung many songs, demonstrated in the streets, we have done all these things and nothing has changed. What more can we do? There is only one way to make an end to this and that is just to blow up the whole thing; everything is better than this.' That is the revolution we have gone through and are still going through in Europe and America:

> 'Cause summer's here and the time is right for fighting in the street, boy ...
> Hey, I think the time is right for valid revolution[41]

In 1968 I came to an American town and they said 'You are the man who is always talking about hippies and revolution and so on, well, that's not here.' I was in the place for three days and after the three days I said 'Did you read in the papers that there are drugs in the school and that many kids were taken to jail – don't tell me it's only in the days when I'm here. You just close your eyes. You just "continue to continue to pretend"[42] that everything is quite all right.'

At that particular place they asked me what I mean when I talk about revolution. I said 'I mean shooting in the streets.' They thought I was absolutely crazy. A couple of months later there was shooting in the streets, in Berkeley, Paris, in many places in the world. Some of those people wrote me a letter and said 'You were right.' At that time I began to understand that I was wrong. Fighting in the street will never work, because the army plus the establishment is just too big an enemy. Throwing stones is not the answer. Then in Amsterdam fifty young people took one of the university buildings for three days and not one drop of blood was spilt – but since that day we have been working very hard in Holland to have a completely new law for higher education. This was the new way of revolution.

So much has changed in the last ten years that we have actually almost had a revolution. Yet some young people are still dissatisfied and frustrated. That is why after this great wave of revolution we now have a counter-wave of romanticism. Part of this current is a man like James Taylor, who says: 'Won't you look down upon me Jesus, you've got to help me to make a stand.'[43] What is he talking about when he says 'Jesus'? Somebody asked him and he said: 'Of course I don't believe in the historical person Jesus. When I say Jesus I mean the good thoughts and good feelings that people give to me.' He takes the connotation without the definition: forget about the real Jesus, but the word 'Jesus' has such a nice connotation.

So first there was a generation of really desperate people and they had hope that they could change things. And then came the revolutionaries and they said 'Let's just destroy everything,' because they knew that this would be the only way to change things. And now there is a post-desperation generation who are in double despair for they even despair whether their despair will ever lead to anything. They are the new bourgeois. The old bourgeois said 'Give me peace and quiet' – that is what the new bourgeois say as well. The old bourgeois said 'Let me live in my way' – that is what the new bourgeois say as well. Basically it is not so different – even though now anything goes and in the past nothing did go – basically it is the same: 'Let's have peace, let's make a beautiful world, won't you look down upon me, Jesus.'

Four possibilities

I want to end with a question. I began with a scheme that represented the old world view, with a triangle in it to symbolize the triune God. Then people came and deleted God. We saw what that has led to. The big question now is: What does all that has happened tell us? What does it mean? Is there a historical causality that acts as link between getting rid of religion and running into the problems we have run into? Or is there another possibility? If there really is a God, what do you think he says about this? Just read your Bible and it will be clear that he says: 'I am not going to be put out of the door, I am coming with my judgment.' There may be more to the last three centuries of Western history than just historical necessity: perhaps God has come in judgment.

What about the future? There are four possible possibilities. The first is that the leftist revolution will win. Sometimes I feel they will win when I see how many young people are reading Marxist books and are leaning in that direction. As they will be in leading positions in twenty years' time there is a great chance that we will have a slow-paced, bloodless, leftist revolution. You must understand that if the leftists should win there will certainly be a kind of dictatorship. The leftists want to make a perfect world. Let's take the traffic problem in Amsterdam. In order to solve it, the leftists are going to write and ask everyone to put down at what time they have to be at which place and from where they will come. They will put all these things in a computer and then tell everyone exactly how fast they may drive and which route to follow, and if everyone does that the traffic will move very quickly. But you must understand that along the road there will be soldiers and if anyone is a second too late, he or she will be taken off the road. There will be no freedom. And if you are going to stand for freedom, beauty, humanity and justice then there is no place for you in that world. Maybe you will be killed or placed in a concentration camp. I have only one thing to add here: I hope to meet you there.

Another possibility is that the rightist counter-revolution and the establishment will win. If you are a Christian this is an even more difficult situation, because these people will pat you on the back and tell you that it is great that you are a Christian and that they really need you and want your support. That is what happened in Hitler's Germany and that is what is happening in the counter-revolutionary country of Greece. This too will be a dictatorship. And again, if you stand for freedom, humanity, beauty and righteousness there will be no place for you and you will end up in a concentration camp. And again, I hope to meet you there.

Are there are no other possibilities? Yes, there is also the possibility of a real reformation. That is what we pray and work for: for a new grasp of reality, a new starting point to build a new world upon. This will not be easy. If the Holy Spirit would come and breathe over the world to bring a reformation and blow away the dust from all the good books that have become so dusty, do not think things will be different overnight, because the books still need to be read and things still need to be changed. It is a long way back to real reality; we have lost so much. It will be hard work, hard thinking, hard praying, and our life will be at stake. But maybe the Lord will give this to us. Is there no other possibility? Yes, there is a fourth possibility and that is that the Lord Jesus Christ will come back tomorrow – that is the best possibility.

What is Reality?

Inexhaustible meaning

What is reality? And how can we understand the reality we see, the world we live in? These are very important questions, close to my heart. My experience is that the things I deal with in this lecture are very, very difficult. If it takes you twenty years to understand them, you are very quick. I have no solutions to the problems I am raising. It is something that we have to work on, for many years to come. In fact it is the task of the coming generations – plural – to reflect on these questions. If we are able to answer them, we will have found the key to the solution of a lot of the problems and tensions in our Western culture.

Let me begin with an example. Think about the time of our grandparents. How did people in the nineteenth century go on holiday? They would take the train to Basle, change trains to Luzern, change to a small local train and eventually they would stop at a little station where they would disembark. The man of the hotel that they were going to visit would be there waiting for them, just as he had done over the past 25 years, for every year they would go to the same hotel. When they reached the hotel they would say, 'We know that dinner is at six o'clock, so we still have a little time to go for a walk.' They would walk down the same path they had walked for many years, and when they came back they would say how lovely it was to see all those nice places again. They would also say that they missed a particular tree, and the man would say, 'Yes, last year in November we had a big storm and it blew the tree down.' They would grieve for that tree, the hotel owner and our great-grandparents together.

I am telling you this because in the past things like this really did happen. People went to places again and again, and because they went there so often they began to know the reality of the place. So much so that they began to love a particular tree and could shed tears over it not being there anymore. For them it was like a little hole in the universe. Something was missing. Reality is not simply there; we have to get to know it and enter into it. The deeper we go into it, the more we know and understand it, the more we begin to love it, the more real it becomes and the more we will shed tears when it is not there anymore.

We could say that reality is fact plus meaning. A tree is the facts we know about a tree, its atoms and so on, plus their meaning. But it is not totally correct to put it like this because facts come from another framework of thinking. I rather should say that reality is meaning. For what is a fact? A fact is that which we all agree on. If a fact is what we all agree on, then it seems obvious. What I have learnt though is that one word we always have to be very careful about is 'obvious'. When someone says that something is obvious, we may expect a most questionable statement. Reality is meaning; it is meaningful. I could say many more things about the tree: that it has meaning in itself as it is created by God, and that it has many functions, for a tree can be used by birds, we can sit in its shadow, we can cut it down for wood. The tree has many functions but is also more than its funtions. The tree has its own meaning. This meaning is inexhaustible, so manifold that we will never totally grasp it. If we talk about the mountains where these people had their holiday, then it is such a strong reality, with such deep meaning and diverse content, that even if these people went there for a thousand years they would still find out new things. And every time it would become more interesting.

Opening eyes

We do not know what we see, which is the common view of our time, but rather we see what we know. Why did these people walking down the path behind the hotel see that the tree was not there? Because they knew the tree. Somebody else who went there would not have missed the tree because he or she did not know that there had been a tree. If I send several people into a room for several minutes and afterwards ask them what they saw, then a person who knows a lot about furniture will tell you about the different types of furniture in that room. Another person who knows a lot about wallpaper will talk about the wallpaper. Others will only see the books and if they know a lot about theology they may be able to tell exactly to which particular theological school the owner of the room belongs. So we see what we know.

That means by implication that we do not see what we do not know. Does that mean that we are caught: we see what we know and will never see more? No, because we can expand our knowledge through seeing creatively. If we look very attentively and use our imagination, we can expand our knowledge. For instance, say, someone gives you a clock. You do not know much about clocks, and you are interested to know how it works. You open it up but you cannot see how the alarm works. Then you examine it very carefully and use your imagination: if that thing there goes like this, then that will go like that and therefore it rings. As soon as you have seen it, you know it and will never forget it again.

There is a very interesting true story about an old lady who every year for 25 years flew from America to Amsterdam to look at the *Nightwatch*. Somebody else came to look at the painting and they started to discuss it. He said, 'That girl is so intriguing.' She said, 'Which girl?' For 25 years she had come to look at the *Nightwatch* but had never seen the little girl. The man said, 'The girl over there', and from that moment on she would never again not notice the girl, because she now knew the girl was there. Why did she not see her before? Because she was not looking creatively. It is part of the task of the visual artist to open our eyes and to teach us to see things that we did not see before by making them visible. In their own ways that is also the task of the writer and the philosopher. As thinking beings we can all add to the knowledge of humankind and open the eyes of someone else. We could say that teaching is opening eyes.

Santorio

Our reality has changed. That anecdote about how people used to go on holiday, for instance, tells about a time that is past. Nowadays we all drive 5,000 miles for our vacation. We seem to run so fast in order to try and grasp some reality. But as soon as we are somewhere and begin to settle down and know things, we run away again. We flee from reality; we try to get in touch with it yet we are afraid of the contact. Maybe because reality is too strong – just as in *The Great Divorce* by C.S. Lewis people who newly arrived in heaven could not even lift one apple because it was too heavy. It was too strong a reality. In the same way the reality we live in is too strong for us twentieth-century people. My question is: Why?

In all the history books we can read that a big change has taken place in Western history and that the new era began somewhere after the Middle Ages, roughly speaking between 1300 and 1650. That means it took 350 years. It was a very deep change. Before that time the world was different from after that time. We, as Christians, in a way belong to the era before the change, yet in another way to the one after, as we have been completely brainwashed by the new understanding of reality that, and this is crucial, took reality away from us. We know less about reality; we have lost reality. We could say that my great-grandparents, with their type of holiday, still belonged to the old world and that the final stage of the great change took place quite recently with the revolution of our century.

To make clear what has changed I want to tell a fascinating story. In 1614 a man called Santorio, a very clever doctor in Venice – who spent his whole life measuring things and working on the problems I am discussing here – published the book *De Medicina Statica Aphorismis* ('Aphorisms on medical statistics'). When this book was published, it was read by all the leading scientists of that time and they all said that Santorio was crazy. Some said he should be put in an asylum, others that the Inquisition should investigate him as he was dangerous. Nobody even tried to check whether what he had said was right, as they were all utterly convinced that he was wrong. Now, this is what Santorio did. He took a chair and put it on a very big scale. There was a table in front of the chair which was not on the scale. Early in the morning he put a woman on the chair after she had just woken up and gave her breakfast. Something amazing happened. What happened? The scales showed that she became heavier. Everybody said this is impossible, we all know that in the morning when you wake up you are heavy and then you eat breakfast and become lighter. That is why you eat breakfast and drink tea or coffee, to get rid of the heaviness of sleep!

It shows that we all have become materialists who count the number of atoms, and that before 1614 people thought differently. This is part of the change that took place between 1300 and 1650.

Galenus, Mundinis, Vesalius and Harvey

The following tale is the same story, only a bit more complicated and important. It is a story about the heart. What is the heart? The Bible teaches us that we should love the Lord our God with all our heart. The heart is the source of life. Out of the heart come all the good and bad things we do. When you love somebody you lose your heart, and you can give your heart to someone. Galenus thought about the heart in the framework of ancient medicine. What he said is very hard for us to understand, just as it is difficult for us to grasp why you should become lighter when you eat breakfast. Galenus said that there is a kind of liquid produced in the liver, which goes from the liver to the heart, and in the heart hot air is added to it which comes from the lungs (there is a kind of little stove there that burns and makes the air hot) and in this way spirit is added to the liquid – spirit in the sense of being alive and full of spirit (the Latin word *spiritus* means air as well as spirit). Now this system explains everything perfectly, provided that you never look inside the body. For instance, what happens when you get excited? Your heart begins to beat more quickly and you turn red and a fire starts to burn in your eyes, because there is more spirit. When you are a bit sick and very tired, you get white because the heart ticks slowly and there is not much blood and spirit coming from the heart.

But then they began to dissect bodies, exactly in 1300. That is one of the reasons why I said that the change began in 1300. Mundinus, a professor in Bologna, was the first person to do anatomy. According to the old system of Galenus there is blood going from the one chamber of the heart to the other one, which means that there has to be a hole between the two parts of the heart. Mundinus wrote about the hole even though there is no hole. But you see what you know – they knew there was a hole, therefore they saw one. They could very easily have found out that it was not there, but then their whole system would have fallen down. But then Vesalius, the greatest anatomist who ever lived, published his book around 1550. When it was published, he did not get good reviews. Quite to the contrary. He was very heavily criticized, because one of the things he said was that there is no hole in the heart. He was the court physician of the king of Spain, and the king did not want to see him any more. He was almost put in prison and he died in poverty because nobody was interested in the strange things he was saying. People were very strong in their convictions at that time in history – as they are nowadays. If you say you do not believe in the evolution theory or the subconscious you are considered out of your mind. Because those things are considered 'obvious'. No, they are not obvious; they have question marks.

In 1628, 328 years after 1300, Harvey published his book. Harvey was a physician in London and he spent his whole life working on a system. He taught this system to his students, and they said that he should publish it. But remembering Santorio and Vesalius he first refused. After much pressure he agreed to write a little booklet. It seems to be very dull and very technical, but in the booklet he explains that the old system does not work, and then he talks about the large and the small systems of blood circulation. In the small one the blood goes through the lungs and picks up air; and in the large one blood goes through the body. This means that there have to be two seperate chambers in the heart. In the course of his discussion he says that 'in the name of God' – it is the only moment in the book he gets excited – 'you must understand that the heart is a pump.' He uses exactly those words. The heart is a pump, the pump of the blood circulation. This means that after the change we are admonished to love the Lord our God with all our pump! That is the change and that is the problem of the new era.

How do we reconcile the new with the old? I do not want to throw away what has been discovered since 1300. I do believe that in the body the heart is a kind of pump. Nevertheless I do not think it is silly to say that we have to love the Lord our God with all our heart. Yet I do not want to say that in that case the heart is only a symbol – at least, not if 'symbol' is taken to mean something that it is not so important, because symbols are important and embody the true meaning of things. So, what is the heart? How can we reconcile the attainments of science with the Bible – or Genesis 1 with the evolution theory? These are the type of questions we have to answer if we want to solve the problems of our age.

Before the change

Owen Barfield wrote a book *Saving the Appearances*. Science is saving the appearances: it sees something and tells you how it works and explains what you see. The term was much used in the Middle Ages. In this book Barfield discusses various ways of 'participation', which also is a very old term. In ancient paganism everything was participated reality, which means that gods and spirits participate in it. That means that a stone is not just a stone but that it is loaded with a kind of power. There are powers in water, in trees, etc. That is why there were idols, which are statues charged with higher powers. The Bible tells us exactly the opposite, it tells us that God created the world. Which is a very liberating concept, because if our reality is created, it is not participated, which means there are no powers or gods in it. The sun gives us life and warmth but is not a god. It is a creature. That is why we can investigate it. We do not need to be afraid. We are free to use and explore things.

The medieval system knew some participation. It was a Christian system but not completely so. It was vitalistic which means that they believed that there is a kind of living power in things. If we nowadays talk about power in physics, we actually use a medieval term. In the Middle Ages people always talked about the quality of things, and their thinking was substantial, not functional. That means that they always asked the question: What is the substance, the deep reality of the thing before me? Not, how does it work? We always ask how things work and never what they are, because that usually is too difficult to answer. What is electricity? Every scientist will answer, 'Who cares what electricity is, this is how it works.'

As to the interpretation of the Bible and literature, medieval people distinguished between a literal sense, a moral sense, an allegorical sense and an anagogical sense. They would say that the symbolical is the same as literal, for it is the symbolical that expresses the essence and substance of things. We still think in this way when we see a flag: it is impossible to seperate the cloth with its colours and stripes from the meaning of a flag. But on the whole the material and the symbolical have become two different things for us.

Many people think – I do not know where the myth comes from – that people in the Middle Ages believed the earth to be flat. But at that time everybody knew the earth to be a ball. The earth is a ball and around that ball run the moon and the planets and the sun and then far away there is a very big circle, or sphere, and that is where the stars are. The question was, what was behind the furthest sphere? Aristotle believed in this system, but he became very nervous when he was asked that difficult question and so he would evade it. But for medieval Christians it was very easy to answer that question: when you get behind the furthest sphere, there is God. The beautiful thing about medieval thinking is that there is a second system that has God in the centre, and around him there are spheres with cherubs, seraphim, archangels and angels, and at the periphery, furthest away from God, where it is almost dark, there human beings live. God is in the centre and whether human beings are just outside or just inside the City of God, that was the point of discussion. Of course still further away than humankind was matter, so far away that nobody talked about it. So there are two systems that belong together, that are one, two sides of the same coin: the physical system with the earth at its centre, and the other system with God at the centre. A beautiful world system.

A new way of seeing

Then comes the new system, a new way of seeing emerges. In the Renaissance people for instance begin to portray things as they see them whereas in the Middle Ages they painted them in symbols. In medieval painting you have a tree symbol, but now artists start to paint the tree as they see it. But the new way of seeing is not only limited to art, it slowly changes the whole way of thinking.

The Reformation tried to counter the new movement and work out another system, a more biblical one. In a way we are still searching for it. The Middle Ages had made a division between nature and grace. In the Renaissance people started to disconnect nature and grace so that the natural realm could be freely developed. The Reformation tried to bring nature and grace together again and, moreover, to take away the division between the two. For the real division is not between a higher and a lower reality but between the Creator and the creation. The Reformation began to understand that everything is one and that God is involved with all of reality, not just with the realm of grace: that, for instance, God acts in history and that Christ came to make us human, not to make us Christians. The Reformation made out a case for the fullness of reality and the fullness of humanity.

The Reformation, however, was not able to turn the tide and the new humanistic theory was developed further till we come to Descartes and Locke, the two great philosophers of the Enlightenment. Things are now viewed as autonomous, separate from God. People now start from autonomous human beings who use their reason and reflect upon an autonomous nature in which eternal laws apply, laws like two and two is four. Whatever you are, Roman Catholic, Protestant, Muslim, atheist, it does not matter: two and two is four. It is an eternal truth. When Descartes said that for the first time, around 1620, everybody laughed and said: 'Descartes, you know that the only thing that is eternal is the word of God. Everything else is transitory. It is silly to say that two and two is four is an eternal law. It is probably a true fact, but that is all. It is not very important, and certainly not eternal.' But for Descartes it was very important: his own brain and the so-called eternal laws were the only things he could be certain of.

Then Locke came and popularized this type of thinking, which is based on this: we know what we see. So reality is a big X, we do not know anything about it. And then the perception lines reach our eyes and we, with our brains, make the ideas and the reality inside of us. This means that the people of the Enlightenment made their knowledge of reality dependent on their seeing. In this way their knowledge became reduced and they ended up with a reduced world view. Many things were taken away. Think about Elijah, for instance, when he prayed for rain. He sent his servant up the hill and told him to look out for clouds. Well, the boy saw clouds and he said: 'Look, God is doing what he promises!' Now we would say: 'I see forms, which in my brain I deduct to be clouds, so I am going to tell my boss there are clouds coming.' That is all we can say. Experience has taught us that rain usually comes out of clouds, so we know rain is coming. But that God is implied is something one can never see. Can one prove it? So we have reduced our understanding of reality in many, many ways.

Reduced reality

What is the result of this new understanding of reality? First that there is no participation. God or spirits have nothing to do with reality, because things exist there objectively. That means: they are there, even if God or we are not there. Bacon said that research should be done as if things are machines. We have to treat the world like a machine, namely completely objectively. Therefore people began to talk about creation as a watch. God created the world as a watchmaker makes a watch, and then he went away. And now the whole thing runs as it runs. There is no freedom in it, it just runs; we are all caught in a big machine called nature.

That also implies that now everything is neutral. Of course you can have your religion; if you want to pray, please do; if you want to go to heaven, please go. But if we talk about important things like economy, politics, science or true knowledge we just use our perceptions and our brains. This was a very deep change in thinking. Moreover, we are all brainwashed. And maybe the heaviest brainwashing has taken place in history writing. All history writing is done in this vein: Mr A did this and Mr B did that and then this happened; but no one tells you why, what the motives of these people were which were probably religious motives. And so you get the feeling that people did what they did because they did it. We also think that a photograph, which is an image of reality taken by a machine, is a true image that belongs to the same neutrality.

The eighteenth century, the time of the Enlightenment, was also the time of pietism, which is the root of Anglo-Saxon evangelicalism. The pietists still thought in the framework of nature and grace, and therefore they left the whole area of nature to the world. In other words, they were quite happy to discuss science using only their perceptions and brains, because to them science belonged to the realm of nature. This meant that they never fought the battle that should have been fought at that time.

In the medieval system God is in the centre with spheres around him and in the most outer sphere, matter is located. Medieval thinking started with God, and the rest is his creation. No, said the Enlightenment, the only thing that is really real and certain is matter. Matter became the starting point of Enlightenment thinking. That is why you get heavier when you eat breakfast; that you get lighter is subjective and uncertain, but that you get heavier is objective and true for everybody. The only things that are certain are the facts. But facts are reduced reality. Atoms are an abstraction of an abstraction. Human being is an atom, an atom that looks at its own navel, a queer atom that invented God. We now start with the atoms and end with God.

Peter Gay says about Diderot, who was among the great men of the Enlightenment:

> Eighteenth-century thought had liberated man from his filial dependence on God. He had made him part of nature. But the philosophical anthropology of the French philosophes, which promoted man from servitude to God, ironically enough demoted him at the same time: from his position a little lower than the angels to a position among the intelligent animals. While man seemed on the point of conquering the worldly domain through his critical intelligence he was faced with a second expulsion from his terrestrial paradise. And this time the avenging angel was man himself!

People thought they had come of age and have become their own god, but they ended up being just animals. Diderot was very worried about this.

People knew there was something wrong and that this new system would kill them. Exactly at the moment that Harvey said that the heart is a pump, heart mysticism started, the devotion of the Sacred Heart of Mary and Jesus. People tried to save the heart at the moment it was lost. Modern people try to fill the gap. The modern art museum is one big cry of protest: 'I am a human being! It is crazy, it is irrational, it is unsubstantiated, but nevertheless human being is human being.' What we see is the crisis of human beings crying out that they are human. Another thing is that if the only real things are the atoms, then everything else is of people's making, including moral systems and state systems. But if they are only made by people, we can change them if we do not like them. The Marxist revolutionary thoughts of making new structures come out of this idea. Reality is just our thought forms projected onto the world outside.

Susanne Langer, a fascinating writer, has written a book in which she discusses these things. She says: 'The new way of looking at the world is not the result of science. Science is rather a result of a new way of looking at the world. And the real change is the new way people look at reality.' She continues,

> Modern man has this attitude towards the world: the complete submission to what he conceives as hard cold fact. And therefore to exchange fictions, faith and constructed systems for facts is his supreme value. Hence his periodic outbursts of debunking traditions, religious or legendary, his satisfaction with stark realism in literature, his suspicion and impatience of poetry. And perhaps on the naïve and critical level of the average mentality the passion for news.

News gives us the 'neutral' facts, but in fact we are manipulated by the facts, because the news gives us only the facts. What she says about the satisfaction with stark realism is very interesting, especially if you think about the books that have been written over the last twenty to thirty years with such explicit descriptions of sex. Why in the past was it not described like this? For two reasons. Firstly, because it was too loaded with meaning, so strong a reality that one cannot describe it. And secondly, because there was no need for it. Why should you describe it? People would have felt that the almost pornographical descriptions of today were too far below reality. That is not what happens, for there is a very strong encounter between two people that eludes description.

Also, according to Susanne Langer, the conflict is not between faith and science but between faith and a new faith, a new understanding of the world with science as the source of revelation. If for instance I say that I do not believe in the evolution theory, people say, 'But science has proved it.' What has science proved? And what does the proof mean and what are the implications? But if someone says 'Science has proved it,' everyone bows to that and it is the end of the discussion. Because then we know the facts. But I say 'no' to that.

Science falsifies reality

Now I come to the main point of my whole lecture: if you accept the methods and principles of modern science, the Bible is not true. Two years ago I was in a group of very good friends of mine, very fine Christians, and I said that same sentence. Ten minutes later one of my friends said: 'But you said the Bible is not true.' Because it is considered obvious that the principles and methods of modern science are true. And I say: 'No, it is exactly the reverse.' I say, the Bible is true and therefore I have great questions about the principles and methods of modern science. Note that I am very careful not to say 'the results of modern science'. If modern science has developed let's say plastics, I have to accept plastics. If modern science has told me there is blood circulation, I accept blood circulation. It is very hard not to do so. But I do not accept the principles and methods of modern science. I feel they present us with falsifications of reality.

When I say: 'If you accept the principles and methods of modern science, the Bible is not true,' I could equally say, 'Homer is not true' or 'the Koran is not true.' They are not true because they are all fairy tales without any meaning. All literature is thrown overboard because it does not have any meaning, and then the Bible, which is more than just literature, is certainly out. It is a conflict between two different world views, two understandings of the world. These things are not just difficult problems that philosophers may deal with, they are realities of life. There is a lack of motivation among students. Why? Because reality is not interesting. Why is reality not interesting? It is just a heap of facts, without meaning, without participation in anything. We all know the permissiveness, that there are no norms anymore. People can do as they like. The natural human urges are the only real things. I think that Bob Dylan has phrased it very beautifully when he sings about a 'thin man'. Modern people have no reality within them anymore.

I think this is also one of the reasons why people take drugs. Drugs lower our understanding of reality and then reality is not a threat. Because whatever we think about reality, real reality is still there. Real reality becomes something very strange and sometimes it is too strong. That is why we drive so fast during our holidays and why we never stay so long. Because reality is too loaded. It is in discordance with our understanding of reality. Also, there is no participation and therefore we have so much difficulty in the area of politics. My great-grandfather said: 'I love the queen.' Why did he love the queen, a person he never saw in his life? He loved her because she was the centre of the nation. He loved the nation because it was something of a unity that he could participate in. There were values implied. Today we say: 'No, everybody is equal, the queen is just another woman.' Barfield writes this about social equality: 'We are equal precisely in the regard that we are independent, alienated and isolated from each other.' We are equal as long as we are isolated from each other. But when we begin to meet each other, our differences and our particular qualities, i.e. our inequality, come forward. And then we begin to make a unity, because we know that this job should be done by this person and that job by another person with different qualities. That idea of equality is also why people have started to do something very crazy: they investigate rats to find out how human societies work!

Rediscover reality

To sum up: what is the problem? That we have to refind, or rediscover, reality. We must understand that much is involved. It means also understanding suffering, it means understanding what pain means and what death means. If we understand reality and begin to love it, then pain comes in; we may weep over the tree without being sentimental. We have lost that understanding because we have so little reality. To be a Christian means to go into reality, we have a task here. The Bible gives us a real grasp on reality; it gives us much more than propositional facts. In fact, the Bible does not give us any facts (by the modern understanding of facts) because it tells us the truth about things. It teaches us a mentality, an attitude, and it gives us a way of understanding the world. And it is not an old world view, but it shows us the world in its deepest sense, in its deep meaning. Polanyi has written a very important book, which we all need to read, called *Personal Knowledge*. Because truth and understanding are personal and we have to try to get away from objectivity, for it is depersonalised. What is truth? Christ said: 'I am the truth' and he told us to do the truth. So truth is not something static, an objective statement about a factual world outside, but it is something in which we ourselves are involved. It is personal and it is in relationship to God.

Truth, reality, life, love, beauty, righteousness and freedom are such great words that we can barely define them. They are the deepest realities possible, much deeper and more basic than two plus two is four. These are the realities we try to grasp in order to understand the world. Even if we never will be able to define them scientifically or objectively we can say many things about them which are true and important.

To end a question: What is water? Water is the beautiful waterfall with its beautiful sound, and if you look up you see the sun, and you will see a rainbow appear. But water is also the bad smelling ditch. Water is the rain that hits you in your face. Water is the great seas, mighty and powerful. Just a few weeks ago everybody in Holland was trembling because there were big storms and the question was, would the water go over the dikes? That means death, destruction, drowning, danger. But water is also the water that you give to the thirsty. Water is all these things and many more. Poets have been writing about it since the beginning of history and they have not exhausted the knowledge of water! No, say modern people, we will tell you what water is: it is H_2O. That is the problem that we must consider and try to solve. Yes, water is H_2O, but nevertheless it is much more. The heart is a pump, but nevertheless I still want to be able to say that I love the Lord my God with all my heart.

Genesis 1: Creation versus Evolution

Christians and science

For many years I have found myself in discussions about Genesis 1, a topic much debated amongst the old as well as the young. One day it occurred to me that perhaps there is something wrong in the way we pose the problem. Therefore I will not focus primarily on the exegesis of Genesis 1 or the evolution theory, though I will say a few things about both, but I will rather try to find out which ideas and presuppositions lie behind the debate. It is my hope that by clarifying where the real differences and problems are, we will be able to obtain better answers.

The Genesis 1 dispute began somewhere around 1700, when people concluded, erroneously as we know today, that the Egyptian civilization started further back than 4000 BC. Some people in the seventeenth century – maybe that is where the problem really began – had laid down that the earth had been created in 4006 BC on 23 May, a date as precise as that. Happily there was a very clever theologian who made a new calculation and found out that Creation had taken place not in 4000 BC but in 6000 BC and thereby he saved the situation. But in the meantime people had found out that the Chinese civilization goes back beyond 6000 BC and so they had to change again, and from that day onwards they had to accommodate their views again and again.

In the eighteenth century geologists and palaeontologists started to find many strange things like shells on tops of mountains and bones of animals that no one had ever seen. Because of that the liberals of those days, who did not call themselves liberals but rather *philosophes*, or followers of the Enlightenment, became highly critical of the Bible and started to look for new solutions. Thus two parties were formed. One explained the shells on the mountains as a result of the flood that was recorded in the Bible and held that the strange bones belonged to animals that lived before the flood. The other party maintained that these phenomena were not caused by a flood but rather by volcanic eruptions. At that time, around 1800, the debate was won by the people who pointed to the flood.

After 1800 I see two lines. The first line is that of the Bible-believing Christians, who, especially in Britain, which at that time was a centre of science, were mostly pietists. All their emphasis was on having devotional times, reading the Bible and living moral lives, which meant that they never went into deep theological or philosophical reflections. Because of that they had no antidote against the new science and the Cartesian philosophy that was its breeding ground. Their counter-offensive remained on a too superficial level. They just said that science had to be wrong, because the Bible said something else or they tried to adapt the findings of the scientists to the Bible. Unfortunately they hardly did any research themselves.

The second line is that of the scientists. Most of those scientists were not antichristian. They were not trying to prove that Christianity is wrong, but they were for instance High Anglicans going to church on Sunday and being good scholars the rest of the week. Yet as they investigated, they found that the Bible agreed less and less with the results of science, and they slowly discarded the Bible.

Why did that happen? Why did the Christians who went into geology let go of the Bible? This happened because of the Cartesian principles that were applied in the investigations. The basis of the new scientific approach was formulated in the eighteenth century by the geologist James Hutton in the uniformity principle, which involves 'the exclusion of all causes not supposed to belong to the present order of nature'. Which means that if I find shells on the top of a mountain, I will not suppose that in a time past on this mountain lived animals that carried shells on their backs. Rather I know that shells belong to sea animals, so there must have been a sea there or some other explanation along those lines has to be found. That is obvious and I do not see any reason why as a Christian I should not accept that. However, the uniformity principle implies something more, namely the exclusion of *all* causes not supposed to belong to the present order of nature. In other words, never talk about God, never talk about miracles. There may have been a disaster like a flood, but of course only in a limited area, not covering all of the earth.

Why then did these scientists, even though they were church members, adopt the uniformity principle? The answer is this: because all of them accepted the nature and grace duality scheme. They all considered nature to be autonomous and grace to belong to the realm of the church. The nature and grace duality comes out of the Middle Ages, it was fought by the Reformation yet when the Reformation lost its force it came back again and we have to fight it still today. The implication of the nature and grace scheme is that nature is de-christianized, even within the Christian framework, and so it was easy for these scientists to discard the Bible when they were researching nature, because to them the Bible had nothing to do with nature. The Bible might have had something to say about their religious activities but not about their scientific research.

As I said, the Reformation opposed this way of thinking. It is due to its influence that seventeenth-century scholars like Newton, Boyle and van Leeuwenhoek approached their scientific work in a much more integrated way. Van Leeuwenhoek, who invented the microscope and was the first human being ever to see a drop of water through its lens, wrote an article that began like this: 'I always thought that God created the world, but now I know that God created two worlds.' He understood that in his scientific work he was investigating the greatness of God's creation. In his book on religion and the rise of modern science, Professor Hooykaas shows that Christians were very much present at the beginnings of Western science. The first geological investigations, for instance, had been conducted by Christians. Hooykaas once told me how, when lecturing at a theological seminary in Scotland, one evening after the session he was leaning against a cupboard and then said, 'Have you ever realized that the first geologist worked at this seminary?' Somebody answered, 'That rings a bell, look in the closet.' So they opened the doors and found that it was full of stones, which had been kept there even though nobody knew (tellingly enough) why they were there.

Darwin

Then we come to Darwin, who came from an orthodox Christian background. He started out as a theology student, dropped out and became a strong antichristian. People who turn away from the Christian faith often do not only have an emotional need to fight it, but also an intellectual one, as they have to disprove the answers given by Christianity. One of the first questions they need to deal with is this: If there is no God, where does the world come from? Thus we can understand why a man like Darwin, more than anyone else, tried to find an answer to that question.

Darwin made his travels in 1836 and very soon after his return he wrote his book. Then he kept it in his drawer until 1864. He did not want to publish it as he was afraid of all that it might occasion. After much pressure from his friends he finally did bring it out, and after it was published many people sent him letters. Then he wrote to some of his friends, 'I'm baffled because I have no answers.' He was asked again and again: 'If you are right that the world evolved from one cell, then this very first cell must have been very complex, as the possibilities for the evolution of all that came afterwards must have been built into it – how do you account for that?' And Darwin had to admit that he could not.

Even though today the evolution theory is generally held to be true, there are many scientists who have great problems with it. One of their most forceful voices is Polanyi, a leading scholar in England, who has written a book in which he says that the evolution theory is impossible as it comes down to this, that you must have a computer making a computer – the same problem Darwin was facing. There had to be a force, however it be, that was greater or higher than what came into being. The evolution theory is still a hypothesis, yet the popular science books speak as if it has been proved. In the *Time Life* series, for instance, you get nice little drawings of the 'tree of life' that starts with atoms and ends with human beings evolving out of apes. Everybody knows this tree, but the specialists know that there are many leaps in it for which there is no proof. Our real enemy is not true science but popular science with an inbuilt antichristian bias.

Truth

Now, just visualize two people sitting side by side with the first page of the Bible on the table in front of them, reading about the seven days of Creation. One is a scientist who says that it is wrong; the other is a Christian who says that is true. Who is right? What is true? There is, however, a question that precedes these questions, namely: What do you mean when you say this is true? Usually people do not talk about that, they all accept the same kind of truth and therefore there is a problem. Christians as well as non-Christians both define truth as that which is factually true, that which is true according to the definition of modern science. Yet modern scientists base themselves on Cartesian principles, which are in themselves already antichristian, so obviously science will give us antichristian truth. Because of this the scientists will always win because they have the truth on their side by their definition of truth. According to their definition of truth Genesis 1 is not true, and according to their definition of truth the Christian who piously says that Genesis 1 is true, makes a crazy statement.

Many people are aware of this and have sought a solution to this problem. Liberal Christians, for instance, have come to see Genesis 1 as not true in the scientific sense yet true in a spiritual or symbolic sense. There never have been an Adam and Eve, yet they do believe that Adam and Eve have fallen. But that is symbolic truth. By way of the story of the Fall, God is teaching us something, comparable to Christ's teaching us through his parables – they are not factually true yet contain symbolic truth.

Now my question is: What is truth? What is a good criterion for truth? Let's begin with modern naturalistic truth, which started with Descartes. He said: 'I am because I think,' which means I am autonomous, there is nothing outside of me that I have to obey, and I am dealing with an autonomous nature which is guided by eternal laws like two and two is four. These laws are eternal because they always have been true and always will be true, whatever you believe or whoever you are. I would say that they are not eternal laws for they are created laws: God created them. And nobody knows whether on the new earth two and two will still be four. In a way I do not care because it is not so important. But for Descartes the laws of nature and mathematics are central truths – those things that are clear and distinct, that can be understood with one's brain and found out by experiment.

When you start to investigate the world on the basis of these principles, everything changes. Formerly everybody believed that there is a God, who created the world with norms and laws, angels and devils, humans, animals, plants and, lowest of all, things or matter. But if I believe only those things that are clear and distinct, I have to let go of God. Can you do an experiment to prove that God exists? Angels and devils go as well. And the things that are without any doubt, the factual things, matter, become the most solid of all. Before Descartes you could even discuss whether matter was being; in a way it was non-being, it was too low, but now it becomes the basis of life out of which plants and animals and human beings evolve, and finally these humans create for themselves a God. It is a complete reversal in thinking. Everybody today thinks like this, including you and me, even though we know we should not be thinking like this as Christians, and so we get into a kind of tension because we do not believe what we believe. Therefore many people ask, 'Does God exist?'. That is where our time puts the question mark.

Matthew I

How does the Bible see truth? It states first of all that Christ is the truth. Not matter but Christ. If the Cartesian searches for eternal truth, we can point to Christ and his word. Everything else is secondary, also his creation which in its present form will come to an end.

To trace how the Bible deals with truth, let us take a look at Matthew 1, the first chapter of the New Testament, rather than the first chapter of the Old, as there are less emotional overtones attached to this chapter even though it confronts us with the same problem as Genesis 1. Matthew 1 begins like this: 'The book of the genealogy of Jesus Christ, the son of David, the son of Abraham. And Abraham was the father of Isaac and Isaac was the father of Jacob and Jacob was the father of Judah,' and so on. A few verses later, 'and David was the father of Solomon by the wife of Uriah, and Solomon was the father of Rehoboam,' and so on. Then verse 12 states: 'After the deportation to Babylon Jeconiah was the father of Shealtiel,' and so on, and then it ends in verse 17 with this: 'All the generations from Abraham to David are fourteen generations, and from David to the deportation to Babylon fourteen generations, and from the deportation to Babylon to Jesus Christ fourteen generations.' This is how Matthew started out his propaganda pamphlet, which he wrote in order to convince the Jews that Jesus Christ was the promised Messiah of the Old Testament. Now if I write a pamphlet to prove something, I am not going to start with some statements that everybody knows to be wrong. Who would take the trouble to read any further? I would be even more careful to tell the truth if I knew that all these Jews could very easily verify my words. Yet if you look it up in the Old Testament, you will find that Matthew's genealogy is not right. It is simply not true that from Abraham to David were fourteen generations, neither from David to the deportation to

Babylon, and so on, for some of the names have been left out. What Matthew 1 proves is that my thinking is different from Matthew's, and that he and his contemporaries (and the Bible) had a different criterion for truth than we do.

The key to this difference is to be found in Matthew's usage of the number fourteen. At this point I have to bring in a little detour about the use of number symbolism in the Bible, though we need to be careful not to read too much into it as some people have done. Three is the number of God, four is the number of the earth, twelve or three times four is the number of the covenant, God dealing with the world, and in line with this there are twelve tribes of Israel and twelve apostles. People in biblical times were very much aware of the meaning of these numbers. It may come as a surprise to many of us that there were not really twelve tribes of Israel, in reality there were thirteen as Joseph had two sons, Ephraim and Manasseh. But when you read through the Bible, you will find that the writers of the Bible always by some device or another get rid of one tribe. In Revelation 7, for instance, where the 144,000 are sealed as the servants of God (12,000 of each tribe of Israel), Dan is forgotten. But to them it was more important that there were twelve tribes than to be factually exact, because there is something that is more important than factuality. Another number that occurs often is the number 40. The Jews were 40 years in the desert, Moses was 40 days on the mountain, Jesus Christ was 40 days in the wilderness. Now, when I say that the number 40 is a symbolic number and means trial, I do not mean to say that Jesus was only symbolically in the wilderness, no he was really there and he was really tempted. But maybe it was only 39 days, maybe 41 or 42, who cares? Another example is Jesus saying that he would be in the grave for three days, but he was there even less than two days – just count, from Friday evening until Sunday morning, that is less than two times 24 hours.

Matthew opens his Gospel by stating that there were three times fourteen generations from Abraham to Christ. In this way he first of all tells us that there were real people involved in the birth of Christ, people whom everybody knew were far from perfect. David was an adulterer, and out of this adultery Solomon was born, and Rahab was a prostitute. And these men had to go to bed with their women and copulate with them and out of this real-flesh context the next generations were born. And Christ came into the world with all the pain of childbirth. But by his use of numbers Matthew also tells us something else, namely that God was at work in this very human history. Three times fourteen is three times two times seven: three is the number of God, two is the number of affirmation (you always need two testimonies), and seven is the number of holiness. In other words, this line of descent is not only human but it is also a holy line. Thus Matthew changes the facts in order to bring out the reality of the facts. Modern people have a problem here because to them a symbol is something that is not true. But a symbol is actually very real, the most real reality, and accordingly we can speak about real symbols or symbolic reality.

To say this in another way: facts are nothing, for facts by themselves are meaningless. If I say that at this moment a piece of lead is flying through the air in Chile, you say 'So what?' If I tell you that this piece of lead is a bullet that is about to kill the dictator, that makes a big difference because now there is a meaning attached to the fact. In order for a fact to become meaningful there has to be fact plus meaning. What modern people try to do is to have meaning without fact. They say, 'Jesus Christ rose from the dead,' but who cares whether he ever really did? But if you do not have the reality, what do the words mean? One cannot have meaning without facts. Reality consists of fact plus meaning – they belong together – and that reality is made clear by real symbols. That is what we find in Matthew 1.

Genesis 1

If we now go back to Genesis 1 again, it is obvious (and I do not think that Moses and his contemporaries ever had any problem with this) that it is not a factual description. It is rather an interpretation. It gives us more than the facts. It tells us for instance that God said that it was good. That means that there was beauty, that the birds were made in such a way that they do not only fly according to the natural laws of aerodynamics but also according to something which we call beauty. And it means that there was meaning and that it was a meaningful world – not a factual world, though there had to be a real creation. Genesis 1 is not only a myth through which God is teaching us something. I do not care for myths because myths are meanings without facts. There really was a creation. What Genesis 1 makes very clear is that one thing was created after another, which is confirmed by geology and palaeontology: there are different layers with different types of vegetation and animals and so on. How did that happen? Nobody knows; nobody was there.

The Bible gives us an interpretation by saying that God created the world, which gives us an answer to the question of how the world came into existence, a real answer. It tells us that the sun, the moon, the stars have been made by God for us, and that we should not make them into gods and adore them. It tells us that history did not begin with Adam and Eve but a long time before them, as God first prepared for us an earth full of riches such as coal and oil, vegetables and fruit trees, and animals of many kinds, a world full of wonderful possibilities. Everything was created according to its kind, which means that a male and a female lion do not produce little zebras or snakes but little lions. We would all be very surprised if this were different. Yet this is a principle God laid in creation. The evolutionists take these things far too much for granted.

The evolution theory

The evolution theory is an answer to this question: How, if there is no God, has this world come about? The question itself is already secularized. There is something strongly religious about the evolution theory; it is not something neutral. Diderot, one of the philosophers of the Enlightenment, wrote in his *Encyclopedia* in his entry on human being, 'There is no difference between humans and animals and plants and things.' Why did he say that? Because he wanted to make an antichristian statement. Certainly it was not a proved statement; nobody could prove that, and we still have difficulties proving it. The evolution theory states that in the beginning there were atoms and after long stretches of time humans came into being. Long stretches of time are needed in order to jump over all the unanswerable questions.

The evolution theory compares the development of an embryo to the evolution of human beings: in the same way that the early human embryo is a kind of fish, humankind have also gone through a fish stage. It is, however, not at all surprising to me that there is a structural similarity between the developing embryo at a certain stage and fish, or even between fish and crocodiles or birds and buffaloes, because they are all created by God; they all bear the mark of God's style and his style has unity. So between all types of animals there are great similarities. They can all move, eat, reproduce, and they all have senses: they are all made according to these four very basic principles. Because both the embryo and fish live in a liquid medium, there quite obviously may be structural similarities between them. But this is not an evolutionary similarity.

On the other hand, there are many examples of evolution that we have to say 'yes' to. Some animals have in the course of time grown bigger or become smaller, even human beings have changed in that way. Few of the women today could wear the dress of an eighteenth-century woman, because people have become bigger since then. There are changes, there is some evolution, and there is no problem with that. The problem arises when people make a jump from one kind to another, when they say it is possible to go from crocodiles to birds, that atoms finally evolved into human beings in one continuous line. There is no proof whatsoever for all the inbetween stages involved.

I also have a philosophical objection to the evolution theory: I do not believe that there can ever be a new structure unless the possibility for that structure was there first. In order for birds to evolve out of crocodiles, there first must have been the possibility to have birds. The big question is where the possibility for the structure comes from. If the whole world evolved in an autonomous way, this could never have happened unless life in all its forms first was a possibility. You can throw millions of substances together, but you will never get life unless you hit on the principle of life, which then had to be pre-existent. Where does the principle of life come from? The evolution theory is simply too small an answer to too big a question. Some scientist once took a computer and tried to find out whether a world like ours could ever have been made by chance. Very obviously the machine said 'no'. How could a little machine answer such a huge question? Yet it shows that it takes just too much faith to believe that this whole world with its very complex structures could ever have come into being by chance.

In the books on evolution one finds that it is always personalized. When one looks at a documentary film about nature, the narrator says, 'Nature made it like this.' Who is nature? What is nature? Is it a what or a who? People write about nature as if scorpions were thinking, 'What shall I do, shall I put my mouth on top of my head or underneath my brains?' as if they were personal beings making conscious decisions.

There are many questions that are never answered by the evolutionist. For instance, Why do birds sing? Why do we have beauty? Why do we have variety? Or Why has evolution not gone wrong? Koestler in his book *The Ghost in the Machine* does consider humankind as a failure of evolution. His solution is that if we all take drugs for thousands of years, a new kind of being might evolve that will not have all the great problems we have. That is his argument, and I think he is right if you share his starting point.

Much proof is put forward for the evolution theory, at least enough facts to make it seem sensible. There are good reasons for it, because for two centuries or more people have been searching in that direction. All possible proof for one direction has been gathered, while all the proof that does not support that direction has been discarded. I know a man who has found many things that do not fit the evolution theory – like bones of certain types of animals in the wrong layer – but he never gets a publisher for his findings.

Fullness of reality

The biblical vision is much deeper and richer than that of the scientists, as it talks about the fullness of reality. As to the first chapters of Genesis we may ask whether Adam and Eve really lived. My answer is 'yes'. And did they really eat that fruit? Again, I would say 'yes'. But if you would ask me if it is really important whether they actually ate the fruit, I would say that it is significant only because it was loaded with meaning as an act of disobedience. The disobedience is the important thing.

The biblical creation narrative involves much more than facts only, it also accounts for beauty, love, righteousness and other such qualities. It tells us that our world is not a closed box but an open world, open to its Creator, open to be developed and open to all investigation. In Psalm 136 we read of God's great deeds in history, which means that we can pray to him today and he will do something tomorrow. That is the real uniformity principle of our world, that God will never change and that the earth will always remain, due to God's covenant with Noah. The biblical account also leaves room for miracles, not only in the sense of the blind being healed but also in the sense of birds flying south in the winter and returning to the exact same spot in the summer.

The evolution theory also never talks about the curse and creation's groaning. However, nature is not just factually there but it is in travail and waits for the children of God to be revealed (Romans 8). These are not just symbolic images but reality: there is death and decay. Nature in the biblical view is never neutral. It can either proclaim God's great glory, as the mountains do in Psalm 19, or it is subjected to futility and slavery to corruption. If the evolutionists are right about the development of the world, then there has been no Fall. That means that there is no answer to the question where evil comes from but, rather, that evil is built into this world. But that implies that evil is also built into humanity. If that is true, there can never be any redemption. Those are the far-reaching consequences of the evolution theory.

My conclusion is therefore that we should never try to synthesize the Christian and the evolutionist views. We should not try to baptize the evolution theory in order to be able to speak to the world. If we do so, we will have nothing left to say, for we will have given away our Bible. We cannot take Genesis 1 out of the Bible, because it is very central to what we believe that 'You created all things, and by your will they were created' (Revelation 4:11). Genesis 1 is a key to understanding reality and it makes a big difference whether we accept or reject it. The principle behind the evolution theory is in itself unchristian, which means that the discussion is not between faith and science but between faith and faith: between faith that says 'yes' to God's revelation because it makes us understand the world and faith that says humans are autonomous and able to find truth themselves. To me, however, the answers given by the evolution theory are too limited to match the magnitude of the questions posed.[44]

To Do the Truth in Art

Beauty

Truth, love, beauty, and reality are all closely linked to one another. Truth and love are intimately connected, just as beauty and reality are. Hence it is possible to speak about truth in art, and the beauty of reality. The beauty of something is always related to its meaning. A tree, for instance, is beautiful, because it is so wonderfully made to fulfil various functions. A tree, a mountain, a river all have a meaningful place in the ecological structure of reality. Yet we cannot say that their meaning is identical with their function. Their meaning is much more than their structural function.

The beauty of nature as God's creation shows God's style, which is endless in variety and yet of great unity. There is an unbelievably great diversity of animals, which however share a small number of common qualities such as movement, perception, feeding and breeding. Perception takes place by way of sight, hearing, smell, taste and touch. On the basis of just a few of these very simple principles, boundless variation is achieved. There is also great diversity within one kind. When you walk in a wood consisting of thousands, maybe millions of trees of the same type, you will still find that each tree has its own individuality. They are all the same yet different. These differences are partly caused by their position: is a tree located on the border of the wood, where it gets a lot sun or wind, or is it overshadowed by a lot of other trees? Or does it stand on a little hill so that it has bent itself in order to fit its place? Every tree has a meaningful place within the whole of the wood. All of creation fits beautifully together.

But it is not only in nature that beauty can be found. Not much thinking has been done in this area, though some passages in Calvin's writings deal with it. He says that beauty not only pertains to nature but also to human life. An act of love is beautiful, as well as a group of people showing internal love and harmony. The hippies are right in using the term 'beautiful people'. This does not mean that they will win all the beauty contests, because that is another kind of beauty, but this term refers to an inner kind of beauty, which is again closely tied to the meaning of our acts and behaviour.

Also as to the beauty of art, humanly crafted beauty if you like, meaningfulness is an important criterion. An ornament, playful forms on a book cover or patterns on a tapestry can be very beautiful if they are fulfilling a function, if they are in the right place in the right way. An abstract play of forms can be fascinating yet meaningless, unless it is functional in a particular context. On Dutch television we have an abstract intertwining of forms as a bridge between programmes, which as a connecting piece is very beautiful and meaningful. If you would expand it and make it into a two-hour-long show it would lose its meaning.

Apart from ornamental art there is also art that is meant to express something. This art too, at least before our times, was never made for its own sake but always had a function. It was always made to have a meaningful place in a larger structural totality. Take, for instance, the three fountains by Bernini on the Piazza Navona in Rome, one of the greatest places in the world. These fountains were not just conceived as eloquent configurations of sculptures, but they were conceived as fountains. Monuments in the central city square in honour of a king or founding father may be another example, as they are made to express something of the country and its past for future generations. Posters are made to announce particular shows or advertise certain products. Yet when the show has left town or the product has been discarded, somebody may come and take the poster home. The poster is beautiful and meaningful exactly because it has a message. Altarpieces, frescos, decorations, pillars and capitals in a building, mosaics on a floor, garden sculptures, cabinet paintings all have their meaning as functional things while their function also specifies their beauty. A Mozart minuet, for instance, is not just charming music, but it is a dance, which means that its rhythm has meaning and charm as a dance rhythm. Still, just as with posters or portraits, the beauty of the minuet remains even if its original function ceases to be important.

There is a norm in all of the given examples. The artist has to think about the place and function of a work, as they give it its meaning. Art has to be related to its place. There are for instance many types of music, such as chamber music, marches, and concert music, and each of these kinds of music is beautiful in its own setting. It would be totally out of character if a drum band played one of the *Brandenburg Concertos* at a big parade. On an occasion like that a Sousa march would be preferable. The same thing applies to literature. There is a meaningful place for fiction and fantasy while significant messages may be imbedded in them. But there is also a place for entertainment, for horror stories, which some people read in their beds because otherwise they do not sleep well, or for Elvis Presley's voice to wake them up after a good night's rest.

Reality

Even the seemingly afunctional can be very functional and meaningful, for these qualities entail much more than just utility. In our houses we have lots of things that are completely useless: on the mantelpiece we may have a little sculpture of a leaping horse or a prehistoric shell on the windowsill. We surround ourselves with many of these useless objects, yet they can be very beautiful even if they are useless, because they have meaning. Can we live without piano sonatas? I believe we can, yet maybe we cannot because piano sonatas have a place.

Many of the things we put in our homes are figurative: a cat, a dog, a landscape, a still life, human beings in all kinds of relationships. It is very strange that people seem to have a need to have around them exactly what they know well. What do people in Vancouver hang on their walls? Faraway coasts or the sunny beaches of the Mediterranean? No, none of that. They have pictures of the immediate surroundings of Vancouver. I came to know Vancouver just by looking at these pictures, which showed all the beautiful spots. Why do many of us have a portrait of our wife or husband on our desk or our wedding picture on the wall? Why do farmers have pictures of cows? We tend to surround ourselves with depictions of what is well known and dear to us. Maybe they are so dear to us exactly because we have them hanging on our wall. We may love a certain landscape just because there was a great song or a lovely story about it. The songs, the legends, the true stories all go into the landscape, and then the artists come and make pictures of it and in this way they give it even more meaning and make it even more dear. The artists help us to build up an emotional contact with the world around us and to enlarge our intellectual understanding of it. Art works into life: reality is discovered, opened up and conquered, attention is focused, and love is deepened.

Every work of art is a meeting point of reality as it really is and reality as we see it. Our judgment of a work of art is led by these two things as well. We often like a work of art because our view and understanding of something is affirmed by it. But that is not enough, there also has to be a relationship with reality as such. We want a work to be real and true. In this tension between our view, the artist's view and real reality, all appreciation and appraisal of art takes place. Quality plays a role as well, but if we talk about art that is presupposed. If a work of art has no quality there is nothing to discuss. High quality is only a presupposition to take works seriously. Medieval art theory never spoke about quality either.

Although there always is a relationship between art and reality, there is not necessarily a direct connection. Artists often do not give expression to their daily experiences. Schütz, one of the greatest composers, made works of great serenity in the midst of the Thirty Years War, one of the most horrible wars that was ever fought in Germany. Seventeenth-century Dutch art flowered precisely during the war with the Spanish. Everybody says World War I changed the world, but if you look for artworks that directly express this war you will find very few indeed. It was perhaps a catalyst to bring out something new like Dada. How is it possible that artists can make a still life in their studio while outside there is shooting in the streets without that being an escape? Maybe revolution and war are just the things of the day, while art is more tied up with spiritual history and a deeper reality. The relationship to daily life is only important insofar as it deepens the understanding of the artists and the quality of their work.

Art today

What about today? Many contemporary voices say art has to be up to date and in close contact with modern life. Is modern art the art of today? When I look at the present art scene (in its widest and proper sense) I first of all see popular art: the musical, the detective story, the illustration in the magazine, the cartoon, television show, etc. Many of these types of popular art have forms that are based on styles of the past, especially of the late nineteenth century. Impressionistic pictures are still made, which are not totally like their nineteenth-century prototypes but do come close. Is the quality of this popular art necessarily low? I do not think so. *West Side Story,* the detective stories of Dorothy Sayers or a film like *Mary Poppins* are certainly not to be looked down upon as low art. The strange thing is that we are all so brainwashed that we do not consider these things to be the art of today, they just happen to be here today. People often refer to them as commercial, sentimental, superficial – an escape. But that does not need to be the case. There is popular art that falls into a separate category, distinct from low art or nonsense art.

McMullen, in his book *Art, Affluence and Alienation,* introduces the term 'necro art', denoting concert programmes consisting of Bach, Beethoven and Bartók, expositions of Rembrandt and Rodin, plays by Shakespeare and books by Jane Austen and Dickens. Is it not strange that we have all this art of the past still with us as a living art? This is not some general problem that can be found in all times, but it rather says something about our time. People in the past also looked at art of their past, but they did so much less than we do today. We swallow any style and any kind of art, anything goes, maybe as a kind of refuge from the storm of the art of our own day.

It is very odd that, although we all extol Bach and Rembrandt, if someone dares to make a piece of art or music in the line of these old masters, the artist is denounced as being foolish and his or her work dismissed as non-art. We go to the museum and we admire the many wonderful portraits of the past, but it is very hard to find a contemporary portraitist. Between 1900 and 1940 a great break took place in our culture which, for instance, meant the loss of portraitists. The portraitists that are still there either make popular art or covers for magazines like *Time*.

The third category of art that is around us today is twentieth-century art. I intentionally use the neutral term 'twentieth-century art'. This art is no longer naturalistic but makes use of a new style, a new way of depicting, derived from a new understanding that art is a language. We could call it expressionism, if the term is used very broadly. We could call it neoclassicism, but of a new kind. A Maillol is unlike any sculpture that was neoclassical before, and the difference is what I would call its expressionistic quality. It is the change from the Middle Ages to the Renaissance in reverse: they went from forms that pointed beyond themselves to a kind of naturalistic rendering and now we have gone from naturalism to forms that symbolize something. The subject matter of most twentieth-century art is normal reality, working in the tradition of realism. In this category fall the school of Paris between the two world wars, Matisse, Stanley Spencer, Nash, Maillol, Epstein, in music Stravinsky, not his newest period but before that time, Milhaud, Britten, Bartók, New Orleans jazz, the architecture of the Rockefeller Centre, writers like T.S. Eliot and maybe Hemmingway. What about more contemporary examples (from around 1970)? This type of art is still around though it is getting weaker. We can mention the sculptor Manzú, parts of Coventry Cathedral, tapestries, films, and in literature C.S. Lewis and Tolkien. Maybe the Beatles, Bob Dylan and Leonard Cohen also belong here. In general this art does not ask for heated discussions, it is appreciated by the many, it is less extreme than modern art, less difficult, more normal and more human.

Is this really the art of our times? Do these artists tone their work down in order to reach the public, maybe even for commercial reasons? Are the values they stand for empty? Are they bourgeois? These questions need to be asked, as honest questions, not as rhetorical ones. These artists stand beside the stream that is the strongest in our time, for they just want to make works that are beautiful and good. To me that is what an artist ought to do. Maybe the critics just do not dare to consider this better or more important than modern art; they have to be 'with it' otherwise the snobs will turn their backs on them.

Then we come to the modern art of Picasso and so on, of which the roots reach back to the seventeenth and eighteenth centuries. Modern art is the flip side of the growth of science and technology which imprisoned people in the box of scientific reason and took away human freedom. It is a desperate jump out of the box in order to assert human freedom. Modern art shows either the horror inside the box or the beauty outside it. You can make a beautiful castle on the edge of a deep abyss, which is full of slimy, dangerous creatures, and never look down into it – that is what people in the line of Mondrian do. But some do look down and what you see there you can paint either abstractly as the abstract Surrealists do or more precisely as is done by Surrealists like Dali. Pop also shows the negative side, but not always; it can be twentieth-century art as well. When people dare to look down into the abyss of lost freedom, of a rational world turned irrational, of the strange and dangerous, then they find that built into this art is often protest and, politically speaking, anarchism.

Modern art is driven by the slogan that art has to have a connection with its time. It is very interesting that in the nineteenth century the progressive artists said exactly the opposite: they tried to make art autonomous and for art's sake, which meant art that was elevated above all matters of morality and that could go its own way. Art was separated from its own times with the unhappy result, however, that no one had any need for art anymore. But now art has to be relevant and committed again in a desperate attempt to restore to art a meaningful place. Yet, when I look at modern art, is there really any connection with the world in which I live? When we look at the pictures of these people who say they are committed, we cannot find any trace of their commitment. They do not talk about Vietnam or racial relationships or anything like that. What is the relationship between Picasso's heads of women that he made around 1940 and the war that was just beginning? Even his *Guernica* shows suffering and despair, but not that particular village in Spain or the bombing. It talks about the human predicament and the tragedy of violence, but not about a specific war. Modern art breaks taboos, challenges bourgeois values and heralds the end of humanism, but does it really reflect our time? When I walk around in the modern art museum, do I see the twentieth century?

Truth

Is modern art true? My answer is 'yes' and 'no'. 'Yes', it is twentieth-century in that it speaks of existentialist angst, despair, meaninglessness, absurdity, the things the philosophers of our time talk about as well, the failure (*échec*) of humanism. We have come to realize what it means to live in a world without a God. Values have lost their foundation; there is emptiness, alienation; we are threatened by technology: all these things are true. William Barrett in his book *Irrational Man* says that 'Modern art begins and sometimes ends as a confession of spiritual poverty. When mankind no longer lives spontaneously turned towards God or the supernatural world, the artist too must stand face to face with a flat and inexplicable world'. Yes, in this sense modern art gives voice to the problems of our time.

But at the same time we have to say 'no', modern art has nothing to do with the twentieth century and the problems of our day. It hardly ever speaks about concentration camps, race problems or social injustice. Modern artists do not dare talk about things like that, because then they might become propagandist, and they would also have to use imagery and enter the realm of what they would call 'non-art'. What they rather express is a negative experience of reality. It is an interpretation of reality, a view, a spiritual attitude, a revolutionary activity.

So is modern art true? Yes, it is true as an expression of a minority, as an articulation of their spiritual agony, not mine, maybe not yours. Even if it is true for many, it still is just a view. There are many people – also artists – who have another view. Is that not why people keep on asking me to explain modern art to them? If sixty years after an event people still need it to be explained to them, that means either that the people are extremely stupid or that the event is something very strange. This leads us to the more general question of truth in art. Already in 1840 Ruskin said that truth in art is a matter not of imitation but of faithful statements about a fact in history. In my view truth is related to structure, norm and meaning. First, what is structure? It is the way something is build up and how it relates to a larger whole. When you make a cast of someone and colour it in a very naturalistic way, have you then depicted that person? I do not think so. What you have done does not say anything about this person; you have not told us anything about his or her particular structure. When an artist with just a few lines says something about the way someone moves or behaves, then it becomes truth. The paintings of historical events may be a good example: a painter may give all the facts and details of a certain historical situation, but they remain meaningless if the artist does not clarify the structure of the situation, namely its significance in the course of history. It is reported that Luther never said, 'Here I stand, I cannot do otherwise,' when he was called before the emperor. Yet these words very clearly reveal the structure of Luther's actions, so the truth is that Luther did say these words there on that occasion, even if in factual history he never did. Though I am not at all a modern theologian, I do think the Bible often does the same thing. It tells us the meaning and the structure of events rather than what actually happened. You can even trace quite a few mistakes in the Bible if you read it from a modernist perspective of truth, which is factuality. But the Bible does not talk about the facts, it talks about much more; while taking the facts into account – it is not a leap into spirituality – it talks about the meaning of things, which is much more important than the little facts.

Art (except naturalism) speaks about the structure of things. It shows us more than the eye can see, more than a camera can record. Structure is always related to norms. When you are sketching a landscape, for example, and at a certain moment a deer jumps over the road, you may finish your sketch with a deer. Is that true or false to the situation? You include it because it belongs to the structure of the wood that there are animals. So you paint the wood how it should be, not just how you saw it at a certain moment. When you see an ugly heap of rubbish in the foreground of your landscape, are you going to include it in your picture, yes or no? I would say 'no' because it does not belong; or you may include it just to show that it does not belong.

So structure is related to norm, and norms are closely related to meaning. Things become meaningful if they are according to the norm and they lose their meaning if they are not according to the norm. Sin always destroys meaning. A meaningful relationship that took years to build up can be destroyed by just a few sinful words. Or an act can be positive, according to the norm, and then it will be constructive. If you visit a newly married couple and you comment on how beautiful their love is, you will strengthen the reality of their love. A historical act loses its meaning if it is not shown in its relationship to the norm, the good or the evil. That is the problem with our so-called neutral news reporting, which just tells us what happened but never whether something is good or bad.

The structures and norms are universal and given by God in Creation. They are there to be used by us as possibilities. Love in a community, for instance, is not just given to us but is something we must create. It is a possibility, we can be beautiful people, but we have to give form to this possibility. We have to make it concrete, for the universal structures and norms never exist as universals but always in specific, concrete and individual forms. Reality is always the concrete realization of a given possibility. Take America. Columbus landed in America once and then people opened up its possibilities with the (mixed) result of the present USA.

In art, truth is always incorporated in the style and the given form which show our understanding of the norms and structures. Art lays bare the structure of things. The reality of these things, however, is not once and for all the same but is shaped by people in history. It is a dynamic reality.

Why do we paint nudes? Nudes are not part of our everyday reality; there are no nudes walking in the streets. They portray something which is not so much socially true as it is true in a deeper sense. Nudes are painted because through them we gain a deeper understanding of our humanity, and something of the beauty of life can be opened up to us. Nudes can also be lies, however, being either pulled down and pornographic or lifted up and idealistic.

To do the truth

We as human beings have to conquer reality, we have to reconquer our relationship with reality again and again. Why should any boy or girl ever compose another love poem? All the love poems that needed to be made have already been made? Just take a book and select one, why should you want to write a new one? Because you want to talk not about past loves but about *your* love. You have to reconquer the reality of love, to rediscover its structure and to realize the possiblity, it is never just a matter of course. Therefore art in all ages talks about the same old thing and we have never finished with the subject. Not only because we can always discuss a new facet but also because the reality itself is dynamic; the old is always new and the new is always a modification of the old.

Also the cursedness of our world, sin and judgment belong to the realm of truth. In art too we can never by-pass these things, unless we want to end up with empty idealism, sentimentality and a lack of strong reality. The tragic results from the conflict between our fallen state and the structure or norm of how we should have been, form the tension between our longings and desires and the boundaries of what is possible. We always have to bring this into our art somehow for the art to be true, really true. If we do not, we minimize the battle for truth against sin and evil. That is why when I make a landscape I need to show how we have polluted reality, otherwise my painting will be idealized beyond recognition and truth. Sin makes a lie out of reality and takes away freedom. That is why we have to fight for truth, which means taking a stand for the norms, opening the God-given structures, seeking true freedom. That is what it means to do the truth, a term used in John 3:21. Many people think truth is just a matter of definition, but truth is rather a matter of doing. Descartes said that truth is that which is autonomous and always true. He talked about eternal truths, using as an example that only one straight line is ever possible between two points. The Christians in his time laughed heartily when he said that, because what does it have to do with truth? Truth is something completely different. The Cartesian straight line is a fact, for sure, but whether it is true depends on one's conception of truth.

Doing the truth is to work according to the norm, but it will be without meaning if it is done without love. Without love it is without truth and therefore a lie, Paul says in 1 Corinthians 13. Truth is always relative to Christ as Love incarnate, Creator, King and Redeemer. These are not just nice Christian phrases but words about the only solution to the problems posed by modern art, which is a new gnostic art. The gnostics say this world is a rotten world, it is a lie, and in doing the lie they are breaking down reality. We have to understand that our truth and their lies are related to the same thing, namely to Christ, to whom they say 'no' and we say 'yes'. To do the truth is to build up, to serve the good, to show the fruit of the Spirit, to have the mentality that Christ preached in the Sermon on the Mount. We should, for instance, hunger and thirst for righteousness, which means that we should show up evil as evil, and ugly as ugly; yet we should do so with compassion and love.

Doing the truth also concerns giving art its right place and making art in accordance with the function it has to fulfil. Art does the truth in the unity between form and subject matter, and in the choice of a style that expresses what the artist wants to say about a subject in the best possible way. Truth in art includes the fantastic, for fantasy can be very true. Our art, moreover, has to honour God, yet let's be very careful not to use his name in vain. It may not honour his name to use it again and again. To honour God is to show the world as an open world with hope, redeemed by Christ from the curse of the Law (Romans 7). If Christ had not come, the gnostics and modern art would be right: it would be a curse to be part of this world and a hell to be human.

Choice

I believe that my concept of truth is a biblical one, and to back this up I will give some quotes from the Bible. First John 3:12, where Christ talks about doing the truth and doing evil, words I use as well. Peter says in 1 Peter 3:10–11: 'He that would love life and see good days, let him keep his tongue from evil and his lips from speaking guile, let him turn away from evil and do right. Let him seek peace and pursue it.' To do the truth is not just to show the ugliness, it may equally well be to cover up sin. I recently read about a school where one of the teachers homosexually abused one of the boys. This man was slowly and gently removed from the school, without letting everybody know why. After he died, it came out in the open. The man who wrote the article blamed the school for not making the facts known at the time, but in promoting openness in cases like this we might in fact be promoting the sin, so that we are breaking things down and doing the lie instead of the truth. The same applies to art.

John says in 1 John, 'If we claim to be without sin, we deceive ourselves and the truth is not in us.' Truth here is not conceptual truth. Goodness and truth are very much akin in the Bible, as we see in Proverbs 8:7, 'My mouth speaks what is true, for my lips detest wickedness.' Therefore it is not so strange that Christ says 'I am the truth.' He does not say 'I'm true, I'm a true concept, it's a fact I do exist.' No he says 'I am the truth,' by which he means that he is working in love towards the good.

When we connect art with truth, are we then bringing art and morals together and saying that art is basically moral and not aesthetic? My answer is 'no'. Art has little to do with moral precepts and rules. And art certainly does not become good art when it is morally right. But art as art and in the way of art is about beauty, truth and the opening up of reality. Art is never only about morals; it is about much more than morals. The artistically meaningful never stands apart from love, truth, life and creation.

A last question: Can we as Christians make modern art, in the sense of John Cage, Hockney, Bergman or Kienholz? Can we make abstract paintings of red and blue or pure as white? My answer should be clear by now: no, we cannot, because modern art comes out of a view of life that is not compatible with ours. This, however, leads to another question: Can we be different? I think we can but it is far from easy, because truth is never easy. In a way this lecture is a struggle with the problems involved. Yet there is enough going on in contemporary art that we can tie in with. We do not need to be modern in order to be up to date. Above all, we need to be honest. We need to do the truth, build up, in a way that is appropriate for today. I am not asking anyone to go back in history: that would be silly. Are we willing to stand alongside the bigger stream and take our place, maybe just in a little side-stream? I am thinking here about one of the last verses of Revelation: 'Let the evildoers stay evil, and the filthy stay filthy, and let the righteous do right, and let the ones who are holy keep themselves holy.' That is the choice we need to make.

Hermeneutics of Art[46]

One of the questions that puzzle most people involved with art is the question of interpretation. In my lectures (particularly the ones with slides) I do interpret art and often people come to me afterwards and ask, 'How do you know?' In the following I want to try and formulate an answer. I will start with a number of basic and very important thoughts in the introduction. The second part goes into the negative as it deals with why we ask this question and what has caused the problems in our thinking in this area. The third part is positive again as it searches for a different approach.

Introduction

Is there any certainty in our interpretation of art? The first and foremost assertion I want to make is that nothing is certain in this life. All our human thinking is limited and open to correction. The Bible is full of this. Vanity of vanities, this is our knowledge. When we think we know something, the next generation comes and wipes it away again. We see as in a mirror. One of the most beautiful chapters in the Bible is the end of Job, where God takes Job by the hand and says, 'Now, look.' And God shows him creation and says, 'Do you understand the clouds, the waves, the rivers and the sea?' Twentieth-century people might say, 'Of course, we understand. It is H_2O and it has this kind of a cycle.' But even when we have investigated water and know its cycle and what it is made of, we should still stand in awe, because in the end we do not understand it. The more we go into it, the more complex even these simple things become. And Job says in the end: 'I don't know.'

There is only one thing that is completely certain, and that is God himself. God is not relative, but everything else is. What we call reality is his creation and as such dependent on and referring back to God. Jesus says, 'The Word remains in eternity. I am the truth, the way and the life, the beginning and the end, the alpha and the omega.' Only he and his words are certain. But what we say, what we think, what we know, all of that is not certain. This very important assertion is basic to all our understanding.

The second point we need to make is that nevertheless there are many things that are completely certain. It is certain, for instance, that I am sitting here on a chair and that there are people in this room. I call this our naïve knowledge, while by 'naïve' I mean pre-scientific or pre-philosophical. We all live on a naïve level. That means that we take things for granted, even if they have not been philosphically ascertained, and that we are not doubting everything.

Of course we can make mistakes. You can walk behind somebody and think it is a woman, and later find out it is a man. We make all kinds of mistakes, but we know that we make them. And we know that we can ascertain things in our everyday experience. I may be very certain that I am sitting in this room in Hornton Place. Maybe later on I will find out that I have been dreaming that I was here, when I wake up and say, 'It was only a dream.' But when I wake up, then I know that it was a only dream. Even then there is certainty.

Our more conceptual type of knowledge is based on this naïve type of knowledge. No scientist, no philosopher can ever live without naïve knowledge, because that is what they refer to. If as an art historian I stand before a painting of Rembrandt, I have my naïve experience and knowledge of that Rembrandt. As a scholar I will ask all kinds of questions: When was it made? How was it made? What does it mean? These questions are in themselves scientific questions, but they are always referring back to my first naïve experience. Because if I was not completely certain that there was a painting and that it represented a man on horseback, it would be silly to ask why the man is on horseback or why the horse is black. This is also true of the scientist who deals with the physical world. No scientist can say that water is H_2O, unless he or she knows water before trying to analyse it. That is basic to our knowledge. So, we are very certain of this world, which is the world in which God placed us.

Nothing can be done without this basic form of knowledge, which comes prior to any science or scholarship. I emphasize this so much because one of the great myths of contemporary Western culture is that nothing is certain unless science makes it certain. I completely reverse that statement and say: it is our knowledge and science that are not certain, while it is very certain that we are here and that there is a world outside of us and that there is a Rembrandt that depicts a man on horseback.

My next assertion (the third point) is that our view and understanding of reality are based in our faith. Our faith colours our vision, it determines the way we look at the world. If people say to me, 'But the way you look at things is tied up with your faith and the tradition of which you are a part,' then I say, 'Yes, my naïve way of seeing and understanding things is a coloured vision.' We all look through tinted glasses. We should not be dismayed by this, because it is simply part of being human. Yet, while everyone has his or her particular faith and background, we do have our humanness in common. We differ from each other similar to the way tea differs from coffee: both are 95 per cent water and the remaining 5 per cent gives them their unique taste and colour. We as people are 95 per cent human and 5 per cent our own colour. Christians may be coffee and humanists tea, but we are all largely water.

In science [which in my usage of the word includes philosophy, the humanities and all scientific endeavour] we think about reality. But the world we think about – this was the second proposition – is the world we know through our naïve knowledge. The difference between Christian and non-Christian science therefore is that each thinks about different worlds. God gave us his revelation as a key to understand this world. Christians use the key and see the world through those glasses. They, for instance, know there is a God who created this world. The difference between Christians and non-Christians is that they see different things because they look in a different way. If you read a book by any art historian, you will very soon know whether the author is a Roman Catholic or a Protestant or a humanist.

And this brings me to the next point, namely that it is one of the great miracles of reality that there is discernment. (A miracle in the Bible has to do with the wonderful way in which the world is made; it is, for instance, a miracle that the birds sing in the morning, and that they know when to go to the South and when to return, etc.) We can know that we look through tinted glasses and we can discern that somebody else is looking through a different set of glasses. That means that we know that we have our presuppositions and that other people have theirs. Sometimes it is difficult to discern our own and to get out of them. But we are not caught in a hermeneutic circle as many think today: How can you really know anything, because you have your presuppositions, and you look at things from your presuppositions, but you also read your presuppositions from the things you are looking at? I would say that philosophically speaking this is a very difficult problem to tackle, but that I know from my own experience that I can know whether a work is by a Roman Catholic or a humanist. I can make mistakes there. Nothing is certain. I stated that at the beginning. But one of the basic miracles of human reality is communication. We can understand it when somebody says or makes something, and that exactly is art. Of course, sometimes we don't understand and we know it, that is part of our humanity. I may stand before a painting and say, 'Well, this might be made by a Roman Catholic, I admit that there are many possibilities of making mistakes, I know that I don't know. But I do know that this is a painting and that Mary is the subject matter and that . . .'

Our vision is coloured. Nobody is without colour. Yet it is one of the great quests of people today to be colourless.

The quest for certainty

Where does this quest for certainty come from? Why are my students always so frightened when they find out that I am saying these things? After having studied with me for some time they always come to me with a big question: 'Do you really mean that everything is subjective?' They are always very shaken to find out that I am fighting for subjectivity in knowledge. And I answer, 'Of course, everything we say is human and therefore subjective.' But the 'of course' is hard to accept, because everybody wants to be certain and to have objective certainty. And my big question is, 'Why?'

I think that the source of this desire to be certain is that modern people want to be autonomous. They want to look at a world without God. They want to have certainty within creation and base themselves on something in reality. However, twentieth-century people have only one certainty left and that is that there are atoms. The interesting thing is that people who look through superstrong microscopes do not see atoms; when enlarged like that, the atoms become waves and 'evaporate'. So, in the end, even the certain thing becomes uncertain. And I would say, 'Obviously so,' because nothing is certain in this world. You cannot make an idol out of material things, you will always fall down. But even so – and this is the real quest of humanity, this is our being fallen, this is our sin – we want to have certainty outside of God. We do not want to accept God's revelation and say, 'Thank you Lord, this is the key to understanding the world.' Science is a human invention in order to search for certainty outside of revelation. It is the myth of our time that this is possible. It is the great slogan of modernism that knowledge is power. We want to know, and the more certain our knowledge, the greater our power.

When I want to know how I can be certain, one question will become most important, and that is the question of epistemology. This is the great change that occurred in our culture and at the beginning of modern science, that people started to put epistemology first and ontology second. They wanted to first think about knowledge and then about being as they wanted to make sure that what they said about being was based on true knowledge. But in fact, it is the other way around. You can never have an epistemology unless you first have an ontology. If you do not know that you are, how can you know that you know? I just read a very deep discussion of Kant which stated that Kant smuggled in ontology in order to be able to start with his epistemology. When he begins with 'How can I know through pure reason?' this presupposes that there is pure reason. That is why I said first of all 'God is.' That is completely certain and all other certainties follow.

Descartes was searching for certainty. He asked, 'Of what can I be really, really certain?' So he prays to Mary – he was a devout Roman Catholic – and says, 'Mary, I promise I will go on a pilgrimage, if you show me a point that I can be completely certain of.' And then he has his vision and makes his pilgrimage and writes his book *Discourse on Method*. When you read this book, which is written in 1637, you will find that the absolute point of certainty for him is: 'I think and therefore I am.' In other words, I can never get out of this that I think. I would say, 'Obviously so,' because that is one of my own assertions, that one of the things we are completely certain of is that we think. But I would never make that a starting point, because you can only be certain about this if you first have the other statement, that there is nothing that is certain and true in itself because it always has to be God's truth. The interesting thing is that Descartes knew this as well. He added a second statement 'and God is' as he knew that the first point is not completely certain. He needs God in order to make sure that what he thinks is true. But if you really analyse it, you will see that his God is based on his own thoughts, and not his thoughts on God. This is the change we need to fight.

Thinking became the starting point, which according to Descartes needs to be clear and distinct. Yet when measured by his own standards we have to say that what he said was certainly clear, but it was not distinct; it was all muddled thought. Descartes's system does not even stand the test of his own principles.

Descartes wants to have autonomous thinking about an autonomous world. That is why he began to talk about 'two and two is four'. We have all heard the argument that whether we are a Christian or a humanist, we all agree that two and two is four. At this point we should be very critical, because this is the crux of Cartesian thinking. It means that 'two and two is four' is an eternal law, and that it is true independent of who you are and who God is. When Descartes said these things for the first time, everybody laughed because it was so obvious that he was wrong. We are so brainwashed now that everybody agrees that he was right. But we must understand that he was not. Why did he want to have 'two and two is four'? Because he wanted to get God out of the picture and start with autonomous human being, which you can only have if you have autonomous nature, eternal laws of nature that stand on their own.

Galileo brought in a second characteristic of modern thinking. In the Middle Ages (as C.S. Lewis's *The Discarded Image* makes very clear) everybody knew that the world is round and that around it the stars and planets are circling. Now these planets move in strange ways. How can we account for this? Or, in medieval terminology, how can we save the appearances? For that is what our theories do: by explaining they try to save the appearances. Medieval scholars developed several complex calculations to account for the movement of the planets. Then Galileo comes with a new system and says, 'It's very simple if you make one basic assertion, and that is that the sun is in the centre and not the earth.' Everybody said, 'Hurray, now we have a better theory.' But then Galileo added something, 'And it is really like that, the sun is really in the centre.' And then they all said no, because Galileo made an enormous jump by stating that our theories about reality are reality itself. Yet it is exactly on that assumption that all our science is based, even though the really advanced scholars of our time know that this is not true. So we should be aware that science gives us no more than theories about reality. Whether they are true or not, who knows?

Then Locke wrote his *Essay Concerning the Human Understanding* (1690), a book that was very popular and influential in its time, comparable to Darwin's writings in the nineteenth and Freud's in the twentieth century. It is the book that changed the world. He says, 'All knowledge is based on sensation and reflection.' There are sensation or perception lines coming from the outside which we receive and on the basis of these lines we make ideas inside our mind. Outside is a big X we do not know anything about. But out of this big X happily some perception lines come which are arranged by me in space and time. So, there is not a woman sitting there, I do not know what is sitting there. I only know that some lines are coming to me, and that I arrange them in space and time into a woman. I call it a woman but, of course, that is my idea.

We could summarize Locke's proposition as follows: we know what we see. In that way he has reduced knowledge to only what we can ascertain by your senses. Anything that is outside of our senses, we do not know. Can you prove that God exists? Of course not. Do angels exist, or the Devil? Old fairy tales no one believes in anymore, not even most Christians. So that was the next step: while for Descartes, God was still somewhat part of the picture, Locke completely chased him out. Locke provided the basis for a humanistic theory that takes its departure from human being. The very first day we enter college or university we are brainwashed with the neutrality postulate, the basic principle that we ought to be neutral. We ought to look for the facts, the things we can see, weigh and measure. We ought to think as if we had no 'colour'. Colour is fine for our private lives, but when we are in the classroom we should talk as neutral beings. And that is because God needs to be kept outside the door. They always say, 'But we are neutral?' I answer, 'You are not neutral, for your neutrality system itself is not neutral.'

Art as the obscure

Where is art in this system? Art, of course, is not in this system, as it is not clear and distinct. Art is not something that can be weighed or measured. I always get this horrible question, 'How can you prove that this painting is beautiful?' The only answer is that this question is wrong, because it comes out of the Cartesian-Lockian framework and within that framework there is no answer to this question, because on that basis there is no proof.

In books on art you will always find the assertion that Baumgarten was the first aesthetician. However, Baumgarten was not the first one, because we have in fact a library full of books on art before we come to Baumgarten. Just think of Plato and Aristotle. But based on modern principles, Baumgarten is the first. Based on mine, he is the beginning of the end. Bonsanquet, who wrote an introduction to aesthetics that has been used by many generations, places Baumgarten in the line of Descartes, Spinoza, Leibniz and Wolff. And it occurs to Baumgarten 'to prefix to the Wolffian logic and method of clear knowledge a prior science or method of sensible or obscure knowledge, and that's aesthetics'. Aesthetics, in other words, is in principle obscure knowledge. 'Baumgarten is thoroughly consistent. Inductive logic and the theory of space and time both belong to the doctrine of clear knowledge. But the subject of aesthetics is obscure conception as being obscure. That is a knowledge in the form of feeling and remaining in that form.' To modern aesthetics the arts are a form of unclear and indistinct knowledge.

So, if people ask me the question, 'How do you know your interpretation is right?' they all have in the back of their minds: Baumgarten said that art is in principle unclear. It means that Baumgarten was a Cartesian with a minus before it, because Descartes was talking about things that are clear and distinct and Baumgarten about those that are unclear and indistinct and therefore can never be proved. If that were true, I would quit tomorrow. Why should I think about art any longer?

Peter Gay deals with the Enlightenment and its relationship to art in the second of his two deep and very well researched books on that time called *The Enlightenment, the Science of Freedom.* He says, 'Scientific thinking is exactly the stripping away of theological, metaphysical, aesthetic and ethical admixtures that had been a constituent part of science since the Greeks. Scientific philosophers of the eighteenth century treat these admixtures as impurities, as survivors of earlier stages of consciousness.' And people are still trying to get these impurities out of the way. As soon as you have a moral judgement on a work of art, they say, 'You are wrong. That's moral.' As a critical person, you do not talk about that.

> Every scientific discovery weakened the hold of theological explanation, metaphysical empathy, and aesthetic considerations. The orbits of the planets were neither beautiful nor ugly. The law of gravitation was neither cruel nor kind. Observed irregularities in the skies proved nothing about divine activity. When it thunders, God is not acting. Every improvement of scientific terminology or mathematical formulation further liberates the scientist from old antropomorphic conceptions of the world and reduced to irrelevance many of the old questions.

Nature is not beautiful and Paul is mistaken when he says, 'Look at the world and you will understand God.' Eighteenth-century people have transcended this, because now they are intelligent apes. And intelligent apes do not look at nature to find a God, because apes do not have religion.

According to the standards of modern science, the Bible is not true. And because to me the Bible is true, I have a big question about modern science. There are implications, because modern science is made to exclude God. Whenever people tell you that you are old-fashioned because you still believe in the Bible, you should answer, 'No, I'm not old-fashioned, but I do have a different epistemology and a different starting point. Your faith is different from my faith.'

We are asked to be objective, to be factual, which means that we base ourselves on those things that are autonomously there, outside of God or human being. Does the planet Venus really exist, as an entity in itself, completely autonomously? Yes, it does. But we have to add: and it does not mean a thing. What is meaning in the modern line of thinking? Meaning is what we add to it. Venus has no meaning, we add meaning to it. It is completely objectively true that there is a heap of atoms which we call Venus. Now, I may say that Venus is beautiful, but that is something I add to it, because that is not a fact and you can never prove it. In this way we have killed reality. All meaning is only my interpretation. Outside of me, this is what Kant said, things are just things in themselves, without meaning.

C.S. Lewis goes into this as well: 'The advance of knowledge gradually emptied this rich and genial universe [of pre-modern times]. First of its gods, then of its colours, smells, sounds and tastes.' All these are taken from the world, they are transferred to the subjective side of the account. They are classified as our sensations, our thoughts, our images, our emotions. 'The subject becomes inflated at the expense of the object. But the method does not end here. The same method, which has emptied the world, now procedes to empty ourselves.' And so he comes to the conclusion that the subject has turned out to be as empty as the object and we have ended with nothing.

Susanne Langer, one of the main aestheticians today, has a chapter in her recommendable book *Philosophy in a New Key* (1948) called 'The fabric of meaning'. She says,

> The desire to construct a world picture out of facts superceded the older ambition to weave a fabric of values, in which things and events were intepreted as manifestations of good and evil, related to powers, wills, minds, but not essentially to each other ... The new facts were not the real destroyers, but the new eyes that saw them ... We have inherited a naïve faith in the substantiality and ultimacy of facts. Facts are our very measure of value ... To exchange fictions, faiths and 'constructed systems' for facts is Modern Man's supreme value. Hence his periodic outbursts of 'debunking' traditions, religious or legendary, his satisfaction with stark realism in literature, his suspicion and impatience of poetry, and perhaps on the naïve and uncritical level of the average mentality, the passion for news.

The loss of meaning

In his book *Saving the Appearances,* Owen Barfield writes about similar things to what his friend C.S. Lewis talks about in *The Discarded Image.* In his book we find many quotes of Milton, because Milton in his *Paradise Lost* was the last man who summed up the old world view. Milton shows us what the world looked like before modern science killed it: things of beauty are still beautiful and do not need proof in a way in which you can never prove it. In order to explain what has happened, Barfield uses the term 'participation'. The old pagan people considered trees, clouds and mountains to be loaded with divinity, to be participating in the god or gods (or the gods were participating in them). That is why you had dryads and so on. The world was charged with meaning, in the sense of divine meaning, deities, spirits and demons. People did not just go and take water out of a well. They first had to appease the demon of the well. And the water was loaded with meaning, it was a godly drink out of which comes life. It revives you when you drink it. Why? Not because the liquid level of your body is restored, as modern people would say, but because there is real power in the water. In a way the ancient pagans were right: reality is laden with godly meaning.

The wonder of biblical thinking, however, is that everything participates yet nothing is made into a god. Genesis 1 tells us that the sun, the moon, the clouds and the trees are all creatures, which means that they participate. They are not simply there, they are not autonomous, they are made by God. Thunder is not just thunder, but sometimes God is in the thunder, as is stated in the book of Job. And lightning is made out of electricity, but that is not what lightning is. I am very interested in the scientists' statements that the sun is made of hot gasses. But when they say that the sun is only hot gasses, then I protest because they have left out everything that is valuable. The pagans who bowed down to the sun as their god were not foolish. If God is forgotten, then the sun is a god. But the Bible says that the sun is not a god but a creature, and that God gave it to us. And sometimes we pray, 'Lord, please let some cloud come to hide the sun, it is too scorching.' This is participation in the biblical sense.

Medieval participation is somewhere in between the biblical and the pagan participation. Things were laden with meaning. Then comes modern thinking and all participation is destroyed. Things come to be seen as just things in themselves and because of this we have lost so much.

In his book *The Changing Nature of Man,*[47] J.H. van den Berg deals with the changes that occurred at the end of the Middle Ages. In 1300, he says, people began to open up human beings in order to do research. They also investigated the human heart. According to the old system the heart is the centre of life, as we have to love our Lord with all our heart. They had developed a theory about the heart that agreed with their concept of the heart as the centre of life. The theory implied that there was a hole between the left and the right sides of the heart. Then they began to dissect the heart, and what did they see? They saw a hole, and they went on seeing a hole for the next 250 years till Vesalius said in 1550 that there is no hole. They were very angry with Vesalius and he was almost put in jail. Why? Because he was killing something. There were deep implications. Seventy years later, in 1620, Harvey researched the blood circulation and said, 'And therefore, by God, I conclude that the heart is a pump.' What was lost? The participation and the meaning of the heart as the centre of life. This was the change.

If we want to turn the tide of modernism this is the problem we need to solve: how to say that we love the Lord our God with all our heart and at the same time say that the heart is a pump. Both are equally true. Modern science tells us we live in unparticipated nature, in a reality without God, without beauty, without love, without all qualities worth living for. Its answers are too small, because it leaves out too much. Can we bring God and participation back into the Cartesian framework again? No, we cannot, because it was conceived precisely to exclude God. We cannot baptize the Cartesian line, because it was made to never be baptized.

Modern science constructs reality on the basis of our thoughts about it. The first man to do the same in art was Masaccio. By using perspective, he constructed a world which was just like the world you see outside, but it was his own construction. Who were the first people to depict unparticipated nature? Look at the Renaissance pictures and you will see the world as the eye sees it. A Madonna? She is just a woman with a baby. How do you know it is the Madonna? Because a woman sitting with a baby in a landscape had been a Madonna for many centuries. But that is our interpretation, after all, we only see a woman. So, we start with our senses and try to reconstruct what we have seen with our senses, which is unparticipated nature, and then we ourselves need to add the meaning. That is why the title of the painting becomes so important. Semiology or semiotics today are based in the same epistemology, as people hold that things in themselves do not mean a thing but that we give them meaning by inventing words for them.

Artists like Masaccio spearheaded these developments. It is my dream that artists today will be the vanguard of a new epistemology and thinking.

Meaning

When we now come to this lecture's third part in which I want to try and formulate my own position, the first question we need to answer is: What is reality? Reality is not an accidental heap of atoms but reality is loaded with meaning. We do not just add this meaning, but the meaning is there and we try to grasp it. We could take the example of a tree or water[48] and all their qualities and functions. They are so full of meaning that words fall far short to express it all. This reality is there and is given to us, and our task is to open it up and to realize its possibilities. That can be done by working in it or just by looking at it and trying to grasp the fullness of the meaning that is there. Just think of our great-grandparents who went on holiday to the same place every year and got to know and love the big, beautiful tree near the hotel and wept when a storm had blown it down. They loved the tree, not because of something they had added to the tree but rather because of something they had discovered about it. They did not just have their subjective feelings, but these qualities were there and they had come to know them.

The reality we have to open up is also a cultural reality, which is given to us as a possibility. It is our task to realize the possibilities. If I had gone to where London now is a very long time ago, there would have been nothing there. But there were possibilities to build a city and people discovered them and now they have been realized. Every day there are new possibilities that need to be realized and old things that need to be forsaken.

We can, however, never realize the possibilities without sinning and making wrong decisions. It is a world scarred by people in which we live. This means that when I talk about reality I can never leave out human being. Reality without human being does not even exist. Yet modern science wants to know the world as it is without people and without God. This is impossible, and some modern scientists know that it is out of the question. Their metaphor, not mine, is this: 'If you want to investigate a dark room, you can only do this by taking a lamp with you. But at the moment you put on the light, it is not a dark room anymore. So you can never investigate a dark room.'

We can also talk about the possiblities as norms and structures that are put in the world by God and have to be positivized. A good example of this is music. Jubal was the first man to take a reed and blow on it and make a little melody. Of course he did not invent anything, he only discovered the possibility of melody, as God gave the structures for melody. The amazing thing is that these structures are open structures, there are different ways in which they can be worked out. For instance, there are two places where writing was invented: in the West, in Egypt and Phoenecia and so on, people began to write horizontally; but the Chinese began to write vertically and created a very different system.

If we, however, try to make something into a structure or law which is not a law, we will always end up with tension. What is wrong just cannot be called right. I once was talking about this when somebody said, 'Yes, but in different societies people have different laws. Cannibals collect the heads of other people, and they enjoy this. To them it is a law that it is a good thing and it works just fine.' I answered, 'No, I don't believe it, because murder is murder, and that is never just fine.' Very interestingly, that same person came to me three weeks later and said, 'I have been reading a book about headhunters and I found out that every boy who has been headhunting for the first time experiences trauma that lasts for weeks or months. Some never get over it because it was so horrible.'

We know reality only very partially; no one is able to grasp the fullness of reality. That means that when you make a statement about something it may be very partial, you may have missed quite a bit, but that does not mean that you have been wrong. Yet it is commonly held today that if you do not know everything, you are not right. In my opinion you never know everything. Hence it is possible that when two people make a film about London, these films may be very different and yet both may be right, as the reality of London is so complex that nobody can grasp it fully. I would even be able to discern through what kind of glasses each of the filmmakers looked at London.

So, true knowledge may be only partial knowledge. Of course, there is also untrue knowledge by which you are contradicting reality, for you cannot just say anything. Not everything can be said, even though there can be two different statements about something that are both true. I do not only think of superficial facts here. The facts are endless. Nobody can know all the facts. But I have in mind a deeper kind of knowledge of the true nature of things, which is more than the facts and which gives meaning to the facts. That there are so many cars in London, does not tell me anything about London. But what the traffic jams mean to the mentality of the Londoners, does tell me something about London.

We always talk about reality, and reality is given to us in our naïve experience and knowledge. That means that all our knowledge is a posteriori. Descartes and Locke etc. were looking for a priori knowledge, 'I think therefore I am.' Everything was there, however, before we began to think. Prior to that is God, who made the world. There is no a priori knowledge because God is always prior to us. The best theory about reality is a theory that interprets all the things that are present as part of God's creation. The more facts and meaning we grasp in our theory, the better our theory. If it is a real good theory, we will also be able to explain why some other people had a different theory and why they made certain mistakes.

The truth we search for will always be subjective, even if we try to do it well. Truth is a relational concept. Truth is not in me, nor is truth out there. There is no true North Pole (even though it is there, whether I am there or not), but I can only say the truth about the North Pole. Truth is always relational, subjective and personal. Because when I look at something, I do not only look at it through my own glasses, but also with my own past and personal history. This should not disturb us, because our understanding of reality, the truth we propose, is always personal. The first letter I received after my book on modern art was published said it was a very nice book, but also very personal. And my first reaction was: 'Oh this is all wrong, because I do not want to tell everybody what I see and understand but I want to talk about the truth.' But after thinking about this I said: 'No, truth cannot be but personal.'

Let me give an example, as I know that I am going against modern scholarship here. I can give hundreds of hours of lectures on Rembrandt without any problem. I can tell you when he was born, which paintings he made, who influenced him and on and on, and after all those hours I will not have said anything about Rembrandt. But at the moment that I say, 'Now look at this Rembrandt, isn't it beautiful and meaningful,' and I go into it and try to really understand it, then I cannot avoid saying who I am because I dive down into the painting and have my personal talk with Rembrandt and I come up again and give you a report of my talk. And unless we go in depth and are willing to stand as one person before another, we will not be able to say anything but that the painting is so many inches by so many inches, from such and such a date, on such and such a subject. Then we end up saying nothing. If we want to say something meaningful, it has to be personal. But must truth not be objective? No, truth is personal and relational; it means you with your personality say something about something outside of you. What you say should be true, of course. Though it is coloured it does not mean that you can say anything.

This means that in all scholarship discussion is essential. When I write a book, or somebody else writes one, they are discussed in the classrooms, at conferences, in books and articles, and that is the way scholarship works. It is a continuous discussion between persons. There is no neutral science. We can collect facts. But facts as such mean nothing. They become important only when we use them in our interpretation in order to gain true knowledge. People today are very afraid of these things. Historians do nothing but publish annotated sources with clever translations of, for instance, thirteenth-century texts, but no one reads such texts in order to try and understand the thirteenth century. I believe we should fight against this scientific reduction of reality to facts only. If we reduce it to facts, we can go on collecting facts into eternity. But to what end? They give no insight.

Causing ripples

Truth is active, because it sets us in motion. Christ said that we have to *do* the truth. Truth is not something that is simply there outside of us and that we can discover. What we can discover outside is reality, and we can say something about it that is right, and that is what we call the truth. But when we discover the truth about something, we will start to act upon it. When I find out that a horse is an animal that I can tame to ride upon, I will begin to use a horse to cover distances too great to walk. As soon as I say something about something, I am already pointing it in some direction. If I say that rhythm in music is important and powerful, the next person who comes along may begin to develop rhythm because it affects us so deeply.

I often say that we see what we know.[49] This implies that all education is the opening of eyes. When we are taught something, we will start to see it and begin to work with it and open it up. To give an example in art history: around 1900 Wölfflin set forth some principles with an eye to looking at art, and he distinguished the linear, the plastic and the painterly. Nobody today is able to look at a painting without seeing the linear, the plastic and the painterly as we all have been taught to discern these qualities and we see what we know. Now we pass these principles on to our students and we open their eyes. In doing so we make them familiar with a tradition of interpretation, which is the accumulation of human experience.

What is style in art? Style is the making visible of a person's meeting with reality. Art shows us a person's understanding and knowledge of reality, which is personal truth and knowledge. The artist communicates this knowledge in an iconic way, by means of an iconic language. Style has, of course, to do with beauty as well, but I focus on language here as that is most obvious when we talk about interpretation. By means of the iconic, artists express their view of reality and show their understanding of the structure of reality. They see what they know and bring this into their paintings. When artists make a portrait, they paint what they know about the person before them. They can also talk about much more complex concepts with the help of symbols and metaphors. They always give more than the facts, more than the eye can see. And again: this is not passive but active, because in doing so they open up reality and make other people see it.

The great miracle is that when I stand before a painting all these things do communicate. The artist told us what he or she knew and we understand and see. Sometimes we have to learn the language, sometimes we have to grow in understanding of what people in a particular time were looking at and why and how they were expressing that. How, what, why, these are the questions we always ask, which means that when we stand before a work of art, we have a dialogue with the maker of the painting. Via the work of art we have a discussion about reality. When we stand before a landscape by Rubens, we say: 'Rubens, you have seen a landscape, the interesting thing is that I can see what you saw and that I can see what is right and deep in your work and where you missed the point.' The wiser and deeper we are, the more chances we have to see mistakes. A doctor may see that the woman in the painting has one rib too many. Or a connoisseur of boats may see that the ship in the drawing could never sail because a certain rope is missing. They know better than the artist. Artists only tell us what they know.

Our discussion with the work of art is in fact not a dialogue but a quadralogue between the work of art and reality and two viewers. I prefer to have two viewers because discussion is so essential. We talk with each other about what the artist did in relationship to reality. It is crucial to go to a play or movie together with others, because then we can sit down during the intermission and talk about what we have seen. In this way we begin to 'chew the cud', just like cows. And in this re-chewing is the digesting: in the discussion we begin to really understand and savour what we saw.

What about certainty, how certain can we be that our interpretation is right? That is a difficult question, but that is the question. Note that I have said that there is no certainty at all. Yet, looking at a work of art is like a mathematical equation with many unknowns. I may not know why the painter did it like this, what the subject is or the reality the painting talks about. But there are also many knowns. I see it is a painting, I see its colours and shapes and that it depicts a landscape in an expressionistic style, etc. Now there is a rule in mathematics according to which one can never solve an equation with more unknowns than knowns, but if there are an equal number of both, then one can solve it and fill in all the unknowns. In art I can usually find the solution, because most of the time there are enough knowns.

There is something which sometimes makes it very difficult to fill in the knowns and that is sin. Artists may be hiding something, or they may, for instance, pretend that they are very devout. I may sense that they made their works in a particular way only in order to avoid the Inquisition or to get a good commission. Can I prove it? Sin really breaks down communication and makes it hard to find a final solution. Then there is also my own sin, that I sometimes do not want to see something. Even so, while keeping this in mind we can speak about an artwork in a sensible way and with a certain amount of certainty. We can never say everything about a work of art and our knowledge will always be partial. But even being partial, it can be true and very meaningful. And precisely because our knowledge is partial, discussion constitutes the heart of the interpretation of art. We can never write the final book on Rembrandt, but we can write a good book that will add to the discussion. It may be such a good book that some of the older books will become obsolete. But undoubtedly tomorrow someone will write again, not because we were foolish or wrong but because the reality we talk about is so large and loaded with meaning.

Discussion is not just a sophisticated activity for the cultural elite but it is vitally important and immensely meaningful. Of course, some discussions are more worthwhile than others. We can lose ourselves in obscure details, for instance. Significant discussions, however, will have their impact on today's cultural reality. When we talk about art, we are not doing something snobbish without any meaning; rather, by discussing art we are working in this world. Because that is cultural life. Discussion is culture. Discussions shape views which may lead to action. If people today are going to the Alps as tourists it is because Turner made visual poems about them and writers like Shelley, Keats and Goethe wrote about them. But their writing came out of many unrecorded discussions which nevertheless were very active.

It is the task of the art historian to take part in the discussions that constitute contemporary culture. Art history is not just a nice hobby. It is a one-sided interest, but in talking about art we work in the world of today. In line with this I consider it my calling to go around the world to talk about art. There is a poignant Zen poem that says:

> He jumped in the water and he caused no ripples.

It is the dream of sinful humans: to do anything with no consequences. But I say, there are consequences and our work is meaningful, loaded with meaning. Even our standing in front of a Rembrandt is causing ripples. The ripples may be smaller than those generated by the speech of an important politician. But my little ripple may go on and there may be other ripples joining it and together they may build up into a big wave that will sweep away modern thinking and create a breaker of renewal and reformation.

Ultranaturalism [50]

A new view of reality

The old painters, roughly before 1750, painted the world on the basis of their knowledge of things. When they depicted a king, they painted the idea of a king, which represented the reality of kings as it existed outside of them. After 1750, due to the new epistemology, reality was reduced to what is seeable and we can experience with our senses. Perception lines reach our eyes and this perception is ordered in our heads into ideas about reality. There are no ideas or universals outside of us; they are only inside of us as a construction of our own minds. Fragonard painted around 1750, at the point of change. If we interpret his painting of the sculptor with his muse in the old way, then we say that the muse inspires the artist by showing him in a vision the sculpture he is going to make. If we interpret it in a modern manner the muse, who is now a little personification, makes an idea come up in his head and he projects it from the inside out. Before the break people had visions, after the break they have hallucinations. It is a complete reversal.

When Jan van Eyck painted a Madonna, he did not need to use a model as he based his depiction on his knowledge of the Madonna. A nineteenth-century painter of a Madonna only knows what the eye can see, so he paints a nice and lovely Italian girl with her bambino and calls her the Madonna. He can only copy particular girls acting as the Madonna. There is a great difference between Jan van Eyck and the nineteenth-century painter. When you can only copy reality, because what you see is the only source of reality and there is no other way of knowing it, there is an alienation built in. You do not know the Madonna anymore. She is gone.

Around 1830 Delacroix, who speaks about these things in his diary, longs to paint just like the old painters. What he can do is make a very precise portrait of his model, Miss Rose, because that is what he sees, but what he wants to make is something like a Titian or Rubens, and in order to do so he begins to stylize or idealize the portrait. These are new words: stylize and idealize. Titian or Rubens never stylized or idealized, but that is what Delacroix does now so that his works look like the old paintings. In fact he uses some tricks because he does not know how to paint like the old masters. It was one of the difficult problems he wrestled with.

The new understanding of reality began with the Enlightenment, when reality was conceived of as a big X that via light beams (perception) enters the box of our minds. A box, light, big X, they all call up associations with the camera. From the Lockian epistemology it was an easy step to the camera, which was invented around 1840. The next step is that a man like Delacroix runs to the shop to buy one of these new photographs and comments that the photographic machine makes much better pictures than we do. We have the tendency to distort in our mind the images that reach us via perception, but the camera presents us with images that are completely objective. This is a new conception of reality and objectivity: the ideal becomes that we look at reality as if we were a machine.

This means that in 1850 Millais, an English painter, had to ask a woman to pose for him in order to make his *Ophelia*. And that she had to float in a bathtub for days on end, because that was the only way the artist could paint Ophelia. If you look at this painting very carefully you still see the traces of the bathtub.

Just a few years later Manet takes a step further by not painting a great subject like love and beauty inspiring man but, in a naturalistic way of painting asking for realistic subjects, just a very ordinary and dubious luncheon on the lawn. People in Paris were shocked, because it showed things as they are, objectively.

In his book *Transformations in Late Eighteenth-century Art*, Rosenblum discusses another painting by Manet:

> Indeed by the 1860s the definitive assault was made upon the idea that a work of art could exist primarily as a conveyer of absolute moral values. In 1867 Manet had painted the death of the ill-fated Austrian Archduke Maximillian who's execution at the hands of a Mexican firing squad on a sunny June morning in 1867 was considered a barbarous outrage for civilized standards of political morality. Yet Manet conceived this horrific event in terms that evoke no moral standards at all. There is a kind of moral anaesthesia, an emotional nullity that at least for mid twentieth-century spectators is perhaps more moving because it is now more true than the older art.

Rosenblum ends with this, 'Just as Manet had destroyed so many other fixed values of the Western tradition, Manet annihilates once and for all any excepted system of Christian or classical morality; as such Manet's painting introduces the moral conditions, or rather the absence of them, that still prevail in Western art and history.'

The cornerstone for the permissiveness of today was laid at this moment in history. It is the end of morality and absolutes as they were conceived of in earlier times. Susanne Langer in her book *Philosophy in a New Key* sheds light on this development as well, when she says that

> The attitude of modern man towards the world is the complete submission to what he conceives as hard, cold fact ... Where a former age would have judged persuasive oratory largely on its origins in God or the Devil, i.e. in the right or the wrong camp, we profess to judge it on the merits of alleged facts, and fall to the party that can muster up the most spectacular cases.

A new mentality was born based on a new way of understanding reality.

Cold facts

When in 1635 Van Dyck painted Charles I, he did not portray him sitting on his throne with his crown and other royal paraphernalia, because in that setting it would have been very difficult to make the king look really kingly. Instead he painted the king while he was hunting, implying that if the king already looked so regal while he was only hunting, how royal and imposing he would be when he was really acting as king. In that way he idealized this Mr Charles up into the King of England. When in 1870 Gerôme made a painting of Frederick the Great, he also portrayed the king in his hunting clothes. But here the king is not idealized up; rather, he is idealized down. Instead of making the king look really kingly, his kingliness is destroyed.

When artists become objective conveyers of the perception lines that reach their eyes, they no longer paint what they know. They can only copy what is right in front of their eyes, as reality itself has become alien to them. Their models could be interchanged for pieces of marble or plastic of the same proportions and colours and it would not make any difference, the resulting paintings would be exactly the same. In a way these paintings have become completely abstract, for the knowledge and therefore the reality of whatever is painted is gone.

The etching *The philosopher* of around 1890 by Max Klinger, a German painter, brings out another point. In this work we see a man looking at a landscape. There is a woman in the foreground who represents his inspiration. This philosopher soon finds out, however, that he is basically looking at himself, as in a mirror. If it is true that all reality is just our interpretation of the perception lines that reach our eyes, landscapes do not really exist. Landscapes are our own invention, which means that, when we look outside and say that there is a beautiful landscape out there, we are saying something that we have made ourselves. That means at the moment we start to look for objective reality, everything becomes subjective. The objective and the subjective become the same; they are two sides of the same coin.

Slowly we have moved towards a world that has become devoid of all moral and other absolutes. Where could people still find the lost values? In the museums, in the paintings of the old masters. Because of this the old paintings get a new significance and weight in the nineteenth and twentieth centuries. But what do you do when you cannot believe in these values anymore, when to you they are subjective, humanly conceived relics of the past? You can do two things. You can blow up all the museums and destroy all the old pictures. But you can also go about the latter in a more subtle way, which is what Marcel Duchamp did by adding a moustache to the *Mona Lisa*. In this way he tore down all the values that are built into that painting. It is very telling that the picture by Duchamp has been very popular in our century, which means that people see it as a statement of twentieth-century truth.

A very popular painting made in 1911 by Anders Zorn depicted a nude girl standing in the water. The artist portrayed her like that because in ages past the nude had been a recurring subject to represent love or beauty, but now it is just a naked girl standing in the water and we can only feel sorry for her as she has to stand in the cold water for no reason at all. Around the same time Picasso also painted a nude. Picasso's picture consists of very beautiful lines and feminine forms, but also here the meaning of the woman or the nude as a metaphor is totally gone. In fact these two pictures mean exactly the same, which is almost nothing. The same can be said about a sculpture by Maillol of a woman's torso. Never before did any sculptor make a thing like this, just a torso. These three works sum up the situation at the beginning of the twentieth century.

In the same year (1911) Kandinsky published not only his book on the spiritual in art but also an article in which he put forward that in the old art there always was an equilibrium and harmonious relationship between the artist and the reality he was representing. But today, he continues, this old equilibrium is gone and we are left with two possibilities: either we depict the reality as we see it in a very precise manner or we make pictures that are totally abstract. However, he says, when we paint exactly what we see, we must understand that this realism is basically abstract. Realism is abstraction. And when we make a totally abstract picture, it is basically realistic, which means that abstraction is realism. In order to make this clear Kandinsky compares a painting with a page in a book. We can look at the forms of the letters that are on the page. We see round forms, standing forms, lying forms, square forms, small forms, big forms and we can enjoy their beauty. Or we can read the letters. But we can never do both at the same time.

This last part of Kandinsky's argument can also be explained like this: in the Lockian epistemology we had the big X of reality, and the perception lines that come into the box of our mind. Now we cut off the perception lines exactly at the moment they enter the box. Then we have on one side the perception lines as precisely as possible without the intervention of anything subjective, which means total objectivity. That is what naturalism tries to do. But we can also look at the other side, namely at that of the box or our mind, where we make fantastic geometrical forms. Here we find abstraction, as these forms are the reality without the perception. Yet, both sides are essentially the same as both are no reality and both are abstract. It means we can have either the ultranaturalistic, as naturalistic as can be, abstraction or the mind-made abstraction.

In the eighteenth century art became Art, with a capital A. Kant said that art is by definition that which is totally without any use. For example, a rail in the railroad is a very useful thing, it is not a work of art. Now I take this rail, twist it and make a knot in it and hang it from the ceiling. Then it is a work of art, because it has become completely useless. This is exactly what Marcel Duchamp started to do with his Ready-Mades around 1918. His *objects trouvés* are totally unusable and therefore are works of art. What are they? Naturalistic? Of course they are naturalistic, nothing can be more naturalistic than the things themselves. But if somebody would say, 'No, these objects are totally non-figurative, they don't represent anything,' that is equally true. So they are abstract works of Art, with an enormously big capital A. They are totally abstract in the sense of non-representational and totally abstract in the sense of ultranaturalistically natural.

Ultranaturalism

Jumping to the 1960s and 1970s we come to a painting by Norman Rockwell of around 1960, in which we see a man in a museum standing before a picture by Jackson Pollock. Is this Jackson Pollock painting, as part of Rockwell's work, naturalistic or is it non-figurative? It is both at the same time as it is a naturalistic representation of something that is totally non-representational. The same can be said about a picture of the New York artist Howard Kanowitz which gives a naturalistically very precise rendering of a minimal art sculpture. Also in a work consisting of a bronze cast of two beer cans (Jasper Johns's *Painted bronze II* from 1960) the difference between naturalistic and abstract is annihilated. On the one hand it is very precise and naturalistic, on the other it is totally abstract.

In the *Great American nude*, a series of mixed media tableaux made in the early 1960s by Tom Wesselmann, we see a real table and chair, a real heating element, a real telephone and a painted woman on a painted bed. Can I also say a real woman on a real bed? Are the table and the telephone not really abstract? What is more abstract or what is more real? We find that the most real things become abstract. The distinction between naturalism and abstraction becomes completely blurred.

What is the most beautiful spot around the place where you live? Just print 10,000 questionaires and hand them out and put the results in the computer and out comes the most beautiful landscape. The only twentieth-century way to know whether something is worthwhile is by statistics. In line with this George Deem made a painting called *Statistical landscape* (1969), a collage of a number of very famous paintings, a Hobbema in the top corner, several Corots and other well-known pictures. In the third row we see a still life, but after all a still life is also a landscape: a little landscape on a table. He also included a nude girl, but after all a nude is only the hills and dales of a woman, what is the difference? Remember that a landscape does not exist; it is always a human interpretation.

As in the last painting in this type of modern art we often see that in one way or another older art is copied. It is as if the only reality these artists know is the art reality. They seem to be more inspired by old art than by reality itself. Picasso, for instance, has made many interpretations of the famous *Las meninas* ('The maids of honour') of Velasquez. Another artist copies an old work in three ways within one painting: on the left-hand side in the style of Picasso, in the middle naturalistically, and on the right-hand side in the style of a cartoon. Style always was a conveyer of the way an artist understood reality. By way of this painting this artist says that there is no one way to understand reality. Our interpretations are just patterns we impose on it, as the Structuralists say as well. We can interpret reality any way we want.

Mati Klarwein, a painter from Vienna who later went to work in the United States, makes a painting called *Abstract vision in form of a Spanish landscape*. By giving the work this title he emphasizes that, even though the work depicts a landscape, it is abstract. When we put another painting from the same year next to it which consists of a red square on a blue square, we have to conclude that both are equally abstract. The one shows the forms of a Spanish landscape as they reach our eyes by way of rays of light and the other one shows the mathematical forms that inhabit our heads. They both mean the same as they both lack any reality, whether they use the forms that we perceive or the forms that shape themselves inside our brain.

Domenico Gnoli makes a huge painting depicting a button, again naturalistic yet abstract. Another artist portrays a middle-class woman. However, he has left out her arms and legs. At the left- and right-hand sides of her body the cloth goes on, which makes the painting more abstract. In a way she is there and not there. Why did the artist not show anything more than just this part of the body of a woman who might have been his mother? Is it not because he is saying that humanity is dehumanized and that we have lost real humanness? I believe there is a kind of protest implied here. The artist shows the meaninglessness of something that we know to be meaningful. In a way we are hurt because the woman is treated as if she were nothing. We can easily accept this of a button, but it is much more difficult to accept of a woman. This is the soft protest that is inherent in many of these ultranaturalistic paintings. They show meaningful things as if they were meaningless, and exactly that tension is an important part of their meaning.

In 1970 Kanowitz made a work in which we see a city through a window. However, while looking at the work we soon discover that the city is made by a stencil. Of course it does not make any difference whether there is a city a couple of miles away or whether there is only a stencil behind the window, the light beams that reach our eyes are the same. Actually, there is no real window either; everything is just a drawing.

A painting by Malcolm Morley shows a soldier in front of an arch. It is, however, not a real soldier in front of a real arch, it is a painting after a souvenir you can buy at Keypoint West. It is a painting after a souvenir after a photograph after a soldier. Being this far removed from the real soldier, it has become totally abstract.

Another painting is obviously made after one of these glossy photographs in certain kinds of magazines. It is even more precise than a photograph, as for example the stitches on the trousers of the girl are rendered in more detail than any photographic machine could record. And just because it is so objectively precise it becomes totally abstract and meaningless. In the same line the Swiss artist Franz Gertsch made a painting after a slide made with a flashlight.

Philip Pearlstein paints models. Not nudes, not women, but models. Being a model means that you have to lie down many long and tedious hours in order to be painted. So Pearlstein portrays tedious and bored bodies. Roughly 150 years earlier Delacroix makes a portrait of Mademoiselle Rose and it worries him that he can only paint what his eyes can see. Now Pearlstein makes this and it strikes us as very human because, even if these bodies have no heads and so on, after all they're human forms. They are totally abstracted forms, yet they are more human than many of the other works I dealt with. This shows how much we have lost in the course of the years. I say 'we' because we should never say 'they', it is 'we', all of us, for we are all deeply influenced by television, radio, photography, magazines, artworks, films, etc. We are all brainwashed into this new view of reality, and even with the greatest effort we may hardly succeed to get out of it. It is not just their problem, it is our problem. These ultranaturalistic works do not just represent their reality, they may just as well represent ours. Let us be careful.

Christianity and Music

Should we aim to be a subculture?

Implicit in the lecture 'Rock and Protest' above was the question: 'What are we as Christians going to do with this music?' This question I now want to deal with in an explicit way, though I will not focus on rock music only.

The topic 'Christianity and music' is part of the larger subject of 'Christianity and culture', which can be divided into two parts: firstly our own cultural forms and secondly our relationship with the culture around us.

Firstly, our own cultural forms. To be human is to be a cultural being, there is no other possibility. If you decide to live in a cave with no warm clothes and to eat only soup and bread, then you might say that you have fled culture. But I would say that you have made your own kind of culture, a very ascetic culture but still a culture or a particular style of living. Culture is a style of living: the way we do things, the things we look at, the things we love, the things we do not love and put outside of our orbit. We cannot escape being cultured, because we are human.

Many evangelicals look quite negatively at culture. That is their culture, to be negative about culture. For this very reason we at L'Abri have felt that we ought to try to make a small contribution towards change. That is why we have a concert as part of this L'Abri conference in the USA, and we do not see it as a little added extra, a little ornament or diversion. No, it is something very much at the heart of everything we have to say. We were approached by someone who asked, 'Why do you have this? What does a concert have to do with Christianity?' I would say, 'Everything! It's our lifestyle.'

The next important point to make when we think about Christianity and culture is that we should never aim at being a subculture. In a way it is unavoidable to become a subculture. As soon as you have a group of people together who have their own customs, you have a kind of subculture, which in itself is not something bad. But I think we should not aim for it; the Christian's task is to be part of all of culture. What we do is not for our friends but for the world, the nation, the culture in which we are placed. Christ said, 'You are the salt of the world.' He wants us to be 'salting salt', so that we can act in conservation against corruption. We fight against corruption, we try to keep things healthy, try to give taste to things, not just for our own circle but for everybody. We fight for righteousness and justice in the world around us. It may mean that by doing so we become a subculture. If we feel that everybody around us is doing wrong and therefore we try to do things in a better way and nobody listens to us, then it obviously means that we are different. And we should not be afraid of that. We should not be afraid of being a subculture, but we should never strive to be one.

As an example: about six or seven ago all of a sudden the miniskirt came in. Two months later all Christian girls had miniskirts and I had the feeling that this was just a bit too easy. I do not feel that Christian girls should always be two years behind the fashion, that is not what I am asking. But a miniskirt in those days certainly meant – and this was said clearly by all the people who were involved, including the ones who designed it – that a woman is available all the time. So it is not out of prudishness that I am saying this, but because of that context. If you do not want to be available like that, then you have to ask yourself whether you can wear such a piece of clothing. We cannot just follow all the trends, and we should not try to. We should in fact try to be ourselves.

In Western history Christians for a long time set the tone, working for the wellbeing of everybody. The morals we have in Western Europe, Canada and the USA have their roots in Christianity – maybe not in Christianity only, but Christianity undoubtedly had a strong impact on them. In a way, these were Christian countries. Of course never perfectly so, and it does not mean that everybody was a Christian, but if monogamy is in the laws of all our Western countries, then we must say that this comes from Christianity. But today things are changing and Christians are becoming a very small minority, certainly the Bible-believing Christians.

Misplaced optimism

Being a small minority, how should we act? More than ever, we should read the Old Testament, particularly the prophets, because they were speaking into a similar situation in which a nation that formerly had been God-fearing was falling away from God. There was a little group who still believed, 7,000 who did not bow. They called out to the others, 'Return to the Lord and be blessed.' I believe that we should do the same. It is not in the first place our calling to evangelize but to be prophets and say, 'Turn back to the Lord. If you don't, God will come with his judgment.' Zephaniah said it like this, 'Come together, hold assemblies, oh shameless nation, before you are driven away like drifting chaff, before there comes upon you the fierce anger of the Lord, before there comes upon you the day of the wrath of the Lord.' Then he goes on, turning to those who believe, 'Seek the Lord, all you humble of the land, you who do what he commands. Seek righteousness, seek humility; perhaps you will be sheltered on the day of the LORD's anger' (Zephaniah 2:1–3).

Firstly, seek righteousness. It is very difficult for young people today to have a different lifestyle from everybody around them. The social pressures are very great. But yet this is what we are called to do, to be righteous. This is not just to be old-fashioned, of course, it can be done in new ways. Secondly Zephaniah summons us to seek humility, which means that we have to accept that we are a minority and that we are not going to change the world. We are not going to say, 'Just follow us and everything will be okay,' because that is too optimistic. We must realize that even if tomorrow everybody would turn around and become Christians, we need at least two generations, if not more, to build up what has been broken down.

In the New Testament Peter's first letter also addresses people who are believers but live in a non-believing world. Christians at that time were a very small minority as well. Peter tells them that it is quite possible that they may end up in jail, but that they should not be afraid. In Dutch L'Abri we always say to people who want to become Christians, 'Do you realize that within ten years you may be in jail or in a concentration camp?' In the largest part of the world the situation is like that. Even very near to us, in Spain, it is not so long ago that boys of 18 years of age who had to go into the army for one or two years had to go to Mass every Sunday morning, and at the moment of the transsubstantiation they had to present their arms. If you were a Protestant you could not do that and would have had to spend your term in the army in jail. So we are in an exceptional position in that we can still talk freely in our countries, but it may not stay that way. Let us be humble.

Keep the good things

Now we come to the question of the Christian and the culture outside, the non-Christian culture. The Bible teaches us that we should not be contaminated by the wrongs of the world and not follow the ways of the world. By 'world' in this sense is meant the sinful world. But the Bible says as well that we should not be afraid to investigate everything and keep the good things. We are not meant to withdraw. The Bible very interestingly never talks about culture in a negative way. The culture of the world as such is not negative. The Scriptures do not teach us that everything produced by non-Christians is intrinsically bad. When Solomon made his temple he called an architect from Tyre who certainly was a pagan. But he was a good architect. Revelation 17 even talks about Babel, the personification of the evil world, the centre of all antichristianity, as a city full of beauty and riches, a place where the women wear beautiful gowns. The Bible does not say that what comes out of the world is therefore bad. Rather it teaches us to listen, and to look around us, and to keep hold of the good things.

Paul writes in the first letter to the Corinthians, 'All things are lawful for me, but not all things are helpful. All things are lawful for me, but I will not be enslaved by anything.' All things are allowed but we have to try and see whether they are positive. There is a strong emphasis in the whole Bible, but particularly in Paul, on freedom. It was Paul's life's work to say two things: that salvation is the finished work of Christ plus nothing and, closely tied to this, that there is freedom. He verbalizes this very beautifully in Colossians 2, where he starts out by saying, 'See to it that no one takes you captive through philosophy and empty deception, according to the tradition of men rather than according to Christ' (v.8). He says this with a view to the gnostics. Then he sums up very concisely what the gospel means: the forgiveness of sins, the renewal of life, and the triumph over evil. And then he goes on in Colossians 2:16, 'Therefore, let no one pass judgement on you in questions of food or drink, or with regard to a festival, or a new moon or a Sabbath.' He says, 'Therefore, you are free.' He continues, 'If with Christ you have died to the elemental principles of the world, why do you live as if you still belonged to the world? Why do you submit to regulations, such as "do not handle, do not taste, do not touch" in accordance with the commandments and teachings of men?' Do not let yourself be put under all sorts of rules and regulations again, do not let this freedom be taken away from you, for that goes against the very gospel!

It is our mentality that counts

Keeping this in mind, we can talk about our lifestyle. Being a Christian means that you believe in certain creeds and dogmas. There is nothing to be said against those things; they are important and have a place in our lives. But being Christian is not just to adhere to a theological system but also to have faith, to trust and love the Lord and to walk with him. It is a mentality and a lifestyle that come out of our love for him. Christ never talked about dogma, and in the Sermon on the Mount, where we find his basic teaching, he does not say, 'If you become a Christian, this is what you have to do.' He rather talks about a mentality. To give some examples, in Matthew 5 we read, 'You have heard that it was said to the men of old, "You shall not kill. And whosoever kills shall be liable to judgment."' Jesus does not say this old teaching is wrong, but he says it is not enough, and thus he continues, 'But I say to you that everyone who is angry with his brother shall be liable to judgment and whoever insults his brother shall be liable to the council. Whoever says "you are a fool" shall be liable to hell.' In other words, we should not go by a legalistic yardstick and think we have committed murder only when somebody lies dead on the floor; no, we are already wrong when we are angry with somebody else. Because that is a wrong mentality and it is the mentality that counts.

We are not only adulterers when we share our bed with the wrong person; no, says Christ, if you look to a woman in a way of wanting her you have already begun your adultery. Note that he does not say: 'And therefore keep women out of your sight.' He puts the blame where it belongs, with the lusting person. Because of that this text has been one of the most liberating texts in the world. That women can be sitting in this room at this present moment is possible because of what Christ said there, otherwise they would not be here, they would be in a harem or would walk around covered by veils because men were looking at them only as sex objects. So Christian life is a mentality, not a set of rules.

To have faith is to live in a certain way. Whatever your beliefs or convictions, they will show forth in your life. Very often we make a separation between a person's spirituality and his or her life. A person's spirituality is considered to be something private, whether he or she believes in Christ, Buddha or Marx. But beliefs are not just private, they come out in our lives. I have found a metaphor to clarify this. If I have in front of me a number of glasses, one with coffee, one with tea, one with wine, one with cola, what is the difference between them? The difference is very slight indeed, because they all contain 95 per cent water. Only 5 per cent is different, nevertheless they vary greatly in taste and colour. In the same way, when you are a Christian, you are 95 per cent human and 5 per cent Christian. But the 5 per cent is not something we can shove aside as irrelevant, because that is our particular taste and colour. Also the Marxist is 95 per cent human, and because we are all human we have much in common. Yet the 5 per cent leads to decisive differences in our lifestyles.

Music makes the person

What can we say about music as part of our Christian lifestyle? Music is the environment we create for ourselves. Music is not something that we just have in common with everybody. It is not the 95 per cent, it is the 95 plus 5 per cent. The first thing I do when I visit your home is to look at your records, because they tell me who you are. In Dutch we have the expression 'the clothes make the man,' which means that we know a person by how one dresses. Music likewise is an expression of our selves. We do not listen to just anything but choose the music we make and listen to, for there is an intrinsic connection between the music with which we surround ourselves and who we are.

I do not suppose to find when I go through your records that there will be only hymns – we cannot live by hymns alone. There will be all kinds of music. If I see that there is some medieval, Romantic and modern music in your collection, then I know that you are somebody with a wide interest in this world and that you want to know more about other outlooks on life, because music is like coffee, tea or cola. We listen to our contemporaries in their musical expression and we get to know them through that. All the wisdom and foolishnesses of people of the past and present come to us through their music.

If we listen to Beethoven it does not mean we necessarily agree with Beethoven and that Beethoven's colour is our colour. It means we think it worthwhile to listen to what he has to say. If we listen to a sad passage in Beethoven's music we will hear not only his expression of grief, but we will also be confronted with his view on grief in relationship to his starting point as a humanist. That means that if I listen to his music I have a kind of discussion. Listening to music is entering into a dialogue.

People have often asked me what kind of music they should play in a coffee bar with evangelistic purposes. I always say, 'This is very important, maybe the most important, because by the music you play anyone who enters that coffee bar will know who you are.' That does not mean that you should be playing hymns all the time, but it means that you have to make choices. Some types of music cannot be played there, because they are inappropriate. Some music may at first hearing seem unsuitable but may turn out to be different from what you first thought once you have really listened to it. It takes time to make good choices. You have to try out various types of music and live with them for a while. Think about them. Dialogue.

The influence of music

If we make music part of our environment, the question arises what influence music has on us. We need to make a distinction here between live music and music that is played on the radio or gramophone. There is a great difference between listening to a record and being at a live performance. One can listen to the radio all day long, but one cannot listen to a band for that long, especially not if one does not really feel 'at home' with their music. That would be just too much. Live music has a much stronger impact.

We should not exaggerate the influence of music. It is not that big. When we listen to a modern record, we do not end up completely brainwashed like modern people. On the other hand, music does have an impact and it does matter what music we listen to. In fact, to think that music or a movie does not affect us in any way is not being too optimistic but rather too pessimistic. Think about it: someone has a great idea and works it out in a film script and finds ten million dollars and then many people work very hard for a year and at the end it comes to the screen. Do you think that all those people would be willing to spend sweat, blood and tears though it would have no impact at all? Of course it has an impact. Dr Schaeffer always quotes this short Japanese poem,

> He jumped in the water and he caused no ripples.

That is Zen Buddhism. But as a Christian I say, 'You jump in the water and whether you want it or not, you cause ripples.' We all cause ripples because human life is meaningful.

Of course, some types of music are more influential than others, and the influence also varies for different people. I know a fellow who spent a short period, half a year, on the drug scene. He has been out of it for four or five years now. He says, 'If I put on a Pink Floyd record, it has an immediate effect on me. I do not wash myself anymore; I do not tidy the room; I stay in bed in the morning and I have to scramble back again; it costs me days and days.' That music has a very strong influence on that particular fellow who has been part of that scene. Maybe on other people it does not have such an impact, because they do not have the same associations. Music that is or that has been very dear to our hearts may be very influential. Then we need to be careful and we may need to discipline ourselves. But we cannot make general rules; we cannot say 'This is good and that is bad.' Our calling may also play a role in this: if we want to meet and understand other people, it may be good to listen to their music. We are free to choose what music we want to listen to, yet we should be responsible for our choices. If some images or books or music pulls us in a sinful direction we better leave them aside. Some people can read things that are much too strong for others, but the latter may be able to read other things again that are too strong for the former. So, each person has his or her own responsibility. We should always ask ourselves: can we stand before the Lord in these things? But it is not a matter of little rules. That is why Paul said, 'Try it out, and keep what is good.'

The debasement of entertainment music

Two or three centuries ago, before the great break in Western culture that took place with the Enlightenment, there was a unity in culture. If you happened to live in Leipzig around 1725 you would go to church on Sunday morning and there you would hear the latest cantata of Bach as part of the liturgy. In the afternoon the same people would go to the market place and there would be a brass band playing dance music, and they would enjoy it. In the evening in their homes they would make some chamber music or maybe they would go to a formal concert, where organ or violin concertos were played. All these types of music were understood by everybody and they were all part of the general culture. For different occasions, however, there were different kinds of music. They had a word for that in those days, which we have forgotten, namely 'decorum'. Decorum means that things need to be appropriate to a situation. If you have a parade you are not going to have an orchestra lead it playing a Beethoven symphony, because that is out of place. You'll have a brass band playing Sousa, music that is suitable and enjoyable in that particular situation.

At the time of the Enlightenment, art and music were made very High. When Beethoven walked in the street, he wanted the emperor to lift his hat first for him, because he was more important, he was the high priest and great prophet of culture. If people listened to his music, they had to be very silent, because now they were listening to revelations from the depths of the soul of humanity. So-called serious music became very important and elevated and at the same time entertainment music became very unimportant and low. Which meant that since that day no real composer or good musician has wanted to work in the entertainment world. The result was on the one hand High-culture Romantic music that very few people listened to and on the other hand low-culture entertainment music that became more and more banal and debased.

Around 1900 it had become so unbearably silly and dead (surely part of the death of our culture!) that something had to be done. People looked for an 'iron pill' to revive this music. The only people in the Western world who had not taken part in this cultural development were the African-Americans, because they had not been able to get a proper education. Their entertainment music was still strong. And again and again white people said, 'We want to have that music, because it's alive,' and within ten years that particular type of music (ragtime, jazz, blues or rhythm-and-blues) would be streamlined and commercialized and as dead as a doornail again. The same thing happened with rock-and-roll and later with the Beatles, Bob Dylan and the protest songs. Mammon always took over and killed it again. Just tune into your radio and you will hear what I mean. It is one of the great problems of our culture that we have such a low kind of entertainment music. Happily there were black people around who gave us at least some kind of renewal.

Rock and pop

This brings me to a little booklet that I have wanted to review for quite some time but have never found the time to do. It is called *A Big Beat, a Rock Blast*, written by Frank Garlock. On the cover it says, 'Mr Garlock is a favourite of young people, because he is in tune with young people and their needs. A faculty member at Bob Jones University. A regular speaker, etc. His lectures have produced lasting results with as many as a hundred decisions for Christ being made in a single service.' And these poor kids, after making their decisions for Christ, went home and destroyed their records. This booklet really makes me mad, because the author is completely indiscriminate. He talks about Bob Dylan and pop music, which is just light music, as if they have the same strength and impact. 'Yes, I believe that we can definitely conclude that rock-and-roll is not only a symptom of the problems of teenagers of this generation, but also part of the cause.' Yes, I do agree. But then he goes on, 'You know a person by the company he keeps,' the old saying says. And if any music has been guilty by association, it is rock music. It would be impossible to make a complete list, but here are a few of the associates of rock: drug addicts, revolutionaries, rioters, Satan worshippers, dropouts, draft dodgers, homosexuals and other sex deviates, rebels, juveniles, criminals, Black Panthers, White Panthers, motorcycle gangs, suicides, Satanists, voodooists, communists in the United States, paganism, lesbianism, immorality, promiscuity, free love, free sex, disobedience – civil and uncivil, sodomy, venereal disease, discotheques, brothels, ordeals of all kinds, night clubs, strip joints, filthy musicals such as *Hair*', and on and on the list goes, ad nauseam. 'And just add powerless Christianity,' he concludes.

When I read this, I think, 'Have you really gone into this? Do you know what you are talking about?' You cannot just lump all those things together. The worst is that Garlock is also racist in his argumentation. For instance, he says, 'All one needs to do is to go and make a trip to the place where rock-and-roll has its roots: to Africa and the South-American Indians. There's a certain ceremony which often goes along with this type of music: voodoo rituals, sex orgies, youth sacrifices, Devil worship, so know the direction in which we as a nation are heading!' That is nonsense and it is a racist statement. Why should Indian or African music be any less? Maybe the Africans and Indians are cola, maybe they are strong rum, but nevertheless they are human. We should never talk like this.

Then he quotes an article about a certain Mrs Dorothy R. in Denver who did an experiment with rock music and potplants. Within a month all plants exposed to rock music died. The suggestion is that rock music has an automatic destructive influence on us, that for human beings exposed to rock music it may perhaps take two months to die . . .

'Why is this music so strong?' Garlock asks, and he answers: 'It has taken the elements of tension out of the blues, hot and cool bebop, swing, honkie-tonk, Latin-American and African dances, ragtime, black-faced minstrels, dixieland and jazz, and it has combined them all into one style: overloaded with tension.' And I would say 'yes', if you listen to the music from the beginning of the twentieth century till now you would hear ever greater tensions. And if you have lived with this music and grown with it, then the tension is quite natural. Because if you want to make something that is strong you find that after you have played it many times it is not strong anymore. In order to be strong, it has to get stronger. That was even true of classical music in its development: orchestras grew larger, organs expanded, and so on. Until you have gone too far and then you look for something more restrained again. That's cultural development, in every place and in every age.

If we do not understand this it is because we have never grown along with the development. It shows that we have been completely alienated from the world around us, and we have lived not just as strangers in the biblical sense but in a much deeper sense. We have not been living in our own town but have become complete outsiders. As outsiders we have no right to judge. It is like going into a foreign culture and eating unfamiliar food. You cannot say it does not taste well. You can only say that you have to get used to it, and that you do not understand the subtleties of that particular food culture yet.

Garlock's conclusion is, 'Don't listen to this music, break your rock records and listen to classical music.' But this is wrong thinking because it fails to have an eye for decorum. Classical music is concert music. We cannot expect our kids to listen to concert music, let's say to the symphonies of Beethoven, all the time. If you are in a social group together and you want to drink and talk, then Beethoven is out of place. Even Bob Dylan is out of place. You have to look for music that fits the occasion. You cannot say forget about rock and go to classical music, because those are two completely different worlds. It is part of our culture that we do not understand these things. It is also part of our culture that there is such a great gap between those two worlds which is interpreted as the 'generation gap', but I think that much more is at stake. Garlock fails to see that this music is an expression of a spiritual situation and that we should not just look at the music but also at the causes of the music, at the state of our present culture and at the modern mindset. When Garlock talks as if there is some conspiracy against the Western world to corrupt it by introducing free sex, drugs and rock music, then this is simply too superficial and crazy to even think about. He never answers the real problems, he does not even begin to discuss them.

To come to a conclusion: we have to be aware of the problems of our time and try to fight the spirit of the age, also in the area of music. All music is coloured, reflecting the specific spirituality of the person who made it. However, when we listen to music we do not automatically embrace the colour of its maker but we rather enter into a discussion with it. It is important that we try to understand the music of our time. We cannot say that all contemporary music is wrong; rather, we should say that some of it is wrong – not all rock and pop are wrong, but some of it is wrong. Whilst we should be very careful not to be tainted by wrong influences, yet we are free to test the music around us and to keep what is good, and perhaps even to work towards music of our own that is just as lively and good as the best examples, yes and maybe even better.

The Christian Artist

Calvinism and art

What do we mean when we talk about a 'Christian artist', not only with respect to Christian artists in our time but also to those of the past? In many books you will find that Protestants never were interested in the arts and that they never achieved anything in this area. Is that correct? Bach, Handel, Rembrandt and many other great artists, were they not Christians? Is that an aspect of their art that is unimportant?

Let us look at Dutch art, for instance. For many years I held the view that Calvinists never produced any art in the Netherlands and that this was not right. I discovered, however, that Dutch seventeenth-century art has a stronger connection to Calvinism than people usually think and that historically speaking it is simply not true that Calvinism was negative towards the arts. Calvin himself never made one negative remark about the arts as such. He did criticize particular artistic manifestations, a certain way of dancing that he deemed too wild or erotic, for instance. But that does not mean that for him dancing was out, it only means that for him some kinds of dances were out. Even of this type of remarks we do not find that many. Calvin considered artists to be people with an importance of their own because he looked at them as craftsmen. He viewed them in the same way as he would a shoemaker or a furniture maker, and not as highly gifted geniuses as some other people around that time began to look at them.

When the Spaniards came to the South of the Netherlands (which is now Belgium) in order to restore it to Roman Catholicism, the Calvinists had to flee. Among them were learned men who had studied in Geneva under Calvin, so these people were true Calvinists who had become Calvinist by choice. They fled to the north, to Holland – they are the ones who brought Calvinism there – and they fled to the east, to Germany, particularly to the area around Heidelberg which is called the Pfalz. The ruler of that area was also a strong Calvinist. He followed the Heidelberg Catechism, which is still used in the Reformed churches in the Netherlands. He gave those refugees from Belgium a village of their own, which soon grew into a small town. It is very interesting that this town, called Frankenthal, which is near Worms and still exists today, very soon became an art centre that produced tapestries – tapestries with scenes on them to be used as wallhangings. Particularly in the history of landscape painting Frankenthal has been very important as many of its citizens later moved to Holland and played an important role in the Dutch landscape art of the seventeenth century. Many Dutch seventeenth-century artists were strong Calvinists, not just churchgoers but active in many ways. They did not have a problem with art. Nobody ever discussed it; nobody ever said anything against it.

Pietism and art

The question remains where the negative attitude towards the arts comes from that can be found amongst many Christians in the past and in the present. Puritanism was sometimes negative towards the arts, but it is pietism which has always opposed the arts. In pietism the Christian life is narrowed down to the faith aspect of life, to piety and devotion. Pietism has had many different colours in different periods of history. There were pietistic tendencies in the Middle Ages; the Methodists in England in the eighteenth century and onwards were pietists; and also in eighteenth-century Germany there was a strong pietistic movement. The evangelicals are the Anglo-Saxon pietists of today. To the pietist mind being active in this world means that you have to do something for the Lord, save souls or evangelize. Many evangelicals have a bad conscience because they are teachers, shoemakers or artists for they do not consider that to be Christian work. There is a dichotomy in their life because everything that is not Christian in a narrow sense, devotional or directly active in the Christian sphere, is considered worldly and negative by them. It belongs to the world. Calvin, however, would never say that everything outside of the church or the Christian community is the world, he would say those things are also God's world. When you make shoes or paintings you are working as a Christian, and you have to do it well and you have to do it in order to serve society. But to the pietist mind the arts fall outside the Christian sphere – they rather belong to the world – though to some the arts become acceptable if they are part of evangelism or worship.

Calvin never held the opinion that artists should paint only Christian themes. In fact, the tapestries from Frankenthal show us mostly wood scenes and landscape scenes, and only sometimes biblical themes. For the Calvinist all of life belongs to our service of God. We live in the covenant and God is concerned with everything we do; even our sleeping is part of our Christian life, because God takes care of us.

But Calvinism was influenced by pietistic ideas, so that after 1650 the Calvinists' appreciation of the arts diminished. On top of that they increasingly felt that the direction art was taking was not quite their direction, so that in the course of years the break between the Calvinists and what happened in the world of art became bigger. However, art was never rejected as absolutely by Calvinists as it was rejected by the pietists.

The first pietist was perhaps Bernard of Clairvaux. St Bernard lived in the twelfth century, a period when Christianity was at a low tide and the church and the world were in chaos. Then St Bernard came and said that people had to turn back to Christianity. To him that meant going back to the monastery and thus he founded the new monastic order of the Cistercians. Bernard was the first person in Western history to say that there should be no paintings or sculptures in the churches. So the Cistercian churches are very bare, there are no stained-glass windows, no sculptures and no paintings. Around the same time there was another man in France who said exactly the opposite. He wanted fabulously big churches with as much gold and glitter as possible. His name was Suger and he is the founder of the Gothic style. Dissension arose between St Bernard and Suger which became so strong that the king eventually brought them together to sit down and discuss it. They worked out a kind of compromise: Suger promised to tone down a bit, and Bernard promised not to speak too strongly against Suger's churches. It is very interesting, however, that also the Cistercian churches are very beautiful. They are bare but they have beautiful proportions. St Bernard was not against beauty but against artistic adornments.

The next man in this line, who in a way was a pupil of St Bernard although he never met him, is St Francis of Assisi. St Francis founded a new monastic order again, the Franciscan order, and he too was seen as someone who was there to save the church. One of the first things he said was, 'No embellishments in the churches, no sculptures and no paintings.' However, when you go to Assisi you will find the San Francesco there, the central church of the Franciscan order. This church is very famous and important in the history of art precisely because of its paintings. How is this possible? This could happen because, very soon after St Francis, there developed two streams in the Franciscan order and the stream that did want art in church was backed by the pope (and for this very reason you will see depictions of the pope all over Assisi).

Gnosticism, stoicism and cynicism

Where do pietism and its particular outlook on the arts come from? Pietism developed under the influence of ideas that stem from three different sources outside of Christianity. These influences go way back in history: they are gnosticism, stoicism and cynicism.

Gnosticism was a movement in the time of Christ. Paul and John fought against the gnostics who held that this world is bad because it was created by a bad God and that human beings are caught in this bad world and have to try and get out of it. If you bring these ideas together with Christian thinking, which soon happened, then the bad God becomes the Old Testament God, i.e. Jehovah, and the good God becomes the New Testament God, i.e. Christ. You get a tension, which you sometimes still find today. Also for gnostic Christians the world is bad, so they do not touch it, they get out of the world and do not take part in it.

These ideas were strengthened by two other influences which originated in Greek antiquity. Firstly, that of the Stoics, who said that human beings have an immortal soul and that the body is unimportant. You may be tortured or killed, anything may happen to your body as long as your immortal soul is okay. Only the soul counts. An emphasis on the saving of souls comes from that as well as the fact that many evangelicals go through this world just waiting to die in order to have their immortal soul with the Lord.

Secondly, the influence of the Cynics. The name 'cynic' comes from the Greek word for dog. They called themselves 'the dogs' because they had a total contempt of all forms of culture – culture was just a façade to them to cover up who we really are. Most of you may have heard of the Cynic Diogenes, who lived in a barrel. There is an anecdote about him according to which Alexander the Great – not just any little king but the greatest king – came to visit him. Diogenes did not leap to his feet and bow down to the great king. No, he remained seated in the front of his barrel as Alexander the Great began to talk to him. But Diogenes only said, 'Could you move on a little, you are standing in my sunshine.'

It is not the Bible that speaks in a condemning way about our involvement with art and culture, but it is a Christianity that has been influenced by ideas that come from foreign sources. In the past only the pietists adopted this anti-culture position, but today it has become quite a strong movement, particularly in Anglo-Saxon countries.

The role of faith

If you read books on the history of art you will soon discover that it is very difficult to find out whether somebody is a Christian artist. Artists will be discussed at great length but no mention will be made of their faith. The reason for that is that since the Age of Reason we are not supposed to talk about faith because what a person believes is unimportant. The Age of Reason proclaimed that the only way we can work is by using our brains and senses, the rest is sheer subjectivity. It is fine if you want to have this or that belief, but then that is private.

In history books we are told what people did, but not why they chose a certain course of action. And very soon someone says that of course it was because of money and then everything is explained on the basis of economic forces. It is almost impossible to tell a present-day historian that somebody acted in a certain way because he or she was a Christian. Why did people go on the Crusades? I would say because they were Christians, even if they may have been mistaken. St Bernard was a fervent preacher for the Crusades and certainly there were Christians who thought it important to go to the Holy Land in order to liberate it from the Muslims. Today people say that they went there for economic reasons, but that is a Marxist interpretation. Some may have gone for economic reasons, but then they were the hypocrites who used Christianity for their own good. It is a falsification of history to say that was the only reason, just as it is a falsification of art history to never tell us whether an artist is a

Christian. Recently I found that Moreelse, a Dutch painter in the early seventeenth century, was a Calvinist, and a very strong one. He played a role in the politics of those days. If I now look at his paintings, which portray little shepherdesses and so on and which are even a bit erotic, then I begin to understand that maybe I was looking for something totally wrong when searching for a Calvinist artist.

Faith does play a big role in every person's life, whether Christian faith or faith in something else as a non-Christian. Non-Christians also have their ideals and beliefs. It is telling, for example, that when you come from America to visit Europe you are advised to go to the centre of European culture which, so you are told by the five big stars in your guidebook, is Florence. If you go to Florence you will see the works of Michelangelo, Raphael, Botticelli and all those great artists of the Renaissance. But what your guidebook does not tell you is that that type of Renaissance art is only to be found in Florence and not in other places, not even in Siena, which is just an hour by train from Florence. So the Renaissance was not something European with Florence as its capital, but what happened in Florence happened nowhere else: it was a humanist centre where the ancestors of the people of the Enlightenment were to be found. What you are in fact visiting is the birthplace of modern culture, just as Christians go to the Holy Land to visit the place where Christ was born.

We should also keep in mind that religion in the past was part of belonging to a certain community. Faith was not something completely private as it is today. The city of Amsterdam, for instance, decided in 1574 to leave Roman Catholicism and become Protestant. Most people did indeed become Protestants, while some kept on going to a Catholic Church and others just went without much inner conviction. But the community as such became Protestant. Why is the canton of Vaux in Switzerland a Protestant canton? Because at the time of the Reformation the parliament in Lausanne organized a dispute in which Farel had to defend the Calvinist position against someone who represented the Roman Catholic Church, and they discussed it for a couple of days while the people of the canton listened, and at the end there was a vote and the people voted for the Protestant position and the canton became Protestant from that day onwards. In those days faith was not such a personal thing or, rather, it was also personal but not in an exclusive way; it was a communal thing as well. So in the books of those days you may read remarks like 'by the grace of God' or 'with God's help', which are not just hypocritical or traditional phrases but they also do not necessarily mean that the person in question was such a confirmed Christian.

The communal character of Christianity means that in a way all art before 1700 (when the Enlightenment began) was Christian. Of course you had foolish and wise, deep and superficial, committed and uncommitted Christians, orthodox ones and those with crazy views,

Christians of all shades and colours. But everybody believed in God, without exceptions. Even during the Enlightenment when Christianity was shaking and the Bible was just an old book, they all said, 'You can believe anything you want, but you cannot be an atheist. If you are an atheist, you are a dangerous person and you have to go to jail.' Tradition was so strong that even then it was impossible to say you did not believe in God.

Today there is a collective faith as well. It is the belief in neutrality which has its roots in the eighteenth century, when science and so-called facts were declared neutral and faith was marginalized as private. You will never hear on the radio or the news that Mr X died in the Lord, or that God in his anger punished a country or that he blessed another. But in the seventeenth century that was the most natural thing in the world. If there had been radios then, people would have said, 'God dispersed the Armada and we praise and thank him for that.' Today we would say that the fleet was smashed against the rocks by a great storm; Christians too would say that because that is our communal neutrality. We live in a pluralist society, which means that one's belief is private.

The Christian artist

But of course the faith of artists does play a role when they express themselves in their work. Like everybody else, artists live within the framework of their times, so that they have much in common with every other person: language, ideas, traditions, history, the problems of the day and so on. We all live in that same framework, a huge system that nobody can completely assess in all its ramifications, a framework which we call 'our times'. But as Christians we are a little bit different from everyone else (no one totally fits the system) and there are some things in that framework that we do not accept and some things that we add to it. Thus Christian artists will be a little bit different from other artists and it is precisely the difference that counts.

The Germans have been teaching that culture is driven by a kind of spirit, called the *Weltanschauung* (world view). Also Americans use the German word, because there is no English word with exactly the same meaning. However, in the past no one ever talked about *Weltanschauung* – it is a concept that comes out of German Romanticism and particularly from Hegel. In this view there is an impersonal spirit that influences the actions of people and drives the times. Nobody, however, can define this spirit and nobody knows how the driving comes about; it is something mysterious, which mystifies rather than enhances our understanding of art and culture.

What then is a Christian artist (or Christian scholar or shoemaker or any kind of professional)? The Bible teaches that we confess with our mouth what we believe in our heart. There is an inside and an outside aspect to our faith and they are one. There is not a mysterious spirit that somehow influences what we do, no there is very direct connection between our faith and our actions. If all was fine there would be a total unity, but living in a broken world our mouths may say something different from what our hearts believe to be true. Yet with our mind and spirit we grasp things and out of that comes a mentality, a way of dealing with things, the mentality Christ teaches us in the Sermon on the Mount. The Bible teaches us not just knowledge and facts but wisdom, and on the basis of that wisdom we act.

Now we should not make this too individualistic. When I am sitting here, I am a person acting out of my own personality and my own knowledge and wisdom, speaking with my own mouth about what is burning in my heart. But I also stand in the tradition of the teachers I have listened to, of the papers I have read, of the church I have been part of that has a history going back to the sixteenth century and even further, to Paul. Nobody is just an individual; even though we act individually we are always part of a bigger community.

A Christian artist is an artist who works out of a Christian spirit and understanding. That understanding may be deep or shallow, wise or foolish, for Christians have no insurance that they will never make mistakes or be sinful. Nevertheless it makes a difference whether an artist is a Christian or not because there is a connection – imperfect though it may be – between his or her faith and work. This conclusion may seem quite obvious and simple. Yet in the course of the years I have had many discussions answering many confused and wrong questions about these matters. What I have tried to do is rephrase the questions and point out the direction in which we may look for answers. As Christians we often have too easily followed the world in its idea of *Weltanschauung*, while the Bible offers us so much wisdom and knowledge about human actions including our creativity.

The Problem of Christian Themes in Art

Natural and supernatural

The problem I want to deal with in this lecture may be summed up in the two following artworks. A depiction of the Storm on Lake Genezareth from around AD 1000 shows us Christ in a boat with his disciples when a storm arises. In this Ottonian miniature we do not see any water, the boat seems to float in the air. It is a strange, non-naturalistic picture. This does not mean that the artist did not look at nature at all. He has for instance definitely observed what sails look like in a storm. The supernatural however is very strongly underlined here. You do not doubt for one moment that something special is happening, and even if all these halos were not there you would immediately understand that this is a situation beyond common reality. In the same way as the Bible tells us that what happened on the lake, when Jesus calmed the sea, was not ordinary but rather very special. On the other hand, if we had been eyewitnesses it would have appeared completely normal.

Rembrandt made a drawing of the same theme. At least that is the subject that is traditionally ascribed to it. But it could just as well have been any boat on a lake in Holland in the seventeenth century and not a specific biblical subject. Here we have the supernatural depicted as totally natural. But this is not really satisfactory either. In short, this is the problem: the Scriptures tell us about episodes in Jesus' life that were not everyday, but if we try to bring out the supernaturalness in our art we may miss the point, for the Bible also stresses that these events took place in ordinary day-to-day reality.

Early solutions

How did early Christian art solve this problem? In a way it avoided it. It did not depict Christ in an overt way but rather in symbolic ways, for instance by portraying him as the Good Shepherd among the vines. In this case we have two symbolic connotations: Christ as the Good Shepherd and Christ as the Vine. Every Christian would understand the intended meaning. It is often suggested that symbolism was used in early Christian art in order to hide the Christian content in surroundings that were hostile to Christianity, but this particular image is from the fourth century and it would have been common knowledge by then that these were Christian symbols. Among the themes depicted were also Daniel in the Lion's Den, as a reminder of the way in which God helps people, or Jonah in the Whale, as a reference to Christ's resurrection. These are all clear biblical images though of a very specific kind.

Roughly between AD 300 and AD 1000 a different type of Christian representation came into being. In a twelfth-century tympanum above the door of Autun Cathedral in France we see a portrayal of the Last Judgment. At that time Christ is commonly depicted with a big halo all around him, a mandorla. It refers to Christ as the great King of heaven and earth who will be the judge of all. We see some people go into heaven and some into hell. Underneath this we read: 'Behold this image of the Last Judgment and our Lord Jesus Christ and be afraid.' Christ is the stern judge here and the real gospel, the grace of God is not represented. Also in Byzantine art Christ is depicted as the great ruler. Imagine yourself standing in a church looking up to the mosaic in the apse and then you see this magnificent, huge figure looking down upon you. He makes an act of blessing with his fingers, but in fact he is very severe – not someone you would be drawn to at all but rather someone you would be afraid of. That is also why Mary starts to be represented, becoming more and more prominent until she becomes almost everything. By bringing in Mary, the Holy Mother, the Compassionate, the grace of God and the tender side of the gospel are brought back into the picture again.

The Baptism of Christ was very early on taken as one of the main themes of Western art as this is the instant in which the Trinity becomes manifest. We see Christ being baptized, above him the dove and higher still God the Father. The *Baptism of Christ* made in 1108 in Liège in the eastern part of Belgium contains one of the earliest depictions of God the Father as a human being. We see Christ here with what looks like a miniature mountain of water around him, which stands for the Jordan. In a twelfth-century miniature from Limoges in Southern France we see the Jordan represented by two ancient river gods. They hold a cauldron out of which water flows, which proceeds to make a pattern of a mandorla around Christ. The mandorla emphasizes the deity of Christ, which corresponds with the significance of this unique moment in which Christ is visibly shown to be the Son of God. This particular theme with its emphasis on Christ's divinity presents Jesus to us as someone who is very far removed, and very different, from us. It stresses the supernaturalness of Christ just as this is commonly underscored in early medieval art.

In this respect a change begins to set in with Gothic art. Christ becomes more human, less the great King and Judge. He is still a lofty personality, but at least he is human and not just far off. The earlier art had as its drawback that it put too much emphasis on the aloofness of Christ which led to the devotion to Mary, but now another type of problem comes in. This may be demonstrated in a painting by Duccio of the Betrayal of Christ by Judas from around 1300. Christ taken prisoner is just like anybody else taken prisoner, at least from a visual point of view. In a deeper sense of course there is more. The dilemma now is how to bring this 'more' into the picture. Duccio has done it like this: he puts Christ in the middle, he gives a halo to him but not to the other figures, and he gives him a different type of cloth, in red and blue with a golden edge.

Then a big step is taken by Giotto, who brings in human psychology. He makes Judas look into the eyes of Jesus at the moment he betrays him, and you see that Judas knows that even though he may have won in the sense that Christ is taken prisoner, in reality he has lost. Christ looks at him and says 'Judas, you know what you have done.' This is the moment when Judas steps out on the road to suicide. Here we see a man who has betrayed a great leader and then meets the leader and is defeated by his great personality. It has become a very human story. In a way it was a very human story: Christ is human and Judas is human and in this sense the painting is true. But at the same time it may have become too human, and something was lost. The issue was heavily debated at the time.

Renaissance tensions

In 1414 Jan van Eyck paints the *Baptism of Christ*. We see a beautiful landscape with, as a small detail in the middle of the painting, the baptism of Christ. To do justice to this work we must add, however, that this is the first landscape ever painted. Jan van Eyck was perhaps the greatest genius in the history of painting as he was the first to see and depict a castle and its reflection in the water. We even understand that this is an evening landscape, for we see the sun setting. This may somewhat make up for the fact that Jan van Eyck made so little of the Baptism of Christ and the representation of the Trinity. But at the same time we have a bad feeling, because the special significance and the holiness of this event is totally lost. The fact is that the first person to realize this was Jan van Eyck himself. He tried to bring back something of the holiness in a symbolical way. For instance, the castle may not just be a stronghold along the river Jordan but it may have had some specific connotations – Bethlehem or Jerusalem or the City of God. With Jan van Eyck we never quite know where the symbol ends and reality begins.

What was the answer of the fifteenth-century Italian painter Piero della Francesca? He was a true believer and did not like it that the deity of Christ and the reality of the Christian message suffered due to the humanistic and worldly tendencies of his time. How would he paint the Baptism of Christ?[52] To emphasize the importance of Christ he makes him stand in the middle, and we see John the Baptist, some angels and a few other people who are going to be baptized. Now try to imagine that these figures were not there. What would be left of the painting would be a very fine landscape. This is the second reality in the picture. But this reality appears in a much smaller scale than the reality of the biblical event, which means that Christ is not standing in a river but rather in a little stream that hardly wets his feet. By way of these differences in size della Francesca tried to find a solution. However, we may lose more than we gain this way because Christ is now outside of everyday reality. Della Francesca's solution rather concurs with the division of reality into the two realms of nature and grace that is prevalent in Roman Catholic theology and philosophy. Nature is the landscape and grace is the baptism scene, and they are two separate realities that do not intermingle.

Bellini, another Renaissance painter, works in a quite different way. In his painting of the Transfiguration of Christ of around 1500 we see Christ with Elijah and Moses and the three disciples. We know this because Bellini sticks to the traditional composition for this theme. If he would let go of that nobody would understand this picture anymore; there would be just six figures. There is nothing in this painting that tells us that this is a very special occurrence, when Jesus appeared as a God-like figure radiating light. There is no light coming out of Jesus here, there is nothing supernatural at all in this painting. This of course is the other extreme: here we are left with only the natural.

The problem of how to depict the biblical themes created an increasing tension in fifteenth-century art. It is one of the keys to understanding the art of that time. It was Raphael and his generation who gave a new answer, which paved the way for sixteenth-century art and the Baroque. In Raphael's depiction of the Transfiguration we see Christ with Moses and Elijah floating in the air. They are truly supernatural. There is a clear division between heaven and earth, the supernatural and the natural, while the dividing line is often represented by clouds, which are symbolic clouds. But Raphael does not stop there, he also incorporates the story following the transfiguration in which Christ goes down the mountain and then meets some of the disciples who complain that they could not drive out the demon that had taken possession of a boy. Christ says that he will do it if only they will have faith enough. So in this painting we also have a disciple pointing up to Christ as the one who is going to bring the solution. Here we have a very clear contrast between the natural and the supernatural, between nature and grace. This was a real solution to the problem, even if it raised other ones.

Reformation and Counter-Reformation responses

The pose of Christ in Raphael's painting is very much like that of a classical sculpture, but it is also exactly like the posture of Christ in a woodcut of the Resurrection which Dürer made in 1510, a couple of years earlier. Even if the subject matter is not exactly the same, it presents the same problem: Christ not simply as a human being, but Christ as God. That is why Raphael could use this woodcut as the prototype for his painting of the Transfiguration. In this woodcut of the Resurrection, Dürer opts for the same solution as Raphael. He uses clouds to underline the supernatural character of the risen Christ. I have good reason to think that Dürer really understood the problems involved and was very aware of the implications of what he was doing. The symbolism he uses to bring out the extra-ordinary is always very apt and to the point.

When we look at the risen Christ of Dürer we see that he is a very solid personality, it is the same Christ whom, a couple of days later, Thomas could touch and whose wounds he could feel with his fingers. The risen Christ was a person of real flesh and blood, material reality. A few years later Grünewald portrays him contrary to this, rather like a ghost rising out of the grave. In Grünewald's painting of the Resurrection the fleshness of Christ is totally absent; his Christ has become entirely supernatural. For Grünewald material reality is bad in itself, which is however a mystical rather than a biblical conception.

A theme that came up and spoke to the hearts of people in the time of the Reformation was the Conversion of St Paul. It then also became a subject loved by Roman Catholic artists, for they liked the mixture of the supernatural and the natural that this theme presented. In the sixteenth century for the first time, artists began to use biblical themes in order to say something else with them than their commonly accepted meaning. They use or rather misuse the subjects they were expected to portray in order to put a question mark behind them. In a depiction of the Conversion of St Paul, which was made in Bologna in 1560, we see Paul lying on the ground as a kind of ballet dancer. The rein of the horse has been decorated with a very beautiful design, which of course has nothing to do with the reality of this event. The artist plays with the traditional elements of the theme in strange ways that cast doubt on the reality of the story. This is Mannerism, a type of art that is very close to modern art. The next generation, working in the spirit of the Counter-Reformation, says 'no' to this. In a work by Carracci, one of the great renewers standing at the cradle of Baroque art, a comment on this Mannerist painting is given, and there you see a Paul who really fell on the ground and a real staggering horse and reins that are not particularly beautiful.

Caravaggio, another renewer of Roman Catholic art around 1600, paints a Conversion of St Paul which is very realistic, naturalistic even, though he does make use of supernatural light. The horse is very commonplace, just standing there. This is typical of the movement in which Caravaggio took part. Carracci is more traditional; Caravaggio is more renewing and daring, so daring even that many people in his time did not like him as they felt he made things too natural.

Rubens's *Conversion of St Paul* is more like Carracci's again, though adding much movement. There are three staggering horses, not just one, and Christ is coming down from the sky. Rubens makes it into a grand and dramatic event in order to underline its supernatural character. The figures are rather superhuman, endowed with more life, muscle and movement than we ordinarily possess. In his portrayal of the Passion, Rubens depicts Christ as classical antiquity would portray Apollo. This classical way of rendering the body is employed as a means to praise Christ. This is the heroic Christ, God triumphant. It is an exegesis of Christ, not as a normal being but as a supernatural being. It was the greatness of the Baroque that they tried to find ways in which to bring out the supernatural aspect of the biblical themes, yet at the same time there can be the criticism that it became a bit too out of this world. A man who shared this view was Rembrandt.

Seventeenth-century Dutch directions

When Rembrandt makes a picture of the Passion, he paints Christ as a weak, normal human being with a body of no classical beauty at all. When Jesus is taken from the cross, it is a real dead body, ugly to look at. This is Rembrandt's comment on Rubens's painting of the Passion. But Rembrandt's answer raised questions that asked for a solution as well.

In Rembrandt's etching of Christ on the road to Emmaus we see Christ standing on the road with two of his disciples as they ask him to join them for a meal in the house nearby. Apart from the more traditional clothing, there is nothing special about Christ. He is just a man. Yet we know that it is Christ. How does Rembrandt bring this out? In two ways: firstly he draws trees behind Christ to give a suggestion of a halo; secondly he emphasizes the figure of Christ by pictorial means. By accentuating the side of the house by means of dark strokes he creates a rhythm in this etching of disciple-Christ-disciple-house with the downbeat on Christ and the building. Christ moreover stands in the middle of the little group of people with the other two looking at him, which makes him stand out as most important. Here we see the supernatural portrayed not in the medieval or Baroque sense of the anormal or supernormal but here the supernatural is very normal yet at the same time extranormal, which is in line with the way the Bible tells it.

When Rembrandt depicts the Resurrection we see two very solid angels. It makes us wonder whether angels are really that substantial and material, quite the opposite to the way Grünewald approached the supernatural. These angels have such light in them that the soldiers are fearstricken and blinded, just as the Gospels tell us. Rembrandt uses this light here, as he does more often, to represent the presence of God. In a pictorial way again he brings out the supernatural.

The different states of Rembrandt's etching of the Crucifixion show us that he really struggled to do justice to this very special event and that he was not happy with his solution. He erased and changed things in the various states. What he tried to do was to depict the Crucifixion, including all the darkness and suffering. Perhaps this is beyond our human capacity and imagination. Rembrandt at least felt he did not succeed. But this feeling of failure may be exactly his greatness, as it shows that he really took the subject matter very seriously. This sense of inadequacy may also be the reason why we do not find many paintings of religious subjects in Dutch seventeenth-century art. These Dutch painters who came out of the Reformation felt that the Baroque way of portraying the supernatural as superhuman was incorrect. If Paul was not an ordinary person like you and me, the whole message of Paul would have no meaning for us, it would only have meaning for superhumans like St Paul. Precisely because he was a weak human being just like us, his words have meaning for us. This discussion with the Roman Catholic Baroque art around them probably made the Dutch opt for the view that it is impossible to depict biblical themes. If you want to do it well, you will always fall short, and the more supernatural you make it, the more you will miss the point.

The Dutch artists rather painted still lifes, landscapes and genre scenes instead, which also was a solution to the problem. These paintings are not just like photographs, they are much more. They do not just represent what one sees. To paint them the Reformation was necessary, a deep spiritual vision of the visible reality, a spirituality that knows that this reality does not stand in itself. They could only be painted on the solid base of the Reformation and its understanding of the Bible and reality. So these are real Christian pictures, maybe even better solutions to the problem of making Christian pictures than the *Crucifixion* of Rembrandt. They depict the reality God places us in. Not the biblical reality of the past but the reality the Bible talks about, here and now. These pictures would not have been possible without the freedom that Paul talks about in his letters.

I would like to illustrate this with the painting of a mother and her sick child by Gabriel Metsu. This is a completely unique picture, there is nothing like it in history. It is so unique exactly because you have a mother and a sick child and nothing else. It is not a Madonna, it is not a supernatural being, it is just as normal as can be. There may be other pictures with similar themes, but they are either too sentimental or too shallow. The beauty of this picture is also in the design – it has some Mondrian-like traits – but there is much more to it. This is a great depiction of human reality, of real love, love of a mother for a child, of care and compassion, yet without sentimentality, without great movement, without the presence of classical heros or kings. It is as everyday as can be, yet it has real grandeur. This is something that is hardly ever reached, and in my opinion this could only come out of the

Reformation. To make something like this, you need a solid faith and the fullness of the gospel. You need a real humanness that does not make humans too great in the humanistic sense or too small in the modern sense of the debasement of human being.

Nineteenth-century snapshots

We now skip over the eighteenth century to the nineteenth. We then enter a totally different world. Here we get paintings like the one of around 1840 of a melancholy girl going towards an older woman, maybe her mother, to ask for help, and this woman looks up in a more or less praying attitude to something which is hanging on the wall in the corner of the picture. We could say that what happens between the four edges of the frame of the painting in a way stands for the reality of the painter and his time. What this painting tells us is that the great Virgin Mary is like an old print on the wall. She is not real. There is no picture like this before 1800. Something like this could have been portrayed before, but then Mary would really have appeared. She would have come into the room and probably she would have been very large and the human figures tiny in comparison. Here there is only an old print of Mary at the very edge, almost outside of the picture. What is real in this picture are the people who have faith. There is only faith left; the reality of what people have faith in is only a print.

In the religious pictures of the nineteenth century we seldom see Christ or biblical stories, we just see the faith of people. God has gone out of the picture. What is painted now is women sitting in a church somewhere in Tirol, as in the painting *Three women in church* by Wilhelm Leibel of 1878.

The Englishman John Everett Millais painted *The carpenter's shop* in 1848, a revolutionary work at the time. What was new in this picture was the brightness of its colours and its subject matter. Millais adhered to High Anglicanism, which was very liberal. What he depicts here is a real biblical reality: Christ as a child in the house of his parents. Of course he does not paint something as horrible as the Crucifixion but he portrays the sweet story of Jesus as a boy, helping his father Joseph in his carpenter's shop. Anne, the mother of Mary, is also present and the little boy has wounded his hand and his mother says 'Oh son, have you hurt yourself?' And there comes little John the Baptist carrying water to wash away the blood. There are also sheep watching the scene. You know who are the sheep, I presume – that is you and me. What this painting shows is that you need a biblical base to understand reality, otherwise you lose it and you end up with sentimentality.

The next two paintings make it even more clear what was happening. Holman Hunt went to the Dead Sea and there at the edge of the sea he painted a goat while he had his gun at his feet, because it was a very dangerous place at that time. It took him three months to paint the goat. When he came back to England he exhibited the painting but nobody seemed to understand that he meant this animal to be a scapegoat, the goat who takes our sins into the desert. It is a very biblical picture about the heart of Old Testament salvation, but there is nothing about that in the picture, which shows only a goat standing beside a sea.

In 1864 Ciseri, an Italian painter, made his *Ecce homo*. It is a very important picture, one of the masterpieces of this period. The painter was a really talented man. Let's try to understand what he does in this painting. We can see that it is an Ecce Homo. But he does not make Christ look at us, as is normally done in paintings of this subject, because then there would be a relationship between Christ and us. Jesus is not standing in the centre either, so all artistic devices are used not to draw attention to Christ. So we ask ourselves: what is the subject of this work? What is this painting about? Maybe it is about the wife of Pilate, who has been to Pilate but he would not listen, and there she walks back very sad and afraid of the future. But she is not really prominent enough to be the subject. We see a man standing there with his chest in front of two others, so he must be really important. But his whole position makes us understand that he is not important, that he is just a soldier. Standing in front of this picture you will find that within five minutes you are discussing whether the reconstruction of the Jerusalem is done correctly. Very soon you forget the actual subject and you're just looking at Jerusalem in the year AD 33. What about Jesus? He is in the centre but he stands with his back towards us. It is an artistic law that when you look at the back of a figure you do not see the figure but you just see the space around it. Is that the real subject matter: space?

I can also come to this picture in another way. I can understand how it was made: say I have a camera and travel back to the year AD 33, rush into the palace of Pilate by the back door and go 'click'. The painting is then like a photograph of the actual event. I refer to the camera here because it was invented around the same time and because it makes no choices, just like this painting. It is void of human decision, of human understanding, of biblical understanding. It just records what we might have seen. Ciseri was a liberal Roman Catholic. His art is not tied at all to biblical Christianity. What always amazes me is that especially in fundamentalistic evangelical circles you find this type of art, again and again, in their Bible illustrations and Sunday school pictures.

Sunday school pictures

Not so long ago I found this next work in a gallery in Bologna, Italy, where it was made around 1840. It is very cleverly drawn and it is in exactly the same style as so many Sunday school pictures. It shows Ruth reaping. It is a sentimental painting of a beautiful woman. The artist depicts her half in the nude and makes her very sensual, which attracts our attention to everything that it should not attract attention to. Whether she really was virtuous or not is difficult to decide. Certainly looking at this picture it becomes something debatable. If you look at her hand, there even are submeanings which are almost pornographic. Some of the illustrations in our own Bibles may be like this. They have nothing to do with a biblical understanding of reality but rather with a liberal and humanistic one. It is very strange that exactly this type of painting, which is commonly considered to be the lowest point of art history, has been exalted as the model for the depiction of biblical scenes. Even still today.

In a German painting of around 1880 of Christ and the two disciples at Emmaus, the only way to make Christ be Christ is to make him a very sentimental figure with a beard and dressed in feminine clothes. He needed to be made into such an odd figure, because Christ does not fit the naturalness of the naturalism of the nineteenth century as he does not belong to naturalistic or positivistic reality. He does not look strange in a seventeenth-century picture. Here he is not natural anymore but naturalistic, because the natural no longer stands on the firm base of the gospel and the Reformation. Here the reality of Christ has been lost, he has become a strange being.

The next picture is even more sentimental, taken from a recent Pentecostal magazine. You buy this for one-and-a-half guilders in Holland and then you can have Christ on your wall. It is made by a man who took one of these courses on learning to draw in four weeks, and when he had gone through all the techniques he went home and made this very clever picture, with all the gimmicks and all the little tricks. He moreover copies the nineteenth-century pictures. This sentimental nothingness is called Christ. If this is the Christ of twentieth-century evangelical or orthodox Christianity, then we are really poor people and we can understand why we are not taken seriously.

In the illustrations of a Dutch children's Bible, Christ is portrayed almost like a ghost. Do not think that the artist was not talented. He was very talented and a serious Christian as well. But he did not understand that he was looking at the wrong examples, ones that stem from a type of Christianity that has lost the gospel and sees only the material side of things. I want to emphasize that we cannot take this too seriously, even if it only concerns Sunday school pictures. We must understand that when our children grow up they either cling to this type of Christ, and then they become these bourgeois type of Christians, or they become antichristian, and want to beat up everything that is 'Christian', by which they mean this. We have to say that we agree, let's beat it out of the world and seek to portray a Christ again who is a real reality.

Twentieth-century diversity

Next we come to a painting which is a comment on the *Last Supper* of Leonardo da Vinci. Christ is sitting at the table with the disciples, but Christ's head is not there, just his body. Through the body of Christ we can see a boat on a lake. So the painting says that the real thing is the boat on the lake and the rest does not exist, is mistaken for reality. This work has nothing to do with Christianity. We must understand that the artist, Salvador Dali, was making this on purpose to deceive Christians. The more Christians would say that this is a great painting, the more Dali would laugh and say how silly these people are. He read some of the writings of St John of the Cross, and some other mystical books, and then was considered a deep thinker and a Christian, but in reality he still was the old Dada and Surrealist painter making fun of Christianity. He was fighting the Catholicism he had seen in his youth in Spain, where probably a reproduction of Leonardo da Vinci's *Last Supper* had been hanging in the room of his catechism classes. He hates this picture and by distorting it he has found a way to hit back at last. We really must talk about it in this vein because there is nothing more in this painting.

Gauguin depicts the Crucifixion as something of the past, though the women in his painting still have faith in it. To him it is a kind of folklore, interesting, nice to make a picture of. It does not represent anything he believes in.

So, are there any twentieth-century renderings of biblical themes to be found that avoid the naturalism of the nineteenth-century *Ecce homo*, the insincerity of Dali or the folkloristic fascination of Gauguin? I could point to a Passion made by Manessier, a French, Roman Catholic – probably from the modernist stream – artist. Maybe his Passion is too abstract, maybe it is just about passion, human suffering in general and not about the Passion, but at least he tries to do something new. The Spanish painter Saura did a series of Crucifixions. He is known for his awful human figures that communicate hatred of human beings. He says that in his *Crucifixiones* he tries to give a picture of human suffering. Whether we like them or not, maybe they were the best pictures of the Crucifixion that were made in this period of history. Then there is the French painter Léger, who made a whole series of windows of biblical themes. He is not a Christian painter but a man who was honestly trying to solve the problems that the subject matter confronted him with. In the *Deposition* he steers clear of naturalism; he tries to make a beautiful design that stands on its own and at the same time says something more. In a way it is shallow, it has more of a nice design than it has depth of meaning. Perhaps it shows the shallowness of our time, which as victims of our age we cannot evade.

Why could Christians not make good pictures of themes like this? Because the problem of how to render biblical themes still needs to be solved. It is really too optimistic to say that just because we are Christians we have deep insight. We have to fight with all our being to get just a little grain of insight. Maybe it was easier for people of the seventeenth century because of the great tradition of their time. We have to win their understanding back, one little step at a time. And if we have to learn from non-Christians how to do it, well let's be honest and take our lesson.

I have not given a solution; probably a solution cannot be given unless this generation is going to work on these problems together. Maybe Rembrandt can point the way, though we can never just copy his work. Maybe the solution will be the still life, maybe the mother with child.

Predestination

Ephesians 1

'Praise be to the God and Father of our Lord Jesus Christ who has blessed us in the heavenly realms with every spiritual blessing in Christ.' This is how Paul starts out the passage in his letter to the Ephesians that deals with our election before the foundation of the world (Ephesians 1:3–14). Paul begins with God. God has blessed us. God has taken the initiative and has bestowed good on us in ways that exceed all human imagination even before he created the earth.

'For he chose us in him before the creation of the world to be holy and blameless in his sight.' This text is often interpreted as if predestination would mean that long before we were born, God chose us, you and me, but not him and her. I do not think that is the way these verses should be read, and neither did Calvin with whom my view corresponds on this issue.

God predestined us, which means that long before our existence God was already preparing things for us so that we would be blessed. The 'us' is not to be understood individualistically here as if pertaining to you and me as individuals, but it refers to the church, first to the people Paul was writing this letter to and, as it applied to the church at that time, also to us.

What makes predestination such a difficult concept to us is that it asserts on the one hand that we are predestined to accept God as our Lord and Saviour, while on the other hand it also affirms that we are free to choose for or against him. Predestination is not within the bounds of our logic, something we can understand if only we think things through consistently. However, that our choice is predestined is part of our experience. As Calvin explained: when you preach to ten people, there will be five who say 'yes' and five who say 'no', and the five who say 'yes' all say, 'Isn't it great that God has given me this great gift of faith?' All believers know that it is not to their own merit that they have accepted Christ, but that the Holy Spirit somehow inwardly prepared them to open themselves to the message.

I have often been amazed that as a youngster I never came into contact with people who led me into wild ways, for that could easily have happened. Maybe God was already working in my life so that later on I would not have to go through the difficult and painful process of adjustment. All I can do is thank him for that. It was not because I was such a great person but because he protected me. It is not our choice to believe in God but 'in love he predestined us to be adopted as sons through Jesus Christ, in accordance with his pleasure and will' (verse 5). Predestination can never be divorced from grace.

Determinism and freedom

As to his view on predestination Calvin has often been accused of merely following the Stoics of antiquity who held that everything in this world is determined. The Stoics were materialists who believed that the world consists of the material only which is subject to the law of cause and effect. There are also many people today who think like that. Positivism holds that everything is determined on the material level, and that humans are conditioned furthermore by their social surroundings. If I were clever enough I could have predicted that you would be reading these words at this very moment.

Calvin always refuted this charge of Stoicism by answering that he could never be a Stoic, as he believed in a God who is there and who acts so that there is more to this world than just cause and effect, and that, moreover, the Bible speaks very clearly about human freedom. It was part of Paul's very life's work to stress the centrality of freedom. We are free because we do not have to earn our salvation by our good works. We do not have to justify ourselves in the face of God, we do not have to prove ourselves in the face of other people, we are free to move, unhampered by a system of holy rules.

How do we reconcile this freedom with the predestined route of our lives? We first of all have to affirm that God is the great God Almighty. If he wills something to be, it is. He spoke, and the world was. He sent Christ, and the way to reconciliation was opened. He will come with his Last Judgment, and the scroll of Life will be read. God is the all-powerful Master of the universe and we can only say 'amen'. Yet the Bible also affirms that there is total freedom. We are free to act, there is no determinism, there is no God directing us to go left or right. It is precisely our humanity that gives us that freedom. Animals act according to their instincts in beautifully prefigured ways. The Bible reminds us how fantastic it is that the stork knows where to go in summer and winter. But humans are free to move in their own ways. They are even free to choose whether they want to love God, yes or no. Adam and Eve were advised not to eat from that one tree, yet they were free to do so. God never said they could not do that, he only said they should not do that, because it would be very foolish. And even after they had eaten from this foul fruit God did not take away their freedom. He said, 'No, I made you human; you are going to be human.'

The question of determinism versus freedom has been a hard one for philosophers of all times, because whether we choose for one or the other, we are always wrong. When we say that everything is determined, everybody objects because it is our experience that we are free: we can move where we want and we are free to make choices. But when we say that we are totally free, that also goes against experience because we know that we cannot do everything. We encounter the same dilemma in Ephesians 2:10, where we read that 'We are God's workmanship created in Jesus Christ to do good works which God prepared in advance for us to do.' We do good works in our freedom as Christians, yet God has prepared them for us. In Philippians 2:12–13 Paul exhorts us to work out our salvation with fear and trembling, for it is God who is at work in us, both to will and to work. Again, a logical paradox, for it is completely our work but it is completely God's work as well.

Can our actions be predestined and free at the same time? Is there an answer to that question? In a way we do not need an answer because the Bible does not explicitly give us one. That is just the way things are; we experience and accept it. When we, for instance, pray for people we do not pray that God will take control over their actions and take away their freedom. Rather, we ask God to lead them to do in freedom what is good for them. God apparently can do something and yet not take away freedom. How is that possible?

Two answers

Maybe this question is too big to answer, yet I will present two attempts to formulate an answer, Francis Schaeffer's and mine.

Schaeffer says this: when we read the Bible there are a number of things we just have to accept as they are beyond our comprehension and ability to investigate. One is that God created the world. Nobody can go back to the time of creation and stand behind God, look over his shoulder and see how he fashions the heaven and the earth out of nothing. We cannot grasp how that was ever possible, but we accept it and thank God for it. A second point is that Christ is both God and a human person at the same time. Again, we cannot understand it, we simply have to accept it. A third point, which is maybe the most difficult of all, is that God is one yet three. We are not polytheists, we have one God and one God only, and yet this God is three. We cannot explain it, it goes beyond logic. Yet every time we deviate from the biblical position we find that we loose something because then we take away from God's Godness and make him more of a human size and shape.

The fourth point is the one we are discussing here: God is 100 per cent the boss, and nevertheless people are also 100 per cent free. We could understand it if it were 95 per cent God's acting and 5 per cent our own, but it is blasphemous to say God does only 95 per cent because he is 100 per cent in control. How much freedom do we have? Not just 5 per cent, but 100 per cent: 100 per cent human freedom. We do not have the freedom of a bird, we cannot fly, we do not have the freedom of an atom or an angel. We only have human freedom, but we have it for the full 100 per cent. If we choose for God, it is a totally free choice, not only 5 per cent free; that goes against experience. So it is 100 per cent of God and it is 100 per cent of us. According to Francis Schaeffer there are four things we have to accept: that zero equals one (creation), that one equals two (the two natures of Christ), that one equals three (the Trinity) and that 100 per cent plus 100 per cent equals 100 per cent. And when we accept those four points, the whole Bible becomes a clear and rational book that is in agreement with our everyday experience. Not a book in which strange and crazy things happen that never happen otherwise. Now, in all other religions or philosophies one always has to accept 20 or 200 points. In Christianity there are only these four.

I have searched for a different way of explaining the fourth point. In the eighteenth century the deists compared God to a watchmaker and his creation to a watch, a perfect super-watch. The stars and the planets and everything else in this world work like wheels within wheels within wheels. God made this big watch and then he withdrew and let it tick on by itself. The watch is an image of complete determinism. We do what we do because that is how the watch is made. However, the mistake of this image is that it makes God too small because our great God Almighty, the One who according to the Jews is beyond all naming, created this world as a watch which not only runs on time but in which at the same time all the wheels are free to move as they wish.

In God's watch everything has its own type of freedom to choose. Even atoms can make choices, as Heisenberg found out. If you take, for example, one gas and you mix it with another gas, then 50 per cent of the gas makes a new chemical substance and 50 per cent does not. If you should follow one particular atom, you would never be able to predict whether it would be in the one 50 per cent or the other 50 per cent. So atoms obviously have a choice. An atom's freedom is very limited, of course, but it does show that the totality of the universe runs on freedom. Everything is free and everything is in flux, but nevertheless there is no chaos. If we would make a watch and all the little wheels were free, the watch would not even run for one second. A machine is always totally predetermined. When one wheel is a little loose, it stops. But God makes all the wheels free and it still keeps on running. It is already beyond my understanding that God could make this universe, even more so that he could make it out of nothing, but it is completely beyond me that he could make it in such a way that everything dovetails perfectly while yet free.

Implications

Calvin wanted to emphasize God's sovereignty in opposition to the position of the Roman Catholics of his time who, due to humanistic influences, had given humans too big a say in the work of redemption. Calvin stressed that it is first and foremost God's grace and predestination that lead us to Christ, that God first sends the Holy Spirit to work in us before we ever turn to him. For Calvin this was cause for great thankfulness and adoration, and not for fear of a God who accepts and rejects human beings at will. It was rather the Calvinists of a later date who distorted Calvin's view in that direction, but his own viewpoint was totally scriptural and very beautiful. Calvin did not claim to fully understand it all. Neither do I, because I cannot explain what I cannot explain. I can only explain to you that it is beyond explanation. It is, however, not irrational but only beyond human logic.

Calvin underlined the authority and greatness of God, yet he emphasized at the same time that this inconceivably great God is first of all a gracious God and that precisely because of his greatness he can be a personal God who is involved in the lives of each one of us. He is not so big and therefore so far away, but he is so big and therefore so close to each one of us. He knows us all intimately. He hears us when we pray. It makes sense to pray to him for other people, because he can act in people's lives. He can make your friend drive a little bit faster so that he or she just misses the plane that crashes on the road. Or maybe he made him or her forget something and turn back home in order to get it. If you go into the stories of people you will find that these things do happen.

That God is at work in people has implications for the evangelist as well. Schaeffer once told me that when he had just become a pastor, he worked very, very hard. He was always completely exhausted. Why? Because when he was talking to somebody, he felt he had to convince that person. If he was not able to do that, he felt it was his fault that the other person did not accept Christ. But then one day he found out he had been wrong. That is not the way to do it. After all, nobody can make anyone else a Christian; that is beyond us. So what do we do? Well, if God calls us to speak to somebody we try to give the best possible answers, but at the same time we pray that God will work in that person's heart so that whatever we say right will make itself felt and continue to work, and whatever we say wrong will have no impact. We acknowledge that it is first of all God's work rather than our work. Then the pressure is gone and because of that it is not so exhausting.

It may be a logical contradiction, yet there are many examples in our own lives as well as many instances in the Bible which testify to the reality that we freely choose our own course of action, while at the same time it is God who makes us take that course. On the day of Pentecost, Peter gives a long speech in which he points out that there are many prophecies in the Old Testament that predict the coming of the Messiah. At the height of his speech Peter says, 'Now, don't you understand that Jesus was the predicted Messiah, to whom happened exactly all the things that were prophesied, who died on the cross and was crucified?' And then he continues, 'Why did you do it? How could you kill the Son of God?' So he says in one and the same sentence that on the one hand it was all according to God's prophecy and that on the other hand they were responsible because they did it. And nobody told Peter that this was a crazy and impossible thing to say, because they all knew that it was true.

We are 100 per cent free and therefore 100 per cent responsible for our deeds, even though God is at work in our lives as well. We also have no certainty that we will never take a wrong turn because God is taking care of us. We are not above temptation, and it is not impossible to fall away. So we have to be careful. When we become lazy in our faith, we may find that after two or three months we are sliding away. I have found in my own life and in the lives of others that when we are heading in the wrong direction, God always puts signs on the road and warns us that this is not the way to go. But some people are stubborn and just push the signs aside and after one or two years they find that they are completely on the wrong track and then they look back and see how foolish they have been, just like the prodigal son in the parable. Some may find the way back, but there may be others who do not turn back. I can never say that God chose me and because of that it is impossible for me to go astray. But on the other hand it would be crazy not to thank God in my songs and prayers that he gave me my faith and that he keeps me from falling, that in a way he does it for me, so that I do not have to choose, because I would be too weak and too foolish to make the right choices. That again is logically inconsistent, but it is the glorious experience of God's children. Thank God that when we work out our salvation with fear and trembling, the great God of grace does come into our lives to work in us both to will and to work.

Love is the End: Sermon on 2 Peter

The salutation

Even though Peter started out as a fisherman and even though he complained somewhere in his letters about the difficulty of Paul's letters, we should not conclude that he was a rather illiterate, simple-minded man. Not only was he called to be one of the leaders of the early church, but he is also a man who could write in a very logical and intelligent style, as we read in this letter. Peter begins his Epistle with a rhetorical phrase, in the style of those days and very compact. He first introduces himself, Simon Peter, and then states to whom the letter is addressed: '*To those who have obtained the faith of equal standing with ours in the righteousness of our God and Saviour, Jesus Christ.*' So he addresses himself to people who know the Lord, and if we know the Lord this letter is also directed to us. The introduction ends, as was the custom in those days, with a benediction: '*May grace and peace be multiplied to you in the knowledge of God and of Jesus our Lord.*' This is not just a beautiful religious phrase used here only because it was a tradition to start letters this way, but to Peter it is also reality itself and therefore he continues to explain these words in the following section.

Life and godliness

He continues: '*because his divine power has granted to us all things that pertain to life and godliness through the knowledge of him who has called us to his own glory and excellence.*' Central here are life and godliness, which God makes possible for us through our knowledge of him. There are many places in the Scriptures where life is mentioned because it is the very heart of what God is talking about in the Bible. God gives us life; he wants us to live; he is a God of life. That life is the opposite of corruption and death. Paul also writes about that in Romans 8:10,11: 'But if Christ is in you, although your bodies are dead because of sin, your spirits are alive because of righteousness. If the spirit of him who raised Jesus from the dead dwells in you, he who raised Christ Jesus from the dead will give life to your mortal bodies also through the spirit which dwells in you'. This life is not only life in the future, but it is also life now. It begins now, just as Jesus said that those who accept him go from death to life. We are raised with Christ and made new men and women, so that we may have life.

The second thing God makes possible for us is godliness, which is the fruit of this life that God has given to us. It means walking in Gods ways. Galatians 5:22 makes clear that the fruit of the Spirit simply is love, joy, peace, patience, kindness, goodness, faithfulness, gentleness and self-control. This life and godliness, says Peter, are given us through the knowledge of him who called us to his own glory and excellence. The knowledge of God is not a theological or theoretical knowledge, even though that is also important, but it is a knowledge that God gives us through the Scriptures, so that we know who he is not in a philosophical way but in a personal way: knowing what he wants and what kind of a person he is. Immediately connected with it is that we get to know ourselves as well, because we are made in his image. We need to know who God is and what he wants us to do in order that we may have life and show the fruits of that life. This knowledge is the basis of life and godliness.

Divine nature

Peter goes on: *'by which he has granted to us his very precious and great promises, that through these you may escape from the corruption that is in the world because of the passion and become partakers of the divine nature'.* So there is an opposition here: on the one hand there is life, which God wants to give to us, and on the other hand there is corruption, from which God wants us to escape. Corruption is in the world because of passion and covetousness, because of the things we want. But in the Tenth Commandment it says 'Don't covet this and that,' because it leads to sin and sin leads to death. So, God is helping us to escape from corruption in order that we, as the text continues, may become partakers of the divine nature. There have been many people who have woven great theories around these words, but they simply mean that we will start to show the image of God. In the text in Romans 8 that we just read we find the same idea: we are one with the Lord, Christ is in us, his spirit dwells in us, and that means we partake in his divine nature and escape corruption.

The letter continues *'For this very reason make every effort to supplement your faith with virtue, and virtue with knowledge, and knowledge with self-control and self-control with steadfastness and steadfastness with godliness and godliness with brotherly affection and brotherly affection with love.'* It begins with 'for this very reason', because God is a great God who has given us life and the fruits of life, who has taken us out of the world of corruption, and for that reason we have to make every effort. God is not dealing with us as puppets or robots; he does not just flick the switch and off we go. No, God has given us those things, and then he wants us to do something with them as human beings, in freedom, every person in his or her own way. He wants us to work with our own gifts according to our own personality in order that our personality may be realized. That also means that we do not work in order to gain a good relationship with God or to work out our salvation; it works quite the other way around: because we are saved and God gave us a knowledge of himself, that is why now we can work

God's scaffolding

Then Peter begins to talk about what I call God's scaffolding: *'so supplement your faith with virtue, virtue with knowledge,'* and so on, and it ends with love. Usually we think about love in a much too sentimental way, as some kind of feeling. That is easy in a way. But love is not soft; it is something very strong that also asks an effort. Love is the end, not the beginning. Peter urges us to begin with faith and build it up from there in order that we may come to the point where there is real love. We have to put all our effort into it. It begins with faith. Faith is something very simple here. It is not a kind of mystical quality, but faith just means that we trust in the Lord, that we listen to his word and accept it because we know that when God says something, it is good. And then we get to virtue. Virtue is a fruit of faith, for we can only grow in virtue if we know and accept what God wants us to do. There is a beautiful text in Proverbs 2 in which you also find this relationship between faith and virtue:

> My son, if you receive my words and treasure up my commandments with you, make your ear attentive to wisdom and incline your heart to understanding, yes if you cry out for insight and raise your voice for understanding, if you seek it like silver and search for it as for hidden treasures, then you will understand the fear of the Lord and find the knowledge of God. For the Lord gives wisdom, from his mouth comes knowledge and understanding, he stores up sound wisdom for the upright, he's a shield to those who walk in integrity, guarding the path of justice and preserving the ways of this saints. Then you will understand righteousness and justice and equity, every good path.

Also here we find that we should begin to have faith in the Lord by accepting what he has to say to us, because that is the beginning of wisdom, and then we will know what is righteous and what virtue means. First faith, then virtue.

The third thing our text mentions is knowledge. The humanists have always said that knowledge leads to virtuousness, but the Bible says that we first have to listen to and do what is right and then we will understand. Let me give an example: if a thief becomes a Christian and is told that he should not steal, then he or she understands that, 'Okay, God says I should not steal.' But only gradually he or she will begin to understand why God has said that, and why it is not good to steal. God's commands are not something strange; these things are part of the world itself, and the world is better and we are better if we do not steal. So, as the person does God's will, he or she gradually grows in an understanding and knowledge of right and wrong.

Only when we have that understanding can we come to the next point, which is self-control. It is very difficult to control yourself, but if you have come to see why you should restrain yourself, it is much easier. And if you have gained self-control, then of course it is not just for one day but it should become something continuous, so that steadfastness grows out of it. There has to be endurance in doing what we know is right, because not to do something one day but to do it the next day in a way does not mean a thing, but to go on doing something makes us strong and reliable people. And that then leads to godliness, which means that people see that this is indeed a fruit of the Spirit. So godliness comes only when we persist in living in a certain way, when we have an understanding of right and wrong so that we can control ourselves not only once but persistently. Then it will start to show and become godliness. We see that one thing is built on top of another, and we cannot just reverse that sequence. It is the way we are built, the way God made those things to function in our lives.

Love

When we have come to godliness, it will show: we become like light from a candle. Only then can we come to mutual affection, because only then can we recognize one another as children of God. And then, as the last step, we can begin to love. Love is the end of the line. We often make love so sentimental and easy, but Peter says here that it is not something we just do. Rather it is the end of a long process. He also makes clear that we first need to grow in love for the people near to us, and that it is only from there that we can move on to love people who are far away. If our fundraising for the people in Africa and so on is not built on something that also happens at home, it becomes an empty gesture. We first need to show that we really know what it is to love people, our friends and family, and then the love for our neighbour will be the fruit of that. So when God commands us to love him and our neighbour as ourselves, he is not telling us to have a nice feeling inside but rather to work with all our effort in order to realize it.

Then we come to the next verse: *'For if these things are yours in abundance, they will keep you from being ineffective or unfruitful in the true knowledge of our Lord Jesus Christ.'* If we have indeed acquired these qualities, then we can start to really accomplish something in this world and to become a readable letter from Christ. Many people want to do great things for the Lord, but often forget that they have to begin at the beginning, to have faith and then virtue and to build that up until they have true love, and then maybe they can do something for him. For then they will be effective and fruitful, as Peter's letter states. There is so much ineffectiveness and unfruitfulness because people start out from the wrong end.

A sequence like the one we just studied is found not only here in this passage but in many places in the Bible. It is remarkable that these sequences go contrary to contemporary, also Christian, philosophy and psychology. We tend to think differently. In Matthew 24 we read that in the last days, because wickedness is multiplied, love will grow cold. We probably would have written the opposite: that because love grew cold, there was wickedness in the world. No, says Jesus, wickedness increase and therefore love grows cold. In Romans 5:3–5 we find another sequence: 'We will exult in our tribulations, knowing that tribulation brings about perseverance; and perseverance proven character; and proven character hope; and hope does not disappoint, because the love of God has been poured out within our hearts through the Holy Spirit who was given to us.'

The beauty of that particular passage is that it ends with the reassurance that God will not disappoint us. When we begin to work and put our effort into growing according to his will, then he will never leave us disappointed but will truly fill our hearts with love.

Part IV

HANS ROOKMAAKER: AN OPEN LIFE

by LAUREL GASQUE

Preface

In the spring of 1977, I was living in Edinburgh. The sun was shining beautifully through the windowpanes of my little flat in Rose Street when I answered the telephone on Monday 14 March. My delight in the day and at hearing Marleen Rookmaaker's voice soon jolted into a dark shadow of shock and sadness as she told me that her father had died in the early evening of the night before. It hardly seemed possible that he could have slipped away from all of us so suddenly.

Sorrow softened as I listened to Bach's wonderful cantata, *Gottes Zeit is die allerbeste Zeit* (BWV 106) – 'God's time is the very best time . . . In him, we die at the right time, as he wills.' Then memories flooded in.

My husband, Ward, and I treasured our friendship with Hans. There had been so many memorable and enjoyable times with him and with Anky and the family. We had had opportunity to see him in all sorts of surroundings: from the intimacy of our home in Vancouver on extended visits as our houseguest to Dutch and Swiss L'Abri as well as in British, American, and Austrian settings. Publicly and personally, professionally and privately, there was no contradiction. He was completely himself. He did not try to ingratiate himself through small talk or chitchat. But he did have a great sense of humour. I think Ward is the only person I ever saw who could make him laugh heartily at himself. We loved the fact that he did not take himself seriously every second of the day.

We also almost killed ourselves suppressing our laughter on one occasion at seeing Hans trying to be as tactful as possible in giving his opinion of a work of art one of our colleagues had invested a considerable amount of money in at his wife's disapproval. He was obviously looking for Hans's endorsement to justify his expenditure and confirm his good taste. When Hans was not immediately forthcoming, he finally asked, 'What do you think?' There was a significant interval of silence. There we all were, including our colleague and his spouse and children, waiting with bated breath to hear Hans's expert opinion. Fiddling with his pipe a bit, he finally looked around at all of us and then at the painting and said, 'Well, it really should be entitled, "Tunnel of Love". It would be best if you put it under your bed.'

But writing the biography of a mentor and friend is not simply about warm personal reminiscences. Over the course of writing this brief biography, I have had to ask myself many questions about what it means to give a textual account of someone's life with fidelity to the remaining documentary evidence as well as the highly personal memories (including my own) of those still living.

By turns I have been challenged, humbled, and awed by the life of a person who was neither famous nor obscure by worldly standards. Here was someone who lived a relatively ordinary life of influence in the middle of the twentieth century. The upsurge in biography today often goes hand in hand with catering to curiosity about celebrity and the hunger of the public to know the foibles of a famous person's life. Few famous people in any age can be what one might call typical of their time.

Yet we desire deeply to know the lives of people and long for figures who represent their ages. Perhaps the main reason the Bible is still the world's bestseller and we name so many of our children after its cast of characters is that it is a book of biographies, giving powerfully rendered, unvarnished and distilled lives of people who made a difference for good or ill.

Biographies help give us our moral place in history as we participate through identification with or reaction against those we read about. Biographies also overcome the arbitrary distinctions and artificial divisions we make when thinking or writing about history. At best, if crafted well, they can synthesize a personal perspective with a wider view of the events of a period that inspires us to try to understand another time or to live well in the present.

The struggle to achieve a moving narrative while remaining faithful to written evidence and personal recollections is not easy. It provides a great temptation for the biographer to move subtly to create a form closer to fiction than the more limited telling of a life based almost strictly on what can be corroborated.

Out of complete sincerity and desire for Hans Rookmaaker's name not to fall into oblivion, the late Linette Martin made an important first attempt to share his life soon after he died by publishing a biography in 1979. For that, anyone who values the life and work of H.R. Rookmaaker must be grateful. Despite inconsistency regarding chronology, some historical inaccuracies, and elements of invented narrative, anyone who writes a biography after her work stands on her shoulders and owes her a debt of appreciation. In the latter part of her book, she was able brilliantly to capture Rookmaaker's colloquially voiced speech on the page of a written text. A voice, we do not hear in quite the same way in his recorded lectures or his letters. It is so authentic that we can ever be grateful for her dramatist's gift and forgive her for her factual errors.

The purpose of another biography has been to link Rookmaaker to his works and his ongoing influence as well as to try to correct a number of inaccuracies. There has also been an attempt to elaborate the important influence of some people and perspectives in shaping his life and outlook that were overlooked previously.

In his own right, the life and thought of J.P.A. Mekkes, Rookmaaker's most important mentor and a key post-World War II Dutch Reformational thinker, still needs to be made available to English-speaking audiences. Further reflection on the relationship of Hans Rookmaaker and Francis Schaeffer in their missional dynamic to the so-called hippy generation would also be helpful. It would also be useful for a historian of Christianity to explore the bridge between Rookmaaker's life and thought and the current generation who have been influenced by him in their art or thinking or written work.

I am more than painfully aware of many names that are missing from this account of the life and influence of Hans Rookmaaker that could be mentioned. No biography can encompass a whole life. The next biographer perhaps can craft it even more inclusively now that we have the published *Complete Works* available in accessible form.

I am reminded of Hans's playfulness. Walking up a pavement with his family and with our family, he would rush ahead of all of us and say, 'Three steps forward and two steps back!' and have us all doing the same thing down the street with people looking at us as if we were crazy. What a life lesson in hope! There are setbacks, but buck up, we are also, by God's grace, going forward. At many instances along the way in life and work, and writing this biography, I have been reminded of 'three steps forward and two steps back', not by abstract admonition but by the remembrance of the act of charging up and down an ordinary street in a normal neighbourhood, three steps forward and two steps back.

No biography can get it all right. The aim of this biography has been simply to say that an 'ordinary' life can make an incredible difference.

Acknowledgments

First and foremost, I would like to acknowledge my deep gratitude to the subject of this biography. Hans Rookmaaker never failed to encourage me intellectually and spiritually through friendship or to inspire me to independence of vocation by his creative example and serious conversation. Through his generous gift of time in viewing art and architecture, listening to music, and in discussing vigorously, extensively, and openly issues of culture and meaning with me, he gave a dimension to my education that I could never have obtained by formal means. Hans's complete confidence in the indissoluble relation between art and reality and his wise understanding of their inter-relatedness have enriched my thinking and, indeed, my life.

It has been an honour and privilege to write the brief biography of someone who has contributed so much to so many lives, including my own. For this invitation I thank Marleen Hengelaar-Rookmaaker and Pieter Kwant. I am humbled by the confidence they have placed in me to undertake this task.

I have benefited greatly from the generosity and trust of the Rookmaaker family in allowing me to have access to family records, documents, letters, photos as well as Hans Rookmaaker's annual appointment agendas. Sadly Anky Rookmaaker-Huitker died on 10 February 2003, as this account of her husband's life was being completed. Throughout the process of research and verifying details, she kindly assisted as she could until only a few weeks before her death. I shall always appreciate the extended interview I was able to have with her in July 2001 in Ommen, her welcome then, and her hospitality on many other occasions. I also value the opportunity I had many years ago to meet both of Hans's sisters, Door Haver Droeze and Hannie Rotgans, who were my dinner partners at a family occasion I was invited to join. Less than a year before her death in 2002, Hannie allowed me to interview her in her home in The Hague. Door passed away in 1989.

Again, I give my thanks to Marleen Hengelaar-Rookmaaker. She has been patient beyond measure and indefatigable in answering questions and tracking down or correcting information for me. I am grateful for help with the history of *Redt een Kind* (Save a Child) from her husband, Albert Hengelaar. I am also appreciative of their gracious hospitality and extraordinary helpfulness when I have been in the Netherlands. Their warm friendship has heartened me at every stage of my work.

Special thanks must go to Jaco Bauer for her unwavering help in translating many documents and letters from Dutch. Her grace and good humour during long hours of working together have sustained me when I thought we might not ever get through some materials.

The staff of the Special Collections of the Buswell Memorial Library at Wheaton College (Wheaton, Illinois, USA) – David Malone, Head of

Special Collections and College Archivist; David Osielski, Reference Archivist; and Keith Call, Assistant Archivist – are all owed my thanks for their outstanding help as I worked through the Hans Rookmaaker Papers in their custody. I am also indebted to Graham Birtwistle and C.A. van Swigchem of the Free University of Amsterdam for a record of the history of the Department of Art History. I thank Graham Birtwistle for answering many other enquiries as well.

I would like to extend my appreciation for photographs appearing in the biography taken by Sylvester Jacobs, John Walford, and Peter Smith. I also gratefully acknowledge the help of the Documentatiecentrum at the Free University in tracing photographic material.

Many, many people have open-heartedly shared their memories with me or open-handedly assisted me with valuable information in this project. I am sincerely grateful for their help. They are: the late David Alexander, Pat Alexander, Chris Anderson, Philip Archer, Thena Ayres, Jeremy Begbie, Elaine Botha, Ned Bustard, Raelene Cameron, Bettina and David Clowney, Tyrus Clutter, Eleanor DeLorme, Meryl Doney, Harry van Dyke, Bill and Grace Dyrness, Joyce Erickson, Eduardo Escheverria, Lindsay Farrell, Roger Feldman, David and Susan Fetcho, Don Forsythe, Rudi Fuchs, Sharon Gallagher, Nigel Goodwin, Erica Grimm-Vance, David Hanson, Bruce Herman, Irving Hexham, Eugene Johnson, Marc de Klijn, Jason Knapp, Ed Knippers, Roel Kuiper, George Langbroek, Barbara Lidfors, Ranald and Susan Macaulay, Mary Leigh Morbey, David Muir, Karen Mulder, Laurie Nelson, Gerard Pas, Albert Pedulla, Ted and Cathy Prescott, David Porter, Wayne Roosa, Dan Russ, Phil Schaafsma, Edith Schaeffer, Dal and Kit Schindell, Rachel Smith, Betty Spackman, Frank Speyers, T. Grady Spires, Barbara and Jonathan Stanfield, Alva Steffler, Norman Stone, Charles Twombly, Maria Walford-Dellù, Murray Watts, Graham Weeks, and Shorty Yeaworth.

Many friends and colleagues sustained me during this endeavour in ways that defy categories that I have already mentioned. I wish to acknowledge their support. Friends who have been at my side are: Joy Gratz, Pat Henneman, Mary Frank, Julia Popp, Chris and Jeannie Houston, John and Debbie Bowen, Don and Maureen Bennett, Ruth and Ken Smith, Jerry and Jane Hawthorne, Susan and Steve Phillips, David and Lucia Gill, Don and Edie Tinder, Leona DeFehr, Jim and Diane Alimena, Elizabeth and Jim Gladden, Bob and Julie Fredericks, Peter and Frances Shaw, Ruth and Paul Pitt, John and Babby Schwarz, Grace Irwin, Janet and Jeff Greenman, Brian and Lily Stiller, Ruth Ericson Byrholdt, Betty Bennett, Soo Inn Tan, Earl Palmer, Luci Shaw, and Greg Wolfe. I would like to give particular thanks to some of my International Fellowship of Evangelical Students (IFES) and Inter-Varsity Christian Fellowship of Canada colleagues who have encouraged me to write: Lindsay and Ann Brown, Jim Berney, Barb Boyt, and C.P.S. (Pat) Taylor. The solidarity of these friends and colleagues has been an enormous encouragement.

Elria Kwant, my constant communicant with Piquant, has been wonderful in helping me bring to birth this biography. The depth and breadth of her spirit in prodding me on has been singular. She has been the skilled mid-wife in bringing this book to life. I give her my heartfelt thanks for her perseverance throughout the long labour.

Last but not least, I would like to thank my dear, long-suffering family for all their care. Though I have been tense to live with at times, they have more than tolerated me and lived good-naturally with 'Hans' as an adopted member of our family as I have written a narrative of his life. I thank my mother, Doris Sandfor, who lives in our home, for many a delicious dinner that took me away from obsessively thinking about the next sentence I should write to family fellowship and a wider perspective. Many times while writing, I have thought of my daughter, Michelle Gasque, as a small child giving Hans Rookmaaker a very respectful and wide berth as she encountered him, especially going up or down stairs. She was not exactly afraid of him, but knew instinctively as a child that he was not someone to fawn over small children. This probably left a much more distinct trace on her memory of him than the many houseguests in our home who tried to sidle up to her. She has cheered me on from the outset and cared for me touchingly all along the way. To my husband, Ward Gasque, I express deepest thanks for all his skilled help and sound advice, from dealing with the smallest detail to taking in an understanding of the whole scope of the task I was involved in. Words can hardly convey the depth of appreciation and feeling I have for his constancy and care and concern that I bring my work to completion well.

Laurel Gasque
Camano Island, 2003

1
Impact

Hans Rookmaaker's life spanned a mere fifty-five years (1922–1977). Those years were situated symmetrically in the midst of the twentieth century. He completed the first half of the course of his life in the years 1949/1950. Incandescently, he was gone by 1977.

Since his death the arts scene amongst Christians of almost all traditions and denominations in Europe and North America has changed significantly. In New York City, the Bible Society now has a serious art gallery. The National Gallery in London marked the year 2000 with an extraordinary exhibition of images of Christ sponsored by two major trusts willing to back such an arts event, despite the considerable embarrassment that some art historians still seem to have about Christian subject matter. Over the past thirty years Christian rock music has matured considerably lyrically and musically. Christians in the Visual Arts (CIVA) is an established organization linking and creatively supporting a wide network of Christian artists in all fields of the visual arts. *IMAGE: A Journal of the Arts & Religion* serves as a beacon of hope for many writers and artists as it speaks credibly from a perspective of faith commitment to a wider culture beyond the boundaries of religious institutions. In Scotland the Leith School of Art was founded and in the Netherlands a Christian art academy was established as a result of Rookmaaker's own efforts.

A generation ago these kinds of developments and resources that we have begun to take for granted simply did not exist. In North America the marginalizing and minimizing of the arts were not just a condition of the church but also of a pragmatic culture that viewed the arts as a luxury rather than a necessity. In Europe the situation was different. The wider culture valued the arts and invested in them more by comparison to their North American counterparts. For many cultured Europeans art, filled with the beauty and greatness of past human achievement, was a surrogate religion. For an extremely influential and highly intellectual minority it became a staging ground for raging anger and discontent, especially after the debacle of World War II and the collapse of confidence in an abiding moral order. On both sides of the Atlantic the church, challenged by a new society and not completely confident of its identity, frequently closed its eyes and ears to culture by ignoring trends or becoming defensive.

With extraordinary openness and human sympathy, and with deep faith Hans Rookmaaker faced these cultural conditions squarely. Not only did many of the arts developments mentioned above not exist a generation ago but they were not fully imaginable. The dynamic impact of Rookmaaker's life and his short life's work made them a lot more probable. Out of all proportion to his length of days he qualitatively influenced key individuals and groups that were to have a remarkable effect on changing attitudes toward the arts in the church and many other institutions.

In 1961 at the height of the Cold War and the great race for space between the Soviets and the Americans, Rookmaaker, not yet a full professor but teaching at the University of Leiden, made his first extended trip to North America. He came not sponsored or invited by churches, though individual friends from his Reformed tradition welcomed him and warmly hosted him, but through a Dutch government funded grant. The purpose of his trip was to make a study of the teaching of art history in the United States.

To say the least, he made the most of this trip. While in the United States he visited virtually every major centre of art-historical study east of St Louis, Missouri, as well as every major art collection from the northeast seaboard to the Midwest. He attended the College Art Association meeting in New York City, where he met many prominent art historians. He took this golden opportunity also to pursue his passion for African-American music and culture. By this time he was an expert in this field and had recently published a book on jazz, blues and spirituals. His diary during this trip is dotted with contacts with leading black figures, such as Thomas A. Dorsey, Mahalia Jackson, and Langston Hughes. Furthermore, he managed to meet a wide range of church-affiliated people, from black Baptists and Dutch Reformed types to a broad spectrum of evangelicals attached to institutions like Calvin College and Wheaton College or organizations like *Christianity Today*. He also travelled to Canada. Afterwards he exuberantly corresponded with an amazing number of the people he had met on his travels.

Rookmaaker continued to deepen his thought and nurture his friendships. By 1968 he was a professor and had formed the Art History Department of the Free University of Amsterdam. He was in full stride. The intervening years had helped prepare him for an increasingly chaotic culture. Often this period is looked back at nostalgically as a gentler more peace-loving time flowing with flower children, happy hippies, when marijuana filled the air and some social issues, such as basic civil rights for black people in the USA, got straightened out. With fading memory the fierceness of the student protest movements that were gaining strength both in Europe and North America have not always remained clear. The massacre under a US combat troop led by Lt William Calley of all 500 civilians of the Vietnamese village of My Lai who showed no sign of resistance inflamed anger as did the entire war. The attempted assassination of Rudi Dutschke, a well-known German student anarchist and activist, unleashed turbulent solidarity demonstrations in Vienna, Paris, Rome and London. Student protest closed down the University of Paris in the spring of 1968 and turned the streets of Paris into a battle zone, imperilling the government. West Germany was launched into a decade of tumultuous internal struggle as radicals gathering around the Baader-Meinhof gang tried to kick-start revolution through violence and terrorism.

During these tumultuous years of student unrest in the late 1960s and early 1970s, few thinkers or leaders were prepared for the hard social, political, and philosophical realities of this era. Many academic and administrative careers were broken in universities across the world. Rookmaaker was not impervious to the pressures on and within his own institution or on himself as an administrator and teacher. But, remarkably, he was prepared spiritually and intellectually for the fundamental challenge of the younger generation's radical quest and the turbulence of the times it helped create, because through the years he had striven earnestly to bring to bear Christian understanding on all the issues of life. He made a huge impact on the lives of students in several countries.

At first glance he looked like an unlikely person to have much to say to a radical and rebellious generation bent on changing not only the university but also society and its mores. A driver's license that he obtained in 1961 during his extended travels in the USA describes him as having brown hair and eyes, weighing 160 pounds with a height of five feet and eight inches. He was not physically a big man or imposing at all. Dressed in an English worsted three-piece suit and smoking his pipe, he appeared a typical, comfortably positioned bureaucrat or professor. He looked more like a bank manager than an art historian. There was not a trace of bohemian manner in his style. On the surface, it was not difficult to suspect him of being slightly out of touch with current trends or contemporary culture.

When the clamour came, however, he was ready. Many times he faced hostile audiences of art students who were astonished to hear this ordinary-looking little professor talking impassionately and intelligently about contemporary issues and trends from a Christian perspective. His courage in facing and discussing the questions of art and morals in society, areas rarely ventured into publicly by conservative Christians, motivated many reluctant Christian students who had compartmentalized their lives to relate their faith to their whole lives and studies in a deep and lively way.

But it was not only Christian students who responded to him. Tony Wales, who in the mid-1960s served on the staff of British Inter-Varsity Fellowship (IVF), said he had seen students and others come to faith in Christ through such lectures of Rookmaaker as 'Three Steps to Modern Art'. Wales also had seen him receive a standing ovation by several hundred students at a London art college following a two-hour-long presentation and analysis of rock and protest music. On that occasion not only did these students of the protest generation show their respect but at the end of the same lecture the chairman of the painting department of the college acknowledged that he now for the first time could understand his own son. Wales also relates Rookmaaker's evident disappointment on another occasion when a lecture he was to give at the Royal Academy had to be moved to a larger hall because the Reynolds Room was bulging with people!

Rookmaaker was a masterful communicator in both Dutch and English. When the lights went down and he started to show slides of great works of art of the past or startling contemporary art and comment on them, his audience was fascinated, whether they agreed with him or not. His lecturing style was highly unusual for a continental professor, as he spoke not from a written manuscript but extemporaneously and with full attentive engagement with his listeners. It was an art form, a performance. Like a jazz musician playing inventively with themes, he would improvise within a given structure (the lecture topic) with mastery and control, skill and intensity. He would bait and shock, amuse and bemuse. A lot hung on the sequence of visual or audio examples he used. The more often he repeated a lecture the richer it got. His material never became stale with repetition because there was always something new, if only in the provocative tone or way he put things.

In the light of day he was equally compelling. Going to an art gallery with him was an exceptional learning experience. He regularly took his own students from the Free University to the many special art collections in the Netherlands as well as on extended excursions to collections abroad, especially to Italy. But he also frequently invited small groups or individuals to join him at the art museum when he spoke at conferences.

He did not feel compelled to look at every painting or work of art when he entered a gallery. He would say, 'Look at the one that draws you to itself.' Or, when he gathered a small group before a picture, he would ask the most obvious question first: 'What are you looking at?' Often there was acute discomfort in the group because such a basic question seemed so self-evident. Suspicion would arise that there must be some hidden agenda behind it to show up their ignorance. Rookmaaker, however, never was naughty nor did he toy with people in this way. He would be playful and provocative for pedagogical purposes. He was always a sincere teacher. Soon everyone in the little group would learn that they genuinely needed to see firsthand what they were looking at. Afterwards this made Rookmaaker's own remarks on the picture all the more rewarding because everyone in the group had started first by seeing it for him- or herself.

Rookmaaker was protective of his little flock of students when visiting an art gallery. He did not take kindly to interlopers whom he did not have a personal connection with. Many of his students relate incidents when a curious visitor would sidle up to the group to hear the interesting things the small dignified gentleman was saying and being told directly by him in a not so gentle way, 'This is a very special art history course. It costs two thousand dollars. Please go away!' Aghast, the intruder would be dispatched. And the small group beamed at being considered so special and exclusive. There lurked beneath an unpretentious exterior a complex personality of immense vitality and not a few surprises.

Rookmaaker brought his own humanity and his understanding of humanity to his scholarship in a conscious way that is unusual for academics. He also sought to help his students bring their humanity fully into their learning and studies. His own words best describe how important the human element was for him in learning and teaching:

> we must judge as human beings, not as an abstract *homo aestheticus*, not as art historians or as artists but with our full human being. ... But everyone may and can judge art. The difference comes between a practiced judgment, based on experience, and the judgment of someone who is just beginning to look. The latter must still learn a lot – in the first place, to see. And that is exactly the situation of our students. We also need to teach them to look as human beings. All of education is concerned with the humanity of young people. The point of departure is their humanity, their young and inexperienced humanity. They need to develop competence in judging, they need to gain experience and insight. They will have to do that themselves. It is all too subtle and too richly multicoloured for us to be able to teach it to them as one teaches a maths sum. But we will have to show them the way. Help them. Pass on something of our experience and our knowledge by which they at least can be guarded from the most obvious misconceptions and dead ends. ...
>
> The student expects that you will judge as a human being. ... a person with conviction, a point of view, a person with a warm heart who can get angry and can also say why you were so moved or became so enthusiastic, can explain why something had such an impact on you. We may talk about works of art, preferably close to the works of art themselves, as long as it is not an argument for argument's sake – so interesting and so cultural – as long as the real commitment is to find the truth, to say the right thing, in order to do justice to the artist, the work in question, and to the students and ourselves as well.
>
> Besides, we can be sure that our work is never perfect. But it certainly can be meaningful. It is possible to work and deal with art and with students in this way. If it were impossible, it would be better never to speak about art again, no, even stronger, to never look at it again. After all, the work proves to be humanly impossible to approach and does not really require our reaction,

the input of our personality. Basically these things are about love for our neighbour and for the truth, because only these can make us free and make our work meaningful. (*CW* 2:134–135)

In 1970, the year Rookmaaker published his best-selling book, *Modern Art and the Death of a Culture*, most students in Europe or North America were not being thought of or educated in this deeply human and personal way. On 4 May that year the world looked on with horror as students, only some of whom were protesters against the bombing of Cambodia (a decision by President Nixon that appeared to expand the Vietnam War), were gunned down by National Guardsmen on the vernal campus of Kent State University in Kent, Ohio. The opening words of Rookmaaker's book perfectly captured the mood of the era: 'We live at a time of great change, of protest and revolution. We are aware that something radical is happening around us, but it is not always easy to see just what it is.' (*CW* 5:5)

He was spot on. Rookmaaker had written a searing account in this work of the dehumanization of life in our times as shown in the rise of modern art. These were threatening words for many who had accommodated themselves comfortably to modernity and contemporary culture, whether they were or were not Christians, or whether they were or were not aware of this conformity. When it came out, *Modern Art and the Death of a Culture* received wide acknowledgement and even acclaim, from a brief notice and review in *Art News* to Malcolm Muggeridge's making it one of his *Observer* Books of the Year for 1970. Muggeridge also promoted it in *Esquire*, where he was also a book review editor. *Modern Art and the Death of a Culture* was a genuine crossover book. It used a single language that was accessible to people whether they had Christian conviction or not. Its success may possibly have inspired its copy-editor at Inter-Varsity Press, David Alexander, to co-found with his wife, Pat Alexander, Lion Publishing, a new press dedicated to a refreshingly inclusive way of communicating with and engaging the public.

In *Modern Art and the Death of a Culture*, Rookmaaker resolutely faced the problematic and polemical character of modern art that denounced the nature and dignity of humanity. In the nineteenth century Nietzsche said, 'God is dead'. In the twentieth century, the most potent stream of modern art implicitly said, 'Man is dead.' Rookmaaker asked the question:

> What has become of people? Miró once painted a picture of a picture. He took a reproduction of a secondary seventeenth-century Dutch picture (it could just as well have been a Vermeer or a Rembrandt) and gave his own reinterpretation. Nothing is more telling. 'Man is dead,' it says. The absurd, the strange, the void, the irrationally horrible is there. The old picture is treated with humour, scorn . . . and devastating irony until nothing is left. As the image is destroyed, so too is man. (*CW* 5:88)

For Rookmaaker this was spiritual combat, not simply a matter of aesthetic niceties or opinions. He was attempting to awaken spiritual sleepers to the idea that modern art was not amoral or neutral but loaded with meaning that conveyed an impact on all of us, whether we ever darkened the door of an art museum or not, because it was an assault on our humanity. The implications were not theoretical but were as practical as how we raise our children, elect our leaders or care for the earth's environment.

A tremendous disruption with past assumptions of Western culture regarding the nature of humankind and reality had been heralded while most people were distracted by the clever allurements of a technological age. Modern artists like Picasso, Miró and Duchamp not only promulgated a view of human beings as absurd but also celebrated it, led the way and propagated it through their works of art. It is widely known that early audiences of this art reacted violently to it. This did not come generally from an informed perspective but out of an intuition at some vague level of being threatened. We may smile at their reaction to the shock of the new and feel mildly superior in being able now to appreciate this art, but Rookmaaker pointed out that only those practising an aesthetic of detachment, interested purely in formal analysis of the work of art, or somewhat naïve viewers not desiring to appear to be philistines could say, 'The new art gives nothing more than a human message, conveyed by new means. . . . [or] artists are expressing their times, and when they live in different times their forms are different.' He remarked further that 'all the while the sometimes obvious content is being ignored. And even when there is an attempt to discuss content, they make it subjective and say "This is how things are seen by this person." In any event, to question the truth of what is stated in art is taboo' (*CW* 5:196). Rookmaaker tackled both the radical implications of meaning in modern art and the studied avoidance to engage that meaning.

This changing view of human beings, of course, did not happen overnight, or even in the decades at the turn of the twentieth century. Rookmaaker's own doctoral dissertation on Paul Gauguin, perhaps his most influential scholarly work, concentrated on this pivotal period at the turn of the century. However, his *Complete Works* attest that a monumental amount of his thinking went into analysing and reflecting on the gradual transformation of thought regarding the nature of being human that transpired in Western culture since the time of the High Middle Ages. He focused frequently on views concerning human nature as formulated in Renaissance and Reformation thought during the sixteenth and seventeenth centuries, and particularly on the implications of the Enlightenment view of man in the eighteenth century for an unfolding view of modernity that the twentieth century ultimately received as a dubious legacy.

He forcefully engaged these ideas in his essay 'Commitment in Art':

> This new vision of human beings and the world – a result of the development starting with the Enlightenment and continuing through Romanticism and positivism – was first given expression in painting. It happened around 1911: the old view of people having positive contact with reality, a contact already loosened by Impressionism, was totally destroyed. Human being as an absurdity, estranged from the world, which was in itself chaotic, accidental and apparently contingent and hostile, became the painter's new preoccupation. Some artists, like Picasso, began to paint absurd humanity, while others, like Kandinsky, turned to abstraction. In this revolution, this violent destruction of so many established values, much that was deeply anchored in the reality of human life was torn down. A great part of the alarmed public found it unacceptable. Just as people had reacted violently at the beginning of Impressionism, so Kandinsky relates how his abstract paintings had to be cleaned every night at his exhibition in 1912 because the public had spat on his work. The artist was committed and had a message. That much the public accepted and did not deny, but being themselves also committed, they retained the right to reject that message. (*CW* 5:192–193)

Rookmaaker's approach to these issues was not always appreciated and frequently stirred up strong reactions. Often he was (inaccurately, as his *Complete Works* attest) accused of not understanding and dismissing abstract art. He was criticized for focusing too much on the content and meaning of works of art. In an article written in 1972, Nicholas Wolterstorff believed that Rookmaaker looked 'right through the sensory qualities of the work of art in order to discern the message beyond'. Alva Steffler, an art professor at Wheaton College, Illinois, had a similar impression after reading Rookmaaker's writing and becoming personally acquainted with him in the early 1970s, though latterly modifying these views and coming to an appreciation of Rookmaaker's perspective.

No one may have put it in print, but there was a climate of criticism around Rookmaaker that regarded him as a popularizer. Rookmaaker's communication skills sympathetically won him nicknames like 'the pipe-puffing pundit of Amsterdam' and 'the Dutch Kenneth Clark' from some of his peers and colleagues. But in the academy there is often, unfortunately, a price to pay for the ability to communicate with a broad audience. Popularizing is not at all popular with most academics! The assumption is that doing this signifies 'the scholar' is 'lightweight', meaning he or she is not sufficiently serious in undertaking scholarship. Such a person is frequently accused of oversimplifying complexities or even distorting issues for the sake of having an audience, whether this is well-founded or not. Both J.R.R. Tolkien and C.S. Lewis were ostracized to a certain extent by their Oxbridge colleagues because of this prejudice. Dorothy L. Sayers was not tarred with this brush because she was not and did not claim to be a scholar, though her actual achievements belie this. But if the accusation places one in the company of people like the former, it may well be a badge of honour.

Rookmaaker seems to have borne with this well. He had a high degree of personal confidence. While he appreciated the esteem of his colleagues, it does not appear that he had any craven need for their approval. One wonders what his own awareness of his students' appreciation of him was? Did he have any sense of how far some of these inchoate artists and art historians would take his words and work and be formed significantly by them? He clearly basked in their admiration. Perhaps this approbation acted as compensation.

The extent of Rookmaaker's intellectual interests were far broader than usual for an academic. In his own field of art history his writing was not confined to one or two areas of investigation but ranged over the whole course of Western art. At the same time he published works on African-American music and spoke about various cultural issues on public radio. Moving easily from technical philosophy and scholarship to readable, popular journalism, he was what today we might call a natural born public intellectual. Yet he never eschewed or disparaged technical scholarship. In his association with Professor H. van de Waal of the University of Leiden, he helped pioneer DIAL/Iconclass, the most important technical art-historical research tool of the twentieth century for comprehensively classifying art-historical subject matter.

Rookmaaker deployed a broad blend of interests and competencies dynamically. He spoke a good number of European languages and had a reading knowledge of several more. Academically his ability ranged from researching technical scholarship for specialists to communicating many of these findings to a general public. He did both with equal respect. In both speaking and writing he had considerable skill to captivate. None of this, however, was in his case an end in itself to create a brilliant career or achieve acknowledgment, though he became a full professor and received recognition. From the moment he opened himself to fully embracing a biblical faith in Jesus Christ he was on a mission that motivated him until his last breath. The light shed into his life by the true Light of the world illuminated his vision and imbued him with an immense sense of calling to be fully human in a world created by the living God in accordance with his rich reality. Essentially Rookmaaker's aim was to share this fullness of life with others, not in a reductive or one-sided way but in a way that reflected the complexity and completeness of God's sustaining love in creation.

During his lifetime relatively few people who heard him or read his work knew much about the circumstances of his life or the hard won way he had come to be a Christian. Occasionally he would share that he had come to Christ in a German prisoner-of-war camp. But it barely needed being stated explicitly, because anyone with ears to hear could tell no matter what topic Rookmaaker talked about that they were encountering a powerful genuineness based on actual experience. This tacit undercurrent of strength through struggle permeated his style. Undoubtedly this authenticity was key to his impact on an unusually wide diversity of people. He was not everyone's cup of tea or a mass style communicator. He was often playful and implied meaning in a way that encouraged his audience to form their understanding of what he was saying in a way that integrated their thinking with their feeling, but he did not strive to manipulate emotions.

One would expect an art historian to influence other art historians. And Rookmaaker did. What is less usual is for an art historian to have influence on many artists, including musicians and writers. But this Rookmaaker also did. It is rare for an art historian to make an impact on mature scholars and thinkers in other fields. Rookmaaker did this as well. In the 1970 summer school of Regent College (Vancouver, Canada), the distinguished British biblical scholar, F.F. Bruce, who taught along with Rookmaaker during that time, made clear his appreciation for the widening of his horizons as a result of listening to his Dutch colleague. David McKenna, an influential American Christian educator, while president of Seattle Pacific University, desired to come and study with Rookmaaker because he felt that his understanding of culture was compellingly important for an understanding of higher education in the contemporary world. Most rare is it for an art historian to make an impact on ordinary people with no singular interest in art, scholarship or education. Yet Rookmaaker quite often could communicate with people from a variety of walks of life because he was not an aesthete, and his aim was ultimately not simply to inform people about art but to share with others through art the fullness of life and the richness of reality that God created through his love. As a result of hearing or reading Rookmaaker, a sincere housewife could stunningly be awakened to her ingrained bourgeois sentimentality or a businessman suddenly see that it might be a good thing to plant some trees and landscape his parking lot instead of just covering it over in asphalt and cement.

He might infuriate some people on occasion. He was not totally approachable. He would have been the last person on the planet to coo over a baby. He would never have made a politician, trying to get elected. He had his shortcomings and blind spots. He could be gruff. He sometimes became truly angry. Though he never especially sought conflict, he could face it. He passionately sought to do justice to the complexities of any issue, idea, opinion or work of art or scholarship that he encountered. He hungered and thirsted for righteousness. He was not a plaster saint but a man of many complexities and hidden depths.

Hans Rookmaaker's life rang true to reality. He unfailingly engaged his contemporary listeners and readers in refreshing and interesting ways that accorded with the experience of living in the twentieth century. It is all the more of interest for us that so much of his thought is still accessible and has application and relevance for many of the challenges of life in the twenty-first century.

Why is this so?

Who was Hans Rookmaaker?

What formed him?

As we follow the course of his life in subsequent chapters, these are the questions to be engaged.

2
Childhood

Henderik (Hans was his family nickname) Roelof Rookmaaker was born in The Hague, Netherlands on February 27, 1922, an ominous year for what would transpire in the next decades for both Europe as a whole and for H.R. Rookmaaker personally. In this year Benito Mussolini came to power in Italy and remained so until 1943. The Weimar Republic was extremely fragile, stricken by soaring inflation and shaken in the following year by a threatened coup in Saxony and Thuringia, an uprising in Hamburg and the infamous Putsch that Adolph Hitler and his Nazi thugs attempted to stage in Munich. In 1922 the Union of Soviet Socialist Republics officially became federated under a plan drawn up by Joseph Stalin, the general secretary of the Communist Party at that time.

The post-World War I situation of the Netherlands was not especially stable either. Disputed territorial claims, economic crisis, kaleidoscopic shifting structures of political parties and their changing alliances with one another all contributed to numerous governments being formed up until the Nazi occupation of the country in the spring of 1940.

During this period while Germany was heading toward the Third Reich, the huge Dutch colony in Southeast Asia, the Dutch Indies (Indonesia's official name at that time), was heading for a showdown with its colonial masters in a struggle to gain national independence.

In the year of Hans Rookmaaker's birth his father was in Holland on study leave from his post in the Dutch colonial service. For the previous five years he had served as a *Controleur* of the subdivision of Boné in the town of Watamponé in the southern part of Celebes (today Sulawesi). During the years 1920–1923 he eagerly elected to improve his administrative skills by opting for a two-year course offered at the newly created Dutch Indies Administration Academy (*Nederlandsch-Indonesische Bestuursacademie*) in the The Hague.

Henderik Roelof Rookmaaker, senior was born on 21 August 1887 in Batavia, the Dutch Indies (today Jakarta, Indonesia). His father before him, also a Henderik Roelof Rookmaaker (1848–1905), was also a colonial administrator in the Dutch East Indies and attained the office of Assistant-Resident.

A calligraphically designed family tree indicates nine Rookmaaker children born in the late nineteenth century in different places in the Dutch Indies as the Assistant-Resident and his, presumably, long-suffering wife traipsed from post to post around the Spice Islands to work and to live. Hans's father was the eighth child, and the third of four sons. He would surpass his father professionally by taking up the position of a full Resident (the highest administrative office in a major government district).

Theodora Catharina Heitink Hans's mother, was born on 17 March 1890 in The Hague. As far as we know, she had no family links with the Dutch Indies. She was pretty. By family accounts she came from a good but not particularly religious family. As her husband also did not come from a religious background that may have proved to be one of the most important similarities and perhaps one of the few things they genuinely had in common.

After graduating on 20 June 1911 from the University of Leiden, where he had studied in preparation for administrative service in the East Indies, Henderik married Theodora later that summer on 25 August. By October of that year he was back in the East with his newly wedded wife and stationed at Pompanua in southern Celebes. The groom may have returned home to the land of his birth, but not so his bride. The adjustment that the two of them, still in their early twenties, had to make to each other and living as a recently married couple in a culture so radically different from what Theodora had known before was considerable. It seems that she never fully adapted to living in this part of the world.

Soon children were to come. Theodora Catharina (nicknamed Door) was born on 28 November 1912, a little over a year after their arrival in Pompanua. Then two years later Henrietta Christina (nicknamed Hannie) was born on 3 March 1914. By this time Henderik was a Controller of South Boné in Mareq in another part of southern Celebes. He and Theodora were starting to continue the pattern of his peripatetic family of moving every one or two or few years in order take up another colonial administrative position somewhere in this vast archipelago spreading itself from the Indian to the Pacific oceans.

In 1920, after nine years of marriage and living in the Dutch Indies, the Rookmaakers, now with two little girls of eight and six years old respectively, set out to return to the Netherlands. They made the most of their journey, taking five months and visiting China, Japan and the United States on the way. The exquisite charm and beauty of Japanese gardens made a notable impression on Henderik. While we do not know what impressions her travels made on her, Theodora must have greatly anticipated and desired to be back in the land of her birth, where she could resume a way of life she found familiar and far more congenial.

In later years her daughter, Hannie, detailed how difficult it was for her mother to adjust to living in a culture so different from the one she was formed in. The food, rhythms of life and climate always remained alien to her. There is no record of how well she spoke Bahasa, the language of the region. Theodora seems to have constructed her own alternative pattern of life, if not reality, when she lived in the East Indies, right down to preparing Dutch food daily for herself. It must also have been difficult for her as a young Western woman, perhaps pampered at home, not to have the full attention of her energetic and capable husband who increasingly became involved in his work as he advanced in his ability to manage. Hannie could state forthrightly that her parents had a difficult relationship because of these factors. Whether from personal character or conformity, however, there never was a hint or suggestion that they ever thought of separating or dissolving their marriage. The return to The Hague with the birth of a little boy during this stay suggests that the leave literally breathed new life into their relationship, at least for a while.

By 1924 H.R. Rookmaaker, senior was back in the Dutch Indies with his family. He now served as the Controller of a colonial administrative division in the middle of the western part of Sumatra. One imagines that Hans Rookmaaker's first sense of his own personal identity must have occurred around this time, physically and geographically far way from where he was born, on the way to or in a land that was in many ways the polar opposite of the land of his adult years.

Photos of the three- or four-year-old Hans Rookmaaker suggest he was a handful. He is a bundle of energy with a closely shaven head of hair and a barrel of monkeyshines, just waiting to be let loose. In one small but revealing picture his older sister, Door, is obviously trying to hold him still for a serious family photograph while he is totally distracted and attempting to break away from her. It is a telling family portrait. Father Henderik faces the camera intently and frontally, uniformed properly as a colonial official with his pith helmet in his hand at his side. One can almost feel the equatorial heat and glare of the sun in his eyes as he tries to focus them straight at the camera while we might wish he had kept his helmet on. Mother, Theodora, stands firmly at his side, visibly a much stouter woman than she was a decade earlier. She strains her eyes toward the camera without any evidence of regard for her eldest daughter at her side trying her best to keep little Hans (Hansje) literally in the picture. Hannie, the younger daughter, stands before her parents most respectfully, one hand clasping her other. Her face is bowed in shadow. One wonders whether her posture is because of the bright sun shining above or because she is feeling awkward and embarrassed to take this kind of family photo. Perhaps it is both.

Door, ten years older than her brother, became very much his little mother. Other family photos show her keeping an eye on him, holding his hand or standing behind him literally and figuratively. Though she married, she herself never had children of her own. She would outlive her brother by more than a decade, showing concern toward the end of her life for his children. There seem to be more photos of Hans as a child with his father than with his mother. In a photo taken in The Hague of him at the age of ten with his mother, he stands by her side, leaning toward her slightly with a clear expression of apprehension and real anxiety on his face. She faces the camera squarely and resolutely, without even a trace of a smile on her face.

As the baby of the family, Hans was spoiled to a certain degree. Servants abounded in his colonial home to meet his physical requirements more than amply. If his mother was not overly attentive, his sisters adored him. His father, though reserved and not especially demonstrative, clearly took an interest in his son and was proud of him as a boy and a young man. Hans in turn was proud of his father. Throughout his life he often expressed his admiration for the Resident. His father was in many ways a remarkable man. Even by today's standards he can be considered a rather enlightened colonial official. Hans absorbed many of his father's qualities. In his adult years this can be seen in his personal discipline and professional diligence, his willingness to take on responsibility, his eagerness to learn and not inconsiderable organizational skill, and his great love for the beauty of nature.

During his career as a colonial official, H.R. Rookmaaker, senior was recognized for his outstanding abilities. The peak of his career was when he was promoted to become Resident of the Lampong districts of southern Sumatra. There he was active not only in organizing, but taking the leadership in persuading and motivating people from the more populous Java to immigrate to the southern part of Sumatra to develop parts of it barely thought to be habitable. He did not lure migrants under false pretenses. He said it would be difficult for them. They would need to sacrifice. And they would need to pay with hard labour before they received any benefit from their move. In short, it proved to be a successful experiment of indigenous people colonizing another part of the region voluntarily. For this achievement he received the Oranje-Nassau medal from his government.

Before his final departure from his post in Sumatra, Rookmaaker, senior also initiated the protection of the forests. Through his efforts the South Sumatra and Way Kambas National Parks were formed. He tried to convince his colonial colleagues that elephants and other animals needed protected areas to live in in order to be preserved from attack. All of this was quite extraordinary at a time when the idea that it was important to safeguard nature from increasing human incursion was rarely discussed by fellow government officials.

The active interest that Hans's father took in plants and animals created a conscious awareness and appreciation of rare creatures right at home. If a young boy might be expected to find the business of a father boring, a boy could not be indifferent to a father bringing home with him live birds and other kinds of exotic wild animals, many of which had been injured. There is an old snapshot of Rookmaaker, senior dressed in a white suit sitting at a table with an exquisite floral arrangement in a classically colonial setting holding a little rodent-like creature on his arm. His entire concentration is focused on this small furry animal with a long tail as he strokes it ever so gently.

By 1927 Hans's father had become a serious naturalist who loved to explore the rich and complex world of natural phenomena around him. He frequently took his children with him on his explorations. Although Hans was probably too young to accompany his father on his expedition to capture Komodo dragons in 1927, it must have brought an enormous amount of excitement into his home as it was discussed and these largest of the earth's monitor-type of lizards in transit perhaps were viewed by the boy. Systematic scientific study of these giant monitors was just beginning. In total, twelve Komodo dragons were captured and sent to zoological gardens and centres of study in Europe. As these ferocious primordial-looking beasts are huge, on average around two and a half meters long (eight feet) and with long forked yellow tongues that can lash out to more than a foot, it must have been no small undertaking to capture them. Thereafter two newly identified species were named after Rookmaaker, senior: the frog *Oreophryne rookmaakeri* (1927) and the shell *Xesta rookmaakeri* (1930). One of the birds he collected was identified latterly (1948) as a new subspecies and named for him *Mesia argentauris rookmakeri* (incorrect spelling).

In 1929 Rookmaaker, senior was an Assistant-Resident based at Lho Semaweh (Lhokseumawe) on the north coast of Aceh in Sumatra. Part of his official duties had always been to entertain visiting dignitaries. In that year, when Hans was seven years old, his father welcomed Prince Leopold of Belgium (1901–1983) to Lho Semaweh and hosted various events for him, including a rather sumptuous banquet. Five years later the Prince was to become King Leopold III of Belgium. The Belgian professor, Victor Van Straelen (1889–1964), accompanied the twenty-eight-year-old prince. Van Straelen was a noted international naturalist, pioneering conservation and parks in Central Africa as well as in the Galápagos Islands. Family photos and reminiscences emphasize the royal visitor, but the professor's visit may well have had a more lasting impact on and been a formative factor for Rookmaaker's own education regarding natural preservation that he pioneered later in southern Sumatra. For his hospitality and helpfulness in showing the prince and professor around the natural wonders of this part of the world, Hans's father received a Belgian medal of appreciation.

In 1931 the Rookmaaker family returned to the Netherlands on a year's leave. Once again they lived in The Hague. Hans was nine years old. By this time he had had more moves in his life than most people even in present-day mobile Western culture have in a lifetime. His sisters were in their late teens; he was not yet an adolescent. His education through travel and meeting an unusually wide spectrum of people must have outstripped his formal schooling. Hans was a resilient child who learned well despite a constant stream of changing schools and new teachers on two different continents. Intellectually, he was ahead of his age. When his family returned to the Dutch Indies, an experiment of placing him in a class ahead of his age and sending him to boarding school in another part of the island group proved unsuccessful. He may not have had a perfect family, but apparently he appreciated being near them and was a better learner as a result of this security amidst a sea of constant change.

H.R. Rookmaaker's Residency in Sumatra was cut short by ill health. In 1936 he returned to the Netherlands to live in The Hague. The official termination of his Residency occurred in 1937. He may have tried to return to his post briefly, but a heart condition finally forced him into retirement. The Rookmaakers, seniors lived through the war years in The Hague.

With his father's help and counsel Hans opted to make an important educational choice. Instead of going to a gymnasium for a classical education with Latin and Greek, he chose the five-year course of a technical high school in Leiden. With constant moving about, life had never been exactly convenient for Hans. Now the uncertainty of his parents' future in regard to his father's health and professional life left the family at loose ends concerning their son's schooling. Finally, a difficult decision was made for Hans, to live temporarily with relatives in Leiden while he went to school there.

Hans's high school education next led him to Den Helder, the famous Dutch naval college located at the far northwestern tip of the Netherlands, where the best and brightest were enrolled to be apprenticed to serve the future of their country.

Meanwhile, somewhere along the way this emerging youth fell in love with African-American music and opened himself to it. He began to amass a collection of records of the blues, jazz and spirituals that in his adulthood would become one of the most important sources in Europe for this kind of music. There is no evidence that he was a particularly rebellious youth asserting himself by taking up this type of music, though in later years he personally exhibited great empathy for youth who were full of protest and who gravitated to styles of music that were guaranteed to offend the bourgeois sensibilities of their parents.

Music and dance were in the air of this era. On both sides of the Atlantic and beyond, young people and not so young people kicked up their heels and danced, desiring to become expansive after the economically lean years of the 1920s in the wake of World War I. A marvellous snapshot of Rookmaaker, senior from the 1930s shows him playfully and exuberantly bursting out in an *olé* of a flamenco or going along for a real run at a rumba. His son joyously followed in his father's footsteps when it came to enjoying this kind of fun.

Constant change, cultural complexities, and emotional ambiguities filled Hans Rookmaaker's childhood. He experienced many privileges. He also experienced many uncertainties. Instead of being demoralized by these conditions, he seems to have allowed them to shape his self-confidence, shielding him from a feeling of being too much of an outsider or stranger. As the days ahead would show, this capable and in many ways self-assured child still sought a true home for heart and head and hand to dwell in.

3
Youth

Hans Rookmaaker grew up as a secular young person. It is difficult to tell whether attending a Christian Reformed high school influenced him at all. As a well-meaning official and parent, Rookmaaker pater, definitely not a pious person, could tell his children when they were reluctant to attend church services on important holidays, 'God damn it! You go to church!'

Hans's religious sensibilities would wait to be developed. He described his own religious upbringing in this way:

> I come from a family that can in no way be described as religious. There was no profound opposition to religion. My father did believe that God existed and that the Bible was a worthwhile book – perhaps his grandparents had been Protestants – but that was all. They even forgot to have me baptized. As a boy I did go to a Christian secondary school – because it was such a good one – but I was not in any way reached by the gospel there. It is really remarkable, by the way, how little mission-minded Dutch Christians often are. Apart from one conversation with one of my teachers no one ever tried to tell me anything more of the gospel. (*CW* 2:10)

By the late 1930s when Hans was in his formative teenage years, the world of the Dutch Indies was behind him. The Dutch colonial enterprise was crumbling and a new nation, Indonesia, was slowly coming into existence despite an added struggle of resistance through three years of Japanese occupation during World War II. Hans's father had been one of the last and best colonial administrators, but the paternalistic world he served and the need for men like him were disappearing. No longer able to discharge his duties due to illness, and after a brief stint in the Ministry of Finance, Hans's father ailed on in The Hague on government disability allowance, no doubt astutely observing these changes abroad and perhaps even glad he did not have to deal with them directly. Hans's mother resumed a social life that suited her far more than that in the Dutch Indies.

The young Rookmaaker's interests burgeoned. Intellectually, he was an energetic all-rounder. He did as well at mathematics and science as he did at history and the humanities. He had a special interest in ship design. One supposes his fascination with ships developed in the weeks he had spent since childhood sailing to and from the Netherlands and around the Spice Islands. Based on these interests and the changing situation overseas, a career in the navy probably looked a lot more promising than any consideration of following in the Rookmaaker tradition of colonial civil service.

Hans's real passion, however, was for music, especially authentic African-American music. He was not interested in the modified styles created to cater to a consumerist white audience. From the beginning, he demanded the genuine thing. He listened over and over to the same pieces. Precociously he developed a discerning taste for the nuances of this music and a considerable knowledge of its development. He also became an almost obsessive record collector. He spent any available money he had on them and regularly borrowed from or traded records with his friends.

Physically he was filling out from a somewhat scrawny child to his adult height of five feet and eight inches. A high school photo shows the face of a serious but pleasant-looking young man with dark brown hair and eyes. In somewhat later pictures of him in his naval cadet's uniform he even looks rather dashing.

Although the Dutch navy had officially been in existence since 1488, the Royal Netherlands Naval College at Den Helder was not established until the middle of the nineteenth century. As Den Helder was an important naval base and shipyard, it was decided that this would be an ideal location for educating midshipmen. Its first official classrooms were built in the grounds of the state shipyard. In 1854 it opened with 25 cadets enrolled. In 1939, the last year Hans Rookmaaker was a midshipman (*adelborst*) there and on the eve of the college's closure in 1940 by the Germans, there were 98 naval cadets. It was a select group with its own special traditions. Interestingly, many of the midshipmen at Den Helder managed to escape to England when the German occupation of the Netherlands occurred. There they continued their naval training at a base in Cornwall. A naval institute was also organized at Surabaya in the Dutch East Indies, but it was forced to close in 1942 at the time of the Japanese invasion.

One wonders whether Hans Rookmaaker had a chance or choice to escape in 1940 as some of his fellow midshipmen did. By that time there were compelling factors in his life to keep him close to home and prevent him from running away, even if he had had the opportunity or felt convinced he could have helped the war effort by being outside of the country. Although his sister, Door, by this time had married and was living with her husband in the Dutch Indies, in The Hague he still had a single sister and parents with health problems who concerned him and needed him. But even beyond these important reasons was a factor of far greater significance for the course of his life. Hans Rookmaaker was deeply in love and, though young, had become engaged.

Sometime during those naval cadet years, Hans, who not only loved music but also loved to dance, for want of a date invited or perhaps dragged along his older sister, Hannie, to go out dancing with him one evening when he was at home. Not long after their arrival at the dance club, Hannie recognized an acquaintance of hers across the room.

Hannie liked to take complete credit for introducing her brother to her friend, Riki Spetter, that evening. She also declared it was love at first sight for both of them.

They both met what they thought was their match. Hendrika Beatrix (nicknamed Riki) Spetter was born on 10 May 1919 into a middle-class Jewish family who lived in The Hague. She was one of five children. She had an older sister and three brothers. She was three years older than Hans, but this difference of age usually so discernable in teenage years was probably not too noticeable. By this time Hans was adept at relating to older young ladies. His sisters were respectively ten and eight years older than he was, and they gave him ample observation of their ways as well as tutelage in how make an impression on what in those days was considered the fairer sex.

From photos, personal accounts and her loving letters to Hans while he was in prison, first at Scheveningen near The Hague and later at Langwasser near Nuremberg, we can gain a glimpse of this young woman. Her life was to be tragically brief. She and her entire family, save for her brother, Max, who was in the Dutch East Indies at the time, were swept away by the Nazis.

She was a special person. Although Hans was barely 18 years old, their relationship was not a case of an ignorant, youthful infatuation. Hans was genuinely a mature young man for his age. Riki had some inspiring qualities. Anky Huitker, her friend and clerical office colleague, who later became Hans's wife, knew her and her family well and always maintained an admiration and respect coupled with affection for her.

Riki had sparkle. She was not conventionally beautiful at all but was attractive and exuded personality. Her hair was not quite brown but a dark blond. This we know, for she touchingly attached a lock of it to one of her last letters to Hans. Photos of her rival that of Hans's father doing the rumba. One snapshot shows her holding a perky cat on her shoulder, her arm raised high above her head with some tasty little bit in her hand that the feline is totally transfixed on and ready to devour. She expresses total absorption and joy in this creature's anticipation of attacking its prey. Another snapshot shows her playfully taking a draw on Hans's pipe as she languidly lounges on a day bed. Another picture shows a solemn and domestic side to her. Sitting before the same day bed with batik hangings behind it, slim and serious, she looks intently into the camera as she knits. Her face suggests a certain realistic awareness of life.

Despite the ominous situation of a war on their doorstep, Hans and Riki enjoyed some months of joy and enjoyment in each other's company. They were a convivial couple. There was much coming and going between their homes and their friends' homes. They delighted in listening to music and dancing and talking half the night away – a habit that Hans never grew out of or gave up, if given a chance. But new love and romance would not last long for either of them.

When Den Helder was closed after the Nazi occupation that took place on 10 May 1940 at Whitsuntide (also the date of Riki's birthday), Hans, still technically a commissioned officer in the Dutch navy (*sergeant-adelborst*), transferred to a course in engineering at Delft Technical University. This was much nearer his family and his fiancée, all of whom continued to live in The Hague. Despite occupation there was still some regularity in the daily pattern of his life until 4 March 1941. On that day he was arrested for possession of *deutschfeindliche Flugschriften* ('anti-German literature').

It came about that one of his lecturers at the university, René Donker, had passed on to him a pamphlet entitled *De vrije Katheder* ('The free podium'). He had been caught with this in his pocket. Along with Donker and two other defendants he had to stand trial nine months later in December 1941. He was the youngest of the four of them. He seems to have been in custody the entire time from March to December 1941. That meant missing the best part of an academic year. Although it is ambiguous, it seems that the two and a half months he was sentenced to for his 'crime' was assigned retroactively. Nevertheless, he still had spent six and a half months in jail, as it seemed, for nothing.

During that time Riki and his family worried about him greatly every day. Mostly his father, Hannie, and Riki wrote loving communal letters to him asking what they could do or send to him. He was allowed to write notes and letters to his family. And they were able to answer and send him some essentials of survival, such as his toothbrush, extra blankets, and books. It must have been both hard and odd to have him incarcerated in the maximum security prison of Scheveningen, right on their doorstep in The Hague, without being able to see or visit him.

At this point, time was a lot more precious than any of them probably realized. After Hans's release from Scheveningen Prison there were to be only five months before commissioned officers like him were commanded by the Nazis to report in Breda, a city historically associated with the Royal Netherlands Military Academy. That call came in April 1942. From this centre, Rookmaaker was dispatched with a group that became *Oflag* 67 (*Offizierslager für kriegsgefangene Offiziere* = 'POW camp for officers 67'). They were sent to Langwasser in the southeast environs of Nuremberg in Bavaria.

From the time that Hans had returned from the Dutch East Indies to the Netherlands in 1936, his life began unfolding at a rapid rate. He was forced to grow up quickly. He had to make difficult decisions about his education. He had to deal with dramatic experiences in his life that he chose to embrace and ones that he had no control over whatsoever. The gravity of life and his own serious nature were beginning to open him to the realities of a spiritual and religious dimension to his life that he never had fully acknowledged or engaged before. The days ahead would change him and the conditions of his life forever.

In the meantime Riki kept up a courageous spirit. She had remained constant in her loyalty to him while he was in Scheveningen Prison. She had written to him consistently, also when he was being held in Germany. Her letters are filled with endearing sweetness, but without sentimentality. At the same time she also took on a major amount of responsibility in caring for her sick mother. She tried to enjoy herself and reported to Hans about going here and there, to this one and that one's house to talk and listen to music. She tried to hunt down special rare records and books that he was looking for. In a letter of 6 July 1942 she wrote:

> My dearest,
>
> The book *From Socrates to Bergson* that you wanted me to get for you is not available any more ... [regarding] records I was in the shops, but no good ones are coming out. I am anxious to hear from you. How often can you write? I walk to the mailbox every day, but there is nothing from you. Patience is supposed to be such a beautiful thing, but I don't see much in it.
>
> Your always loving,
>
> Riki

Gradually the Nazi regime was becoming more and more of a daily repressive reality for Jews in the Netherlands. Public transport was not available for Jews and Riki had to walk everywhere, including to her work. Negotiating the quotidian necessities of shopping meant daily errands took doubly long. It became a major undertaking to go over to the Rookmaakers, seniors' home and discuss with them Hans's situation and the news of the day or to sit down all together to write a letter to him.

More and more social events happened at her own parental home. Her friends thought that coming to her home would be more convenient than her having to walk a long way or alone to their homes. Although she was a welcoming and hospitable person and she seems to have had an open family, it became a burden to always have to be the host, no matter how well meaning her friends' intentions were for her benefit.

The last letters that she wrote to Hans were positive, even as she faced the unthinkable and the unimaginable. Her spirit never wavered. Her maturity was exemplary. She also showed herself to be spiritually-minded. On 10 August 1942, she wrote to Hans: 'I am reading a lot in the Bible, but [there is] much that I don't understand and you must explain it when you return.' There is also evidence in her letters that she was beginning to pray.

By the end of the third week of August 1942, Riki's family, except for one brother who at that time was in the Dutch East Indies, was taken from The Hague and sent first to a detention centre in Westerbork in the Drenthe province in the north of the country, midway between Zwolle and Groningen. Afterwards they were transported to Auschwitz, where they were killed by the Nazis.

When Riki could no longer write, her friend, Anky Huitker, whose family courageously hid Jewish people in their home during the war, sadly informed Hans of what had taken place. Apparently Hans had written to Anky beforehand to ask her to buy some flowers for Riki as a favour for him. Anky wrote:

> Dear Hans,
>
> Finally, I'll answer your postcard. I was glad to hear from you. I took care of the flowers, and she was very happy …
>
> [But the] news now is very sad. Riki … with her whole family was moved on 18 August to Drenthe (Assen). Riki felt terrible to leave The Hague, but [it was] a big comfort that they all went together. She kept up her courage [and] put on a brave face. I have to say she probably can't write to you, but she will think of you all the time. If ever [it is] possible, she will write. I really admire Riki in the last weeks – how she handled all this difficulty. She was the strongest of the family.
>
> Riki asked at the last moment that I should write that you should not be anxious because she feels she has inner fortitude. She was unbelievably competent.
>
> As soon as I hear from her, I will let you know. But, [I think] it will be long, because they cannot write to us …
>
> Many kind greetings from all here who know you,
>
> Anky

The monstrous insanity and oppression of Nazi ideology and war wiped out this promising young life as it did so many other innocent lives. Only gradually did Hans come to understand and realize the magnitude of his personal loss. Hans's sisters felt that at some level he probably never recovered from the crushing blow of losing Riki. It was a double loss. At the same time he experienced the premature loss of his own youth.

4
Conversion and Calling

Almost the first thing Hans Rookmaaker did when he returned after the war to the Netherlands was to place advertisements in newspapers in several Dutch cities asking if anyone had seen or had any knowledge of Riki Spetter, who had been seen last at Westerbork on 18 August 1942. Although what Anky Huitker had written to him regarding Riki being taken away by the German occupiers had not reassured him that he would hear from her, it had understandably left the door open for some hope. It was a hope that Hans carried with him through the rest of the war years.

Riki's last letter to Hans was addressed to him at a field post address (*Feldpostadresse* 45667). This was a different address from the one she had been writing to at Nuremberg-Langwasser just six days earlier, on 4 August 1942.

Shortly after Hans's call in April 1942 to report with other commissioned officers to Breda, he was transported with a group of his fellow officers to the very centre of the fanatical *Führer* cult at Nuremberg. It was here that the infamous Nazi Party Rally Grounds, designed in 1934 by Hitler's favourite architect Albert Speer, were located. A camp zone southeast and adjacent to the Party Rally Grounds from 1939 on served as a prisoner-of-war camp. This was Langwasser (today a suburb of Nuremberg), where *Oflag* 67, Rookmaaker's designated camp, was located.

Up until 1943 inmates at this camp laboured for the city of Nuremberg on the construction of the Party Rally Grounds. Hans probably spent most of the summer there. After breaking its non-aggression pact with the Soviet Union by invading its vast territory in June 1941, Germany was almost completely strapped for a work force. Every able-bodied person was serving in the armed forces in an insane war that was being battled on several fronts. Whether serving major industry or pet projects of the *Führer*, forced foreign labour had become part of Nazi party policy.

From the change of address on Riki's letter to Hans on 10 August 1942, it seems she must have heard from him that he was being moved from Nuremberg-Langwasser. Over a month later Hans began sending letters to his family from a camp unit that was designated *Stalag* 371. It was situated in Stanislau in the historic region known as Galicia, an area that is part of the western Ukraine. Although considered a territory of Poland from 1919 to 1939, this place was part of the German-occupied Soviet Union when Hans was there. Today this city, nestling amidst the northeastern foothills of the Carpathian Mountains, is known as Ivano Frankivsk. Until 1962 it was called Stanislau, when it was renamed to honour the Ukrainian poet Ivan Franko (1856–1916). Many if not most of the prisoners of *Stalag* 371 were Dutch.

From an incident that took place on 4 June 1943 in Saxony at Colditz Castle, a notorious special maximum security prison reserved for elite foreign prisoners, we know of an attempted escape by Dutch inmates that linked them to *Stalag* 371. They chose that date because they knew they were soon going to be moved to Stanislau. The link between Colditz Castle and Stanislau and the Dutch is interesting. Hans may have stayed there temporarily on his way to Stanislau when Riki sent him the German field post addressed letter.

At any rate, by June 1943 when the Dutch contingency from Colditz Castle arrived in Stanislau, Hans already had been there for nine months. He was to stay there until sometime in February 1944. In the 17 or 18 months that Hans was at Stanislau, a profound transformation that had begun in Nuremberg, or even earlier, took place in his life.

From reading between the lines of Riki's letters, Hans seems to have started a serious reading and consideration of the Bible. In an essay published in 1967 he wrote that he had started thinking seriously about spiritual matters

> after the German invasion of the Netherlands in May 1940. I then went to study in Delft, to await the end of the war. In those days I began to think more seriously about matters, and sometimes I had the feeling that God could play an important role in our lives. But only when I, along with other professional officers, was made a prisoner of war and landed in a camp near Nuremberg did I begin to think about seriously reading the Bible. There were no other books available and, as a civilized man with cultural interests, I thought it would be good to know something about it. As I was reading, I gradually came to the conviction that the Bible reveals the truth to us. (*CW* 2:10)

The relatively long stay of over a year at Stanislau allowed Rookmaaker more time for sustained thought and reflection.

> I spent a lot of time thinking about the Christian faith, but read very little about it. Apart from this I made good use of the time. Gradually, especially after our POW camp was moved to Stanislau, more books became available. One man had this book and the next, another. I read philosophy, psychology, literature and especially the history of literature; in short, from all sorts of fields in the humanities. I also continued to work clandestinely to finish my training as naval officer while we officially had the opportunity to continue studying through Delft University; I even sat exams. I did all the mathematical subjects. (*CW* 2:10)

Gradually the young officer and diligent student was going beyond merely educating himself to become a more cultured person to making a definite decision about the future course of his thinking and, indeed, about who he personally was becoming. At Stanislau he apprenticed himself to mastering the Bible. The curious, abridged version of the Dutch Bible that he had at his disposal during this time is marked and cross-referenced in a range of handwritings that suggests the wide range of his emotions during these months. It reflects a mind that remembered the content of the Testaments, Old and New, as they related with each other and made an impact on him. It shows an ardency and intense engagement in a personal way with the Scripture that continued to be borne out all through his life.

The very first lines to be underlined in this Bible deal not with a possibly abstract doctrine of the 'nature of man' that might be expected to be derived by an intellectual from Genesis 1:27 but with a text that would have been existential for him then in regard to his desire to be married. It is the text: 'Therefore a man leaves his father and his mother and clings to his wife, and they become one flesh' (Genesis 2:24 NRSV). Cross-referenced with this is Paul's great exhortation in Ephesians 5:25–33 for husbands to love their wives, just as Christ loved the church and gave himself up for her.

Rookmaaker read the Bible in a personally participative way. This did not mean he read it subjectively. He faced hard and difficult passages and let them judge him. In a sense, he let the Scripture read his life as much as he read the sacred text.

While still a prisoner of war he wrote two documents that in many ways presciently foreshadow the task and mission of the rest of his life. 'Prophecy in the Old and New Testaments' (*Betreffende de Profetie*) is the first. 'Aesthetica' is the second. Both are carefully written in the hand of someone who knows how precious a piece of paper is when you do not know where the next scrap might come from. Not a space is wasted in these student-like composition books of approximately 80 pages.

On 19 September 1943, Rookmaaker movingly dedicated his study of the Old Testament prophets to Riki. In it he explores his reading of Scripture in order to understand how the Old Testament/Hebrew Bible is related to and fulfilled in the New Testament and how prophetic utterances might have contemporary meaning. This endeavour seems to have undergirded his other studies on a wide range of subjects during his time at Stanislau. Other than 'Aesthetica', begun almost two years later, it appears to be the only record of systematic studies made while a POW that he endeavoured to preserve and brought back with him to the Netherlands after the war. Towards the end of his time at Stanislau, Hans came into contact with a person who proved to be one of the most influential and faithful friends of his life. The relationship almost certainly did not start on a peer basis. Johan Pieter Albertus Mekkes (1897–1987) was 25 years older than Rookmaaker. Mekkes was a convinced Christian and a deeply intellectual man. He was a professional army man and ranked as a captain in the ground forces. At exactly the right time, Mekkes appeared as a mature and willing guide for this inchoate autodidact.

As Hans did not seem to be aware of his presence at Stanislau before the second half of 1943, it may have been that Mekkes arrived at *Stalag* 371 with the elite Dutch group that arrived some time in the summer of that year from Castle Colditz in Germany. They both were not to remain at Stanislau for much longer, for the Soviets were starting to push the Germans back on the eastern front. At the end of 1943 or possibly at the very beginning of 1944, *Stalag* 371 was evacuated to Neubrandenburg, a city north of Berlin and about halfway to the Baltic in Mecklenburg-Lower Pomerania. Hans's correspondence confirms he was in Germany by 24 February 1944. Meanwhile, Mekkes and Rookmaaker wasted no time in becoming acquainted.

To attain the rank of captain, Mekkes must have had exceptional leadership qualities and ability to develop and educate younger men. A photo of him when he was probably in his sixties suggests he was an urbane man. His letters to Hans show a man of great warmth and character. Mekkes, too, was a self-learner. He started his doctoral studies in philosophical law even while he was in the army. He must have naturally admired Hans when he saw how eagerly this young officer desired to learn. It must have also intrigued him that Hans was inclined to study both Scripture and philosophy, precisely his own interests. Hans in turn knew that here was someone who could help him. Here was a mentor who could cultivate his interests and talents to new and higher levels as well as confirm his growing conviction of the truth of the Bible and the Christian faith.

Rookmaaker told of meeting Mekkes in his essay, 'What the Philosophy of the Cosmonomic Idea has Meant to Me':

> During that decisive time, I was introduced to Captain (later Professor) Mekkes. It was just at the time that we were being evacuated to Neubrandenburg. I heard about Dooyeweerd from Captain Mekkes and started to read Dooyeweerd's book [*De Wijsbegeerte der Wetsidee*, 1935–1936]. Rather, I devoured it. For I discovered, right from page 1, that someone was speaking who started with precisely this question [of whether there would be a place for philosophy within Christian belief], and offered a clear solution, namely that being a Kantian and being a Christian were irreconcilable but that, nevertheless, the Christian has a clear task, also as a philosopher ...
>
> Having once taken this step, I learned a lot from Captain Mekkes, and through him I was further inducted into the Philosophy of the Cosmonomic Idea. We had very many discussions, and in this way I was shaped as a scholar. (*CW* 2:11)

Rookmaaker refers here to the work of Herman Dooyeweerd (1894–1977), a professor of the Philosophy of Law at the Free University of Amsterdam. The particular book he read is known in English by the title *A New Critique of Theoretical Thought*. Dooyeweerd was a powerful thinker who followed in the Dutch Neo-Calvinist tradition of the renowned Abraham Kuyper (1837–1920). A key component of his thinking was something that he believed Kuyper had missed, namely the need for a Christian philosophy to give a clear analysis of the foundations of old and new systems of thought in order to make way for an authentically biblical world view that could challenge the presuppositions of twentieth-century culture.

Dooyeweerd's astonishing intellectual range and detailed investigation attracted Rookmaaker immediately. The Philosophy of the Cosmonomic Idea became for him precisely the tool to help him think systematically and critically from a Christian perspective. It also helped him settle on his calling as a scholar.

At Neubrandenburg in 1945, Hans hastened to start his second special study after the one he had done on the Hebrew Prophets at Stanislau. Under the tutelage of Mekkes, he began writing a systematic work applying Dooyeweerd's approach and entitled it *Aesthetica: structuuranalyse van het muzikale kunstwerk*. This brought together in an amazing way all of his major interests and passions: music, philosophy, and a biblical world view.

Soon after he returned to the Netherlands, Hans was baptized at a church in The Hague and became a member of the Reformed Churches (*Vrijgemaakt*/Liberated). His 'catechism' had been an unusual combination of intensive personal Bible study and Dooyeweerdian philosophy. He also started his scholarly career. Faithful Mekkes continued to stand by him and help the budding scholar shape his essay in aesthetics into an article that was published in *Philosophia Reformata*.

Rookmaaker realized later how his struggle to come to faith and to grapple with the Bible in many ways recapitulated the struggle of the early church to come to its historical orthodox position. When Hans Rookmaaker became a Christian, he committed himself to a firmness that would not be undermined by nebulous ideas of a liberal kind. He passionately stated his view:

> I do not think it is possible that someone can come to know God and his Son through the Bible and then end up as a liberal. If one is confronted with the biblical truth, as I was in those days, then it is a question of accepting or rejecting it. The Bible is either true or not true: there is no alternative. Of course, nobody who is going to read the Bible in this way, even if he or she does not accept it, will deny that there are beautiful words in it, wisdom and insight, but such a person will also see in the end that this not the issue. The Bible comes to us, and came to me, with the demand to accept the gospel as a joyful message, God as Father and hence also his Son as Saviour. That is not to say that a person, such as I was at that time, pondering everything the Bible was telling me and trying to understand the biblical world picture ...

did not see any problems. On the contrary, I still find it rather striking that at that time I personally experienced a dogmatic struggle, similar to the struggle of the early church, and finally came to an insight that turned out to be called 'orthodox biblical Protestant'.(*CW* 2:11)

One might be tempted to assume that this sort of Bible belief coupled with a philosophical system structured in a hierarchy of 'modal law-spheres' was a readymade formula for a rigid form of Fundamentalism. It is not that this cannot happen (about the rigidly Reformed, Rookmaaker learned soon enough), but it would be a serious mistake to say that this combination had that effect on him. With his own words he states that what he found Dooyeweerd saying was 'that the Christian's thinking is not closed off, but is actually opened up'. In a striking way he discovered for himself a classical Christian formulation of Anselm following Augustine: *credo ut intelligam* ('I believe in order that I may understand'). Something dynamic and clarifying had happened to his thinking that he was convinced gave his ideas a firm intellectual foundation while allowing them to roam and range and soar over the whole wide world.

During the darkest days of the war, Hans Rookmaaker experienced the light of new life in Christ. While physically confined and captive in Germany, he became spiritually and intellectually liberated. Amazingly his conversion translated almost seamlessly into a calling for his life's work and mission. A new assurance of identity, however, did not automatically transfer into a crystal clear idea of a career path or the formation of a family based on a reunion with a much loved fiancée. He still had an arduous apprenticeship before him to find his way professionally and to grow into a maturity upon which a marriage could be built.

5
Family and Career

Weaving the strands of life together again after the war was not simple. These years were active, full and complex ones for Hans.

He knew for almost the entire time of his imprisonment that Riki Spetter, his Jewish fiancée, had been taken away with her family from The Hague to the province of Drenthe in the north of Holland; nevertheless, he continued to hope and to write letters to Riki via his family during all that time. Only in January 1945 did he admit how 'sad that we cannot write letters to Riki anymore, but understandable.'

Prior to this he was full of hope. His longing was palpable. He shared the whole gamut of his life with her, despite not knowing whether she would ever even see his letters.

> O, Riki, when will we be together again to talk, to talk about things that are so dear to our hearts and about what you cannot say and express so easily in a letter? I hope you still read the Bible regularly and that you still have peace and trust in God. I pray always that He will give you His grace so that you can have faith in Him. [2 April 1944]

> My dearest Riki, I just listened to my record of the violin concerto of Beethoven. How wonderful now and then to enjoy music. Later, we will listen together to concerts and records. A cat has just given birth to kittens in the barracks. We are taking care of the mother. The kittens, of course, [are being taken care of] by the mother ... I am lately occupied with a Christian philosophy ... Later, I will explain it to you when we can talk again. Luckily, there is someone here in the camp who has studied this philosophy and can give guidance in this subject. I always hope you can find peace and trust in God. I am so happy that we talked about this the last day were together. I hope it is still like that with you. [22 April 1944]

> Dearest Riki, ... There will be an end to this war. We will come together again ... I hope and always pray that you can endure and find that God may give you faith from which you can draw strength and power. [27 December 1944]

The Russian offensive had continued to push westward since the time Rookmaaker and Mekkes and their fellow prisoners were hastily evacuated from Stanislau in the western Ukraine to the overcrowded POW camp at Neubrandenburg about 100 kilometres north of Berlin. By mid-January 1945 the Russians had swept into Poland, occupied Warsaw, and were pressing to Germany's East Prussian frontier. In March and early April the Germans marched some groups of prisoners from Neubrandenburg west toward the Elbe and others north toward

Rostock. Apparently Hans was one of those who remained until rag-tag Russian soldiers, probably the 70th Army of the 2nd Belorussian Front, occupied the poorly supplied camp on 28 April 1945 and theoretically liberated it. But there were still problems. The Red Army harassed some of the ailing prisoners, and there was some indentured service for a time as the occupation of the surrounding area was secured. Food and medical shortages were acute. Eventually (it is not clear how) Hans made it home to The Hague after the European armistice of 8 May 1945. The Netherlands had been liberated prior to this on 5 May.

The last part of his captivity probably was the worse in terms of physical deprivation. His letters from Stanislau and Neubrandenburg reveal a surprising amount of abundance for wartime. Before leaving Stanislau he sent a suitcase filled with tobacco, chocolate, Nescafé and other foodstuffs to his family in the Netherlands. He felt they needed it more than he did! Camp authorities ordered the inmates to get rid of anything they were not prepared to carry. Hans decided he would be glad to carry his winter coat with him. These luxury items that he packed in his suitcase to send home seem to have been sent by the Red Cross or other international charitable agencies. During his time in POW camp, he received food and various items from a number of places in the world, including Argentina and America. While he was at Neubrandenburg he also had his family send him some of his favourite jazz records.

Rookmaaker acquired an amazing education while in POW camp. He worked on a wide range of the humanities, including the Greek and Latin he had missed by not attending a classically oriented gymnasium for his high school education. He also studied technical subjects. He had his family send him all sorts of specialized books pertaining to the type of studies he had been doing at Delft Technical University. He even officially sat exams in mathematics and other scientific subjects. Clandestinely he also pursued his training as naval officer. And, of course, there was his intensive study of Scripture and the Christian philosophy known as the Philosophy of the Cosmonomic Idea, pioneered by Herman Dooyeweerd.

Riki had written to Hans: 'I am reading a lot in the Bible, but [there is] much that I don't understand and you must explain it when you return.' There seems little doubt that this sober plea and his love for her propelled the serious and systematic study of the Hebrew prophets and God's way with Israel that he started at Stanislau. She inspired the beginning of his investigation, and he dedicated it to her. She was also present at the conclusion. Simply at the centre of the back cover of the notebook he used, he drew two capital R's, for Riki and Rookmaaker, that he symmetrically linked with the crossbar forming a visual double entendre for HRR.

On Hans's return to The Hague and even before trying to find Riki, he had to address the dramatically changed circumstances of his own immediate family and his country. The armistice with Germany was just two days short of exactly five years of German occupation of the Netherlands that had begun on 10 May 1940. He had spent most of those years in detention, first for nine months at Scheveningen Prison near The Hague and afterwards slightly over three years in at least three different German POW camps. His brother-in-law, Gerard Rotgans, who managed to be abroad during the war, had written to him at Neubrandenburg to say that he could 'barely imagine how Holland look[ed]'. During the last months and days of the war, life in Holland was extremely grim, especially with shortages of food, fuel and medical supplies.

The first grave reality that he had to face was that his father had died in his absence. The war years had taken a terrible toll on the former colonial official. Eleven days before Rookmaaker, senior's death on 31 January 1945, Hans had written from Neubrandenburg:

> It is freezing here all the time in these last months, but luckily not too much because the heating here is so-so. How is everyone's health? I hope you can get through all the difficulties. ...I hope the food parcels will arrive soon. ... I am very glad you received the last package I sent to Holland. Now I hope everything finishes soon. [20 January 1945]

Sadly, Hans's father did not live to see his son return home nor the defeat of Germany and the end of its brutal occupation of his country. His health had been compromised from the late 1930s when he was forced into an early retirement after a couple of attempts to resume his career. The war only undermined his health all the more. For unknown reasons, the Rookmaakers had to move to another house in The Hague during the wartime. They also experienced hunger and cold. Apparently after the strenuous activity of chopping firewood, Rookmaaker (*Pappie*) died of a heart attack at the age of 57.

Hans's mother (*Mammie*) was 55 years old when he returned. She was a sorrowing widow and had lost the pillar of her security and the compass of her family life. Physically she showed stamina and survived the war years relatively well, but mentally she exhibited signs that she was not fully emotionally stable. It was inevitable that she would look to her son for support and make demands, perhaps not totally conscious, on him. By this time, both of his sisters, Door and Hannie, were married. This alleviated him at least from being the only responsible adult male in the family. His siblings and their spouses, however, were scattered. Door and her husband, Dick Haver Droeze, had spent the war in the Japanese occupied Dutch Indies. Armistice there did not come until later, at the beginning of September 1945, nearly three months after it had been declared in Europe. Hannie's husband, Gerard, was abroad. All of this meant that a great deal of responsibility was still placed on the shoulders of a young man of 23.

The big question loomed over him: Where was Riki? He placed advertisements in the newspapers in The Hague, Amsterdam, Utrecht and Leeuwarden to see if anyone had been in contact with her or knew of her whereabouts since she was last seen in Westerbork in August of 1942. He must have felt increasingly crushed as no response to his campaign to find her materialized, including asking around the old network of mutual friends who remained from pre-war days.

The changed external circumstances of his country and his family and personal life perhaps were not the most drastic challenges Hans faced on his return home. He had changed radically, more profoundly than he himself may have been aware of at the time. It was a shock to his family, especially his adoring sisters, to find that their beloved brother had returned filled with religion and talk of Christian philosophy. They knew their Hans was clever and loved to study. They knew he had found solace in his studies during his detention. But they were not prepared for the fact that a significant part of his passion for learning had led him to a vigorous faith informing everything he thought about and wanted to do with his life. As his family had no particular religious heritage, his fervency seemed to them like fanaticism. In the following years shock transmuted to anger. Hannie and her husband, Gerard, tried to reason Hans out of his stance. Until her last days Hannie showed considerable resistance and hostility to her brother's beliefs.

Meanwhile, he was acquiring a new spiritual family that expanded exponentially for the rest of his life. The father of that spiritual family was Captain J.P.A. Mekkes, who had wisely mentored Hans at Stanislau and closely guided his study of a Dooyeweerdian approach to Christian philosophy at Neubrandenburg. Mekkes did not abandon him when they returned to Holland, but kept in regular touch with him and nurtured him in every way, spiritually and intellectually, and probably emotionally as well, by his firm friendship.

Presumably it was Mekkes who helped him find a church where he could be baptized. Because soon after his return to the Netherlands, Hans was baptized, confirmed and became a member of the Reformed Churches (*Vrijgemaakt*/Liberated). He later related that, while his older sisters had been baptized as babies, his parents had totally forgotten to have him baptized as an infant. Mekkes also quickly helped set him on his way academically by encouraging him to develop and elaborate his thoughts on aesthetics that he had begun to set down at Neubrandenburg. These were brought to fruition and published in two parts in the Calvinist journal *Philosophia Reformata* (1946–1947).

Hans's commitment to the church and his new Christian family did not supplant all of his former friendships. As he tried to re-establish relationships, one person stands out above all others in her openness to Hans and her openness to the faith that he had found while a prisoner of war. This was Anna Marie (nicknamed Anky) Huitker (1915–2003).

Anky was seven years older than Hans. Before the war she had also been a part of his circle of friends and a close personal friend of Riki's. Anky and Riki worked in the same clerical office. They may have become friends at work. Anky knew Riki's family well and socialized with her brothers. When as a mutual friend of Riki and Hans she considerately reported to him in late August 1942 that Riki and her family had been taken away by the Nazis, she had no idea in mind that her relationship with Hans would ever deepen beyond what it was then.

After the scourge and affliction of the war, a new reality emerged. So many loved ones were dead or gone. There was no going back to the good old days, even if they could be called that. There were choices. One could go crazy or become cynical and/or radicalized. One could also squarely face the new terms life set forth and try to continue to live in as positive and healthy a way as possible. Both Hans and Anky, individually and eventually mutually, gradually did just that. Rather than run away from the new conditions of their lives, they embraced them and moved forward cautiously and circumspectly.

Anky Huitker was a completely different type of woman and personality from Riki Spetter, but of no less character. She was born on 10 August 1915 on the sugar plantation, Sindanglaoet, located near the city of Cirebon on the north coast of Java. In 1908, three years before Hans's parents were married, her parents, Leendert (nicknamed Leen) and Maria Helena (nicknamed Lien) moved there. At Sindanglaoet, Anky's father managed the sugar refinery located on the plantation. Anky joined an older sister, Adriana (nicknamed Addy), who had been born in 1911. Their parents were members of the Dutch Reformed Churches (*Hervormde Kerk*), the major Protestant denomination in the Netherlands that dated back to the sixteenth century, when the northern provinces of the Low Countries revolted against Spanish rule. The symmetry of Anky's and Hans's experience of their earliest years in the Dutch Indies extends to her parents' neglecting to have her baptized as a small child. Perhaps the colonial environment did not lend itself to this sort of conscientiousness or conformity.

Business and management must have been naturally inculcated in the Huitker family. After the family's return to the Netherlands when Anky was still a child, she gravitated in her adolescence to organizational work and found employment in office work. Without a doubt, her true métier was to be an entrepreneur as would be evident later in her life. She was a person who knew how to get things done. She was petite and wholesomely attractive. She was multilingual, bright and quick and determined when she sensed a challenge. She was a woman of practical intelligence, but not an intellectual. She also was not a conventionally domestic type of woman, though quite able to manage a household adeptly. She had remarkable tenacity, especially for causes she believed in.

An amorphous family adherence to Protestantism did not give Anky or her sister, Addy, clear spiritual direction for their lives. After the Great War, thoughts of inevitable human progress and perfection that had insinuated significantly into European thought were severely shattered. The theological liberalism of the churches was on a tremendous roll, undercutting clear commitment to a historical understanding and affirmation of the Christian faith. There was a virtual vacuum in constructive ideas for fresh spiritual or political and social life at this time. Into this void, the West opened itself in an exceptional way to Eastern thought. The Huitker sisters were sensitive and open to these trends of the time.

In the years between the wars, they found their way to Castle Eerde near Ommen, where the famous mystic, Jiddu Krishnamurti, had been invited in 1926 by Baron van Pallandt to make his European home and where thousands flocked to hear him speak. Dutch radio broadcasted his talks. Addy and Anky came from nearby Lemelerveld, where they had first lived after returning from the Dutch Indies and where they still had relatives that they visited. It was only half an hour at most by bicycle to Eerde to see and hear the charismatic young man known as 'The Star of the East' whom Theosophists claimed was the reincarnation of Jesus. There was considerable excitement around the activities at the castle.

Addy, as the older sister, seems to have been influenced more by the atmosphere surrounding Castle Eerde. She kept pictures of herself taken with Krishnamurti. Anky never forgot the experience of being there either. She would have been only 14 years old when Krishnamurti dramatically announced before an astounded audience of mainly Theosophists that he renounced that he thought or ever considered himself to be a reincarnation of Lord Maitreya, whom most of them believed had been an earlier incarnation of Jesus.

After this admission, the Krishnamurti following at Castle Eerde at Ommen dwindled. A few years later, Baron van Pallandt resumed the proprietorship of the castle and made it available from 1933 to Jewish children fleeing persecution by the Nazis, a cause that the Huitker sisters had great sympathy with and which could well have been an important reason why they maintained an attraction for and sympathy with Eerde and never forgot it. It could also have been part of what inspired them to their courageous activities of protecting Jews during the war. Castle Eerde and the camp at Westerbork (known as the Dutch 'Gateway to Auschwitz'), locations originally developed as well organized refuges for Jews fleeing Nazi Germany, were, with cynical pragmatism, commandeered malevolently by the Nazis after their occupation of the Netherlands and taken over and used as penal/transit camps for the duration of the war.

Hans and Anky resumed their acquaintance in a gradual and natural way following the war. They both had a concern to find Riki, fiancée and friend. They both had experienced a great deal of hardship and uncertainty during the war years. Anky was no stranger to Nazi terror. In different but equally true ways, Anky's spirit matched Hans's. The Huitker family valiantly united to resist the Nazi occupiers and courageously conspired together at great personal risk for each of them to hide Jews in their home for the duration of the war. Without a let up they lived under constant strain for years. After the war, Addy married Leo Wolff, one of the *onderduikers* who had hidden in their home. A certain nervous tenseness from these years of unwavering vigilance never totally left Anky, though she could, as occasion arose, relax and enjoy herself. From terrible tensions and disintegrated dreams fine filaments of mutual understanding and respect incrementally grew into strong cords of love and commitment between Anky and Hans that were to sustain them for the rest of their lives.

Anky was spiritually hungry and open as she began to see more and more of Hans. He, of course, was eager for her to find the reality of faith in Jesus Christ that he had discovered while a prisoner of war. The message that had fallen on closed ears in his family, she slowly received with warmth and sincerity as he shared it with her and engaged her questions. She did not rush into faith or take it lightly. Though they were in contact soon after the war and presumably talked about issues of belief then, it was not until probably sometime in 1947 that her commitment to the Christian faith was clear and defined. She still waited until 1949 (the year in which she and Hans were married) to be baptized and to become a member of the Reformed Church (*Vrijgemaakt*/Liberated) in Amsterdam.

Hans and Anky showed admirable restraint in their developing relationship. They enjoyed each other's company and companionship, and they were each growing in their Christian faith. They spent time with each other naturally and with ease. Although it seemed likely that Riki had died at Auschwitz, they had no conclusive proof of this. Their reluctance to rush their relationship bore strong signs of having been motivated by respect for someone they both honoured and hoped would somehow appear. Neither Hans nor Anky ever learned that Riki died at Auschwitz on 30 September 1942, shortly after she was taken away. Stalwartly they carried on with their lives and did not make special demands on each other, or life in general, for that matter. Anky continued in her office work. Hans pursued his further studies.

Hans's love of learning only increased through his discovery of his love of God. As immediate as his finding Christian affiliation on his return to The Netherlands was, so was his seeking a place where he could continue his education. Thus in 1946, without skipping a beat and with hardly a cent to his name, he enrolled as a student at the University of Amsterdam.

In many ways it was easier for Hans to know his calling as a scholar than it was for him to find the right subject to study, one that could lead to a meaningful career that would provide support for the family he one day hoped to have. Issues that are often the last for a serious scholar to acknowledge were ones that Hans confronted at the outset, even before he had started his university studies.

Czeslaw Milosz, the acclaimed Polish poet and University of California at Berkeley professor, a slightly older contemporary of Hans, points out in his own intellectual and spiritual self-portrait: 'A man must abide somewhere, a physical roof over his head is not enough; his mind needs its bearings, its points of reference, vertically as well as horizontally.' Often it is in the midst of particular studies that have captivated interest, or even afterwards, that a scholar finds his or her intellectual abode. Milosz is an example of someone who eventually consciously and confidently found his abode in the Roman Catholic Christian tradition.

With his conversion Hans rather recognized immediately his spiritual and intellectual dwelling place to be in a biblical and Reformed tradition. The Christian philosophy of Herman Dooyeweerd was confirmed for him by its high degree of congruence with Scripture, especially in its understanding of God's law perceived in the broadest sense of its co-inherence with the structure of reality. He had not discovered this philosophy and then read it all back into the Bible. Quite the reverse was true. His reading of the Bible prepared him to recognize a way of thinking that could open up biblical insight into the world, scholarly disciplines and normal human activities. He was not entrapped or enslaved by this philosophy but, rather, set free. Instead of being scattered in his thinking, he was given aid to think rigorously in a systematic but dynamic way, across categories, without losing his intellectual or spiritual footing because he had a place to stand. However, for all its benefit to him, it did not provide him with a tidy formula for a career. The questions remained: What specifically was he going to study? What kind of career would his choice create?

Detachment was not a characteristic Hans Rookmaaker exhibited. He was always engaged personally in what he thought and did. In *Aesthetica: structuuranalyse van het muzikale kunstwerk*, the study he began at Neubrandenburg, he managed to pack all his passions for music, philosophy and a biblical world view into his formulation. Long before one talked of 'personal knowledge' in the Polanyian sense, Hans was intuiting this. Dooyeweerd's philosophy rescued him from Kantian incertitude regarding knowing and alerted him to questioning radically the objectivity and neutrality of any subject, including science. Being personal in one's approach to knowledge did not mean being subjective or creating truth, as in some postmodern trends, but acknowledging one's personal participation in the process of knowing. Hans needed a subject he felt close to.

Dooyeweerd also made Hans aware of how easily almost any area of human endeavour can become a substitute for religion. In the all-consuming task and fascination of graduate and doctoral studies, many a scholar becomes more the worshipper of his or her subject than its steward or servant. Hans cast about to find a field he could serve.

Music had been his passion. He loved classical music and African-American music, and he knew a great deal about both. Musicology seemed to him an ideal subject. In high hopes of pursing the history of music, he was disappointed when he was told that he did not have the technical prerequisites required for this study. Independently he had studied Greek and Latin, subjects he knew would be required, but he did not realize he needed to be able to play a musical instrument competently to be admitted to a degree in musicology. Ironically, for all his knowledge and appreciation of music, Hans could not make music. For that matter, he could not sing or even carry a tune in the midst of voluminous support during congregational hymn singing. Thus it was that he eventually turned to the study of art history, a subject that he was more than adequately suited to and one that permitted him quite compatibly to continue his serious and abiding interest in African-American music history.

Hans needed to attend to practical matters before he launched into his newfound academic field at the University of Amsterdam. He applied for and was granted a discharge from his commission as a naval officer. He also supervised his mother's move from The Hague to Amsterdam, where he installed her in a flat they shared. At about the same time Addy Huitker married Leo Wolff and moved to Amsterdam. Following this event, Anky and her parents also moved to Amsterdam. In terms of convenience this meant that Hans and Anky were able to see much more of each other.

As though life was not full enough with the responsibilities of study, home and church life, and his growing involvement with and love for Anky, Hans took on the further task of starting a group for Christian students from the Free University and the University of Amsterdam. After beginning his studies, he quickly discerned the need for Christian students, especially those coming from his church, to have strong support in the midst of a university environment that frequently was hostile to their faith and was inclined more to uphold a secular humanism. Hans was intrinsically mission-minded. He understood that taking a Christian message into the world was as much about sharing it stratigraphically, throughout the academic disciplines and professions at home, as it was about spreading it geographically, abroad. Gathering together students from the Reformed Churches (*Vrijgemaakt*/Liberated), he gave leadership and helped to pioneer the formation of the *Vereniging van Gereformeerde Studenten in Amsterdam* (VGSA). This fellowship encouraged friendship that nurtured Christian maturity through Bible study and reflection, bringing biblical thought to bear on the issues of life and learning. For the rest of his studies and for the rest of his career, Hans in one way or another supported VGSA and its mission. In appreciation, he in turn was honoured by being made a lifelong member.

In 1948, Anky began administrative work in Amsterdam that suited her and brought a friendship to her and Hans that would make a deep impact on both of them and take them to activities and places they could never have dreamed of then. Apparently through church links, she had found a job working for the organizing committee preparing for the first and founding assembly of the International Council of Christian Churches (ICCC), 11–19 August 1948. Under the leadership of Carl McIntire (1906–2002), who had started the Bible Presbyterian Church in 1938 and the American Council of Churches in 1940, delegates from 58 churches representing 29 countries came together to witness to the Lordship of Jesus Christ and to protest against the establishment of the World Council of Churches (WCC) that was to occur (19 August – 4 September 1948), also in Amsterdam. In McIntire's eyes and probably in the eyes of most of the delegates to the ICCC, the WCC represented the arch-fiend of liberalism.

Hans was only 26 and not exactly an experienced churchman at this stage, nor was he an official delegate to the ICCC meeting. He was a full-time university student who checked in intermittently with the young woman working in the office, namely Anky Huitker, whom he had recently asked to marry him. Later comments by Hans suggest that he did attend some of the sessions. Short of pestering Anky, he was eager to have her find any Americans at the assembly who might know something about African-American music and be willing to talk with him about it.

In the midst of her administrative duties, Anky saw a fair amount of an approachable American who spent time in the ICCC office making special arrangements for various sessions. He had impressed her, and she thought he might be the right man for Hans to speak with. So it was on an evening in August 1948 when Hans accompanied Anky back to her office for her to do some more work that they unexpectedly ran into Francis A. Schaeffer (1912–1984), the very person she wanted Hans to meet, busily working away there. Little did the three of them know at that time the great influence they would have on each other or how their futures would be woven together for the benefit of many people they did not yet know or who were not even born then.

Immediately upon being introduced, Hans respectfully asked Schaeffer, ten years his senior, if he had some time to speak with him. Anky remembered Schaeffer looking at his watch and telling Hans he could spare about half an hour. Then they disappeared to talk. Anky never saw Hans for the rest of the evening. When she saw him the next day she asked whether he had had his questions answered. She was amazed to hear that he never even got round to asking them because he and Schaeffer had streaked straight into an extensive discussion of modern art and its presuppositions that did not end until 4:00 a.m.!

The year before the inauguration of the ICCC in Amsterdam, Schaeffer had spent three months travelling throughout Europe as a representative of the Independent Board for Presbyterian Foreign Missions and as the American Secretary for the Foreign Relations Department of the American Council of Christian Churches. He had recently moved to Lausanne, Switzerland with his wife, Edith, and their three young daughters, primarily in order to establish a ministry called Children for Christ. Along with this work he also collaborated from his European base of operations in the formation of the ICCC.

Less than a year after the ICCC assembly in Amsterdam, Hans and Anky were married. If meeting Francis Schaeffer sparked a key event in Hans's life, it also did that for Anky, for whom hearing Schaeffer preach in a way that was understandable and edifying during those days of the ICCC in 1948 contributed greatly to her Christian growth and maturity. As they prepared to enter into the most solemn and momentous commitment of their lives, Anky was probably more acutely aware than Hans was of their lack of family Christian heritage and the need for resources to sustain mutual solidarity for a lasting marriage. Schaeffer's encouragement could well have been what she needed in her spiritual development to help her feel prepared to take such a serious step.

On Wednesday, 1 June 1949, Hans and Anky were married at a civil ceremony attended only by their immediate families at the Town Hall of Amsterdam. A small church service followed later in the week. The little gathering consisted basically of the elders of the church, a few friends from the congregation, and members of the VGSA. The bridal pair was so impoverished that they walked from their little loft in the Huitker's house to the church for the ceremony. Afterwards there was no party, though they did manage to scrape up enough cash to spend a honeymoon in France, visiting Paris, Versailles and Dijon.

In 1949 European economic recovery from the war was still shaky. Hans and Anky were extremely vulnerable financially, as were their families and most of their peers. Hans found the funds to travel to France and tide them over by selling a valuable stamp collection that he had inherited from his grandfather. Happily, he was able to find income by becoming an art critic for *Trouw*, a daily Dutch newspaper with a strong Calvinist readership coming out of the Kuyperian Christian Reformed (*Gereformeerde*) tradition. In 1949 he also passed his *kandidaats* examination (equivalent to a bachelor's degree) and received an appointment as an assistant to Professor I.Q. van Regteren Altena (1899–1980), a connoisseur and specialist in the art of the sixteenth and seventeenth centuries and one of the editors of the prestigious art-historical journal, *Oud Holland*.

Hans wasted no time getting started on both his further studies and a family. As Anky was well into her thirties when they married, they were happy to learn a few months into their marriage that they were expecting a child. As the new baby gestated, so did the new scholar.

Being a graduate assistant had its advantages besides helping to cover fees. First of all, it allowed Hans to see more of his professor in action. Secondly, it allowed him to receive more attention from his professor. Thirdly, it gave him invaluable experience in teaching even as he was learning. Van Regteren Altena taught his students to look meticulously at works of art in order to get thoroughly acquainted with them. He also emphasized at the same time the study of them in their art-historical context. Though he wore this lightly in later years, Hans was given an excellent apprenticeship in connoisseurship by his professor, who at the time of his studies was also the Director of the Print Room of the Rijksmuseum. Hans's art-historical education was founded on constant exposure to original works of art under expert guidance.

To this erudite and classical formation he added an extraordinary self-education in contemporary art. His reviews for *Trouw* required regular visits to art exhibitions and museums all over the country and occasionally abroad. Although many of the shows he saw were of older art, there was also a burgeoning of modern art to be seen. The young man who had independently cultivated a discerning taste for the nuances of African-American music and a considerable knowledge of its development now applied these same kinds of sensibilities to understanding the visual art of his own era. As both the history of jazz and modern art are now established academic subjects, it needs to be pointed out that when Hans began writing about these subjects in the early 1950s, they were not universally recognized as scholarly subjects. His own contribution in this area, at least in The Netherlands, helped them gain serious attention.

Hans was building his unique blend of competencies. Alongside his technical expertise in art history and firsthand familiarity with contemporary art, he was beginning to hone his ability to communicate with a wide public without pandering to the lowest common denominator of his audience. Furthermore, he was thoroughly imbued with biblical understanding that did not remain locked in a text but dynamically sought a horizon in everyday life.

In his reviews, his style was simple and direct. He knew how to hook his readers' interest in his first paragraph, if not his first line. He always informatively gave historical, cultural or religious background information that aided his analysis. Without a hint of patronizing, his reviews registered warmth and an undisguised desire to teach and persuade his audience to take action. They are studded with exhortations to: 'take a closer look,' 'go see,' 'take a trip,' 'hop on a train.'

The fashioning of Hans's career and communication skills was well underway when he faced the steepest learning curve that he had encountered up to that point in his life. In Amsterdam, on 15 July 1950, he became a father for the first time. Hans and Anky welcomed a healthy baby boy on that day and named him in the Rookmaaker family tradition of father and grandfather, Henderik Roelof (Hans/Hansje as he was subsequently nicknamed). Hansje cleverly managed to make his appearance into the world on the date of Rembrandt's birth in 1606.

The new little creature fascinated Hans, but he was not quite sure what to do with it or how to relate to it. Being the slightly spoiled baby in his own family had not helped him have natural intuition for this new situation. His somewhat emotionally distant relationship with his own parents was also an impairment.

After a break of slightly less than three years, Leendert Cornelis (nicknamed Kees), born 21 February 1953, closely followed by Maria Helena (nicknamed Marleen), born 26 August 1954, joined their older brother Hansje. Both of these children were also born in Amsterdam. This time, however, names were chosen from the Huitker side of the family with Kees being the namesake of his maternal grandfather and Marleen that of her maternal grandmother. Though Hans loved his children dearly and was solicitous of their welfare, he still was not adept at relating to small children and left them almost completely in the hands of their mother as he focused on his studies and writing.

Hans was by no means hopeless as a father. Gradually as the children grew up and he could converse with them, he worked as hard as he could to understand them. Although not emotionally demonstrative, he could be playful and warmly humorous with them. Even if he was not home every evening for a meal, he was faithful in having some family time with them each Sunday afternoon as well as making sure there was an annual vacation. Sometimes during vacations, however, family time was not separated from his personal and professional interests. There was always something he was interested in seeing either on the way or while the family was on holiday. Revolt occurred. Marleen distinctly remembers a period of time when she refused to go into art museums.

In teen years, when many parents try to clamp down strictly on their offspring, Hans wisely listened to his children and left them free to find their way. They continue to respect him for this. Hans never rebuked them for the length of their hair, the clothes they wore or the music they listened to. He did not send all his children to Christian schools. Although Hans, junior did attend a Christian school, Kees and Marleen did not. Hans, who as a teenager had been more than an avid, almost obsessive record collector, had great sympathy with the importance of serious popular music giving direction in his children's lives. They in turn kept him in touch with current trends even as he was able to show them some of the roots of rock music in jazz and the blues. Hans and Anky did not convey their beliefs and values to their children so much by overt lessons or preaching as by their inherent character and quality of life.

Hans's stamina for work in the 1950s was staggering. As his young family was growing, so was he academically. In the same year that Kees was born (1953), he received his *doctoraal* (equivalent to a master's degree) in art history from the University of Amsterdam. When he completed his degree, his assistantship also came to an end and, though still writing one or two articles a week for *Trouw*, he needed to regroup and find more income to support his family. For the next three years he took up teaching high school at the Spinoza Lyceum in Amsterdam. All the while he and Anky faithfully supported their church, encouraged students and hosted a regular Bible study group.

But it was hard going. Because Hans and Anky had not grown up in the church, they felt to a certain extent like outsiders. Anky, especially, felt disappointed and spiritually dry. People outside of the church, her parents for example, were often more humane than those inside it. A bright spot was their flourishing friendship with Francis and Edith Schaeffer, whom they met with on the Schaeffers' periodic visits to The Netherlands.

Anky took particular interest in their ministry to children and the Bible study lessons they prepared for them. When asked by the Schaeffers to help with this work in Holland, Anky found it benefited her as much as it did her own children and their friends who came into her home.

These same years were not easy for the Schaeffers either. In the summer of 1954 their young son, Franky, contracted polio. Early in 1955 the Swiss government notified them that they had to leave the country permanently within six weeks. Astonishingly, a turnabout of this situation occurred through a set of unusual circumstances when they acquired unexpected funding to purchase Chalet les Mèlézes in Huémoz and were allowed to remain in Switzerland. Anky and Hans, who kept in close contact and constant prayer for them, rejoiced at the reversal of events and followed with exceeding interest the transformation of the Schaeffers' ministry after their season of crisis. On 4 June 1955 Francis Schaeffer resigned from the Independent Board for Presbyterian Foreign Missions and inaugurated the informal beginning of L'Abri Fellowship, a work of hospitality and hope that gave shelter to countless numbers of spiritually and intellectually hungry seekers.

In that summer, with three small children aged five and under, Hans and Anky set off to see their friends in Switzerland. Anky never forgot their first visit to Huémoz. Meals were marvellous times of feeding body and soul as they lingered over dinner in deep discussion about all the things that meant the most to her and Hans. It almost made her forget that she had on her hands three small rascally Rookmaakers, as full of energy as their father had ever been as a child. She appreciated Mrs Schaeffer graciously doing her best to cater to these little creatures when they turned up their noses at ice cream and cakes and called for bread and milk. Monolinguals can have little comprehension of how bewildering it is for children to be surrounded by a swirl of adults speaking a language other than their own. All three Rookmaaker children seem to have survived their initiation into English by subsequently learning to speak it with exceptional fluency.

Hans and Anky came away from their visit to Huémoz spiritually refreshed and inspired, despite being a little ragged around the edges from managing their healthy young brood on such a long excursion. Not too many months later they decided to cut to the quick and go for a future that would prepare Hans to engage at the highest levels the kinds of seekers that came to a place like L'Abri. In 1956 Hans finished his work with *Trouw* and turned his focus full-time to obtaining a doctorate in art history, at the same time struggling with his burning desire to write a book on jazz, blues and spirituals.

Hans drove himself harder than ever. He was back at the University of Amsterdam with his old professor, van Regteren Altena. He loved the art of the sixteenth and seventeenth centuries, but he felt a tremendous pull toward understanding the art of the century in which he lived. He was convinced by everything he had experienced so far in his life that the crisis of the modern condition, which had reaped chaos and devastation for most of the twentieth century, could be understood through modern art, which presented a way of disclosing what was at stake in assuming the validity of modernity's presuppositions. The powers of persuasion that he charmed his *Trouw* readers with must have worked on his professor as he made the case for a dissertation on Paul Gauguin and Synthetist art theories as a critical bridge between the art of the ages, as it were, and what was created in the twentieth century.

Graham Birtwistle, in his fine essay on the shaping of Rookmaaker's thought, makes clear that few established academics at the time deemed modern art a true task for a real scholar. That Hans along with his contemporary, Hans Jaffé, curator at the Stedelijk Museum of Amsterdam, who investigated the De Stijl movement of the 1920s, were allowed to research areas of modern art, affirms that the faculty of art history at Amsterdam was willing to move beyond its reputation for impeccable historical scholarship to a progressive consideration of more recent art. It put Hans in the vanguard of what the Dutch art-historical establishment was willing to concede as serious research.

On the practical side, teaching at a high school, no matter how fine the students were or how prestigious the institution, could not drive forward his scholarship or his career. Providentially he was able to find a new position that undergirded his studies, expanded his art-historical horizons, prepared him professionally to be competitive for a future job market, and provided him with income.

Moving from *Trouw* into his doctoral work, Hans found a position in 1957 as assistant to Professor Henri (Hans) van de Waal (1910–1972) at the University of Leiden while he was still living in Amsterdam. One is tempted to wonder what bonds of tacit sympathy there might have been between Hans and van de Waal, a Jew, who was dismissed from his position as assistant at the Leiden Print Collection with the Nazi occupation of the Netherlands. Van de Waal somehow managed to escape far worse from the occupiers' hands and returned after the war to become both the director of the Print Collection and a professor of Art History at the University of Leiden. The great Polish Catholic Christian art historian, Jan Bialostocki, called van de Waal 'one of the masters of the study of images'.

Although Hans never earned a degree from his work at Leiden nor ever intended to, it is safe to say he learned as much there by assisting van de Waal as if he had earned a second doctorate. As a scholar of Dutch historical iconography of the sixteenth to the eighteenth centuries in its relation to religion, literature and social history, van de Waal pioneered the systematization of iconological groups as they relate to specific typological contexts. This was one of the greatest boons those studying the content and meaning of historical art could have hoped for, as it made collections of art works readily accessible on the basis of subject, not just by artist or more general categories such as landscape, portrait or still life. Working with the thousands of photo cards of artworks amassed by the *Rijksbureau voor Kunsthistorische Documentatie* (RKD/Netherlands Institute for Art History, founded in 1932), van de Waal designed an ingenious system of number/letter/code classification called the Decimal Index of Art of the Low Countries (DIAL) which he presented in 1958. To make his system more easily available to international scholars, van de Waal chose English. The system was so successful that an improved and extended version of DIAL which no longer focused only on Dutch art was published in 1968. It is called the Iconclass System.

During most of the decade of the development of Iconclass, Hans was van de Waal's righthand man at Leiden until his own appointment as Professor of Art History at the Free University of Amsterdam. Rookmaaker's loyalty is confirmed in his correspondence. He did not want to run away from his work at Leiden and leave his older colleague in the lurch. At pains to give proper closure to his time there, he recruited and trained his successor, amidst preparations to take up his own post. One assumes this was Leendert D. Couprie, who eventually succeeded van de Waal and went on to edit and complete the Iconclass system when the scholar of images died in 1972. Rookmaaker's calendars show he continued to keep in regular contact with Couprie well into the 1970s after van de Waal's death.

While Rookmaaker shows evidence of being influenced by art historians such as Hans Sedlmayr, Erwin Panofsky and Ernst Gombrich, a less explicit but much deeper influence may have been van de Waal. The deviser of DIAL/Iconclass may not be as well known as those other scholars are, but he was equally as great and, in many ways, a more multifaceted scholar and educator. The model van de Waal provided

Rookmaaker with in their close working relationship should not be overlooked as an important influence on him. Van de Waal kept up cordial collegial relations with many leading art historians, including Panofsky and Fritz Saxl of the Warburg Institute in London. He founded a special collection on the History of Photography as one of the divisions of the Leiden Print Collection. He was an outstanding lecturer and much loved as a teacher by his students, both of art history and other disciplines. He was committed to art education for young people, a concern that led to his being made the Dutch delegate to UNESCO seminars on the role of museums in education. R.H. Fuchs said of him that, 'the history of art, in his experience, was not just an area of human endeavour to be documented, mapped, analyzed and interpreted. To him it meant, above all, the opportunity to study how individuals function within their culture, and, conversely, how a culture nurtures and shapes an individual.'

Those familiar with Rookmaaker's own breadth of interests should not have trouble seeing how van de Waal's approach would have appealed to him and implicitly influenced his emphasis on the content of art in its cultural context and given him ideas about the scope of what can be included and brought to bear on the understanding of works of art. Fuchs's further description of van de Waal helps us see this better.

> [Van de Waal] remained aloof from the doctrinaire and the bullying. In an ancient Jewish tradition, he was not a teacher *of* a discipline, but a teacher *for* individuals. That is why he firmly refused to conduct a course in methodology; he instinctively felt that by doing so he would limit his students' personal freedom and hinder the development of their individual talents. He did, though, conduct a graduate seminar in what he called *beeldleer* - the 'general science of images', related to art as linguistics is to literary texts. Definitely not a methodology or a theory of art, van de Waal's *beeldleer* was more like a systematic inventory of everything that conditions a work of art, from the properties of paint to iconographic codes and from the history of frames to the history of taste. *Beeldleer* precedes methodology; it deals not with schematic structures but with concrete, particular facts.

Van de Waal's decision to set up DIAL/Iconclass in English may also have influenced Hans's decision to go the harder route and write his dissertation on Gauguin in English so that it could reach a wider academic audience. As doctoral research goes, he completed his work in record time, especially considering that he was holding down a job to support his family as well as working on writing another book at the same time. At 4:00 p.m. on 7 July 1959 he went to his *promotie* (graduation ceremony) at the University of Amsterdam. He got there by the skin of his teeth.

The successful candidate for the *doctoraat*, H.R. Rookmaaker, and his dear wife who had supported him all the way by keeping the home fires burning and typing his drafts and their corrections, must have been greatly relieved. This time after the ceremony there was a party. Van Regteren Altena, Hans's professor, wrote the next day to say thank you for the enjoyable, presumably expansive, meal and evening he had had with him and Anky and others after the official conferring on of the doctoral degree.

In *Synthetist Art Theories*, Hans's dissertation on Paul Gauguin, he broke new ground for the study of the dynamics of thought and artistic practice at play at the inception of modern art. Sifting through a monumental amount of nineteenth-century French art theory, selecting, translating and analysing pertinent texts, have won Rookmaaker regard for decades. To this he added an analysis of Gauguin's contribution as a major figure who fought for the artist's freedom to find new forms apart from any previously held established tradition, conceived an understanding of the iconic character of the visual arts (that is, colour and line representation of the visible world could express what is unseen but equally as real) and created a new and higher value for the decorative aspects of art.

In the days before Rookmaaker's *promotie* all of his hard work and original research hung in the balance. The committee from the Faculty of Arts and Letters was not convinced that he had written a text that was in comprehensible English. Hans was the first to admit that his English was not perfect. Yes, he had made the decision to write in English. Days before he was to defend his work, he was asked in a threatening way to translate everything into Dutch. Seeing this problem coming, he had called upon his friends, who came to his rescue. Both Calvin Seerveld and Francis Schaeffer wrote letters to the committee, stating that though *Synthetist Art Theories* was not written in perfect English, it was clear as scholarly discourse in English and that they should approve his dissertation. Schaeffer, in his letter, added that not only had he read the manuscript, he had had a Cambridge scholar who was visiting him also read Rookmaaker's writing and both agreed that it could be understood. That may have clinched it for the committee. It surely added further bonds to an already established friendship, as well as a deep debt of gratitude to Seerveld for help in the hour of need.

One has the sense that Rookmaaker sought his PhD in the way one would a union card or a valuable ticket to a game or concert. He was interested in his subject and knew it added to knowledge about the emergence of modern art, which he was passionate about understanding. But completing this goal over these years was not the all-consuming end to which he was willing to sacrifice his soul and other interests or commitments in his life as often happens with graduate students on a trajectory to having a brilliant career. He remained committed to VGSA, his involvement with L'Abri deepened, he spoke at churches and conferences and student groups, he remained faithful to his circle for Bible study and continued writing his book on jazz, blues and spirituals. Though he was quite serious about his research, one almost has the feeling that his dissertation was a nuisance he had to get through in order to do other things that his broader vision of mission and life called him to.

Near to his heart was a project that he had dreamed of and nurtured for a long time. This was his book, *Jazz, blues, spirituals* (1960). Even as he was in the last throes of writing his dissertation, he was lining up details regarding publication permissions for this book. It must have been the book he had wanted to write since he was a boy.

In 1958, prior to the completion of Hans's doctorate, the Rookmaaker family moved to Leiden. By the time of the publication of *Synthetist Art Theories* and *Jazz, blues, spirituals*, they were domestically well established there. As he settled into teaching at Leiden and working with DIAL/Iconclass, Hans seems to have known, however, that he would not be spending the rest of his academic career there. By this time there is also the sense that he liked the intensity of doing many things at the same time. Soon he applied for and was granted funding by the Dutch government to travel to the United States for the purpose of learning how art history was taught there. It provided a special opportunity to spy out the land to see if he might have a professional future there. Professorships in art history were much more limited in number in the Netherlands than they were in North America.

On 27 August 1961, the day after his daughter Marleen's seventh birthday, Hans flew to New York, where he was welcomed by Harry Schat, a Dutch friend of his living in New Jersey. Harry was a multilingual businessman with an ardent bent for Reformed theology. Hans and Anky had known him for years. In fact, he was the son-in-law of Dominee Meester, the minister who had baptized Anky. Harry was a born organizer and helped get Hans on the road immediately, first to Toronto and then all around the eastern USA. Until 14 December, when he flew back to the Netherlands, he kept up a gruelling pace, meeting literally hundreds of people, visiting every major art collection from the northeast seaboard to the Midwest, attending the College Art Association meeting in New York City, contacting dozens of prominent art historians and seeing at least 20 college and university campuses. He also took this opportunity to make connections with numerous leading figures from the African-American community.

He returned home nearly physically exhausted, but mentally restless. He went back to his regular routines of teaching, rounds of speaking and, with Anky, commitment to L'Abri; but soon he was inquiring about all kinds of job possibilities in the USA and asking his American friends for their advice regarding the academic credibility of various institutions and which ones would be better to have a position at. He cast his net so wide that he was even willing to teach philosophy (a field he had no professional qualification in) rather than art history. In one or two instances, such as at the University of Rhode Island, his negotiations became quite advanced. Probably gnawing at the back of his mind was how in future days he was going to support his family adequately continuing on only a lecturer/assistant's salary and that he ought to make contingencies for their provision. He had sold his grandfather's stamp collection when he needed to. He also was willing to sell some of his rare records, if need be. He made little on his writing or speaking. The Rookmaakers were by no means comfortably off during this time of their lives.

It is questionable whether Rookmaaker really wanted to leave the Netherlands, except for pragmatic reasons. Possibly he also hoped that, if rumour spread that he was about to be hired for a job in America, he might appear more valuable at home and some people would not want to lose him.

Whether or not that was the case or in his mind, in late 1963 or early 1964 Rookmaaker was approached by academic representatives of the Free University of Amsterdam who came to his home in Leiden with an invitation for him to become the founding professor of a new department of Art History. Abraham Kuyper, the Dutch Calvinist theologian and political leader, founded the Free University in 1880. It was 'free' in the sense of free from both church and state control as an independent institution. It was also where Herman Dooyeweerd taught. As Rookmaaker had never relinquished his active participation in the circles that regularly studied Reformational thought, particularly Dooyeweerd's, he and Anky accepted the invitation almost immediately. At last he had found a place where he could be faithful to his calling as he furthered his career. He could create and contribute something new within the Dutch Calvinist ethos that often shied away from serious engagement with the arts.

In the middle of 1964, the Rookmaakers moved from Leiden to Diemen, a suburb of Amsterdam not far from the university. Hans was happy working at the Free University and, at last, for the family to own their home. There was an atmosphere of energy around the big city. An added bonus to the move, especially for the children, was the proximity of Grandma Huitker and Aunt Addy and Uncle Leo. They lived just ten minutes away by bicycle, which made it easy for the younger members of the family to see their relatives. Aunt Addy was a good cook and she and her husband were warm and hospitable people.

The children liked going regularly to the Wolff-Huitker home on Wednesday afternoons and also for *Sinterklaas* (5 December, St Nicholas Day, when the Dutch traditionally exchange gifts).

Although Anky and Hans did not see eye to eye with Addy and Leo on every matter, they had a cordial relationship with them. Leo was one of the directors of a leading socialist publishing house (*Arbeiderspers*).

Addy was active in volunteering for socialist political causes. They were devoted to each other and, with no children of their own, were generous toward the Rookmaaker children.

The relationship on the other side of the family was still quite ruptured. Hans grappled with varying degrees of estrangement from his siblings for the rest of his life.

It must have pained him not to have close communication with his sisters, whom he had been so near to as a boy and adolescent. They still could not get over the religious commitment he had made and the reinforcement of this in their eyes by his marrying someone who held the same convictions equally firmly. Hans never flagged in his constancy of concern and support for the care of his mother. Whether she was aware of her son's activities and attainments remains uncertain because of her increasing dementia. But she lived to the day her son had become a full professor and bestselling author. At the age of 81 she died quietly in The Hague on 12 July 1971.

By this time Hans had been at the Free University for seven years. He was stretched by additional demanding administrative duties, which he never had had to the same degree at Leiden. He steadily attracted students and the art history department grew.

Internationally he was in high demand as the one of the most articulate Christian spokespersons in the world for the arts.

Hans and Anky's support of L'Abri Fellowship also continued to deepen with every passing year. They had a constant flow of seekers through their home. They urged many to go to Swiss L'Abri. Many of these found they felt lost there as the community at Huémoz expanded rapidly in the early 1970s when word spread around the world of its unique atmosphere. The Rookmaakers desired to build up an indigenous Dutch L'Abri to serve the growing numbers coming to them for counsel. From the late 1960s onward they poured enormous effort into this task. And, as though Anky did not have enough to do with this work, out of a vision to feed the hungry and clothe the naked, she set out to found an international charitable agency to support orphans and poor children, called *Redt een Kind* (Save a Child), an organization that has grown and continues to serve. Hans fully supported his wife's humanitarian and entrepreneurial endeavours.

The years of crafting a career and forming a family had been arduous but blessed with twists and turns and full of surprises that Hans could never have surmised when he returned to Holland after the war. There still were heartaches, but there was an even greater abundance of joy. The tapestry of his life was rich. He had a fine family, a career that perfectly matched his calling and a widening circle of genuine friends.

6
Friendships

In the last decade of his life, Rookmaaker's friendships both at home and abroad burgeoned. Amidst the extensive and intensive activities of administrating, teaching, writing, speaking, and travel, he managed to maintain a high level of consistency in his commitment to his friends, old and new.

The domain of friendship may have been where he was most open. This is surprising because his demeanour was reserved and he appeared somewhat wary in encounters with new acquaintances. His conservative clothing and pipe puffing reinforced a feeling of his keeping his distance. North Americans often felt intimidated by his Continental professorial bearing. In this way his style was not 'friendly' at all.

Rookmaaker's openness to other people was more profound and far-reaching than immediate amiability. Superficiality was not a part of his make-up. The war and his conversion had set a significant standard for the meaning of friendship, its costliness and its mystery. Looking more closely at some representative friendships and also at some of the circles where he found friendship enables us to see him in ways that otherwise might be overlooked or not evident.

Foundational for all Rookmaaker's postwar friendships was J.P.A. Mekkes, who never ceased to be concerned for Hans's welfare from the time he met him in Stanislau POW camp to his sudden death in 1977. (Mekkes lived to be 90, dying 10 years after Hans.) Erect and dignified, Mekkes knew how to be more than a regimented military man or a precise philosopher; he knew how to be a warmhearted, faithful friend.

In speaking and writing, Rookmaaker's own reluctance to be overly autobiographical inadvertently has given the impression that Mekkes merely served as a catalyst to his conversion, providentially entering his life, encouraging him to pursue scholarship after the war and afterwards seemingly disappearing from his life. This is far from the case.

It is moving to see Mekkes marching along with Hans through the rest of his life. Hans, in his turn, was not only a receiver of this rich gift but also a generous giver of friendship to Mekkes and many others. In June 1945, not long after both of them had returned to Holland from Neubrandenburg, Mekkes wrote to console Hans regarding not finding Riki and his almost certainty that she was not alive. He also rejoiced with Hans going on to pursue formal studies, and he wished him to have peace once again.

In late May of 1959, Mekkes wrote of his happiness at hearing that Hans's *promotie* for his doctorate was moving forward and that all the conversations they had had in the barracks had not been wasted. He also stated his disappointment and regret at not being able to attend the ceremony because of ill health and his doctor's orders for him to go away for six weeks of curative rest. Rounding out the message the old soldier wrote:

> But our road goes on, and I hope we will [travel] together faithfully for a long time. I hope you have a vacation afterwards. It is good for your family to do this. I didn't do it enough. Now that you have this high point of hard work behind you, you must relax. Greetings to Anky.
>
> A handshake from your marching companion and colleague,
>
> Mekkes

When Mekkes returned from his cure, he and his wife were delighted to find a beautiful flower arrangement sent by Hans and Anky to welcome them home. He let Hans know how much he appreciated the thoughtfulness and effort of this gesture at a time when he must have had many things to think about. He also communicated that he was reading Hans's dissertation by 'spoonfuls'.

On it went. He cared about all the facets of Hans's life. Mekkes immediately sent his congratulations to both Hans and Anky when he heard that Hans had been nominated as Professor of Art History at the Free University. He was thrilled that Hans could extend an application of the Philosophy of the Cosmonomic Idea into another area of scholarship and that he was finding his life's work unfold in this way. He was glad Hans could pass his position at Leiden into good hands. He wondered if Hans's mother could grasp her son's achievement, how the children were handling the changes, and whether the family had found the right house to live in.

Although Mekkes undoubtedly influenced Rookmaaker intellectually, the thread of Mekkes's abiding influence in his life was spiritual and most detectable perhaps in the value Hans placed on friendship and the effort he was willing to expend on the quality of a relationship. Hans's friendship with Mekkes did not require frequent personal meetings to sustain it. It was simply a fact of their lives. They loyally remembered each other whether it was a birthday here or the publication of a book there. If Mekkes's handwriting became feebler over the years, his friendship did not! They shared a bond that broke boundaries across traditional barriers of friendship that enriched Hans immeasurably and ultimately aided him in his relatively few years to be an enormous hope and help to others.

Mekkes was of the generation of Herman Dooyeweerd and Dirk H.Th. Vollenhoven, all of whom were also of the generation of C.S. Lewis, Owen Barfield, and J.R.R. Tolkien. They all had experienced the First World War. Mekkes met Rookmaaker with the authority of an experienced higher-ranking officer and informed mentor when Hans was a mere midshipman imprisoned during the Second World War. Although Hans eventually became a faculty member and theoretically equal colleague of both Dooyeweerd and Vollenhoven at the Free University and knew them both, he never experienced their friendship in the same personal way as with Mekkes. There was always a gulf with these luminaries as between initiates and a neophyte, teachers and a student. Mekkes shared his experience with Hans, but not in a paternalistic way. It is to Mekkes's credit that he did not allow differences of age (25 years), rank or expertise to prevent him from transforming an inherently unequal relationship into bonds of reciprocal friendship and collegiality. He did not try to dominate his protégé but released him into a wider world. Mekkes must have understood deeply that Jesus had called his disciples, including himself and Hans, to be friends, not servants or slaves. Hans, for his part, had unfailing respect coupled with love and affection for this unique friend whose ardent adherence to theoretical thought never prevented him from its application to real life and the nurturing of living relationships.

The most well known and celebrated of Rookmaaker's friendships was with Francis A. Schaeffer. At the height of both their public lives in the late 1960s and early 1970s few people would have noticed that there was a decade of difference in their ages. The impression was of two highly different personalities with distinct callings focused on a common mission. In appearance the languorous Alpine guru, dressed in long woollen stockings and corduroy trousers fastened at the knee suitable for mountain climbing, contrasted dramatically with the dapper little Dutch professor, neatly dressed in his three-piece suit and smoking his pipe. Like complementary colours, each giving a distinct hue, they contrasted but also exhibited an organic underlying affinity. This produced a potent dynamism when they appeared together, as they often did, at L'Abri conferences held in North America and Europe during these years.

Any self-consciousness of the age gap between them must have diminished quickly. From the start, Hans, the younger man, was prompting the arts education of the older man as he talked with Schaeffer about the meaning of modern art far into the night on the occasion of their first meeting in 1948. We do not know whether Schaeffer was looking for this kind of intellectual conversation partner. He came to the exchange with Rookmaaker prepared in a way that few, if any, postwar American missionaries to Europe were. He was a regular visitor to art galleries and museums. The rich legacy of European culture was not lost on Schaeffer, and he knew that art mattered in understanding contemporary Continental society as it related to his unfolding ministry in Europe. Hans, for his part, already had entrée into a circle of serious discussion regarding Christian philosophy and cultural matters that Mekkes had introduced him to before he met Schaeffer. The arts, however, were not fully on the agenda of these Reformational thinkers, although Abraham Kuyper had addressed the place of art in a Calvinist life system in a rectorial address at the Free University (1888) as well as in his famous Stone Lectures on Calvinism given at Princeton Theological Seminary in 1898. Schaeffer must have been familiar with the Stone Lectures from his Reformed theological education in America, and this could well have opened him to further consideration of the arts when he arrived in Europe.

Almost immediately both of them recognized a meeting of minds in the neglected area of Christian reflection on the arts. This domain established their intellectual reciprocity and personal relationship. It by no means defined it or prescribed it. Over the course of the next thirty years their friendship would widen and deepen, be tested and flourish.

From a conventional point of view, they were unlikely candidates for the kind of closeness and camaraderie they developed. Schaeffer was American. He was older. He had experienced World War II at a safe distance. He was an ordained minister. He and his wife had come to Europe for the purpose of ministry to children who had experienced the trauma of war and uncertain postwar conditions. He first was Bible Presbyterian, one of several fundamentalist offshoots from the Presbyterian Church in the USA that started with J. Gresham Machen's secession in 1929 from Princeton Theological Seminary to form Westminster Theological Seminary in Philadelphia. In the 1950s Schaeffer had moved, however, in an evangelical direction when he joined the greater portion of Bible Presbyterians who, opposed to Carl McIntire's narrow leadership, formed the Reformed Presbyterian Church, Evangelical Synod (today part of the Presbyterian Church in America). He was educated, but by no means a scholar.

Rookmaaker, on the other hand, was European. He was younger. In the midst of the upheaval of a terrible war, he had become a Christian. He was more interested in philosophy than theology. He had just become engaged and was still finding his career path when he met Schaeffer. While he too was a member of an offshoot Reformed group (*Vrijgemaakt*/Liberated, formed in 1944/45), his circles in the Netherlands by no means mirrored those in the USA. Smoking and drinking were not considered taboo. Nor were these Calvinists in Holland entrenched as exclusively in theological debate as Schaeffer's American confrères were; many were actively exploring new intellectual terrain opened up by Kuyper's wide-ranging thinking that a Calvinist understanding applied to all realms of life and learning and not just to the theological or ecclesiastical. Furthermore, Rookmaaker had a much more academic bent than Schaeffer.

If they exhibited stark contrasts, they also evidenced strong convergences. Both Schaeffer and Rookmaaker were committed to being faithful to Scripture in its full-orbed holy ordonnance. They also shared a broad missional vision of seeing both individuals and society transformed by the reality of a living and loving God active in the world. If Schaeffer was an evangelist who was an intellectual, Rookmaaker was an intellectual who was an evangelist. Many came to faith through both of them. Neither of them fit the standard profile of an evangelist or an intellectual. Both of them blew apart the common prejudice that being biblical and theologically orthodox meant being culturally irrelevant.

The spiritual hunger of the West that was evident in the appeal and growth of Eastern religions between the world wars resurged in the 1960s. As the passionate urge to political reform was often linked to Marxism and left-wing politics, the religious element appearing in a myriad of forms in the striving for reform during these times often has been overlooked or obscured in hindsight as historical interpretation has stressed the rise of various socio-political movements such as civil rights, feminism and environmental concern. Some ministers (most famously, Martin Luther King Jr) gave key leadership to these causes even as they did in previous centuries to the struggle to abolish slavery and open the way for women's rights. Yet most ministers only observed these occurrences from the sidelines and preached from the safety of their sanctuaries, not truly knowing how to discern the trends of the times or what to do with such an unruly heterodox mixture of belief and protest. Mentors, guides and gurus were in demand. Many, if not most of them, proved less than reliable. There was also a great longing for community.

Schaeffer and Rookmaaker, despite their different backgrounds, were both able to see that the spiritual quest of the younger generation was not focused only on the religious sphere but also was creating unrest in other areas of cultural life and experience. Their friendship had prepared them in a remarkable way to meet these conditions.

Although their relationship had been sparked initially by intellectual exchange, it was not limited to this realm. Their friendship soon became a rich and complex mix of four people and two couples, all sharing a vision of serving rather than careerism. In a reminiscence of their friendship, Edith Schaeffer looked back in 1977, after Hans's death, to the time they had all met before L'Abri Fellowship had ever even been thought of. She remembered how she and Fran had helped Hans and Anky get bed linens for their first home as rationing was still a fact of life in Holland and made it difficult for a young couple to buy enough basic household goods to get started. Before the establishment of L'Abri, the Rookmaakers joined with their friends to start Children of Christ classes in Europe and supported them when the Schaeffers were in deep difficulties and it looked like they would have no future in Switzerland.

When Swiss L'Abri was formed in 1955, the Rookmaakers were some of the Schaeffers' first guests. The ethos of hope and hospitality they experienced with their friends strengthened the bonds of their appreciation and inspired them to continue and expand their own reception of students and seekers (many of them artists) into their home. The conversations with the Schaeffers may also have been the providential prompt that mobilized the Rookmaakers' resolve for Hans to complete a doctorate. Hans and Anky were struck by how much more prayer there was at L'Abri in comparison with the Dutch Christian circles they were familiar with. Not only did the Rookmaakers become members of the work of L'Abri in Switzerland but they also exerted themselves at home, so that the momentum from their efforts eventually grew into a full-fledged L'Abri Fellowship in the Netherlands. By 1971 a huge welcoming, white eighteenth-century farmhouse (*Huize Kortenhoeve*) at Eck en Wiel in the agriculturally rich province of Gelderland was purchased through the L'Abri Foundation of the Netherlands (*Stichting L'Abri Fellowship Nederland*). The widening circle of transforming friendship begun in the Rookmaaker home (first in Leiden and then in Amsterdam) could no longer be hosted there, due to lack of space, and a new stage in the work of L'Abri in Holland burgeoned forth that would shape the Rookmaakers in Hans's last years almost as much as they shaped the work.

Character and conviction were more at the root of Rookmaaker's and Schaeffer's firm friendship than complete intellectual similitude or the parallel shaping of their thought. Schaeffer had the utmost respect for Herman Dooyeweerd, but he also admitted he had been virtually untouched by his formal philosophy. A key component to Schaeffer's apologetic strategy was the presuppositionalist theology of Cornelius Van Til (1895–1987, a professor of Theology at Westminster Theological Seminary), who in turn had drawn upon Kuyperian critical thought for his formulations. In a letter to Hans in 1967, Schaeffer marvelled that although their thinking had developed independently it flowed in a similar direction. Spiritually and intellectually they were in essential agreement, yet there was space, an openness in their relationship that allowed for differences and breathed vitality for hundreds, and probably thousands, of young people seeking renewed direction for their lives.

One has sympathy for the tension that Rookmaaker must have felt knowing that his contemporary Dutch friends had done more robust theoretical thinking than his American friend and his offshoot tradition had. But it was also true that his more precise thinking Reformed confrères had often neglected actual application of their rigorous reflection to contemporary missional engagement in the culture of the day.

Both Rookmaaker and Schaeffer shared a courageously wider view of the world that was not based on a slavish adherence to a cramped consensus of academic opinion or credentials for its interpretation. They both had a bold confidence backed by considerable experiential learning that transcended a need to have academic respectability. They did not mean to flaunt this. They had a mission that was not advanced by finicky correctness for every detail being covered before a word could be said on a subject. Justifiably and unjustifiably, they were often criticized for lack of precision or for generalizations they made about subjects they had little expertise in. Generally, Rookmaaker was more cautious. While the scholarly establishment felt constrained to contain and maintain discrete fields of knowledge and research in the university, students were seething to know how knowledge applied to their yearnings for a different world. In short, they hungered after wisdom as to how they should live. Both Schaeffer and Rookmaaker movingly identified with their spiritual and intellectual longings and communicated this compassionately.

Perhaps because L'Abri Fellowship was outside of formal establishment structures, it created a subversive appeal apropos of the period that was extremely attractive to those seeking holistic meaning in an age of fragmentation. L'Abri (meaning 'shelter' in French) gave, and continues to give, refuge literally and figuratively to an enormous number people. It should not be forgotten that it is also a Fellowship, a company and community of friends. L'Abri did not arise from clever leadership using strategic planning to tailor a ministry to meet the needs of the perceived spiritual market of the time, but out of abiding friendship, not only between Schaeffer and Rookmaaker and their spouses, but a host of others as well who worked and frequently struggled to build community rather than a well-oiled organization.

The authenticity of Rookmaaker and Schaeffer's partnership appealed powerfully to students in the 1960s and 1970s. They had a significant track record of loyalty to each other. Schaeffer encouraged Hans in his doctoral work. When Rookmaaker's dissertation was challenged for being written in stilted and stylistically awkward English by his university committee and threatened with rejection, Schaeffer, along with Calvin Seerveld, came valiantly to his defense so that an exception was made by the committee and the objection dropped.

Meanwhile Rookmaaker, the veteran journalist, urged Schaeffer to write, whether he had impressive terminal degrees behind his name or not. In the famous student protest year of 1968, book after book began to flow from Schaeffer. But only he and Hans and a small circle were aware of the adversity in which these publications had arisen. At the beginning of 1967, Schaeffer was depressed and shared what a difficult time it was for him. For sometime he had been under siege by a small, but adamant sector of Reformed adherents in America with strong links to the Netherlands who were attacking him theologically and philosophically. Much of their criticism centred on Schaeffer's embracing of American evangelicalism. They also censured Schaeffer because they thought he was out of touch with American culture after living in Europe for twenty years. His final failure seemed to have been that in their opinion he did not understand sufficiently Reformational thinking as rendered by Herman Dooyeweerd and others associated with his generation of Dutch Christian philosophy. These people were also alarmed by what they construed as Schaeffer's overweening influence on Rookmaaker. They let Hans know this with intense persistency, as though they desired to drive a wedge between him and his friend. This placed Hans in a difficult position and jeopardized some relations of longstanding that he valued and did not want to declare a choice about. He was dismayed by the sharp tone and unloving attitudes of the accusations he heard against his colleague.

Rookmaaker ultimately refused to be intimidated by these tactics and took his stand with Schaeffer. He wrote in a letter to Cornelius Van Til on 10 May 1967 on how irrational he found the attacks on Schaeffer and how much he appreciated the Westminster theologian's not endorsing the views expressed by Schaeffer's critics. He further explained how his friend had developed his thinking and his own terminology in communicating with a generation that did not lay stress on theological doctrine, which if it had been mentioned would have scared them away from listening. Schaeffer's strategy, he said, was developed 'on the battlefield' in discussions with young radicals, existentialists, or angry young men, or Christian students on their way to losing their faith because of the pressures of present-day culture. It aimed to convince young people that a biblical Christianity was both relevant and required special commitment.

In covering the criticism of Schaeffer, Rookmaaker wanted to communicate clearly to Van Til that Schaeffer had recently received a friendly welcome from his Dutch Reformational circles. At the end of February and the beginning of March 1967, Schaeffer spent nearly a week with Rookmaaker at the Free University. During this time Schaeffer gave a formal lecture on the background and spiritual principles of modern philosophy that Rookmaaker considered, not surprisingly, in line with Dooyeweerd's thinking. Hans reported to Van Til as well that Schaeffer had had an extended personal visit with Dooyeweerd and that it had gone well. No doubt Hans was hoping Van Til would broadcast all of this on his side of the Atlantic.

Even before this visit Rookmaaker's friends and colleagues at the Free University could have been in little doubt about the impact Schaeffer had had on him. Amidst the opening remarks of his inaugural address as Professor of Art History at the Free University on 28 May 1965, Rookmaaker directed special words of appreciation to Schaeffer for being there. On the occasion of this significant milestone in his own career, he went on record as to what their relationship meant to him by saying:

> It seems to me a token, not only of our friendship but also of our spiritual unity, that you have come from Switzerland for this occasion. Since the first

time we met, in 1948, we have had many long talks about faith, philosophy, reality, art, the modern world, and their mutual relations. I owe very much to these discussions, which have helped to shape my thoughts on these subjects. I want to express my deep gratitude, and consider it a great honour and joy to be a member of L'Abri Fellowship. (*CW* 5:167)

Rather than being hostile to his friendship with Schaeffer, as a very small vocal minority in America was, Rookmaaker's Calvinist friends and colleagues in Holland by and large were ambivalent. Rookmaaker himself perplexed them enough. Whether it was his non-religious upbringing, the influence of the American Schaeffer, his particular personality traits, his sense of mission or a combination of the above, he did not conform to their expectations of a conventional Dutch professor.

The journalistic spirit of Abraham Kuyper lived on in Rookmaaker. Hans was a born activist and communicator, two things academics rarely are. Before both his professorship and popularity abroad, he travelled around the Netherlands, glad to give talks and lectures to student groups, in churches or at other special events. He enthusiastically and creatively conveyed his expertise in art history and/or African-American music combined with his religious convictions and outlook to captivated audiences. Some felt this activity came close to self-promotion and was unbecoming for a serious scholar. Money was not the motivation, because he received little honoraria from these efforts. More to the point was the frequent absence from the Reformed mindset of an appreciation for domestic missional engagement. Hans never forgot that there was virtually no attempt to take the opportunity to inform him of the faith at the Christian secondary school he had attended as a boy.

Rookmaaker's blending of his friendships with his work and with a sense of mission was as disconcerting for some as it was inspiring for others. Few handled better both of these possible feelings than Hans's exact contemporary, C.A. ('Bert') van Swigchem, a friend and colleague of longstanding. Van Swigchem was much more of an insider in Calvinist circles than Hans was. Academically he had begun his career as a historian and later transitioned to the study of architectural history. He had a position at the Free University many years before Hans did and understood perhaps better than anyone else how a department of art history might be introduced there. In fact, in some respects his work was so significant in getting the department underway that he probably deserves to be called the co-founder of it as he was there from its inception in 1964/1965, standing shoulder to shoulder with Hans.

Van Swigchem and Rookmaaker respected each other's views, whether they agreed or not. This translated into something that is rarely found: a frank relationship that was equally warmhearted. In a letter to van Swigchem dated 6 April 1961, well before they were colleagues, Hans wrote to say how much he appreciated van Swigchem's response to the book he had just written (*Kunst en Amusemement/*'Art and entertainment', 1962). Not everything he read in the letter was to his liking, but the warmth of appreciation for the care with which van Swigchem had engaged with his work was evident. An exchange of honest thoughts, exhibited here, shows in hindsight that they both bore exceptional qualities of character to work realistically and effectively with each other later on. Hans reflected the security of their association when he wrote:

> Dear Bert,
>
> Thank you for your letter. I appreciate that you tell me what is on your heart.
>
> I did not know at first what to do with your critique. You ask for a completely different book: How To Look At Art. I will do that later.
>
> [First] I do not think that you read the times right. Your objections are not relevant in my experience ... There is a crisis and there are signs that want to be solved by a more direct Christian way of living.
>
> [Second] You suggest that I do not have a good feeling for the Reformed public. That is why I wanted you to read it – to make it better and more relevant [there].
>
> ... You do not really say a lot about the text regarding my analysis of modern art and contemporary culture. Do I take this positively or negatively? Do you [also] mean I am not allowed to speak of The Apocalypse? I believe only in this way can one see clearly into the situation.
>
> ... Your letter has stimulated me to review the whole process, and I am grateful. I can accept your critique because on a deeper level we agree ...
>
> Again thanks.
>
> > Hans

Van Swigchem admired Rookmaaker for his many initiatives and extensive professional and personal network of contacts. Hans was on excellent terms with the art-historical establishment in the Netherlands. That made life easier for both of them. When their department resources were minimal, their students were welcomed without a word to use the library of the University of Amsterdam and elsewhere. Hans brought repute to the new art history department through his research. Van Swigchem appreciated not only how strategic it had been for Hans to write his dissertation in English, but how rare it was for a Dutch dissertation ever to find its way into a new paperback edition as had been the case with *Synthetist Art Theories* (published as *Gauguin and Nineteenth Century Art Theory* in 1972). When they did not have enough students to begin with, Rookmaaker created a museum assistant's certificate programme that did not require prerequisites. The enthusiastic response filled classes and proved to be a recruiting ground for more students later. In the team effort they were, van Swigchem seems to have been a catalyst for other students to move over from history to study art and architectural history. Through their shared ideals and ideas they formed a special professional partnership that created a good working environment as staff were added to the department.

Maintaining this kind of balance was not easy. Although Hans may have felt disappointed that his colleague whom he admired was not interested in L'Abri Fellowship, van Swigchem was undoubtedly right not to get involved and convolute their relationship further. The distance between them probably made for a better friendship. Van Swigchem could more readily interpret needs of students coming out of typically Calvinist homes. He could also better see gaps in the day-to-day administration of a department that Hans overlooked as he became increasingly committed to activities abroad. Tensions arise in all close working relationships. Van Swigchem gave Rookmaaker the credit for their good relationship, but one suspects his own modesty and patience contributed a considerable amount to it as well.

No other friend had a better grasp of Hans's diverse networks in the Netherlands, Great Britain, the USA and Canada than the American-born Dutchman and aesthetician, Calvin Seerveld. They met in the 1950s, when Seerveld was in Europe pursuing graduate research in aesthetics in Italy, Switzerland and the Netherlands.

The vague beginning of their relationship is belied by its uniqueness in the constellation of Hans's friendships. Seerveld cannot remember exactly when they met. He recollects with clarity, however, the impact it made on him as a young foreigner and scholar attending his initial meeting of the Association of Reformational Philosophy in Holland. These meetings, which Hans faithfully went to virtually each year, usually met at the famous American Hotel located in the heart of Amsterdam. Seerveld vividly remembers the night he flung open the door of the grand ballroom, eager to enter the gathering. A huge, dense cloud of smoke, hovering a metre thick above the heads of the crowd seated in the high-ceilinged room, hit him! Before the evening finished, he was also struck by the amazing mélange of people who were there – not just scholars and teachers but also ordinary church people with a concern for good and godly thinking and education. Rookmaaker could have been there. Seerveld could well have met him at such a meeting.

Seerveld remembers that early on while he was a poor graduate student living with, almost off, his wife's family in The Hague, Hans introduced him to Henk Krijger, a painter with whom he eventually became a much closer friend. If Seerveld had come to a major rescue job in defending the acceptance of Rookmaaker's dissertation in 1959, Hans in 1958 at least came to Seerveld's aid in a minor way by being the first person ('the friendly questioner') out of four to begin the interrogation for the defense of his dissertation in comparative literature and philosophy at the Free University. It was probably this history that made Hans bold enough to ask Seerveld to help him.

At Seerveld's viva, Hans's appreciation for jazz found an unusual opportunity for application. Although Rookmaaker was barely literate at that time on Benedetto Croce (1866–1952), the subject of the thesis, he managed to improvise and elaborate his questioning extensively for considerably longer than required, in order to take up time for the arrival of the next interrogator, K.J. Popma (1903–1986), a renowned Calvinist philosopher, classicist and novelist, who was nowhere in sight! As Hans was looking around longing to wind up his riff, to everyone's relief the erudite and somewhat eccentric Popma appeared. The absent-minded professor had taken a train to the wrong destination, but now he was there and all could proceed accordingly.

Rookmaaker and Seerveld became much closer during the course of Hans's first extensive trip to North America in 1961. At that time Seerveld was teaching at Trinity Christian College, a small undergraduate institution coming out of the Reformed tradition, located in Palos Heights, a suburb of Chicago. Hans stayed at Seerveld's home for a week in October of that year and 'bach'ed' it with him while Cal's wife was away visiting her relatives in the Netherlands.

Sharing improvised meals and driving around the Chicago area together to visit various colleges and art collections gave them ample opportunity for expansive conversation that they previously had not had the opportunity for. Without Seerveld as navigator and chauffeur, Rookmaaker may never have made it to his cherished visits to both Mahalia Jackson's church and to her home. The enormous collection of tapes and records of the Chicago-jazz expert John Steiner dazzled them both. Another evening they took off to hear the powerful trumpet playing of Bob Schoffner in a Chicago club. Today all of this seems innocent and natural for two professors of art theory and art/music history to be doing with their time. But in 1961 these were unusual activities for those teaching or giving lectures at evangelical or Reformed Christian colleges. The natural entrée Hans had into African-American circles also shows the breadth of his personal relationships, not merely the breadth of his personal interests.

The bonds of friendship were definitely deepened between Rookmaaker and Seerveld through their time together in Chicago. They shared a strong sense of calling for the cause of the Christian faith in their academic disciplines. Rookmaaker trusted Seerveld as a person he could confidently and confidentially share his professional aspirations with and seek honest help from. In the midst of his extended season of restlessness after returning from his trip to North America, Hans asked for Seerveld's advice. In straightforward language Seerveld exhorted him to stay at Leiden until something could open up at the Free University. The Free, in his opinion, was the best place for Hans to make an impact. Taking a position at a second-tier secular university or a Christian college in the USA was far less strategic in terms of long-range and lasting influence. Looking at all of this afterwards and its seemingly self-evident nature, it is easy to lose sight of how sound Seerveld's counsel was not only for his friend's best interests but also for the promotion of Christian scholarship.

While they both worked out of a thorough knowledge of Neo-Calvinist philosophy and endorsed an enormous amount in each other's vision and thinking, there were always significant running differences between them on aesthetic matters. Foremost was the dissimilarity of their approaches in understanding what constitutes the core meaning of the aesthetic sphere. Rookmaaker stood with the venerable tradition of 'harmonious beauty' being key to the aesthetical dimension. For Seerveld the centre resides in 'allusiveness'. The essence of art for the latter is its parabolic character and quality of multivalence. Intellectual differences never daunted their appreciation of each other. Iron sharpens iron. They had hoped to teach a course together at the Institute for Christian Studies in Toronto in the summer of 1977. Rookmaaker's death in March of that year prevented the plan they had long thought of from being fulfilled.

Schaeffer and Seerveld aside, it is amazing that Rookmaaker cultivated so many warmhearted and meaningful friendships in the Anglophone world. Other than professional contacts in the art historical world, which were considerable, Hans's personal and cultural conditioning was a lot more tough minded and generally sophisticated than most of the people he came to know in Britain and North America. Most Continentals of his ilk would have probably been expected to look on the attitudes he often encountered either as outdated or provincial, if kindly disposed, or dismissed as ignorant, if not so kindly disposed. One can only return to his perennial openness in not completely prejudging people or situations to appreciate the breadth and depth of the friendships in the English-speaking world that he developed.

Schaeffer was his vanguard, interestingly enough, in Britain. By the mid 1960s, Schaeffer was speaking regularly at British universities, often in conjunction with the local Inter-Varsity Fellowship (IVF) Christian Union. There were also L'Abri conferences taking place. Rookmaaker was a great hit at these. It did not take long for the word to spread that he could intelligently and honestly critique a work of art. Eager artists filled with fear and trepidation at what they might hear from him brought their work for him to view at these gatherings.

The dainty pietism of much of British and American evangelicalism was antithetical to Rookmaaker's brand of realism. Younger artists and a number of progressive IVF staff workers in Britain knew in him they had a friend and ally they could trust. They were ready for something more authentically engaged with their experience of life. They loved and respected him for his colourful and vigorous style in tackling and trying to understand the manifestations in Western culture that robbed people of their full humanness. The so-called stuffy British were the least reserved of his fans and affectionately dubbed him 'Rooky'.

The evangelical establishment on both sides of the Atlantic, however, was more wary of him. Inter-Varsity Press in the UK questioned him as to whether it was necessary or wise to use paintings of the nude to make his points in a book he was planning to write for them. They considered it a serious problem. It might be fine in the context of an art college, but not proper at all for ordinary parishioners into whose hands it might fall as the press intended to see that his book was distributed as widely as possible. Fortunately, it fell to the lot of the talented and diplomatic editor, David Alexander, to work with Hans to bring forth the book we know today as *Modern Art and the Death of a Culture* (nudes and all!) – probably the first true crossover book IVP ever published.

While Rookmaaker may have had a broad grin like the Cheshire cat when he smiled, he was not a domesticated animal but rather an untamed one that disturbed the insecure and empowered the semi-confident. He was deliberately provocative:

> You took Christian standards for granted. The young people said to you, 'Why do life [in] this or that way?' and you said, 'Never bother me with questions; just do it.' But they are intelligent young men and women. They have looked at the world and they have made up their own standards. You say we should fight pornography? Yes, we should fight pornography, but remember it only came this far because we Christians were not there when we should have been there. Now the battle is lost and we can only clean up the battlefield. So do not say 'Wicked young people sleeping with each other,' but say 'Wicked Christians who did not explain well when the questions were being asked.'

Urging Christian people to wake up and shake off a couple of centuries of sleep was not an easy or appreciated task.

In 1966, after Rookmaaker's article, 'Letter to a Christian Artist', appeared in *Christianity Today*, he became embroiled in a running controversy with its editors as he tried to challenge them to think critically about the kind of art they were publishing in its pages. The case in point was regarding reproductions of the work of a contemporary American artist of religious themes that Rookmaaker thought made *CT* look ridiculous in the eyes of outsiders and whom the editors defended as being fine work by a leading American artist. The issues and attitudes here were (and are) far more important than the names of those involved. Rookmaaker's frank response was more blunt than customary and startling:

Even if [this artist] is a real Christian, [he] is not an artist that can be talked about seriously as an artist. If this is Christian art, it would mean that we Christians have no art, probably not even the mentality or will to have art at all. It would prove that Christianity is in principle not compatible with art. ... the *Head of Christ* is a complete failure and as subject matter – it is difficult as such – far above the possibilities of the artist. ... The second one, the weeping woman, is again a complete failure – it did not even succeed in being sentimental ... a young man making these would have a hard time getting entrance to any academy, and really not because people do not like Christian work or only accept modernist art. ...

I personally feel that either my own work – to promote the cause of Christian endeavour in the arts, both critically and creatively – is a hard necessity, meaning that it seems to be much harder than I ever thought it would be, or my work is hopeless, and I better stop doing it. ... I really mean it – that if this is Christian art, I should stop working for it, and if this is real art in the line of Rembrandt, I should never like to think of art anymore. You must believe me that this is a *cri de coeur*, as I am sure I am not alone. Those to whom I showed these works here in Holland all reacted as I do.

I am perfectly aware that things cannot be changed anymore. I am not asking you to publish this – you can if you wish to – but I simply had to write this to unburden my conscience and to warn you against experiments in this line. I am really sorry for your work, which has now been stained by it. I'm sure, without your realizing what was happening.

Sincerely Yours in Christ,

Hans Rookmaaker

Christianity Today's editors stereotypically declared this artist had to be good because he graduated from 'the leading art school in America' and his name was listed in *Who's Who in American Art*. The leadership at the publication suggested that people simply respond to works differently and obviously had no desire to prolong a discussion on the topic of art. Rookmaaker tenaciously chewed on his art bone, coming back again and again to suggest something very important was at stake that they should treat with utmost seriousness. In late January 1967 he wrote:

The strangeness of modern art is partly due to an attitude of protest against pictures like these and what they stand for. So if we defend them, our case must be strongly [grounded]. I feel the protest is right, but the antichristian direction it takes and the resulting absurdity is horrible. We Christians must search and work towards a new and fresh art, twentieth-century and biblical, without compromise or synthesis with worldly streams.

Hoping to meet you, and sincerely yours in the Lord,

Hans Rookmaaker

Church audiences who trashed modern art were stunned when he turned to them and said: 'How can you say that modern art is ugly when you worship the Lord in a building painted like *this*?' The response Rookmaaker sought from evangelicals gradually came, somewhat more quickly in Great Britain than in the North America. Rookmaaker's toughness did not merely take ideas seriously but people just as much, if not more seriously. He was not out to score intellectual points but to nurture relationships that could work for realistic change in the world, nothing too high-falutin. 'Compare van Goyen with work of Claude or any of the Italianate painters. They present a world you can never have. It is good to have dreams but if the quality of that dream is forced it will only lead to frustration. We must dream towards an attainable end.'

Linette Martin tells of a student who complained on a beautiful day of not having a swimming pool nearby as Rookmaaker stood with him. Rookmaaker immediately retorted with not a little anger: 'If you think like that you will never enjoy life! You will always be frustrated and you will never make the most of opportunities around you! There is so much to enjoy. If you think only of what isn't there, you'll never be happy!' Words like these were characteristic of a man who knew what it was like to reconstruct most of the dreams and desires of his life after a devastating war. His shock tactics were not meant to harm but to stir to life 'the living dead' of our age.

Rooky was a breath of fresh air, or more precisely, a special aromatic air, as he wafted his pipe while making gallant gestures to punctuate points when he spoke. For those with a real nose to smell, his aroma lingered with them long after in a life-giving way. Here was a real personality who could inspire others to think and encourage them to dream attainable dreams they never dared think of before. He was remarkably transparent in his relationships. Although there was often rich reciprocity in his closest friendships, they brought him little worldly advantage. He simply knew how to be a friend who never ceased caring for his neighbour, even if he often expressed it pungently and provocatively.

7
Passions

Hans Rookmaaker's words left unforgettable echoes in the ears and hearts of his hearers. His convictions were completely and creatively united with the manner of his expression. Beneath his ordinary appearance was a potent subterranean quality of controlled intensity that infiltrated his expression, giving it an implicit evocativeness. The discrepancy between the conventional 'packaging' and the restrained force of feeling below the surface of his speech charged his communication with a tangy quality. Not all people were prepared for the robustness of his style. He could exclaim, for example, 'All truth is relative,' and send his devout listeners into shock until with impeccable timing he resuscitated them by supplying the predicate, 'to Jesus Christ.'

Rookmaaker displayed considerable personal professorial dignity, but academic aloofness played no part in his expressive style or the content of his work. The secret of Hans's ability to engage the imaginations of so many struggling with the issues of the arts, culture and belief was that his own imagination was thoroughly engaged. His leading themes were not mere abstract ideas but passions that came from hard won experience. His way of knowing was participatory. In his own life he integrated the intellectual, emotional, and volitional to a high degree and did not drive a wedge between the physical and spiritual realms.

Since the Enlightenment, formal education has focused almost exclusively on the cultivation of the intellect, neglecting the feelings and the will. Somehow Rookmaaker managed to educate his feelings commensurately so that they made a remarkable bridge between his ideas and his sense of action. His formative years in a non-Western culture and early and continuous exposure to jazz and other forms of African-American music were probably also influential in catapulting him away from being a predictable professor.

This could also have influenced his aptitude for a qualitative appreciation of history. History viewed in this way suggests that over the course of time human nature does not necessarily remain static. Not only do ideas and events change, but people also change. An important interlocutor for him on this subject was Jan Hendrik van den Berg, a learned historian of psychiatry, who was especially cognizant of the cultural and historical rootedness of phenomenological psychology. His book, *Metabletica, of Leer der veranderingen: beginselen van een historische psychologie* (published in English in 1961 as *The Changing Nature of Man*) detailed with abundant historical specificity directions and intuitions Hans's thinking was already heading toward. Hans was deeply immersed at the time in the rich visual documentation for an understanding of subject matter in art being gathered by the Iconclass project in which he was involved at Leiden. Van den Berg did not create his outlook but seems to have confirmed his own understanding of the cultural and historical embeddedness of thought. Personal correspondence in 1961 and 1962 confirms their mutual appreciation of each other's work, although van den Berg's perspective was more broadly humanistic rather than specifically Christian.

Both van den Berg and Rookmaaker were ahead of their times in their critique of modernity. In *Metabletica,* van den Berg described the changing relation between adults and children over the centuries in the West that has led to an increasingly prolonged infantilization and adolescence, delaying the taking on of adult responsibilities by young people. Van den Berg observed a web of attitudes and events surrounding childhood synchronically rather than simply tracing a discrete line of explicit exposition on childhood diachronically. Simply put, childhood had been extended since the Renaissance. It was not possible to read some kind of law of uniformity regarding the rearing of children back into history. There were qualitative differences and changes. This made an impact on contemporary practices of parenting and education and many other areas of life that most people never reflected on and took completely for granted. Hans immediately could see the application of this approach to other spheres. Culture surrounded art, and art also was a lens into viewing culture and philosophical ideas.

Van den Berg liked the way Hans linked art with the art of living, but he also was academically savvy enough to know that specialists in art history were not apt to agree with his approach. He found it refreshing that Hans had the courage to articulate his convictions with clear language more than he felt he himself did.

This qualitative approach to history meant that art was not simply an illustration of the past. Although art was independently justified, it was not autonomous and offered a means to interpret the culture and philosophical beliefs systems it was a part of. Rookmaaker was not particularly interested in systematic or philosophical theology. He was a serious lay reader of the Bible with a perspective more sympathetic to biblical theology. The thematic unity of the biblical writings fascinated him and exhibited for him not merely the cleverness of human writers but the Authorship of God, who continued to love, live, and work in history. At times to the point of polemicizing, Rookmaaker maintained the authentic world view underlying seventeenth-century Dutch art was a biblical one consistent with Scripture. In a strict sense he did not do theology through art; that is, he did not exegete art primarily for theological meaning. But he also did not do theology of the arts as was and is so fashionable; that is, he did not talk about art from the perspective of theological conceptions and generalizations of an abstract nature. He was geared to understanding the meaning embedded in the works of art themselves rather than interpolating theology into the arts. Rookmaaker was, however, an important precursor of the 'theology through art' approach because he sought cultural, philosophical and, to some degree, biblical insight through individual, concrete works of art rather than taking works of art as a pretext to explain ideas. (This is explained further in chapter 8.)

Rookmaaker was also a precursor of the now more widely spread understanding of art monuments as historical documents that can supplement the textual record and bring to light new insights of times past that ordinarily might be overlooked without their consideration. Already in the 1950s as an art critic he could write:

> Then there is the strange and very beautiful crucifix from Brunswijk, carved a century or so later during the mid-twelfth century by Master Imerwald. Indeed, one aspect of the appeal of these sculptures is that they are amongst the earliest examples (still) in circulation. One of the oldest figures of the Madonna we know originates from a church in Essen. It is a wooden sculpture covered in gold leaf and dates back to the tenth century. It is important and interesting both for art historians and church historians, even though most of us will not find it particularly attractive. (*CW* 1:234)

No examination of Rookmaaker's view of history can omit the formative and substantial influence on him of the thought and writings of Guillaume Groen van Prinsterer (1801–1876), archivist and historian to the Dutch monarch. As a deeply believing man, Groen sought to articulate and evaluate underlying assumptions influencing events by the light cast on them by Scripture. Hans found affinity with this approach and seems naturally to have come to a similar practice during the process of his conversion.

He especially valued two published works by the royal historian. The first, a handbook of Dutch history (*Handboek der Vaderlandse Geschiedenis*, 1846), Hans declared 'one of the most wonderful books on history that I have ever read' (*CW* 6:175). ' On the basis of the documents he was working with, Groen felt compelled in this book to re-write the history of Holland from a Calvinist Christian perspective. In it he took issue with a secularist interpretation promulgated by Enlightenment writers that denigrated the Protestant influence of the House of Orange on the creation of the Dutch republic. This work became a textbook in schools and established a new way of looking at the origin of the nation that valued its Reformation heritage. The second work, *Ongeloof en Revolutie* ('Unbelief and revolution') was delivered originally as a series of lectures in 1847 on the topic of the French Revolution. Hans felt that Groen's exposition of the implications of the antithetical principles animating the Reformation and the French Revolution read not only as history but also as prophecy.

Rookmaaker was passionate about this kind of history that stepped beyond detachment into life. It had a ring of reality to it that abided with him. Groen, on the basis of his historical study, called for action, even though he considered himself more of a theorist. The unbelief that drove the French Revolution, expunging God from every sphere of society and the state, was still alive and causing consequences that did not lead to freedom but to new forms of bondage. Presciently, for example, Groen predicted the disruptiveness and destructiveness that the unfettered expansion of a revolutionary drive for unlimited individual rights would have upon an understanding of the nature of justice. His distinct anti-revolutionary stance led the way for his most famous follower, Abraham Kuyper, a man of action, to translate historical analysis into a popularly based political party, supported by grassroots lay citizens in the Reformed tradition who had felt disenfranchised prior to that time. In 1879, three years after the death of Groen van Prinsterer, the Anti-Revolutionary Party (ARP) was formed under Kuyper's leadershipto bring a practical application of belief into political, social and cultural life in the Netherlands.

In 'A Dutch Christian View of Philosophy', Rookmaaker identified himself wholeheartedly as a student of Groen and Kuyper and paid tribute to their vision and achievement:

> [T]hey understood that Christianity is not just religion, Christianity is not just the church, Christianity is not just a good feeling in your heart because you are saved and going to heaven but Christianity is all of life and it is the covenant. We walk with God and he is taking care of his people and we should walk in his ways and look at the world with an open Bible and use the key that the Bible provides for us to understand the world, everything, not just religion but everything. And they talked about this and they founded a political party. This party was called the Anti-Revolutionary Party, which meant that they were anti the spirit of the French Revolution, which is the Enlightenment, which is autonomous human being, which I always talk about because I too am a pupil of Groen. (*CW* 6:176)

Biblical and historical understanding intricately intertwined with Hans's passion for freedom, another continuous theme in his life and works. He would shake his head and express with his entire body a heaviness and disappointment at the lack of freedom he found in the church and amongst Christians. He ached in befuddlement and frustration at the contradiction of his believing brothers and sisters in this area as he heard preaching that proclaimed that Christ sets people free, but saw a legalism that inhibited believers and held them back from being preserving salt and purifying light in their society. Knowing there can be no genuine creativity and authentic art without freedom, he grieved visibly for young Christian artists experiencing this restrictive environment.

Freedom, true intellectual and spiritual liberation, was the capstone of his own conversion. How would any Christian want to forfeit it? He had come to experience this freedom while in physical captivity in a Nazi POW camp. This freedom was embedded entirely in an understanding of the living reality of Jesus Christ and his servant Paul's exposition of this truth. Freedom captivated Rookmaaker's imagination and set him on a creatively constructive way of life. Authentic freedom, as he knew it, means to be able to develop as a human creature in accordance with reality. We see how basic and biblical this understanding was for him: 'I simply cannot accept – on the contrary, it strikes me as unscriptural – that when a person becomes a Christian she or he must be inhibited and lose their freedom. No, the Christian's portion is life – instead of death – and freedom, being truly human'(*CW* 3:336).

His feeling for freedom contrasted with legalism as much as it did with a prevalent permissiveness without rules or norms that contemporary culture promoted. The latter led to libertinism rather than true liberty, creating ever greater tyranny and despair. He stated over and over again in many variations that Christ died not to make us Christian but to make us human. Being fully human meant being fully free.

Hans could be outspoken, but rarely was he ready to call down a judgmental opinion on others or, for that matter, on himself. David Muir, a British professional storyteller, remembers one occasion when Rookmaaker was asked if it was inconsistent to be a Christian and a smoker. Hans immediately pulled out his pipe from his pocket and put it in his mouth as he contemplated his answer. His reply (as Muir remembers): 'God has a distinct record of accepting burnt offerings from those who really loved and feared him, and I am certainly one. If there perchance comes a whiff of tobacco from any light I give out, well, let's leave God to his judgments and us to our obedience to his calling of and for us.'

Hans's humanity may have been perplexing to the less alive. For believing artists, bursting with life, he was a revelation. At the beginning of his artistic journey, Muir knew this to be true and calls him today 'a man who really knew what it is to walk that straight and narrow way and while doing so giving us a great example of how to walk in moral and aesthetic freedom and enjoy it at the same time'.

At the heart of who Hans was, was a passion for beauty. As a theme in his works, it is ubiquitous. Harmonious beauty stands for him at the centre of the aesthetical sphere and is woven into the fabric of all of creation. Yet beauty alone did not define art for him. His love of beauty did not make him a reverent devotee of beauty as such or a prissy aesthete. He was vehemently against aestheticism, an attitude that insisted that beauty was the most important aspect in art and/or life to which everything should be subservient. He looked for loveliness that goes unnoticed in the ordinary surrounding us everyday. The writer and editor, Sharon Gallagher, has a vivid recollection of being exhorted by Hans during a visit by him to Berkeley, California in 1972, to walk home each day by a different route so that she could see afresh the beauty that surrounded her all of the time. A simple suggestion became an avenue to enhanced living for her that she has bid others try.

Seventeenth-century Dutch art was a celebration of the beauty of the ordinary in common life and served as example par excellence of the treasures of the quotidian. In many ways it epitomized the quintessence of Rookmaaker's aesthetic values. Some have thought his dedicated appreciation of it captivated him to a degree that diminished his ability to regard, even understand, the art of other times, especially the modern period. This, however, would be a serious misreading both of his spirit and his works, which copiously show his positive engagement with art of all periods and also with some non-Western art.

This is not to deny that he had a special attachment to the art of the Golden Age. He did. And it came naturally and straight out of his spiritual kinship with the tradition of Groen van Prinsterer and Abraham Kuyper.

Rookmaaker, though a student and admirer of Kuyper, was not an uncritical recipient of everything the latter said, especially his pronouncements on art in his Stone Lectures (1898). But he agreed when his fellow Dutchman and distinguished modern pioneer of the integration of learning and life stated the influence of Calvinism on Dutch art at its most glorious effulgence:

> under the auspices of Calvinism, the art of painting, prophetic of democratic life of later times, was the first to proclaim the people's maturity. ... [N]on-churchly life was also possessed of high importance and of an all-sided art-motive. Having been overshadowed for many centuries by class-distinctions, the common life of man came out of its hiding-place like a new world, in all its sober reality. ... the idea of election by free grace has contributed not a little toward interesting art in the hidden importance of what was small and insignificant. If a common man, to whom the world pays no special attention, is valued and even chosen by God as one of His elect, this must lead the artist also to find a motive for his artistic studies in what is common and of everyday occurrence, to pay attention to the emotions and the issues of the human heart in it. ... Thus far the artist had only traced upon his canvas the idealized figures of prophets and apostles, of saints and priests; now, however, when he saw how God had chosen the porter and the wage-earner for Himself, he found interest not only in the head, the figure and the entire personality of the man of the people, but began to reproduce the human expression of every rank and station.

The towering Protestant visual interpreter of the Bible, Rembrandt van Rijn, managed to bring home the prophets and apostles to the world of seventeenth-century common life and to render an encyclopedic cast of everyday characters as participants in holy history. In his preoccupation with biblical subjects, Rembrandt was unusual as the trend of his century was more toward an exquisite naturalism represented through landscape, portraiture, genre interiors and still life, rather than biblical subjects. Furthermore, superb artists such as Jan van Goyen, Jan Steen, Johannes Vermeer, amongst Rookmaaker's favourite artists, were Roman Catholic. Confessional status was not the issue. Calvinism in a deep and rich way, Kuyper and Rookmaaker believed, had pervaded the whole culture in Holland in the seventeenth century so that everyone was the recipient of its liberating benefits whether they were technically Catholic or Protestant. Life had been qualitatively immensely enriched for everyone. Rookmaaker pointed out particular ways in which he thought this was so:

> Jan van Goyen made us see the particular beauty and the characteristics of the structure of our great rivers, Paulus Potter (and many others) depicted the Dutch cattle, Van Ostade helped us to better appreciate the colourful country life, and so on. Especially the painters of later times – since the fifteenth century – have taught us to see (as a result of the nature of their art). Did Heda not show us the beauty of a glass which reflects light, did Kalff not open our eyes to the amazing reflections of light on silver? The paintings of our seventeenth century are, each in their own way, 'iconic' songs about the beauty of God's creation, poems about the joy of this earthly life – very sober and realistic, and without denying the effects of sin and the fall. (*CW* 4:228)

Rookmaaker was no aesthete, but he was wonderfully discriminating, looking ardently for beauty in the small and inconsequential. As he travelled, he loved villages and out of the way places, not just big cities and glitzy galleries. In Switzerland and Austria the aesthetic brought forward by seventeenth-century Dutch art allowed him to see the wise use of land in the integration of farm buildings within the landscape in a way that beautified it and added charm to it. But in the United States and Canada, it led him to observe a more appropriative and instrumental use of land that often led to the scarring and ugliness of the landscape, though it was as inherently beautiful as anything in Europe. Nothing was generally added that graced it. Of course, he was aware that some of the same values he saw written in the landscape of North America were also coming to Europe.

The art of seventeenth-century Holland gave Rookmaaker a place to stand aesthetically parallel to his firm footing philosophically in the tradition of Calvinist thought. Far from restricting him, this aesthetic gave him enormous scope. A few of the things it helped him love were: clarity, modesty, restraint, decorum, splendour without ostentation, simplicity without bareness, humanity, warmth, expressiveness without emotionalism, playfulness, humour, elegance, faithfulness to nature without slavish realism, and charm. He admired the minimalist elegance of much of modern art, especially in its application to contemporary design. His sensibilities had no trouble leaping from the pristine vast spaces of whitewashed church interiors by Pieter Saenredam (1597–1665) to the bare essentialism in the geometrical abstract style of Piet Mondrian (1872–1944).

Linked to Hans's fervent attachment to beauty was his appreciation and high view of women. He may well have been living in another universe, certainly another age, in how he expressed this in his comportment. In his day and today the cold trivialization of sex and absence of transcendence in most people's lives, makes it difficult to describe the qualitative complexity of his expression of eros, but it was there and very real.

Rookmaaker was no ladies man, but he loved women – not just beautiful women. Despite his unexceptional exterior, through his restrained intensity, he had a powerful effect on women because he was truly both interesting to them and interested in them, their ideas and sensibilities. He could equally irk and run off young women who fawned and were sentimental and thought creating candlelight settings was the essence of charm. He would literally turn on the highest-powered light that he could find when this happened! There were nudges and winks on occasion when he took interest in a young woman as he shepherded her around an art museum, but his interest did not translate into transgression. He was well aware of the wealth of experience he shared with his wife, Anky, that was a treasure never worth losing. He also supported her in a career of philanthropy that did not take off until she was in her fifties and was justifiably proud of her achievements. He knew his strength and credibility in communicating came from commitments he had made, particularly in marriage.

He was neither romantic nor puritanical. Agape and eros were not pitted against each other in his personality, but embraced in a way rare for our times. In this way he lived like Bach, no man to go about town womanizing but not frightened at weaving sexuality into the spiritual meaning of his cantatas in a way that is still surprising, if one really reflects on the content of his texts. Two of Hans's favourite Bach cantatas exemplify an eroticism that is foreign to our own times, but as natural a way of being for Hans as it was for Bach.

In the first, 'O Everlasting Fire, O Source of Love' (*O ewiges Feuer, O Ursprung der Liebe*, BWV 34), a cantata Bach had written for the wedding of a pastor, he had little trouble later seamlessly recycling it with minimal changes for Pentecost, remembering the coming down of the Holy Spirit in tongues of fire on his bride, the church, after Jesus' Ascension. The second, 'Wake, Arise, the Voices Call Us' (*Wachet auf, ruft uns die Stimme*, BWV 140), a cantata for the last Sunday in the calendar of the Christian year before Advent, speaks of a wedding. Its biblical anchoring in the parable of the ten virgins (Matthew 25:1–13) compresses eschatological preparedness with the expectant intimacy of a bridegroom about to consummate his marriage. The duet aria sung by the soprano and basso is a joyous celebration of bliss in union even as it is an allusion to words in the Song of Solomon (2:16; 6:3):

> Soprano (Bride/Soul): *My friend is mine,*
> Basso (Bridegroom/Jesus): *And I am thine*
> Both in union: *Let love bring no division*
> Both at the same time, but not in unison:
> Soprano (Bride/Soul): *I will with thee on heaven's roses pasture*
> Basso (Bridegroom/Jesus): *Thou shalt with me on heaven's roses pasture*
> *Where pleasure in fullness, where joy will abound*

In the 1970s the siege mentality of pious evangelicals was evident in the area of sexual mores, even as a proactive engagement on the way to social justice was often sadly lacking. Between the secular proponents of sexual promiscuousness and the backlash from pulpits propounding all-encompassing agape at the expense of eros, Rookmaaker may not have stood entirely alone, but he was isolated and threatening in his own way in this area, particularly to some insecure British types consumed with concern about 'the permissive society'. Sexuality was not a topic he spoke on explicitly. But it was one he knew a great deal about as it was related to the subject matter of much of the art he dealt with. All those nudes he talked about made some nervous. Because he could exegete through art the qualitative changing nature of sexual relations over the centuries, he was able to understand the degradation he found in his own day. But it also helped him handle it healthily with hope, suggesting a better, more biblical way rather than reactive fear. He modelled something valuable in this area equally for the sexually indulgent as much as for the sexually judgmental.

Beauty and love in the widest and deepest way went together for Hans. He said:

> To speak of a beautiful act is thus to my mind not a metaphorical use of terms. Because the act was in obedience to the Second great Commandment, to love our neighbor as ourselves, it could also be beautiful, in the sphere that for want of a better word we refer to as the aesthetic.

> Loveliness is something we should seek, says the Lord. That speaks for itself: it is inappropriate for believers who desire to love their neighbours and to be salting salt to go through life snarling and growling! ... Although in reality matters are sometimes uncannily tangled up in a hopeless knot of sin and wretchedness and goodness and beauty, it is remarkable to see how love can ennoble someone's face, so that someone who is not very attractive by nature can still be regarded as very beautiful, as having a kind of beauty that is not based directly on the harmonious proportion of shapes but that is all the

same striking. On the other hand we can sometimes see very beautiful women whose beauty is hard and pitiless, cruel in sensuality – think of many photos of film stars and of women in advertisements. One is confronted often enough with this sort of 'ugly beauty'. (*CW* 3:101)

Hans would probably not have been an easy personality to define in any age, but he was especially not so in one that relegated matters of meaning to a reductive understanding of history and eschewed the Bible on the basis of a prejudicial cultural reception of it rather than a firsthand reading of its text. It is only possible to intimate that he reflected and embodied, not only with his words but also with his entire being, a rejection of what he considered to be an intellectually and spiritually impoverished culture and a frequently effete expression of Christian faith within it. His passion for modern art was positive and central to his work, not because he agreed with the message of meaninglessness and absurdity in much of it but because it gave an accurate reading of the times that few were willing to face, whether they called themselves Christian or not.

Rookmaaker was an exceptionally integrated person, full of contrasts, polarities and tensions. He was earthy and sensuous, but also spiritually minded and sober; rough-hewn and refined; fierce but gentle; courteous, yet capable of being rude. At times it was difficult to know whether he was being playful or profoundly serious. He would lead his hearers to anticipate being amused and then suddenly, when they started to laugh, say gravely, 'You should not laugh, you should weep!' He was no pietist, but he was a man of deep piety and sincerity.

His passions were many – many more than have been suggested here. His aesthetics took deep roots in everyday reality. He imbibed 'the fullness of life' and shared it to the utmost. For him Bach could have written his little ditty: 'On land, on sea, at home, abroad, I smoke my pipe and worship God!'

8
Legacy

The last years of Hans Rookmaaker's life were filled with incessant activity as he met his commitments at home and travelled extensively abroad. Then, in a mere moment, at the height of his influence and impact, all was suspended in an instant. At an unsuspected hour on a day beginning to bud into spring in March 1977, his earthly life was over.

In their shock and sorrow, Hans's family were inspired to choose a profoundly appropriate text from one his favourite books of the Bible, The Revelation to John, to announce his death. It read: '"Blessed are the dead who from now on die in the Lord." "Yes," says the Spirit, "they will rest from their labours, for their deeds follow them."' (Revelation 14:13b)

In fifty-five years (exactly the same number of years allotted to his spiritual ancestor, John Calvin), Rookmaaker's work in this world was completed. The legacy of his labour has followed; and, in many ways, it is only getting underway twenty-five years after his death. His work continues not only to benefit believers of all denominational stripes who are active in the arts but also to honour the Calvinist tradition he identified himself with.

Ordinarily, scholars influence other scholars in their field through their research and writings; but the reach of Rookmaaker's impact on others expands well beyond academic art-historical circles, through both his writings and personal contacts to include artists and musicians, poets and publishers, filmmakers and philosophers, and even a few theologians and educators in other areas. While the exceptional diversity of his impact reflects Rookmaaker's many interests, it also refracts a personality of complexity and a character not easily classifiable by convenient categories, sacred or secular. Rookmaaker did not have star attraction, as popularly understood; but he did have appeal for people from a wide spectrum of society. He was under no illusion about his capacity to captivate everyone he encountered. But he was aware that there were some few whom he truly could communicate with and be of help to.

Those who possessed a desire or a capacity to nurture their imaginations toward goodness were drawn to him like bees to honey when they read his books or heard him speak. He might not have articulated his basic aim in these terms, but this was what he was after and accounts for the amazing diversity of individuals from different nationalities he managed to interest, his appeal across disciplines and professions, his credibility with women as well as men, and his persuasiveness with a younger generation coming along today.

For those who connected with him, he was more than a masterful teacher: he was an inspirer. He had phenomenal power to motivate. British artist and art educator Peter Smith writes: 'It is no secret that, like many others, I came across Rookmaaker at a crucial time in my life. The list of those who are still active in the fields of the Arts in the broadest sense, let alone other disciplines, who would admit to some kind of debt to Rookmaaker is ... long. Rookmaaker's biblical and Reformational thinking about the Arts re-located many of us in a fuller and richer world with the freedom and responsibility to serve Christ beyond the confines of Pietism.'

'Hans Rookmaaker not only talked about history. He made history.' That is the estimation of the American art historian Rachel Smith (no relation to Peter Smith), who is too young to have known Rookmaaker personally but who discovered his writings as an undergraduate before embarking on her academic career. The history she refers to is the conversion of attitude toward the arts that he was so significantly instrumental in causing amongst conservative Protestants, a change that opened the way for someone like herself, coming from a Reformed church background, to take up the arts with impunity and embrace them with joy as one of God's greatest gifts to humanity.

The change Rookmaaker helped so notably to create did not come dramatically or through any systematic agenda that he promulgated, but rather softly and steadily, through a contrapuntal weaving of his biblical vision and voice with his personal relationships as he pursued his profession as an art historian and calling as a Christian to integrate his faith with his learning.

While Rookmaaker's influence has developed slowly and subtly over the course of time through those on whom he has left his mark, the actual pace of his life in his last decade was very fast even by today's electronically driven standards for speed, and this contributed to his astounding impact on people. The qualitative contribution he made to the lives of so many individuals and organizations during these years represents a staggering personal emotional and spiritual investment that is still paying artistic and scholarly dividends.

From the late 1960s until his death, Rookmaaker gave massive energy to mentoring a whole host of people. Not all of them were his official students. Single-mindedly, he directed his academic career in the service of his calling in a way that went beyond narrowly defined notions of professorial duty and frequently ran counter to administrative expectations at his university. He may be admired for this; he may also be criticized for this. It may have caused him at times to neglect some of his official students.

Rookmaaker's relationship with Graham Birtwistle, one of his first foreign-born graduate students and today an Associate Professor in Modern Art at the Free University of Amsterdam, contains many aspects of the complexities of Hans's last years as well as his authenticity of spirit in encountering the issues facing his students and dedication in sustaining personal relationships.

By the time that Birtwistle heard of the name Hans Rookmaaker, 'the Flying Dutchman' (a name given to him by Linette Martin) was just beginning to flit from the Netherlands back and forth to Great Britain routinely. In 1961, Rookmaaker had taken his first grand tour of North America, but the days of his comings and goings to North America regularly were still ahead of him. Birtwistle first got wind of the peripatetic professor, both by reputation of his personal appearances in the UK and his scholarly repute, as he was transitioning from being a student in art history and English literature at Manchester University to lecturing in art history at Leicester Polytechnic.

An intellectual ride with Rookmaaker was always interesting. As with so many others, it began with a bumpy start for Birtwistle. While Birtwistle was a believer when he met his future mentor, almost by accident, on a visit to L'Abri Fellowship in Switzerland, he was not prepared to concede many of his own deeply held personal preferences in art, which tended to a subjective Romanticism, or to assess the intellectual assumptions of his educational formation critically in light of his Christian beliefs. Rookmaaker listened to him and challenged him intellectually and spiritually on these fronts in a way that he had never known before from his religious upbringing or formation afterwards.

The seriousness with which he was taken and the cogency of Rookmaaker's thinking contributed to his reassessment of his previous ideas. So much so that he decided to go to the Netherlands, learn Dutch and study for a doctorate in art history with Rookmaaker, a decision that eventually led to his current appointment.

But the story of Birtwistle is not so straightforward. His initial reaction to Rookmaaker represents a pattern. Many, on first engaging Rookmaaker's thinking, especially his utterances on modern art, did and do dismiss him and his ideas summarily. One often hears thoughtful people, many of whom are practicing artists, reject his work because they perceive that he did not understand modern art, that he hated it and wanted only to see contemporary art that looked like it was made for, if not in, the seventeenth century. In their view, abstraction was anathema for him. Rookmaaker's provocative style and unwillingness to bow to the fashionable trends of the times only made him all the more susceptible to bracketing his views and considering him reactive and out of touch rather than seeing him as offering a broader and deeper, boldly sophisticated, critique. Although it is understandable how some have stayed at this stage of engagement with Rookmaaker's thought, it is unfortunate that they have missed his philosophical criticism of modernity and confused it with a dismissal and damnation of modern art.

For the man who formed the foundations of his thinking in the furnace of World War II, the stakes were high. Ideas reflected in modern art were not just neutral or nice, coincidental concepts. They were loaded with philosophical presuppositions as to the meaning of reality. When art institutions went out of their way to evangelize, one might say, for the cause of modern art, there was more happening than just making the general public aware of new art. In Rookmaaker's judgment, they were preaching and making propaganda for a view of reality totally antithetical to the acknowledgement of a creational order given by a loving and living Creator. It was '[r]eality ... experienced as an alien power, irrational, strange, imprisoning humankind with its laws ... They experience their own lives as meaningless accidents and feel they have been thrown into a sick reality' (*CW* 1:321).

Rookmaaker had come near to walking down the same road himself in the chaos of war until he became convinced of a richer and deeper way of experiencing life in Christian freedom. He longed for others to know such fullness of life. He understood the temptation of this route; and, in many ways, he had tremendous compassion for those captivated by their alienation and seduced by modern art as a surrogate religion. Rookmaaker took modern art with absolute seriousness. He decried Christians who dismissed it and ignored it. For him, it was a key indicator of the condition of the times. He saw value and a certain achievement in Picasso's rejection of Enlightenment thinking, but he was not beguiled by the creed the artist went on to promote in its place. He also could appreciate modern art's breaking down of the dogma of naturalism espoused by much of nineteenth-century academic art that in its own way distorted reality as much as any art of the twentieth century.

Rather than a specific style or particular spiritual pedigree, Rookmaaker was looking for evidence of the affirmation of our humanity situated in meaningful reality in contemporary art. His deep appreciation of the art of Georges Rouault's dark, yet redemptive, vision is a case in point to disabuse those who believe that he never had any appreciation for the art of the modern era. He could acknowledge the beauty in an abstract painting by Jackson Pollock. But the arrogance of wilfully trashing a world still filled with evidences of God's glory despite sin and evil incensed him. Still, he was aware that '[i]f modern art is sometimes oppressive and negative in direction, then we as believers [also] bear some of the responsibility' (*CW* 4:370-371).

Graham Birtwistle, along with many others, learned that Rookmaaker was not an intransigent opponent of modern art but rather a critic with whom one could have a meaningful dialogue, one that could open up understanding on both sides of a conversation. Birtwistle was not side-lined into writing on some 'safe' and approved area but dealt with art that Rookmaaker had little liking or personal sympathy with, to say the least. His doctoral dissertation took up a re-evaluation of

COBRA (acronym for Copenhagen, Brussels, Amsterdam), a movement as well as a style of post-World War II art, deriving highly charged abstracted imagery from prehistoric, primitive or folk sources of art. Rookmaaker took his students seriously as intellectual partners who could bring insight to him even as he sought to instruct them. He was not the kind of professor one dare not cross with a different opinion or perspective. He might not agree, but he would listen and question in a way that engendered growth and maturity in the thinking of his students. He could release his students to become who they were supposed to be. They did not have to be little clones of him.

Many students like Birtwistle became his friends. In this way much leads back again to J.P.A. Mekkes, Hans's wise mentor who knew how to grow reciprocity and collegiality out of differences in age and status and understanding. Mekkes mediated the mystery of mentoring to him well.

In the spirit of Mekkes, Hans also became the kind of person who saw promise in people before they completely recognized their own giftedness. Mekkes wrote when Hans received his doctorate that it pleased him to address him with a title he had always seen before his name. Rookmaaker often looked penetratingly into a person's potential in the same way that Mekkes gazed into his.

One of the most dramatic instances of Rookmaaker's talent scouting skill was with John Walford, who presently is Professor of Art History at Wheaton College (Illinois). In the late 1960s, Walford was a young man living in London and trying to find himself and a purpose to live for. Although he had studied law for four years out of a sense of obligation to his family, his heart was not in it. He loved poking around art galleries and antique shops and began to dabble in buying and selling paintings, though there was no particular appreciation of art in his background.

In a conversation with a friend, Walford mentioned he had just bought a seventeenth-century Dutch painting. Immediately his friend suggested that he ought to meet Professor Rookmaaker and ask him about the picture. Little did he know what he was getting himself into. Rookmaaker not only responded to him, he turned up on his doorstep, unexpectedly, the morning after he and his friends had had an expansive evening in his flat. The dapper Dutch professor did not seemed bothered at all by the disarray of the young man's dwelling. As unpromising as an encounter like this might have seemed, it was the beginning of a course of care for Walford that would transform his life and give him a vocation.

By the time Rookmaaker met John Walford he was no stranger in Great Britain and knew dozens of young artists up and down the country. He frequently spoke at L'Abri Fellowship conferences at Ashburnham Place in Sussex. Meryl Fergus (later, Doney), who served in the late 1960s as a Travelling Secretary for British art colleges with Inter-Varsity Fellowship (today UCCF) and her successor, Tony Wales, were nearly worn out from accompanying the Dutch dynamo around to speaking engagements at universities, colleges, and various conferences. After these events they would then usually stay up nearly half the night with their guest speaker while he discussed ideas with students into the early morning hours over coffee or drinks in their digs or some other establishment that stayed open.

Rookmaaker drew close and was particularly encouraging to a number of young artists in the British Midlands. Today most of these artists have well-established reputations. Paul Martin, painter and printmaker as well as skilled in ceramics and sculpture, teaches at the Leith School of Art in Edinburgh and regularly receives commissions for his artwork, which has taken a direction informed by his adherence to the Orthodox Church. Martin Rose is a distinguished portrait painter with work hanging in the National Portrait Gallery (London). Kate Rose, printmaker, teaches art, as does her husband, Martin, at the Birkdale School (Sheffield) and has work in the collections of The Arts Council of Great Britain and the Sheffield Art Galleries. Meryl Doney, who also benefited greatly from his personal encouragement, has gone on to become an art impresario. With her husband, Malcolm, she co-hosts The Art Room (theartroom.net), a project to promote the work by artists who revel in paint and provide rich aesthetic nourishment for daily living rather than recondite ideas for cognoscenti. She has also co-authored with Malcolm *The Oxford Children's A to Z of Art* (1999). Meryl has written literally dozens of books on arts and crafts, serves on the research and development team of the Hayward Gallery on London's South Bank, and is involved in producing a major forthcoming exhibition entitled 'Presence: Images of Christ for the Third Millennium' (2004), to be located at several English cathedral sites.

Superficiality was not in Rookmaaker's vocabulary. He exhibited incredible quality in his personal relationships, even as they expanded exponentially. He did not forget about the young fellow back in London who was not an artist but who loved art, namely John Walford. From studying law, Walford had moved to teaching school. When Rookmaaker met up with him again, he bluntly told him he was wasting his time at teaching and that he should develop his God-given interests and come to study art history with him in the Netherlands. Walford was stunned at the thought. Could he not study art history in England, in his own mother tongue? Birtwistle seems to have been the one who challenged him by asking whether he would be willing to study theology with an atheist? His compatriot convinced him that being taught art history based on materialist suppositions was not much different. Finally, Walford braced himself to learn Dutch and submit himself to an invaluable apprenticeship of not only learning the academic requirements for a career in art history with his mentor, but a mission to cultivate a love of the arts in the church which would lead to a renewal of making art amongst Christians.

From Rookmaaker's well-planted seed of insight into Walford's talent, a thriving and fruitful tree has grown. John is the author of a major book on the great seventeenth-century Dutch landscape artist, Jacob van Ruisdael (Yale 1991), and *Great Themes in Art* (Prentice-Hall 2002), an important general history of art textbook, creatively structured thematically as well as chronologically in order to engage students in reflecting through art on spirituality, the self, nature, and the city. In turn, Walford has poured out his Rookmaaker inheritance on his talented student James Romaine, who confidently careens along writing crisp, culturally engaged art criticism even as he engages in serious art-historical research. Romaine's *Objects of Grace: Conversations on Creativity and Faith* (Square Halo Books, 2002) brings together, without a whiff of self-consciousness, the dynamic interaction of faith and art in the lives of ten very different types of artists. In an essay he wrote entitled, 'Creator, Creation, and Creativity' in *It was Good: Making Art to the Glory of God*, edited by Ned Bustard (Square Halo Books, 2000), Romaine exegetes and illuminates the power of Michelangelo's biblical vision to be vital down to our day and to honour the Giver of all gifts even as multitudes of people mill about the Sistine Chapel viewing his magnificent art. The legacy of Hans Rookmaaker lives on in the freshness and fidelity of work like this. Nor is it coincidental that Ned Bustard, the publisher of Square Halo Books, has been deeply influenced by Rookmaaker. After reading *Modern Art and the Death of a Culture,* Bustard says that for a decade he kept this tome on his nightstand, as it was one of the few credible books he could find linking being an artist and a Christian.

When Graham Birtwistle and then John Walford arrived in Holland to study with Rookmaaker, they encountered several worlds that their professor already inhabited and that they needed to discover. Hans did not have to go abroad to find an audience or following, though perhaps the prophet was not always appreciated as much as he might be in his own land. He was a man in motion, incredibly involved in the life of his profession, country, causes and church.

One of the first of his Dutch worlds that students like Birtwistle and Walford saw was Rookmaaker's university world at the Free University of Amsterdam. Hans was well connected in the art-historical world both within Holland and abroad. His conversation rarely indicated these connections, but his letters and diaries show that he corresponded and/or met with many of the leading figures in art history of his day, such as Erwin Panofsky, Frederick Hartt, Jan Bialostoki, Linda Nochlin, and Herschel Chipp, to name but a few. He could have well found a position elsewhere than at the Free. He kept abreast of the ongoing research regarding the photographic documentation of the subject matter of art history at Leiden University, where he had formerly held a position, and liased consistently with L.D. Couprie who was involved with this project. Today at the Free University there are still boxes and boxes of photos for this type of research that Rookmaaker collected. Further, he seems to have kept his hand in the International Association of Art Critics (AICA), founded in 1948/1949 to evaluate art criticism in relation to art history and to consider the responsibility of those who write on art in relation to artists and to the public. Administrative duties in his art history department, the university senate, and his own lectures plus excursions with his students to local art institutions and abroad were more than enough to keep any mortal occupied.

To occupy him further, however, there were growing unpleasant tensions within the department at the end of the 1960s and into the 1970s that everyone, students and staff, were aware of. While Rookmaaker had developed the department along with Bert van Swigchem and was drawing some of its best students, a significant sector of Dutch students was not happy. Many students were vocal in pointing out that they considered he spent too much time abroad, at L'Abri or with the 'Rookies', his international students, even neglecting his scholarship. One can sense the confrontational spirit of the time in the 'Interview by Art History Students from the Free University'. On these points he defended himself as needing to have awareness and contact with the wider world and to be hospitable to strangers and help them feel welcome. Still, even 'Rookies' like Walford and Birtwistle wanted to see him devote himself more to scholarship.

Amidst these tensions he was not a paragon of perfection and probably was too reactive and not completely tactful. He had little sympathy for a trend he saw in many of the students at the Free University, moving away from appreciating the University's rich Reformed heritage and demanding a less specifically Christian education. He was in a painful bind. He had won his way to faith in the hardship of war and held dear every Christian principle that the Free University was founded on. Many of these students came from comfortable and typically Calvinist homes and were impelled in a diametrically different direction. They wanted out and not into Christianity (as they conceived it) and often associated it with authoritarianism and bourgeois morality. In Hans's mind they were trying to throw away the most important treasure in his life and did not understand how much he was a co-belligerent with them in regard to wanting to overthrow hypocrisy and exploitation.

Nevertheless, Rookmaaker, had students in abundance, even if they were not all 'official' students. Mature Dutch students, such as Marc de Klijn and Hans van Seventer, who were formally enrolled (as we shall see) did get his message in a way that transformed their thinking and gave them clear direction for their lives. Ultimately, there were no concrete walls around Hans's classroom or lecture hall. He soared in a less structured setting, a creative context that he played off as he taught. He seemed to be learning simultaneously as he was teaching, right where he was – driving along (he loved his Volvo and never let its service lapse), looking at a landscape, walking through a gallery or partaking of a meal at *Huize Kortenhoeve* at Dutch L'Abri.

Bert van Swigchem, his colleague, puts his finger exactly on Hans's leading teaching motif when he identified him as a bridge builder. More than anything he desired that there be a bridge between people, on one side, who recognized a Christian oriented understanding of art history and theory with people, on the other side, who wanted to be Christian-oriented makers of art. Without this open spirit, Hans Rookmaaker simply would not have been Hans Rookmaaker! His legacy attests that many, many people found Rookmaaker not only to be a bridge builder for them, but indeed a veritable bridge himself.

For years, over and beyond his official academic activities, he travelled around the Netherlands speaking to all and sundry groups. His annual daybook agendas are filled with commitments showing how he crisscrossed the country from Groningen to 's-Gravenhage, from Amsterdam to Enschede to address gatherings and give lectures. Rookmaaker remained passionate about music and communicated memorably about it. From the titles of his talks noted in his dairy, there was quite a Dutch demand for topics like 'Blues and Spirituals', 'Jazz', 'Black Music', and 'Rock and Protest'. In these years he also edited and annotated the *Classic Jazz Masters* reissued for the Riverside Series of Fontana Records.

Rookmaaker's calendars are also dotted with recurrent appointments to attend showings of films at various locations. For many years he contributed to national public life by serving on the Netherlands Film Censorship Board (*Nederlandse Filmkeuring Kommissie/NFK*). This by no means meant just a simple jaunt of an afternoon or evening to see a movie or two. Rookmaaker wrestled intently with the issues of morality and censorship. His consciousness of the Calvinist heritage of the Netherlands made him immensely aware of the tradition of intellectual freedom and even an unusual toleration for pluralism going back to the seventeenth century in his native land. For example, he affirmed and was proud that René Descartes (1597–1650) had been able to live and work and think freely for twenty years in Holland, whether he agreed or not with that philosopher's thought. Freedom must be delicately balanced with responsibility and the welfare of the public.

Rookmaaker did not have a readymade Christian reaction to film, or for that matter, to television and radio broadcasting. He scorned the attitude of Christians who righteously opted out altogether from seeing television or viewing films. It was better to have a voice in these matters, even if collectively made judgments were not always completely correct. As a potent element of our culture, it was a part of our Christian calling to give guidance in the area of the media and also for young people to have an exposure to them that was critically and constructively tempered so that they could be inoculated, as it were, against their most pernicious effects. Proactively he participated in creating programmes on the radio, such as a series on African-American music, as well as supporting the general efforts of both Protestant networks (*Nederlandse Christelijke Radio Vereniging* in the mid 1960s and the *Evangelische Omroep*, which he helped to establish after its inception in 1970) in the Dutch pluralist broadcasting system. He also desired to see Christians making films that were life-affirming without avoiding difficult issues. (That part of his vision is probably only now beginning to take place.) Censorship was not just about sex but also about violence and sentimentality. It boggled his mind that North American viewers could be outraged at sex and nudity, yet tolerate before their eyes a steady stream of mayhem and obscenity consisting of horrific violence and saccharin sentimentality.

Although in the Netherlands today there is virtually no censorship of film – with discretion left to distributors and broadcasters on a voluntary basis to judge suitability for children – one must not be tempted to believe that Rookmaaker's work in this area was totally in vain. He knew public morality could not be legislated, but it could be shaped and was being shaped rapidly, especially through new media. The situation of reviewing films provided an important impetus for him to articulate thoughts about the media and its technology that he may not have otherwise done. It is not an exaggeration to say he pioneered in his own way every bit as much as Marshall McLuhan, his famous contemporary, in opening up understanding between the arts in popular culture and in so-called High culture.

Although not unanimously appreciated by all of his students at the Free University, Rookmaaker's commitment to contemporary cultural engagement in the light of biblical understanding did not go unnoticed by a number of thoughtful Dutch students and artists coming to critical junctures in their careers in the late 1960s and early 1970s. With the realities and issues of this generation close to his heart, Hans began to stir the Calvinist establishment to a fuller appreciation of art. He challenged them with the notion that art was as formidable a shaper of culture as the political, economic, and scientific spheres that they had integrated already into their lives. Those who only hear the polemical voice of Rookmaaker, singing the glories of the greatness of Calvinism's influence on the arts, especially the art of seventeenth-century Holland, need also to hear the critical voice of Rookmaaker calling the tradition to reform and to elaborate an understanding of the arts. While it was untenable to believe that Calvin and the Reformation had been entirely negative regarding the arts, he clearly recognized the history of the Reformed tradition had a mixed record *vis à vis* the arts. With genuine anguish he speculated on how many people with artistic talents and frequently young might have been driven from the church, and even from Christ, by an oppressive cultural impoverishment due to a lack of clear affirmation of art in Calvinist churches. With conviction he worked to build structures and organizations to transform this situation by helping to found the art history department at the Free University of Amsterdam (1964–1965), co-founding and being the first chairperson of the Christian Cultural Study Centre (*Christelijk Cultureel Studiecentrum/CCS*, 1964) leading eventually to the establishment of the Christian Academy for Visual Arts (*Christelijke Academie voor Beeldende Kunsten/CABK*, 1978) in Kampen, continuing the cultivation of the work of L'Abri Fellowship which he and his wife, Anky, had planted in the Netherlands in the late 1950s, and supporting initiatives in broadcasting and publishing in his homeland.

His call for change rang true. He was constructive and credible by his own commitment to labour in establishing structures to make a difference. Building on the outlook of people like Abraham Kuyper, Guillaume Groen van Prinsterer and Willem Bilderdijk, Rookmaaker also crafted a vision of a particular kind of Dutch aesthetic sensibility. Deeply embedded in reality and in love for all of creation in every detail, he perceived a perspective disclosed by biblical contiguity that was neither ecclesiastical nor secular. For him it was manifest by:

> Great freedom and openness to the entire creation, love for great and small, awareness of a certain hierarchy of values, avoidance of pomp and circumstance, sobriety that on the one hand avoids all idealization and on the other brooks no glorification of sin, emphasis on the human without heroizing while nevertheless acknowledging the importance of inward and outward struggle and taking an interest in the more intimate aspects of human relations – all this is ever the fruit for art of an approach to life nourished by the Scripture. (*CW* 4:379)

Further along these lines, he endorsed the Kuyperian conviction that Calvinism helped open up art to the value of the seemingly unimportant and the beauty of the quotidian and the humble landscape of his native land. In a reflection on seventeenth-century Dutch landscape, he wrote:

> There was no longer any need to travel, to linger on mountains or wander in forests, to glorify the ruins of antiquity. And there was even less desire to violate that reality by romanticizing or poeticizing it (thereby turning it into something contrived). The 'ordinary' became relevant, meaningful, important. Out of a profound respect for this land (graciously given back to them by God, so that they could live in freedom), out of a deep reverence for this divine creation, out of a true love for reality in all its beauty and uniqueness, this art was born. (*CW* 4:167)

Eventually Rookmaaker's extraordinary exposition of the ordinary could inspire artists who lived as far away as Oklahoma or Ontario to see significance in their own settings. But, closer at hand, in Holland he was influencing a future generation on several fronts by being relevant to the present, critical of the past, and giving some hope for the future.

Marc de Klijn, Dutch artist and author, cherishes Rookmaaker's preserving effect on his life spiritually and intellectually. Marc was born in 1939 into a non-religious Jewish home. During the war his parents, with him as a small child in tow, managed to survive by being *onderduikers* who hid in homes at various addresses throughout the country. Many years later he began reviewing his parents' increased self-awareness of being Jewish after the war, as well as his personal losses, including the death of his mother just as he was completing his school examinations and going on to study graphic design in Basel, Switzerland. On returning to the Netherlands in 1966, Marc took up the study of art history and philosophy in Amsterdam as he worked as a freelance designer; he also realized that he was in a mental crisis as to his personal identity and purpose for living. The turbulence of student unrest all around at the time contributed further to his explorations. Through contact with L'Abri Fellowship in Switzerland and with Rookmaaker at the Free University and L'Abri Fellowship in Holland, Marc found his way to belief and was baptized in 1971. He became a member (as Graham Birtwistle had) of the same denomination that Hans belonged to after 1968 (*De Gereformeerde Kerk Vrijgemaakt Buiten Verband*).

Over the course of the years, Marc de Klijn has been a dedicated custodian of Hans Rookmaaker's legacy. He has done this through the development of his own artistic work, writing and teaching – supporting all endeavours to disseminate the thought and published works of Rookmaaker. His own achievements are considerable. He regularly exhibits his art and has his work reviewed. He is the author of many articles and several books on topics such as the influence of Calvinism on landscape painting, art and religion, and issues of faith. He has translated into Dutch an essay on topography by Eric Gill (1882–1940), an artist whose work Rookmaaker admired. He has written a book on the Shoah (forthcoming 2004) in which he engages controversial contemporary interpretations of the horrendous suffering of the Jewish people during World War II.

De Klijn taught for some years at the Christian Academy for Visual Arts (*Christelijke Academie voor Beeldende Kunsten*/CABK, 1978) in Kampen. He continues to maintain a studio in Kampen, but more recently he has supported an initiative of the Christian Artists Association for Visual Artists (*Christian Artists Vereniging voor Beeldende Kunsten*) with links to a broader arts organization, Christian Artists Association (*Kunstenbond*-CNV or CA for short), with headquarters in Rotterdam. Somewhat confusingly, the Christian Artists Association for Visual Artists is also called CABK. It represents an aspect of a wider attempt by CA to found a European Academy for Culture and the Arts based on a non-traditional educational model of mobile academic modules rather than a full-blown traditional system of formal programmes anchored in one physical location. In the case of the visual arts, special seminars are arranged, some of which occur along with a host of other seminars in music, performance, media arts and writing during a huge annual event sponsored by CA in Doorn, not far from Utrecht. In 2003 an intensive seven-day summer session in drawing and painting took place in the Carmelite Cloister at Drachten in the northern part of the country. As the older CABK follows a more institutionalized model of education for full-time students, the newer CABK seems sighted on being flexible and serving part-time students and working artists, as well as on restoring a healthy relationship between the church and art.

Britt Wikström, a Swedish-American sculptor living in Holland, is another artist influenced by Rookmaaker who has brought his work to bear on the CA. She has been key to bringing a strong sense and presence of the visual arts to CA. The CA, founded and assiduously developed since 1980 by Leen La Rivière, concert promoter and tour organizer with a knack for speaking and writing about creativity, music and the arts, at first focused its annual seminar with subsidiary workshops on music followed by dance, mime and theatre. La Rivière affirmed the importance of the visual arts and was welcoming to Wikström to help to pioneer this domain by drawing other outstanding artists for exhibitions and workshops. However, the reception of the visual arts in CA has not always been smooth. The stable place that they now seem to have in the organization probably can be traced back by a thread of credibility due to Rookmaaker's influence on the work and outlook of artists of the stature of Britt Wikström who are contributing to the maturing of this facet of the work of CA.

Rookmaaker's imprint is stamped all over Art Revisited, an enterprise created by Hans and JoAnn van Seventer to promote the work of artists who love reality and are devoted to a painterly depiction of common life and objects without slavish realism. Their media company, located in Aduard, near Groningen in the north of the Netherlands, published books, prints and fine art cards (until 2002). They are also involved in making documentaries, mainly on themes related to the arts. Filmmaking is the fulfilment of a longstanding dream for Hans.

The van Seventers, both formal and informal former students of Hans and for some years senior workers at Dutch L'Abri, have been drawn close to a core of artists who met each other through Rookmaaker's work as a professor of Art History at the Free University. A common chord was their appreciation of his exposition of the link between a work of art and an artist's beliefs and world view. This group designated itself The Zwiggelte Group, because they gathered often to discuss ideas and share their work at the van Seventer's and member artist, Jan van Loon's farm in the small village of Zwiggelte near Westerbork.

In 1982 their work was presented together in an exhibition entitled 'Reality Revisited', organized by the van Seventers and accompanied with a text written by JoAnn. 'Reality Revisited' travelled in that year to the United States and introduced the work of Pit van Loo, Jan van Loon, Henk Helmantel, Rein Pol, Jan van der Scheer and Jan Zwaan to a North American audience.

Today these artists (except Pit van Loo, who died in 1991) are all going strong in the Netherlands and have been joined by others inspired by a similar outlook. Their mutual affiliation with each other is quite loose now, except through their representation via reproduction by Art Revisited. All of them exhibit their original works regularly at galleries around the country and some of them attract collectors from abroad.

Henk Helmantel's painting is rightly in high demand as it comes off his easel. His work genuinely invites comparison with the great Dutch masters in technique and sensibility, but after that only a superficial look at his work would suggest that he is only trying to emulate the art of a bygone age. He is *sui generis*. His composition, scale and sparseness set him apart and show him to be a contemporary painter who is continually nourished by his artistic and spiritual heritage.

Van Loon's work expressively embraces the everyday world, from wine glasses to landscapes, dynamically ranging stylistically between naturalism and abstraction. For Rein Pol realism is more than a laborious substitute for a good photograph. His painting is quirky. One can find in it everything from elegant musical instruments to pig parts in formaldehyde. He also is a masterly portrait painter. Jan van der Scheer takes off in other directions. Inspired especially by Japanese art, van der Scheer paints exquisite watercolours with subjects ranging from oriental objects to plants and animals. Jan Zwaan is the son of a painter. When he was young, his father frequently took him with him as he painted *en plein air*. To this day he is dedicated to working outdoors. But it does mean painting quickly in the constantly changing moist climate of the Low Countries. His painting reflects his intoxication with light and texture.

Rookmaaker was ready to move on when he felt vision was lacking. Conversely, where he viewed vision was strong, he stayed the course (e.g. L'Abri Fellowship). When the Christian Cultural Study Centre (*Christelijk Culturreel Studiecentrum/CCS*) became less focused in terms of its Christian purpose (in his eyes), he could take interest in helping develop and supporting the Christelijk Studiecentrum ICS (International Christian Study Centre), which began in 1970. Today this centre carries on in a direction that Rookmaaker would no doubt be pleased with. As part of the Impact Network, it dynamically relates to multiple initiatives, including publications (*IMPACT* and *CAHIER*), an informative and attractive web site (http://www.impactnetwerk.nl), lecture series, student groups, and annual conferences that seek to challenge and equip those aged 25–40 to be faithful followers of Jesus Christ in their personal and professional lives, in communal life together, and in public. It is also affiliated with the International Fellowship of Evangelical Student (IFES), the umbrella organizations linking independent evangelical student movements around the world. Amidst ongoing study groups that it sponsors for lawyers, social workers and other professionals, ICS plans to host a special study group (2003/2004) on 'The Complete Works of Hans R. Rookmaaker' and celebrate a Hans Rookmaaker day on 1 November 2003 (All Saints Day).

Wim and Greta Rietkerk, much loved friends of the Rookmaakers and their gifted co-workers at Dutch L'Abri since 1974, steadfastly continue this work in the Netherlands, even as Wim over the years has also pastored a church and chaplained university students. Students and seekers still come to *Huize Kortenhoeve*, the big white, welcoming eighteenth-century farmhouse at Eck en Wiel, set in the orchard heartland of Gelderland, to be quiet, to listen to recorded lectures, and to reflect creatively – in short, to retreat in order to go forward with renewed vigour. That the vitality of Dutch L'Abri continued after the death of Hans Rookmaaker is no better validated than in the publication of his *Complete Works*. In 1986/7 Pieter and Elria Kwant spent a year there that seemed uneventful and unpromising, though in the course of it there increasingly arose a silent prayer in Pieter to do something with his life that would serve to build up others and honour God. He attests this inchoate longing and supplication years ago gave him the desire to see Rookmaaker read widely again. Though Pieter and Elria never knew Hans personally, they experienced him in the freshness of his writings. According to Elria, 'He is always very "present" in his writings – never just cold facts!' After considerable experience working with established publishers behind them and ongoing, Pieter and Elria launched their own press, Piquant, in 1999. The focused intent and scope of their commitment to serving those who serve the arts through their list is unprecedented amongst Christian publishers.

In 1974, when the Rietkerks became full-time workers at Dutch L'Abri, Hans was happy to announce that they would be joined part-time by Henk Geertsema, a talented young assistant professor from the Free University who was willing to divide his time between teaching some courses at the university and being their co-worker. Henk was someone who knew L'Abri Fellowship well, both in Switzerland and Holland. As a student of theology and philosophy he benefited from being able to sharpen his intellectual skills through the mentorship of both Rookmaaker and Schaeffer. Henk was a theologian (an expert in the theology of Jürgen Moltmann) and a specialist in Marxist philosophy, a combination that Hans saw as especially suited to the needs and concerns of young people at L'Abri at that time. The promise Rookmaaker saw in Geertsema led to what some might consider a reckless career move on Henk's part, moving from a full-time university position to being a half-time Christian worker alongside teaching some courses in philosophy; but this move has today been vindicated. Geertsema is recognized as a distinguished philosopher, whose writings range over such topics as modern culture, the human character of knowing, humanity in scholarship, faith and life, and the meaning of freedom for the study of the social sciences. Prof. Dr H.G. Geertsema now occupies the Dooyeweerd Chair of Philosophy at the Free University of Amsterdam, as well as serving as *bijzondere hoogleraar* in Reformational Philosophy at the universities of Groningen and Utrecht.

Rookmaaker's academic mentoring was not lavished only on men. Dr Mary Leigh Morbey is Associate Professor of Culture and Technology at York University in Toronto. She possesses an eye-popping resumé of awards and publications. Her writings span such subjects as cybercolonialism and world musea, electronic technologies and the visual arts, and gender, and are on the forefront of scholarship on technology and culture.

Mary Leigh does not hesitate for a second to acknowledge that Hans Rookmaaker was a major shaper of her life in her early twenties when she studied with him in the faculty of Art History at the Free University (1973–1976), receiving her doctorandus degree there in 1976. She says:

> As my professor, he literally taught me how to 'think' in deeper and more nuanced ways, and did this in a most gentle and supportive manner. He did not differentiate between male and female graduate student at that time in the early 1970s as many in the academy did. This was most helpful to my development and I imagine the development of other female students with whom he worked.
>
> As a Christian scholar, he continually pressed the meaning and purpose of life given to Christian believers and this has subsequently shaped all aspects of my life: my marriage, family, academic/scholarly work at every institution I have served whether it be Redeemer University College or York University.

She also appreciates that Rookmaaker introduced her to Calvin Seerveld, who mentored her further, especially around carefully crafting her scholarship. In sum, they both have left their legacy in teaching her how, in turn, to mentor her students Christianly.

One must not forget the academic achievements of Rookmaaker's children either. A visit to The National Library of the Netherlands in The Hague will find publications of all three of his children there. Both of Hans's sons, Hans, junior and Kees have doctorates from the University of Utrecht. Hans, junior dedicated his book, *Towards A Romantic Conception of Nature: Coleridge's Poetry Up to 1803* (1984), to the memory of his father, 'whose ideas and love of learning have always been a source of inspiration to me'. Inspired by stories his father shared of the serious naturalist and environmental pursuits of his colonial administrator grandfather, whom he never knew, Kees has gone on to be a world authority on the history of zoos and the rhinoceros in captivity and has several books to his name. Kees has also written on his grandfather's expedition to Rintja in the Dutch Indies in 1927, to capture twelve of the largest of the earth's monitor-type lizards, known as Komodo dragons. Marleen has made her mark in pioneering serious reflection from a Christian perspective on popular music. She has also taken on the mammoth task of gathering all her father's works together, seeing to their translation into English, and editing them. All of this is a testament to their father's inspiration as well as to their filial respect for him.

Most of the Americans and Canadians who were influenced by Rookmaaker were introduced to him in the 1970s when he increasingly gained a public presence and profile in North America. He had written articles for *Christianity Today*, published his bestselling book, *Modern Art and the Death of a Culture* (IVP, 1970), and was highly visible as a close associate of Francis Schaeffer. From 1970 to 1977, the year of his death, he travelled each year except 1971 to North America. During these years he forged many friendships with individuals as well as links with Christian institutions in both the United States and Canada.

A few North Americans who were in Reformed circles or who were living or travelling in Europe learned of him in the 1960s. Calvin Seerveld was an exception. He had met Rookmaaker in the late 1950s when he was living in Holland. T. Grady Spires, Professor of Philosophy (Emeritus) at Gordon College (Wenham, MA), was in touch with Rookmaaker from the time of his first visit to the USA in 1961. In the mid 1960s he collaborated on translating 'Let's Sing the Old Dr Watts: A Chapter in the History of Negro Spirituals,' which appeared in *The Gordon Review* (1966). Grady also tried to recruit Rookmaaker to teach at Gordon, but there was not enough institutional will at that time at Gordon to do this. Grady's abiding friendship with Hans strengthened his tenacity to make the arts more visible at Gordon and eventually put them on the college's agenda in a serious way. Gordon College now has an impressive faculty of art and a well-equipped arts centre in its own building. It also gives an institutional home to Christians in the Visual Arts (CIVA), the premiere place in North America for Christian artists, art teachers, critics, collectors, and other lovers of the visual arts to come together from across the whole denominational spectrum to be encouraged to excellence in their work and faithfulness to Christ in their daily walk. Although CIVA was not founded out of a direct impulse related to Rookmaaker, many of its earliest leaders as well as some of its present leadership found their formation significantly shaped by him and/or his thinking.

Ted Prescott chairs the Art and Theatre Departments at Messiah College in Grantham, PA. He is a sculptor and art critic with many prestigious commissions and literary credits to his name. Ted has also been a president of CIVA. The affirmation that Rookmaaker gave to him and his wife, Catherine, a gifted portrait and landscape painter, was incisive.

In the autumn of 1970 the Prescotts went for six months to L'Abri in Switzerland. They were filled with enthusiasm for their newly found faith and deeply affected by the counter-cultural revolution of the 1960s. Ted was a newly minted MFA in sculpture and trying to figure out what he was supposed to do. Both Prescotts had many doubts and insecurities around what they were doing and where they were going. Then Francis Schaeffer arranged for them to spend time with Rookmaaker. When it was time for Hans to return home, they drove him to the airport in Geneva. In a characteristic gesture that he would make on many occasions with many people, he suggested to them that they could stop at the municipal museum of Geneva on the way. His humour and vitality affected them. His ideas were totally new and removed from what they had received as students. They were challenged. Equally as characteristic of Rookmaaker, he encouraged them to find their own way and not accept everything he said as being from on high.

As their time to return to the USA approached, they longed to linger in Europe. Hans invited them to stay in Holland and even found inexpensive accommodations for them. Ted was stunned when Rookmaaker arranged for him to have an interview with the Ministry of Culture in the Netherlands regarding studying art restoration. Even more amazingly, after the interview the ministry was willing to have the Dutch government send him to Italy for two years to gain competencies, if he could wait six months for a new fiscal year. However, their coffers were completely depleted and they had to head home. But before their departure, Hans arranged for them to spend an evening in a charming thatched-roof house near the river Amstel with some of his students. On that memorable occasion, they met someone who subsequently became their deep and lifelong friend, namely, John Walford. Although they may have wondered what their life would have been like had they spent two years in Italy, little did either they or Walford know then that John would come to spend his entire teaching career in America.

As theology was not Rookmaaker's forte, we can now see from this point in time something that probably would have surprised him greatly. That is, his enrichment of theological education through people bringing fresh perspectives to this field through the arts. The list is sizable.

Bill Edgar, a musician and a professor of Theology at Westminster Theological Seminary (Philadelphia, PA), was immensely appreciative as a musically gifted young man, beginning his undergraduate studies at Harvard, to find someone like Rookmaaker, who was interested in genuine jazz the same way he was and who generously gave him old jazz recordings in 1962. Subsequently Edgar has written books in both English and French relating music to Christian understanding.

In 1967 Thena Ayres, Assistant Professor of Adult Education and Dean of the Summer School at Regent College and then a recent university graduate, met Rookmaaker at L'Abri in Switzerland and soon cemented a friendship with him by meeting him accidentally again shortly afterwards in Rome in an art gallery while he was on excursion there with his art history students. Spontaneously Rooky invited her to come along with the group. Italian art and opera, guided by a Continental professor and his energetic students, was a heady and inspiring mix for a young woman from western Canada. Thena was struck immediately by the fact that he related his scholarly learning to his Christian understanding. Furthermore, she saw that his perspective on the visual arts engaged the dilemma of being modern – alone and alienated from God. She also noted how he encouraged artists and went out of his way for his students; qualities of mentoring that she, like Mary Leigh Morbey, has absorbed into her own practice of teaching.

In 1967 William Dyrness was a theological student in his last year at Fuller Theological Seminary in Pasadena, CA, and had heard of the Dutch art historian through Francis Schaeffer. In that year Bill wrote a letter to Rookmaaker to explore the idea of his coming to study with him, explaining that he did not want to leave the field of theology but wanted to see if theology could enrich his understanding of aesthetics. After an interlude of study in Amsterdam with decisive direction from Rookmaaker, Dyrness eventually went on to complete a doctorate on the art and theology of Georges Rouault at the University of Strasbourg in France. Also of great benefit to him as he was setting out were the other young scholars, such as John Walford, Maria Dellù (today Dr Maria Walford-Dellù), and Graham Birtwistle, whom Hans introduced him to. As a professor of theology and an academic administrator whose career has taken him from Asia Theological Seminary in the Philippines, New College Berkeley (Berkeley, CA) and full circle back to Fuller, Bill Dyrness continues to make a monumental contribution to theology and the arts. In the 1960s the arts were nowhere on the theological horizon of Fuller Seminary. Today they are highly visible, with a centre devoted to them and an annual arts and film festival to boot.

Rookmaaker's influence on the direction of the arts at Regent College was formative. The whole conception of Regent College was innovative. In 1969, when it was founded, there was not another post-graduate theological institution that was aimed specifically at equipping lay people rather than ministers or theologians with a theological education. Although the arts were not a conscious part of the agenda of the new endeavour, there was great openness from the founding faculty, particularly James Houston and Ward Gasque, to the arts as a vital impulse within the community.

Prior to coming to Vancouver to help establish the college, Ward and Laurel Gasque were living in England. At that time they had opportunity to host Francis and Edith Schaeffer in their home in Manchester and also to attend a spring conference of L'Abri Fellowship at Ashburnham Place in Sussex in March 1968. There they were introduced to Hans Rookmaaker and were immediately impressed by his academic sophistication and utterly refreshing approach to thinking about art and culture and Christian belief in contemporary society. Following the conference they were delighted to join him on one of his inimitable walking art history courses at the Tate Gallery in London. After that the Gasques could hardly wait to sign him up to teach at a Regent College Summer School.

So it was that Rookmaaker became a featured part of the Regent College Summer Schools (1970, 1972, 1974). Further incentive for him to come to Vancouver was his friendship with Thena Ayres, who by that time had returned from Europe and her graduate studies at Covenant Theological Seminary in St Louis and was on the staff of Inter-Varsity Christian Fellowship in Canada. Thena was a great supporter of the fledgling college and was excited that the arts would be encouraged so substantially by having someone of Hans's stature leading the way. Other friends living in British Columbia were the poet Hannah van der Kamp and artist Robert Main. When Hannah and Robert married, they made sure it was in the summertime when Rooky was around. Enthusiasm abounded and in 1970 on Hans's first stint at Regent, he brought Anky, Hans, Kees, and Marleen with him to Vancouver for a summer holiday that went down in the family annals as truly memorable.

Rookmaaker's summer sessions at Regent were legendary. The peppery little professor with the pipe might say almost anything to provoke a good discussion. Jaws sometimes dropped at images he showed at his slide presentations. He could be tough on his projectionists, too. One of the survivors of this experience was Dal Schindell, then a student at Regent College who was also an artist. After Rooky, there was no turning back for Dal. As soon as he could scrape up the funds he was off to England to continue his studies at Sheffield Polytechnic, where he soon became a member of the H.R. Rookmaaker inspired artists' group there that harkened back to the days when Hans was shepherded around the British Midlands by Meryl Doney and Tony Wales. Other unsuspecting Regent Summer School students to come under the influence of Rookmaaker have been Roger Feldman, Wayne Roosa, Mary Ellen Ashcroft and Betty Spackman. In 1970, New York artist Chris Anderson flamboyantly flew into Vancouver simply to meet Rookmaaker.

As a result of meeting Rookmaaker, Feldman left studying theology and devoted himself to becoming a sculptor. Presently he is Professor of Art at Seattle Pacific University. Wayne Roosa is an art historian teaching at Bethel College (St Paul, MN) and author of numerous publications. His forthcoming book is entitled, *The Quiet Heresy: Biblical Themes in*

Contemporary Art. Mary Ellen Ashcroft also teaches at Bethel College. She is a professor of English literature and a prolific author herself. Spackman is an artist who has gone on to exhibit her work in Canada, the Netherlands and Austria and to teach for many years at Redeemer University College (Ancaster, ON) and now at Trinity Western University (Langley, BC). Anderson has received many grants and awards for her work and it is held in over fifty public and corporate collections. She has exhibited her painting work in the USA and abroad and taught at many institutions, including Regent College. Schindell has ended up back at Regent College, where he serves as Director of Publications, Director of the Lookout Art Gallery, and Instructor in Christianity and Art in a programme at the college that is burgeoning. Formerly, Regent College Summer School students under Rookmaaker, Roosa and Ashcroft have returned to Regent a number of times to teach a new generation of summer school students there.

Whether teaching at a summer session, giving special lectures or going to a conference sponsored by L'Abri, Rookmaaker always managed to squeeze an enormous amount of travel in between his destinations when he was in North America. Philadelphia artist Bettina Clowney remembers spending a whole day with Rookmaaker at the National Gallery of Art in Washington, DC, as well as a visit to the Philadelphia Museum of Fine Arts. Although her work has taken off in some directions that she feels Rookmaaker would have considered 'mystical' (she has studied icon writing with the Russian iconographer Vladislav Andrejev for a decade), she says he was very influential in her life and art. When she met him, she was a new Christian, and a very dedicated painter and student of art history. His dry humour delighted her. She comments, 'His enthusiasm and deep humanity and humility impressed me. He heard my aspirations with emotional generosity [and gave me] huge permission [to seek] truth, life, and God in my work . . . to be myself with my work and with God.'

Art historian Lee Hendrix, Curator of Drawings at the J. Paul Getty Museum, met Rookmaaker through L'Abri connections in Tennessee as she was completing her undergraduate years at Vanderbilt University. After foundational graduate studies with Rookmaaker at the Free University, she was well prepared to do a doctorate at Princeton University on the Flemish late Renaissance painter, Joris Hoefnagel, and to continue to an outstanding scholarly career. In Calgary, Alberta in 1975, Dutch-born Canadian artist Gerard Pas caught up with Rookmaaker after hitchhiking his way across half of Canada to meet him. By Pas's own admission, he pushed the provocative and even distasteful in his art so that even after considerable spiritual transformation he still shocked many people by some of his habits of language and life. But as Bettina Clowney discovered, he too found that Rookmaaker looked and listened at a deeper level to his aspirations.

Rookmaaker was not shocked and seriously engaged Pas in an intellectually nuanced way so that he could be free as a Christian to pursue complex issues in his art without superficiality or simplistic solutions.

In the early 1970s in the midst of the free speech movement at the University of California at Berkeley, Sharon Gallagher, film critic and editor of *Radix* magazine, felt tremendously heartened when Rookmaaker came to Berkeley to 'support the troops' there who were seeking a third way between the radical right and the radical left – a way that showed committed Christians were also radical in the sense of going to the roots of their faith in seeking social justice and embracing the arts for the benefit of all. Hans gave informal talks and a lecture on the UCB campus. Sharon interviewed him for publication. Berkeley performance artists Susan and David Fetcho found Rookmaaker's honesty and humanity reassuring in its spontaneous expression. Being in Berkeley gave Hans a strong dose of what the dynamics of protest were like at America's most influential public university.

But, Rookmaaker was to have an impact and develop interests even farther afield than Berkeley. In 1970, Kefa Sempangi, a Ugandan artist whom Hans had invited to study with him, arrived at the Free University. Hans had met Kefa on one of his visits to the UK. The young Ugandan had been doing post-graduate studies at the Royal College of Art in London. Hans and Anky welcomed Kefa and his wife, Penina, with warmth and hospitality. They were eager to learn more about Africa from the Sempangis. Hans soon asked questions about art and culture in Africa to gain a better understanding than he would have had solely by reading scholarly texts. Kefa was a firsthand informant. Understanding art in contemporary non-Western cultures was a significant area of enquiry that Hans was developing before he died. This subject also interested Bill Dyrness, who had come with broad missional interests in art and culture to study with Hans earlier.

When Kefa and Penina returned to Uganda in 1971, Hans and Anky did not forget them. They supported Kefa in his academic work in the Fine Art Department of Makerere University (Kampala) as well as the benevolent work he took up for street children during the time of severe oppression under the terrorist regime of Idi Amin. And, in 1974, they enabled the Sempangis to leave their country and find refuge abroad until they were able to return in 1979. During the depths of the brutality of Amin's tyranny in Uganda, Hans was unable to visit his student's homeland, but he did visit Kenya. In 1976 he accompanied Anky on a trip she made there in connection with her *Redt een Kind* work. This opportunity gave him a brief but rich experience of Africa. Travelling with Anky gave him an advantage to see African life and culture more from the perspective of a participant than he would have had as a conventional visitor. Coming less than a year before his death, his first direct encounter with African culture in context was only beginning to fertilize his reflection on art and faith in the non-Western world.

In Hans's time at Swiss L'Abri, he may not have been aware of another African student who listened attentively and deeply to all that he had to say. Kwame Bediako, a Ghanaian, destined to become one of Africa's foremost theologians, sat rapt for a week at Hans's feet in Huémoz. Bediako went on to earn doctorates in French literature from the University of Bordeaux and in theology from the University of Aberdeen. Today he is noted for penetratingly exploring the experience of African identity as it embraces the Christian faith. He serves as the Director of the Akrofi-Christaller Memorial Centre for Mission Research and Applied Theology in Akropong-Akuapem, Ghana and is a minister of the Presbyterian Church of Ghana with a worldwide reputation as an interpreter of African culture and Christianity. Bediako honours Rookmaaker's work and acknowledges its influence on him at a seminal stage in his development. He feels he is doing for Africa what he believes Rookmaaker was attempting to do for Western culture. Following in the footsteps of Abraham Kuyper and other distinguished Reformed thinkers, Bediako will be giving the Stone Lectures at Princeton Theological Seminary in the autumn of 2003.

Rookmaaker's impact in Great Britain has been touched on already, but it deserves to be looked at again as it continues to grow. Peter Heslam writes, 'It is Hans Rookmaaker . . . who was largely responsible for establishing the Kuyperian tradition in Britain . . . and inspiring a whole generation of Christian art students with his vision of thinking about the arts, and indeed practicing the arts, from a committed Christian perspective.' While broadly speaking, what Heslam says is true, there was also prepared ground for Hans when he planted his seed of Neo-Calvinism in British evangelical circles primarily associated with Inter-Varsity Fellowship (today, UCCF). Several factors contributed to these favourable conditions.

First of all, when Rookmaaker arrived on the scene in Britain in the late 1960s, biblical and theological scholarship by evangelical Christians was gaining credibility. Foremost among these scholars was F.F. Bruce, the John Rylands Professor of Biblical Criticism at the University of Manchester. He had been one of the founders of both the Theological Students Fellowship and the Tyndale Fellowship for Biblical Research, groups that gave a sense of confidence to a new generation of evangelical scholars, and was one of the authors of the earliest influential scholarly and non-technical books that were being published by Inter-Varsity Press. Although he was neither a Presbyterian nor a Calvinist in the strict sense, Bruce had recently taken over the editorship of *The Evangelical Quarterly*, described as a 'Journal for the Defence of the Reformed Faith'. When Bruce and Rookmaaker came to know each other at Regent College in 1970, there was instant mutual respect and warmth between them. At the same time, there was a renewal of Calvinist theology in the UK, pioneered by the study groups called by Martin Lloyd-Jones and later dominated by J.I. Packer, and the reissuing of older Calvinist works by the Banner of Truth.

Secondly, coupled with this changing intellectual climate amongst evangelicals was an eager audience poised for just the resources Rookmaaker could bring to them. The evangelical literature coming off the press focused primarily on biblical and theological studies rather than on issues of contemporary life and culture. Thus, there were leaders of the younger generation, people like Meryl Doney, Tony Wales, and David and Pat Alexander, who were ready to leap from the margins of cultural discourse to direct engagement. Rookmaaker brought the right blend of intellectual substance, along with missional dynamism, that they were looking for, but could hardly have believed existed before they saw Rookmaaker in action. They also loved the fact that he blew away with the smoke from his pipe the sentimental pietistic cant and niceties that evangelicals were prone to and cut to the real issues at stake in the culture. Each of the individuals mentioned above went on to careers in writing and publishing that greatly broadened the scope of Christian publishing in the UK.

Thirdly, and perhaps most importantly and decisively for Rookmaaker's introduction to the UK, was a group of friends with a Reformational outlook in Britain who connected directly with Dooyeweerdians in the Netherlands. Key amongst this group was David Hanson, today a physician specializing in ear, nose, and throat and a keen Christian layman living in Leeds. David says he knew about Rookmaaker before he met him through his connection with the highly prized Riverside Classical Jazz recordings as well as by the reputation of his other writings, the contents of which were conveyed to him by his friends who read Dutch.

Rookmaaker seems to have invited himself to Britain. In 1966 Hans wrote to David Hanson that he would like to come and stay with him and 'would you please find some art students, artists, art teachers [for me] to talk to?' David is still not sure who had given Hans his name – possibly J.D. Dengerink or Henk van Riessen, Dutch philosophers whom he knew. As Hanson sprang into networking to make arrangements for Hans's visit, little did he realize what an important gateway he was providing for Rookmaaker's influence in Great Britain. Of longterm significance was the contact he made that paved the way for Hans to visit the Birmingham Art College, where he met Peter Smith, Kate and Martin Rose, and Paul and Sandra Martin, who at that time were students there. As noted above, members of this group have become well-established artists. Without in the least being slavish, their work is still attuned to the philosophical and artistic implications of what Rookmaaker was saying and continues to say through his works.

Rookmaaker's direct influence on Hanson was strong. He calls it 'a powerful factor in moving me further and further away from dualist pietism'. He persuaded Hanson that 'the missionary position' was of small consequence unless it was linked with commitment to be a transforming presence in civic society, professional life, and one's own neighbourhood. In turn, the Reformational and Kuyperian perspective conveyed by Hans has helped to inspire David and his wife, Ruth, who holds a post-graduate degree in psychology, to develop this perspective within the West Yorkshire School of Christian Studies (WYSOCS).

The multiple trips Hans made to England each year in the last decade of his life called for a lot of juggling and the utmost economical use of his time when he was in the UK. In the late 1960s a small interest in the arts was beginning to blossom amongst evangelical Christians. The actor Nigel Goodwin was filled with passion to see performers, artists, and musicians with strong faith in the practice of their professional lives. In November of 1967, he met Rookmaaker on a visit to L'Abri in Switzerland. His relationship with Hans never faltered as he learned from him, and his friendship with him became deeper with every passing year.

Prior to 1967 only a few art students in Birmingham associated with the Reformed tradition seemed to know about Rookmaaker. While Rookmaaker's name was closely associated with Francis Schaeffer, he did not come to Britain riding on his coattails. L'Abri Fellowship was not even formally established in Britain at the times of Hans's early visits. It did, however, have a small study base in a house church in Ealing in the west of London. Nigel nurtured friendships there with Sylvester and Janet Jacobs and Linette and Joe Martin, whom he had met in Switzerland. They had strong interests in the arts. Sylvester was an American photographer. Linette was a dancer and writer. Later she wrote the first biography of Rookmaaker (*Hans Rookmaaker: A Biography*, IVP, 1979), but even before that, Sylvester's story of encountering hostility and rejection as a black person growing up in the United States (*Born Black*, Hodder & Stoughton, 1977). Colin Duriez, author and literary entrepreneur, had also been with them at Swiss L'Abri in 1967.

Momentum was mounting. After accompanying Rookmaaker to Birmingham, Meryl Doney was introducing him to ever widening circles of students. In 1968, Inter-Varsity Fellowship (UCCF) sponsored a major conference on vocation in Keele. Rooky was the featured speaker and proved to be the galvanizing element. He provoked thinking and was a catalyst to action. Increasingly, art students were gathering and Rookmaaker was speaking at conferences in different parts of the country. From 1968 onwards, larger events and longer-term ventures were embarked on.

Meanwhile, Nigel Goodwin's vision matched the concern of a group of Christians that included Ciff Richard, who had recently come to faith, in desiring to see a meeting place where those active in the arts could talk and laugh, weep and work, and pray. In 1971 Nigel joined forces with these friends in establishing the Arts Centre Group (ACG). Nigel, newly married, worked with his wife Gillie in directing the operations and hosting events at the ACG's first location in Kensington. Later the ACG moved to premises in Waterloo, with The Old Vic and The Young Vic theatres close by, and Nigel and Gillie were gradually released after painstaking pioneer labour to a broader ministry that enabled them eventually to travel more and be of encouragement to countless artists around the world. ACG saw a host of extremely talented people being influenced by Rookmaaker at the threshold of their careers in the arts come through its doors. Some of them were: Norman Stone (filmmaker), Murray Watts (director and writer for theatre and film), and Malcolm Doney (artist and author).

The ACG continues to provide support to Christian artists and includes a mentoring programme and a quarterly magazine called *ArtsMedia*. The editor, David Porter, and his wife, Tricia, who is a professional photographer, were both encouraged to make the arts their life's work through their early and formative contact with Rookmaaker. As an expression of their esteem for Hans, their book, *Over the Bent World*, an introduction to the life and work of Gerard Manley Hopkins, was dedicated to him.

Other organizations to arise that were influenced by Rookmaaker were the Institute for Contemporary Christianity in London and *Third Way* magazine. Thirty years ago the Greenbelt Arts Festival started primarily as a Christian music festival with about 1,500 young people stomping in soggy Suffolk fields. In the 1980s up to 30,000 would come. Located today at the Cheltenham Racecourse, thousands still show up (many of them the mature youth of yesteryear with their children) for a celebration of the arts through exhibits, workshops and seminars, concerts, and corporate worship. This event shows the lifting of the stigma and suspicion of the arts amongst conservative Christians as well as a broadened understanding and appreciation of cultural engagement in the UK these days. Founding father of the festival, John Peck, a poet and pastor, relished the work of Hans Rookmaaker and Francis Schaeffer. Peck also lends his wisdom to Christian Artists (CA) in the Netherlands.

Two other initiatives that bear an influence of Rookmaaker in the UK are the Leith School of Art (LSA) in Edinburgh and the Theology Through the Arts (TTA) project, now a part of the Institute for Theology, Imagination and the Arts (ITIA), a new research unit, based at the University of St Andrews with links at the University of Cambridge. Philip Archer, artist and principal of LSA, attests that Rookmaaker set them on a path that they continue to travel. Eleven years ago after the tragic deaths of Mark and Lottie Cheverton, founders of the school,

Philip was invited to head its administration. While Archer knew Rookmaaker, he is glad to have Paul Martin teaching alongside him who knew him better. Paul believes, 'Rookmaaker was one of the most important influences of the 1960s and 1970s beginning the work of "justifying the ways of God to man" through the arts.'

Jeremy Begbie, theologian and musician, the creative shaper of Theology Through the Arts, is not only one of a sizable list of theological educators influenced by the thought of Hans Rookmaaker, he is himself a sizable industry in theology and the arts! Begbie spearheads research colloquia, publishing projects, experiments in artistic creation as well as the supervision of graduate research students in theology and the arts; he also does a great deal of public lecturing and scholarly writing. Today, the TTA project he launched at the University of Cambridge is more like a movement – a movement to think differently about the arts in relation to theology. It turns the abstraction of a theology of the arts that tends to wander off into woolly vagueness on its head, and brings into focus a genuine respect for concrete works of art and artistic practices that can be theologically explored and exegeted with precision for their intellectual meaning, cultural relevance, and spiritual discovery. In this lies one of the most important affinities TTA has with Rookmaaker's thought. One might almost say that it took a Jeremy Begbie to come along to give a name to the approach to the arts that Rookmaaker was a master practitioner of. Neither the breadth of Rookmaaker's intellectual interests and cultural concerns, nor his deep regard for philosophical issues, ever took him away from the concrete and the specific, from cultural analysis or philosophizing through the consideration of particular works of art embedded in history or present reality. He never took works of art as a pretext for explaining or illustrating his ideas or theories. Begbie's discussion of Rookmaaker and art in his book *Voicing Creation's Praise* (T & T Clark, 1991) is a key document in placing Hans's work in the context and tradition of Dutch Neo-Calvinism.

Besides Begbie, many other musicians have felt the influence of Rookmaaker. Ric Ashley, Professor of Music and Composition at Northwestern University (Evanston, IL), has spent extended time in the Netherlands and studied Hans's works in Dutch. In respect for his time at Dutch L'Abri and the benefit of Rookmaaker's conversations with him, Peter Anthony Monk, a contemporary composer, dedicated one of his works to him. More popularly oriented musicians have also appreciated him. In 1985 Garth Hewitt, sometimes described as a British activist-troubadour counterpart to Bruce Cockburn, dedicated his album *Alien Brain* to Hans. The late Mark Heard, perhaps one of Christian rock's most respected singers and writers, clearly expressed his appreciation for Rookmaaker. Hans's impact has reverberated long for British poets and writers Steve Turner and the American-based Steve Scott as well.

How does one sum up the influence of Hans Rookmaaker's life? Several impressions of the man and his work stand out. First and strikingly, there was his refreshing modesty, lack of pretension, and willingness to be a servant of the arts and artists, and in this, a servant of Christ and his church. This set him apart from many of his academic peers who were sequestered in their professional work. Secondly, there was his love of life, all of life: music, art, good food and drink, good conservation, new experiences, new friends. Thirdly, he had the ability to discern the gifts that young men and women whom he met along the way possessed and to encourage them to move in the direction that would best develop their God-given gifts, giving them freedom to be themselves. Fourthly, he was a willing mentor to many young adults, both scholars and artists, in a wide variety of vocations. It is especially noteworthy that he mentored a remarkable number of women as well as men. This was unusual for his time, as it is perhaps even today. Fifthly, he was a bridge builder, linking the scholarship of art to the work of artists, celebrating all of the arts and developing a broad mastery of different eras and disciplines, communicating effectively with both scholars and the general public. Sixthly, he sought to reclaim the arts for the Reformed Christian faith. Although there is still much land to be possessed, the contributions of Rookmaaker's intellectual and spiritual children and grandchildren bear witness to the progress that has been made in the past half century and give much hope for the next. Seventhly, he was committed to living and thinking as a Christian in the midst of the world rather than in a cloistered sectarian shelter. And he challenged all who came under his influence to do likewise.

In the first three months of 1977, Hans had been busy as usual. The first of January was a special day, not just because it was the first day of the year, but also because the Chapel in the Barn at Eck en Wiel was dedicated, and Edith and Fran Schaeffer were there from Switzerland to help celebrate this occasion. It was the last time they were to see Hans. Just a few days later, Hans was off to the USA. For many years he attended a gathering for the Association for Reformational Philosophy at this time of year. But he did not do this in 1977. Eleanor DeLorme, a friend who is an art historian at Wellesley College in Massachusetts, remembers that she and her husband drove him to the airport for his flight back to Holland. Soon he was going full tilt back into university life, and yet at a bit of a remove from it, as he and Anky had been living in Ommeren, not far from L'Abri at Eck en Wiel since 1975, and it was necessary for Hans to commute. Happily, however, he enjoyed overnighting when he did go into Amsterdam with Graham Birtwistle, who had taken over the Walfords' charming cottage near the Amstel. He had plans to go to Edinburgh in May and then in July to Canada to teach in Ontario and possibly go on to Vancouver.

On Sunday morning, 13 March, the Rookmaakers went to church in the newly dedicated chapel at L'Abri. Wim Rietkerk preached. The air was crisp, and the day was quiet. They went home for a peaceful afternoon. But Hans did not feel well. By 8 p.m. in the evening he was gone, dying with an expression of surprise and delight without any sense of horror.

From the time of his conversion Hans was practicing prophetic preparedness: 'Watch therefore – for you do not know when the master of the house will come, in the evening, or at midnight, or at cockcrow, or in the morning.' How like his beloved Bach cantata, *Wachet auf, ruft uns die Stimme.* Or, *Gottes Zeit is die allerbeste Zeit.*

On Wednesday, 16 March, Hans's funeral took place in the pre-Reformation church in Eck en Wiel. Wim preached on '"Blessed are the dead who from now on die in the Lord." "Yes," says the Spirit, "they will rest from their labours, for their deeds follow them."' (Revelation 14:13b) – the text chosen by his family and cited at the beginning of this chapter. Hans's request for his funeral was honoured with Mahalia Jackson's rendition of

> Soon one evening, I'm going home to live on high ...
> 'Gonna move on up a little higher ...
> It will be howdy, howdy and never goodbye.

Hans was buried in the small cemetery in Eck en Wiel. His gravestone is simple and completely open in the middle – a fitting memorial for an open life.

Appendix I: Chronology

1848   Henderik Roelof Rookmaaker (1848–1905), grandfather of H.R.R., born. Later became an Assistant-Resident in the colonial administration of the Dutch East Indies.

1887   August 21. Henderik Roelof Rookmaaker, senior, father of H.R.R., born. Later became Resident in the colonial administration of the Dutch East Indies.

1890   March 17. Theodora Catharina Heitink, H.R.R.'s mother, born.

1897   J. P. A. (Johan Pieter Albertus) Mekkes, mentor and friend of H.R.R., born.

1911   H.R. Rookmaaker, senior graduates from the University of Leiden with studies colonial administration.

        August 25. H.R. Rookmaaker, senior marries Theodora Catharina Heitink.

1912   November 28. Theodora Catharina Rookmaaker, H.R.R.'s sister, born.

1912   January 30. Francis A. Schaeffer born.

1914   March 3. Henrietta Christina Rookmaaker, H.R.R.'s sister, born.

1915   August 15. Anna Marie (Anky) Huitker, H.R.R.'s wife, born in Sindanglaoet, Indonesia.

1919   May 10. Hendrika Beatrix (Riki) Spetter, H.R.R.'s fiancée, born.

1920   The Rookmaaker family returns to The Hague for H.R.R., senior to pursue further studies in colonial administration

1922   February 27. Henderik Roelof Rookmaaker born in The Hague.

1924   The Rookmaaker family resumes living again in the Dutch Indies.

1927   H.R. Rookmaaker, senior goes on an expedition to capture twelve Komodo dragons on Rintja in the Dutch Indies.

        H.R. Rookmaaker identifies a new species of frog (*Oreophryne rookmaakeri*).

1929   H.R. Rookmaaker, senior becomes Assistent-Resident at Lho Semaweh (Lhokseumawe) on the north coast of Aceh in Sumatra, Dutch Indies.

1930   H.R. Rookmaaker identifies a new species of shell creature (*Xesta rookmaakeri*).

1931   The Rookmaaker family returns to The Hague for a year's leave.

1932   H.R.R. living once again in the Dutch Indies.

1936   H. R. Rookmaaker, senior retires to The Hague due to ill health. H.R.R. is becoming an avid and discriminating collector of recorded African-American music.

1937   H.R. Rookmaaker, senior's official Residency in the Dutch Indies terminated.

1938   H.R.R. is a midshipman (*adelborst*) at the Royal Netherlands Naval College at Den Helder.

1940   H.R.R. is engaged to Hendrika Beatrix (Riki) Spetter.

May 10. The German occupation of the Netherlands.

1941   March 4. H.R.R. arrested for possession of anti-German literature and held in Scheveningen Prison in The Hague until December.

1942   April. H.R.R., as a commissioned officer, ordered by the Nazis to Breda and immediately incarcerated and transferred to a POW camp at Langwasser near Nuremberg.

August 18. Riki Spetter is last seen at Westerbork.

September 30. Riki Spetter dies at Auschwitz. (A fact H.R.R. never knew during his lifetime.)

By the autumn, H.R.R. incarcerated at Stanislau (today Ivano Frankivsk) in western Ukraine.

Japanese invasion(s) of Dutch East Indies.

1943   H.R.R. meets J.P.A. Mekkes in Stanislau POW camp in late summer.

September 19. H.R.R. dedicates to Riki Spetter his study of the Old Testament Prophets, *Betreffende de Profetie*.

1944   February H.R.R. transferred to a POW camp at Neubrandenburg in northern Germany

1945   January 31. H.R. Rookmaaker, senior dies of a heart attack in The Hague.

May 5. Liberation of the Netherlands.

May 8. Armistice in Europe.

Summer. H.R.R. makes his way back to The Hague.

September 2. Armistice in the Pacific.

August 17. Indonesian independence declared.

1947   H.R.R. founds the Vereniging van Gereformeerde Studenten te Amsterdam (VGSA).

H.R.R. is engaged to Anky Huitker.

August. H.R.R. meets Francis Schaeffer in Amsterdam.

1949   H.R.R. passes his *kandidaats* examination (equivalent to a bachelor's degree).

June 1. H.R.R. and Anna Marie (Anky) Huitker married at Amsterdam.

	H.R.R. starts writing art criticism for *Trouw*, a daily newspaper.
1950	July 15. Henderik Roelof Rookmaaker, son of Hans and Anky Rookmaaker, is born at Amsterdam.
1953	February 21. Leendert Cornelis (Kees) Rookmaaker, son of Hans and Anky Rookmaaker, is born at Amsterdam.
1954	August 26. Maria Helena (Marleen) Rookmaaker, daughter of Hans and Anky Rookmaaker, is born in Amsterdam.
1955	February. Francis and Edith Schaeffer threatened with expulsion from Switzerland. The inauguration of the L'Abri Fellowship. Summer. The Rookmaakers and their three children spend six weeks with the Schaeffers in Switzerland.
1956	H.R.R. stops writing for *Trouw* and turns his focus full-time to obtaining a doctorate in art history at the University of Amsterdam.
1957	H.R.R. begins teaching at the University of Leiden. The Rookmaaker family moves from Amsterdam to Leiden
1958	Hans and Anky formalize their connection with the Schaeffers as the representatives of L'Abri Fellowship in the Netherlands.
1959	July 7. H.R.R. receives his doctorate from the University of Amsterdam.
1960	Publication of *Jazz, blues, spirituals* (Zomer & Keuning).
1961	H.R.R. makes his first visit to the United States and Canada on a Dutch government grant to research the teaching of art history in North America.
1964	H.R.R. is invited to be Professor of Art History at The Free University of Amsterdam. The Rookmaaker family moves from Leiden to Diemen, near Amsterdam.
1965	May 28. H.R.R. gives his inaugural address, 'The Artist as a Prophet?', as Professor of Art History at The Free University of Amsterdam. H.R.R. begins traveling regularly to Great Britain through links with L'Abri Fellowship and Inter-Varsity Fellowship (now UCCF). Anky Rookmaaker founds *Redt een Kind* (Save a Child), organization in support of orphans and poor children in India and Africa.
1970	H.R.R. publishes *Modern Art and the Death of a Culture* (IVP) H.R.R. begins traveling regularly to North America after teaching in this year at a summer school at Regent College (Vancouver, BC Canada).

	December 20. Malcolm Muggeridge makes *Modern Art and the Death of a Culture* one of his Observer Books of the Year.
1971	Dutch L'Abri is founded.
	July 12. Theodora Catharina Rookmaaker, H.R.R.'s mother, dies in The Hague.
1975	Hans and Anky Rookmaaker move to Ommeren.
1977	March 13. H.R.R. dies in Ommeren.
	March 16. H.R.R. buried at Eck en Wiel.
1984	May 15. Francis A. Schaeffer dies in Rochester, Minnesota, USA.
1987	J.P.A. Mekkes dies.
1989	Theodora Catharina (Door) Haver Droeze, elder sister of H.R.R., dies.
2002	Henrietta Christina (Hannie) Rotgans, younger sister of H.R.R., dies.
2003	February 10. Anky Rookmaaker, widow of H.R.R., dies at Hardenberg.

Appendix II: Sources

Notes to Preface

The late Linette Martin wrote a brief study of the life of H.R. Rookmaaker shortly after his death, entitled *Hans Rookmaaker: A Biography* (London: Hodder & Stoughton; Downers Grove: IVP, 1979). Until now, this is the only book-length biography that has written on him. Recently, Graham Birtwistle has written a succinct entry on 'Henderik Roelof Rookmaaker (1922–1977)', in the *Biographical Dictionary of Evangelicals*, edited by Timothy Larsen (Downers Grove and Leicester: Inter-Varsity Press, 2003), pp.563–565. Birtwistle has also contributed an essay on 'H.R. Rookmaaker: The Shaping of his Thought' in the first volume of the *Complete Works* (*CW* 1:xv–xxxiii). Jeremy S. Begbie's *Voicing Creation's Praise* (Edinburgh: T. & T. Clark, 1991), pp.127–141, offers a perspective on Rookmaaker's aesthetic as it relates to the neo-Calvinist tradition. A list of writings commenting on the work and thought of H.R.R. is included in this volume (*CW* 6:434–446).

Primary documents for the life and work of Hans Rookmaaker that have been consulted extensively in preparation of this biography include: *The Complete Works of Hans R. Rookmaaker* 1–6, edited by Marleen Hengelaar-Rookmaaker (Carlisle: Piquant, 2002–2003), which were in process of being edited as I was writing; Hans Rookmaaker Papers in the Special Collections of the Buswell Memorial Library, Wheaton College, Wheaton, Illinois, USA (see Appendix B at the end of this volume); papers, photographs, letters, official documents, annual appointment agendas, in the possession of the Rookmaaker family. In the interests of readibility, liberty has been taken to make minor stylistic changes to some of the letters without changing the meaning.

From 1970 to 1977 I had serious and sustained personal conversations with H.R.R. in Vancouver, Seattle, Amsterdam, Eck en Wiel, Lausanne, Huémoz (Switzerland), Mittersill (Austria), London, and other locations in the UK. During this time I had the opportunity of hearing H.R.R. lecture in many different contexts. I have also had extensive personal communication with members of the Rookmaaker family and a multitude of his former students, friends, colleagues, associates, and others who have been greatly influenced by him.

Notes to Chapter 1

The American Bible Society Gallery is located in mid-Manhattan (1865 Broadway, New York, NY 10023, <www.americanbible.org/gallery>). On the

2000 exhibition of images of Christ at the National Gallery, see Gabriel Finaldi et al., *The Image of Christ* (London: National Gallery Company Ltd, 2000), a catalogue of the exhibition; Neil MacGregor with Erika Langmuir, *Seeing Salvation: Images of Christ in Art* (London: BBC, 2000); and 'Nigel Halliday Talks to Neil MacGregor', *Third Way* (March 2000), pp.17–21. On the development of contemporary Christian rock music, see John J. Thompson, *Raised By Wolves: The Story of Christian Rock & Roll* (Toronto: ECW, 2000). See the websites of Christians in the Visual Arts, <www.civa.org>, *Image: A Journal of the Arts & Religion*, <www.imagejournal.org>, Christelijke Academie voor de Beeldende Kunsten/CABK, Kampen, <www.huygens.nl/21000_frame.htm>, and Leith School of Art, Edinburgh <www.leithschoolofart.co.uk>.

Sources of information on the life and travels of Rookmaaker in this chapter include: his annual appointment agendas, letters and papers in the Special Collections at Wheaton College and in the possession of the Rookmaaker family. His book, *Jazz, blues, spirituals*, was originally written in Dutch (Wageningen: Zomer & Keuning, 1960) but is now available in English in *CW* (2:157–311). Quote from Tony Wales is from his obituary, 'H.R. Rookmaaker', *Third Way* (1/6 [24 March 1977]), p.10. The review by Michael Shepherd is from the British journal, *Art News*, in 1971; I have a copy of the review with a note from H.R.R. indicating the source, but I have been unable to locate exact issue and page number. Muggeridge lists *Modern Art and the Death of a Culture* as one of his four nominations for Books of the Year for *The Observer* (20 December 1970), p.17; see also *Esquire* 75 (March 1971), p.16.

The quotations from Rookmaaker on 'the new art' and 'new vision of humanity' come from his essay on 'Commitment in Art' (originally published in *Art and the Public Today* [Huémoz-sur-Ollon: L'Abri Fellowship Foundation, 1968], pp.5–21 = CW 5:188–203). H.R.R.'s study on Gauguin was published as *Synthetist Art Theories* (Amsterdam: Swets and Zeitlinger, 1959); rev. ed. Published as *Gauguin and 19th Century Art Theory* (Amsterdam: Swets and Zeitlinger, 1972) = *CW* 1:3–227. Quotation from Nicholas Wolterstorff is from his article 'On Looking at Paintings: A Look at Rookmaaker', *Reformed Journal* (February 1972), pp.11–15. Information from Alva Steffler is based on personal communication with the author (November 16, 2002). J.I. Packer dubbed H.R.R. 'the pipe-puffing pundit of Amsterdam' in 'All That Jazz', *Christianity Today* 30/18 (December 12, 1986), p.15. Michael Shepherd (in his review quoted above) described him as 'the Dutch Kenneth Clark'. On Decimal Index of Art of the Low Countries (DIAL)/Iconclass, see <www.iconclass.nl>. F.F. Bruce's comments are from his article 'Regent College, Vancouver', *The Witness* (Nov 1970), pp.418–419. David McKenna's letter to H.R.R. is in Wheaton Special Collections. Testimonials of housewife and businessman were oral comments to me by Regent College summer school students.

Notes to Chapter 2

Information contained in this chapter is based on extensive interviews with members of the Rookmaaker family and review of family papers and photographs. On a visit to Indonesia in 1981, I verified some details of H.R.R, senior's administrative tenure in the Dutch East Indies by consulting with the authorities in Jakarta who were then the custodians of the documentation of the former colonial administration. L.C. (Kees) Rookmaaker, 'The life of H. R. Rookmaaker (1887–1945), pioneer of nature conservation in the Dutch East Indies,' *Säugetierkundliche Mitteilungen* 41/1 (1998), pp.2–6. Family sources date the birth of H.R.R., senior in 1887; however, some government sources give the year of his birth as 1888.

Notes to Chapter 3

The quotation from the elder H.R.R. to his reluctant children was given in a chapel talk by Hans Rookmaaker at Regent College in 1972. On this same occasion H.R.R. mentioned that he learned all his theology from Jelly Roll Morton! The substance of the material contained in this chapter was again obtained from conversations with the Rookmaaker family and from papers, letters, documents, and photographs in their possession. A short history of the Royal Netherlands Naval College at Den Helder is contained on their website <www.kim.nl/rnlnc/htm/rnlnchistory.htm>.

Notes to Chapter 4

Details for this chapter stem from personal letters of Hans Rookmaaker, his family, and Riki Spetter. Information concerning the internment camp at Langwasser near Nuremberg is found on the website of Stadt Nürnberg <www.museen.nuernberg.de/english/reichsparteitag_e/pages/bauten_e.html>. Information concerning the movement of Dutch prisoners from the POW camp at Colditz Castle to Stalag 371 at Stanislau [Ivano Frankivsk, Ukraine] in June of 1943 came from <www.geocities.com/schlosscolditz/colditz.html>. L. Martin and others have incorrectly located Stanislau in Poland. Even today, Stanislau is still the German identification of Ivano Frankivsk. The four longish quotations from Hans concerning his internment are from his reflections on the history of the Cosmonomic Idea (see *CW* 2:10–12). The original manuscripts of *Betreffende de Profetie* and *Aesthetica* written in prison are in the Special Collections at Wheaton College. The former document is found in *CW* 6:19–119 as 'Prophecy in the Old and New Testaments: God's Way with Israel'. The Bible Rookmaaker used was the so-called 'Utrecht Translation' by H. Th. Obbink and A. M. Brouwer of 1942. 'Aesthetica' was first published in two parts in *Philosophia Reformata* (1946–1947) and is found in *CW* 2:24–79 as 'Sketch for an Aesthetic Theory based on the Philosophy of the Cosmonomic Idea'. Herman Dooyeweerd's major philosophical work that gave Rookmaaker a framework for his work as a Christian scholar is the three volume *De Wijsbegeerte der Wetsidee* (1935–1936), which was later expanded and translated into English as *A New Critique of Theoretical Thought*, 3 vols (Philadelphia: Presbyterian and Reformed Publishing Co., 1969). On Dooyeweerd, see J. Begbie, *Voicing Creation's Praise*, pp.106–126. The collected works of Dooyeweerd are being translated into English and published in two, multi-volume series under the general editorship of D.F.M. Strauss through the Dooyeweerd Centre at Redeemer University College in Ancaster, Ontario, Canada and published by Mellen Press. For information about the publications, visit the website of the Dooyeweerd Centre at <www.redeemer.on.ca/dooyeweerdcentre>.

The history and names of the variety of Reformed churches in the Netherlands are confusing even to those who read Dutch. Rookmaaker found his spiritual home with a group of congregations that had broken away from the *Gereformeerde Kerken in Nederland* (GKN), founded by Abraham Kuyper and associates near the end of the nineteenth century, in 1944 to form the *Gereformeerde Kerken* (*Vrijgemaakt*, GK(v)). In 1966–1967 the GK(v) experienced its own schism, leading to the founding of the Reformed Churches (Liberated, Unconnected), today the Netherlands Reformed Churches (NGK). Rookmaaker sided with the NGK, which has close links with the Christian Reformed Churches in the USA and Canada. See *The Reformed Family Worldwide*, edd. Jean-Jacques Bauswein and Lukas Vischer (Grand Rapids: Eerdmans, 1999), pp.383–394. Roel Kuiper and Marleen Hengelaar-Rookmaaker were helpful in clarifying the date and details of the schism.

Notes to Chapter 5

Details for this chapter are dependent on personal letters, papers, documents, and oral information from Hans and Anky Rookmaaker and their family. On the liberation of Neubrandenburg, see <www.aiipowmia.com/wwii/wwiiwkgrp.html>. On Rookmaaker's intensive study of the biblical prophets and also the work of Dooyeweerd and the Philosophy of the Cosmonomic Idea, see notes on chapter 4 (above). My last conversation with Hans's sister, Hannie Rotgans took place in July 2001. See also notes on chapter 4 (above) on the Reformed Church. For Rookmaaker's earliest work on aesthetics, see *CW* 2:24–79. Much information concerning Anky Rookmaaker and her family is found in her chapter, ' Lifting Up Holy Hands', in Lane T. Dennis, ed., *Francis Schaeffer: Portraits of the Man and His Work* (Westchester: Crossway, 1986), pp.153–162. On Castle Eerde and the story of Krishnamurti, see <www.nevenzel.com/eerde.htm>. Information concerning the date and place of Riki Spetter's death was obtained from the Center for Research on Dutch Jewry at the Hebrew University of Jerusalem, see <http://www.snunit.k12.il/sachlav/dutch/maineng/search.html>. The quotation from Nobel Prizewinner Czeslaw Milosz is from his book *The Land of Ulro* (New York: Farrar, Straus and Giroux, 1984), p.152. Reference to '"personal knowledge" in the Polanyian sense' refers to Michael Polanyi's classic work, *Personal Knowledge: Towards a Post-Critical Philosophy* (New York: Harper & Row, 1964). On the work of Dooyeweerd, see notes on chapter 4.

I am indebted to Marleen Hengelaar-Rookmaaker for information on the history of the VGSA. Interestingly enough, she was the first woman president of the group when she was a student at the University of Amsterdam. It is also where she met her husband, Albert Hengelaar. On the International Council of Christian Churches, see *The Reformed Family Worldwide*, pp.705–706; and D. K. Larsen, 'Carl McIntire (1906–2002)', in *Biographical Dictionary of Evangelicals*, pp.393–395. On Francis and Edith Schaeffer and the work of L'Abri Fellowship, see C. Duriez, 'Francis August Schaeffer (1912–1984)', *Biographical Dictionary of Evangelicals*, pp.582–585; and Lane T. Dennis, ed., *Francis Schaeffer: Portraits of the Man and His Work*. The majority of Rookmaaker's exhibition reviews for *Trouw* are contained in *CW* 1:229–361, but some are also included in *CW* 4:461–479 and *CW* 5:361–379.

Detailed bibliographical information on Rookmaaker's doctoral dissertation, *Synthetist Art Theories* (1959); rev. ed., *Gauguin and 19th Century Art Theory* (1972) = *CW* 1:3–227 is contained in notes to chapter 1 (above). On van Regteren Altena, see the electronic *A Biographical Dictionary of Historians, Museum Directors and Scholars of Art (DAH)* <www.lib.duke.edu/lilly/artlibry/dah/regterna.htm>. Graham Birtwistle's essay is found in *CW* 1:xv–xxxiii. On De Stijl movement, see H.L.C. Jaffé, *De Stijl, 1917–1931: The Dutch Contribution to Modern Art* (Amsterdam: Meulenhoff, 1956; repr. 1986). See Jaffé's obituary of H.R.R. in *Lier en Boog* (Jan 1978), p.82. Jan Bialostocki's comments on van de Waal is in his review of van de Waal's *Drie eeuwen vaderlandsche geschied-uitbeelding, 1500–1800: Een iconologische studie* (1952) in *The Art Bulletin* 52 (1971), p.264. On van de Waal, see *DAH* <www.lib.duke.edu/lilly/artlibry/dah/vandewaalh.htm> and R.H. Fuchs, 'Henri van de Waal, 1910–1972', in *Simiolus* 6/1 (1972/73), pp.5–7. On the RKD, see <www.rkd.nl/frame-e.htm>. On DIAL, see notes to chapter 1. Information concerning Seerveld and Schaeffer's writing to H.R.R.'s dissertation committee is contained in letters, which are in the Special Collections at Wheaton College. For information on *Redt een Kind* (Save a Child), see <www.redteenkind.org/en/>.

Notes to Chapter 6

On Mekkes, see 'Bij het sterven van prof. Dr. J.P.A. Mekkes', *Nederlands Dagblad* (29 July 1987). On Vollenhoven, the colleague and brother-in-law of Dooyeweerd, see 'Vollenhoven, Scriptural Philosophy, and Christian Higher Education', by John H. Kok <http://home.planet.nl/~srw/vollen/volkok.htm>. On Schaeffer, see notes to chapter 5 (above). On Abraham Kuyper, see J. D. Bratt in *Biographical Dictionary of Evangelicals*, pp.351–354; Peter S. Heslam, *Creating a Christian Worldview: Abraham Kuyper's Lectures on Calvinism* (Grand Rapids: Eerdmans, 1998); and *Kuyper Reconsidered: Aspects of His Life and Work*, eds. Cornelis van der Kooi and Jan de Bruijn (Amsterdam: VU Uitgeverij, 1999). Kuyper's 1898 Stone Lectures at Princeton Theological Seminary were published in Dutch and English in 1889 (Amsterdam, London, Edinburgh and New York). Since 1931, Eerdmans has had the copyright for the English edition of *Lectures on Calvinism* and has kept the book in print until today. On the various American Presbyterian groups to which Schaeffer was connected, see *Reformed Family Worldwide*, pp.522, 532, 534, 537. On the spiritual hunger of the West in the 1960s, see Camille Paglia, 'Cults and Cosmic Consciousness: Religious Vision in America in the 1960s', *Arion* (Winter 2003) <www.bu.edu/arion/paglia_cults00.htm>. On the Dutch L'Abri, see <www.labri.nl/> and <www.labri.nl/home_en.htm>. On Cornelius Van Til, see J.M. Frame in *Biographical Dictionary of Evangelicals*, pp.682–684. Van Swigchem wrote a brief history of the department of art history of the Free University in 2001, to which I was kindly given access courtesy of Graham Birtwistle. Information about L'Abri, the Schaeffers, and the Rookmaakers comes from correspondence in Special Collections at Wheaton College as well as L'Abri family letters in the possession of the Rookmaaker family. Comments of Rookmaaker concerning Schaeffer in his inaugural address are included in the introduction to *Art and the Public Today*, p.3 = *CW* 5:167. Rookmaaker's *Kunst en Amusemusement* (Kampen: J.H. Kok, 1962) is translated into English as 'Art and Entertainment', *CW* 3:1–131. Information concerning Seerveld and Rookmaaker is based on personal conversations and letters in Special Collections at Wheaton College. *Modern Art and the Death of a Culture* (London: Inter-Varsity Press, 1970) is found in *CW* 5:1–164. Both David Alexander and H.R.R. expressed warm appreciation for their collaborative relationship. In fact, in recognition of the fact that Alexander had been so helpful in the copy-editing of his English style, Rookmaaker went so far as to suggest that his name should be included on the title page, but Alexander demurred. Rookmaaker confessed: 'He greatly improved my English style while retaining my voice!' Rookmaaker's 'provocative' quote on Christian standards comes from L. Martin, p.146. 'Letter to a Christian Artist' is now in *CW* 3:209–213. The quotation, 'How can you say modern art is ugly when you worship the Lord in a building painted like *this*?' is taken from *Arts & Minds: The Story of Nigel Goodwin* by David Porter (London:

Houghton and Stoughton, 1993), p.109. Quotes on van Goyen and to student come from Linette Martin, p.138.

Notes to Chapter 7

As we move into the era of more recent history, more and more of the details are dependent on personal interviews, informal conversations, and personal correspondence (both 'email' and 'snail mail') with participants in the story, in addition to the usual written documents contained in the Rookmaaker Archives of the Special Collections at Wheaton College and in the possession of the Rookmaaker family.

J.H. van den Berg, *Metabletica, of Leer der veranderingen: beginselen van een historische psychologie* (Nijkerk: Callenbach, 1956); E.T. *The Changing Nature of Man* (New York: Norton, 1961). The phrase, 'theology through the arts', represents a movement that has been spearheaded by Jeremy S. Begbie, see <www.theoarts.org>. On art monuments as historical documents, see Margaret R. Miles, *Image as Insight: Visual Understanding in Western Christianity and Secular Culture* (Boston: Beacon Press, 1985). On Groen van Prinsterer, see Harry Van Dyke, ed. and trans., *Groen Van Prinsterer's Lectures on Unbelief and Revolution* (Jordan Station, ON, Canada: Wedge Publishing Foundation, 1989), pp.39–83. Translation is available in electronic form at <http://capo.org/gvp.htm>. The quote from Kuyper is from his *Lectures on Calvinism* (Grand Rapids: Eerdmans, [1931] 1976), pp.165–166. Experience and quotation from David Muir was passed on to me in a communication from Elria Kwant (April 2003). Recollection of Sharon Gallagher was communicated to me personally (March 2003). For a contemporary discussion on the visual arts in Calvinism see Paul Corby Finney, ed., *Seeing Beyond the Word: Visual Arts and the Calvinist Tradition* (Grand Rapids: Eerdmans, 1999).

Notes to Chapter 8

I have had more than one occasion in recent years to be in personal contact with or to have communication from the majority of the individuals mentioned in this chapter. Some I have known for a considerable amount of time. I have expressed appreciation in my acknowledgments to those who have provided me with helpful information; hence, it would be too tedious to repeat the names of these individuals in the notes. Rather, I will seek to offer literary documentation of a few specific details and will reserve the bulk of the space here to list websites with which the individuals and organizations mentioned are associated. In many cases, the interested reader will be able to learn a great deal about the work of the people and groups that have in some manner been influenced by the life and vision of Hans Rookmaaker.

Comments by Peter Smith are from a review of Rookmaaker's *Complete Works* 1-2 for *ArtsMedia* 3 (Autumn 2002, conveyed to me in electronic form). The observations by Rachel Smith were made in a personal communication at the Christians in the Visual Arts biennial conference (June 2003). Information from and concerning Graham Birtwistle has been by way of recent email and fax exchanges as well as personal conversation since we were students in England in the late 1960s. Rookmaaker's positive evaluation of the art of Georges Rouault is in *CW* 5:236-239. Information on John Walford is from articles in the *Wheaton Record* (25 September 1981): *Wheaton* alumni magazine 15/6 (2002), pp.20-21; an audiotape produced during a visit of Anky Rookmaaker and Marleen Hengelaar-Rookmaaker to the Wheaton College campus (1985); and personal communication. Rookmaaker corresponded with Panofsky about his work on Michelangelo (*CW* 4:73-101), met Frederick Hartt in Italy, received a visit from Bialostoki in Amsterdam, and corresponded with Nochlin and Chipp. The interview by art history students at the Free University is found in *CW* 3:496-501. H.R.R.'s use of the example of Descartes as an illustration of tolerance and intellectual freedom in the Calvinist heritage is found in his Westminster discussions on television and film (*CW* 3:455-459). Susan Snell, 'History of CA', (2000), <www.continentals.nl/downloads/HistoryCA.pdf>, gives an overview of Christian Artists Association. *Reality Revisited by Six Dutch Painters,* by Hans van Seventer and JoAnn van Seventer (Zwiggelte: The Zwiggelte Group, 1982) documents the early work of Dutch artists influenced by Rookmaaker. Quotation from Mary Leigh Morbey is from an email message (June 2003). On Sempangi's early work, see his book, *A Distant Grief* (Glendale: G/L Publications, 1979). For Kwame Bediako's vision, see his *Theology & Identity: The Impact of Culture Upon Christian Thought in the Second Century and Modern Africa* (Oxford: Regnum Books, 1992). Peter Heslam's comment is from his essay on 'A Theology of the Arts: Kuyper's Ideas on Art and Religion', in *Kuyper Reconsidered* (Amsterdam: VU Uitgeverij, 1999), p.25. On Nigel Goodwin, see the biography by David Porter (mentioned in notes to chapter 6). David and Tricia Porter, *Over the Bent World* (Carlisle: Paternoster Press, 1999). Comment from Paul Martin is from a personal letter to the author by Philip Archer (May 2003). Some of the information concerning musicians influenced by Rookmaaker was obtained from Thompson's *Raised By Wolves* (see notes to chapter 1); others come from personal knowledge.

Website Links for People and Organizations Mentioned in Chapter 8

Names are listed in the order in which they are mentioned in the narrative. I was unable to find a web link for the people mentioned but not listed.

Peter Smith, artist and educator, Kingston College, UK
<www.kingston-college.ac.uk/d>

Rachael Smith, art historian, Taylor University
<http://www.tayloru.edu/upland/academics/departments/visualarts.html>

Graham Birtwistle, art historian, Free University of Amsterdam <www.vu.nl>

John Walford, art historian, Wheaton College
<http://www.wheaton.edu/homeArt.html>

Paul Martin, artist and educator, Leith School of Art
<www.theartroom.net> and <www.leithschoolofart.co.uk>

Sandra Martin, artist and educator, Leith School of Art
<www.leithschoolofart.co.uk>

Martin Rose, artist <www.theartroom.net>

Kate Rose, artist <www.theartroom.net>

Meryl and Malcolm Doney, authors and impresarios, The Art Room
<www.theartroom.net>

James Romaine, author and art historian
<http://squarehalobooks.com/oog.htm>

Ned Bustard, artist and publisher, Square Halo Books
<www.SquareHaloBooks.com>

Marc de Klijn, artist and author
<www.solcon.nl/langeveld/keerpunt/k/klijn-marc-de-schilder.htm>

Hans and JoAnn van Seventer, publishers, writers and producers
<http://www.defilmderedding.nl/content/aanzet.html>

Nederlandse Christelijke Radio
<http://info.omroep.nl/ncrv/home?nav=ijcgFsHtGPJqK>

Evangelische Omroep <www.eo.nl/home/html/home.jsp>

Christelijk Academie voor de Beeldende Kunsten/CABK
<http://www.huygens.nl/21000_frame.htm>

Christian Artists Vereniging voor Beeldende Kunsten (CABK)
<www.continentals.nl>

Christian Artists Association (Kunstenbond-CNV or CA) <www.continentals.nl>

Leen La Riviére, impresario <www.continentals.nl>

Jan van Loon, artist <www.stoneart.nl/realisten/vanloon.html>

Henk Helmantel, artist <www.helmantel.nl>

Rein Pol, artist <http://www.stoneart.nl/realisten/pol.html>

Jan van der Scheer, artist <www.galeries.nl/mnkunstenaar.asp?artistnr=4314&vane=1&sessionti=340898117>

Jan Zwaan, artist <www.galeriebakker.nl/pages/kunstenaars/JanZwaan>

Christelijk Studiecentrum ICS <www.impactnetwerk.nl>

International Fellowship of Evangelical Students (IFES) <www.ifesworld.org/defaulthome.asp>

Wim and Greta Rietkerk, senior staff, Dutch L'Abri <www.labri.nl>

Pieter and Elria Kwant, Piquant <www.piquant.net>

L'Abri International <www.labri.org>

Swiss L'Abri <http://www.labri.org/switzerland.html>

British L'Abri <http://www.labri.org/england.html>

H.G. (Henk) Geertsema, philosopher, Vereniging voor Reformatorische Wijsbegeerte <http://home.planet.nl/~srw/home.htm>

Mary Leigh Morbey, art historian, York University, Canada <www.edu.yorku.ca:8080/~mmorbey/home.htm>

H.R. (Hans) Rookmaaker, rector, Christelijk Gymnasium Sorghvliet, The Hague <www.sorghvliet.demon.nl>

L.C. (Kees) Rookmaaker, Special Advisor, International Rhino Foundation <www.rhinoresourcecenter.com/>

Marleen Hengelaar-Rookmaaker, editor, LEV <www.labri.nl> and <www.piquant.net/PDFs/Rookmaaker_cat.pdf>

Calvin Seerfeld (emeritus), Institute for Christian Studies
<www.icscanada.edu/faculty/index.shtml> and
<www.seerveld.com/tuppence.html>

T. Grady Spires (emeritus), Gordon College <www.gordon.edu>

Gordon College, Art Department <www.gordon.edu/academics/art/>

Gordon College, Center for Christian Studies <www.gordon.edu/ccs>

Christians in the Visual Arts <www.civa.org>

Ted Prescott, artist and educator, Messiah College
<www.messiah.edu/departments/art/>

Catherine Prescott, artist and educator, Messiah College
<www.messiah.edu/departments/art/>

Bill Edgar, musician and theologian, Westminster Theological Seminary
<www.wts.edu/faculty/faculty-htstudies.html#edgar>

Thena Ayres, educator, Regent College <www.regent-college.edu>

William Dyrness, theologian, Brehm Center, Fuller Theological Seminary
<www.fuller.edu/brehmcenter/>

Regent College Spring and Summer School Program
<www.regent-college.edu>

Ward and Laurel Gasque, educators <www.koinos.org>

Laurel Gasque, author, and lecturer
<www.twu.ca/news/news_detail.asp?NewsID=241>

Hannah Main-van der Kamp, poet
<www3.sympatico.ca/voxfeminarum/bios.html>

Dal Schindell, artist and educator, Regent College
<www.regent-college.edu>

Roger Feldman, artist and educator, Seattle Pacific University
<www.spu.edu/depts/fpa/>

Wayne Roosa, art historian, Bethel College (MN)
<www.bethel.edu/college/acad/dept/art.htm>

Mary Ellen Ashcroft, educator, Bethel College (MN)
<www.bethel.edu/college/dept/english/faculty.html>

Betty Spackman, artist and educator, Trinity Western University
<www.twu.ca/news/news_detail.asp?NewsID=241>

Chris Anderson, Painting Fellow, New York Foundation for the Arts
<www.chrisandersonart.com> and
<http://nyfa.org/nyfa_artists_detail.asp?pid=96>

Bettina Clowney, artist and spiritual director
<http://thegalleriesatmoore.org/gmslide/search.cgi?code=2655>

Lee Hendrix, curator of prints, J. Paul Getty Museum <www.getty.edu>

Gerard Pas, artist <www.gerardpas.com>

Sharon Gallagher, editor, *Radix* magazine
<http://www.radixmagazine.com/>

Kefa Sempangi, artist and Member of Parliament, Uganda
<www.ambrosiafinearts.com/galleries/kefa_sempangi.html>

Kwame Bediako, theologian, Akrofi-Christaller Memorial Centre, Ghana
<http://www.ocms.ac.uk/regnum/detail.asp?book_id=8>

David and Ruth Hanson, educators, West Yorkshire School of Christian Studies <www.wysocs.org.uk/why_wysocs.html>

Nigel Goodwin, actor, Genesis Arts Trust <www.tradeandtryon.com/gat/>

Sylvester Jacobs, photographer and educator
<www.weeks-g.dircon.co.uk/SylvesterJacobs.htm>

Linette Martin, author (deceased)
<www.parable.com/nrb/item_1557253072.htm>

Colin Duriez, author and publishing consultant
<www.renew.org.uk/spck/cat/author.php?3192>

Arts Centre Group <www.artscentregroup.org.uk>

Norman Stone, filmmaker
<www.wheaton.edu/learnres/ARCSC/collects/sc13/bio.htm>

Murray Watts, theatre and film director and author <www.ridinglights.org>

David Porter, author <www.porterfolio.com>

Tricia Porter, photographer <www.porterfolio.com>

London Institute for Contemporary Christianity <www.licc.org.uk>

Third Way magazine <www.thirdway.org.uk>

Greenbelt Arts Festival <www.greenbelt.org.uk>

John Peck, pastor and promoter of the arts <www.greenbelt.org.uk>

Philip Archer, artist and educator, Leith School of Art <www.theartroom.net> and <www.leithschoolofart.co.uk>

Theology Through the Arts, Cambridge and St Andrews <www.theolarts.org>

Institute for Theology, Imagination and the Arts, University of St Andrews <www.st-andrews.ac.uk/institutes/itia/index.htm>

Jeremy Begbie, musician and theologian, Cambridge University <www.theolarts.org/people.html>

Ric Ashley, musician and educator, Northwestern University <www.intervarsity.org/followingchrist/tracks/arts/leaders/>

Garth Hewitt, musician <www.garthhewitt.com>

Mark Heard, musician (deceased) <www.mh.rru.com>

Steve Turner, poet <http://www.lion-publishing.co.uk/authors/meet_steve_turner.htm>

Steve Scott, author, Arts and Media Group, Warehouse Christian Ministries <www.gaylen.com/resume/sresume.html>

Eleanor DeLorme, lecturer and curator, Davis Museum, Wellesley College <www.wellesley.edu/PublicAffairs/Profile/af/edelorme.html>

Notes to Volume 6

Part I: God's Hand In History

1 Included in part II of this volume, as 'Prophecy in the Old and New Testaments: God's Way with Israel'.
2 The material included in 'God's Hand in History' are: a series of audio cassettes on 'God's Hand in History', a series of audio cassettes on 'Revelation', and a typed sermon on Malachi. The audio cassettes are in the L'Abri library including one that was lost and subsequently re-recorded by H.R.R. for Colin Duriez.

Part II: Articles and Interviews

3 Thomas à Kempis, *Imitation of Christ*.
4 The British Israel Movement (which identifies the British nation with the ten lost tribes of Israel – ed.).
5 H. de Greeve.
6 Willemse.
7 H. Bavinck, *Christendom en wijsheid van het Oosten* [Christianity and oriental wisdom].
8 'Mann hässt nicht, solange man noch gering schätzt, sondern nur wenn man gleich oder hoher schätzt', *Jenseits von Gut und Böse*, No. 173; see also No. 251 on the Jews, and further No. 250.
9 World War II was at its height as Dutch naval officer Rookmaaker typed away at this manuscript in the German detention camp in Stanislau.
10 The modern state of Israel was established in Palestine in 1948, subsequent to the writing of this manuscript.
11 *Kerkbode van de Gereformeerde Kerken in de Provincie Noord-Holland* 7, 1 (1951) pp.1–2.
12 P.K. Keizer, 'Paarlen voor de zwijnen', *Gereformeerd Gezinsblad* (August 4, 1951).
13 Excerpts from a talk held for the Bible Clubs of the 'Het Tehuis' congregation (*Nederlands Gereformeerd*) in Groningen on March 13, 1970.
14 *Opbouw* 4, 14 (1960) pp.111–112; originally published in *Ruimte* 6, 3 (1960).
15 *Christenen Doorgelicht* (Stichting Interlectuur, 1974) pp.45–52.
16 Rookmaaker refers here to the division between the Liberated Reformed Churches and the Reformed Church that occurred during World War II.
17 i.e. The Belgic Confession, Heidelberg Catechism and Canons of Dort, together with the appended Apostles' Creed, Nicene Creed and Athanasian Creed.
18 See *The Dust of Death* (Downers Grove, Il: InterVarsity Press, 1973) ch. 10: 'The Third Race'.
19 This lecture was assimilated into chapter 4 of *The Creative Gift*; see *Complete Works* 3, part II.

20 See *Complete Works* 3, appendix to 'The Creative Gift'.
21 Grand Rapids: Eerdmans, 1972.
22 The use of 'istic' in Dooyeweerdian terminology generally signalizes the absolutization of the aspect under discussion.
23 *Boekenbeeld, Maanblad van het Christelijk Lektuur-Centrum,* 1972, 1.
24 See *Complete Works* 1: 'Gauguin and Nineteenth-Century Art Theories'.
25 See *Complete Works* 2: 'Jazz, Blues and Spirituals'.
26 See *Complete Works* 3, part I.
27 See *Complete Works* 5, part II.
28 This interview with Hans Rookmaaker was conducted on 30 November 1971 by Colin Duriez during an arts weekend for students organized by the UCCF. It followed a public lecture Rookmaaker gave at the Royal Academy, London, a few days earlier in which he had pointed out that it is content, and not style, that is the key to understanding the modernity of modern art. The interview was subsequently published in the magazine *Crusade* (April 1972) pp.27, 41. This is a slightly expanded version of the published interview containing additional material from the recorded interview.
29 Kant is a German philosopher (1724–1804) who helped to frame all the problems of modern thought. Dooyeweerd's main work (*A New Critique of Theoretical Thought*) is aimed at answering Kant by presenting an alternative 'post-critical' philosophy.
30 *Right On* 4,4 (Berkely, 1972) p.7 (this magazine is now called *Radix*). The interview was conducted by Sharon Gallagher.
31 The 'box' refers to the universe when conceived of as a closed mechanistic system – Sharon Gallagher, ed.
32 This interview about Billy Graham for the Oral History Programme on Trans-World Radio was conducted in August 1971 by Jan J. van Capelleveen and Mrs Lois Ferm.

Part III: The L'Abri Lectures

33 Louis Armstrong and his Hot Fives: 'I'm not rough'.
34 Bob Dylan: 'My back pages'.
35 Leonard Cohen: 'Story of Isaac'.
36 Paul Simon: 'Sound of silence'.
37 Paul Simon: 'Patterns'.
38 Rolling Stones: 'Everybody needs somebody to love'.
39 Leonard Cohen: 'Tonight will be fine'.
40 Velvet Underground: 'Heroin'.
41 Rolling Stones: 'Street fighting man'.
42 From Paul Simon's 'Flowers never bend'.
43 James Taylor: 'Fire and rain'.
44 In conclusion H.R.R. quoted from James Weldon Johnson's *God's Trombones, Seven Negro Sermons in Verse* (New York: The Viking Press, 1927) the poem 'The Creation'. Cf. Complete Works 2, pp.227–229.

45 This lecture was given to the Fellowship of Christians in the Arts, Media and Entertainment in London in October 1970. It was the first time H.R.R. gave this particular lecture, which to him at this stage was still more a programme than a finished result. He said: 'It is what I want to work on in the following years, and I hope that others will begin to think along with me, ask questions, give criticisms, and add things, so that something may evolve that could be very important.'

46 Lecture given in Kensington, England to the Arts Centre Group on December 14, 1974.

47 1956; original title: *Metabletica.*

48 See the 'Westminster Discussions' in *Complete Works* 3; see also the lecture on 'What is Reality?' below.

49 See the lecture on 'Reality' below; see also in *Complete Works* 2: 'Art, Philosophy and our View of Reality'.

50 On the recording of this lecture the first part of the lecture (probably the first 30 minutes) and the last part are missing due to recording mistakes. The main argument of the lecture is, however, still intact. As this lecture shows what H.R.R. was engaged with in his final years and as it is very likely that this material would have been included in the book he was working on at the end of his life (see in volume 4: 'An Unfinished Manuscript') the editor has tried to present the remaining material as lucidly as possible. The lecture was based on a slide-show.

51 This is a combination of two lectures, or rather of two different versions of the same lecture, namely: 'Christianity and Music' and 'Christianity and Art'.

52 See *Complete Works* 3, plate 4.

Appendix A: Bibliography of Published Writings about H.R.R.

Note that entries are arranged chronologically.

Articles about H.R.R.

Author unknown, 'Vluchtig portret' (interview with H.R.R.). *Trouw* (around 1958).

Author unknown, 'Kunsttheorieën der synthetisten.' *Trouw* (July 1959).

H. de Jongste, 'Een belangrijke promotie.' *Mededelingen van de Vereniging voor Calvinistische Wijsbegeerte* (September 1959), pp.3,4.

Author unknown, 'Vol verwachting van 'n spreker over jazz.' *H.D.* (April 14, 1961).

Author unknown, 'Causerie over jazz in Wilhelminakerk.' *H.C.* (April 14, 1961).

W. Meijer, 'Over de normen in de kunst.' 1,2. *Nederlands Dagblad* (1962).

H. Wiersma, 'Dr. Rookmaaker strijdt voor nieuwe gereformeerde levensstijl'. *Spiegel* (June 29, 1963), pp.44–45.

A. Zijlstra, 'De christen en de cultuur.' *Gereformeerd Gezinsblad* (May 17, 1965).

Author unknown, 'De kunstenaar een profeet?' *Gooi en Eemlander* (May 28, 1965), p.3.

Author unknown, 'Prof. Rookmaaker aan V.U.: Negeren van kunst is onmogelijk.' newspaper unknown (May 29, 1965).

Author unknown, 'Prof. Rookmaaker sprak voor A.R. Oegstgeest.' *NLC* (February 1966).

K. Vollmans, 'De geest van de revolutie, de mens van de wetteloosheid.' *NUK* (February 1968).

Author unknown, 'Bourgeoismentaliteit sterft nooit uit.' *Zwolsche Courant* (March 1, 1968).

Author unknown, 'Professor Rookmaaker zoekt meer in Beatles-songs dan er inzit.' *Parool* (October 26, 1968).

A. Landsbury, 'The Absurdity of Man.' *British Weekly* (December 6, 1968).

P. Cousins and A. Long, ' "Rook" on art.' *Crusade* (April 1970).

M. Robinson, 'Will there be Martyrs?' *The Vancouver Sun* (July 11, 1970).

D. Dijksman, 'Prof. Rookmaaker ziet heil in rock en beat tegen de ontkerstening.' *Haagse Post* 36 (1971), pp.18–19.

M. Ozmer, 'Man Trapped in a Closed System, Dutch Art History Teacher Says.' *The Chattanooga Times* (March 19, 1971).

W. Edgar, 'Book review. H.R. Rookmaaker: Modern Art and the Death of a Culture.' *Christianity Today* (May 1971), p.844.

Author unknown, 'Geloof opnieuw integreren in leven van alledag.' *Nieuwe Haagse Courant* (September 1, 1971).

Author unknown, 'Nog meer boekjes óver het geloof zijn niet nodig.' *Trouw* (September 1, 1971), p.5.

W. Edgar, 'Book review. II.R. Rookmaaker: Modern Art and the Death of a Culture.' *Westminster Theological Journal* 34 (1972), pp.179–183.

N. Wolterstorff, 'On Looking at Paintings: A Look at Rookmaaker.' *Reformed Journal* (February 1972).

G. van der Walt, 'Moderne kuns aftakeling van menslike waardes.' *Litografiese Bylae tot die Oosterlig* (December 10, 1974).

Author unknown, 'Kunstwerk ontmoeting van kunstenaar en medemens.' *Reformatorisch Dagblad* (January 4, 1975), p.2.

Author unknown, 'Christenen moeten kunst scheppen vanuit bewogenheid.' *Friesch Dagblad* (February 21, 1976).

G.M. Birtwistle, 'In memoriam prof. Rookmaaker.' *Trouw* (March 15, 1977).

Author unknown, 'Prof. H.R. Rookmaaker onverwachts overleden.' *Reformatorisch Dagblad* (March 15, 1977).

W.G. Rietkerk, 'Ter herdenking van prof. dr. H.R. Rookmaaker.' *Opbouw* (March 25, 1977), pp.92–93.

M. de Klijn, 'Bij het heengaan van prof. H.R. Rookmaaker.' *Opbouw* (March 25, 1977), pp.92–93.

Gratia, 'Prof. Rookmaaker, de christen en de kunst.' *Friesch Dagblad* (March 1977).

J. Bulens, 'Bij het heengaan van Hans R. Rookmaaker.' *Kunstzinnig* (March 1977), p.21.

H. Algra, 'In memoriam prof. dr. H.R. Rookmaaker.' *Friesch Dagblad* (March 1977).

T. Wales, 'H.R. Rookmaaker.' *Third Way* 1,6 (March 1977), p.10.

P. Clowney, 'Dr H.R. Rookmaaker.' *Christian Graduate* (U.C.C.F., June 1977), pp.47–48.

H.G. Geertsema, 'In memoriam.' *Beweging* 41, 2 (April 1977), p.20.

C.A. van Swigchem, 'Bij het heengaan van prof. dr. H.R. Rookmaaker.' *VU Magazine* (April 4, 1977), p.39.

C. de Jong-Ofeissen, 'Prof. dr. H.R. Rookmaaker als "baas".' *STUK* (publication of the art history subfaculty at the VU), (April 1977).

G.M. Birtwistle, 'In memoriam.' *Philosophia Reformata* 42, 1 (1977).

P. Smith and H.G. Geerstsema, 'Hans Rookmaaker: An Appreciation.' *IARFA Journal* (1977).

Author unknown, 'Twee nieuwe christelijke academies.' *Centraal Weekblad* (October 8, 1977), p.3.

H.C.L. Jaffé, 'In memoriam H.R. Rookmaaker.' *Lier en Boog* (January 1978).

W. Edgar, 'Book review. H.R. Rookmaaker: Art Needs No Justification.' *Westminster Theological Journal* 42 (1979), pp. 203–208.

C. Rijnsdorp, 'Rookmaaker en het programmatisch christendom.' *Trouw* (January 9, 1979).

L. Gasque, 'Hans Rookmaaker: A Biography – A Review Article.' *Crux* 16, 2 (June 1980), pp.24–29.

W. Edgar, 'Book review. H.R. Rookmaaker: The Creative Gift.' *Westminster Theological Journal* 55 (1983), pp.473–475.

Author unknown, 'Two Men – One Vision.' *Sound* (June/July 1984).

Th. Peppink, 'De relatie Evangelie en kunst bij de kunsthistoricus prof. dr. H.R. Rookmaaker, 1, 2.' *De Wekker* 94, 95 (December 1984, January 1985), pp.80–81; 109–110.

J. Leaf, 'Not Forgotten or Passed Over, the Treasured Lives of Hans and Anky Rookmaaker.' *Strait* 18 (January 1985), p.21.

J.I. Packer, 'All That Jazz.' *Christianity Today* 30, 18 (December 12, 1986), p.15.

B. Hyatt, 'Letter.' *The Cut* (Arts Centre Group), (Autumn 1989).

A.J. Koekkoek, 'De kritiek op de moderne kunst bij Evert van Uitert en Hans Rookmaaker. Een vergelijking van hun inaugurele redes.' *Radix* 17, 3 (1991), pp.160–170.

W. and G. Rietkerk, 'Rookmaaker en l'Abri.' *Opbouw* 45, 24 (December 2001), p.489.

G. Birtwistle, 'Het internationale gezicht van H.R. Rookmaaker.' *Opbouw* 45, 24 (December 2001), p.490–491.

M. de Klijn, 'Rookmaakers blijvende inspiratie.' *Opbouw* 45, 24 (December 2001), p.491–492.

B. Wikström, 'Een korte reactie.' *Beweging* 65, 4 (December 2001), p.12.

H. Helmantel, 'De blijvende betekenis van Rookmaaker.' *Beweging* 65, 4 (December 2001), p.13.

J.J. Burger, 'H.R. Rookmaaker.' *Nader Bekeken* 9, 1 (January 2002), p.27.

T. Ramaker, 'Rookmaaker: Art Needs No Justification.' *Impact* 3 (May 2002), pp.29–30.

T. Goudriaan, 'Rookmaaker, een internationale eye-opener.' *Reformatorisch Dagblad* (June 10, 2002), p.15.

Author unknown, 'Rookmaaker 1, 2' (Kunstgrepen). *Reformatorisch Dagblad* (September 23, 2002).

D. Porter, 'His Very Speaking Likeness.' *Now* (October 2002), p.18.

P. Smith, 'The Complete Works of Hans Rookmaaker.' *The Artsmedia Journal* 3 (ACG, Autumn 2002).

G.M. Birtwistle, 'Henderik Roelof Rookmaaker.' *Biographical Dictionary of Evangelicals* (IVP, Leicester England / Downers Grove USA 2003), pp.563–565.

P. Smith, 'The Complete Works of Hans Rookmaaker Vols 3 & 4.' *The Artsmedia Journal* 6 (ACG, 2003)

Reviews of books and record series by H.R.R.

P.A. Hekstra, 'Synthetist Art Theories.' *Opbouw* (October 1959), pp.228–229.

J.W. Mojet and D.M. Bakker, 'Kanttekeningen bij twee kunsthistorische dissertaties (van Rookmaaker en Stellingwerff).' *Sola Fide* 13, 5 (1960), pp.17–24.

Author unknown, 'Jazz, blues en spirituals.' *Disco Discussies* (March 1960).

Author unknown, 'Jazz, blues en spirituals.' *De Gooi en Eemlander* (October 11, 1960).

Author unknown, 'Platen en plaatjes' (about *Treasures of North American Negro Music*). *Elsevier* (October 22, 1960).

D.K., 'Treasures of North American Negro Music.' *Luister* (November 1960).

R. ten Kate, 'Nothing but the Blues.' *Disco Discussies* (November 1960).

H.K., 'Nieuwe studie over jazz, blues en spirituals.' *Friesch Dagblad* (November 26, 1960).

J. Wisse, 'Jazz, blues en spirituals.' *Elsevier* (November 1960).

D. Oman, 'Jazz, blues, spirituals.' *Sola Fide* (September 1960).

D. Oman, 'Supplement to previous review.' *Sola Fide* (November 1960).

M. de Ruyter, '"Jazz, blues, spirituals" boek vol inconsequenties.' *Parool* (October 14, 1960).

K. Deddens, 'Jazz-blues-spirituals.' *Gereformeerd Gezinsblad* (October 19, 1960).

R.N., 'Jazz, blues, spirituals.' *Trouw* (October 22, 1960).

Author unknown, 'Op zoek naar schoonheid in Jazz, Blues en Spirituals.' *Signaal* (November 1960).

Author unknown, 'Kundige gids in jazzwereld.' *Leeuwarder Courant* (November 12, 1960).

Author unknown, 'Jazz Blues Spirituals.' *Idil* (November 25, 1960).

Sas Bunge, 'Jazz, Blues, Spirituals.' *Prisma-Lectuurvoorlichting* (December 1960).

A.D.G., 'Jazz, Blues en Spirituals. Boek dr. Rookmaaker met te subjectieve inslag.' *Het Vaderland* (December 6, 1960).

Author unknown, 'Jazz-Blues-Spirituals.' *De Gelderlander* (December 2, 1960).

Cornet, 'Weer een boek over jazz 1, 2.' *Christelijk Gymnasiaal en Middelbaar Onderwijs* 38 (1961), pp.499–503.

Author unknown, 'Jazz Blues Spirituals.' *Mens en Boek* (Katholieke Centrale Vereniging voor Lectuurvoorziening in Nederland), (January/February 1961).

M. Lok, 'Jazz, Blues, Spirituals.' *Poortwake* (Gereformeerde Meisjesvereniging Nederland), (February 10, 1961).

J.W. Scheurer, 'Jazz, blues, spirituals.' *Jong Gereformeerd* 4 (March 1961), pp.733–734.

J. Wit, 'Jazz Blues Spirituals.' *Wending* 15, 12 (March 1961).

H.J., 'Een pijnlijke vergissing.' *Salvo* (Katholiek Weekblad voor de Nederlandse Strijdkrachten), (March 6, 1961).

v. G., 'Jazz, Blues, Spirituals.' *De Open Deur* (March 17, 1961).

J.M., 'Jazz-blues-spirituals.' *Kerkbode van Noord Holland* (March 18, 1961).

Author unknown, 'Jazz, blues, spirituals.' *N.R.C.*, Boek vandaag (Date unknown).

J. v.d. Burgh, 'Jazz-Blues-Spirituals.' *Kerkblad voor de Gereformeerde Kerken (vrijgemaakt) in de classis 's-Gravenhage* (date unkown).

A. Groeneveld, 'Jazz, Blues en Spirituals.' *Libertas ex Veritate* (April 1961), p.187.

A.v.D., 'Jazz, blues, spirituals.' *Philips Koerier* (May 20, 1961).

Author unknown, 'Wat is echte jazz?' *Wij houden van zangen* (May/June 1961).

Author unknown, 'Misverstanden rond de jazz.' *Overijsselse en Zwolse Courant* (May 19, 1961).

Author unknown, 'Eenzijdig boek over jazz-muziek.' *Friese Koerier* (June 23, 1961).

A. Huizinga, 'Jazz, blues, spirituals.' *Calvinistisch Jongelingsblad* (September 1, 1961).

Author unknown, 'Enkele vragen over jazz.' *Calvinistisch Jongelingsblad* (October 13, 1961).

B. Broeren, 'Jazz-Blues-Spirituals.' *Jeugd en Evangelie* 4, 3 (1962).

Author unknown, 'Jazz: van oerwoud-dreun tot modern ritme.' *Nieuwe Provinciale Groninger Courant* (August 8, 1962).

Author unknown, 'Kunst en Amusement.' *Hervormd Amersfoort* (December 7, 1962).

Author unknown, 'Kunst en Amusement.' *Delftsche Courant* (December 7, 1962).

Author unknown, 'Kunst en Amusement.' *Rotterdamsch Nieuwsblad* (December 8, 1962).

G.D. Jonker, 'Twee soorten liefde en de "Carcer Terreno".' *Mededelingen van de Vereniging voor Calvinistische Wijsbegeerte* (December 1962).

L.D. Steefel, Jr., 'Synthetist Art Theories.' *The Art Bulletin* 45 (1963), pp.168–169.

G.T. Rothuizen, 'Kunst en Amusement.' *Sermo* 10, 4 (January 1963), pp.6–7.

J. Bosch, 'Kunst en Amusement.' *Opbouw* (January 11, 1963), pp.302–303.

Author unknown, 'Kunst en Amusement.' *Gereformeerde Kerkbode voor de classes Barendrecht en Dordrecht* (January 12, 1963).

B., 'Kunst en Amusement.' *Hervormd Apeldoorn* (January 12, 1963).

Author unknown, 'Christelijke visie op kunst en amusement.' *Zondagsblad* (January 19, 1963).

Author unknown, 'Kunst en Amusement.' *Hervormd Leeuwarden* (January 25, 1963).

J.W.v.H., 'Kunst en Amusement.' *Correspondentieblad De Christelijke Onderwijzer* (January 30, 1963).

Author unknown, 'Kunst en Amusement.' *Leidse Kerkbode* (Gereformeerd Synodaal), (February 1, 1963).

Author unknown, 'Kunst en Amusement.' *Christelijk Gymnasiaal en Middelbaar onderwijs* (February 2, 1963).

C. Huizinga, 'Kunst en Amusement.' *Calvinistisch Jongelingsblad* (February 8, 1963).

W., 'Kunst en Amusement', *Ons kerkblad* (Gereformeerde Kerken in de classis Arnhem), (February 16, 1963).

W.G.d.V., 'Kunst en Amusement.' *Petok-ja* (February 1963).

K.v.Duinen: 'Kunst en Amusement.' *Polemistes* (February 1963).

W.C.F. Scheps, 'Kunst en Amusement.' *Kerknieuws* 20, 1019 (March 9, 1963).

J. Kwekkeboom, 'Een deskundig vakman, maar geen goede gids.' *Daniël* (March 15, 1963), p.144.

J.v.d.M., 'Kunst en Amusement.' *Stentor* 17, 10 (S.S.R. Utrecht, March 15, 1963).

Author unknown, 'Kunst en Amusement.' *De Wekker* 72, 20 (March 15, 1963).

Author unknown, 'Kunst en Amusement.' *De Geldelander* (March 18, 1963).

C. Rijnsdorp, 'Het boek van Rookmaaker.' *Gereformeerd Weekblad* (March 29, 1963), p.302.

M.V., 'Kunst en Amusement.' *De Zondagsbode* (Hervormd Kerkblad voor Maassluis e.o.), (May 24, 1963).

Author unknown, 'Kunst en Amusement.' *Gereformeerd Kerkblad Haarlem* (June 8, 1963).

Author unknown, 'Kunst en Amusement.' *Ons Kerkblad* (Gereformeerde Kerken in Utrecht (January 10, 1964).

B. Molenaar, 'Kunst en Amusement, 1–6.' *De Sleutel* (September 1964 – April 1965), pp.271–273; 302–304; 47–49; 78–80; 141–146; 167–170.

D.S.-B., 'Georgia Tom Dorsey.' *Jazz Journal* (December 1964).

J. Postgate, 'The Legendary Bix Beiderbecke.' *Jazz Monthly* (December 1964).

S.T., 'Bix Beiderbecke.' *Jazz Journal* (December 1964).

G.M., 'Blind Blake.' *Jazz Journal* (December 1964).

P. Oliver, 'Georgia Tom ... and Friends.' *Jazz Monthly* (December 1964), pp.25–26.

G.E. Lambert, 'New York Jazz Scene 1917–1920.' *Jazz Monthly* (January 1965).

K. Harrison, 'Georgia Tom and Friends;' P. Oliver, 'Blind Blake Blues in Chicago;' and 'Honky Tonk Train.' Journal unknown (date unknown).

Author unknown, 'Honky Tonk Train.' *Jazz Monthly* (Januaty 1965).

Author unknown, 'Blind Blake, Georgia Tom.' *Jazzbeat* (January 1965).

Author unknown, 'Kunst en Amusement.' *Evangelisch Luthers Weekblad* (January 16, 1965).

J. Schrier, 'Historische jazz-opnamen in Riverside's Classic Jazz Masters.' *Luister* (May 1965), pp.200–202.

Author unknown, 'De kunstenaar een profeet?' *Vaderland* (May 29, 1965).

Author unknown, 'Is de kunstenaar profeet?' *Leidsch Dagblad* (May 31, 1965).

R. van Reest, 'De kunstenaar een profeet?' *Gereformeerd Gezinsblad* (July 22, 1965).

J. van Noort, 'In het grensgebied van kunst en amusement' (over filmvorming). *School en Huis* (November 1965, pp.174–176).

S.H. Spanjaard, 'Kunst en Amusement.' *Hervormd Weekblad* (January 20, 1966).

P. van Loo, 'Boekbespreking: De kunstenaar een profeet?' *Philosophia Reformata* 31 (1966), pp.182–192.

Author unknown, 'De kunstenaar een profeet?', *Haagsche Courant* (January 17, 1966).

L.J. Schalekamp, 'Jazz, Blues, Spirituals.' *De Nederlandse Krijgsman* 78, 1678 (April 1967), p.71.

R.E. Baker, 'Art and the Public Today.' *The Gordon Review* 11, 4 (1968), p.259.

M. Shepherd, 'Review of Modern Art and the Death of a Culture.' *Art News* (1971).

J. Pridmore, 'God's Gift of Art.' About *Modern art and the Death of a Culture. CWN Group* (January 29, 1971). In November and December 1971 three extracts of *Modern Art and the Death of a Culture* were published in *CWN Group*.

Author unknown, 'Modern Art and the Death of a Culture.' *Christian Book News* (Autumn 1970).

Author unknown, 'Death of a Culture.' *Crusade* (October 1970), pp.12–13.

Author unknown, 'Modern Art and the Death of a Culture'. *Weekend Scotsman* (December 5, 1970).

M. Muggeridge, List of Books of the Year. *The Observer* (December 20, 1970).

D. Wollen, 'Prophets of Despair' (about *Modern Art and the Death of a Culture*). *Methodist Recorder* (January 7, 1971).

Author unknown, 'Modern art and the Death of a Culture', *The Harvester* (January 1971).

R. Andrew, 'Modern Art and the Death of a Culture.' *Spectrum* (January 1971).

Author unknown, 'Modern Art and the Death of a Culture.' *The Reaper* (February 1971).

M. Muggeridge, 'Books.' Review of *Modern Art and the Death of a Culture. Esquire* 75 (March 1971), p.16.

Author unknown, 'Modern Art and the Death of a Culture.' *Christian News* (March 1, 1971).

C. Boddington, 'Modern Art and the Death of a Culture.' *English Churchman* (March 12, 1971).

Author unknown, 'Since the Enlightenment' (about *Modern Art and the*

Death of a Culture). *The Tablet* (April 10, 1971).

W. Edgar, 'Review of *Modern Art and the Death of a Culture.*' *Christianity Today* (May 1971) p.844.

C. Sutherland, 'Modern Art and the Death of a Culture.' *The Living Church* (June 6, 1971).

M. de Klijn, 'Modern Art and the Death of a Culture.' *Opbouw* (June 4, 11, 18, July 2, 1971).

B. Rietveld, 'In de spiegel van de kunst.' *Centraal Weekblad* 19, 25 (June 1971).

M. Selman, 'Modern art and the Death of a Culture.' journal unknown (July 1971).

R. Kirk, 'Alternatives to Decadence' (about *Modern art and the Death of a Culture*). Various newspapers in the USA (October 1971).

D.J. van den Berg, 'Modern Art and the Death of a Culture.' *Tydskrif vir Christelike Wetenskap* (1972).

W. Edgar, 'Review of *Modern Art and the Death of a Culture.*' *Westminster Theological Journal* 34 (1972) pp.179–183.

Author unknown, 'Modern art and the Death of a Culture.' *The Iliff Review* (Spring 1972).

N. Matheis, 'Modern Art and the Death of a Culture.' *International Reformed Bulletin* (Winter 1972), pp.49–51.

H. Amelink, 'Macht en onmacht van de twintigste eeuw.' *Opbouw* (January 1975).

E. van Donselaar, 'Macht en onmacht van de twintigste eeuw.' N.B.L.C. lektuurinformatiedienst, Den Haag (date unknown).

v. Esch, 'Boekbespreking: Macht en onmacht van de twintigste eeuw.' *Radix* 1,3 (1975), pp.171–174.

Author unknown, 'Y a-t-il un art chrétien?' (about *L'Art moderne et la mort d'une culture*). *Jeunesse Liberée* 44 (1975).

M. Lahellec, 'L'Art moderne et la mort d'une culture.' Journal unknown (1975).

Author unknown, 'L'Art moderne et la mort d'une culture.' *Vie Protestant* (1975).

P.S. 'L'Art moderne et la mort d'une culture.' *Christ Seul* (1975).

A. Venditti, 'L'Art moderne et la mort d'une culture.' *Etudes Evangeliques* (Faculté Réformée d'Aix en Provence), (date unknown).

P. Brouwer, 'Macht en onmacht in de 20ste eeuw.' *Nieuw Nederland* (December 1975).

W. Edgar, 'Review of *Art Needs No Justification.*' *Westminster Theological Journal* 42 (1979), pp.203–208.

Author unknown, 'The Creative Gift.' *Radix* (March/April 1982).

R. Beechick, 'Creativity: "In" for the 1980s' (about *The Creative Gift*). *Success* (Spring 1982).

E. Myers, 'The Creative Gift.' *CSSH Quarterly* (Summer 1983), pp.22–24.

W. Edgar, 'Review of *The Creative Gift.*' *Westminster Theological Journal* 55 (1983) pp.473–475.

J.D. Tangelder, 'Needed: A conscious effort to establish Christian culture'(about *The Creative Gift*). Journal unknown (date unknown).

N. Shaw, 'Modern Art and the Death of a Culture.' *Monthly Record* (December 1994).

V. Byfield, 'Whither Christian Art? About *Modern Art and the Death of a Culture. Western Report* (March 13, 1995), p.37.

I. McKillop, 'Modern Art and the Death of a Culture.' *Alpha* (April 1995).

Theses about H.R.R.

Th. Peppink, 'Evangelie en kunst.' Doctoraal scriptie/ M.Th. thesis. Kampen, 1980.

R. Cameron, 'A Study of Rookmaaker (influences on him, his works, as applied to art education in Australia).' M.A. thesis, Perth, around 1980.

C. Meier, 'Aspekte einer Theologie der Kunst bei Hans Rookmaaker.' M.Th. thesis. Basel, 1986.

M. Otter, 'Christelijke visies op kunst uit de twintigste eeuw.' Doctoraal scriptie/ M.A. thesis art history. Amsterdam: VU, 1989.

Articles that include discussions of the work of H.R.R.

Author unknown, 'Kerstnummer Drukkersweekblad.' *Pen en Pers* (January 1961).

Author unknown, 'Prenten Aad Veldhoen "zinneprikkelend"?' *Leidsch Dagblad* (December 12, 1964).

E. Hoffmann, 'Symbolismus und die Kunst der Jahrhundertwende.' *Neue Zürcher Zeitung* (August 24, 1969).

J.M. Houston, 'The Christian and the Arts in Contemporary Society.' *The Witness* (April 1969), pp.140–141.

F.F. Bruce, 'Regent College, Vancouver.' *The Witness* (November 1970), pp.418–419.

K.L. Poll, 'Geestelijke strijd.' *NRC Handelsblad, Cultureel Supplement* (February 12, 1971).

Author unknown, 'Evangelisatie-congres: Morele kick voor eenzame werkers.' *Bijlage Leeuwarder Courant* (September 4, 1971).

Author unknown, 'Evangelisatie vereist training, zegt rev. Gilbert W. Kirby.' *Haarlems Dagblad* (September 18, 1971).

G. Hoffman, 'Waking up to Reality; A Report on the European Congress on Evangelism.' *Crusade* (October 1971), p.32.

H.M. Conn, 'What is Religious Art?' *The Presbyterian Guardian* (Summer 1972), p.78.

M. Fergus, 'Peter Smith – Just an Ordinary Painter.' *Salt* 1 (Autumn 1974).

M. Fergus, 'From Birmingham: kunst van jonge Engelse christenen.' *Ad Valvas* (V.U.) (December 6, 1974), p.12.

S.T. Kimbrough, 'The Art of Re-presentation.' *Pacific Theological* Review (Winter 1975).

Gratia, 'Christenen en kunst' (about the C.C.S.). *Friesch Dagblad* (1976).

Author unknown, 'Arts Festival Highly Successful.' *Bulletin of Westminster Theological Seminary* (1976).

C. Forbes, 'Affirming the Arts.' *Christianity Today* (February 13, 1976).

K.C. Harper, 'Francis A. Schaeffer: An Evaluation.' *Bibliothecasacra* (Dallas Theological Seminary, June 1976).

B. de Jong, 'In plan christelijke academie beeldende vorming komt tekening.' *Trouw* (September 2, 1976).

J.M. de Jong, 'Enkele kritische opmerkingen over christelijke moderne kunst.' *Radix* 3, 4 (1977), pp.218–229.

Author unknown, 'The Rookmaaker Lecture, The Truth about Romanticism.' Festival 7 (Arts Centre Group), (Autumn 1977).

C. Rijnsdorp, 'Schaeffer als culturele Jeremia.' *Trouw* (December 14, 1977).

G.M. Birtwistle, 'Boekbespreking: Willem L. Meijer, Kunst en maatschappij.' *Radix* 4, 3 (1978), pp.177–179.

C. Lynn Hostutler, 'Walford Stresses Dignity of Art.' *Wheaton Record* (September 25, 1981).

D.T. Koyzis, 'Herman and Francis.' *The Reformed Journal* (August 1982).

N. Halliday, 'Where There's Art There's Meaning, the Significance and Obscurity of Modern Art.' *Third Way* (June 1983), pp.16–18.

A. Chaplin, 'Monk Music.' *Strait* 21 (1985).

R. van Woudenberg, 'Abstractie, kennis en kunst, een gesprek met G. Birtwistle en P. Blokhuis.' *Beweging* 50, 5 (October 1986), pp.91–94.

A.M. Rookmaaker-Huitker, 'Persoonlijke herinneringen aan Francis Schaeffer.' *Bijbel en Wetenschap, Schaeffer Special* (May 1987), pp.121–123.

L. Gasque, 'The Religious Sensibility of Paul Gauguin.' *Third Way* (April 1989). Also translated into Italian as 'Gauguin: Apparenzae Introspezione,' Certezza [Rome] (Settembre-Ottobre 1991) pp.13–16.

A.J. Koekkoek, 'De vloek van de schoonheid. Een verkenning in de esthetica van de Wijsbegeerte der Wetsidee.' *Radix* 19, 2 (1993), pp.109–127.

A.J. Koekkoek, 'Moderne kunst en christelijke verantwoordelijkheid.' *Radix* 20, 2 (1994), pp.108–125.

W.L. Meijer, 'Wat die wind betekent.' *Radix* 20, 2 (1994), pp.126–130.

J. Bulens, 'Christelijk Cultureel Studiecentrum, 1964–1994 dertig jaren.' *Schering en Inslag* 7, 4 (1994), pp.8–18.

K. van Noppen, 'Kunst en de dynamiek van deze tijd, Marc de Klijn in gesprek met G. Birtwistle.' *Cahier* 21, 8 (ICS, June 1994).

R. Kuiper, 'Het gedecimeerde studentenleven.' In R. Kuiper and W. Bouwman ed., *Vuur en vlam. Aspecten van het vrijgemaakt-gereformeerde leven, 1944–1994* (Amsterdam, 1994).

G.M. Birtwistle, 'Filosofie van de kunst en de esthetica.' In R. van Woudenberg (ed.), *Kennis en werkelijkheid. Tweede inleiding tot een christelijke filosofie* (Amsterdam, Kampen 1996), pp.342–370.

A. Amelink, 'Waarom Kuypers denken ook nu nog grote openheid verdient.' Interview with Peter Heslam. *Trouw* (1998).

P.S. Heslam, 'A Theology of the Arts: Kuyper's Ideas on Art and Religion.' In C. van der Kooi and J. de Bruijn (eds.), *Kuyper Reconsidered: Aspects of his Life and Work* (Amsterdam, VU Uitgeverij, 1999) pp.13–29.

P.S. Smith, Foreword to C. Seerveld, *In the Fields of the Lord* (Carlisle, Piquant/Toronto, Tuppence Press, 2000).

G.M. Birtwistle, 'Wegwijzers voor christen-kunstenaars van nu.' Review of H. Brand and A. Chaplin, *Art and Soul. Beweging* 65, 4 (December 2001), pp.43–45.

T.R. Tjerkstra, 'De eerste acht jaren van de VGSA volgens de notulen. Een summa notularum.' *Heen is de tijd, vijfenvijftig jaar vereniging VGSA-VCSA* (VCSA publication 2002), pp.7–15.

F. van der Wal, 'Gun talent een carrière.' *Impact* 3 (May 2002), pp.28–29.

Books that go into the work of H.R.R.

L. Martin, *Hans Rookmaaker, A Biography*. Hodder and Stoughton, London, 1979.

C. Seerveld, *Rainbows for the Fallen World*. Toronto Tuppence Press, Toronto, 1980.

T. Dean and David Porter (eds.), *Art in Question*. Marshall Pickering, Basingstoke, 1987.

J.S. Begbie, *Voicing Creation's Praise*. T & T Clark, Edinburgh, 1991.

D. Porter, *The Story of Nigel Goodwin*. Hodder and Stoughton, London, 1993.

H. Brand and A. Chaplin, *Art and Soul: Signposts for Christians in the Arts*. Piquant, Carlisle, 2001.

J. Douma, *Over beelden en beeldenstormers*. Kok, Kampen, 2001.

W.A. Dyrness, *Visual Faith: Art, Theology and Worship in Dialogue*. Baker Academic, Grand Rapids, 2001.

Appendix B: Hans Rookmaaker Papers at Wheaton College

Holdings in the Special Collections of the Buswell Memorial Library (Wheaton, Illinois, USA)

I Biographical & Bibliographical Notes

Box I.1
 Biography
 Curriculum Vitae
 Customs Declaration
 Driver's License
 Listing of Books and Articles on Art
 List of Publications
 Provisional Bibliography for H.R.R.

Box I.2
 3x5 index cards

Box I.3
 3x5 index cards

Box I.4
 3x5 index cards

II. Correspondence

A. By Date

Box II.A.1
 1945–1965

Box II.A.2
 1966–1970

Box II.A.3
 1971–1973

Box II.A.4
 1974–1975

Box II.A.5
  1976–1986

B. By Category

Box II.B.1
Correspondence from 1951–1956, divided into divisions from A–Z

Box II.B.2
  Art History 1962–1975
  The Encyclopedia of Christianity
  Music 1963–1964
  Reissues: Fontana Riverside
  Ruimte 1951–1954
  Ruimte 1955–1956

Box II.B.3
  Study-trip to USA Sept–Dec 1961, Book and gram. Negro music
  Study-trip to USA Sept–Dec 1961, Personal info and materials
  Study-trip to USA Sept–Dec 1961, Lectures
  Study-trip to USA Sept–Dec 1961
  Study-trip to USA Sept–Dec 1961, Conferences
  Study-trip to USA Sept–Dec 1961, Travel documents
  Undated – English
  Undated – English
  Undated – non-English

III Manuscripts [English and Dutch]

A. Negro Spirituals/Blues

Box III.A.1
English
  1. Early Negro Bands in New York
  2. St Louis dates
  3. The History of Negro Spirituals and Gospel Songs
  4. The Spirituals and the Blues – review of book by James H. Cone
  5. Teksten bij de lezing over 'Blues' op 1 Maart 1955 / Texts of songs played during the lecture about blues on 1 March 1955

General
  6. Beat, Rock and Protest
  7. Rock

Dutch
    8. Afrikaanse Negermuziek
    9. Afro-Amerikaanse volksmuziek
    10. Blues, Satirical Songs of the N. American Negro – foreword H.R.R
    11. Instrumentale muziek van de N. Amerikaanse neger
    12. Jazz, blues, spirituals
    13. 'Laughing to Keep From Crying' – foreword for Frank Boom
    14. Negro-Spirituals
    15. De Negro-Spiritual
    16. Tapes geestelijke muziek circa 1960

B. Jazz

Box III.B.I
English
    1. Bach and Oliver
    2. A Bird's Eye View on Jazz History
    3. Crescent City White Jazz
    4. King Oliver's Creole Orchestra
    5. Piron's New Orleans Orchestra

Dutch
    6. Jazz
    7. Jelly-Roll Morton
    8. Swing

C. Art

Box III.C.I
English
    1. Are There Norms for Art?
    2. Art-History Method
    3. Art, the Christian and . . .
    4. The Artist as a Prophet (English translation of speech by H.R.R.)
    5. Aurier
    6. Autonomy, Heteronomy, and the Function of Art
    7. Charity in 17th-century Art
    8. Christian Creativity
    9. Christianity and Culture
    10. The Christian and the Arts Today
    11. Commitment of Artist, Commitment of his Public (speech by H.R.R.)
    12. God's Hand in History
    13. Iconography and Iconology
    14. Life's Questions

15. Principles for Christians Who Want to Work as Artists
16. Relationship between Japanese and European Culture
17. A Turnabout in Aesthetics to Understanding
18. Youth in Revolt – Youth in Trouble – Who is to Blame?
19. Youth – interview with H.R.R.
20. The Word of God and the Criticism of Art
21. General
22. First draft of a book dealing with the history of art – no title

Dutch
23. Achtergrond en oorzaak van het kerkelijk en ethisch conflict
24. De actualiteit van de oude kunst
25. Afval en zonde
26. Afval, zonde, oordeel
27. Art
28. Art. voor *Calvinistisch Jongelingsblad*
29. Beat en protest
30. Beauty
31. Betreft: Symposium 'Christianity and Art' – Sept 1978
32. Calvin Seerveld
33. Christian Art
34. Concept
35. Creativiteit
36. Creativiteit in liefde en vrijheid
37. Crisis in Values in Contemporary Art
38. Cultuur en revolutie
39. De Franse schilderkunst in de 14e eeuw
40. Eduard von Hartmann
41. Een museum der muziek
42. Enige aspecten van het kunstwerk
43. Ensor en andere groten
44. Esthetica
45. Evangelisatie onder kinderen
46. Forrer, Ooms en Frank in Utrecht
47. Frankrijk
48. Gauguin
49. Gereformeerde studieclub
50. Triptiek van Keulse meester omstreeks 1350
51. Gods ambassadeurs in Zwitserland

Box III.C.2
Dutch
1. Het aesthetische in de ontsluitingsrelatie
2. Het Congres der Internationale Raad van Kerken
3. Het klassicisme in de kunst
4. Wij en het Koninkrijk Gods

5. Correspondence
6. De moderne mens
7. Is Moderne Kunst waar?
8. Klassieke aesthetica
9. Knelpunten in het omroepbestel
10. Kunst, de christen en
11. Kunst en ontspanning op radio en televisie
12. Kunst en vrijheid – 1966
13. Anema's Boek
14. Missa Luba en Missa Bantu
15. Moderne kunst – 1959
16. Natuur en genade in de laat-middeleeuwse schilderkunst
17. De Nederlandse kunst van de 17e eeuw
18. Neo-Gotiek
19. Noodzakelijkheid en praktijk van een christelijke wetenschap
20. Nota over onze kerk – najaar 1973
21. Ons spreken
22. Over het beoordelen van kunst
23. De R. van S.S.R.
24. Rotterdam
25. Schilderijen zien
26. De schilderkunst van de veertiende eeuw
27. Schilderkunrst der 19e eeuw
28. Symbool
29. Thema – Motief – Stijl
30. De tijd waarin wij leven
31. Van Christus getuigen ... vandaag
32. Verslag van de Reis van dr. H.R.R. naar de USA
33. Wat de W.d.W. voor mij betekend heeft
34. Wetenschap, Aesthetica, Kunst
35. De zeventiende eeuwse kunst in Florence
36. Zijn er normen voor kunst?
37. Partial manuscript
38. Partial manuscript
39. Partial manuscript
40. Partial manuscript

German
  41. Theologie der Kunst

IV. Published Articles [English and Dutch]

A. Journal Articles

Box IV.A.1
Dutch – Jazz
1. Amerikaanse volksmuziek op zijn best
2. Antibes
3. Bennie Moten's Kansas City Orchestra
4. Clarence Williams. *Signaal*, March/April 1960
5. De definitie van New Orleans jazz
6. Het einde van een tijdperk
7. Jazz en de 20e eeuw
8. Jazz en klassiek. *Ruimte*, 23 April, 1955
9. Jazz en Wij. *NCRV Omroepgids*
10. Jazz is Music. Jelly Roll Morton. *Signaal*, June/July 1959
11. Jazz vandaag. *Signaal*, November 1960
12. King Olivers klassieke jazz
13. New Orleans jazz – George Lewis. *Signaal*, October 1959
14. New Orleans, Ken Colyer en wij
15. Nieuwe New Orleans Jazz
16. Original Dixieland Jazzband
17. The Second Line

Dutch – Negro Spirituals/Blues
18. Blind Lemon Jefferson
19. De betere spiritual-platen. *Sermo*, November 1959
20. Drie E.P. Amerikaanse negermuziek. *Signaal*, Jan/Feb 1969
21. Gospel concert. *Signaal*, November 1959
22. Gospelsongs
23. Henry Blackman. *Signaal*, June/July 1960
24. Het lied van de neger in Amerika
25. Het neger-volkslied
26. Hollerin' and Cryin' the Blues
27. Ida Cox
28. I'm Going to Live the Life I Sing About
29. I'm Going to Live the Life I Sing About. *Signaal*, March 1959
30. De kerkelijke Negro-Spiritual. *NCRV Omroepgids*
31. Negermuziek uit Noord-Amerika. *NCRV Omroepgids*
32. Op bezoek bij Mahalia Jackson. *Signaal*, April 1962
33. Preachers and Congregations. *Signaal*, February 1960
34. Spirituals en gospel songs. *De Christenvrouw*, Sept. 1965
35. Spirituals in concertvorm
36. The Spirit of Memphis Quartet. *Signaal*, April/May 1959
37. De Stem van haar volk: Ma Rainey

38. Twee kerkdiensten in Harlem
39. Velerlei jazz. *Tot Hoger Peil*, December 1956
40. De Vocalion serie
41. Voices of Victory
42. Volksliederen van N. Amerikaanse Negers

Other
43. Jan van Goyens kunst, *Signaal*, February 1961
44. Bach en Mozart. *Signaal*, May 1961
45. Hoe reizen wij? *Signaal*, May/June 1962
46. Nieuwe kunst in Den Haag. *Signaal*, January 1961
47. Normen voor kunst en amusement. *Signaal*, January 1963

Encyclopedia Articles
48. Saenredam
49. Seurat
50. Steen
51. Surrealisme
52. Synthetisme
53. Symbolisme
54. Tintoretto
55. Toorop
56. Velasquez
57. Vermeer

Box IV.A.2
Dutch
1. *Ad Fontes*, 1964–1966
2. *Beweging*, 1973, 1976, 1977
3. *Calvinistisch Jongelingsbladen*, 1950–1952, 1956, 1959?
4. *Christelijke Encyclopedie*, 1960
   Moderne Kunst, Picasso, Reformatorische Kunst, Rembrandt, Rubens, Schilderkunst, Spirituals
5. *Correspondentie Bladen v.d. Calvinistische Wijsbegeerte*, 1948–51,1953, 1955, 1960, 1967
6. *Ikon*, 1974
7. *Informatie*, 1969
8. *Kerkbode* v.d. Geref. Kerk in de provincie Noord Holland, 1948, 1951
9. *Mededelingen v.d. Vereniging.v.d. Calvinistische Wijsbegeerte*, 1964, 1967
10. *Reformatie*, 1952, 1953
11. *Ruimte*, 1954, 1957–58
12. *Signaal*, 1960–64
13. *Sola Fide*, 1959, 1962, 1964
14. *Stijl*, 1952–1954
15. Miscellaneous published writings in Dutch

Box IV.A.3
English
1. The Absurdity of Man; Modern Art & The Search for Meaning
2. Aesthetics, Art, Beauty. *Baker's Dict. of Chr. Ethics*, 1973
3. Art: A Hedonistic Pastime or a Gift of God. *Decision*, Nov. 1983
4. Art and Crisis. *Genesis*, June 1976
5. The Artist Needs No Justification. *Broadsheet* Arts Centre Group/No. 3
6. Art, Morals, and Western Society. *Beyond Aesthetics*, 1976
7. Art Needs No Justification. *Genesis*, 1975
8. Art, The Christian and *Enc. of Christianity*, 1964
9. Beat/Rock and Protest, 1967
10. Cezanne, Boy in the Red Waistcoat. *Eternity* [not by H.R.R.]
11. The Changing Relation Between Theme, Motive, and Style (incl. mss)
12. Charity in Seventeenth-Century Art
13. Christian Creative Activity. 1968
14. Christian Creativity. *Salt*, 1970
15. The Christian Critique of Art. *The Calvin Forum*, 1952
16. Christianity and Art. *Bulletin...Suid-Afrikaans*, 1970
17. The Comics. *His*, 1972 [not by H.R.R.]
18. Crisis in Values in Contemporary Art, 1972
19. Culture & Revolution (incl. mss). *Christian Scholar's Review*, 1971
20. Culture and Revolution. *Credo*, April/May 1968
21. Definition: The Art of Painting. *Christian Enc.*, 1960
22. Dutch Painting During the Golden Age, 1965
23. Eternity Article #1 *Eternity*, 1971 [not by H.R.R.]
24. Eutychus and His Kin. *Christianity Today*, 1966
25. From Eliza to Odetta. *Philips Music Herald*, 1964–1965
26. Iconography and Iconology, 1964
27. The Image of Man in Modern Art, 1964
28. Interview w/ Rookmaaker. *Crusade*, April 1972
29. Interview w/ Rookmaaker. *Right On*, 1972
30. Let's Sing The Old Dr Watts. *The Gordon Review*, 1966
31. Letter to a Christian Artist. *Christianity Today*, September 1966
32. Mahalia Jackson, A Personal Tribute by H.R.R.
33. Modern Art & Gnosticism. *Zeitschrift für Ästhetik und Allgemeine Kunstwissenschaft*
34. On Culture, 1964
35. *Philosophia Reformata*, 1954
36. The Philosophical Climate Today; Faith & Thought, 1967
37. Principles for Christians Who Want to Work as Artists. *Opbouw*, 1966
38. Symbolism in Painting. *Signs of the Time*, 1966
39. Truth in Art. *Salt*, Autumn 1970

Appendix B: Hans Rookmaaker Papers at Wheaton College

40. Youth in Revolt: Youth in Trouble, European Congress of Evan., 1971

Box IV.A.4
Dutch
1. Barokkunst. *Ad Fontes*, May/June 1965
2. Beat-Protest en Revolutie. *Syllabus*, Jan/Feb 1970
3. Betekenis der Kunst
4. Christus en cultuur [not by H.R.R.]
5. Diepte en breedte van de kunstgeschiedenis. *Ikon*, 1974
6. Een reis naar Zuid-Duitsland. *Ruimte*, January 1955
7. Enkele opmerkingen over de cultuurstaat. *Regelrecht*, April 1965
8. Evangelisatie? *Ruimte*, June 1960
9. Georges Rouault. *Ruimte*, Sept. 1954
10. Grondprinciples van christelijke artistieke arbeid
11. Het begin van onze grote landschapskunst. *Ruimte*, January 1955
12. Het Christelijk Cultureel Studiecentrum (incl. mss). *De Gereformeerde Vrouw*, Feb 1966
13. Het Nederlandse landschap omstreeks 1600
14. Hoe reizen wij? *Ruimte*, March 1955
15. Interview met Prof. Rookmaaker. *Areopagus*, Jan/March 1969
16. Jeugd in opstand; Trans World Radio
17. Kerstmis en kunst. *Signaal*, December 1962
18. Kunst en amusement. *de Sleutel*, June 1965
19. De kunstenaar een profeet?
20. De kunst van de 15e eeuw. *Ad Fontes*, February 1965
21. Patinier. *Gereformeerd Cultureel Maandblad*, October 1953
22. Persschouw. *Opbouw*, July 1960
23. Persschouw. *Trouw*
24. *Philosophia Reformata*, 1946
25. *Philosophia Reformata*, 1947
26. Principes der negentiende eeuwse kunst *Ad Fontes*, October 1965
27. Rembrandt's wijsheid
28. Stijl en levens- en wereldbeschouwing. *Nieuw Nederland* 1946–48
29. Tentoonstellingen en nog wat. *Ruimte*, August 1954
30. Twee soorten liefde en de Carcer Terreno
31. De vrouw in de kunst. *Aksent*, December 1963
32. Waarom moderne kunst? *Ruimte*, December 1954
33. Waarom moderne kunst? *Ruimte*, February 1955
34. Waarom moderne kunst? *Ruimte*, May 1955
35. De werkelijkheid, wijsbegeerte, kunst en wij. *Beweging*, Feb. 1976
36. Wij lazen

B. Newspaper Columns

Box IV.B.1
Dutch
1. *Opbouw*, 1957–1972
2. *Trouw*, March 12, 1949–December 12, 1956

Box IV.B.2
Dutch
1. Bijbelclubs – enkele opmerkingen. *Opbouw*, 1963
2. Cultuur en revolutie. *Opbouw*, August 1968
3. Dansmuziek en Jazzkitsch. *Calvinistisch Jongelingsblad*, Jan. 1952
4. Over het beoordelen van kunst. *Calvinistisch Jongelingsblad*, Oct. 1950
5. Een brief en nog wat. *Opbouw*, 1963
6. Het lied van de neger in Amerika. *Calvinistisch Jongelingsblad*, Sept. 1951
7. Hugo van der Goes: Portinari-Altaar
8. Jazzkunst en Jazzkitch. *Calvinistisch Jongelingsblad*, January 1952
9. Kunst en schoonheid in deze wereld (incl. mss). *Calvinistisch Jongelingsblad*, May 1950
10. De kunst en wij. *Woord en Wereld*, December 1964
11. De Kunst van de 20e eeuw. *Calvinistisch Jongelingsblad*, 7 July, 1950
12. De Kunst van de 20e eeuw. *Calvinistisch Jongelingsblad*, 14 July 1950
13. Omgordt de lendenen van uw verstand en weest nuchter. *Reformatie*, Sept 1952
14. Onze zeventiende eeuwse kunst, 1951
15. Oorsprong en toekomst van de Creatieve Mens
16. Over het beoordelen van kunst. *Calvinistisch Jongelingsblad*, Oct. 1950
17. Over het beoordelen van kunst. *Calvinistisch Jongelingsblad*, Nov. 3, 1950
18. Over het beoordelen van kunst. *Calvinistisch Jongelingsblad*, Nov. 10, 1950
19. De reformatie en de kunst
20. Wij en het Koninkrijk Gods (incl. mss). *Calvinistisch Jongelingsblad*, October 1951
21. Zoutend zout zijn (incl. mss). *Calvinistisch Jongelingsblad*, Nov. 1951

V. Lectures and Sermons

Box V.1
English
    1. Art-historical: June 16, 1974 1/10
    2. Art-historical: July 4, 1974 2/10
    3. Art-historical: July 5, 1974 3/10
    4. Art-historical: July 6, 1974 4/10
    5. Art-historical: July 7–9, 1974 5/10
    6. Art-historical: July 10, 1974 6/10
    7. Art-historical: July 11, 1974 7/10
    8. Art-historical: July 12, 1974 8/10
    9. Art-historical: July 13–15, 1974 9/10
    10. Art-historical: July 17–18, 1974 10/10
    11. Art Needs No Justification
    12. Authority and Permissiveness
    13. Christianity and Culture
    14. The Element Water
    15. Jazz, Twenties
    16. God's Hand in History
    17. The Spiritual in Art in the Past and the Present
    18. The Threat of an Anarchist Revolution Today
    19. Rough drafts of lectures
    20. William Blake, Milton

Dutch
    21. L'Abri, evangelisatie
    22. Beat, rock, protest
    23. Kunst en waarheid
    24. Kunst en vrijheid
    25. Protest en kunst
    26. Sermons
    27. Malachi 3:13–18
    28. 1 John 4:7–26

Box V.2
    29. General lecture notes
    30. Lectures/conferences/exhibitions featuring Rookmaaker

VI. Photographs

Box VI.1
    1. H.R.R., sr. 1927
    2. H.R.R. as a child in Indonesia

3. Family Portrait 1932
   4. H.R.R. circa early 1930s
   5. Riki Spetter
   6. H.R.R. 1939
   7. H.R.R. with father, 1940
   8. H.R.R. 1942
   9. H.R.R. and Anky on wedding day
   10. H.R.R. and family, 1962
   11. H.R.R. with Mahalia Jackson
   12. Professor H.R.R.

VII. Research Notes [Dutch]

Box VII.1
Research Notes divided into divisions from A – QR

Box VII.2
Research Notes 1–4
Research Notes general
Research Notes – Stanislau Prison
Research Notes 1946–1947
Research Notes 1946–1948

VIII. Legal/Financial Documents
Contract for Book on Albrecht Dürer

IX. Secondary Materials

A. Scrapbooks On Music

Box IX.A.1
   1. Collection of materials on blues/jazz/gospel circa. 1956–1958
   2–19. Divisions from A – Z
   20. Arabic Records
   21. News Clippings

B. Jazz Articles [by other authors]

Box IX. B.1
Dutch
   1. Ich Bin Ein Radchen in der Richtigen Maschine

2. Jazz in verdrukking
3. Jazz: van oerwoud-dreun tot modern ritme
4. Le Jazz est-il Mort?

C. Negro-Spirituals/Blues/Pop Articles [by other authors]

English
5. The Birth of the Blues
6. Blues Community Singing Blues Here

Dutch
7. De Gospel-Song
8. Negro Spirituals
9. Negro Spirituals. *NCRV Omroepgids,* January 1956
10. Spirituals
11. De sterren zijn zo vermoeid. *Zaterdag,* September 1967
12. Welke kant wil die Frank Zappa eigenlijk op?
13. Zo gaat het ook niet elke dag

Pop
14. Pop en sex. *Nederlands Studentenblad,* May 1970
15. Pop en subcutuur: Tegenmilieu of Escapisme? *Student,* April 1970
16. Popmuziek Jaarboek. *Parool,* September 1967
17. Popscore. *Zaterdag,* February 1970

D. Articles In English [by other authors]

Box IX.D.I

1. Agony Rock. *Beat Instrumental,* May 1971
2. An Evening Spent at Joni's. *Time,* December 1974
3. Art Criticism. *Interchange*
4. At the Where? *Time,* June 1970
5. Bad Trip. *Time,* November 1968
6. BBC Ban Mick Jagger's Wilde Film
7. The Beatles/Their New Incarnation. *Time,* September 1967
8. Dave Brubeck Unveils Oratorio on Jesus. *Christianity Today,* March 1968
9. England's Elvis: Gut Emotions. *Time,* December 1977
10. Exiled Pastor Speaks of Persecution. *Calvin College Chimes,* Nov. 1974
11. The Girls of Hair. *Playboy*
12. The Gulf of Spirit, Science. *Boston Globe,* July 1975
13. The Human Being in Beethoven. *Philips Music Herald,* 1969
14. Improvising on the Beat. *Time,* July 1974
15. James Taylor: One Man's Family of Rock. *Time,* March 1971
16. Jazz. *Time,* March 1968
17. Jazz Goes to College. *Time,* June 1971

18. Jesus Christ Superstar. *Life*, May 1971
19. Jesus Christ Superstar Rocks Broadway. *Time*, October 1971
20. Jesus in a Pop Culture
21. The Jesus Revolution. *Time*, June 1971
22. Last Trumpet for the First Trumpeter. *Time*, July 1971
23. The Lonely Music of a Man Called Muddy. *Chicago Tribune Magazine*
24. Linda Down. *Time*, February 1977
25. Memorable Songs For Our Times. Mayday Music Inc., 1971
26. Mick Jagger. *The Sunday Denver Post*, July 1972
27. Monk Music
28. Music. Maclean's, June 1972
29. The Necessity of Music
30. The New Jazz. *Newsweek*, December 1966
31. Newport in New York. *Time*, July 1972
32. Playboy Interview: Allen Klein. *Playboy*, November 1971
33. Playboy Interview: Elton John. *Playboy*
34. The Playboy Music Hall of Fame. *Playboy*
35. The 1969 Playboy All-Star's All-Stars. *Playboy*, 1969
36. The 1976 Playboy Music Poll. *Playboy*, 1976
37. Pop Records: Moguls, Money, & Monsters. *Time*, February 1973
38. Religious Concerns Over-Dominate Festival
39. The Road to Respectibility (1927–1930); Arrow in the Blue
40. Rock as Salvation. *The New York Times Magazine*, August 1968
41. Rock as Passion. *Time*, November 1970
42. Rock: The Revolutionary Hype. *Time*, January 1969
43. Schools: A Jewel of a Julliard. *Time*, October 1969
44. Songs in Praise of Birds, Bees, and Birth Control. *Philips Music Herald*, Summer/Autumn 1967
45. The Stones and the Triumph of Marsyas. *Time*, July 1972
46. Student Balances Liberal Arts Education with World-Wide Concert Performance. *Wheaton Record*, February 1967
47. Underground Comes Up on Top. *Philips Music Herald*, Winter 1968/9
48. William Law (1881)
49. Winter Preview

E. Record Album Covers [photocopies]

Box IX.E.1

1. Treasures of North American Negro Music, vol. 1–15 (missing 11, 13, 14)
2. Album Information
3. Miscellaneous Album Information
4. Classical Jazz

F. Christian Artists & Associations

Box IX.F.1
1. L'Abri
2. AICA
3. Association for the Advancement of Christian Scholarship
4. Calvinistic Philosophy/Calvinism and Culture
5. Christian Film Education; Film board/inspection, misc.
6. Christian Film Education; Film board/inspection, 1963–1965
7. Christian Film Education; Film board/inspection, 1966–1970
8. David Reece

Box IX.F.2
1. The Emissary. *Collegiate Scene Magazine*
2. EO Evangelical Broadcast
3. European Congress On Evangelism
4. Fellowship of Christians in the Arts, Media, and Entertainment
5. *The Gordon Review*
6. Institute for Christian Art
7. International Association of Art Critics
8/9. *Koers*
10. Loorthians
11. Vereniging van Gereformeerde Studenten te Amsterdam
12. General

Box IX.F.3
1. Material on CCS from 1964–1977
2. CCS – undated
3. CCS – Chr. Kunstacademie
4. CCS – Van Tienenweg 37 Diemen

G. Reviews [books and records]

Box IX.G.1
1. *Synthetist Art Theories: Genesis & Nature of Ideas on Art of Gaugin and His Circle*, 1959
2. *Jazz, blues, spirituals*, 1960
3. *Kunst en amusement*, 1962
4. *De Kunstenaar een profeet?* 1965
5. *Modern Art and the Death of a Culture*, 1970
6. Malcolm Muggeridge, 1970–71
7. *The Creative Gift: Essays on Art and The Christian Life*, 1981
8. Nothin' But the Blues
9. Fontana/Riverside, Record Reviews
10. Book Announcements
11. Spirituals and Blues, by Cone

H. Articles about Rookmaaker

Box IX.H.1
1. The Absurdity of Man. *British Weekly*, December 1968
2. Affirming the Arts
3. Alien Brain
4. All That Jazz
5. The Art of Representation. *Pacific Theological Review*, Winter 1975
6. Arts Festival Highly Succesful. *Bulletin of Westminister Theological Seminary*, 1976
7. The Creative Gift. *CSSH Quarterly*, Summer 1983
8. The Christian and the Arts in Contemporary Society. *The Witness*, Apr. 1969
9. Dr. H.R. Rookmaaker. *Christian Graduate*, June 1977
10. Francis A. Schaeffer: An Evaluation. *Bibliotheca sacra Journal*
11. Hans Rookmaaker: A Biography. *Crux*, June 1980
12. Hans Rookmaaker: An Appreciation
13. H.R. Rookmaaker. *Third Way*, March 1977
14. Letter. *The Cut*, Autumn 1989
15. Master Painters' Work Shown To Couples Club
16. Not Forgotten or Passed Over. *The Greenbelt Newspaper*, 1984/85
17. Our Looking at Paintings: A Look At Rookmaaker. *The Reformed Journal*, Feb 1972
18. Our Calling to be Critical. *Loog*, May 1972
19. Paper on Hans Rookmaaker. *ICS*, 1978
20. Paul Clowney
21. Readers Respond. *The Reformed Journal*
22. Regent College, Vancouver, Nov 1970
23. 'Rook' on Art. *Crusade*, April 1970
24. The Rookmaaker Lecture; Festival, Autumn 1977
25. Two Men, One Vision. *Sound*, June/July 1984
26. Waking up to Reality. *Crusade*, October 1971
27. Walford Stresses Dignity of Art. *Wheaton Record*, September 1981
28. What is Religious Art? *The Presbyterian Guardian*, Summer 1972
29. Will There Be Martyrs? *The Vancouver Sun*, July 1970
30. Yet Another Leaflet on Student Protest. Birmingham College of Art and Design Christian Fellowship, October 1968

Box IX.H.2
Dutch
1. Arabische en Berber-Muziek. *Het Vaderland*, March 1951
2. Barok Rome
3. Beweging zonder naam. *Music & Art Magazine*, December 1985
4. Bij het heengaan van Hans R. Rookmaaker; CCS
5. Bij het heengaan van Prof Dr. Rookmaaker. *VU magazine*, April 1977

6. Bourgeoismentaliteit sterft nooit uit. *RW. Courant,* March 1968
7. Boekbespreking. Overdruk uit *Radix*
8. Bulletin; February, 1975
9. Christenen moeten kunst scheppen vanuit bewogenheid. *Friesch Dagblad,* Feb 1976
10. Clarence Williams. *Signaal,* June/July 1961
11. De Christen en de cultuur. *Gezinsblad,* May 1965
12. Die Moderne Kuns Aftakeling van Menslike Waardes; Litugrafiese Bylae Tot *Die Oosterlig,* December 1974
13. Dr H.R. Rookmaaker. *Friesch Dagblad,* February 1976
14. Dr Rookmaaker strijdt voor nieuwe gereformeerde levensstijl. *Spiegel,* June 1963
15. Een belangrijke promotie. *Mededelingen v.d. Vereniging voor Calvinist. Wijsbegeerte,* Sept 1959
16. Evangelisatie – congres: Morele kick voor eenzame werkers; Bijlage *Leeuwarder Courant,* September 1971
17. Evangelisatie vereist training, zegt Rev. Gilbert W. Kirby; Erbij, *Haarlems Dagblad*
18. From Birmingham: Kunst van jonge Engelse christenen. *Ad Valvas,* Dec 1974
19. Geestelijke strijd. *NRC Handelsblad,* Cultureel Supplement, Feb 1971
20. De Geest van Revolutie, De Mens van Wetteloosheid; NUK, Feb 1968
21. Geloof opnieuw integreren in leven van alledag. *Nieuwe Haagse Courant,* Sept 1971
22. Macht en Onmacht in de 20ste eeuw
23. Helende Beelden. *Music & Art,* April 1988
24. Het boek van Rookmaaker. *Gereformeerd Weekblad,* March 1963
25. In de spiegel van de kunst. *Centraal Weekblad,* June 1971
26. In Memoriam, H.R. Rookmaaker. *Beweging,* April 1977
27. In Memoriam Prof. Dr H.R. Rookmaaker. *Ad Valvas,* March 1977
28. In Memoriam Prof. Dr H.R. Rookmaaker 1922–1977
29. In Memoriam Prof. Rookmaaker. *Trouw,* March 1977
30. In plan Christelijke Academie Beeldende Vorming komt tekening. *Trouw,* Sept 1976
31. Is de kunstenaar profeet? *Leidsch Dagblad,* 1965
32. Jazz en evangelielied. *Jong Gereformeerd,* March 1961
33. Kanttekeningen bij twee kunsthistorische dissertaties. *Sola Fide,* '60
34. Kerstnummer Drukkersweekblad. *Penin Pers,* January 1961
35. De kunstenaar een profeet? *Gooi & Eemlander,* May 1965
36. Kunst en amusement. *Sermo,* January 1963
37. Kunst en amusement. *Polemists,* February 1963
38. Kunst en amusement. *School en Huis,* November 1965

39. Kunstwerk Ontmoeting van Kunstenaar en Medemens. *Reformatorisch Dagblad*, Jan 1975
40. Literatur und Kunst. *Neue Zuricher Zeitung*, August 1969
41. Liturgie van de Samenkomst bij het overlijden van Rookmaaker
42. Macht and onmacht van de 20e eeuw
43. Macht en onmacht van de twintigste eeuw. *Opbouw*
44. Negeren van kunst is onmogelijk. *Zaterdag*, May 1965
45. Nieuwe studie over jazz, blues en spirituals. November 1960
46. Nog meer boekjes over het geloof zijn niet nodig. *Trouw*, Sept. 1971
47. Onder de regenboog. *Opbouw*, January 1963
48. (On) Kruid. *Friesch Dagblad*
49. Over de normen in de kunst. *Gereformeerd Gezinsblad*, June 7, 1963
50. Over de normen in de nunst. *Gereformeerd Gezinsblad*, June 8, 1963
51. Perspectief; *Mededelingen*. December 1962
52. Persschouw. *Opbouw*
53. Prediking. *De Rotterdammer*, July 1960
54. Prenten Aad Veldhoen zinneprikkelend? LD, December 1964
55. Prof. Dr H.R. Rookmaaker. *Lier en Boog*, January 1978
56. Prof. Dr H.R. Rookmaaker als 'baas'. *Stuk*, April 1977
57. Prof. H.R. Rookmaaker onverwachts overleden. *Reformatorisch Dagblad*, March 1977
58. Prof. Rookmaaker, de christen en de kunst
59. Prof. Rookmaaker sprak voor A.R. Oegstgeest; NLC, February 1966
60. Prof. Rookmaaker ziet heil in rock en beat tegen de ontkerstening. *Haagse Post*
61. Professor Rookmaaker zoekt meer in Beatles-songs dan er inzit. Parool, Oct 1968
62. Prof. Rookmaaker: Christenen mede schuldig aan extreme kunst. April 1965
63. Promotie H.R. Rookmaaker
64. De relatie evangelie en kunst bij de kunsthistoricus Prof Dr. H.R. Rookmaaker. *De Wekker*, December 1984
65. De relatie evangelie en kunst bij de kunsthistoricus Prof. Dr. H.R. Rookmaaker. *De Wekker*, January 1985
66. Riverside's Classic Jazz Masters. *Luister*, May 1965
67. Rooirok en Rookmaaker
68. Rookmaaker en het programmatisch christendom. *Trouw*, January 1979
69. Schaeffer als culturele Jeremia. *Trouw*, December 1977
70. Ter herdenking van Prof. Dr. H.R. Rookmaaker. *Opbouw*, March 1977
71. Treasures of North American Negro Music. *Luister*, November 1960
72. Twee nieuwe christelijke academies. *Centraal Weekblad*, October 1977

73. Van de Leden; Christelijk Gymnasiaal Middelbaar Onderwijs, Mar. 1961
74. Vluchtig portret
75. De weg tot ontwaking en opbouw: een Calvinistisch cultureel congres. *De Rotterdammer*, February 1953

French
76. L'Art Moderne et la Mort d'une Culture; A Tranvers les Revues...
77. Les Grandes Soirees du Mouloudia et du V.S.M.; Alger-Soir, Aug 1947
78. Y a-t-il un Art Chretien; *Jeunesse Liberée*, 1975

I. Manuscripts by Others

Box IX. I. I
1. Collected Poems
2. Evangelie en Kunst, door ds. Theo Peppink
3. Kort overzicht over de geschiedenis der wijsbegeerte; College-dictaat van Dr D.H.Th. Vollenhoven, January 1947
4. Kort overzicht over de geschiedenis der wijsbegeerte; College-dictaat van Dr D.H.Th. Vollenhoven
5. Inleiding Encyclopaedie der Rechtswetenschap; Dr H. Dooyeweerd
6. Pat Cook
7. Professor Mekkes
8. Science in Christian Perspective

J. Media

Box IX.J.I [in X.B.I]
Photographs
1. Bunk Johnson
2. Brunswick Record
3. The Colossi of Memnon
4. The Damnation of Faust
5–6. Emily Addie Jones White
7. Fall of Icarus
8. Jelly Roll Morton
9. Jelly Roll Morton
10. Kid Ory & Jazz Band
11. King Oliver's Creole Jazz Band, 1923
12. Kunst en Amusement
13–18. Monnickendam
19. Modern Art and the Death of a Culture
20. Ptah of Memphis
21. She Had A Heart After All

22. Sonny Terry
23. They Call It Jazz

Glass Plate Positives
   English Song Lyrics; Richard Dering, Alfred Deller Consort

X. Free University

A. Student Papers

Box X.A.1
1. The Abstract Society
2. An Approach to the Problems of our Culture
3. Aspects of the Blues Tradition
4. Bomb Culture
5. Brief Analysis of the Naked Society
6. Christianity in Art
7. Christian Art in Asia: India, China, Japan, and Philippines
8. Christian Letters to a Post Christian World
9. The Church at the End of the 20th Century
10. Death in the City
11. The Dialectics of Liberation
12. The Dialectics of Liberation
13. Eros Denied
14. Ethics In A Permissive Society
15. Faut-il Bruler Sade?
16. Feminine Mystique, Betty Friedan
17. The Feminine Mystique, Betty Friedan
18. Future Shock, Alvin Toffler
19. The God Who is There, F. Schaeffer
20. Literary Artist Remembers the Future: Time, Dickens, & Little Dorrit
21. Loss of Self in Modern Literature and Art
22. The Making of the Counter Culture
23. Manchild in the Promised Land, C. Brown
24. The Meaning of Perspective in The Quattrocentro
25. The Naked Society, Vance Packard
26. One Flew Over the Cuckoo's Nest
27. Pascal et Voltaire: La Lumiere Steinte?
28. The Permissive Society: Fact or Fantasy?
29. The Recovery of Harmony: Poetry of Wallace Stevens
30. The Secular City
31. The Secular City
32. Subjective Values and Scientific Objectivity

33. The Symbolic in Art
34. Time and History
35. Thoughts About a Very Bad Picture
36. The Touch of Ingmar Bergman
37. Twentieth Century Cultural Problems
38. Twentieth Century Cultural Problems
39. The World as Image

B. Bibliographies & Course Outlines

Box X.B.1
General
1. Aan de deelnemers aan het doctoraal werkcollege Beeldende Kunst I
2. Aanvulling bibliografie 19de eeuwse iconografie
3. Bibliografie Barok kunst
4. Bibilografie 2de Blok – 1150–1500
5. Bibliografie 4de Blok – 1750–heden
6. Bibliografie 18de eeuw
7. Bibliografie 19de en 20ste eeuw
8. Bibliografie Renaissance
9. Bibliografie Renaissance in Florence
10. Bibliografie voor de werkgroep Ikonografie van de 19e eeuw
11. Blokprogramma Sept–Dec 1975, 2de Jaar Middeleeuwen
12. Blokprogramma Sept–Dec 1975, 3de Jaar Barok
13. Christianity and Art
14. Christianity and Culture, 1974
15. Course on 20th Century
16. Documentatie excursie Bourgondië
17. Enige 17de eeuwse geschriften over kunst
18. Iconografie 1975–76 – 2de en 3de jaars studenten
19. Kunsthistorische terminologie
20. Literatuurlijst 1e blok Middeleeuwen Architectuur
21. Literatuurlijst 1e blok Middleleeuwen Beeldende Kunst
22. Literatuurlijst voor de Architectuur van de 19de en 20ste eeuw
23. Paper – onderwerpen Barok
24. Suggesties voor paperonderwerpen Ikonografie, 2de en 3de jaars
25. Tentamen Theorie en Geschiedenis der Kunstgeschiedenis

Course Outlines
26. Betreffende de Studie Voor de Akte M.O. Pedagogiek, 1963–1964
27. Confrontation with the Revolution, 1970
28. Dutch Painting During the Golden Age, 1965
29. Werkcollege Hermeren, 1976

Regent College

30. Modern Art and the Death of a Culture – summer course
31. Summer Session 1970
32. Summer Session 1974 address list
33. Twentieth Century Cultural Problems, July 3–21, 1972

XI. Unknown

Box XI.A.1
1. Addresses/Business Cards
2. Art Historical materials
3. Book Reviews
4. Correspondence, undated
5. Index
6. Lecture notes
7. Publication Notes: *Gauguin and 19th-century Art Theory*
8. Publication Notes: *Jazz, blues, spirituals*
9. Publication Notes: *Modern Art and the Death of a Culture*
10. Publication Notes
11. Royalties
12. C.C.S
13. Cultuurpolitiek
14. Het Beleid op het gebied van kunst en cultuur
15. Ontwerp Christelijk Cultureel Congres
16. Profetie
17. UNIE – School met de Bijbel

XII. Media

A. Audio Tapes
1. A Dutch Christian View on Philosophy I
2. A Dutch Christian View on Philosophy II
3. De taak van een christenkunstenaar
4. Gods hand in de geschiedenis I
5. Gods hand in de geschiedenis II
6. Gods hand in de geschiedenis III
7. Rookmaaker: Music Lecture
8. Culture as Creation of Life Form
9. Spirituals and Gospel Music I
10. Spirituals and Gospel Music I
11. Comments on Art and Culture I
12. Comments on Art and Culture II

Appendix B: Hans Rookmaaker Papers at Wheaton College

13. Comments on Art and Culture III
14. Comments on Art and Culture IV
15. Comments on Art and Culture V
16. Comments on Art and Culture VI
17. Comments on Art and Culture VII
18. Christianity and Culture I
19. Christendom en cultuur I
20. Christendom en cultuur II
21. Blues I
22. Blues II
23. Wat is werkelijkheid? (What is Reality?)
24. Toward a Christian View of Culture I
25. Toward a Christian View of Culture II
26. Jazz I
27. Jazz I
28. Hooglied (Song of Solomon)
29. Evangelisatie (Evangelism)
30. Kunst behoeft geen rechtvaardiging (Art Needs No Justification)
31. Is kunstgeschiedehis een hobby? (Is Art History a Hobby?)
32. Gezag en vrijheid I
33. Gezag en vrijheid II
34. Beat and Protest I
35. Beat and Protest II
36. Kunst en waarheid (Art and Truth)
37. Romeinen 7, 8 (Romans 7–8)
38. Creativiteit (Creativity)
39. Eva's Dochteren I en II (Eve's Daughters)
40. Eva's Dochteren III (Eve's Daughters)
41. Openbaring (Revelation)
42. Art Needs No Justification I
43. Art Needs No Justification II
44. Genesis I
45. Genesis II
46. 2 Petrus 1:1–11 (2 Peter 1:1–11)
47. Ultra Naturalisme (Ultranaturalism)
48. Moeten we modern zijn I
49. Moecten we modern zijn II
50. Moeten we modern zijn om eigentyds te zijn
51. Tolerantie (Tolerance)
52. John Walford discussing Hans Rookmaaker, 11/7/85
53. What is Art?
54. Jazz and the Christian
55. Three Steps to Modern Art
56. Beat Music I
57. Beat Music II

Publisher's Afterword

It has been an immense honour to be involved with the publication of *The Complete Works of Hans Rookmaaker*. Our vision for this project was kindled in 1986, when we spent a year at the Dutch L'Abri and became aware of the ongoing influence of Hans Rookmaaker through the many people he had inspired so profoundly.

Marleen expressed her willingness to undertake the immense task of editing her father's works. Pieter next pursued the project as publishing director of Paternoster Press, but it was not until Piquant was conceived in 1999 that the *Complete Works* could become a reality. Despite many pitfalls and our own lack of experience, we praise God that we can now celebrate their completion.

Much joy has come from the artwork by Marc de Klijn which has appropriately given these volumes a distinctive character. Alongside Marc's contribution we have to mention the cover designs of Jonathan Kearney, who personally supervised the printing of the jackets!

We thank Stichting Pro Religione for their generous grant, which has enabled the production of volumes 5 and 6 and is subsidizing a set of the *Complete Works* in the libraries of 70 key Bible colleges and theological faculties in the Majority World.

The Piquant vision behind the *Complete Works* is straightforward: to make the sharp insight and powerful encouragement of Rookmaaker available to a new generation of readers. Christians in the arts today are by no means the rare birds they were in Rookmaaker's day. A vast number of Christians now practise and enjoy the arts. But we dare say that wisdom and clarity about how to exercise one's freedom in mature Christian reflection, recreation and artistic endeavour is as difficult as ever.

Our guiding editorial principle has been to produce not a text-literal work but one that is as uniformly readable as possible without distorting the intended meaning – so for example all the writings, including published books, have been edited for gender neutrality. And the NIV Bible text has generally been used. Some repetitions have been deleted. Those who want to do further research on Rookmaaker are encouraged to use the *Complete Works* to identify useful articles and chapters, but they will need to consult the originals for detailed text-critical studies. Contact information for the Buswell Library at Wheaton College is supplied in the editor's preface to this final volume, and Appendix B lists the original manuscripts in the collection at Wheaton College. Complete collections of original manuscripts are also kept in the *Documentatiecentrum* at the Free University of Amsterdam and at the Institute for Christian Studies in Toronto, Canada. Exciting ideas for further study are scattered throughout the *Complete Works* as H.R.R. often indicated very specific topics that would make valuable contributions –

many of these are still lying fallow! As publishers we would love to hear from anyone undertaking further research or writing related to the works of H.R.R.

All to say, enjoy the read. We do apologize for a number of errata – some of which have come to our attention since publication and are listed below. Please contact us by emailing info@piquant.net if you have any further queries or comments.

Pieter and Elria Kwant
Carlisle, UK, 2003

Errata

Throughout spelling should be L'Abri
sp. Masaccio 2:149; 4:48, 306, 307
sp. Berckheyde and van de Heyden 1:255; 4:185
'a thing of beauty is a joy for ever' 3:211; 4:239, 356

The following instances of the word 'motif(s)' should change to 'motive(s)':
1:17 (line 24), 63 (line 10), 67 (line 3 from below), 85 (line 2 under quote), 87 (line 7 from below), 94 (para 2, 3x), 97 (line 9 from below), 101 (line 2), 121 (line 13 from below), 122 (lines 18, 31, 36), 123 (line 14), 124 (line 4 from below), 140 (line 8 above lower quote), 141 (lines 3, 18, 22, 30, 31 below top quote), 143 (bottom line), 144 (lines 6, 7, 17, 19, 29), 145 (line 3 from below), 149 (line 15), 156 (line 9), 162 (line 19), 199 (line 7, 10 under 'Freedom'), 365 note 25 (line 3, 2x), 382 note 317, 395 note 506, 414 note 819, 421 note 884 (line 1); 2:92 (line 1).

1:94, line 8: replace 'experimentalists, tachists' with 'Experimentals, Tachists'
sp. Borobudur 1:196, 198, 201
sp. Susanne K. Langer 1:202
1:230, note: replace 'of which some' with 'all of which'
1:313, line 1: cap 'Negro'
1:341, title: change to 'Experimentals'

sp. Watts's instead of Watts' throughout vol 2
sp. Neubrandenburg (Neu-Brandenburg) 2:11, 12
2:viii, page numbers as follows: *We see what we know* (144), and *Three examples* (148)
2:11, lines 13, 14: change to '... I personally experienced a dogmatic struggle, similar to the struggle of the early church, and finally ...'
2:93, lines 13–15: replace the sentences 'The result is ...This is also a result' with 'That they have let it come to this is partly caused by the theorization of the humanistic world view, into which humanistic philosophy has penetrated in popularized form. This is also the result'
sp. Gustav van de Woestijne 2:90, 104
change 'craftspeople' to 'artisan(s)' 2:111; 4:24,
replace 'Tame' with 'Taine' 2:141
sp. Coca-Cola 2:147
sp. Stephen Foster, 2:181
sp. Tommy Ladnier 2:217
sp. Lil Hardin 2:240
2:266, line 29: replace 'Allan Ramsay' with 'Frederic Ramsey'; sp. (Frederic) Ramsey 2:290, 291, 311, 320, 332, n.266, n.462, n.478
2:297, replace '*Geworfenheit*' with '*Geworfen-sein*'
sp. Bartók (Béla) 2:298; 3:54, 422
sp. Marian Anderson 2:304, 319, 322, 348, 350, 366
2:306, 309: in title and 6x in the lyrics insert 'up' to make 'I'm going to move on up a little higher'
2:319 last line second para sp. 'themselves'
sp. Leonora (Leonore) 2:n.115
2:n.505, insert: A similar article is 'Mahalia Jackson – The World's Greatest Gospel Singer,' *Salt* 1 (Autumn 1974) pp.2–3.
Vol 2, back cover blurb, change '22-year-old Hans Rookmaaker' to '21-year-old Hans Rookmaaker'

insert 'of the Dutch writings' after 'rest' 3:xi
sp. Grandville 3:12
insert 'linen' before 'canvas' 3:12, quotation
change to *Rain, steam, speed* 3:67
sp. Helmholtz, 3:176
3:196, change to: 'The strife of the poet for a new expression, a new poetic value, ...perhaps non-existent reality.'
change 'eves' to 'eyes' 3:202
3:378, in the Volboudt quotation change 'does no longer have' to 'has just as little'.
instead of 'carnality' orig. 'bestiality' (or 'animality')

sp. Rädecker 4:224
sp. Léger 4:270
sp. Veneziano 4:301
sp. Malevich 4:455
4:n.539, 'H.R. Rookmaaker ...'
4:n.592, change to 'that had split off from the Reformed Church in the Netherlands in 1944.'

Complete Contents of all 6 Volumes

Articles/Lectures

Aesthetics: Aesthetic Sphere and Disclosure, the, 2:89–92; Art and Beauty in this World, 4:206–210; Art and Psychology, 4:244–250; Art of Painting: A Definition, the, 4:231–235; Art, Aesthetics, and Beauty, 2:138–142; Art, Philosophy and our View of Reality; Hermeneutics of Art (L'Abri lecture), 6:236–251; Iconic Function, the, 2:114–115; Science, Aesthetics and Art, 2:93–113; Sketch for an Aesthetic Theory based on the Philosophy of the Cosmonomic Idea, 2:24–79; Style and World View, 2:80–88; Symbolism in Painting, 4:235–239; To Do the Truth in Art (L'Abri lecture), 6:225–235

Art History & Art Apreciation: About the Content of Works of Art, 4:3–6; Art and Beauty in this World, 4:206–210; Art as Profession, 4:220–225; Art History at the Free University of Amsterdam, 3:491–496; Art, Morals and Western Society, 4:252–268; Artistic Metamorphosis of the Dragon, 4:189–192; Chinese Landscapes, 4:445–446; Christmas Portrayed in Art, 4:200–202; Depth and Breadth of Art History, 3:481–491; Female Figure in Art, The, 4:192–194; Humour in the Visual Arts, 4:195–200; Is the Photo Natural? 4:446–453; Judging Works of Art (Westminster discussions), 3:414–415; Judging Works of Art, 4:210–218; Learning to See (Westminster discussions), 3:411–414; Learning to See, 4:219–220; Method of Art History, The, 3:479–481; Reproductions, 4:453–460; Symbol of the Fish in the Logo of Opbouw, The, 4:188–189; Three Works of Art, 4:202–205; What is Art? (Westminster discussions), 3:407–411; What is Visual Art? 4:225–230

Art History, Middle Ages: About the Content of Medieval Works of Art, 4:7–10; Art of the Fourteenth Century in France, The, 4:14–52; Ecclesia and Synagogue in Strasbourg, 4:10–14; Landscape from 1380, A, 4:52–55; Les Grandes Heures de Rohan: What Visual Art can Give, 4:55–59

Art History, Fifteenth Century: Art of the Fifteenth Century, The, 4:60–63; Leonardo da Vinci, 4:72–73; Portinari Altar by Hugo van der Goes, The, 4:67–69; Theological Treatise, A, 4:69–72; Two Kinds of Love and the 'Carcer Terreno', 4:73–101; Van Eyck's St Barbara and Life in the Covenant, 4:63–67

Art History, Sixteenth Century: Albrecht Dürer's Theory of the Created Structures, 4:104–107; Dürer's Apocalypse: An Artist's Message to his Contemporaries, 3:237–244; Dürer and Landscape, 4:109–113; Dürer's Melancholia, 4:107–109; 'Expressionistic' and 'Normal' in Altdorfer's Work, 4:116–120; Influence of the Reformation on Art, The, 4:102–104; Patinier, 4:121–125; Resurrection Theme in Sixteenth-Century Art, The, 4:113–115

Art History, Seventeenth Century: Baroque Art, 4:140–143; Beginning of the Great Dutch Landscape Art, The, 4:164–167; Changing Relation between Theme, Motif and Style, The, 4:146–149; Charity in Seventeenth-Century Art, 4:153–161; Dutch Landscape around 1600, The, 4:162–164; Landscape Art of Jan van Goyen, The, 4:167–171; Rembrandt's Wisdom, 4:171–177; Saenredam and Emanuel de Witte, 4:179–181;

Seventeenth–Century Dutch Art: Christian Art? 4:132–140; Theme, Style and Motif in the Sixteenth and Seventeenth Centuries, 4:143–146; Woman in Danger: A Motif in Seventeenth–Century Art, 4:149–153

Art History, Nineteenth Century: Dutch Painting at the Beginning of the Nineteenth Century, 4:185–187; Principles of Nineteenth–Century Art, 4:182–185

Art History, Twentieth Century: Aad Veldhoen: Contemporary Wholesome Art, 5:246–247; Angst 5:217–219; Art of the Twentieth Century, The, 5:219–225; Art or Not Art? 5:287–291; Artist as a Prophet? The, 5:169–188; Commitment in Art, 5:188–233; Form and Content of Modern Art, 5:285–287; Function of Visual Art in our Times, The, 5:279–285; Is Modern Art True? 5:305–311; New Art: Art Nouveau and Jugendstil, 5:209–210; Pondering Four Modern Drawings, 5:225–231; Rouault, 5:236–239; Surrealism, 5:231–236; This Too is our Times, 5:239–244; Ultranaturalism (L'Abri lecture), 6:252–258; Whence do we Come? What are We? Where do we Go? 5:210–217; Wholesome Twentieth-Century Art, 5:245–246; Why Modern Art? 5:261–278

Christians, Artists & Culture: Affluence, the Welfare State and Culture, 3:337–359; Art and Beauty in this World, 4:206–210; Art and Entertainment on Radio and Television, 3:385–403; Art and Lifestyle, 3:375–385; Art and Mission (Westminster discussions), 3:433–435; Art and Politics, 4:250–252; Art as Profession, 4:220–225; Art not Neutral, 4:268–271; Artist as a Prophet? The, (inaugural lecture on assuming professorship at the Free University) 5:169–187; Can we Use Modern and Abstract Forms? (Westminster discussions) 3:423–426; Certainty (Westminster discussions), 3:415–422; Christian and Art, The, 4:355–361; Christian and Art Today (I), The, 4:361–366; Christian and Art Today (II), The, 4:376–379; Christian Art (Westminster discussions), 3:427–430; Christian Artist, The, (L'Abri lecture), 6:269–275; Christian Critique of Art, The, 4:352–355; Christianity and Culture (Westminster discussions), 3:435–444; Christmas Portrayed in Art, 4:200–202; Commitment in Art, 5:188–203; Culture and Revolution I, 5:247–254; Culture and Revolution II: We Live in '1787', 5:254–260; Do we need to be Modern in order to be Contemporary? 5:311–335; Faith and Culture, 3:319–335; How Do We Travel? 4:443–445; Influence of Art on Society, The, 4:372–376; Judging Works of Art, 4:210–218; Learning to See, 4:219–220; Nudity (Westminster discussions), 3:444–455; On Being Salt that Salts, 3:314–319; On Portraying God and Christ (Westminster discussions), 3:430–433; Problem of Christian Themes in Art, The, (L'Abri lecture), 6:276–287; Schematic Summary of the Artistic Revolution (appendix to *Art and the Public Today*), 5:204–206; Some Comments on the Culture State, 3:360–367; Television and Film (Westminster discussions), 3:455–459; To Do the Truth in Art (L'Abri lecture), 6:225–235; We and Art, 4:350–352; Youth in Revolt, Youth in Trouble: Who's to Blame? 3:368–374

Christian Life & Faith: Bible Study Groups, 4:430–435; Child Evangelism 6:120–122; Coming to Conversion – Some Comments, 4:425–430; Evangelization, 6:125–130; Genesis 1: Creation versus Evolution (L'Abri lecture), 6:215–224; International Council of Christian Churches (ICCC), the, 4:413–414; Life's Questions – on Suffering, 4:435–439; Love is the

End: Sermon on 2 Peter (L'Abri lecture), 6:294–298; On Witnessing, 6:122–125; Our Calling in a Postchristian World (L'Abri lecture), 6:163–173; Predestination (L'Abri lecture), 6:288–293; Present Apostasy, The, 4:414–420; We and the Kingdom of God, 4:421–425

Education: Art and We: CCS – The Early Vision, 4:367–370; Art History at the Free University of Amsterdam, 3:491–496; CCS, Towards a Christian Art Academy, The, 4:370–372; Gird your Minds for Action and Keep Sober in the Spirit, 3:460–476; Norms for Art and Art Education, 2:116–137

Music: African–American Music as a Source of Beauty and Historical Information, 2:331–333; African–American Church Service in the USA, the, 2:352–353; African Music as it Really Is: Disenchantment and Confirmation of a Romantic Dream, 2:317–318; American Folk Music at its Best, 2:322–325; Blind Lemon Jefferson, 2:326–328; Christianity and Music (L'Abri lecture), 6:259–268; Folk Songs of Black Americans, 2:330–331; From Eliza to Odetta, 2:318–322; Hollerin' and Crying the Blues, 2:333–336; Jazz and Revolution (L'Abri lecture), 6:185–191; 'Jazz', Jazz and Classical, 2:362–367; Jazz on the Riverboats, 2:372–373; Jelly Roll Morton, 2:369–370; Let's Sing the Old Dr Watts: A Chapter in the History of Negro Spirituals, 2:338–345; Listening to Jazz, 2:359–362; Negro Spiritual in Church, the, 2:345–347; Nothin' but the Blues, 2:336–337; Ory's Creole Trombone, 2:370–371; Poetic Fiction in the Blues, 2:325–326: Rock and Protest (L'Abri lecture), 6:192–202; USA 1961 (trip report on meeting musicians), 2:356–358; Visiting Mahalia Jackson, 2:353–355; Voices of Victory (spirituals), 2:349–350

Philosophy: Art, Philosophy and Our View of Reality, 2:144–150; Basic Principles of the Philosophy of the Cosmonomic Idea, the, 2:3–9; Certainty (Westminster discussions), 3:415–422; Constituent Factors of a Historical Deed, the, 3:247–313; Dutch Christian View of Philosophy, A, (L'Abri lecture),6:174–184; Is Modern Art True? 5:305–311; Norms for Art and Art Education, 2:116–137; Philosophy and Art: Pieter Bruegel, 4:126–131; Philosophy of Unbelievers, the, 2:13–20; Shestov, 5:292–296; Sketch for an Aesthetic Theory based on the Philosophy of the Cosmonomic Idea, 2:24–79; What is Reality? (L'Abri lecture), 6:203–214; What the Philosophy of the Cosmonomic Idea has Meant to Me, 2:10–12

Bibliographies

Bibliography of Published Writings about H.R. Rookmaaker, 6:434–446

Calvinism and Art, an Annotated Bibliography, 4:379–382

Christianity and Art: A Preliminary Bibliography, 1571–1970, 4:382–392

Iconography and Iconology: A Literature Study, 4:239–243

in Gauguin and Nineteenth-Century Art Theory: 1:202; Art and Art Theory in the Naturalistic-Realistic Tradition, 1:209–210; Art and Literature outside the Circle of the Synthetists, 1:211–215; Art, Art Theory and Aesthetics before the Nineteenth Century, 1:203; General Works on Nineteenth-century Art, 1:207–208; Kindred Spirits of the Synthetists, 1:215–218; Later

Literature on Synthetism and the Synthetists, 1:222–223; Literature and Culture in the Nineteenth Century (up to 1885), 1:205–207; Memoirs and Writings after 1900 of Eye-witnesses, 1:222; On Precursors of the Synthetists, 1:208–209; Philosophy and Aesthetics in the Nineteenth Century, 1:204–205; Writings by Gauguin, 1:219; Writings By or About the Synthetists (1885–1900), 1:218–219; Writings Concerning Gauguin after 1959, 1:223–224; Writings Concerning Gauguin, 1:219–221

in 'Hans Rookmaaker: An Open Life', appendix II discusses the author's sources

in *Jazz, Blues and Spirituals*, 2:310–311

in *Modern Art and the Death of a Culture*, 5:162–164

with Articles: Art of Painting: A Definition, The, 4:n.465; Christian and Art, The, 4:n.564; Modern Art and Gnosticism: An Open Letter to Prof. Dr Jan Aler, 5:n.439; Do we Need to be Modern in Order to be Contemporary? 5:n.477

see also the list of materials in the Hans Rookmaaker Collection at Wheaton College (Ill), 6:447–470

Biographies

Hans Rookmaaker: An Open Life (Laurel Gasque), 6:299–430
Hans Rookmaaker: The Shaping of his Thought (Graham Birtwistle), 1:xv–xxxiii
see also the Bibliography of Published Writings about H.R.R., 6:434–446

Books by HRR

Art and Entertainment, 3:1–131
Art and the Public Today, 5:167–206
Art Needs No Justification, 3:315–349
Creative Gift, The, 3:133–244
Gauguin and Nineteenth-Century Art Theory, 1:1–227
God's Hand in History (with Colin Duriez), 6:1–87
Jazz, Blues and Spirituals, 2:155–314
Modern Art and the Death of a Culture, 5:1–164
Prophecy in the Old and New Testaments: God's Way with Israel (Stanislau document), 6:91–119
Synthetist Art Theories, see Gauguin and Nineteenth-Century Art Theory
Unfinished Manuscript, 4:278–311
Contributions to Multi-Volume Works: Art, Aesthetics, and Beauty, 2:138–142

Book/Film Reviews

Basjou's 'Han van Meegeren, the alchemist of Roqueburne', 1:352–355
Buñuel's *Un Chien Andaloux*, 3:190–203
Colmjon's 'The Hague school', 1:289
Garlock's *A Big Beat, a Rock Blast*, 6:158–160
Gombrich's *In Search of Cultural History*, 4:275–277
Kalff's 'Rembrandt and the Bible', 1:264–265
Kalsbeek's 'Faith and science', 3:476–479
Kat's doctoral thesis: 'The prodigal son as literary motif', 4:441–443
Meijer's 'Art and revolution', 5:358–360
Oxenaar's 'The art of painting of our times' and Hess's 'Documents for the understanding of modern art', 5:350–358
Paperbacks about Art, 4:272–275
Prange's 'The god Hai-Hai and rhubarb', 5:341–346
Redeker's 'The days of artistic desperation', 1950, 5:339–340
Rotermund's 'Rembrandt: drawings and etchings of the Bible', 4:177–179
Sedlmayr's 'The revolution of modern art', 5:346–350
Seerveld's *A Turnabout in Aesthetics to Understanding*, 2:151–153
Stellingwerff's 'Origin and future of creative man', 2:21–23
Stellingwerff's 'Reality and religious motive in Vincent Willem van Gogh', 1959, 5:336–338
Van der Meer's 'Rembrandt's gospel', 1:265–266
Van Os's 'Moa-Moa, modern thought and primitive wisdom', 4:439–441

Diagrams

Eighteenth-century world view, 3:63
Genotypes and subgenotypes, 2:33
Seventeent-century world view, 3:62
Stucture of a work of art (aesthetic, visual, iconic), 3:33
Twelve-bar structure of blues songs, 2:186

Discography

updated, in 'Jazz, Blues and Spirituals', 2:312–314

Exhibition Reviews

General: Art Fair in Delft, 4:475–477; Beauty in Miniature: Coins from the Past and the Present, 4:472–473; Dutch Ceramics from 1500–1800, 4:473–474; Dutch Tiles: Applied Art in Arnhem, 4:474–475; English Landscape in Sussex, The, 4:478–479; Eskimo Sculpture: Unaffected Characterization of the Surrounding World, 4:466–467; Hokusai Exposition in Eindhoven, 4:465–466; How do Others see Us? How do We see Them? 4:468–469; L'Italia Splendida: Life as a Feast, 4:477–478; Roman Portrait: Classical Realism, the, 4:462–463; Russian Icons: Mixture of Mysticism and Realism, 4:470–471; Unique Exhibition of Etruscan Art, 4:461–462; Wonderful Chinese Art, 4:467–468

Middle Ages: Alsation Art in Delft I, 1:237–238; Alsation Art in Delft II, 1:239–240; Art Treasures from the Vatican: Early Christian art in The Hague, 4:463–465; Art Treasures of the Lower Rhineland: Grand Culture from around AD 1000, 1:231–233; Beauty from the Middle Ages in the Rijksmuseum, 1:242–244; Burgundian Splendour by Flemish Masters, 1:245–246; From Gothic to Renaissance, 1:236–237; From the Treasuries of the Middle Ages, 1:233–234; Italian Drawings: Breaking with the Renaissance, 1:251–252; Jan van Scorel: Universal Artist, 1:248–250; Leonardo da Vinci: Brilliant and Universal, 1:250–251; Painting in the late Middle Ages, 1:235–236; Portrait in the Old Netherlands, the, 1:246–248; Religious Art in Tournai, 1:244–245; Rhineland's Art in Arnhem, 1:240–242

Seventeenth & Eighteenth Centuries: 120 Famous Paintings in the Rijksmuseum, 1:268–269; Caravaggio's Influence on the School of Utrecht, 1:253–254; Drawings from Two Centuries in the Rijksmuseum, 1:278–279; Dutch Still Lifes, 1:256–157; Fame and Value of a Great Artist: Rembrandt Exposition in Amsterdam, 1:259–262; French Landscape, The, 1:276–277; Gainsborough in Bath, 1:280–281; Goya's Accusations, 1:281–282; Painters of Architecture, 1:254–256; Rembrandt as Graphic Artist, 1:262–264; Rembrandt House in Amsterdam, The, 1:257–259; Rembrandt's Pupils, 1:266–268; Rubens and Antwerp, 1:272–274; Story of the Portrait in the Rijksmuseum, The, 1:269–270; Swiss Graphic Art in the Print Gallery of the Rijksmuseum1:277–278; Three Centuries of Portraits in the Rijksmuseum, 1:270–271; Venetian Art of Painting, The, 1:274–276

Nineteenth Century: Beautiful Nuyen Discovered, 1:288–289; Bresdin: Etcher and Lithographer, 1:298–299; British School of the Hunting Scene, the, 1:295–296; Constantin Guys, 1:292–293; Early Works by Van Gogh, 1:296–297; Hokusai Exposition in Eindhoven, 4:465–466; Hundred Years of Norwegian Painting, a, 1:293–294; James Ensor: a Great Graphic Artist, 1:297–298; Monet: a Mirror of Impressionism, 1:301–302; Nuyen: a Gifted Romantic, 1:287–288; Pier Pander – an Overdue Classicist, 1:290–292; Romantic Painting: Entitled to more Recognition and a little Fame, 1:283; Romantic Painting, The, 1:284–285; Romantic Works from the Nineteenth Century, 1:285–287; Van Gogh: Visual Phenomenon, 1:297; Van Gogh's Contemporaries, 1:299–300; Verster in Lakenhal, 1:290

Twentieth Century: Bart van der Leck, 1:319–320; Beautiful Wood Sculptures of High Quality: Cor Wijker, Spirited and Convincint, 5:365–366; Beauty in

Stone: The Statue as a Symbol of our Times, 5:370–372; Beckmann: Violent Expressionism, 1:308–309; Belgian Art, 1:330–331; Berserik: One of the Best, 1:347–348; Biennale of Modern Sculpture in Middelheim Park, Antwerp, 5:372–374; Christian Art in Amstelveen, 1:352; Collection Urvater in Museum Kröller-Müller, 1:324–325; Comparative Exposition of Modern Art, 1:339–340; Contact Between Art and the Public, 1:355–356; De Stijl in the Stedelijk Museum of Modern Art, 1:318–319; Domela Nieuwenhuis, 1:342–343; Emergence of a Style, 1:358–359; Escher's Graphic Art: Puzzling Cleverness, 1:348–350; Europe 1907, an Important Year for Art, 1:304–305; Experimentals In (or out of) the Stedelijk Museum of Modern Art, The, 1:341–342; Female Compassion in Painting: Käthe Kollwitz, Charley Toorop, and the Joffers, 1:311–312; German Art after 1945, 1:328–329; Graphic Work of Henk Krijger, 1:350; Guggenheim Collection in the Gemeentemuseum, 1:320–322; Healthy French Art, 1:334–335; Henry Moore Searches for a new Kind of Sculpture, 5:363–365; Henry Moore: Creator of Dynamic Forms, 5:362–363; Homage to Lion Cachet, 4:471–472; Humour in Drawing: Mirror of Modern Life, 1:336–337; Italian Art in Museumpark Rotterdam: An Old Tradition Revived, 5:366–368; John Rädecker, Artist of Great Stature: Sculpture as a Portrayal of an Exalted Vision of Life, 5:377–379; Joseph Zaritsky: Chaotic Work without Clear Substance, 1:329–330; Language of Statues – An Exhibition in Sonsbeek Park, Arnhem, The, 5:368–370; Macke: Pure Talent, 1:309; Meritorious Work of Paul Citroen, 1:345–347; Modern American Graphic Art, 1:338–339; Modern Art as National Property, 1:343–345; Modern Italians in the Stedelijk Museum of Modern Art in Amsterdam, 1:312–313; Monumental Arts 1:356–358; Munch: Forerunner of Modern Art, 1:303; Paula Modersohn-Becker, 1:309–311; Picasso of Eindhoven, the, 1:313–315; Picasso's Guernica in Amsterdam, 1:315–318; Poorly Organized Exposition, 1:350–351; Poster Art, a Living Art, 1:360–361; Rodin's Life's Work: Dante's Humanism in Bronze, 5:361–362; Rouault: Modern Christian Art, 1:333–334; Saul Steinberg's Mockery: Nihilistic Games, 1:337–338; Schumacher: Magical and Romantic, 1:327; Sculptures in Park in Groningen, 5:374–376; Surprises in Arnhem: High-Quality Dutch art, 5:376–377; Three Friends who gave Expressions to a Flemish View of Life, 1:331–333; Toorop: Mature Talent in Full Bloom, 1:347; Unbelief as Emptiness, 1:322–323; What is Expressionism? 1:305–308; Willink, Envisioner of Existential Angst, 1:325–327; Works by André Petroff, 1:335–336

Interviews

By Art History Students from the Free University of Amsterdam, 3:496–501
By Marc de Klijn. 6:131–145
By Jan van Capelleveen for Trans-World Radio Broadcast, 6:156–159
By C.A. Delhaas-Kraan and J. Boelema, 6:145–150
By Colin Duriez for *Crusade*, 6:150–153

By Sharon Gallagher for *Right On*, 6:154–156
The Background to Modern (Rock) Music, a Broadcast Interview, 2:377–381

Letters

Christianity and Culture: A Reply, 3:335–337
Modern Art and Gnosticism: an Open Letter to Prof. Dr Jan Aler, 5:296–305
On Art and Entertainment: a Response Letter, 3:403–406
To a Christian Artist, in *The Creative Gift*, 3:209–213
To Betty, on Abstract Art and Abstraction, 4:397
To David, on Popular Music, 4:404–409
To Mr B, on Nudity in Art, 4:397–403
To Peter, on Art and Crisis, 4:393–396

Music/Record Reviews

see notes to *Complete Works* 2, part II, 2:392–401 for records discussed in *Jazz, blues, spirituals*
Bach cantata no.12 & Mozart mass (Bach and Mozart), 2:383–384
Backwoods Blues, 2:325–326
Big Bill Broonzy, Blues Singer, 2:333–335
Blues in the Mississippi Night & Prison Songs – Murderer's Home, 2:330–331
George Lewis New Orleans Stompers (New Orleans Suite, A), 2:373–375
Ida Cox Sings the Blues, 2:328–329
Johnny Dodds with the Dixieland Thumpers, 2:375–376
Les Maîtres allemands des XVIIe et XVIIIe siècles (Sylvie Spycket ensemble, Old Music), 2:382–383
Music from the South: Field Recordings & Country Brass Bands, 2:331–333
Nothin' but the Blues, 2:336–337
Original Dixieland Jazz Band: Historic Recordings, 2:367–369
Roland Hayes Sings (Spirituals in Concert Form), 2:347–348
Series: *Treasures of North American Negro Music*, 2:322–324
The Folk Blues of Blind Lemon Jefferson, 2:326–328
Two Church Services in Harlem, Chrismas Day and New Year's Eve, 2:351–352

Photographs/Plates

see Contents listings in *Complete Works* 2, 3, and 6

Scripture Index to the Complete Works

Genesis

1	2:227; 3:168, 193, 196, 381, 420; 4:305, 6:9, 143, 167, 168, 169, 207, 215, 217, 218, 219, 221–224, 244
1:28	3:152
1:28	3:146
2	3:48, 167; 4:402; 6:9
2:15	3:140, 152
3	3:58, 93, 96, 446; 4:251, 397, 399, 400; 6:82
3:8	6:75
3:15	6:10
3:15, 23	3:148
4:6, 7	6:10
4:17	3:140
6:2	4:206
6:6, 7	2:226
9:1,2	3:146
12:2–3	6:100
17:1–17	6:94
32:28–30	6:101
41:32	6:94
48	6:103
48:9–10	6:100

Exodus

13:21	1:n.1068
15:20	3:20
19:5, 6	6:68
23	3:20
31:3, 4	5:n.130
34:6, 7	6:8

Leviticus

7:18	3:329; 4:63
9:1	6:94
18	3:92
20:2–5	3:102
22:1	6:94
23	3:20
23:40	4:206
26	4:420

Numbers

15:22–25	4:n.596

Deuteronomy

2:5, 9	6:10
4:5–9	6:9
4:25–31	6:9
6:10	3:163
6:14, 15	6:9
8	4:423
8:2	6:84
8:3	6:85
8:17	3:376
8:17–18	3:316
9:4	6:10
12:13–15	4:63
12: 20–23	4:63
15:1–4	3:330
16	3:20
18:22	6:97, 103
20:25	6:100
28	3:268, 311, 316, 376, 379; 4:133,136, 352, 420; 5:25; 6:5, 12
28:8	6:11
28:10, 13	4:140
28:12–68	4:211
28:13	3:180, 319, 384, n.213, n.257; 4:139

28:13, 33	5:n.396	**2 Samuel**	
28:15–21	6:13	7:13–14	6:100
28:17	6:12		
28–30	6:8, 9, 10, 15, 17, 21, 23, 26, 30, 52, 77		
28:60	6:104	**1 Kings**	
29	6:14, 23	8:32–53	6:17
29:4	6:103	8:35–36	6:18
29:5–6	3:n.248	8:66	6:94
29:19–20	3:384	12:28–30	6:18
29:21–27	4:452	12:24	6:103
29:24	6:104	18	6:19
29:25–27	5:227		
29:29	4:452; 5:217; 6:5, 57		
30	3:316; 4:133; 5:277; 6:5	**2 Kings**	
30:1	6:11	6:17	6:130
30:1–10	3:n.272		
30:9	4:136		
30:11	4:136	**2 Chronicles**	
30:11–14	6:14	2, 3	4:350
30:14–20	6:69	34	6:22
30:15–21	6:14	35:18	6:103
32	3:n.123; 6:163		
32:8	6:20		
32:15	3:346; 5:n.15	**Ezra**	
		9	4:415
Joshua			
2:1	2:346	**Nehemiah**	
2–18	2:345	9	4:415
8:3–35	3:92		
Judges		**Job**	
2	6:16	1:22	5:296
2:11–16	6:16	2:10	6:98
3:7	3:163	38	4:138
		40:6	3:173
1 Samuel			
24	3:154		

Psalms

2:2–3	6:106
10	4:326
14:1	5:n.82
18	4:451
19	3:193; 4:451; 6:224
19:3, 4	3:135; 4:451
32:6	2:226
39:12	3:n.45
42	4:292
44	3:192; 6:25, 27
44:9	6:26
44:23–26	3:225
47	2:353
51	5:238
73	3:161, 191; 4:358; 6:27
73:3, 13–15	6:27
73:17	3:225
73:17–20	3:194
81:13	5:n.305
89:46	3:192; 6:48
107	4:451
119:54, 29	3:352
119:105	3:6
136	5:160; 6:223
145	4:451

Proverbs

1:7	6:108
2	6:296
5:18	3:404
5:19	3:92; 4:400
7	4:140
8:7	6:234
8:30	3:200
18:2	3:52; 4:244; 5:273
28:9	4:n.600
28:26	4:209
29:25	3:109

Ecclesiastes

1:13	3:466
2:13	3:20
2:26	3:20
7:16, 17	3:160
8:11	6:29
8:15	3:193
9:7–10	3:20
11:9	3:125

Isaiah

1	3:439; 5:136, n.358; 6:167
1:9	6:103
1:10, 14–15	6:33
1:20	6:34
2	5:224
2:12, 19	6:76
2:21	1:342; 2:113; 5:n.306; 6:108
2:26	3:n.271
5:14, 15	3:192
5:15, 16	3:197
5:20	1:342
5:25	3:192; 5:n.81
9:18	3:219
9:19	6:5
10:5, 6, 12	6:35
10:12	6:103
10:24	6:113
11:9	6:118
11:11	6:103
12:3	2:n.443
13:9, 10	6:74
13:19	3:102, 406
16:14	6:103
19:2	6:112
22:13	3:192
24:4–6	5:n.80
24:5, 6	3:161, 191
24:7	3:125
24:8	3:20
25:28	6:114

28:19, 20	6:70	55:11	4:432
28:23–29	6:174	56	6:105
29:13	2:9, 78; 4:n.565	56:1–8	6:115
29:13, 14	4:n.602; 6:101	56:6–7	6:115
29:14	6:114	57	6:111
30	3:316; 4:n.601; 6:34, 35	57:7	6:67
		57:17	3:192, 224; 5:n.119; 6:48
30:1	4:n.598		
30:15	6:34	57:17–18	6:26, 27
30:18	6:35	59:1	6:115
30:19	6:114	59:15	6:67
30:20	4:420	59:16	6:67
30:26	6:118	61:6	6:68
30:27–33	6:35	62:4	2:n.446
32:3–4	6:117	64:24	6:113
32:6	3:161	66:10	6:118
32:12–16	6:86	66:15–24	6:69
32:15	3:180	66:18	6:68
33:17–24	6:117	66:23	6:115
34:4	6:75		
34:16	6:91		
35:1	6:85, 113	**Jeremiah**	
35:6	6:85		
40:19	3:156	1:3	4:68
42:13	6:111	1:12	6:119
41:17, 20	6:117	2	4:n.601
42:24–25	5:278	2:13	4:416
42:25	3:316; 4:416, 418; 5:n.309, n.323	2:29–30	5:n.309; 6:36
		2:35	4:419
43:5–7	6:114	4:4	3:162, 172
44:9	3:156	5:4–5	6:109
44:16	3:14	6:13–15	3:154
44:22	6:115	6:21	6:101
45:7	6:98	6:22–26	6:113
47:6	6:106	7:18	4:221
47:9	6:111	8:8	4:416
47:10–11	6:111	9:23	4:n.599
48:4–5	6:91	9:23, 24	2:8, 3:401
48:5	4:424	9:24	3:n.261
48:9–11	6:21	15	6:36
49:5–6	6:105	15:1–2	6:36
51:19–20	6:104	15:14	6:36
52:11	6:111	16:1–4	6:113
53	6:66, 99	16:13	6:104
53:5	6:100	21:9	3:n.204
55:8, 9	3:230; 6:97, 115	23:16–19	6:69

23:17	5:n.323
23:18–22	4:418
24:9	6:104
24:10	6:103
25:9	6:104
29	6:23
29:18	6:23
29:8, 9	6:23
30:3	6:114
31:1	6:103
31:20	6:100, 103
31:26	6:91
31:31–34	6:54
32:33	6:117
32:34	6:117
33:14	6:101
33:24, 37	6:101
34:20	6:113
38:18	3:n.204
36:32	6:35
39:15–19	6:37
39:17–18	6:114
44:27	6:104
44:28	6:103
45	3:165, 235; 5:290; 6:36, 37, 49
45:5	3:464, n.204; 4:424
50:4	6:113
50:7	6:104, 110
50:20	6:115
51	4:n.605; 6:23, 24, 110
51:6	6:110
51:7	4:420; 6:24, 110
51:20	4:420; 6:110
51:50	6:96, 110

Lamentations

5	4:13
5:7	6:103

Ezekiel

1	6:63, 92
3:7	4:n.594
3:18	4:420
6:8	6:103
6:8–10	6:38
6:10	3:194
7:24–27	4:420; 6:107
7:25	5:234
7:26	5:n.307, n.323
9:9	6:47
11:13	6:103
12:21–25	6:91
12:27–28	4:418
12:28	6:119
14:21, 22	6:31, 103
14:21–23	3:n.122; 6:38
14:22–23	6:101
16	5:277; 6:80
16:14–15	4:207
18	6:28
18:19–20	6:38
18:30–32	3:n.272
21:7	6:119
21:27	6:119
22	6:24
26, 27	6:111
27, 28	3:142
28:22	6:111
28:6–7	6:113
33:1–20	6:79
33:7–16	6:122
33:8	3:218
34	6:103
34:24	6:114
34:26	5:277
34:30	6:113, 114
36:14	6:113
36:16–29	6:119
36:22–23	6:116
36:25	3:162
36:26	6:114
36:26–28	6:113
37	4:134
37:22	6:114

38	6:112, 117	*3:1–3*	6:117
38:3	6:113	*3:1, 9*	6:113
39:7	6:115	*3:12*	6:112
40:1	6:91		
43:27	6:94		
47	2:n.47	**Amos**	
47:22	6:115	*2*	6:54
		2:13–15	6:86
Daniel		*3*	6:54
		3:4–5	6:113
3	2:n.449	*3:6–8*	4:452
4:30	4:207	*4*	6:44
7	6:67	*4:1–3*	6:21, 22, 44
7:7	6:96	*4:3*	6:35
7:9–14	6:67	*5:13*	3:n.250
7:13	6:67	*5:18–20*	6:74
7:25	6:83, 106, 114	*5:21–24*	4:206
8	6:73	*6:4*	4:n.558
8:10, 11	6:73	*6:5*	4:350
10	6:20	*9*	4:211
11:40	6:113	*9:17*	6:104
12	6:65, 74	*11:1–4*	6:100
12:1	6:20		
12:3	6:74		
12:4	6:65	**Jonah**	
12:7	6:83		
12:10	6:98	*4:11*	3:176
Hosea		**Micah**	
4	3:161	*3:5*	3:224
4:1–3	3:235	*3:4–7*	6:48
5:6	5:n.119	*3:5–7*	6:74
6:6	4:206	*4:2*	6:96
7:7	4:452	*5:1*	6:100
11:1–4	3:224, 6:100	*5:2*	6:101
		6	4:63, 134
		6:1–8	4:425
		6:3	4:350
Joel		*6:8*	3:144
2:1–2	6:109	*7:1–7*	6:78
2:10	6:109	*7:7–10*	3:n.214; 6:49
2:30–32	6:75	*7:7–11*	4:326
2:32	6:103		

Nahum

3:3	6:113

Habakkuk

1:2	6:71
1:13	6:29
2:2, 3	6:30, 119
2:3	4:326
2:14	6:118
3:2	4:68
3:10–11	6:75
3:16	4:452; 6:75

Zephaniah

1:12	3:224
1:12	3:361
2 – 3	3:263
2:1–3	6:261
2:3	3:145, 165, 235; 4:326 5:359; 6:49, 87
3:9	6:115
3:11–13	6:39

Haggai

2:21–24	6:114

Zechariah

1:8	6:91
1:18	6:97
2:7	6:111
3:4	2:n.442
3:4–7	6:114
4:6	6:94, 115, 118
5:1–5	6:115
5:10–11	6:112
7:9–14	4:n.597
8:13	6:115
12:1–9	6:113
12:9	5:295
12:10	6:115

Malachi

1:2	6:45
1:6–7	6:45
2:8	6:45
2:13–14	6:46
2:17	3:192; 6:46
3:2	4:202; 6:47
3:7	6:47
3:10	4:288
3:13–14	4:452
3:13–15	6:39, 47
3:13–16	5:240
3:16	5:359
3:16, 18	4:333
3:18	3:318, 4:420

Matthew

1	5:44; 6:219, 220, 221
4:4	6:85
4:1–11	6:111
5	6:263
5 – 7	4:422, 437
5:1–12	3:n.30
5:4	6:25
5:10	6:86
5:13	3:145, 160; 4:134; 6:8, 52
5:14	6:121
5:15	4:140
6	6:85
6:16	3:119
6:23	5:n.341
6:25–34	3:173
6:33	3:163; 4:136, 351
7:7–12	6:127
7:9	3: n.9
7:11	3:114
7:13, 14	3:164

7:15–20	6:53	24:44	6:118
7:17, 18, 20	3:164	25:10	2:n.444
7:19, 24–27	5:277	25:31	3:145
7:21	4:417	25:37	3:n.46
8	5:366	27:25	6:104
10	6:54	28:11–15	3:224
10:14–15	6:52		
10:23	3:n.251		
10:28	3:172	**Mark**	
10:29	4:352		
10:34	6:87	2:27	3:168
11:28	3:16	7:21	1:342
11:30	3:112; 4:352	7:21, 22	5:n.126
12	3:416	10:28	4:325
12:28	3:n.42	10:28–31	3:163
12:32	4:419	12:24, 25	6:73
13:33	4:135	13:14	6:73
15:1	5:n.132	13:20	4:352
15:11	4:340, 356	13:22	2:113
15:16–20	3:122	13:26	6:73
17:21	3:112		
23	6:8, 53	**Luke**	
23:15	4:429		
23:24	4:418	1	4:201
23:29–30	3:n.273	1:1–4	3:230
23:34, 35	4:418	4	3:148
23:34, 37–39	6:53	7:28	4:419
23:39	6:104, 114	10:17–20	6:83
24	3:164, 230; 4:419; 5:135, 225; 6:298	10:18	6:82
		11:11	3:n.9
24:3	6:69	12:14	4:420
24:6	6:69	12:48	3:n.274; 4:420
24:7	6:71	14:34–35	5:277
24:9	6:87	16:31	4:417
24:12	3:n.255; 4:424, n.565; 5:n.120	17	6:116
		17:10	2:5
24:12–13	6;119	17:21	6:95, 117
24:14	6:105	17: 26–30	4:212
24:25	6:116	21	5:224
24:29–31	6:77	21:12	3:146
24:32	6:99	21:24	6:104
24:32–33	6:118	21: 25, 26	5:306
24:33	4:352	21:25–28	5:233; 6:73
24:36	6:118	21:26	6:107

John

1	3:167
2:22	3:230
3	3:125
3:7	6:95
3:12	6:234
3:19	3:200; 6:113, 116
3:20	2:143
3:20, 21	4:338
3:21	3:175, 230, n.34; 4:286; 5:n.249; 6:233
4:14	2:n.443
5:24	3:162
8:32	3:201
12:6	6:104
12:31	6:95, 104
12:48	2:9; 4:423; 6:116
13:35	3:n.48
14:2	2:n.440; 6:126
14:13	3:228; 6:126
14:16	6:126
15	4:n.568
15:1–8	3:111; 6:125
15:4	3:400
15:5	2:3
15:5, 6	3:200
15:7	3:163
15:9–10	6:126
16:11	3:n.43
17	4:419
17:14–16	3:125
17:15	3:162
17:21	3:384; 4:414; 6:126
17:31	3:n.48
20:27–31	3:230

Acts

1:3	3:230
4:20	3:230
7:43	3:102
8:1, 4	6:125
14:6	4:211
17:26	3:311

Romans

1	3:49, 75, 86, 193; 4:205, 332, n.249; 5:289
1 – 2	3:294; 6:124
1 – 8	6:30
1:18	4:214; 6:36
1:18, 19	3:227
1:20	3:135; 4:451
1:21	5:102
1:24	6:48
1:28–32	3:192
1:32	2:273; 3:50, 76, 376, 379
2	6:105
2:14–15	4:209
5:3–5	6:298
5:5–6	3:109
6	3:145, 162; 4:334, 428, 434; 5:n.125; 6:126, 171
6 – 7	3:429
6 – 8	6:124
6:6	3:111, 125
6:8–11	3:140
6:22	6:126
7	3:125; 5:n.123; 6:234
7:20	3:127
7:21	3:227
7:24–25	3:111
7:25	3:383
8	2:383; 4:357; 6:120, 135, 224, 295
8:1–17	3:111
8:2	3:125, 197
8:9–10	3:n.44
8:10, 11	6:294
8:15	3:172
8:18	3:174, 203; 5:n.71
8:18, 22	3:193
8:19	3:226
8:19–22	5:n.79
8:20	3:137, 139
8:21	3:49, 139
8:21–23	3:124

8:22	3:49	6:12	3:125
8:31–39	4:425	6:12, 10:23	3:125
8:35–39	6:30	6:20	3:125
9:13	6:30	9:20, 10:32	3:125
9:14–29	6:103	10:1–14	6:55
9:20	6:31	10:11	3:218; 4:451
10:2	3:n.277; 4:350	10:23	3:125
10:2–3	3:112	10:23–33	4:66
10:3	4:416	10:25	4:64
11	6:53, 101	12	3:233; 6:127, 141
11:4–5	6:54	12:12	2:3; 4:324
11:11	6:54	12:12–31	3:125
11:11–27	6:116	13	3:162, 171, 366; 4:n.570; 6:234
11:12	6:105, 118		
11:17	2:3	13:4–6	3:172
11:22	6:105	14:1–3	4:420
11:25	6:114, 118	15	3:462
11:25–27	6:93	15:20	3:203, 225
12:17, 18	3:194	15:20–28	6:79
12:19	3:153, 172, 194; 4:424; 5:n.131	15:24	3:136
		15:24–26	4:422
12:19, 20	6:55	15:24–28	3:139; 6:47
13	3:182, 333; 6:176	15:26	6:79
13:1	3:148	15:54	3:49
14:7	6:125	15:58	2:5, 79; 3:314
14:16	3:125		
14:16–17	3:126		
14:17	3:194, 382	**2 Corinthians**	
14:22–23	3:119	3:2	4:428
15:4	2:173	3:6	3:n.10
15:5	3:n.48	4:5	6:130
		5:1	2:n.440
		12:9	3:n.13

I Corinthians

1:23	6:129
1:25	6:97
1:30–31	4:n.599
2:12–16	4:419
3:10–15	5:335
5	3:125
5:9–13	4:423
5:10	3:125
5:11	4:419
5:13	3:106, 153; 5:n.131

Galatians

1:5	3:n.14
2:15	3:230
5:1	3:168, 382
5:22	3:172, 401, n.44; 4:331; 6:125, 126, 294
5:22–24	3:384
5:23	3:200; 5:n.124

Ephesians

1	6:228
1:3–14	6:228
1:10	3:139
2:10	6:289
2:20–22	3:168
3:6	6:105, 115
4:18	2:4
4:27	6:84
4:28	3:76
5:11	2:3; 3:n.266
5:17	3:n.262
6	3:366; 4:363, 431; 5:139; 6:84
6:10	3:476
6:10–18	3:n.258
6:10–20	2:9; 3:15, 381
6:12	3:45, 177, 347, 372; 5:180, 260, n.68; 6:82, 110

Philippians

1:9–10	3:n.268
2:12, 13	3:227; 6:290
2:15	5:240
3:8	4:432
4:5	3:161
4:8	2:273, 297, 381; 3:77, 100, 176, 213, 384, 401; 4:234, 338, 358, 364, 394; 5:140, n.284
4:8, 9	3:200

Colossians

1:13, 14	4:n.566
1:15–19	3:168
1:19	6:99
1:25	6:126
2	3:441; 5:308; 6:171, 262
2:1–5	3:173
2:8	2:3, n.264, n.267
2:9–15	3:227
2:11	3:162
2:11–12	3:111
2:11–15	3:172
2:13, 14	4:n.566
2:15	3:n.43
2:16	6:127, 262
2:16–17	3:113
2:16–23	3:172, 383
2:18–22	4:n.567
2:20	3:172
2:20–22	3:113, 382
2:22–23	3:16
2:23	3:113; 6:130
2:23 – 3:17	4:357
3:1–4	4:n.568
3:5–17	3:384
4:5–6	3:314, n.254
10:1–4	3:225

I Thessalonians

5:1, 4	6:119
5:16	3:112, 20
5:21	3:125, 202

2 Thessalonians

1	3:185
2	3:376, 394; 5:204, 260
2:9	2:112
2:9–11	5:118, n.305
2:10, 11	6:13
2:11	5:n.323; 6:49
2:12	1:342
3 – 4	3:14

I Timothy

2:8	4:452
4:1	4:n.595

4:4	2:72	4:2–3	3:16
4:12	5:n.305	4:7	6:84
6:11	4:n.607		
6:12	6:84		

2 Timothy

1 Peter

1:12	3:n.12	1:13–25	3:476
2:16	3:n.264	1:17	3:n.45
2:26	6:84	2:13	3:314, 188
3	3:185, 376; 5:204, 229, 260	2:15	3:n.252
		3:3	2:142
3:1–4	5:273	3:10–11	6:234
3:4–5	3:379	3:15	6:126
3:5	4:n.607	4:12–13	6:86
3:14–17	5:278	4:17	3:145
3:16–17	2:9		
3:17	3:318		
4	5:229		

2 Peter

4:3	2:286	1:5	3:161
4:3–4	6:96, 106	1:5–7	3:172
4:8	2:n.438	1:7	1:123
		1:19	6:93
		1:20–21	6:92
		2	5:135; 6:294
		2:7	3:349

Hebrews

1	3:167	2:10	3:23
1:2	5:385	2:18–19	6:46
2:1–4	6:54	2:19	3:161, 197; 5:205, n.123
8:10–12	6:54		
10:15–16	3:n.11	3:3, 4	3:192; 5:240; 6:47, 107, 118
10:31	6:8		
11:3	2:346		
12:5–7	3:112		
12:7	3:125		

1 John

12:22	2:n.441	1	3:232, 382
		1:1	5:n.122
		1:7	3:112
		1:8	3:383
		1:10	3:125

James

1:22	3:146	1:16	3:112
1:27	3:118, 320, n.46	2:15	3:n.265
2:19	4:434	2:18	5:308
3:10	n.571	3:8	6:84
4:2	3:n.47	3:18–24	3:119

3:21	3:172	*6:10*	3:225
3:21, 22	5:n.133	*6:11*	6:71
5:3	4:424	*6:12*	6:96
5:3–4	6:125	*6:12–13*	6:97, 105
		6:12–14	5:n.119; 6:107
		6:12–17	6:72
Jude		*6:15*	6:108
10	3:75, 76	*6:15–17*	6:76
		6:16	3:14; 5:n.117, n.306
		7	3:165; 6:220
		7:2,3	6:87
Revelation		*7:9*	3:217
		7:9–16	6:108
1 – 6	3:240	*7:9–17*	2:n.442; 3:226
1:13	2:n.442	*7:17*	3:263
2:1–7	4:419	*8:1*	6:62, 76
2:5	6:55	*8:3–5*	6:77
2:10	2:n.438	*8:13*	3:136
2:12–17	4:419	*8:21*	3:241
2:18–29	6:55	*9*	6:56
2:21	2:226	*9:1–3*	6:108
2:27	6:81	*9:4*	3:n.43; 6:112
3:7	2:n.444	*9:13*	2:n.447
3:16	3:223	*9:17*	6:96
4	3:135, 240; 6:63, 64, 66	*9:20*	5:n.117; 6:109
4:4	2:n.438	*9:20, 21*	1:342; 3:194, 221; 6:56
4:11	3:n.70; 4:378; 6:64, 224	*9:21*	5:n.304
		10:4	6:64
5	3:136, 428, n.123; 6:60, 64, 65, 66, 67, 116	*10:7*	6:31, 57
		11	4:n.130
		11:1	2:n.447
5:1	6:99	*11:3*	4:n.451
5:2	6:99	*11:7–8*	4:n.603
5:5	6:99	*11:11*	6:83, 106
5:7	6:67	*11:13*	6:108
5:9	6:99	*11 – 13*	4:n.340
6	3:165, 428; 6:68, 73, 87	*11, 17*	3:n.128
		12	3:462; 4:423, 424, 189, 230; 6:80
6:1–8	6:68		
6:1–17	6:62	*12:1*	6:101
6:3	6:69	*12:1–6*	6:80, 103
6:4	6:106	*12:3*	4:190
6:5	6:71	*12:5*	3:n.247; 4:202, 422; 5:n.128
6:9, 10	6:71		

12:6	6:83	*18:9–10*	6:111
12:7–12	6:81	*18:10–19*	6:112
12:10–12	6:82	*18:16–18*	3:380
12:13–17	6:83	*18:20*	6:112, 112
12:14	4:352	*18:24*	6:111
12, 13	6:62	*19:11*	6:69
13	3:464; 4:424	*20*	6:105
13:1–3	6:110	*20:1–3*	6:95
13:5	6:111	*20:2*	4:191
13:11–16	6:110	*20:4*	6:95
13:14	6:111	*20:8*	6:112, 113
13:17	4:424	*20:9*	6:117
13:18	6:95	*20:10–15*	3:263
17	3:161, n.128; 6:80, 262	*20:11–15*	6:116
		20:12	2:n.452; 6:99, 116
17:3–6	6:110	*21*	6:118
17:5	6:111	*21:6*	2:n.443
17:15	6:96	*22:7*	6:119
17:16	6:112	*22:11*	3:383, 384; 6:118
17:17	6:112	*21:12*	2:n.453
18	3:161	*21:18–21*	2:n.453
18:4	3:161; 4:n.606	*21:27*	2:n.452
18:8	6:111	*22:14*	2:n.453

Concordance of Names

Aalders 3:336

Abbing, Roscam, *Real Challenges to Christendom* 3:185

Abel 6:10

Abelard 4:32;

Abraham 2:106;3:84, 230, 468; 4:6, 13, 233; 5:137; 6: 28, 30, 86, 101, 132, 219, 220

Adam 2:16, 22; 3:93, 139, 158, 415, 429, 430, 431, 445, 459; 4:128, 144, 147, 397; 6:60, 218, 221, 223, 289

Adam, Paul 1:150

Addams, Chas 1:337; 3:23; 4:199

Aelst, van 1:256

Aerts, Hendrick 1:255

Aertsen, Pieter 4:162

Agucchi 2:141

Ahab 6:19, 53

Aiken, Henry David 5:285

Alba, Duchess of 5:34

Alberti, Leon Batista 4:92, 105, 122, 123, 281, 306; 5:343

Alexander the Great 4:150, 153; 5:37

Alexander, Texas 2:269

Alford, J. 5:331

Alken, Henry Thomas 1:295

Allen Jr, Henry 2:243

Allen, Ed 2:246, 324

Allori, Christoforo, *Judith and Holofernes* 4:148

Altdorfer, Albrecht 4:104, 114, 115, 116–120, 121, 379
Beautiful Madonna 4:104
Flight into Egypt 4:119
St Florian altar 4:119
Alexander's battle 4:119
Danube landscape 4:456

Aman-Jean, F. 1:57, 58, 70

Amerson, Rich of Livingston, 2:158, 182
'Black woman' 2:343

Amos 4:326; 6:20, 21, 74

Amsberg, Claus von 3:393

Andersen, Hans Christian 3:199; 4:320

Anderson, Ed 2:246, 370

Anderson, Marian 2:176, 304, 319, 322, 339, 348, 350, 351

Andrea, de 1:345; 4:262

Andrea, John de 4:262

Andriessen, Mari 4:224; 5:242, 369, 374
Dockworker 5:375

Anema, Sjeerp 5:359

Angelico, Fra 4:90, 142, 465

Anna 4:88

Anquetin 1:188

Anseele, Eduard 1:332

Antonio, Marc 4:261

Antonioni, Michelangelo 5:302
Blow-Up 3:457
L'Avventura 4:266

Antony, St (Anthony) 2:161; 3:320–321

Apollinaire, Guillaume 5:74, 86, 251 302

Appel 1:341, 356; 2:126, 129, 133; 3:14, 103, 119, 380; 4:454; 5:99, 240, 247, 255, 272, 279, 286, 350, 352, n.370; 6:198
'Poeme Barbare' 5:96 (n.86)

Aquinas, Thomas 2:140, 152; 4:27, 32, 52, 297, 304; 5:21

Arcimboldo 4:97

Aristotle 1:143, 153; 2:3, 140, 151, 152; 3:289; 4:4, 10, 27, 46, 297; 5:73, 194; 6:208, 241
Poetics 1:176

Arman, 5:102, 103;
The skeleton of Achilles, 5:103

Armstrong, Louis 2:164, 199, 205, 212, 213, 215, 221, 230, 237, 238, 240–243, 244, 245, 250, 251, 257, 258, 265, 266, 271, 276, 280, 281, 324, 357, 361, 365, 368, 369, 370, 371, 376, *plate 11*; 3:19; 4:347; 6;5:112; 6:189, 190, 191, 192; 5:112

Arnason, *History of Modern Art: Painting, Sculpture, Architecture* 3:413

Arnold, Kokomo 5:112

Arntzenius, P. 5:263

Arp 5:100

Asam, C.D., *The Adoration of St James* 4:161

Asch, van 1:295

Ast, van der 1:257

Astrup, *Night work in the garden* 1:294

Augustine, St 3:144, 422, 435; 4:150, 153, 293, 297; 5:22; 6:62

Aurelius, Marcus 4:150, 153;

Aurier, G.A. 1:5, 9, 10, 65, 66, 76, 87, 91, 93, 99, 100, 114, 117, 128–133, 136, 138, 139, 143, 145, 147, 150, 159, 161, 164, 172, 178, 184, 185, 386; 4:237; 5:213, 344
   Le Moderniste 1:114

Austen, Jane 3:412; 6:228

Averkamp 4:168;

Ayler, Albert, 5:125; 6:198, 199
   'Holy Ghost' 6:198

Baburen 1:254

Baccafumi 1:252

Bach 2: 29, 46, 101, 104, 206, 214, 215, 216, 239, 295, 301, 355, 361, 367, 382, 383–384; 3:19, 20, 54, 56, 108, 122, 234, 354, 388, 395, 397, 403, 404, 422, 436; 4:225, 246, 248, 356, 379, 406, 407, 408; 5:111, 146; 6:139, 189, 228, 265, 269
   Brandenburg Concertos 2:206, 214, 218, 302, 333; 3:21, 28; 4:324, 330, 341
   Cantata No. 12: *Weinen, Klagen, Zorgen, Zagen*, 2:383–4
   Mass in B Minor 3:55, 108
   Musikalisches Opfer, 2:364
   St John Passion 3:108
   St Matthew Passion 2:68; 3:394; 4:258, 330, 341
   Weihnachtsoratorium 4:200
   Wohltemperierte Klavier 2:175/6

Backer 1:267

Bacon, Baron Francis 6:210

Bacon, Francis 2:117; 5:103–105, 192, 198, 202, 288

Bacon, Roger 4:305
   Fragment of a crucifixion 4:458

Badings 2:75; 3:403

Baegert 1:242

Bahr 1:186

Bailey, Buster 2:271

Baj 3:196; 5:96, 318

Baldinucci 4:93, 94, 95, 99, 100, 497

Ball, Hugo, 5:304
   Das byzantinische Christentum 5:304

Balzac 1:25, 26, 27, 30, 32, 56, 83, 106, 118, 121, 131, 143, 154, 184, 411; 5:93, 173
   Etudes philosophiques 1:118
   Louis Lambert 1:27, 32, 138
   Les Lys dans la Vallée 1:28
   Seraphita 1:32, 138, 192, 193
   Un chef d'ouevre inconnu 1:192

Bandinelli, Baccio 4:92

Bandy, Lou 2:75

Baquet, George 2:205

Barbara, St. 4:6

Barbarin, Paul 2:205, 244

Barber, Chris 2:285

Barfield, Owen 6:3, 207, 213
   Saving the Appearances, 6:207, 244

Barnes, Paul 2:370

Barnet, Béla 2:270

Barocci, F., *Martyrium of St Vitalis* 4:158;

Barrett, William 5:124
   Irrational Man, 5:124, 324; 6:230

Barth, Karl 3:333, 472

Bartók, Béla 2:298; 3:54, 422; 6:228, 229

Bartolommeo, Fra 1:252; 4:63
   Madonna della Misericordia 4:156

Baruch 3:165, 464; 5:290; 6:36, 27, 29, 49

Basadella, 5:373

Basie, Count 2:271, 272, 361

Bassano, J., *Parable of the sower* 4:158
Bastien-Lepage 1:8, 9, 43, 364
Baudelaire 1:9, 10, 13, 14, 15, 18, 19–25, 27, 27–31, 33, 37, 40, 45, 47, 50, 55, 58, 61, 62, 63, 64, 67, 68, 71, 72, 77, 83, 86, 88, 91, 92, 93, 96, 100, 102, 109, 111, 114, 115, 119, 120, 121, 124, 127, 129, 130, 131, 137, 138, 139, 143, 144, 148, 150, 154, 156, 157, 158, 161, 166, 167, 175, 176, 178, 179, 183, 184, 199, 226, 369, 372, 388, 393, 425, 427; 2:141; 4:197, 236; 5:32, 34, 173, 176

   Curiosités Esthétiques 1:71, 100, 105

   Fanfarlo 1:20, 24

   Les Fleurs du Mal 1:21, 71, 114

   Salon 1:22, 24, 27, 29, 63, 138

Baudet 3:360

Baudry, *Venus bathing* 1:7

Baumeister, Willy 1:328; 5:177

Baumgarten, Alexander 2:141, 152; 3:414, 415; 6:241, 242

   Aesthetics 4:318

Baxandall, *Art and Experience in Fifteenth Century Italy* 3:413

Beaneveu 4:44;

Beardsley 1:56, 360;

Beatles 3:403; 5:114, 256; 6:187, 193, 229, 266

   'Eleanor Rigby' 3:218; 5:136, 201, 250

   Roll over Beethoven 6:193

   Sergeant Pepper's Lonely Hearts Club Band 5:123, 137, 249

   'She's leaving home' 5:129, 251

Beauvoir, Simone de 5:93

Bechet, Sidney 2:205, 217, 218, 279, 369

Beckett 3:457; 5:125

Beckmann, Max 1.xxiii, 307, 308–309

   Blind man 1:308

   Monte Carlo 1:308

   The night 1:307, 308

   The trapeze 1:308

Bednarik, *Gevaarlijke welvaart* 3:360
Beerling, F. 5:292
Beethoven, Ludwig von 1:127; 3:19, 54, 57, 403, 422; 4:222, 248, 374; 5:361; 6:228, 264, 265, 266, 268; 2:25, 101, 300, 301, 302, 362

   Egmont (*Egmond*) 2:75

   Eighth Symphony 2:28, 66, 333/334

   Fidelio 2:n.115

   Leonora (*Leonore*) 2:n.115

   Missa Solemnis 3:21; 4:222

   Ninth Symphony, 2:73; 3:55

   Quartet Opus 59 No. 2 in E minor, 2:66

   'Wellington's Victory' 2:74

Beggarstaff brothers 5:61
Beiderbecke, Bix 2:221, 222, 250, 266, 368
Belling, Rudolf, *Dreiklang* 2:61
Bellini 1:275
Bellori, *Giovanni* 2:141; 5:194
Bembo, Pietro 2:141

   Asolani 4:86

Benedict, St. 4:203
Benivieni, *Canzone de Amore* 4:86
Berchem, 5:357
Berckheyde 1:255, 276; 4:185
Berenson, Bernard 2:134
Berg, J.H. van den, *The Changing Nature of Man* (Metablica) 6:244
Berger, John, 3:491

   Permanent Red 3:491

Berghe, van den 1:332, 333
Bergman, Ingmar 5:117; 6:234

   Silence, 6:195

Bergson, Henri 2:4, 85
Berkeley 1:125, 158, 159
Berlage, Hendrick P. 2:48, 86; 5:61, 209
Bernard 1:82, 85, 87, 88, 103–107, 107, 108, 109, 112, 114, 115, 127, 128, 129, 136, 140, 143–146, 157, 160, 166, 171, 173, 185, 186, 188, 191, 400,

409, 414, 417; 4:237
Christ in the Olive Garden 1:87
Breton women in the meadow 1:110
Bernard of Clairvaux, St 4:294, 317, 323; 6:270, 271, 272
Bernini, G.L. 2:35; 3:80; 4:193, 195
Saint Theresa, 3:80
Piazza Navona fountains, 2:139; 6:226
Berrington 1:280, 281;
Berserik, Herman 1:xxiii, 345, 347–348; 5:242, 245, 246
Bertini 4:80
Bertram of Minden 1:235
Bertram, Ernst 4:13
Bertrand 1:330
Beyer, de 1:279
Beyeren, van 1:25
Bezalel 3:175, 176
Bigard, Barney 2:244, 247
Bigari, V.M., *Restoration of Bologna to the Vatican* 4:161
Bilderdijk, Willem 4:367, 374; 5:174
Bilders, Johann Warnardus 4:186
Bildus, J.W.A. 1:261
Binnington 4:187
Biran, de 1:22
Bizet 2: 262
'Carmen' 2:262
Blair, Lee 2:370
Blake, Peter 5:106
Blake, William 1:46–48, 52, 53, 55, 69, 377; 5:35, 39, 40, 60, 110, 172, 175, 354
Songs of Innocence 5:40
Blaue Ritter Group, the 5:70, 83
Bledsoe, Jet 2: *plate 23*
Bles, Herri de 4:162
Blesh, Rudi 2:248, 339, 358, 374; 5:99
Bloemaert, A. 4:166;
Bloy, Leon 1:333
Bob, Barbecue, 5:112
Bobby Leecan's Need More Band, 2:235

'Apaloosa blues' 2:235
Bocage, Peter 2: *plate 10*
Boccaccio 5:16
Decamerona 4:144
Bocchi 4:77, 79, 99, 497;
Böcklin 1:165
Boer, de 1:334; 4:476
Boerderelle, 2:86
Boime 3:485
Boisdenier, Boissard de, *La retraite de Moscou* 1:8
Boissard 4:152
Bol, Ferdinand 1:266; 3:108
Bolden, Buddy, 2:198, 199
'Take it away' 2:200
'Bucket got a hole in it' 2:200, 205
Bologna, Giovanni da 4:91, 99;
Bonar, Horatius, *God's Way of Holiness* 3:111
Bonet 1:330
Bonington 1:12, 41, 286
Bonnanus 4:6;
Bonnard 1:191, 304
Bonsanquet, 6:241
Bontemps, Arna 2:319
Boom, van der 4:471
Borchgrevik 1:294
Bornel, Guiraut de 4:27;
Bosboom 1:256
Bosch, Hieronymus 1:244; 2:67; 5:354
Bosch, Jeroen 4:195;
Boschaert 1:256
Both, Andries 2:133
Botticelli 4:62, 141; 5:233, 326; 6:273
Boucicaut master 4:307
Flight into Egypt 4:302
David adoring God 4:302, 303
Boudin 1:301
Bougainville 1:187
Bouguereau, William A. 1:7, 79, 134, 142; 5:51
Satyr and Nymphs 1:7
Brother and sister 1:8

Bourbon, Jeanne de 4:37;
Bourdelle 1:245; 5:372
Bouts, Dirk 1:246, 247; 4:109, 121, 124, 246
Bouveret, Dagnan 1:60
Bovillus 4:83;
Boy, Sonny 2:269
Boyle 6:216
Brahms 3:422; 4:340;
Braque, Georges 1:305, 307, 315; 2:86, 133; 3:345; 5:72, 75, 282, 345, 357
Braud, Wellman 2:369
Bray, Jan de 1:271
Bray, S. de 4:152
Bredius, *Rembrandt's Bible* 1:257
Bree, M. I. Van, *Burgomaster van der Werff offers himself to the starving people of Leiden* 4:161
Bréhier 1:409
Bremmer 1:347
Brès, de 4:453
Bresdin 1:61, 70, 71, 298–299
Breton, André 3:195; 5:272, 300
Breugel 4:125, 126–131, 146, 149, 162, 164
    Christ carrying the cross 4:128, 129
    Mad Meg (Dulle Griet) 4:129
    Tower of Babel 4:129
    Fall of Icarus 4:130
    The parable of the blind man 4:130
Brezhnev, USSR President 6:15
Bridgman, P. W. 5:324;
    Philosophical Implications of Physics, 5:324
Briggs 2:241
Brigitte, St 5:338
Bril, Paul 4:162, 164
Britten, Benjamin 6:229
Broderlam 4:41
Bronzino 1:252; 4:91;
Broonzy, Big Bill, alias Johnson 2:186, 326, 190, 269 292, 303, 314, 326, 333

'Moppin blues' 2:190;
'Black, brown and white' 2:303
'Trouble in mind' 2:314
Brouwer W. C. 1:268; 4:40; 5:209
Brown, Ford Maddox 1:50, 51
    Work 1:51
Brown, Sterling 2:191, 266, 319
Brubeck, Dave 2:275, 276, 297
Brückner, Anton 2:35
Bruegel 1:298; 3:37; 4:121, 125, 126–131; 5:269
Bruin, H. de *Paul in Ephesus* 1:350
Brundy, Walter 2: *plate 10*
Brunelleschi 4:306;
Brunies George 2:220
Brusselmans 1:331
Bruyne, Prof. Dr E de 4:32
Bultmann 5:44, 127
Bun, Paul 5:101
Buning, Werumeus 1:341
Bunk Johnson's Band 2: *plate 20*;
Buñuel, Luis 3:190–202, 505; 5:89–91, 302
    Un Chien Andaloux 3:190, 191, 199, 202
Bunyan, 5:210, 212
    Pilgrim's Progress 5:210
Buonarroti, Lionardo 4:73;
Buontalenti, Bernado 4:73, 91, 92, 93, 94, 95, 96, 97, 98, 99, 100, 499
Burckhardt, Jacob 3:288; 5:297, 307, 326; 4:276; 5:297, 307, 326
Burgh, van der, 5:374
Burleigh 2:319
Burne-Jones 1:53, 54, 55, 56, 57, 58; 5:60, 77
    The golden stairs 1:56
    The mirror of Venus 1:56
Burnett, J.C. 2:26
    'The gospel train is leaving' 2:226
Buxtehude 2:382
Byron 1:63

Cabanel 1:142
Cachet, Lion 4:471–472
Cage, John 5:114, 118, 143, 309, 330; 6:234
　'Four Minutes Thirteen Seconds' 3:170
　Silence 6:196
Cain 3:140–141, 144, 145, 153, 197, 312; 6:10, 35
Caine 3:66, 84; 5:46; 6:10, 35
Caldecott 1:106
Callot 3:67; 4:191
Calvani 5:367
Calvin, John 2:3, 4, 167, 340; 3:5, 6, 100, 101, 144, 324, 337, 435; 4:134, 327, 379, 380, 381, 453; 5:22, 276, 337; 6:174, 225, 269, 270, 288, 289, 291, 292
　Genevan Psalter 3:437
　Institutes 3:98
Cambiagi 4:99
Campigli 1:313
Campin 1:268, 269, 270; 4:39, 44, 53, 121
Camus, Albert 2:113; 3:70, 190; 4:435; 5:73, 87, 93, 125, 279, 300, 324
　The Plague 3:164
Canaletto 1:275, 276
Caravaggio 1:253–254; 4:270, 482; 5:52, 345; 6:280
Carducho 4:311
Carey, Jack 2:204
　'Jack Carey' / 'Nigger no. 2' 2:204
Carey, Mutt 2:200, 204, 370, 371, plate 12
Carlyle 1:3, 32, 35–37, 55, 63, 88, 115, 123, 153, 161, 162, 165, 177, 178, 179, 194, 436, 437; 3:51, 110, 151, 369, 376; 4:237, 238; 5:210–217, 301, 308, 328, 329
　Sartor Resartus 1:115, 193, 437; 3:94, 151; 4:398; 5:210, 301, 328
　On Heroes, Hero-worship, and the Heroic in History 1:177; 5:211
Carmichael, Stokely 5:108, 258

Carr, Leroy 2:186, 187, 269, 323; 4:404
　'Midnight hour blues', 2:187
Carra 1:312, 313
Carracci 3:267; 4:115, 482; 5:345; 6:280, 281
Carrega 1:334
Carrière 1:128
Carroll, *Alice in Wonderland* 4:198;
Carstens 4:11
Casa Lama Orchestra, the 2:257
Cassandre 3:305; 5:81, 317
Cassirer, Ernst 2:141; 4:476
Castagnary 1:8, 40, 42
Castiglione, *Cortegiano* 4:86, 98
Castle, Irene and Vernon 4:337; 6:188
Cati, P. *The Council of Trent* 4:158
Cato, Billy, 2:370
Cats, Jacob 1:279; 4:149, 379, 380
　Sinne en Minnebeelden 4:147
　Houwelijck 4:151
Cavallini 4:296
Celestin's Original Tuxedo Jazz Band, 2:205, 249
Cellini 4:91;
Cézanne 1:81–84, 90, 99, 102, 104, 107, 108, 109, 113, 136, 172, 277, 300, 303, 305, 306, 309, 322, 380; 3:69; 4:149, 185, 466, 482; 5:57–59, 62, 69, 71, 76, 99, 191, 285, 342
Chabot 1:332; 5:85, 315
Chagall 1:314, 315, 329; 3:426; 5:198, 221, 237
Chardin 1:256; 4:319
Charles the Bold 4:46
Charles V 4:37, 42
Chateaubriand 1:121
Chatman's Mississippi Hot Footers 2:233
Chaucer, Geoffrey 2:123
Chavannes, Puvis de 1:80–81, 90, 111, 118, 128, 151, 192, 194, 195
Chenier, André 5:171
Chéret 1:360

Chesterton, G.K. 1: 227;
   The Napoleon of Notting Hill 1:227
Chevreuil 1:77, 78
Chipp, Herschel B. 1:xxv;
Chirico, Giorgio de 1:312, 313; 5:76, 86, 88, 198, 344
Chopin, Frédéric 2:101, 231
Christian Travellers, the, 2:289
Christus, Petrus 1:268
Christy's Minstrel Show 2:181
Cimabue 4:296;
   Madonna 4:260
Ciseri, Antonion, 5:43, 45; 6:284
   Ecce homo, 5:43; 6:248
Citroen, Paul 1:345–347; 5:315
Claeszens, Pieter 1:256
Clark, Kenneth 3:445
Clark, R.E.D. *Christian Science and Belief* 3:176
Claude 1:13
Clement of Alexandria 3:159; 4:293
Cleve, Joos van 1:247
Cobb, Revd 2:357
Cobb, Scott 2:244,
Cobra 1:xxii; 5:99, 100, 197
Coene, Jacques 4:302
Cohen, Leonard, 5:62, 6:164, 165, 195, 196–107, 229
   'Story of Isaac', 6:195
Coleridge, Samuel Taylor 1:55, 165, 394; 3:410; 4:265
   Rime of the Ancient Mariner 1:55, 175; 2:27
Colette 1:245
Colincy, Gautier de, *Miracles of the Virgin* 4:301
Collaert 1:330
Collins, Lee 2:370
Columbus 3:270; 6:232
Comte, Auguste, 1:120, 375; 5:49
Condillac, *Treatise on Sensations* 1:73
Condivi 4:74
Condon, Eddie 2:239, 293

Coninxloo, Gillis van 4:162, 163, 164, 166
   Midas' Judgment 4:162, 163
Constable, Henry 3:31; 4:187, 239
Constable, John 1:12–13, 15, 19, 41, 46, 75, 281, 286; 5:35, 36, 51;
   The haywain, 5:35
Constant 1:341
Conte, J. del, *The preaching of John the Baptist* 4:156
   Baptism of Christ 4:156
Cook 1:187; 4:469
Coolen, A. *Fairytales for Grown-Ups* 1:350
Coornhert 3:326; 4:128
Coorte 1:257
Copernicus 4:305
Copley 5:39
Corinth 3:99, 447;
Corneille, Guillaume, 2:133; 3:59; 5:272
Cornelisz, Cornelis 4:165
Cornelisz, Jacob 1:237, 249; 4:165
   The optician 1:237
Corona, G.A., *St Anthony preaching in Padua* 4:156
Corot 1:41, 42, 80, 198, 277, 301; 4:264; 5:36, 51
Cortona, P. da, *The treaty between Jacob and Laban* 4:160
Cosimo 4:73, 98, 191
Costa, Mendez da 1:347; 5:229, 370, 377
Cottet 1:103
Couldwell, 2:369
Count Basie Band, the 2:271
Courbet 1:6, 8, 20, 39, 40, 42, 43, 50, 96, 169, 188, 189, 299, 301; 3:72; 4:182, 264; 5:36–38, 49, 51, 59, 93, 190, 192, 193
   Stonebreakers 1:51
Courlander, Harold, 2:158, 290, 320, 332, 342, *plate 25*
Couture 1:6, 15;
Couzjin 3:196; 5:376

Cox, Ida 2:230, 328, 329
Coxie 1:248;
Coyler, Ken 2:285
Coypel, C.A., *Don Quixote demolishing the puppet show* 4:155, 160
Cozens 4:265
Cranach 1:270; 3:72; 4:104,119, 120;
    Luther 4:103
    Gethsemane 4:104
Crane 1:54, 56, 106
Crivelli 1:275;
Croce, Benedetto 2:141
Cromwell, Oliver 5:18
Crosby Band, the 2:259, 368
Crosby, Bing 2:362
Crosby, Bob 2:259, 368
Crow, Jim 2:181
Cullen, County 2:319
Cusanus, Nicolaus 4:305
Cuyp 1:255; 4:195, 476
Cyr, Johnny St 2:205, 236, 240, 243, 370
D'Hont 5:369
Dada 3:22, 346;
Dagnan-Bouveret 1:134
Dahl 1:294
    Dresden by Moonlight 1:294;
Dali, Salvador, 3:195; 5:87, 88, 95, 274, 279, 312, 317; 6:229, 286
    Last Supper, 5:95
    St. John of the Cross 3:431; 5:95, 317
Dampft 1:58
Daniel 3:61, 142, 144; 6:20, 63, 65, 67, 73, 74, 82, 276
Daniel, Emma 2:292
Dantan 1:8
Dante 1:52; 4:45; 5:60, 233, 361, 370
    Inferno 3:84; 5:233, 361, 370
    Purgatorio 4:6
Dargenty 1:105;
Darwin, Charles, 1:147, 165; 2:85; 3:176, 187; 5:31; 6:169, 217–218, 241; 5:31, 41

The Botanic Garden, 1:147
Origin of Species, 5:41
Daumier, Honoré 1:38, 79, 85, 111, 188, 189, 293, 337; 3:68, 103; 4:196; 5:38, 51, 57, 95, 242, 243
    Picnic on the Grass, 5:38
    Miserere, 5:95
    Olympia, 5:38
David (biblical) 3:75, 88, 144, 154; 4:6, 68, 133, 175, 350, 451; 6:17, 114, 219, 220
David, Gerard 4:61, 62, 109, 121, 147;
David, Jacques Louis 1:7, 11–12; 3:64, 154, 486; 5:37, 39, 267
    Battle of the Romans and the Sabines, 5:37, 39
    Oath of the Horatii, 4:21, 24, 260
Davidson, John 3:58, 196. 296, 376; 5:68
Davis sisters 2:289, 344, 357
Davis, Blind Gary 2:291
Davis, Miles 2:296, 297
Davis, Stuart 5:281
Day, Doris 2:362
De Stijl, 1:xxi, xxiii, xxiv, 318–319; 3:70; 4: 5:86, 221, 245, 280, 299
Debussy, Claude 1:74, 76, 304; 2:298, 299, 364; 3:54, 108
    L'après midi d'un faun 1:76
    La cathédrale engloutie 1:75, 76
    Les sérènes, 2:74
Decamps 1:15
Deem, George, *Statistical landscape* 6:257
Degas 1:43, 44, 85, 102, 107, 113, 189; 4:182, 184; 5:56, 367
Delacroix, Eugène 1:12, 15–19, 21, 22, 23, 30, 31, 33, 39, 40, 50, 58, 72, 73, 76, 83, 85, 86, 88, 91, 92, 95, 96, 99, 100, 101, 102, 105, 124, 129, 138, 139, 156, 171, 172, 175, 176, 177, 178, 182, 198, 199, 288, 299, 365, 366, 368, 372; 2:84; 3:284; 5:34, 35, 48, 51, 57, 59, 344; 4:182, 187, 223; 5:34, 35, 49, 51, 57, 59, 345; 6:252, 253, 258

Delaroche 1:18, 152;
Delaunay, Robert 1:142, 152, 304; 5:76, 77, 192, 281, 316;
   Eiffel Tower, 5:281, 316
Delilah 4:144, 147
Delvaux 1:331; 3:380; 5:88, 317
   Cyrialide, 1:331
   Penelope, 1:331
Denis, Maurice 1:60, 73, 80, 91, 92, 93, 94, 96, 97, 98, 99, 112, 113, 115, 132, 133–137, 138, 139, 147, 148, 151, 152, 156, 166, 172, 173, 174, 179, 185, 191, 401
Derain 1:307; 5:72, 76, 192
Descartes, René, 2:149; 3:5, 63, 198, 381, 414, 457; 4:87, 135, 282–284, 305; 5:25, 28, 123, 124, 190, 329; 6:145, 163, 209, 218, 219, 233, 239, 240, 241, 242, 247
   Discourse on Method, 6:239
Desdoumes, Mamie 2:200
Desmond, Johnny 3:88
Desnoyer 1:320
Despiau, 5:367, 369, 372
Detaille 1:8
Deutsch, Niklaus Manuel 1:277; 4:117
Dewey, J. 5:172
Dickens 3:21; 6:228
Dideau, Charles 6:156
Diderot 1:44; 3:64, 220, 425; 5:28, 123, 190; 6:195–196, 211
   Encyclopedia 3:182, 454; 5:30; 6:222
Die Brücke 5:63, 64
Diepenbrock 1:60–61
Dilthey, Wilhelm, 2:84, 85; 3:305, 310; 4:78; 5:177, 297
Dine 5:106
Diogenes of Sinope 3:160
Dionysius the Areopagite, Pseudo- 2:140
Disney, Walt 1:235; 5:298
Dix, Otto 4:266
Dixie Hummingbirds, the 2: *plate 24*

Dobbelman 5:374
Dobson, Frank 2:86;
Dodds, Johnny, 2:205, 207, 212, 235, 237, 240, 241, 242, 243, 248, 250, 257, 258, 271, 279, 364, 374, 375–376, *plates 10, 15, 20;* 5:112
Dodds, Warren Babe (Baby), 2:205, 207, 212, 214, 241, 282; *plates 10, 20*
Doesberg, van 1:318, 319, 415; 5:75
Domini 3:83
Donatello 1:291; 4:48
Donne, John 3:435; 4:324
Doorne, van 1:341
Dooyeweerd, Herman 1:xiv, xvii, xix; 2:5, 11, 32; 3:416, 478; 4:25; 5:337; 6:3, 142, 152, 174, 177, 178–181, 184, n.29
   A New Critique of Theoretical Thought 2:44, 57, 68, 77; 6:177
   In the Twilight of Western Thought 1:xxviii
Dorival 1:196
Dorra 1:401
Dorsey, Thomas A. 2:212, 270, 320, 355, 358
Dostoevsky (Dostoyevsky) 3:19; 6:116
   The Brothers Karamazov 3:173, 193; 4:435; 6:97, 108, 111
Dou, G. 4:153
Dougherty 1:180
Doumergue 3:6; 4:379
Douwes 4:476
Dowland, John 5:48, 50
Drayer 1:345
Drielst, van 1:279
Dubuffet, Jean, 2:117; 3:103, 196, 378; 4:98; 5:100, 101, 288
   Le Magicien 4:97
Duccio 4:296; 5:7; 6:278
   Betrayal of Christ, 6:277
Duchamp, Marcel, 5:77, 78, 81, 99, 108, 192, 300, 309, 330; 6:255, 256
   Bride (The change from a virgin to

a bride) 5:77
The King and Queen Surrounded by their swift nudes, 5:77, 81
Nude descending a staircase, 5:77, 78
Mona Lisa with moustache, 6:255
Ready-Mades, 5:78; 6:256
Ducretet-Thomson, 2:351
Dudok, 5:85
Dufay, Guillaume 4:246
Dunbar, Scott and Celeste 2: *plate 9*
Dupagne 1:245
Duranty 1:43, 44
Dürer, Albrecht, 3:19, 22, 61, 204, 237–244; 4:81, 102, 103, 104–113, 116, 119, 121, 124, 126, 141, 163, 174, 200, 239, 248, 249, 270, 363, 379; 5:147, 151, 244, 266, 345; 6:143, 279, 280; 5:147, 151, 244, 266, 345
Apocalypse 3:237–244, 239, 241
Knight, Death and Devil 4:248
The studying Jerome 4:248
Melancholia 4:108, 248
Grosze Passion 4:113
The Revelation of John 4:500
The life of Mary 4:500
Dutrey, Honoré 2:212, 215, *plate 10*;
Dvorák, 2:347
Dvorak, Max 4:51, 78; 5:178, 184, 297
Kunstgeschichte als Geistesgeschichte 3:480; 5:178, 297
Dyck, Van, 1:268, 270, 280; 4:152, 194, 214, 239, 354; 5:18; 6:254
Dylan, Bob 2:378; 3:422; 5:119, 130, 201, 254; 6:158, 164, 187, 193–195, 229, 266, 268
'Ballad of a thin man' 5:5; 6:213
'Desolation Row' 5:136, 250
'My back pages' 6:195–196
Ebed-melech 6:37
Ebreo, Leone 4:86;
Dialighi d'Amore 4:85
Eckhardt 4:29;
Edward the Confessor 4:39

Edwards, Ed 2:208
Eecen, Pauline, *Homo prudens* 5:375
Eeckhout, van der 1:267
Eeden, van, F.W. 'The sun, dying, sank into the sea' 2:28
Eeghen, van 1:278, 279
Effront, Nadine 5:373
Einstein 3:469
Elburg 1:341;
Elckerlyck 4:435
Elenbaas 5:377
Eliade 5:108
Elijah 2:177, 226; 3:144; 4:470; 5:27, 137; 6:19, 21, 53, 54, 209, 279
Eliot, T.S. 5:251; 6:229
Elisha, 6:19, 20, 64, 82
Elizabeth I, Queen of England 2:167; 4:222; 3:437; 5:18
Ellington Band, the 2:257
Ellington, Duke 2:247, 249–253, 257, 265, 293, 294, 356, 365; 3:205, 403; 6:191
'Creole love song', 2:249
Elstrom 1:245
Eluard, Paul 5:199
Emerson 1:165
Empoli, Jacopo da 4:151
Endell 1:186
Engelbrachsten, Cornelius 1:248
Engels, Friedrich 3:301, 313, 327
Engels, Lucila, *Child on stairs* 4:458
Enoch 3:144–146, 197
Ensor, James 1:297–298, 332, 386
La mort poursuivant le troupeau des humains 1:298
Grand view of the Maria Church 1:298
View of the Port of Ostende 1:298
Ephraim 6:103, 220
Epstein, Jacob 5:85; 6:22
Erasmus 3:243, 244, 324
Praise of Folly 3:325
Erigena, John Scot 4:297, 304, 309
Ernst, Max 3:195, 380; 5:87, 88, 89,

197, 198, 317
La femme a cent têtes 4:253
Esau 6:30
Escher 1:348–350; 3:10, 11, 12, 22
  Other world 3:11
Esslin, Martin, 5:134
  The Theatre of the Absurd 3:171
Esterházy family 2:74
Estes, Sleepy John 2:269
Europe, Jim 4:337; 6:188
Evans 1:27;
Eve 2:16, 132; 3:93, 139, 140, 158, 429, 445, 459; 4:144, 147, 304, 397; 6:60, 110, 218, 221, 223, 289
Eversen, A., *Winter in Enkhuizen* 1:283
Eversole, Finley 5:125
Evreux, Jeanne d' 4:35;
Eyck, Jan van 1:236, 240, 246, 247, 248, 268, 269, 270, 366; 2:31, 46, 133, n.20; 3:57, 238; 4:43, 44, 48, 53, 62, 88, 109, 121, 165, 203, 204, 213, 223, 224, 246, 302, 303, 304, 308—309, 310, 342, 361; 5:345; 6:252, 278
  Altar of the Lamb of God 1:248; (*Adam*) 3:446; (*Eve*) 2:132; 4:445; 5:152
  Arnolfini and his wife 1:268; 4:235
  Baptism of Christ 4:303; 6:278
  Heures de Turin 4:58, 303
  Madonna with Chancellor Rolin 4:308
  The man with the carnation 1:268
  Portinari 2:132
  St Barbara 4:63–67
Eysden, van 1:345
Ezekiel 3:452; 6:31, 37, 38, 63, 64
Ezra 4:415;
Faber 3:248;
Fabri, Albrecht 5:198
Fabritius, Carel 1:267; 3:36
Falguière, *Madeleine* 1:8
Faraday 3:176

Farey, Everett, 2:284
Fauves 1:10, 151, 152, 200, 304; 5:62, 29, 94, 179, 237, 243, 316
Fawcett 2:352
  'Blest be the tie that binds', 2:352
Fearnley *Moonlight over Sorento* 1:294
Feininger, Lyonel, 1:332; 2:117; 5:76, 81, 281
Fénéon 1:77;
Fenton, J Johnson, 2:184
Ferdinand 3:387
Ferrarese master *Madonna* 4:308;
Ferrier, Kathleen, 2:362
Feuerbach 1:165
Ficino, Marsilio 1:154, 162; 2:141, 152; 4:83, 84, 85, 86, 98, 100, 238; 5:170
Fiesole, Vincenzio de' Rossi da 4:98;
Filiger 1:112, 113
Fillray 1:337
Fiore, del 1:275
Fisk Jubilee Singers 2:176, 177, 179, 229, 308, 339, 347, 351
Fitzgerald, Ella 2:328
Fitzgerald, Scott 6:185, 187
Five Blind Boys, the 2:304
Flaubert 1:56; 3:321; 5:48, 49, 226
  Madame Bovary 4:261; 5:48
Flaxman 1:291; 5:39
Flinck, Govert, *Isaac and Jacob* 1:267
Fokke, *Moderne Helicon, een droom* 4:196
Fontainas, André, 1:81, 195; 5:214, 215
Fontana *The end of God* Fontana, Lucio, 2:117; Fontana, Lucio 5:103, 118, 143, 192, 198, 320
  The end of God 4:259; 5:103
  Spatial concept 4:259
Forain 1:89
Forge, Andrew, 5:101
Foster, Stephen 2:181, 338, 363
Fragonard 1:41, 276; 5:357; 6:252
Francesca, Piero della , 2:149; 4:307;

3:81, 82, 85; 6:278, 279

Baptism in the Jordan 3:81, 83, plate 4; 4:61, 307

Francis of Assisi, St 3:255, 444; 4:45; 6:271

Franck, César 4:221

Franck, Sebastian 3:326; 4:127, 128, 129, 130; 5:294, 300

Francke, Master *St Barbara Altarpiece* 1:235

Franken, F., *Conversion of St. Bavo* 4:158

Frasconi 1:329

Frederick II 4:27

Freud, Siegmund, 2:98; 3:5, 196, 344, 416; 4:245, 305; 5:31, 86, 172, 222, 272, n.317; 6:166, 196–197, 241

Frey, Dagobert 5:178

Friedrich, Caspar David 1:294; 3:11; 5:234

Frisco 6:188

Froebel 1:226

Fuller, Jesse 2:292

Fuseli 1:48, 278; 3:378; 5:39

Gaddi, Taddeo 4:299

Gainsborough 1:280–281, 295; 5:39

    A market cart crossing a brook 1:281

    Lady Molyneux 1:280

    William Poyntz 1:280

Galenus 6:206–207

Galileo 3:478; 6:240

Galle, Th. 4:149;

Garland, Joe 2:370

Garlock, Frank, *A Big Beat, a Rock Blast* 6:266

Gasset, Jose Ortega y 4:454

    Revolt of the Masses 3:28

Gauckler 1:156

Gaudi 5:61

Gauguin, Paul 2:119; 3:15, 59, 69, 110, 278, 289, 290, 291, 312, 376; 4:238, 440, 441; 5:54–59, 62–64, 84, 103, 191, 214–216, 285, 315; 6:286

    Calvaire 1:97, 134

    Diverses Choses 1:178

    D'ou venons-nous? 1:191

    Vision after the sermon 1:110, 114, 196

    Manau Tupapau 1:189–191

    Noa noa 1:187

Gauss 3:176;

Gautier, Théophile 1:28, 31

Gavarni 1:39, 293, 337

Gay, Peter 3:220; 6:211

    The Enlightenment, the Science of Freedom, 6:242

Geergen tot Sint Jans (of St John) 1:242, 244; 2:82; 5:21

Geffroy, G. 1:57

Gelder, Aart de 1:267; 4:151

    Scenes from the Passion 1:267

Gelder, Aert

George Lewis Group, the 2:281

Géricault, Théodore 1:11, 19, 38; 2:84; 4:182

    Le Radeau de la Méduse 1:38

Germain 1:58;

Gêrome 1:7; 5:51

Gerrasi, 5:258

Gershwin, George, 2:262, 263, 320

    Porgy and Bess 1:227; 2:262

Gertsch, Franz 6:258

Gervix 1:8

Gessner 1:278

Gestel 1:320, 332

Gheyn, de 1:254

Ghiberti 4:48; 5:343

Ghil (Ghill) 1:61, 105, 161

    Traité du verbe 1:161; 4:237

Ghirlandaio 4:67, 69

Giacometti 5:198

Gianbologna 4:100

    Rape of the Sabine virgins 4:148, 502

Gide 1:168; 4:442

Gilbert and Sullivan, *Patience* 1:57; 5:60

Gilchrist 1:53, 55
   Paolo and Francesca 1:53
   Beata Beatrix 1:53
Gill, Eric, 5:85
Gillespi, Dizzy 2:158, 275, 277, *plate 22*; 5:169
Gillray 1:14
Gilpin, *The long driveway in the park of Windsor Castle* 1:295;
Ginsberg, Allen 3:222; 5:108, 254, 258, 260, 309, 330
   'Howl' 3:160, 161; 5:109, 249, 309, 330, 332
Giordano, Luca 4:253
Giorgione
   Venus 4:151, 400
   The tempest 4:155
   Concert champêtre 4:261
Giorgione 3:69; 5:38, 190, 267, 347
   Noah's drunkness 1:275
   Pastoral concerto, 5:38
   Venus 2:133; 3:98; 5:190, 267, 347
Giotto 1:173, 429; 2:134; 3:204, 413; 4:53, 88, 296, 299, 302, 456
   Flight to Egypt 4:301
Girard d'Orleans 4:38
Giuffre, Jimmy 2:298
Gleizes 5:75
Gleyre 1:7
Glynn, Lillian 2:188, 230
Gnoli, Domenico 6:257
Godard 5:300
Goes, Hugo van der 1:246, 247; 4:109, 121; 5:337, 338
   Portinari altarpiece 1:247; 4:67–71, 89
Goethe 1:56, 60, 121, 165; 3:51, 119, 410; 4:12, 265; 5:171, 213
   Faust 4:381
Gogh, Vincent van 1:9, 15, 72, 84–89, 90, 105, 106, 107, 110–111, 113, 181, 189, 226, 290, 296, 299, 300, 303, 304, 306, 310, 325, 335; 2:126; 3:247, 256, 273, 380, 394; 4:22, 382, 482; 5:57, 59, 62, 63, 64, 191, 222, 230, 284, 336–338, 342, 343, 344
   Garden at Etten 1:111
   La Berceuse 1:111
   Pair of shoes 5:147
   Potato eaters 4:224, 260
   after Rembrandt's *Resurrection of Lazarus* 5:285
Golden Gate Quartet, the 2:286, 304, 309, 358
Golding, 5:74
Goliath 4:6
Gollwitzer 3:61, 88
Goltzius 4:149, 151, 165
Gombrich, Ernst 1:13, 14, 26, 28; 2:134; 4:275–277
   The Story of Art 3:413
Goncourt, de 1:64
Goodman, Benny, 2:270, 271, 361; 5:112
Goodman, Paul 5:108, 258
Gorki, Arshile 5:99
Gossaert, Geerten 3:32; 4:442
Gossaert, Jan (Mabuse) 1:247, 248, 270; 4:204, 311
   St Luke paints the Madonna 4:76
Goudzwaard, Bob, 6:177
Gourmont, Rémy de 1:424; 4:237
Goya 1:13–15, 19, 30, 71, 268, 270, 281–282, 366; 3:67, 68, 110, 183; 4:465; 5:33, 34, 38, 39, 48, 51, 147, 190, 303, 357
   El sueño la razón produce monstrous 1:13
   Caprichos 1:14, 281
   Desastros de la Guerra [disasters of war] 1:14, 282; 3:67
   Quien lo creyera 1:14
   Siempre suceded 1:282
Goyen, Jan van 1:83, 377; 2:133, 134; 3:32, 38–41, 61, 62; 4:167–171, 204, 225, 246; 5:11–14, 35; 6:144
   Approaching Storm 3:38–41, *plate 1*
   Village along the river 4:170

Graaf, de 3:8
Graf, Urs 1:277; 4:117
Graham, Billy 6:158
Grandville 1:19; 3:12; 4:198; 5:73
Grant, Bobby 2:232, 326
Graves, Morris 5:355
Gray, 5:39
Greco, El, 2:68; 4:239, 249; 5:15, 186, 266, 254, 367
Greco, Equilio 5:367
Green, Charlie 2:329
Greene, Graham 5:125
Greer, Sonny 2:252
Grieg, Edvard, *Peer Gynt* 2:75
Grien, Baldung 1:240, 270; 4:117
Griffiths, Suddie 2:182
Gris, Juan 1:312
Gromaire 5:85
Gros, Antoine 1:11, 38
Grosseteste 4:305
Grossman, 2:277
Grosz 3:103
Grünewald 1:239; 4:43, 58, 116, 239, 248, 249; 5:20, 147, 184, 303, 354;
  Crucifixion, 5:303
  Isenheimer altar 4:114
  Temptation of St Anthony, 5:147
Guardi 1:275, 276
Guariento 1:275
Guercino 3:46, 47; 4:151; 5:52;
  Elijah in the Wilderness, 5:52
  St. Peter raising Tabitha 4:159
  Presentation of Christ in the Temple 4:159
Guizot 3:103
Guston, Philip, 2:117; 3:196; 5:99
Guys, Constantin 1:39, 292–293
Haan, Meyer de 1:113, 115, 409; 5:214
Haasse, Hella 3:21
Habakkuk 4:68;6:29, 30, 75
Haftmann, Werner, 5:92, 357, 358
  Malerei im 20. Jahrhundert, 5:92

Haggard, Rider, *She* 2:42
Haggart, Bob 2:259
Hals, Frans 1:253, 254, 271; 3:54, 57; 4:137
Hamilton 5:106
Hammacher 5:376
Hammond, John 2:234, 305, 306
Hananiah 4:419
Handel, *The Messiah* 3:118; 4:324, 330
  Water Music 4:324
Handy, W.C. 2:208–210, 230, 231, 251
  'Memphis blues' 2:209
  A Treasury of the Blues 2:209
  'St Louis blues' 2:210'
Hanneman 1:280
Hardin, Lilian 2:212, 240, *plate 11*
Harding, D.E., 5:324
  Hierarchy of Heaven and Earth 5:324
Harnett 4:342
Harris, Noel Chandler, 2:166
Harrison, Jimmy, 2:250
Hartmann, Eduard von 1:153
Harvey, William 6:206–207, 211, 245
Hawkins, Coleman 2:250
Haydn, Franz Josef 2:74; 4:340
  Surprise Symphony 3:396
Haydon 5:39
Hayes, Roland 2:176, 177, 304, 339, 348, 350, 351
  'Little boy, how old are you?' 2:348
Heath Robinson, W. 1:56
Heckel 1:306, 328; 5:64
Heda 1:256; 4:228
Heemskerck, Maerten van 1:248, 249
Hefner, Hugh 5:134
Hegel, Georg W.F. 1:99, 133, 164; 2:21, 141, 152; 3:288; 4:276, 318; 5:124, 307, 326; 6:274
Heide, van der 4:195
Heidegger 1:182, 323; 2:275, 300; 3:13; 5:83, 124, 300, 308, 322
Heine 1:160

Heisenberg 6:291
Helm, Bob 2:284
Helmholtz 1:78; 3:176
Hemmingway 6:229
Henderson, Charles Cooper 1:295
Henderson, Fletcher 2:247, 249, 250, 269–271, 365; 5:112
Hendrik, Wijbrant 4:185;
Hendrix, Jimmy, 1:357; 6:198, 199
Henner 1:128
Henri 1:141
Henry, Carl 1:78, 79, 152
Herod 4:303
Hess, Walter 5:350, 357
Heyden, van de 1:255; 4:185
Heyward, Du Bose 2:262
    Mamba's Daughter 2:319
    Porgy 2:262, 320
Hierck, Huib 1:345
Hildebrandt 1:291
Hindemith 3:403
Hitler, Adolf 3:102, 255; 6:56, 202
Hobbema 4:137; 5:41
Hobbes, 5:28. 30, 123, 133, 189; 6:164, 193–195
    Leviathan, 3:183,Hockney, 6:234
Hocke 4:88
Hodges 1:271
Hodler 3:95; 4:399
    Student putting on his coat 1:278;
Hodler
Hofer 1:328
Hoffet, F. 3:312
Hogginbotham, Wat 2:243
Hokusai 4:348, 465, 466
Holbein 1:270, 280
    Dance of Death 1:278; 4:117
Holmes, Charlie 2:243
Holofernes 4:144, 147
Holthe, Jan van 5:266
    Gevecht, 5:266
Holyord 4:443;
Homer 1:18; 4:469; 5:223
    Odyssey, 2:27
Hondecoeter, Gillis d' 4:164
Honegger 2:298; 3:54
Honthorst 1:254; 4:151
Hooch, Pieter de (Hoogh) 1:268; 4:137
Hoogendijk 4:476
Hoorn, van 5:374
Hooykaas, R. 6:217
    Religion and the Rise of Modern Science, 6:144
Hopkins, Lightnin' 2:292
Horace Silver Quintet, the 2:297
Horatius, 169
Horn, Le, 5:377
Horta 5:61
Hosea 5:135; 6:21, 22, 54, 71
Hot Fives 2:221, 240–243, 245, 283, 370, 376
Hot Sevens 2:240–243, 265, 371, 371, 376
Houckgeest 1:255
Houseman, Victor 2:247,
Housman, A. E. 5:301, 309, 330
Howard, Darnell 2:244, 371
Howard, Fred 2: *plate 23*
Howard, Kid 2:280, 374
Höweler, *XYZ der Muziek* 2:383
Hugh of St Victor 4:294
Hughes, Langston 319, 356
Hugo, Victor 1:19
Huitker, Anky 6:3
Huizinga 4:46;
    The Waning of the Middle Ages 4:32, 46
    De schaduwen van morgen, 6:108, 122
Hulswit, van 1:279
Hume 3:5; 4:254; 5:28, 29, 52, 123, 190, 329
    'Inquiry Concerning Human Understanding', 5:29
Hundertwasser 5:198
Hunt, Holman 1:50, 51, 52, 53, 54,

380; 3:65, 206; 5:45, 60; 6:283
The Awakening Conscience 1:51
Light of the World 4:260
Pre-Raphaelitism and the Pre-Raphaelite Brotherhood 1:50
Scapegoat, 5:45
Hunziker, Frieda 1:359
Hurot 1:182
Hurt, John 4:341
Huss John 3:238
Husserl 5:68
Huszar 1:318
Hutton, James 3: n.219; 6:216
Huxley, Aldous 5:126, 127, 134, 248
    Brave New World 3:222, 392; 5:126, 248
Huyghe, René 1:187; 3:13, 70, 71; 4:454, 460
Huysmans 1:55, 66, 68, 69, 71, 83, 89, 117, 118, 122, 386
    A Rebours 1:66, 68, 69, 71; 3:177
Huysum, van 1:257
Hyckes, R. 2:86
Ibsen, Henrik 2:75
Ignatius of Loyola 3:5
Ingres 1:11, 15, 30, 79, 85, 90, 198, 291, 364; 3:98; 4:223; 5:36, 53, 92, 315, 343
    La Source 4:260, 266
    Odalisque 3:98
Isaac 3:216; 4:233; 6:219
Isaiah 2:381; 3:156, 419, 420, 427, 444; 5:46, 82, 89, 135, 250; 6:8, 33, 34, 35, 51, 67, 70, 74, 174
Israëls, Isaac 1:304
Israëls, Jozef 1:304
J.J. Johnson Quintet 2:297
Jackson, Franz 2:357
Jackson, George Pullen 2:259, 338
Jackson, Holbrook 3:196; 5:68
Jackson, Lewis 2:344
Jackson, Mahalia, 2:305, 306, 308, 322, 342, 344, 353–355, 357, 358, 379, 380, plate 29; 3:56, 115; 5:68, 113; 6:142

'Amazing grace', 2:344, *plate 29*
Jacob, 5:54; 6:100, 101, 219
Jacquemart de Hesdin 4:38
Jael 4:144
Jaffé, Hans 1:xvii, xviii, xxiv, xxvi, 319;
Jaguer 3:378
Jamar A. 1:245
James (biblical) 3:328, 439
James, King of England 3:331
James, William, 2:85
Janis, Conrad 2:356
Janse, A. 3:8, 515 n.270; 6:131
Janson 1:284
    History of Art 3:413
Jansz, Claes 4:167
Jarry, Alfred 5:73, 251, 300
    Ubu Roi 3:190; 5:73
Jaspers, Karl 1:86; 5:124
Jazz Messengers, the 2:297
Jefferson, Blind Lemon 2:185, 260, 327, 333, 334, 343; 5:112
Jeremiah , 2:106, 381; 4:68, 419; 3:419, 420, 444; 5:136, 137, 290, 359; 6:8, 23, 24, 35, 37, 39, 49, 69, 75, 104, 133
Jeroboam, 3:468; 6:18
Jerome, St. 4:10, 13
Joachim 4:88
Joans, Ted 5:169, 171
Job 3:49, 224; 4:437; 6:27, 28, 29, 32, 36, 236
Joel, 5:277; 6:75, 109, 112
Joest, Jan 1:232
Joffers 1:311
Johfra, 5:233, 234
John of the Cross 6:286
John the Baptist 3:83; 4:39, 133; 6:66
John the Good 4:38, 53
John, St 3:81, 135, 136, 172, 238, 455; 4:4, 35; 5:20, 308; 6:52, 55, 60, 63, 64, 66, 67, 70, 72, 75, 76, 77, 271
    Revelation 4:102, 107, 109, 189
Johnny Dunn's Band 2:211

Johns, Jasper, *Painted bronze II*, 6:256
Johnson, Bill, 2:*plate 11*
Johnson, Blind Willie, 2:254, 255, 267, 291, 320, 323, 343, 344; 3:25;
Johnson, Buddy 2: *plate 10*
Johnson, Bunk, 2:199, 205, 281, 282, 283, 307, *plate 10*, *plate 19*
Johnson, Dink 2: *plate 12*
Johnson, Dr, 5:81
Johnson, Fenton J. 2:184, 319
Johnson, Guy, *Negro Workaday Songs* 2:223;
Johnson, James P. 2:258
Johnson, James Weldon 2:227–229, 319, 320
   'The Creation' 2:227–229; 6: n.44;
Johnson, Lonnie 2:231, 269, 356
Johnson, Mainzee 370
Johnson, Merline 2:269
Jolson, Al 2:263
Jonah 3:176; 4:189
Jonas, Hans 5:300, 302, 308, 328
Jones, Jo 2:272
Jones, Mother 2:292
Jones, Richard M 2:212
Joplin, Scott 2:195, 196, 363, 368; 6:188
   'Maple leaf rag' 2:196, *plate 7*; 6:187
Jordan, Raimon 4:27
Jorisz, David 4:128
Joseph 4:58, 174; 6:220, 283
Joshus, 2:345, 346; 3:61
Josiah 6:22, 23
Joyce 3:195
Joyce, James 5:87, 98
   Ulysses, 5:87, 98
   Work in Progress 3:389
Jubal 6:246
Judah 6:219
Judith 4:144, 147;
Julius II, Pope 4:73, 74

Jung 5:86, 175
Kafka, Franz 2:113; 1:308; 5:87, 227, 300, 324
   The Trial 3:103; 5:87
Kahn 1:62, 167
Kalff 4:228
Kalsbeek 3:476–479
Kandinsky, Wassily (Kandinski) 1:xxiii, 152, 186, 315, 320, 341; 3:69, 110, 486; 4:149; 5:53, 66–69, 71, 75, 84, 85, 96, 192, 193, 197, 198, 221, 286, 319, 345; 6:255
   Painting with white surface 1:321
   Klänge: 'In the Woods', 5:69
   Über das Geistige in die Kunst 3:379
   Über die Formfrage, 5:299
Kanowitz, Howard, 5:320; 6:256, 258
Kant, Immanuel 1:22, 152, 153, 159, 421; 2:78, 118, 149, 152; 5:29, 123, 170, 171, 190, 195, 319; 3:5, 327, 477, 478, 486, 487; 4:254, 281, 318; 5:29, 170, 190, 195, 319; 6:152, 155, 239, 243, 256, n.29
   The Critique of Judgement, 2:141
   Critique of Pure Reason, 5:123; 6:178
   Critique of Practical Reason, 5:123
   Kritik der Urteilschaft 1:153; 5:171
   reine Vernunft 2:4
   Träume eines Geistessehers 1:159
Kat J.F. 4:441–443
Keeler, Christine 5:38
Keller, Gottfried 5:301, 309, 329
Kelsey, Revd 2:348
Kemper, Bernet, *Muziekgeschiedenis* 2:40
Kempis, Thomas à 5:20
   The Imitation of Christ, 5:20–21
Kenton, Stan 2:296
Keppard, Freddie 2:205, 211, 368
Ket, Dick 1:257
Keyser, Hendrik de 4:180
Keyser, Thomas de 1:248

Khnopff 1:58
Kid Rena's Delta Jazz Band 2:280
Kienholtz, 5:302; 6:234
Kierkegaard 2:21; 3:327, 478; 5:32, 124
King Oliver's Creole Jazz Band/Orchestra 2:216, 361, 371, 249. *plate 11*, 20; 4:347, 408
Kirchner, Ernst 1:305; 2:133; 5:64, 270
Klages 5:175
Klapper 4:256;
Klarwein, Mati 5:320
   Abstract painting, 5:320; 6:257
Klee, Paul 1:341; 2:216, 276, 294; 3:196; 5:83, 90, 221, 272, 301, 330, 348, 354
Klein, Yves 3:170; 5:143, 192
Klerk, de 5:85
Klimt 1:305; 5:61
Kline 1:321; 5:99
Klinger, Max 3:205
Klombeck 5:40
Kloos 2:68
Kneulman 5:371, 372, 377
Knight, Mary 2:306
Knipperdolling 3:326
Knopf 5:61
Koekkoek, B. C. 1: 283, 284, 286, 287; 4:186; 5:40
Koekkoek, J.H. 1:287
Koestler, Arthur, 5:126
   The Ghost in the Machine, 5:126; 6:223
Kokoschka 5:198, 299, 357
Kolbe 5:369
Kollwitz, Kathe 5:147
   Farmer's war 1:311
Koninck 1:267
Kooning, Willem de 3:424; 5:99, 288
Krans, Erik 2:283
Krijger, Hans 1:350
Kris 5:170
Krop, Hildo 2:86

Krug 1:152
Kruiningen, van 1:359
Krupa, Gene 2:239
Kruseman 4:186
Kuitert 6:149
Kunstadt, Len 2:356
Kupferberg, Tuli 4:267
Kurpershoek *Jonah and the whale* 1:357
Kurz 5:170
Kuyper
Kuyper, Abraham 1:xxviii, 163–166, 225, 411; 2:3, 5; 3:6, 52, 337, 347, 462; 4:102, 367, 402, 422; 5:174, 187, 359, n.181; 6:174, 176–178, 182
   Het Calvinisme en de kunst 4:379
l'Ainé, Moreau 1:41
Lachalier 1:369
Ladatte, E., *Martyrdom of St. Philip* 4:160;
Ladner 4:293, 295
Ladnier, Tommy 2:217, 231, 279, 329
Laing 5:108, 258
Lairesse, de 1:271; 3:354; 4:154;
   Groot Schilderboeck 4:148, 150, 153
Lam 3:196
Lamb, Joseph, 2:195
Lambert, Don, 2:358; 3:378
Lamech 3:140–141,144, 145, 153, 197, 429
Laneville-Johnson Brass Band 2:193
Lang, Eddie 2:222
Langbehn, A. Julius 5:172
Langer, Susanne 2:141; 3:152; 5: n.238; 6:211, 212
   Philosophy in a New Key, 6:243, 254
Lapsey Band 2:193
Lasso, Orlando di
   Todesca 3:24
Latour, Quentin 3:57
Lautréamont 5:86, 300, 330
Laval 1:108, 145, 171

Lawrence 1:286
Lazarus 4:437; 5:90, 285
Léandre 1:89
Lear, Edward 4:198; 5:73
   Book of Nonsense 1:337
Leary, Timothy 3:222
Lebeau, C. 2:86
Lebrun 1:6
Leck, Bart van der 1:xxiii, 318, 319–320
Leckert 1:286
Ledbetter, Huddie, (Leadbelly) 2:260
Leeser, Titus 5:376
Leeuw, Aart van der
   De Gezegende 2:28
Leeuwenhoek, van 6:163, 296, 216
Leeuwens, Will 1:359
Léger 4:270; 5:281; 6:286
Legros 4:443
Lehar, Franz, 2:262, 301, 362; 3:108
Lehmann, Kurt 1:79, 167, 168, 171, 175; 5:374
Leibel, Wilhelm, *Three women in church* 6:283
Leibniz 3:5, 63; 6:242
Leikhert 1:283;
Leiris, M. 5:93
Lely 1:280
   Windsor beauties 4:194
Lessing 1:165
Levitine 1:13
Lewis Robinson Band, the 2:282, *plate 21*
Lewis, C.S. 3:373; 4:271, 300, 329; 5:301, 306, 324; 6:3, 172, 229
   foreword to Harding, *Hierarchy of Heaven and Earth* 5:301, 306, 324; 6:165, 243
   The Great Divorce 6:205
   The Discarded Image 6:240, 244
   The Abolition of Man 4:322
Lewis, George 2:213, 280–285, 293, 307, 344, 374, 375, *plate 21*
   'Burgundy street blues' 2:213

Lewis, John 2:298
Lewis, Lux 2:234, 262
   'Honky-tonk train blues' 2:234, 262
Lewis, Ted 2: 220
Leyden, Jan van 3:326
Leyden, Lucas van 1:237, 244, 248 4:147, 164, 476
   Destruction of Sodom 1:237
   Saul and David 4:148
Leyden, Nicholas Gerhaert van 1:238
Leys, Hendrik 5:42
Leyster 1:254
Lhermitte 1:8, 9, 85, 364
Liechtenstein, 5:106
Liège, Jean de 4:37
Liender, van 1:279
Liernus, *Adoration of the Magi* 1:236
   Madonna in the Rose Bower 1:236
Limbourg brothers 4:43, 44, 48, 302;
   Très riches heures du Duc de Berry 4:58;
Lincoln, Abraham 2:174
Lindsay, John 2:370
Lint, van 1:330
Lipchitz, Jacques, 5:100
Lippi, Filippo 4:67, 69, 141, 308
   St John Evangelist resuscitating Drusiana 4:156
Livius 4:46
Llwyd, Morgan, 5:18
Locke, John 1:25; , 2:145, 146; 4:254; 5:28, 39, 123, 190, 329; 6:145, 209
   The Reasonableness of Christianity 5:28
   'Essay concerning Human Understanding' 5:29; 6:241
Lomax, Alan 2:182, 204, 223, 259–261, 264, 290, 331, 338, 340, 343, *plate 25*
   American Ballads and Folk Songs, 2:23
   'Murderer's home' 2:343
   Mister Jelly Roll 2:264

Lombard, Lambert
   The gathering of Manna 4:157
   The multiplication of the loaves 4:157
Lorenzetti 4:299, 501
   Good and bad government in Siena 4:298
Lorraine, Claude (La Lorrain) 1:13, 41, 42, 276; 5:13, 35, 36
Lot 3:161, 349; 6:86
Louis Philippe 3:103
Louis XIV 3:409; 6:62, 175; 4:24, 253;
Love Jiles Ragtime Orchestra, the 2:339
Lövgren, Sven 1:xxv
Lucebert, 5:279, 300
Lucie, Lawrence 2:369
Luckner 1:329
Luis Russell Band 2:243, 244, 247, 266, 361
Luke, St 2:148, 178; 4:76, 310
Lunceford 2:270
Luther 3:5, 144, 242–243, 283, 324, 325, 337; 4:102, 103, 117, 120, 134, 135, 327; 5:276; 6:107, 173, 231
Lutter, Claude 2:283
Lyttleton, Humphrey 2:283
Macke, August 1:xxiii, 309
   Strolling three-some 1:309
   The green jacket 1:309
Mae, Jessie 2:306
Maerlant, Jacob van 1:237
   Bible in Rhyme 1:237
Maeterlinck, *Palléas et Mélisande* 1:75
Maffei 1:275
Magnus, Albert 4:12, 297
Magritte, René 1:331; 2:117; 5:87, 88
Mahler 3:21
Mailer, Norman 3:187
Maillol, A.J.B. 1:192; 2:86, 87, 117; 5:85, 193, 6:229, 372, 377, 378, 379; 6:229, 255
   Isle de France 2:86; 5:369
Maistrel, Xavier de 1:21

Malachi, 5:90; 6:40, 45, 46, 47
Mâle 4:35, 39
Malevich 4:455; 5:84
Mallarmé 1:61, 62, 75, 76, 90, 105, 117, 118, 125–126, 127, 158, 159, 161, 181, 182, 183, 185, 200, 386, 408, 410, 419; 3:271; 4:236, 237; 5:73, 215
   L'après midi d'un faun 1:75
   Poeme en prose 1:158
Malone, Earl *plate 23*
Malraux, André, 2:122; 3:486; 4:453, 454, 455, 456; 5:182
Manasseh, 6:103, 220
Mander, van 4:145, 165
   Schilderboeck 4:145, 148, 153, 164
Manessier 1:320, 440; 6:286
Manet, Édouard 1:8, 41, 43, 44, 73, 169, 189, 299; 3:262, 263; 4:182, 262, 264; 5:38, 39, 42, 48, 49, 51, 59, 192, 193; 6:253
   Olympia 1:40, 191; 2:133; 3:69, 260; 4:261; 5:38, 190
   Déjeuner sur l'herbe (Picnic/Lunch on the grass) 1:51, 301; 3:260; 4:261; 5:38
Manetti 4:152
Mani-Vehli-Zumbul-Zadi 1:196
Mannheim 3:346
Mannone, Wingy 2:356
Mantovani 4:406
Manzú, 5:367, 374; 6:229
Marc, Franz 1:307, 321; 5:66, 67, 68, 71, 82 302, 304, 309, 330; 6:197–199
   Landscape in Tyrol 1:321
   Tierschicksale, 3:377; 5:83
Marcuse 5:32, 108
Marero 2:374
Mares, Paul 2:219
Marin, John 5:281
Marinetti 3:508;
Marini, Marino 1:313; 3:120, 121; 5:104
Maris, Willem 1:305

Marlowe 3:5; 5:25
    Dr Faustus, 5:25
Marmion, Simon, *Carrying of the cross* 1:237
Marrero, Billy 2: *plate 10*
Marsman, 2:41
Martin, John, 5:40
Martin, von, *Orde en Vrijheid* 3:361
Martini 4:34, 299
    Guidoriccio 4:38, 298;
Marx, Karl 2:4; 3:301, 327, 361, 490; 5:86; 6:170
    Communist Manifesto, 3:301, 313
Mary (biblical) 2:178, 383; 3:241, 408; 5:8, 12, 25, 29, 43, 188, 338
Mary 4:4, 7, 8, 30, 35, 39, 57, 58, 60, 68, 71, 76, 88, 91, 120, 134, 200, 201, 203, 204, 291, 303
Masaccio 2:149; 4:48, 306, 307; 6:245
    St. Peter and St. Paul distributing alms 4:156
    Trinity fresco 4:306
Masalino 4:306
Mascherini, 2:117; 5:367, 374
Masefield, John 3:31, 32
Masheck, Joseph 1:xxxii
Masmines, de 1:268
Masson, 5:87, 89
Master of Flémalle 1:247
Master of the *Heures de Rohan* 4:57, 58, 59
Master of the Virgo inter Virgines 1:242
Mataré 1:328
Matisse, Henri, 1:201, 309; 2:117; 3:99; 4:192; 5:63, 64, 237, 242, 270, 280, 299, 316, 322; 6:229
    Still life with nude 3:69
    Luxury, Calm and Voluptousness 5:63
Matta 3:196, 380; 5:89, 198, 202
Matthew, St 4:79; 5:44, 45; 6:219, 220
Matthews, Artie 2:209
    'Baby seal blues' 2:209
Matthieu, 5:100, 241

Mauclair 1:32, 58, 74, 82, 90, 118, 167
Mauriac 3:21
Mauve 1:85
Maximus, Valerius 4:46
McGee, Revd F W 2:345
McLuhan 5:71, 146, 257, 314
McMullen, *Art, Affluence and Alienation,* 6:228
McPartland, Jimmy, 2:222, 239
Meckenem, Israël van 1:242
Meegeren, van 1:352–355
Meijer, W. L. 5:358–360
Meisonnier 1:8, 134
Meisterman 1:329
Mekkes, J.P.A 1:xvii, xix; 2:11, 12; 6:152, 178
    Philosophy of the Cosmonomic Idea, 2:11
Memling (Memlinck) 1:246, 247, 248, 270; 4:109, 213
Mendelsohn 1:330
Mendelssohn 4:254
Menthe, Ferdinand La, *see* Morton, Jelly Roll
Merian, Mattheus 1:278
Meryon 1:70, 72, 86
Metsu, Gabriel 4:185; 6:282
Metsys, J. 4:151
Metsys, Quentin 1:247
Metzger 5:108
Metzinger, 5:75
Meunier, 5:370
Mezzrow, Mezz 2:239, 279, 369
Micah 3:235, 367; 6:74, 78
Michael (biblical) 3:241; 6:20, 82
Michaud 1:61, 62, 70, 105, 116, 185
Michelangelo, Buonarroti 1:11, 246, 252, 272; 2:123, 134, 141; 3:43, 97, 204, 237, 483, 489; 4:24, 72, 73–82, 83, 91, 94, 95, 96, 98, 100, 101, 213, 214, 222, 239, 345, 346, 354, 400, 455, 488; 5:266, 343, 345, 370; 6:62, 273
    Beau Dieu 4:260
    David 3:100, 237, 446; 4:260,

290, 343; 5:267, 347
   Creation 3:431
   Last Supper. 5:146
   Last judgement 4:270, 279, 346; 5:146
   Pieta 4:346
   St Matthew 4:82
Michelet 1:85, 162; 4:238
Miff Mole's Little Molers 2:222
Miles Davis Quintet, the, 2:297
Miley, Bubber 2:250, 252
Milhaud, Darius, 2:298; 6:229
   La création du monde, 2:75
Mill, John Stuart 5:49
Millais, John Everet 1:51, 54; 5:60; 6:253, 283
   The carpenter's shop, 6:283
Miller, Glen 2:270
Miller, Henry 5:87, 279
   Tropic of Cancer 3:195; 5:87
Miller, Punch 2:373
Millet 1:85; Millet, 5:336
   Sower, 5:336
Mills 2:252
Milton 1:36, 67; 5:214
   Paradise Lost 1:115, 214
Minne 5:369
Mirandola, Pico della 2:141; 5:170; 4:86, 96
   Oratio de Hominis Dignitate 4:85
Miró 1:xxi, 322–323, 356; 2:294; 3:195; 5:84, 87, 88, 89, 198
   Head of a Catalan farmer 1:322
   The eagle flies to the mountains, which have been hallowed out by comets, to proclaim the word of the poet 1:323
   The grasshopper 1:323
Miskotte, *Antwoord uit het onweer* 6:97, 98, 116
Mitchell, George 2:236, 242, 279, 370
Mitchell's Christian Singers, the 2:266
Modersohn-Becker, Paula 1:xxiii, 309–310

   Elsbeth 1:310
   Mother and Child 1:310
   Self-portrait 1:310
   Still life with fruit 1:310
   Woman of the poorhouse 1:310
Modigliani 1:312
Moerenhout 1:187
Mole, Miff 2:220, 222
Momper, de 4:373
Mondrian, Piet 1.xxiii, xxiv, 186, 226, 318, 319, 321, 330, 329, 340, 359, 415, 416, 440; 2:86, 216, n.84; 3:70, 79, 110, 378, 379; 5:74, 75, 81, 84, 86, 106, 220, 221, 245, 255, 274, 279, 285, 286, 312, 319, 322, 343, 348; 4:149, 459; 6:154, 229, 282
   De Stijl 3:70
   Victory boogie woogie 1:340
Monet, Claude 1:6, 74, 75, 76, 289, 301, 304; 2:133; 4:182; 5:51–53, 57, 76, 191
   Canal at Zaandam 1:301
   Cathedral of Rouen 1:302
   Charing Cross Bridge 1:302
   Field with spring flowers 1:302
   Grenouillère 1:301
   Rouen Harbour 1:301
   Seine at Argentueil 1:301
   Street in Normandy 1:301
   Waterlilies 1:302
Monfreid, De 1:192
Monnier 1:39;
Monteverdi 3:23; 4:115; 5:303
   Orfeo, 5:303
Monticelli 1:85, 88
Moore, Bass 2:370
Moore, Henry Spencer 2:117; 5:103, 104, 312, 317, 362–369
   Three draped figures, 5:369
Moore, Mozelle 2: *plate 14*
Moore, Sturge 1:53, 55
Morandi 1:252, 313
Morandini, F. *Christ healing the leper* 4:158

Moréas 1:61, 105, 117, 154;

Moreau, Gustave 1:58, 68, 69, 70, 71, 90, 110, 114, 117, 118, 122, 127, 276, 333–334; 5:237, 242, 284

Les Chimères 1:68

Salomé 1:69

Jupiter et Sémélé 1:69

Moreelse, P. 4:151, 269; 6:273

Morgan, Sam 2:249

Morganfield, Muddy Waters 2:292

Morice 1:32, 63, 64, 66, 67, 92, 95, 96, 97, 109, 116, 117, 118, 119–124, 125, 126, 127, 131, 132, 137, 139, 143, 149, 150, 153, 158, 159, 161, 162, 163, 166, 175, 185, 188, 189, 194, 195, 386, 396, 397, 401, 405, 409, 420, 427; 5:216

La littérature de tout à l'heure 1:63, 124, 132, 149

Noa noa 1:162/4:238

Morland, George 1:295, 296; 5:41

Morley, Malcolm 6:258

Moro (Antonio Mor van Dashorst) 1:248

Morpurgo-Tagliabue, E. 5:195

Morris, William 1:53, 54, 106, 360; 3:30; 5:60; 4:255, 321;

Mortier 1:331

Morton, Jelly Roll 2:208, 211–213, 217, 218, 235–239, 242, 244–246, 248, 251, 254, 257, 258, 264–266, 270, 271, 281, 294, 358, 364, 365, 368–374, *plate 18*; 4:347; 6:190

'Bucket got a hole in it' 2:200

'Jelly roll blues' 2:205, 208

'Doctor jazz' 2:235

'Dead man blues' 2:245

'Harmony blues' 2:246, 251

'Hot water blues' 2:254

'Kansas city breakdown' 2:254

'Black bottom stomp' 2:235, 266

'King porter stomp' 2:270

'Kansas city stomps' 2:364

Moses , 2:278; 3:144, 163, 335, 419, 467; 4:87, 133, 282, 322; 5:26; 6:10, 11, 14, 15, 16, 17, 28, 36, 50, 51, 132, 163, 174, 221, 279

Mosley 2:374

Mostaert, Jan 1:248

Moten, Benny (Bennie) 2:254

Mozart, Amadeus 1:290; 2:60, 206, 301, 334, 383–384; 3:55, 395, 404, 422; 4:221, 222, 225, 340, 348

Figaro, 2:384

Il Seraglio 4:266

Marriage of Figaro 3:55

The Magic Flute (Zauberflöte) 2:384; 3:55; 4:266;

Muggeridge, Malcolm 1:xxv

Müllerschäfe, *There are no Fathers in the World* 3:184;

Munch, Edvard 1:58, 59, 294, 303, 305, 306, 310; 5:62, 197; 6:196

Jealousy 1:294

The kiss 1:294

Puberty 1:303

The scream 1:303; 3: n.108; 5:218

Mundinus 6:206–207

Munro, T., 5:172

Munthé 1:294;

Münzer 3:5;

Murphy, Turk 2:284, 293

Murray, Don 2:221

Muti, Piero di Tomasso 4:95

Nageli, H.G. 2:352

'Blest be the tie that binds' 2:352

Nahmer, van der 5:369, 375

Napoleon, Phil 2:220

Nash 6:229

Natoire, C.J., *Conclusion of the Peace of Taranto* 4:161;

Nebuchadnezzar 3:406; 4:207

Neckham, Alexander 4:487

Neefs 1:255

Nelson, Big Eye Louis 2:280, *plate 10*

Nero 6:59

Nerval, Gerard de 1:121; 4:374
Netscher, C. 4:152
Neuville 1:8
New Orleans Rhythm Kings 2:219–222, 249, 258
Newton, Isaac, 5:39; 6:216
Newton, John 2:172
Nicholas, Albert 2:369
Niebuhr, H. Richard 5:20
   Christ and Culture, 5:20
Nietzsche 2:21, 84, 85; 3:67, 327; 5:68, 86, 243, 290, 301, 309, 328, 333; 6:105, 112
   Der Antichrist, 2:78
   'Geneaology of Morality' 6:109
   Thus Spake Zarathustra 1:402; 5:329
   Umwertung aller Werte, 5:303
Nieuwenhuis, Constant 5:272
Nieuwenhuis, Domela 1:342, 359
Nigg, Walter 4:239
Nixon, President of the USA 5:307; 6:134
Noah 3:380, 468; 4:403; 6:36, 55, 224
Nolde 1:xxiii, 306, 307, 328
   Maria Egyptica 1:307
Noone, Jimmy 2:205, 217, 251, 279
Nordau 5:359
Northolt, Schulte 2:166
Notke 4:191
   St George and the dragon 4:190
Novalis 1:162
Nuyen 1:286, 287–289
   The Duinkerken coast 1:288
   The windmill 1:288
Nuyen 4:187
Occam, William of 4:304, 305, 309
Oholiab 3:175, 176
Oliver, Joe 'King' 2:200, 201, 205, 211–217, 218, 219, 222, 237, 238, 239, 240, 243, 244–246, 247, 248, 249, 250, 251, 252, 254, 257, 258, 259, 264, 265, 266, 274, 280, 281, 282, 284, 295, 324, 357, 361, 368, 370, 371; 6:189;

   'Jazzin' babies blues' 2:220;'Snag it' 2:199, 250, 373, 375, *plate 11*
   'Chimes blues' 2:246
Ollendorff 4:78, 79
Ongenae 1:330
Ooms, Jan 1:352
Orcagna 4:142, 501
Origen 3:159
Original Dixieland Band 6:188
Ory, Edward 2:205
Ory, Kid 2:199, 205, 236, 240, 241, 243–245, 248, 257, 258, 283, 370–371, *plate 12, 13*
Ory's (Creole) Jazz Band 2:211, 371
Os, van 1:283, 288; 4:439–441
Ostade, van 4:40, 174, 228, 476
Ouborg 5:272, 274, 276
Oud 1:318
Ouwater, Albert von 4:122;
Ovid 5:189
   Metamorphoses 4:185; 5:189
Oxenaar, R.W.D. 5:350–357
Pachelbel, 2:382
Paget, Guy 1:295
Palach, Jan 5:130
Palestrina 4:270
Palissy 4:93
Palladio, Andrea 2:35
Panassie 2:279
Pander, Pier 1:290–292
Panofsky, Erwin 1:412; 2:148, 149; 3:413, 497; 4:74, 75, 78, 79, 296, 304, 310, 345; 6:143
Panzera 2:362
Paolozzi 3:196; 5:100, 106, 107
Parenti, Toni 2:356
Paris, Sidney de, 2:369
Paris, Wilbur de 2:293, 294
Parker, Charlie 2:274,275, 277; 6:192
   'Lover man' 2:277
Parmegianino 4:90;
   Madonna with the long neck 4:87, 91

Pater 4:255

Patinier, Herri 4:125

Patinier, Joachim 4:121–125, 373;

Paudiss, Christoff 1:267

Paul, St 2:13, 15, 106, 215, 309; 3:16, 45, 111, 112, 113, 126, 144, 148, 156, 162, 169, 170, 171, 172, 182, 193, 197, 200, 209, 215, 216, 221, 223, 227, 233, 332, 366, 383, 399, 419, 434, 438, 441, 455, 464; 4:13, 67, 128, 359, 370, 415, 419, 434, 5:10, 20, 23, 80, 102, 127, 135, 141, 149, 159, 202, 260, 278, 308, 349; 6: 30, 31, 36, 53, 54, 55, 105, 125, 126, 139, 141, 147, 156, 169, 242, 261, 262, 265, 271, 275, 280, 282, 288, 290, 294

Payne, Richard 2: *plate 10*

Peach, Georgia 2:306, 325 *plate 27, plate 30*

Pearlstein, Philip 6:258

Peavey, Lottie 2:306–308

Pechard, Freddy 2:205

Pechet, Emile 2:202

Pechet, Mimi 2:202

Pechstein 5:64, 299

Peckham, John 4:305

Péladan, Sar 1:58, 60, 66

Pepe, Lorenzo 5:367

Pepijn, M., *St. Elisabeth giving alms* 4:159

Pepys, Samuel, 5:81

Permeke, Constant 1:332; 2:86; 5:85

Perron, Du 5:333

Peruzzi, Baldassare *Presentation of the Virgin* 4:156

Peter, St 3:161, 162, 188, 349, 464; 4:4, 6, 7–8, 57, 133, 348; 5:90, 153, 156, 157; 6:43, 46, 47, 51, 107, 169, 173, 261, 292, 294

Peterson, Oscar 2:293

Petrarch 3:24

Petrelli, G. *Preaching of the Crusade against the Albigensians* 4:160

Petroff, André 1:335–336;

Phalle, Niki de St 5:117

Phebus, Gaston, *Le Livre de chasse*, 4:30, 43, 54

Phidias 1:165; 5:169

Philip III 4:37

Philip the Bold 4:41

Philip VI 4:37

Philips 1:315

Philo, of Alexandria, 2:3; 3:159

Piazetta 1:276

Picasso, Pablo 1:xxxii, 151, 277, 292, 305, 313–318, 328, 356; 2:86, 91, 113, 117, 133, 149, 216, 276; 3:32, 43, 71, 72, 79, 86, 99, 102, 103, 115, 122, 195, 345, 404, 405; 4:218, 270, 357, 454; 5:69–78, 84, 92–97, 99, 101, 104, 142, 143, 150, 179, 183, 186, 192, 193, 198, 199, 200, 219, 220, 228, 231, 237, 241, 247, 306, 312, 315, 317, 318, 323, 325, 345–347, 353, 357, 359, 360, 362

Bathers, 5:95

How to Catch Wishes up the Tail, 5:93

Les Demoiselles d'Avignon 5:179, 360

Guernica 1:315–318; 5:93, 347; 6:229

Head of a woman, 5:323, 199

Portrait of a lady 3:73; 4:192

Picou, Alphonse 2:205, 280

Pieck, Anton 1:294

Pieneman 1:286; 4:186; 4:186; 5:342, 344, 345

Piero 3:82, 83

Pierson, *Israel* 6:103

Pijper, Willem *The Tempest* 2:75

Pilate, Pontius 3:462; 5:43; 6:85, 103, 284

Piper 5:357

Pirenne 4:27

Histoire de la Europe 4:24

Pisanis 4:296

Pissarro 1:6, 56, 81, 82, 103, 127, 136, 289 (Pisarro), 300

Pizat 1:160
Plato 1:5, 65, 143, 153, 161, 162, 165, 372; 2:140, 151, 152; 3:61, 66, 159, 488; 4:238; 5:70, 73, 187, 194; 6:241
> *Phaidros*, 5:169
> *Symposium* 4:83, 84

Platschek, Hans 3:11, 12, 196; 5:101, 306, 325
Plinius 4:105
Plotinus 1:26, 37, 65, 66, 112, 120, 121, 125, 131, 137, 139, 154, 159, 162, 184, 372, 409, 410, 414, 422; 2:140; 3:100; 4:238; 5:170, 171, 175, 180, 182
Pocetti, Bernardo 4:95
Poe, Edgar Allen 1:28, 29, 30, 31–33, 45, 55, 71, 118, 119, 120, 121, 137, 158, 165, 366, 394
> *The Fall of the House of Usher* 3:378

Polak, Bettina 1:60, 192, 380;
Polanyi 6:217
> *Personal Knowledge, towards a Post-Critical Philosophy*, 4:268; 6:213

Pollaiuolo 4:72
Pollock, Jackson 2:129; 5:99, 101, 319; 4:454; 6:154, 256
Pomeroy, Ralph 4:268
Pontormo 1:252
> *Joseph in Egypt* 3:86; 5:17
> *Hieronymus* 4:87
> *Martyrium of the forty saints* 4:87
> *Deposition* 4:87
> *Adoration of the kings* 4:90

Popma, K.J. 3:159; 5:320
Porphyry 1:26
Portinari 4:67
Potter, Paulus 3:57; 4:137, 224, 228; 5:245, 357
Pourbus 1:248
Poussin, Nicholas 1:6, 11, 41, 42, 83, 268, 276, 277, 284; 2:141; 3:47, 64, 68; 4:57, 249; 5:13, 57, 58, 63, 267
> *Landscape with the funeral of Phocion* 5:13
> *Moses strikes the rock* 4:160

Pozieux 1:58
Prange, J. M. 5:284, 341, 342–347, 352, 353
> *De God Hai-Hai en Rabarber* 5:341, 342

Praxiteles, Venus 3:95; 4:399
Presley, Elvis 6:226
Préz, Josquin des 2:334
Price, Mary 2:342, 343
> 'Dark was the night' 2:342

Prikker, Thorn 1:58
Prinsterer, Groen van 1:xxviii, 164; 2:3, 109, 153; 3:280, 337, 472, 175–176, 177; 4:367; 5:41, 247, 248, 254, 259, 260
> *Unbelief and Revolution* 2:378; 3:337; 3:5, 280; 4:186; 5:41, 247, 254, 289, 332, 358; 6:131, 152
> [*Ongeloof en Revolutie* 3:490]
> *Handboek der Vaderlandse Geschiedenis* 3:465; 4:453, 502, 507; 6:131

Procope, Russell 2:370
Prokofiev, *Love of Three Oranges* 4:266
Przybyszewski, 'Mass for the Dead' 6:196
Pseudo-Bonaventura *Meditationes vitae Christi* 4:68
Puccini, 2:262
> *Madame Butterfly* 2:262

Pucelle 4:34, 40
Pugin 4:255
Puvrez 5:369
> *Najade* 5:369

Quellien, J.E., *Healing of the lame man* 4:159
Rachmaninoff 2:263
Rädecker, John 1:xxiii; 4:224; 5:374, 377–379
Rademaker,
> *Waar bleven de 10 stammen Israëls?* 6:103

Radiot 1:65;

Ragas, 2:208
Rahab 6:220
Rainey, 'Ma' Gertrude R., 2:190–193, 230, 267, 322, 326, 327, 328, 329, *plate 17*; 5:112
Ramsey, Frederic Jr 2:193, 194, 266, 290, 291, 320, 332, 339, 342 *plate 26*

   Jazzmen 2:266, 332

Ramsey, Philip Jr and Sr 2: *plate 14*;
Raphael 1:6, 79, 85, 99, 169, 252, 272, 413; 2:134; 3:57, 81, 204, 267, 237, 434, 486; 4:24, 63, 69, 72, 88, 115, 141, 142, 214, 217, 222, 224, 261, 270, 311, 319, 354, 361, 465, 488; 5:36, 153, 263, 266, 345, n.241; 6:199, 273, 279, 280

   Expulsion of Helidorus 4:156

   Madonna 3:81; 4:89, 142

   Stanze della Segnatura 4:102

Rappolo, Leon 2:219, 220
Rauschenberg, Robert 2:117; 3:196; 5:101, 102, 302, 309, 330
Ravel, Maurice 2:231

   La valse, 2:75

Ravenscroft, *Deuteromelia* 4:197
Ravisson 1:269
Raymond 1:179, 180
Raysse 3:196, 199
Read, Sir Herbert 4:118; 5:172
Red Hot Peppers 2:266; 6:190
Redeker, H. 1:66, 347; 3:303, 304; 5:339–340
Redon, Odilon 1:61, 68, 70, 71, 73, 117, 122, 125, 298, 299, 424; 5:73
Reed, Robert (Doc) 2:290, 332, *plate 25*
Reest, Rudolf van 5:174
Regnault, Henri 1:364
Regteren Altena, van 1:xvii, 311
Reimenschneider, Tuilman 4:270
Rembrandt van Rijn 1:xx, 17, 169, 226, 253, 257–268, 270, 271, 335, 356; 3:19, 36, 54, 62, 66, 84, 85, 99, 108, 234, 337, 358, 394, 434, 435; 2:31, 37, 46, 385 n.20; 4:64, 80, 132, 137, 151, 152, 153, 171–179, 200, 222, 239, 249, 270, 324, 465, 466, 482, 505; 5:10, 16, 18, 51, 97, 151, 153, 172, 244, 271, 288, 318, 337, 343–345, 347, 357, n.329; 6:141, 199, 228, 237, 269, 276, 281, 282, 287

   Bathsheba 1:261; 3:97, 98; 4:401

   The blinding of Samson 4:192

   Christ on the road to Emmaus 1:265; 4:324; 6:281

   Crucifixion, 6:282

   Danae, 2:133; 4:401

   Denial of Peter 4:57, 330

   The flight from Egypt 1:261, 268

   Haman and Mordecai 4:172

   The Holy family with angels 1:260

   Jewish bride 3:56; 4:330, 343

   The Fall 5:146/7

   The nightwatch 2:31, 103; 4:172, 173, 279; 6:204

   Paul in prison 1:261

   Resurrection of Lazarus 5:285

Rena 2:280
Renan, Ary 1:45, 70, 118, 376; 3:66; 5:46
Renfro 2:306
Reni, Guido, *Madonna* 4:142
Renoir, Pierre Auguste 1:6, 300; 5:51–53, 76, 191, 369
Rewald 1:401
Rey, R. *La renaissance du sentiment classique* 1:79
Reyer 5:376

   Phoenix 5:376

Reynolds 1:8, 295; 5:39
Ricci, S., *Marriage feast at Cana* 4:160
Riccis 1:275
Rice, Daddy 2:181
Richier, Germaine 3:196; 5:100, 198

   Orage 4:97

Ricketts 1:53, 55

   Oedipus and the Sphinx 1:55

   Daphne and Chloe 1:56

Rictus, J. 5:266
Ridolfi, C., *St. Peter healing the lame man* 4:159
Riegl 4:482
Rietveld 1:318
Rimbaud 1:70, 117; 5:73, 86, 330
Riopelle 4:454
Ripa, *Iconologia* 4:147, 239
Ritschl 1:329
Ritsema, Coba 1:312
Robbia, Luca della 1:291
Robert, Hubert 1:276, 277
Roberts, Snitcher 2:189
Robertson, Suze 1:257
Robeson, Paul 2:176, 304, 319, 351, 366
Robinson, Jim 2:249, 279–282, 374
Robinson, John 5:127
Rocca, La 2:208
Rockwell, Norman 6:256
Rodin, Auguste 2:84; 4:77, 403; 5:361–362, 370, 372, 373, 377, 378
    The gates of hell, 5:361
    Porte d'Enfer 5:370
    La défense, 5:370
    L'Age d'airain, 2:86
    L'éternelle idole 4:401
    The Kiss 4:401
Roelofs 1:261, 284
Rogers, Shorty 2:276, 298
Rohan master 4:304
    Book of Hours 4:303
    Flight to Egypt 4:303
Rolin 4:203
Roll 1:8
Rolling Stones, 5:114
    'Street fightin' man' 5:116
    'Everybody needs somebody to love' 6:197
Romano, Giulio 4:92; 5:17
    Stoning of St. Stephen 4:87
    Fall of the Titans 4:87

Ronner, Henriette 3:11
Rops, Félicien 1:89
Rose, Mademoiselle 5:34
Rosenblum, R., *Transformations in Late Eighteenth-century Art* 6:253
Rosenmuller 2:382
Rosenquist 5:106
Rosenthal, E. 3:19
Rosetti, Dante Gabriel 1:51, 52, 53, 54, 55, 57, 58, 165, 380; 5:60
Rosso 1:252
    Moses and the daughters of Jethro 4:87, 91
Rothko 3:426; 5:99
Rotonchamps 1:118
Rouault, Georges 1:70, 333–334; 2:117; 5:94, 95, 193, 236, 244, 270, 287, 299, 357
    In the Salon 1:333
    Miserere 1:334; 5:95, 237, 238, 242, 243
Rousseau, Jean Jacques 1:75, 165, 187, 196, 286; 3:183, 187; 4:87; 5:65, 123, 133; 6:164, 188, 189
    Rêveries d'un Promeneur Soliatire 1:75
Rousseau, Théodore 1:85
Rowlandson 1:337
Roy, van 1:331
Rubens, Peter Paul 1:7, 11, 15, 17, 169, 254, 268, 272–274, 332; 2:37, 82; 3:27, 41, 57, 96, 97, 98, 99, 387, 408, 450, 451; 4:22, 145, 151, 155, 239, 249, 269, 270, 399, 459; 5:14, 16, 34, 267, 303, 318; 6:249. 253, 281
    Abduction of the daughters of Leuccipus 3:96, 447, 451; 4:143, 150, 400, 401
    Battle of the Amazons, 5:147
    Cimon and Iphigenia 4:144
    Christ carrying the cross 4:158
    Conversion of St Bavo 4:159
    Conversion of St Paul, 6:281
    Death of Dido 4:147
    Garden of love 1:273

Henry IV's triumphal entry into Paris 4:159
Martyrdom of St Livinius, 5:9
Medici cycle 4:253
Raising of the Cross 4:154, 159
The reconciliation of Esau and Jacob 4:159
St Ignatius healing the possessed 4:155, 159

Rublev 1:336
Ruby Braff's Band 2:297
Rucell, Charlotte 2:344
Rueb, Gra 5:375
Rueter, Gerarda 5:369, 376
Ruisdael, Jacob van (Ruysdael) 1:12, 253, 281; 4:54, 55, 137, 169; 5:n.166
Runge, Otto 5:172, 176, 300
Ruskin, John 1:48–50, 51, 54, 179, 180, 192, 378; 3:30; 4:255, 266, 321; 6:231

Modern Painters 1:13, 48
Stones of Venice 3:30

Russell, Bertrand, *Why I am not a Christian* 4:427
Russell, Luis 2:244
Rust, Bryan 2:324
Ruysdael, Salomon van 1:12, 242, 253, 255, n.229; 4:54, 55, 137, 167, 169, 476

The ferry 4:457

Sade, Marquis de 2:117; 3:149, 193; 5:86, 202, 300, 303, 327

Justine 3:177; 5:89

Saenredam 1:255; 4:179–181
Salis, von 4:77
Salviati, Francesco *Visitation* 4:156
Samson 4:144, 147
Samuel 6:36
Sandberg, Willem 1:xx; 3:59, 378 5:178, 249
Sandby 1:295; 4:265
Sanleolinus 4:101
Santorio 6:205–206, 207
Sartre, Jean-Paul 2:113, 149, 377; 3:10, 47, 70, 110, 169, 190, 196, 197, 220, 457; 5:73, 87, 93, 124, 279, 300, 302, 305, 310, 333; 6:164, 166, 199

Huis Clos 3:195

Satie 5:86
Saul 3:154; 6:17
Saura, Antonio, 2:117; 3:196; 6:286
Savage, Reginald 1:54, 56

Behemoth 1:56
Centaurs 1:56

Saverjj, Roelant 4:164;
Savonarola 3:5; 4:62, 63, 86, 141, 308, 311
Sayers, Dorothy 6:228
Schaeffer, Francis 1:xvi; 3:445; 4:425, 435; 5:3, 167; 6:133, 152, 153, 172, 178, 264, 290, 292

The God Who is There, 6:81
Escape from Reason, 6:179

Schamberg, Morton, *God* 5:78
Scheen, P.A. 1:283, 284, 285, 288
Scheffer, Ary 1:283; 4:186; 5:344
Schelfhout 1:283, 284, 286, 287, 288
Schelling, Friedrich 1:152, 164; 2:152; 4:318; 5:171, 175
Scheltema, Tace 1:271
Schelven, van 4:163, 379
Schierbeek 2:116
Schilder, Klaas 4:449; 5:274
Schiller 1:152, 153; 3:51, 410; 5:171, 172
Schippers 3:92;
Schlegel, Friedrich von 2:141; 3:51; 4:254; 5:171
Schlemmer 1:332;
Schmidt-Rottloff 1:307, 328, 340; 5:64, 270, 299
Schoenberg 2: 277, 298
Schoenmaeckers 5:75
Schoffner, Bob 2:244, 357
Schongauer 1:239; 4:111

Christ carrying the cross 1:240
Flight to Egypt 1:240;

Schopenhauer, Arthur 1:32, 33–35,

35, 36, 47, 62, 137, 153; 2:141; 3:51; 5:300; 6:166
Schotel, van 1:279, 286, 287
   Arrival of the British on the Merwede 1:279
Schouman 1:279
Schrofer, Willem 4:457; 5:242, 245, 282
Schubert, Franz 2:176, 366; 4:340, 374
   Die schöne Müllerin 2:187, 330
   'Death and the maiden' 2;334
Schuffenecker 1:82, 100, 109, 113, 115, 199, 402, 403
Schumacher, W. *Portraits of dead birds* 1:327
Schuré 1:138
Schütz, Heinrich, 2:289; 3:20, 40, 194, 435; 4:115, 246, 356, 379; 6:227
   Auferstehungshistoire 3:28
   Historia der Aufstehung Jesu Christi 4:114; *Musikalische Exequien* 2:289
   St Matthew Passion 3:108
   Symphonie Sacrae 3:21
Schwabe, C. 1:58
Schwitters, Kurt 2:117, 5:78, 87
Scorel, Jan van 1:248–250
   Agatha van Schoonhoven 1:249
   Baptism in the Jordan 1:249
   Entry into Jerusalem 1:249
   Holy Kinship altarpiece 1:248
   Madonna 1:249
   Mary Magdalene 1:249
   The Jerusalem pilgrims 1:249
   The twelve-year-old boy 1:249
Scott, Bud 2:2112, 244
Scott, Walter 1:18
Scotus, John Duns 4:293, 304
Sedlmayr, Hans 1:xxix, xxx, xxxii; 5:346–359
Sedric, Gene 2:356
Seerveld, Calvin 1:xxxi; 3:408, 416
   A Turnabout in Aestheics to Understanding, 2:151–153
Selah, Jubilee, Singers, the 2:286
Sénancour 1:62, 121
Séon 1:58, 59
Sermoneta, Siciolante da
   Baptism of Clovis 4:158
Sérusier 1:99, 112–113, 114, 115, 116, 117, 133, 134, 137–143, 147, 148, 151, 153, 172, 173, 179, 181, 191, 197, 403, 409, 414, 415, 416, 440; 5:63
   A.B.C. de la peinture 1:142
Seth 3:144–146,153, 197; 5:35, 144–146, 153, 197, 474
Seurat 1:39, 58, 76–80, 82, 88, 92, 136, 140, 141, 300, 304, 322, 388, 398; 3:69; , 5:56, 57, 59, 62, 63, 191, 285
   Grande Jatte 1:79
   Le Chahut 1:300
Severini 1:312, 313
   The harlequin 1:313
Shaftesbury 4:254
Shakespeare, William 2:208; 3:19, 104, 403; 4:339, 435; 5:150, 299; 6:31, 228; 6:31, 228
   Hamlet 5:150
   Macbeth 3:413
   The Tempest, 2:75
   Twelfth Night 3:23
Sharp 2:259
Shaw, Artie 2:270 5:112; 6:192
Shelley 1:56; 4:265
Shestov, Leo (Sjestow) 3:58; 5:292–296
Shields, Larry 2:208
Sibelius, J.J.C. 2:35
Siegers, Jan Sikko 6:149
Signac 1:15, 60, 76, 78, 79
Simon, Paul 5:33, 51; 6:166, 195–196
   'Patterns' 6:196
   'Sound of silence' 6:195
Simons, Menno, 3:326
Singleton, Zutty 2:356, 369
Sisera 4:144

Sisley 1:6
Skira 4:453, 456
Sloan, P.F. 6:199–201
    'The eve of destruction' 3:370; 5:79; 6:200
Sluter, Claus 1:238, 245, 246; 4:44, 48, 62
    Moses fountain 1:246
Sluyters, Jan 1:305, 307
Smet, Gustave de 1:332, 333
Smith, Bessie 2: 193, 230–231, 266, 267, 327, 328, 329, 336, 354, *plate 16*; 5:112
Smith, C.L. 1:295;
Smith, Charles Edward *Jazzmen*, 2:266, 332, 339
Smith, Clara 2:230, 336
Smith, Joe 2:250, 271
Smith, Mamie 2:230
Smith, Peter 3:427
Smith, Pinetop,2:234
Smith, Ruby 2:336
Snyder, Gary 5:109, 258, 260
Socrates 4:264
Soest, Conrad van 1:236
Solimena, F. *Rebecca takes leave of her parents* 4:160;
Solomon (biblical) 2:139, 401 n.450; 3:160; 6:17–18, 24, 103, 220, 261; 4:133, 144, 147, 207, 282, 350–351
Song of Solomon 4:400
Soto 5:106
Sousa, 4:341; 6:226, 265
Spanier, Muggsy 2:220–222, 239
Sparbaro, Tony 2:208
Spencer, Herbert, 5:49
Spencer, Stanley, 5:85, 299, 315; 6:229
Spengler, Oswald 1:xxvii, xxviii; 2:85
    The Decline of the West, 2:4
Spetter, Riki 3:3, 91
Spinoza 4:135; 5:294, 296; 6:242
Spirit of Memphis Quartet, the 2:209, 288, 289, 305, 344, 345, 350, *plate 23, plate 26*; 4:407, 408

Spivey, Victoria 2:230, 356
Springer 1:286
Sprott, Horace 2:185, 291, 333
    'Music from the south' 2:333
Spycket, Sylvie 2:383
St Edmond 4:39
Staple Singers, the, 2:313, 322 357
Staring 1:278, 279
Stark 2:196
Starlight Gospel Singers 2: *plate 26*
Starr, Alan 5:130
Stearn 2:275; 3:377
Steele, Silas 2: plate 23
Steen, Jan 3:32, 41–42; 4:40, 137, 139, 146, 152, 174, 176, 205; 5:14, 349
    Christ drives the moneychangers out of the Temple 2:68
    Frolicking couple 4:504
    St Nicholas morning 3:84; 5:14
Steenwijks, van 1: 255
Steinbach, Erwin von 4:12
Steinbeck 3:122
Steinberg, Saul 1:337–338; 3:22, 23
Steiner, John 2:357
Steiner, Rudolph 5:67
Steinlen 1:89, 337, 360
Stellingwerff, J. 5:336–338
    'Origin and future of creative man', 2:21–23
Stendhal 1:121
Still, Clifford 5:99
Stomer 1:254;
Strasbourg, Godfried of 4:13
    Tristan and Isolde 4:13
Strauss, Johann 2:75; 3:205; 5:111
Strauss, Richard, 2:35, 362
Stravinsky, 2:277, 298, 361; 5:315; 6:229
Streissand, Barbara, *The Way We Were* 4:449
Strij, van 1:279
Strik, van 4:185
Strindberg 1:303

Strozzi 1:275
Stuart, Rex 2:271
Stubbs, *Anatomy of the Horse* 1:296
Suger 4:345, 346; 6:271
Sullivan, see Gilbert and Sullivan
Superior Band 2:*plate 10*
Surie, Coba 1:312
Suso 4:29
Sutherland, Graham 4:118, 119;
    Green tree form 4:118, 456;
Sutter 1:78
Swayzee, Edwin 2:370
Swedenborg 1:25, 25–27, 30, 33, 46, 47, 109, 154, 160, 162, 411, 417; 4:237, 238; 5:40
Sweelinck 3:435
Swigchem, D van 6:146
Swingle Singers 4:407
Sybrandi, Piet 3:87
Sypher 4:88;
Taine, H.A. 1:36, 93, 120, 177, 437; 2:141; 5:212–214
    L'idéalisme anglais, Étude sur Carlyle, 5:212
Tanguy, Yves 1:113; 5:87, 89, 198
Tapies 3:196; 5:101
Tassaert 1:9
    The unhappy family 3:65
Tauler 4:29
Telemann 2:382, 383; 3:395;
Temple, Johnny, 2:269
Tennyson, Alfred, 'The Princess' 2:28;
Terborch 1:168; 4:137, 476
Terbrugghen, Henrick 1:254
Terry, Sonny 2:261, 262
Tertullian 5:295, 296
Teschemaker, Frank 2:222, 239, 271
Tharpe, Sister Rosetta 2:266, 267, 306, *plate 27*
Thomas, John 2:241
Thorwaldsen 4:13
Tibaldi, Pellegrino 5:17
    Conception of St John 4:157

Tieghem, van 1:150
Tiepolo, G.B. 1:14, 275; 5:357
    The death of Hyacinthus 1:274
    The Gatherine of the manna 4:161
Tillich, Paul 3:59; 5:127
Timmer 1:357
Timothy 3:441; 5:135
Tinguely 5:117, 309, 330
Tintoretto 1:275
    Last Supper 4:155, 157;
    Presentation of the Virgin 4:155, 157
    Miracle of St Mark 4:157
    Baptism of Christ 4:157
    Moses strikes the rock 4:157
Tischbein, Wilhelm 5:173
Tissot 3:65; 5:45
    Crucifixion, 5:45
Titian 1:248, 275; 3:57; 4:151, 195, 214, 354; 5:15, 16, 34, 38; 6:199, 253
    Assunta 4:260
    Danae 4:261
    Venus and Music 4:261; 5:15, 16
Titus, Emperor 6:8, 104
Titze 4:482
Tobey, Mark 2:117; 5:99, 123, 355
Tolkien 3:417; 6:3, 229
Tolnay, de 4:79, 492
Tolstoy 1:56
Tommaso, Niccolo di 5:338
Toorop 1:58, 59, 60, 167, 294, 311, 347, 381; 2:86; 4:224
    Die anarchist 1:60
    The living room 1:347
Toulouse-Lautrec 1:90, 189, 192, 300, 313, 360; 3:205; 4:348; 5:61, n.343
    Woman at the piano 1:300
Towne, Charles 1:296; 2:244
Toynbee 3:365
Toyne 4:265
Trazegnies, Jean de 2:251
Troeltsch, E. 5:177

Troescher 4:44;
Troost, Cornelis 1:271; 4:186
Troyes, Jean de 4:42
Trumbauer, Frank 2:221
Tunderman, J.W. 3:326; 5:292-294
Turner, J. M. William 1:13, 46, 48, 49, 378; 3:410; 4:187, 265, 374
  Rain, steam and speed 3:67; 5:35
Turpin, Tom 2:195
Two Gospel Keys, the 2:292
Tzara, Tristan 5:300
Ulanov, 2:251
Vahli-Mohamed-Zumbul Zadi 1:402
Valadon, Suzanne, *The forgotten doll* 1:311
Valerius, *Gedenkklank* 3:88
Valéry, Paul 1:168
Valkenborgh, Pucas van 4:162
Vallotton 1:60
Vanderburgt, Flip 2:23
Vasarely 5:106, 198
Vasari 4:74, 91
  Vite 4:92
Veen, K. van 2:86
Velasquez 3:72; 4:239; 5:103, 192, 345
  Las meninas 5:93, 257
Velde, Adriaen van der 4:137, 166, 167, 167
Veldhoen, Aad 3:99, 120; 5:242, 246, 247, 282, 357; 4:262
Velvet Underground 3:436; 6:197-199
  'Heroin' 6:199
Veneziano, Paolo da (Venetiano) 1:274, 275
  Madonna 1:274
  Coronation of the Virgin 4:301
Venne, A. van der 4:164
Venuti, Joe 2:222
Verhaeren 1:167
Verhaghen, P.I. *Presentation in the Temple* 4:161
Verkade 1:117, 140, 141, 155;
Verlaine 1:61, 76, 89, 180, 386; 5:213
Vermeer 1:253, 268, 354; 3:27, 36, 354, 432; 4:137, 246, 270; 5:88, 245, 347, 349
  Christ in the house of Mary and Martha 1:254
  Street in Delft, 4:64, 219; 5:347, 349
Vermeylen 4:44
Verrochio 1:251; 4:72
Verschuiring 1:295
Verster 1:257, 290
  Eucalyptus 1:290
  Snow 1:290
  Spring flowers in a glass vase 1:290
  Town hall in Borger 1:290
Verve, de 1:348
Verveer 1:284
Vesalius 6:206-207, 245
Vestdijk 3:21
Veth, Jan 1:257
Victor Sylvester's Metropole Orkest 2:293
Victor, Hugo of St 2:146
Vidaql, Perie 4:27
Vigny, de 1:121
Villette 1:89
Villon 1:252
Vincent, F.A. 4:264
Vincent, Walter 2:233
Vinci, Leonardo da 1:172, 250-251; 2:141; 3:204, 237, 279; 4:24, 72-73, 105, 221, 488; 5:266, 343
  Last Supper, 6:286
  Mona Lisa
Vinckboons, David 4:164
Virgil 3:46, 47
Visscher, Claes Jansz 4:152, 167
Visser 5:371, 375
  Ode to death and destruction, 5:371
  Dying horse, 5:371
Vitalis, Orderic 4:27
Vitruvius 4:105, 123, 208
Vivaldi 3:395

Vivarinis 1:275
Vlaminck 1:304, 307; 5:270
Vliet, van 1:255
Vollenhoven, D.H.Th 1:xvii; 2:5, 151; 3:270; 6:177
Volterra, Daniele da 4:92
Vondel, Joost van den, *Gijsbrecht*, 2:75
Vos, Maarten de 4:147
Vostell, W. 5:108
Vouet 1:6
Voulboudt 3:378
Vriend, J.J., *Nieuwe architectuur* 2:39
Vries, de 1:255
Vuillard 1:76, 191, 304, 310
Wachenroder 1:177; 3:51
Wagner, W. Richard 1:112, 121, 124, 129, 138, 167; 2:35, 40, 66, 84, 89, 104; 4:222
    Die Meistersinger von Nürnberg 2:29
    Gesamtkunstwerk 2:74, 75
Walpole 5:39
    Castle of Otranto 5:39
Wand, A. Hart 2:209
    'Dallas blues' 2:209
Ward, Clara 2:305, 306
Ward, James 3:438
Ward, Vera Hall 2:290, 332
Warhol, Andy 5:106, 302
    Campbell soup cans 4:260
Washington, Sister Ernestine B. 2:306, 307 344
Watteau 1:276, 277; 4:57, 214, 354
    Embarkation for the Island of Cythera 4:374
Watters, Lu 2:284
Watts, 'Doc' Isaac 2:168, 169, 172, 182, 199, 255, 287, 288, 289, 338–345; 4:338, 348; 5:18
Watts, Alan 5:109, 123, 260
Watts, George Frederic 1:57
Weese 4:34
Weissenbruch 1:287; 3:32
Wellershoff, Maria 4:154

Wencelius 3:6, 100; 4:379, 381
Werff, A. van der 4:151
Werner 1:329
Wesley brothers, 2:169, 170, 172
Wesley, Charles 2:171, 342
Wesselman, 5:106
    Great American nude, 6:256
West Benjamin 5:39
    William Penn meets the Indians 4:161
Wet, Chritiaan de 5:229
Weyden, Rogier van der 1:244, 245, 246, 268, 269; 3:238; 4:39, 49, 62, 76, 121, 165, 204, 310
    Birth of Christ 1:246
    Charles the Bold 1:270
    Engagement of Mary 1:246
    Last Judgement 5:147
    Portait of a young woman 1:268
    Saint Luke painting the Madonna 4:204
Whistler 1:379
White, George 2:175, 176, 177, 347;
Whiteman, Paul ('King of Jazz') 2:220, 221, 222, 250, 263, 296; 6:190, 192–193
Wiegman, Matthieu 1:245
Wierix *Ira* 4:149
Wijker, Cor 5:365, 366
Wijngaert, van 1:283
Wilfred 1:193
Wilhelm, Kaiser 5:172
Wille 4:379
Willette 1:337
William of Ockham 5:293
William of Tyrus 4:27
Williams, Johnny Clarence 2:205, 217, 244, 246, 247, 251, 252, 254, 324, 369, *plate 15*
Williams, Mary Lou 2:274
Willinck 1:325–327
    The sémaphore 1:325
Wilson 4:265
Wimes, Jack 2: *plate 8*

Winckelmann, J.J. 2:134, 141; 3:64; 4:21, 264
  Thoughts on the Imitation of Greek Works in Painting and Sculpture 4:263
Windelband 1:153
Winter 1:329
Wit, Jacob de 4:185
Witelo 4:305
Witte, Emanuel de 1:255; 4:179–181
Wittgenstein, Ludwig, 2:141; 3:457
Wodehouse 3:21
Woestijne, Gustav van de 1:245
  Christ in the desert 1:245
  Crucifixion, 2:90, 104
  The Judas kiss 1:245
Wolff 6:242
Wölfflin, 2:134; 4:51; 6:249
Wols 3:11, 196; 5:101, 303, 306, 307, 324, 325
Wolstenholmes 1:295
Wordsworth, William 1:56; 4:265
Wotruba 4:97; 5:100, 369, 372
Wouters, Rik 1:333; 5:368, 369, 372
Wright, Frank Lloyd 5:61
Wright, John Buckland, 5:85, 299
Wyeth, Andrew, *Christina* 4:260
Xenocrates 2:140
Yancey, Jim 2:234
Yeats 1:57, 167
Yerba Buena Jazz Band, the 2:281, 284, 307
Young, Wayland 3:186; 5:39
Zadkine 1:15, 317; 3:108; 5:100, 372, 379
  Demolished city 1:317
Zahn 3:337, 339, 341
Zardis 2:374
Zaritsky, Joseph 1.xxi, 329–330
Zbinden, Hans, *De bedreigde mens* 3:360
Zephaniah 3:165, 361; 6:31, 38, 40, 87, 261
Ziem 1:85
Zola 1:12, 40, 91, 93, 96, 129, 165, 303; 5:49, 270, 271
Zorn, Anders 6:255
Zuidema, S.U. 5:264
Zylstra, *World Politics in the Light of Scripture* 4:502

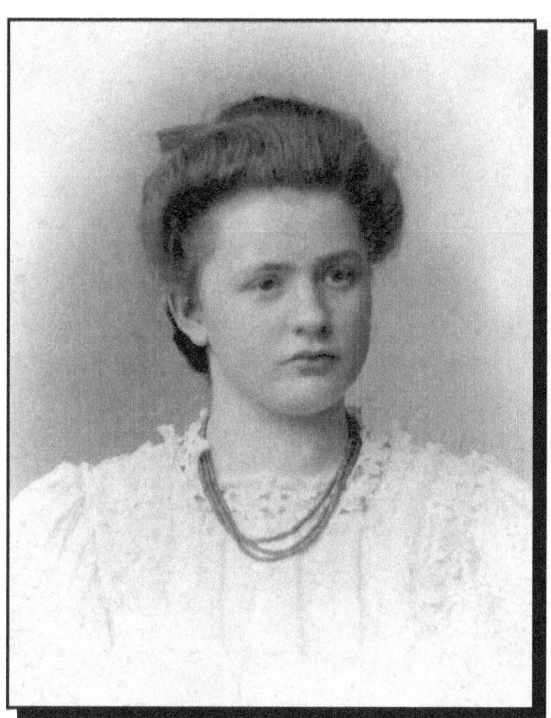

1. H.R.R.'s mother, Theodora Catharina Heitink (1890–1971), at age 16.

2. H.R.R.'s father, Henderik Roelof Rookmaaker senior (1887–1945) in the 1930s exuberantly bursting out in an *olé* of a flamenco. His son would joyously follow in his footsteps when it came to enjoying this kind of fun.

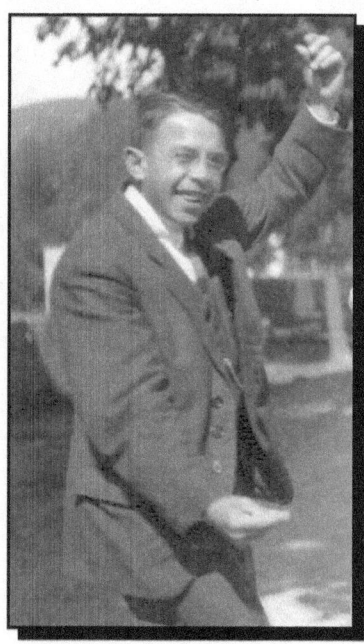

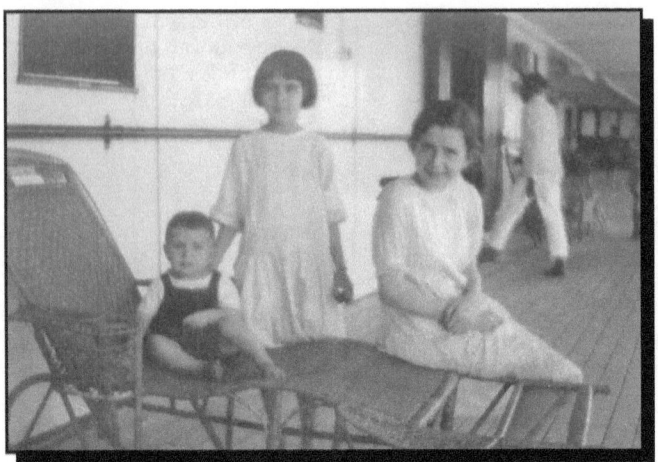

3. One-year-old Hans (Hansje) and his sisters, Door (b.1912) and Hannie (b.1914), on board the *Prins der Nederlanden* in 1923.

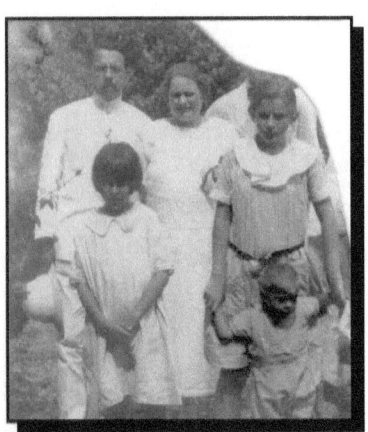

4. A family photograph from 1924 shows Door trying her best to keep little Hansje in the picture, while the equatorial heat and glare of the sun is palpable.

5. The active interest that Hans's father took in plants and animals created a conscious awareness and appreciation of rare creatures right at home.

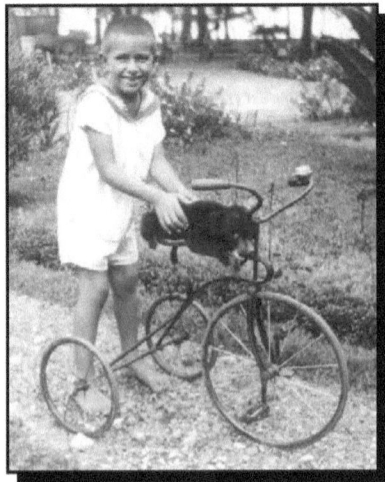

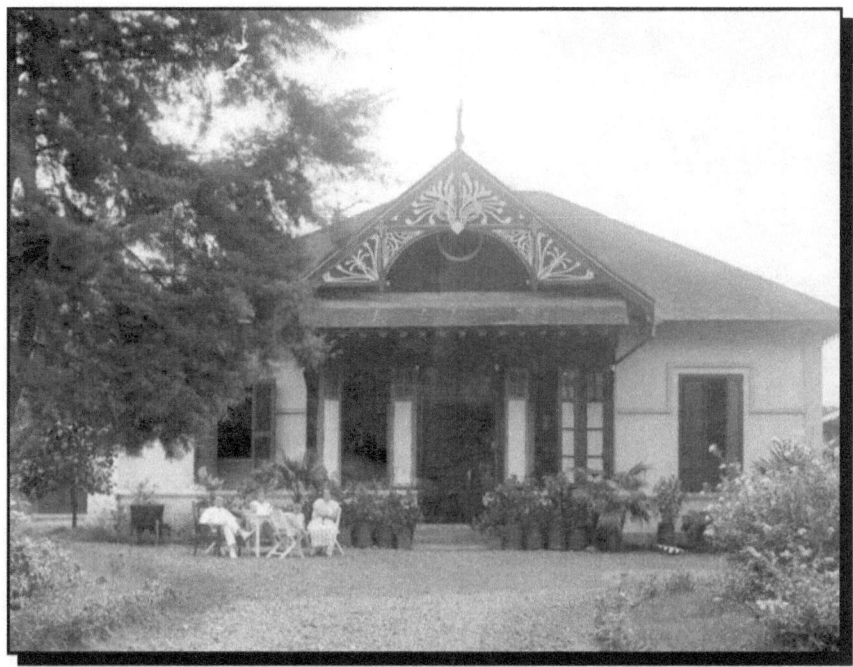

6. The Rookmaaker family home in Sumatra.

7. A family photograph from c. 1926, with Hans's father this time keeping the exuberant boy in the picture.

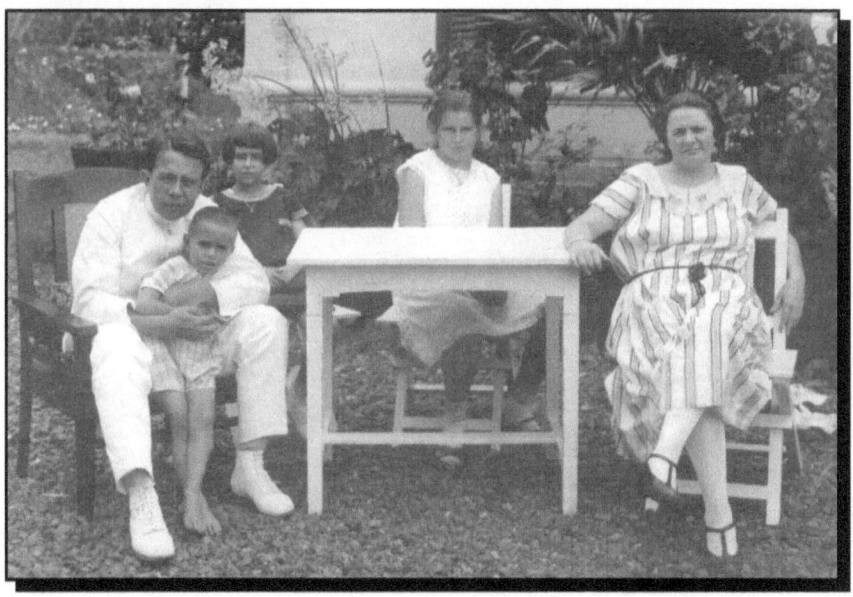

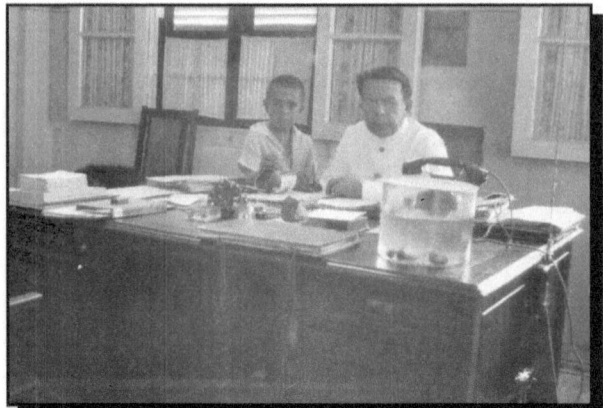

8. Hans was welcome in his father's office, as this photo from 1930 shows. His father clearly took an interest in his son and was proud of him as a boy and a young man. Hans in turn was proud of his father.

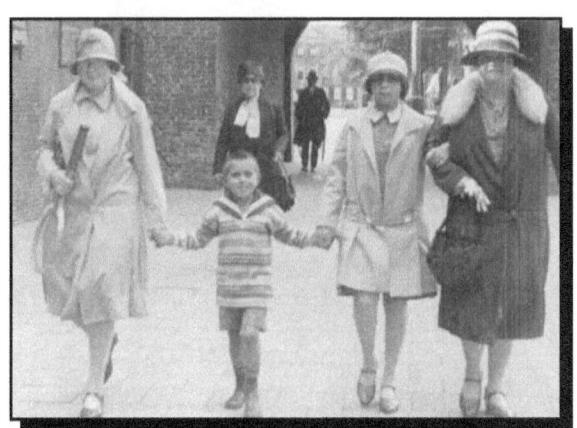

9. Hans with his mother and sisters on leave in the Netherlands.

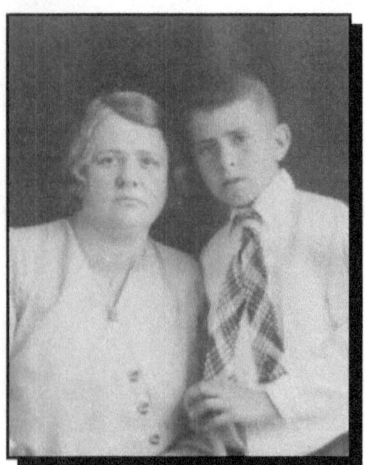

10. A rather anxious-looking Hans with his mother in The Hague, 1932.

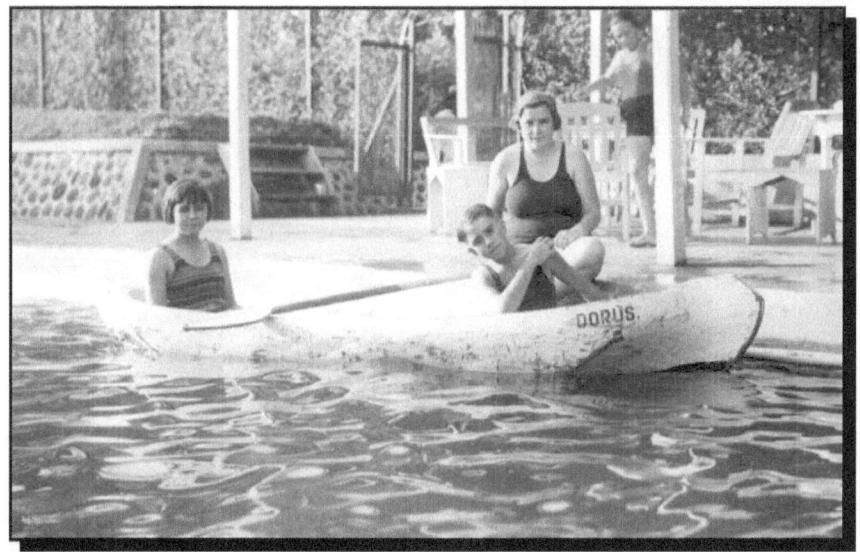

11. Hans's sisters adored him.

12. H.R.R. and his father, c. 1938.

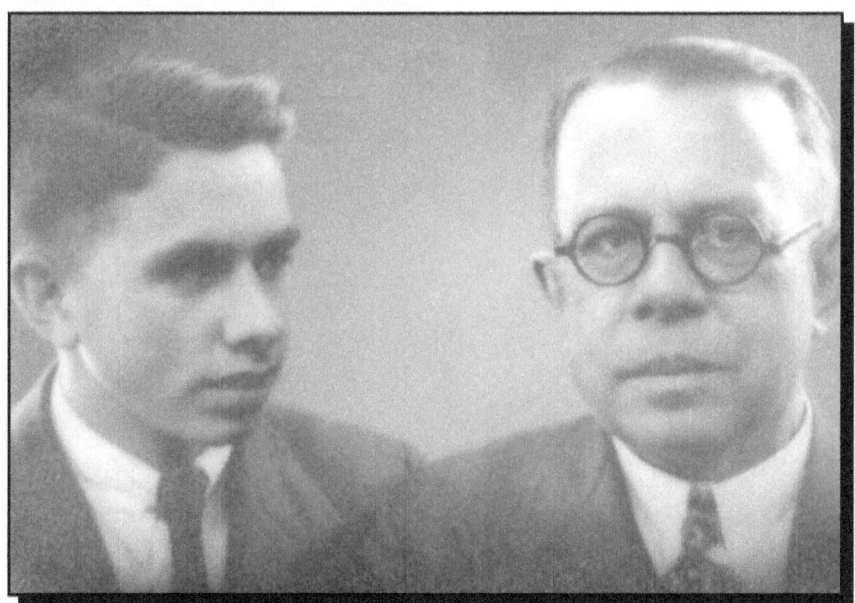

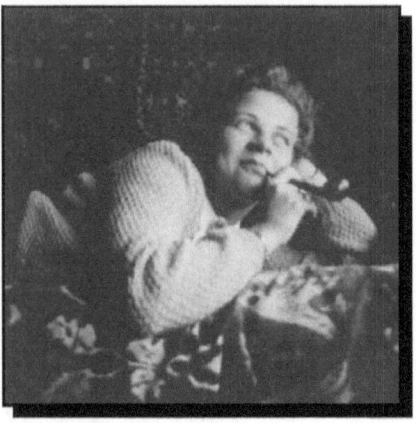

13. Hendrika Beatrix (nicknamed Riki) Spetter (1919–1942) had sparkle! This snapshot shows her playfully taking a draw on Hans's pipe as she lounges on a day bed.

14. Riki absorbed in luring a perky cat with some tasty bit in her hand.

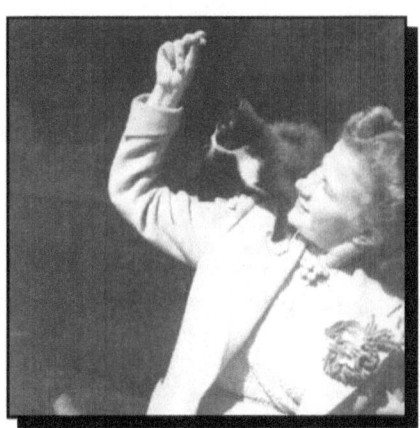

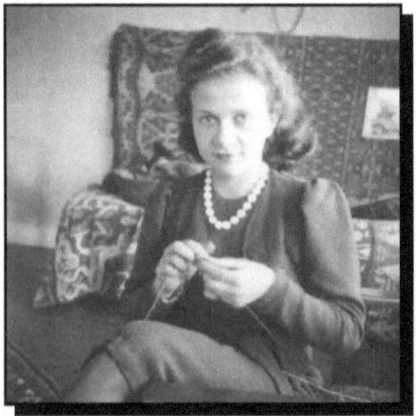

15. This more solemn snapshot of Riki betrays a realistic awareness of life.

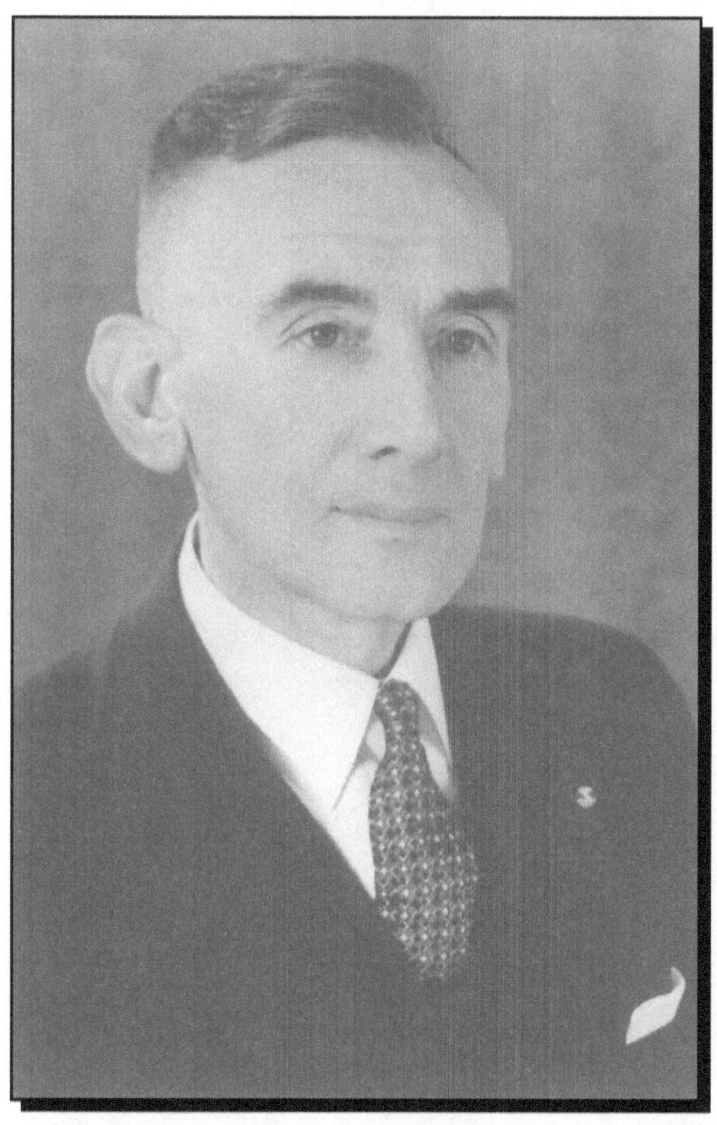

16. Captain J.P.A. Mekkes (1897–1987), whom Hans met in 1943, became one of the most influential and faithful friends of his life. Photograph by Fotostudio Joh. van Hespen, The Hague.

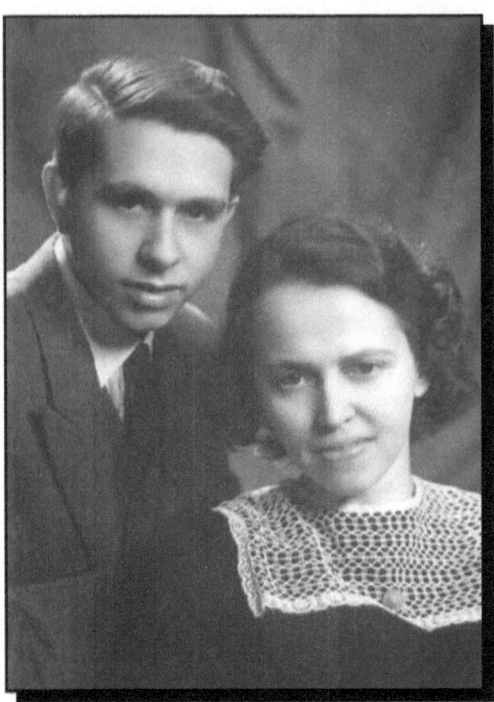

17. In 1948 Hans became engaged to one of Riki's friends, Anna Marie (nicknamed Anky) Huitker (1915–2003).

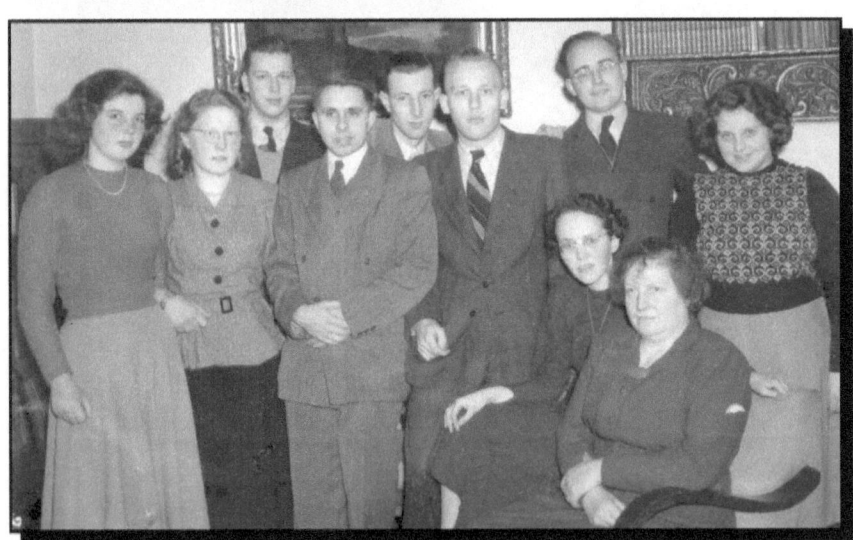

18. As a student at the University of Amsterdam, Hans helped to pioneer the formation of the *Vereniging van Gereformeerde Studenten in Amsterdam* (VGSA), a fellowship that encouraged Bible study and reflection to bring biblical thought to bear on the issues of life and learning. Identified on this photograph are, third from left, am. Trimp, followed to the right by Hans Rookmaaker, Piet Tollenaar, Hans Vrijmoet, Anky Rookmaaker, Tjerk Tjerkstra and far right, Trudy Mackloet.

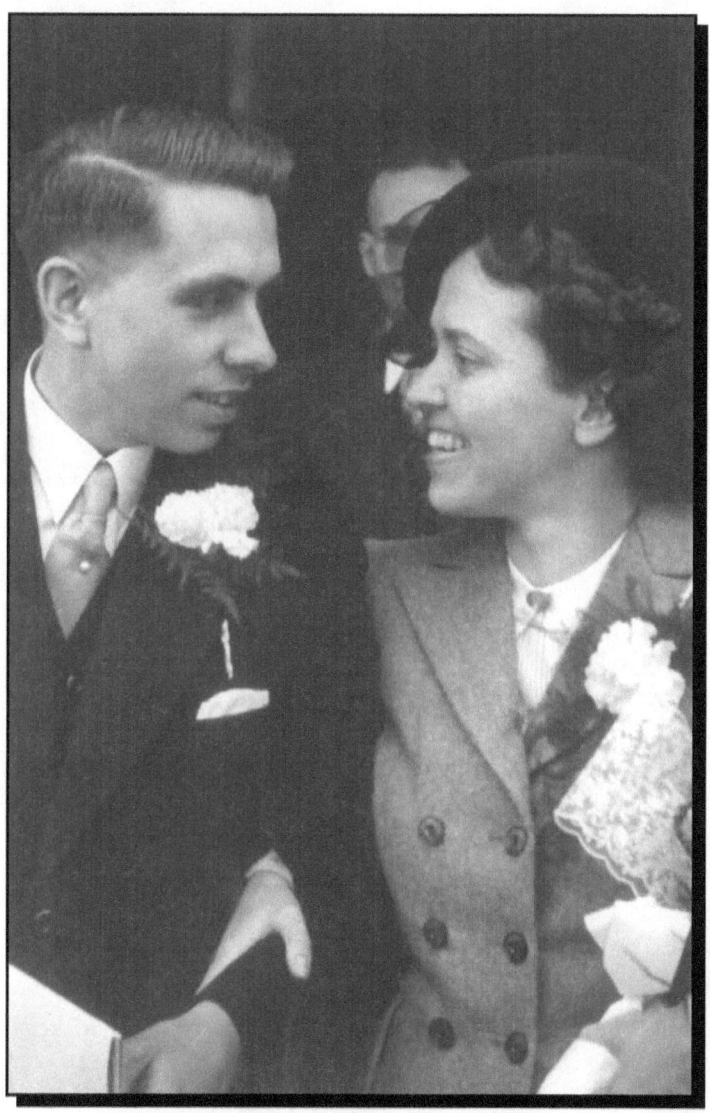

19. On Wednesday, 1 June 1949, Hans and Anky were married at a civil ceremony, attended only by their immediate families, at the Town Hall of Amsterdam.

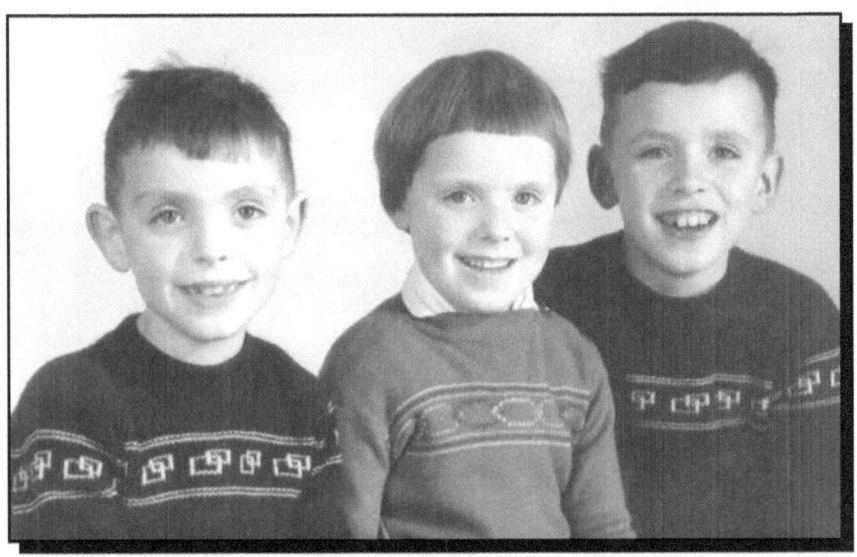

20. Hans and Anky were soon blessed with a family (l. to r.): Leendert Cornelis (Kees), Maria Helena (Marleen) and Henderik Roelof (Hans, junior), who cleverly made his appearance into the world on the date of Rembrandt's birth.

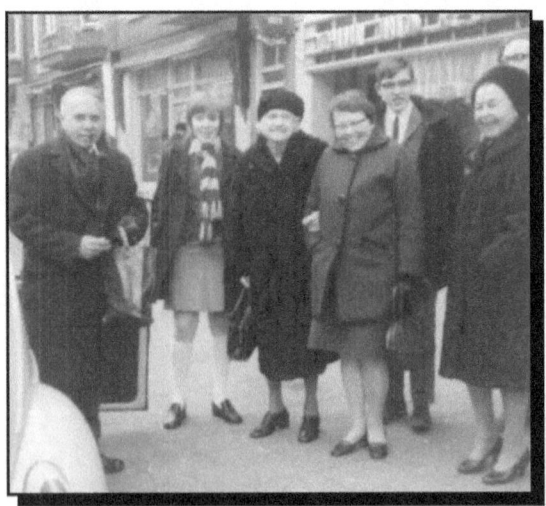

21. Family photograph c. 1966, from left to right: H.R.R., Marleen, Mrs Rookmaaker, senior, Anky, Kees, H.R.R.'s sister Hannie, and Hans.

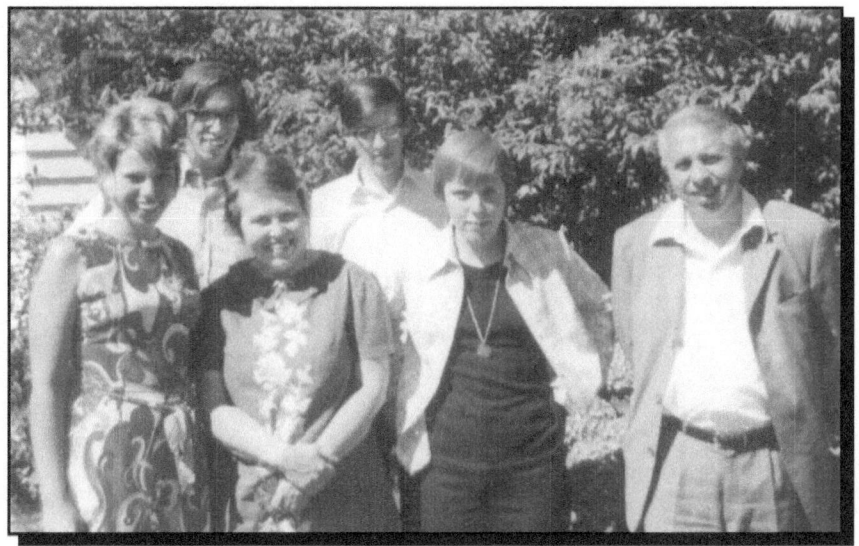

22. The Rookmaaker family on vacation in Vancouver, B.C. in 1970. From left to right: Thena Ayres, Hans, Anky, Kees, Marleen, and H.R.R. Photograph by Laurel Gasque.

23. Some leaflets announcing lectures and H.R.R.'s book, *Modern Art and the Death of a Culture*.

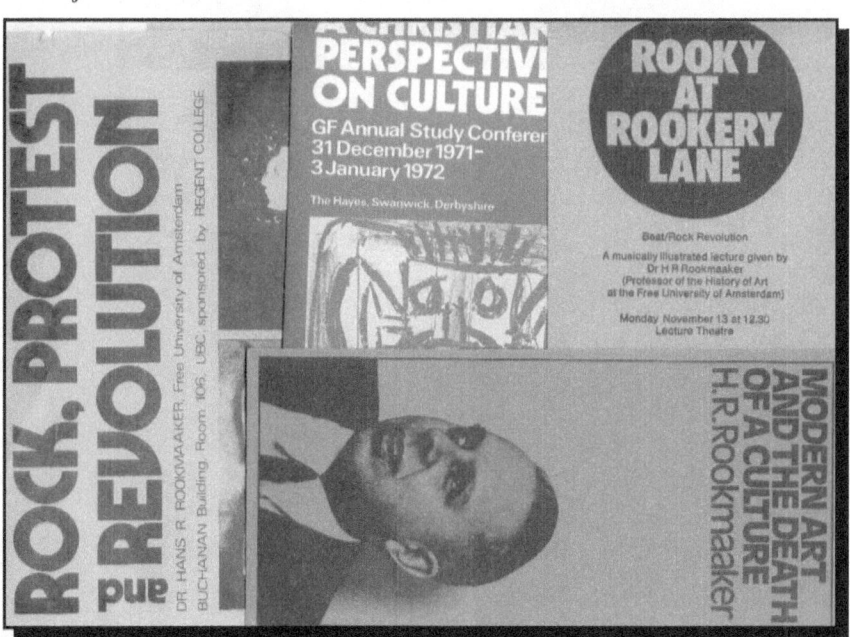

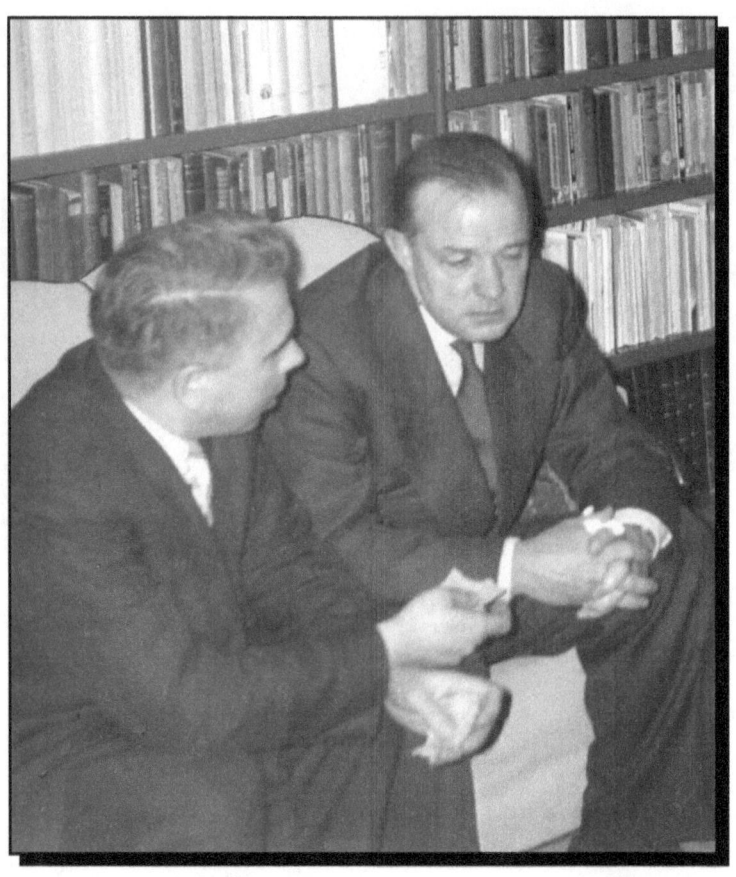

24 & 25. H.R.R. and Francis Schaeffer (above) and Edith and Anky (below) during a visit of the Schaeffers to Leiden around 1960.

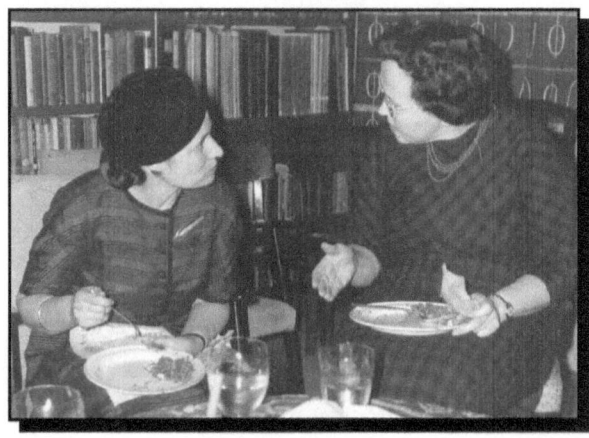

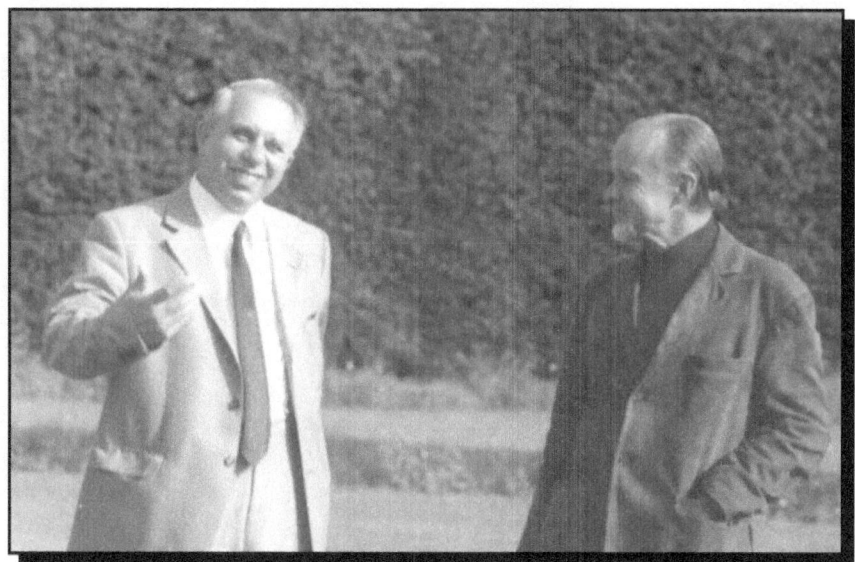

26. H.R.R. and Schaeffer during the 1960s and early 1970s, like complementary colours, each giving a distinct hue, contrasted but also exhibited a deep underlying affinity when they appeared together at L'Abri conferences held in North America and Europe.

27. From the late 1960s onward Hans and Anky poured enormous effort into the task of establishing a Dutch branch of L'Abri. Here they are in conversation with co-worker Wim Rietkerk, 1976.

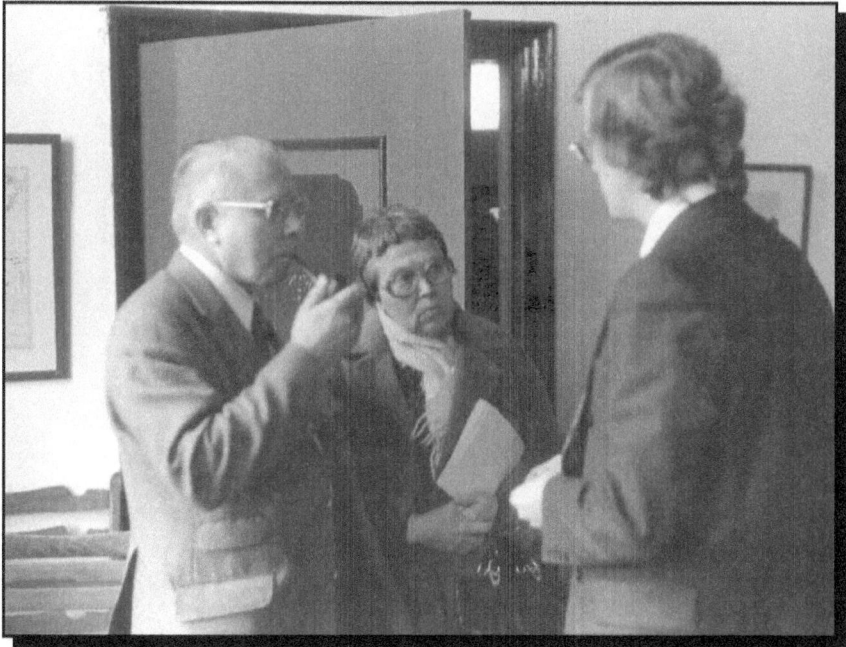

Photograph by Sylvester Jacobs

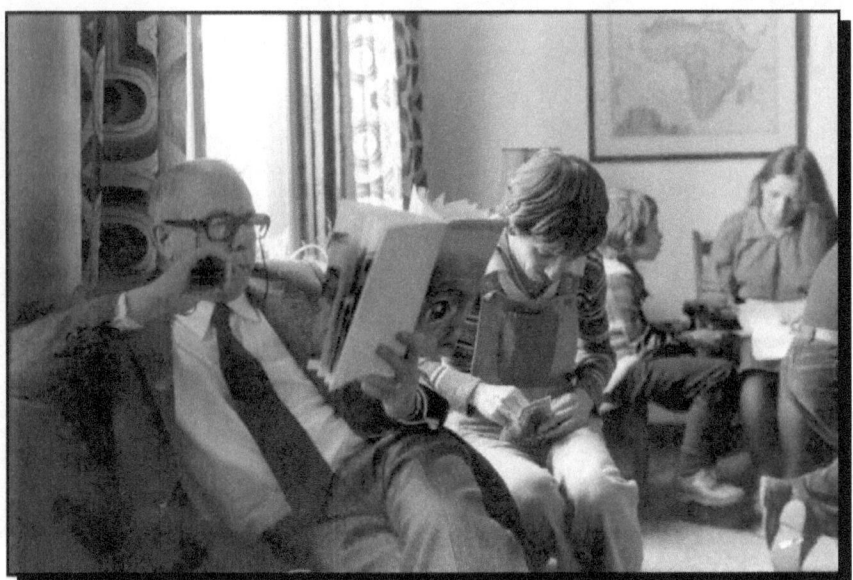

Photograph by Sylvester Jacobs

28 & 29. One student remembers Hans being asked: 'Is it an inconsistency to be a Christian and be a smoker?' To which he reportedly replied: 'God has a distinct record of accepting burnt offerings from those who really loved and feared him and I am certainly one of them. If there perchance comes a whiff of tobacco from any light I give out, well let's leave God to his judgments and concentrate on our obedience to his calling.'

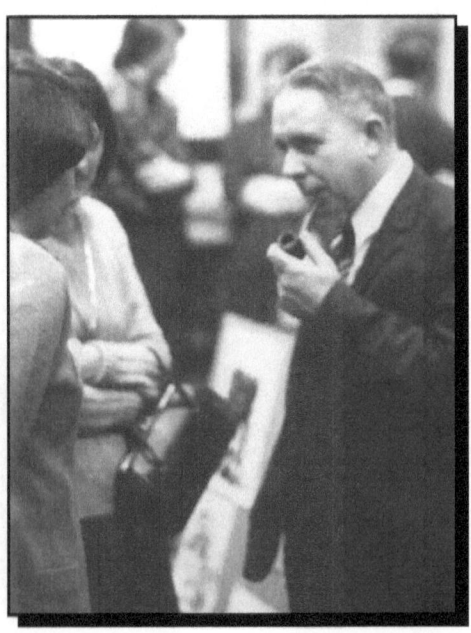

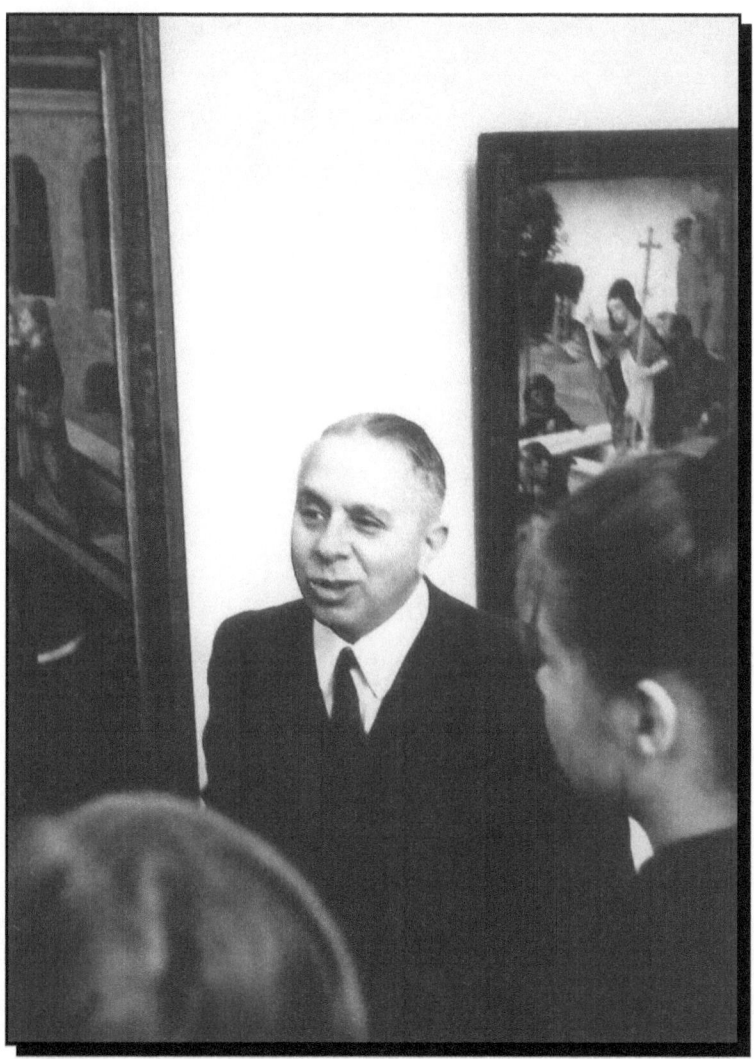

Photograph by John Walford

30. Rookmaaker was protective of his little flock of students when visiting an art gallery. Many of his students relate incidents when a curious visitor would sidle up to the group H.R.R. and Francis Schaeffer, and Edith and Anky, during a visit from the Schaeffers to Leiden around 1960. There lurked beneath an unpretentious exterior a complex personality of immense vitality and not a few surprises.

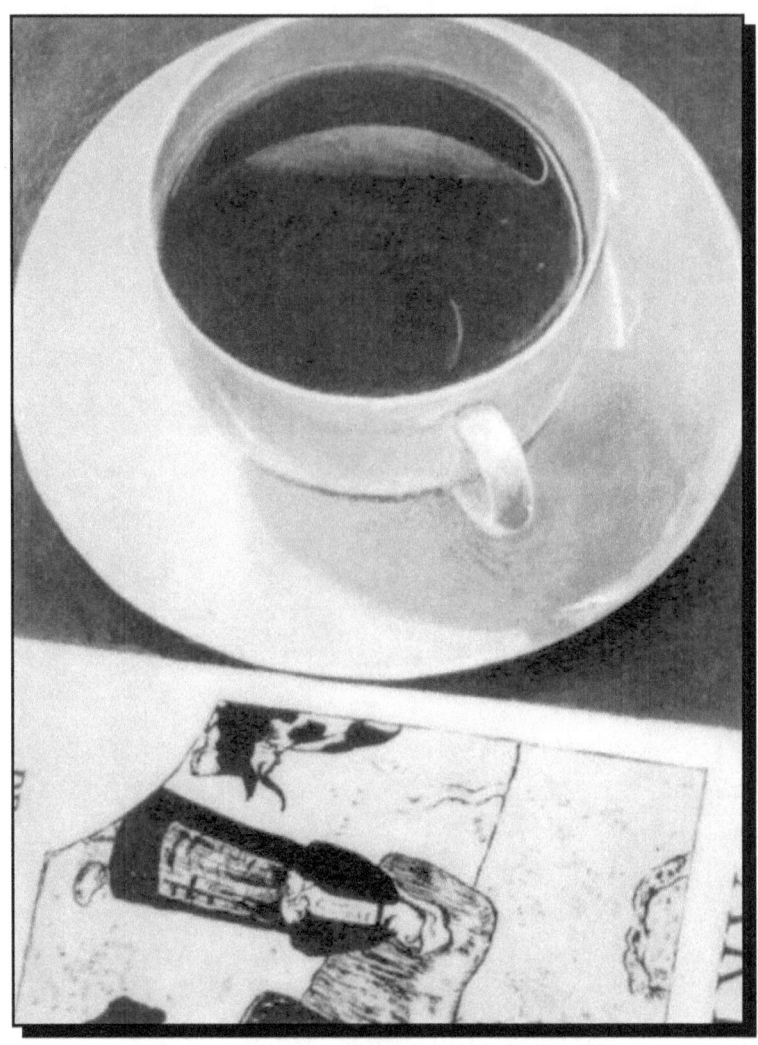

31. Peter Smith: *Black Tea (for H.R. Rookmaaker)*, acrylic, 1977. This painting by a British artist and former student of Rookmaaker expressed poignantly the deep loss many felt at his sudden and untimely death in 1977, Rookmaaker drank black tea and, in looking for a metaphor to express the loss, the artist 'made a cup of tea' for H.R.R. The illustration in the foreground by Gauguin was reproduced on the front page of the Appendix with Notes to H.R.R.'s doctoral thesis, *Synthetist Art Theories* (1959).

www.ingramcontent.com/pod-product-compliance
Lightning Source LLC
Chambersburg PA
CBHW031602210526
45464CB00004B/1391